Table of Contents

Color Coded For Your Convenience

NEW

Select Savings™ Section

Unbelievable offers that more than pay for the book. Turn the page and start saving!

Fine & Casual Dining

Explore dining at the best fine dine and casual restaurants in your area.

Family Restaurants, Informal Dining & Carryout

Enjoy the savings and convenience of your favorite family and quick-service restaurants.

Attractions

Discover the latest movies, live shows, concerts, sports, family activities and more.

Travel & Hotels

Featuring the best-known names in travel, cruises, car rentals, airfare, hotels and more!

Retail & Services

Pick up savings at your favorite national and local retailers.

Find It Fast!

Start Using Your Book Today and Remember to Register at...

www.entertainment.com/register

You Must Register To Fully Activate Your Membership

Activate your membership at
www.entertainment.com/register

You must register to fully activate your membership

Activate your membership at
www.entertainment.com/register

See the Rules of Use at the back of your book for details on using your Entertainment® membership card.

New discounts are added daily and waiting for you on entertainment.com

- 50% off discounts not found in your book
- Ongoing discounts—save again and again with your membership card
- $1,000s in travel savings—hotels, car rentals, cruises and more
- Discount movie tickets—as low as $5.50
- Easy search—see where you can save in your neighborhood

www.entertainment.com/register

Printed in U.S.A.

1106-IN000001

SAFEWAY
Your Select Savings Start Here.
Save $20
SAFEWAY COUPON VALID 11/05 - 1/06
Use your Safeway Club Card to enjoy
$5.00 OFF
Any Grocery Purchase of $50 or more during any single shopping trip.*
*Maximum discount of $5.00 per shopper, per quarter. Valid at all Safeway stores in Maryland, Delaware, Washington D.C. and Virginia. Offer valid Quarterly. *Restrictions apply. See reverse side of coupon for more information.
SAFEWAY COUPON VALID 2/06 - 4/06
Use your Safeway Club Card to enjoy
$5.00 OFF
Any Grocery Purchase of $50 or more during any single shopping trip.*
*Maximum discount of $5.00 per shopper, per quarter. Valid at all Safeway stores in Maryland, Delaware, Washington D.C. and Virginia. Offer valid Quarterly. *Restrictions apply. See reverse side of coupon for more information.
SAFEWAY COUPON VALID 5/06 - 7/06
Use your Safeway Club Card to enjoy
$5.00 OFF
Any Grocery Purchase of $50 or more during any single shopping trip.*
*Maximum discount of $5.00 per shopper, per quarter. Valid at all Safeway stores in Maryland, Delaware, Washington D.C. and Virginia. Offer valid Quarterly. *Restrictions apply. See reverse side of coupon for more information.
SAFEWAY COUPON VALID 8/06 - 10/06
Use your Safeway Club Card to enjoy
$5.00 OFF
Any Grocery Purchase of $50 or more during any single shopping trip.*
*Maximum discount of $5.00 per shopper, per quarter. Valid at all Safeway stores in Maryland, Delaware, Washington D.C. and Virginia. Offer valid Quarterly. *Restrictions apply. See reverse side of coupon for more information.
AA1
Ingredients for life. SAFEWAY

Excludes purchases of alcoholic beverages, tobacco, U.S. postage stamps, Metro Flash Passes or Tokens, Amusement Park Passes, bus/commuter passes, gasoline service sales, money orders, container deposits, Lottery tickets, gift cards, gift certificate sales, all pharmacy prescription purchases, Safeway Club Card savings, Safeway store coupons and sales tax. One coupon per visit. Coupon must be presented with Safeway Club Card. Final grocery purchase is determined after all manufacturer's coupons and electronic checkout coupons and exclusions have been presented and deducted from the grand total at the cash register. Not valid with any other offer. Coupons are not valid for online purchases and cannot be copied or duplicated for redemption.

Excludes purchases of alcoholic beverages, tobacco, U.S. postage stamps, Metro Flash Passes or Tokens, Amusement Park Passes, bus/commuter passes, gasoline service sales, money orders, container deposits, Lottery tickets, gift cards, gift certificate sales, all pharmacy prescription purchases, Safeway Club Card savings, Safeway store coupons and sales tax. One coupon per visit. Coupon must be presented with Safeway Club Card. Final grocery purchase is determined after all manufacturer's coupons and electronic checkout coupons and exclusions have been presented and deducted from the grand total at the cash register. Not valid with any other offer. Coupons are not valid for online purchases and cannot be copied or duplicated for redemption.

Excludes purchases of alcoholic beverages, tobacco, U.S. postage stamps, Metro Flash Passes or Tokens, Amusement Park Passes, bus/commuter passes, gasoline service sales, money orders, container deposits, Lottery tickets, gift cards, gift certificate sales, all pharmacy prescription purchases, Safeway Club Card savings, Safeway store coupons and sales tax. One coupon per visit. Coupon must be presented with Safeway Club Card. Final grocery purchase is determined after all manufacturer's coupons and electronic checkout coupons and exclusions have been presented and deducted from the grand total at the cash register. Not valid with any other offer. Coupons are not valid for online purchases and cannot be copied or duplicated for redemption.

Excludes purchases of alcoholic beverages, tobacco, U.S. postage stamps, Metro Flash Passes or Tokens, Amusement Park Passes, bus/commuter passes, gasoline service sales, money orders, container deposits, Lottery tickets, gift cards, gift certificate sales, all pharmacy prescription purchases, Safeway Club Card savings, Safeway store coupons and sales tax. One coupon per visit. Coupon must be presented with Safeway Club Card. Final grocery purchase is determined after all manufacturer's coupons and electronic checkout coupons and exclusions have been presented and deducted from the grand total at the cash register. Not valid with any other offer. Coupons are not valid for online purchases and cannot be copied or duplicated for redemption.

Ingredients for life.

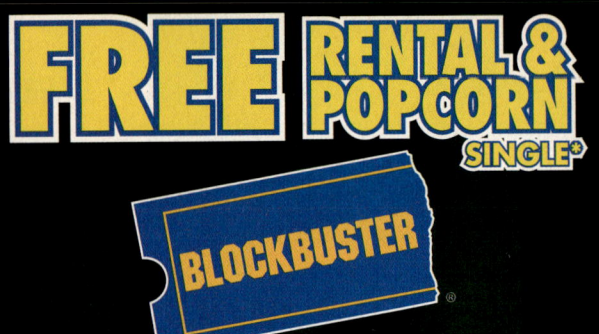

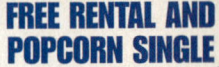

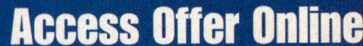

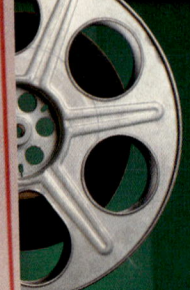

Sign up to receive a free one-month trial of the BLOCKBUSTER Online™ Subscription, with up to three (3) movies out at a time. Offer valid for new customers only; limit one free trial offer per household. You must have Internet access and provide a valid e-mail address and a valid credit card or check card to participate in the free trial or to subscribe to BLOCKBUSTER Online™. If you do not cancel your free trial membership before it expires, the credit or check card provided will be charged the applicable monthly membership fee (plus taxes) beginning on the first day after the end of the free trial and continuing monthly thereafter until canceled. If you cancel your free trial, BLOCKBUSTER Online rentals must be returned no later than ten (10) days past the expiration date of your free trial to avoid additional charges.

Sign up at blockbuster.com and enter promo code pmentpub (promo code is case sensitive)

VALID THROUGH 12/31/2006

Not valid holidays & subject to Rules of Use. Not valid with other discount offers, unless specified. Coupon VOID if purchased, sold or bartered.

Order Form

Each BLOCKBUSTER® Movie Card will be valid for at least six months from the ship date.

Please complete this form with the number of rentals and attach a check or money order made out to: Entertainment Publications, Inc., for the total amount plus shipping and handling of $2.25 for orders valued at $39.99 or less and $5.50 for orders valued at $40.00 or more. Do not send cash. Mail to: Entertainment Publications, Inc.
c/o RENTAL CARDS
P.O. Box 539
Duncan, SC 29334-5390

Entertainment will fulfill the BLOCKBUSTER® Movie Cards and approximately three weeks will be needed for delivery of BLOCKBUSTER® Movie Cards. Movie Cards may not be exchanged or returned for a refund. Call 1-877-814-5292 only if you have ordered more than three weeks ago and have not received your order.

# of rentals		Cost per rental		Total
10	x	3.40	=	$34.00
20	x	3.40	=	$68.00
30	x	3.40	=	$102.00
______	x	3.40	=	$_______._____
		shipping & handling	=	$_______._____
		TOTAL DUE	=	$_______._____

Name: ______________________________

Address: ______________________________

City: ____________________ State: ____________________ ZIP: ____________________

Daytime Phone: (   ) ______________________________

VALID THROUGH 12/31/2006

BLOCKBUSTER® Movie Card is subject to complete terms and conditions found on card. Membership rules apply for rental at BLOCKBUSTER®.

Rent 2 Get One Free BLOCKBUSTER Favorite of equal or lesser value

Free and paid rentals must be in same transaction. Excludes equipment, defensive driving rentals (VHS or DVD) and game rentals. Not valid with any other discounts or offers. This barcode only permits redemption of this coupon one time on one membership account. Limit one coupon of this type per membership account per day. Customer responsible for all applicable taxes and charges associated with rentals. See store for complete rental terms and conditions. This coupon may not be exchanged for cash, sold, transferred or reproduced and must be relinquished at the time of redemption. Any unauthorized reproduction, sale or transfer constitutes fraud. If customer rents multiple movies or games when redeeming this coupon, credit will be applied to lowest rental price. Void if lost or stolen. Cash redemption value 1/100¢. Offer valid only at participating BLOCKBUSTER® store locations. Membership rules apply for rentals at BLOCKBUSTER.

56102A00068

VALID 8/1/2005 THROUGH 1/31/2006

Subject to Rules of Use. Not valid with other discount offers, unless specified. Coupon VOID if purchased, sold or bartered.

Rent 2 Get One Free Movie, DVD or Game rental of equal or lesser value

Free and paid rentals must be in same transaction. Excludes equipment and defensive driving rentals (VHS or DVD). Not valid with any other discounts or offers. This barcode only permits redemption of this coupon one time on one membership account. Limit one coupon of this type per membership account per day. Customer responsible for all applicable taxes and charges associated with rentals. See store for complete rental terms and conditions. This coupon may not be exchanged for cash, sold, transferred or reproduced and must be relinquished at the time of redemption. Any unauthorized reproduction, sale or transfer constitutes fraud. If customer rents multiple movies or games when redeeming this coupon, credit will be applied to lowest rental price. Void if lost or stolen. Cash redemption value 1/100¢. Offer valid only at participating BLOCKBUSTER® store locations. Membership rules apply for rentals at BLOCKBUSTER.

56104R00068

VALID 2/1/2006 THROUGH 10/1/2006

Subject to Rules of Use. Not valid with other discount offers, unless specified. Coupon VOID if purchased, sold or bartered.

Valid now thru November 1, 2006

Up To $8.00 Value

Enjoy a FREE Appetizer or Dessert with the purchase of 2 entrees.

valid anytime

One offer, per party, per visit

See reverse side for details

AA6

Valid now thru November 1, 2006

Up To $8.00 Value

Enjoy a FREE Appetizer or Dessert with the purchase of 2 entrees.

valid anytime

One offer, per party, per visit

See reverse side for details

AA7

Valid now thru November 1, 2006

$5.00 Value

Enjoy $5 off with a minimum purchase of fifteen dollars (excluding tax, tip and alcoholic beverages).

valid anytime

One offer, per party, per visit

See reverse side for details

AA8

BENNIGAN'S

MARYLAND

Greenbelt
6002 Greenbelt Rd.
(301)982-9780

Laurel
14180 Baltimore Ave.
(301)776-4412

Rockville
12276 Rockville Pike
(301)770-2594

Waldorf
35 St. Patrick's Dr.
(301)638-4200

VIRGINIA

Fairfax
11778 Upper Fair Oaks Mall
(703)691-2208

Falls Church
6290 Arlington Blvd.
(703)237-6288

Springfield
6632 Springfield Mall
(703)922-6004

MARYLAND

Greenbelt
6002 Greenbelt Rd.
(301)982-9780

Laurel
14180 Baltimore Ave.
(301)776-4412

Rockville
12276 Rockville Pike
(301)770-2594

Waldorf
35 St. Patrick's Dr.
(301)638-4200

VIRGINIA

Fairfax
11778 Upper Fair Oaks Mall
(703)691-2208

Falls Church
6290 Arlington Blvd.
(703)237-6288

Springfield
6632 Springfield Mall
(703)922-6004

Not valid holidays & subject to Rules of Use. Not valid with other discount offers, unless specified. Coupon VOID if purchased, sold or bartered. Discounts exclude tax, tip and/or alcohol, where applicable.

MARYLAND

Greenbelt
6002 Greenbelt Rd.
(301)982-9780

Laurel
14180 Baltimore Ave.
(301)776-4412

Rockville
12276 Rockville Pike
(301)770-2594

Waldorf
35 St. Patrick's Dr.
(301)638-4200

VIRGINIA

Fairfax
11778 Upper Fair Oaks Mall
(703)691-2208

Falls Church
6290 Arlington Blvd.
(703)237-6288

Springfield
6632 Springfield Mall
(703)922-6004

Not valid holidays & subject to Rules of Use. Not valid with other discount offers, unless specified. Coupon VOID if purchased, sold or bartered. Discounts exclude tax, tip and/or alcohol, where applicable.

MARYLAND

Greenbelt
6002 Greenbelt Rd.
(301)982-9780

Laurel
14180 Baltimore Ave.
(301)776-4412

Rockville
12276 Rockville Pike
(301)770-2594

Waldorf
35 St. Patrick's Dr.
(301)638-4200

VIRGINIA

Fairfax
11778 Upper Fair Oaks Mall
(703)691-2208

Falls Church
6290 Arlington Blvd.
(703)237-6288

Springfield
6632 Springfield Mall
(703)922-6004

Not valid holidays & subject to Rules of Use. Not valid with other discount offers, unless specified. Coupon VOID if purchased, sold or bartered. Discounts exclude tax, tip and/or alcohol, where applicable.

RED HOT & BLUE

Come for the Blues. Stay for the food.

RIBS • BBQ • SOUTHERN ENTRÉES • SALADS

Take Red Hot & Blue home. Visit our convenient take out counter or call ahead and we'll have your order ready.

THEY'LL THANK YOU WITH THEIR MOUTHS FULL.

www.redhotandblue.com

$5 OFF $20

Enjoy $5 off with a minimum purchase of $20 dollars.

Maximum value $5.00

(excluding tax, tip & alcoholic beverages)

Dine In/Take Out only. One coupon per table per visit. No cash value. No reproductions. Good on full priced menu items only. Valid at participating restaurants. See reverse side for locations. Coupon expires 12/31/2006

RED HOT & BLUE

See reverse side for details

AA11

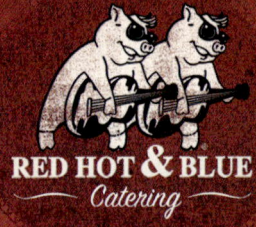

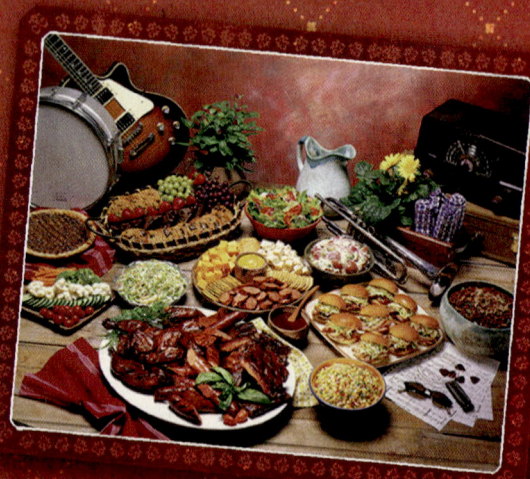

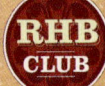

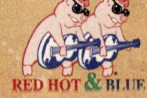

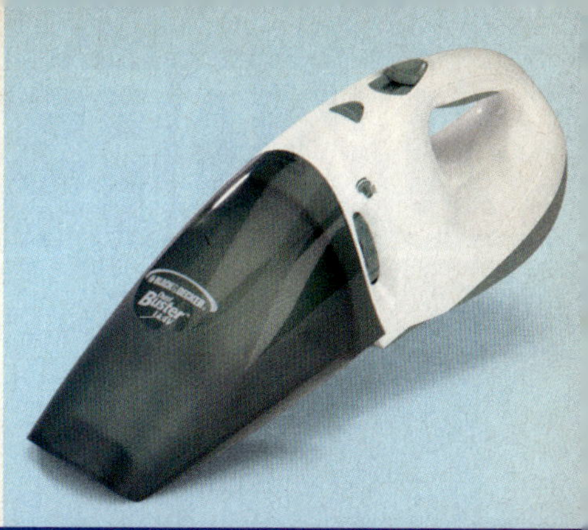

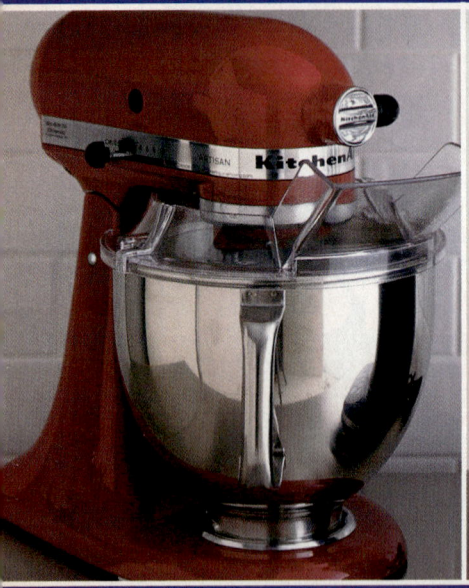

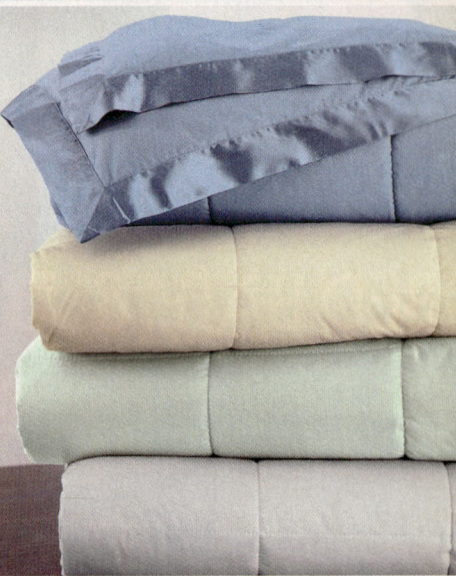

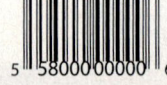

Foot Locker

Lady Foot Locker

kids Foot Locker

*Coupon must be presented at the time of purchase and cannot be used in conjunction with any other coupon, discount offer or associate benefit. Not redeemable for cash. Applicable taxes must be paid by bearer. Cannot be applied to previous purchase, purchase of gift card, Internet or catalog purchases. Valid for one use only. Void where prohibited, licensed or regulated. Valid in the U.S. and its territories only. Some exclusions apply. See store associate for details. Call 1-800-991-6681 to locate a store near you.

Key Code: 96

Subject to Rules of Use. Not valid with other discount offers, unless specified. Coupon VOID if purchased, sold or bartered for cash.

Valid August 1, 2005 thru January 31, 2006

Foot Locker

Lady Foot Locker

kids Foot Locker

*Coupon must be presented at the time of purchase and cannot be used in conjunction with any other coupon, discount offer or associate benefit. Not redeemable for cash. Applicable taxes must be paid by bearer. Cannot be applied to previous purchase, purchase of gift card, Internet or catalog purchases. Valid for one use only. Void where prohibited, licensed or regulated. Valid in the U.S. and its territories only. Some exclusions apply. See store associate for details. Call 1-800-991-6681 to locate a store near you.

Key Code: 96

Subject to Rules of Use. Not valid with other discount offers, unless specified. Coupon VOID if purchased, sold or bartered for cash.

Valid February 1, 2006 thru June 30, 2006

Foot Locker

Lady Foot Locker

kids Foot Locker

*Coupon must be presented at the time of purchase and cannot be used in conjunction with any other coupon, discount offer or associate benefit. Not redeemable for cash. Applicable taxes must be paid by bearer. Cannot be applied to previous purchase, purchase of gift card, Internet or catalog purchases. Valid for one use only. Void where prohibited, licensed or regulated. Valid in the U.S. and its territories only. Some exclusions apply. See store associate for details. Call 1-800-991-6681 to locate a store near you.

Key Code: 96

Subject to Rules of Use. Not valid with other discount offers, unless specified. Coupon VOID if purchased, sold or bartered for cash.

Valid July 1, 2006 thru December 31, 2006

Fine & Casual Dining Index

(Card # is indicated in parentheses)

kids **Great Place for Kids!** NEW **New Merchants Added This Year**

Fine & Casual Dining Index
(Card # is indicated in parentheses)

kids Great Place for Kids! NEW New Merchants Added This Year

Fine & Casual Dining Index
(Card # is indicated in parentheses)

kids Great Place for Kids! NEW New Merchants Added This Year

Fine & Casual Dining Index

(Card # is indicated in parentheses)

kids **Great Place for Kids!** NEW **New Merchants Added This Year**

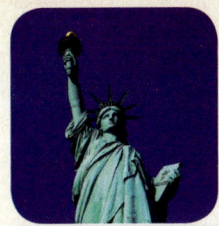

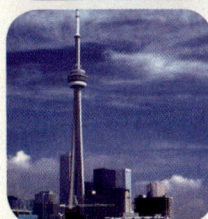

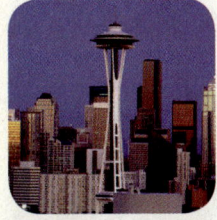

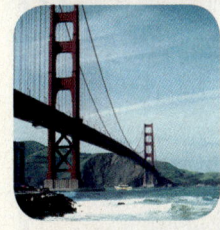

Card No. 3

Up To $25.00 Value

POTOWMACK LANDING®

www.potowmacklanding.com

Enjoy one complimentary LUNCH OR DINNER ENTREE when a second LUNCH OR DINNER ENTREE of equal or greater value is purchased.

Dine in only

valid anytime

Gratuity will be added

Potowmack Landing, a "Contemporary American Fish House", located on Daingerfield Island at the Washington Sailing Marina off the G.W. Pkwy. - features outstanding cuisine including a varied menu of fresh seafood, pastas, steaks & regional specialties along with a spectacular view. We look forward to serving you.

One Marina Dr.
Alexandria, VA
(703)548-0001

entertainment®
entertainment.com

Discounts exclude tax,tip and/or alcohol where applicable
Offers not valid holidays and subject to Rules of Use
Tipping should be 15% to 20% of the total bill before discount

00597298

POTOWMACK LANDING®

Entrees

***Bay Scallop & Pancetta Pizza* …$11**
Sun Dried Tomato Pesto, Bermuda Onion, Gouda, Mozzarella & Asiago

***Grilled Balsamic Marinated Portabello* …$17**
Baby Beet Risotto, Rosemary-Garlic Stewed Tomatoes & Garlicky Spinach

***Half Roasted Chicken* …$18**
Buttered Egg Noodles, Artichokes, Capers, Lemon & Garlic

***White Marble Farms Pork Schnitzel* …$19**
Buttermilk Mashed Potatoes, Today's Vegetables and a Jagermeister Gravy

***Nantucket Cod Ragout* …$20**
Braised Winter Vegetables, Basmatti Rice & Saffron-Tomato Broth

***Chipotle BBQ Glazed Salmon* …$20**
Herb Polenta, Today's Vegetables & Crisp Leeks

***Braised Lamb Shank* ..$22**
Baby Beet Risotto, Garlicky Spinach & Merlot-Thyme Pan Juices

***Grilled Center Cut Swordfish* …$24**
Russian Fingerling Potatoes, Today's Vegetables & Lemon Butter Sauce

***Baked Lobster, Scallop & Shrimp Pot Pie* …$25**
Leeks, Wild Mushrooms, Peas & a Flaky Crust

***Grilled 9 oz Filet Mignon* …$27**
Buttermilk Mashed Potatoes, Today's Vegetable & a Gorgonzola Demi Glace

***Whole Crispy Chesapeake Rockfish* …$27**
Herb Polenta, Rosemary-Garlic Stewed Tomatoes & a Lemon Butter Sauce

***Horseradish Crusted Chilean Sea Bass* …$27**
Buttermilk Mashed Potatoes, Grilled Asparagus & Lemon Butter Sauce

***Grilled Veal Chop* …$28**
Roasted Fingerling Potatoes, Today's Vegetable & a Merlot-Thyme Reduction

Card No. 4

Up To $17.00 Value

Nizam's Restaurant

SUPERB TURKISH CUISINE

www.nizamsrestaurant.com

Enjoy one complimentary DINNER ENTREE when a second DINNER ENTREE of equal or greater value is purchased.

Dine in only

valid any evening

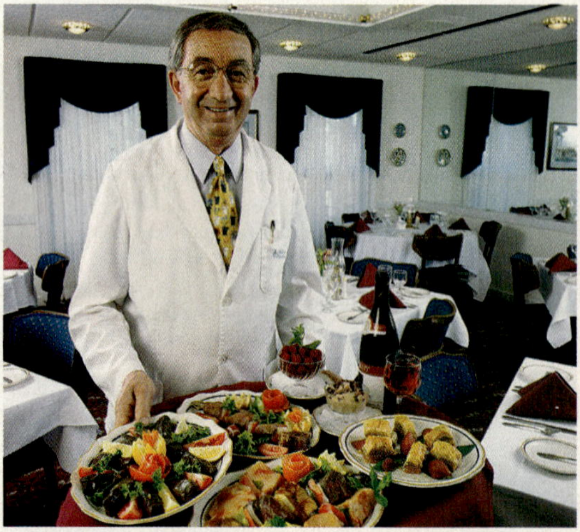

Visit award-winning Nizam's, rated among the Washingtonian's Top 50 & 100's, since 1984. We serve meat & fish kebabs of all types. Don't miss our famous doner kebab served Tues., Fri., Sat. & Sun. evenings. "Even Istanbul has no better doner kebab than Nizam's" raves Phyllis Richman of the Washington Post. We are open daily.

523 Maple Ave., W.
Vienna, VA
(703)938-8948

Discounts exclude tax,tip and/or alcohol where applicable
Offers not valid holidays and subject to Rules of Use
Tipping should be 15% to 20% of the total bill before discount

00627873

Nizam's Restaurant

SUPERB TURKISH CUISINE

Entrées

Yogurtlu Kebab 19.50
A famous Turkish dish layered with sautéed pita bread, yogurt sauce and slices of sautéed beef tenderloin, topped with a fresh tomato sauce.

Manti 16.95
Small pasta stuffed with spiced lean ground beef, served with yogurt garlic sauce and topped with fresh tomato sauce.

Tavuk Shish Kebab 15.95
Marinated chunks of chicken breast, skewered with onions, tomatoes, and green peppers. Served over rice.

Tavuk A'la Sultan 16.50
Chicken breast sautéed with garlic, oregano, fresh tomato and mushrooms, with melted mozzarella cheese on top. Served with rice and vegetable.

Musakka 15.25
An original Turkish dish with layers of eggplant, ground sirloin, and bechamel sauce, topped with cheese au gratin. Served with rice on the side.

Kuzu Incik 21.50
Turkish style lamb shank topped with eggplant, tomatoes, and green peppers. Served with rice.

Tavuk Hunkar Beyendi 16.50
Chunks of chicken breast broiled with onion, tomato and spices. Served over puréed eggplant with rice.

Filet of Broiled Salmon 18.50
Filet of fresh salmon broiled, served with lemon and olive oil sauce, vegetable and rice.

Filet of Red Snapper A'la Bosphorus 17.95
Red Snapper poached with mushrooms, tomato and onion. Served in a casserole dish layered with spinach, white wine sauce, and topped with cheese au gratin. Served with rice on the side.

Karides Shish Kebab 19.50
Jumbo shrimp skewered with onion, tomatoes, and green peppers topped with a light curry sauce. Served with rice and vegetable.

Kilic Shish Kebab 18.50
Marinated swordfish with onion, tomatoes, green peppers and bay leaves. Served with rice and vegetable.

Combination Seafood Shish Kebab 19.25
Marinated swordfish and shrimp broiled on the skewer. Served with rice pilaf and vegetable.

Turkish Shish Kebab (Beef or Lamb) 18.50
Select tender pieces of choice lamb or filet mignon, marinated in the Turkish tradition, alternately skewered with tomatoes, onions, and green peppers, char-grilled to order, served over rice pilaf.

Tas Kebab Beyendi 17.95
Chunks of lamb baked with onion, tomato, and spices, served over puréed eggplant.
Served with rice.

Efes Kebab 19.25
Combination of skewered filet mignon and shrimp, onions, tomatoes and green peppers broiled on the skewer and served over rice pilaf.

Kuzu Pirzola 19.95
Lamb chops marinated in oregano spices and grilled to order. Served with rice pilaf and vegetable.

Karısık Ízgara (Mixed Grilled Meats) 19.95
A selection of choice mixed grilled meats. Served with rice and vegetable.

Abant Kebab 17.25
A skewered combination of beef tenderloin and chicken breast, onions, tomatoes, and green peppers over rice pilaf.

Antep Kebab 16.50
Marinated ground lamb gently spiced, skewered and grilled. Served over sautéed chunks of pita and smoked eggplant, topped with tomatoes and green peppers.

Turkish Shish Köfte 16.50
Marinated ground lamb gently spiced and grilled, served over eggplant puree mixed with kasar cheese with rice pilaf.

Bursa Kebab 16.50
Marinated sliced chicken breast grilled and layered with sautéed pita bread, yogurt sauce and topped with a fresh tomato sauce.

Filet Mignon 21.95
Sautéed with mushroom sauce and grilled to your request. Served with rice pilaf and vegetable.

Eggplant Yogurtlu Kebab 14.95
Layered dish with sautéed pita bread, yogurt sauce and slices of eggplant, topped with a fresh tomato sauce.

Mixed Vegetable Kebab 14.95
Fresh vegetable kebab, marinated and charbroiled and served over rice pilaf with tomato sauce.

All entrées are served with bread, butter and salad with our own vinaigrette dressing.

Card No. 57

PANCHO VILLA
Mexican Restaurant

Up To $14.00 Value

Enjoy one complimentary LUNCH OR DINNER ENTREE when a second LUNCH OR DINNER ENTREE of equal or greater value is purchased.

Dine in only

valid anytime

Enjoy fine dining in a casual relaxing atmosphere. Pancho Villa offers authentic Mexican cuisine along with fast friendly service. When it comes to Mexican dining, we have it all. Let us make your next dining experience UNFORGETTABLE. Open daily.

155 Garrisonville Rd.
Stafford, VA
(540)658-0895

entertainment
entertainment.com

Discounts exclude tax,tip and/or alcohol where applicable
Offers not valid holidays and subject to Rules of Use
Tipping should be 15% to 20% of the total bill before discount

00661645

PANCHO VILLA

Mexican Restaurant

CAMARONES PACHECO 12.50
Five large shrimp stuffed with crabmeat, wrapped in bacon. Served with salad, beans, rice and warm tortillas (your choice of corn or flour). (Sour Cream and Guacamole available upon request)

CARNITAS 11.25
Tender chunks of pork; served with salad, rice, beans, pico de gallo, warm corn or flour tortillas. (Sour Cream & Guacamole available upon request)

CARNE ASADA 11.25
Boneless steak served with rice, beans, salad, pico de gallo, and warm corn or flour tortillas. (Sour Cream and Guacamole available upon request)

CAMARONES AL MOJO DE AJO........ 11.50
Shrimp sautéed in fresh garlic sauce, served with salad, beans, rice and warm corn or flour tortillas. (Sour Cream and Guacamole available upon request)

EL MEXICANO 8.25
Three taquitos, beef or chicken; with salad, beans and rice (Sour Cream and Guacamole available upon request)

FAJITAS TEXANAS
(Chicken-Beef-Shrimp)................................... **12.75**

Specialty Entrees

Mexican Paella
A traditional Mexican dish that includes: chicken, chorizo, shrimp, clams and Mussels in a bed of Mexican rice. Served in its original cooking pot!...$15.95

Mariscada Mexicana
A traditional Mexican dish that includes: clams, mussels, scallops, and a juicy Lobster in a rich seafood broth. Served with Mexican rice.................$19.95

Margarita Chicken & Shrimp
Delicious grilled chicken breast and juicy shrimp smothered in a thick margarita-Lime sauce. Served with rice and a fresh salad..............................$13.95

Russia House

Card No. 78

Up To $20.00 Value

Enjoy one complimentary DINNER ENTREE when a second DINNER ENTREE of equal or greater value is purchased or when dining alone - one DINNER ENTREE at 50% off the regular price - maximum discount $10.00.

valid any evening

Dine in an elegant yet simple dining room & gaze upon an assortment of Russian art depicting life in Russia. Featuring an interesting variety of appetizers, familiar entrees as well as Russian dishes. Our informative staff provides wonderful service. Strolling musicians perform on Friday & Saturday. Lunch is served Monday through Friday. Reservations recommended.

790 Station St.
Herndon, VA
(703)787-8880

00044813

Russia House

Zakuski

Zakuski Platter 8.95
Russian Hors D'oeuvres

Pirozhki 6.95
Puff Pastry stuffed with Meat, Cheese, and Cabbage

Salmon Roe Caviar 9.95
Served over Bliny and Garnish

American Sturgeon Caviar 21.95
Served with Bliniy or Toast and Garnish

Salati

Russia House Salad 4.95
Iceberg Lettuce, Radiccio, Cucumber, Tomato, House Dressing

Classical Caesar Salad 6.95
Prepared Table Side

Noodles

Russia House Noodles and Caviar 15.95
Fettucini topped with Caviar Lemon Butter Sauce

Ghiymya Hinkal 15.95
Pasta, Lamb, and Feta Cheese Casserole

Beef Pelmeni, *Russian Ravioli* 15.95
Cooked in Sour Cream Sauce

Pasta Russa 15.95
Sauteed Mushrooms and Onions over Fresh Fettucini

Ryba

Seafood

Lososina Alexander 20.95
Broiled Filet of Salmon with Champagne Sauce and Caviar

Forel Po-Armianski 18.95
Sauteed Filet of Rainbow Trout, with Artichoke Hearts, and Capers

Zharenaia Ryba Limonnaia 18.95
Sauteed Filet of Flounder with Garlic Lemon Herb Sauce

Shrimp Brochette 19.95
Grilled Shrimp on Skewer over Rice

Rakovinakh Po-Navogordoski 22.95
Sea Scallop, Mushrooms with Sun Dried tomato and White Wine Sauce

Les Entrée's

Basturma, Beef Shish Kebab 19.95
Marinated Juicy Beef Grilled on Skewer over Rice

The Alexander Steak 19.95
Sauteed Pepper Steak with Peppercorn Sauce

Grilled New York Strip 19.95
Served with Garlic Butter Sauce

Grilled Filet Mignon 23.95
Served with Bearnaise Sauce

Steak Nicholeia Flambe 23.95
Butterfly Filet Mignon, prepared Table Side

Bef Stoganov, Beef Stroganoff 23.95
Sliced Beef Tenderloin and Mushroom in a Creamy Sauce

Chateaubiand for Two 59.95
Served with Assorted Vegetables and Bearnaise Sauce

Myaso Po-tatarsky, Steak Tartare 23.95

Golubtsy, Stuffed Cabbage Leaves 15.95
Stuffed Cabbage Leaves with Beef

Kulebiaka Po-Baranina 18.95
Pastry Shell filled with Lamb, Rice, Vegetables, served with Tarragon Sauce

Lamb Shashlyk 15.95
Marinated Lamb on Skewer over Rice

Teliachia Limonnaia 18.95
Medallions of Veal with Lemon Herb Sauce

Telyatina Po Russki 19.95
Veal Medallions with Cream of Mushroom Sauce

Kostitsa de Porc La Gratar cu Muzhdei 15.95
Grilled Pork Chops with Garlic Sauce

Duck Breast with Sour Cherries 23.95
Sauteed Duck Breast topped with Sour Cherries

Georgian Duck 23.95
Sauteed Duck Breast with Russian Style Sauerkraut

Kotlety Po-Kievski, Chicken Kiev 15.65
Baked Breast of Chicken stuffed with Butter Tarragon Sauce

Tsyplionok Tapaka, Chicken Tapaka 17.95
Rock Cornish Hen, Flattened and Sauteed Georgian Style

Juja Kabob, Chicken on Skewer 15.95
Succulent Pieces of Grilled Chicken on Skewer over Rice

Tsyplionok Satsivi, Chicken Satsivi 16.95
Sauteed Breast of Chicken with Garlic and Walnut Sauce

Card No. 13

Up To $18.00 Value

MAMA'S
ITALIAN RESTAURANT

www.mamasitalianrestaurant.com

Enjoy one complimentary LUNCH OR DINNER ENTREE when a second LUNCH OR DINNER ENTREE of equal or greater value is purchased.

Dine in only

valid anytime

Welcome to Mama's Italian Restaurant. Celebrating over 40 years of quality service to Washington, DC. Mama Castro started the business in a small, storefront restaurant in Washington, DC in 1960. Over the past 40 years we have served millions of satisfied customers lunch, dinner, private parties & catered functions. Thank you for your patronage, buon appetito!!

9715 Lee Hwy.
Fairfax, VA
(703)385-2646

entertainment
entertainment.com

00611965

MAMA'S
ITALIAN RESTAURANT

Mama's Famous
ANTIPASTO BAR

Our signature antipasto bar featuring two kinds of homemade soups, dozens of salad toppings, fresh pizza and fresh fruit accompanies all of our entrees

Or You May Enjoy This Treat as an Entree 9.95

TRADITIONAL FAVORITES

Tortellini alla Panna 14.95
Tricolor cheese-filled pasta in a rich, creamy cheese sauce

Lasagna Classico 15.95
With layers of ricotta and meat sauce

Piatto Misto Italiano 16.95
Our popular combination platter of manicotti, cannelloni, lasagna and eggplant parmigiana

CARNE

Prime Rib 18.95
Tender prime rib cooked to order, served au jus with Mama's potatoes and fresh vegetables

Bistecca 20.95
A 12 oz. New York strip steak charbroiled to order, served with Mama's potatoes and fresh vegetables

VITELLO

Vitello alla Parmigiana 18.95
A large breaded slice of veal, dipped in egg batter, covered with layers of provolone cheese and tomato sauce with a side of pasta marinara

Vitello Française 19.95
Veal medallions sauteed in lemon butter and a touch of white wine, served with fresh vegetables and Fettuccini Alfredo

POLLO ALLA MAMA

Pollo alla Parmigiana 17.95
Boneless breast of chicken covered with tomato basil sauce and melted provolone cheese with a side of pasta

Pollo alla Marsala 18.95
Chicken breast medallions sauteed in shallots, mushroom and marsala wine sauce with a side of pasta marinara

PESCE

Gamberetti Fritti 19.95
Shrimp fried in garlic butter, lemon, white wine and fresh parsley, served with fresh vegetables and a side order of pasta marinara.

Calamari Fritti 18.95
Fresh squid sauteed in garlic egg batter, lemon and parsley with a dash of white wine, served with fresh vegetables and a side order of pasta marinara.

Flounder al Horno 19.95
Flounder baked and sauteed in our delicious lobster sauce with a pasta side.

Gamberetti alla Fradiavolo 19.95
Shrimp sauteed in our hot and spicy garlic and tomato sauce, served over linguini.

Card No. 14

Up To $18.00 Value

Stella's

www.stellas.com

Enjoy one complimentary DINNER ENTREE when a second DINNER ENTREE of equal or greater value is purchased.

valid any evening

New American cuisine in a 1946 setting. Our library bar is the perfect place to relax after work while our dining room offers comfortable booths & hardwood chairs & tables to enhance your dining experience. Complimentary three hour validated parking nightly after 5 p.m. Join us at Stella's for a memorable dining experience. Casual, affordable, & delicious.

1725 Duke St.
Alexandria, VA
(703)519-1946

entertainment
entertainment.com

Discounts exclude tax,tip and/or alcohol where applicable
Offers not valid holidays and subject to Rules of Use
Tipping should be 15% to 20% of the total bill before discount

00179503

Stella's

Entrees

Tangier Island Crabcakes

Broiled jumbo lump crabcakes served with fried cheese grits
and a sweet corn-green tomato ragout
18.99

Ahi Tuna with Nishiki Rice

Yellowfin tuna seared rare with wakame and nishiki rice cake-
served with soy ginger butter sauce and fried noodles
18.99

Free Range Chicken

House smoked with jerk spices served with redskin mashed potatoes,
haricot verts and a pineapple mango chutney
17.99

Seafood Linguine

Shrimp, scallops and mussels sautéed with shiitake mushrooms,
and white clam tomato sauce – tossed with linguine and finished with chevre
19.99

Roasted Vegetable Strudel

Roasted zucchini, squash, red peppers, carrots and chevre wrapped
in phyllo pastry and served with red pepper coulis over grilled polenta
15.99

Grilled Salmon

Glazed with an orange reduction and served with jasmine rice and sautéed asparagus
17.99

Pork Tenderloin

Marinated grilled pork tenderloin with sweet Italian sausage basmati rice,
haricot verts and a creamy shiitake mushroom sauce
17.99

New York Strip

Certified Black Angus New York Strip served over redskin mashed potatoes
with broccolini and finished with pinot noir pan gravy
24.99

Filet Mignon

Certified Black Angus filet mignon seared to order, served with béarnaise sauce,
sautéed spinach and a goat cheese potato cake
27.99

Grilled Swordfish

Topped with a chipotle beurre blanc served with roasted potatoes and sautéed spinach
18.99

Card No. 48

SEQUOIA

www.arkrestaurants.com

Up To $17.00 Value

Enjoy one complimentary LUNCH OR DINNER ENTREE when a second LUNCH OR DINNER ENTREE of equal or greater value is purchased.

valid anytime

Overlooking the Potomac River on Georgetown's waterfront is Washington, D.C.'s premier restaurant, Sequoia. Delightful dining in an elegant setting provides unsurpassed views of The John F. Kennedy Ctr. for the Performing Arts, The Watergate & the Historic Virginia Skyline. Join our hospitality M* Card program & visit us at www.arkrestaurant.com.

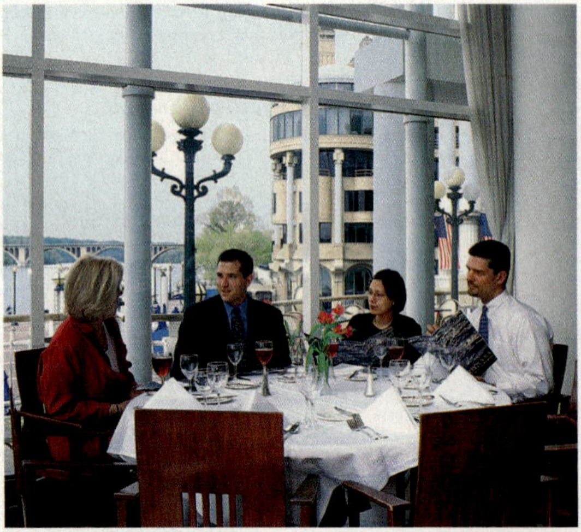

3000 K St.
(Washington Harbor)
Washington, DC
(202)944-4200

entertainment
entertainment.com

Discounts exclude tax,tip and/or alcohol where applicable
Offers not valid holidays and subject to Rules of Use
Tipping should be 15% to 20% of the total bill before discount

00397432

SEQUOIA

RAW BAR

Pristine Oysters on the Half Shell
Chef's selection of the finest oysters available 7.95

Chilled Half Maine Lobster
Accompanied by Sequoia coleslaw 13.95

Grand Sequoia Seafood Platter
A selection of lobster, shrimp, oysters, clams and mussels 28.95

PASTAS

Two Tomato Fedelini Pasta
Sundried and oven roasted tomatoes, topped with seasoned bread crumbs and shaved Grana Cheese 14.95

Gemelli Pasta with Asparagus
Asparagus, mushrooms, tomato and fresh goat cheese in a vegetable broth 16.95

Spinach & Cheese Agnolotti
Agnolotti pasta with sauteed shrimp, bay scallops & garlic pesto wine sauce 18.95

FISH

Pan Seared Sea Bass
With fresh vegetables and tempura potatoes in a Spicy Black Bean Sauce 19.95

Miso Glazed Salmon
Served with wasabi pureed potatoes and sautéed Asian vegetables 18.95

Chesapeake Bay Fresh Blue Crab Cake
Jumbo lump crab cake broiled to perfection 24.95

POULTRY - MEAT

Grilled Corn Fed Natural Chicken
Served with smashed potatoes and fresh vegetables 15.95

Oven Roasted Pekin Duck
Sautéed Asian vegetables, Jasmine Rice 19.95

Colleen's Filet
Char-grilled and topped with a Bordelaise Sauce 23.95

Card No. 25

Up To $18.00 Value

Founders' Restaurant & Brewing Co.

www.foundersbrew.com

Enjoy one complimentary LUNCH OR DINNER ENTREE when a second LUNCH OR DINNER ENTREE of equal or greater value is purchased.

Dine in only

valid anytime

Welcome to Founder's Restaurant & Brew Pub, where we pay tribute to the history of Alexandria by naming our German-style beers after prominent Alexandrians. Chef Winterling's passion for cooking is what makes Founder's a must when you are in the mood for a truely great meal. The food highlights an American cuisine with a Southwestern flavor. We are smoke free.

607 King St.
Alexandria, VA
(703)684-5397

entertainment
entertainment.com

Discounts exclude tax,tip and/or alcohol where applicable
Offers not valid holidays and subject to Rules of Use
Tipping should be 15% to 20% of the total bill before discount

00582225

FOUNDERS'
Restaurant & Brewing Co.

APPETIZERS

Crab and Artichoke Dip...$7.75
Fresh backfin crabmeat, tender artichokes and roasted red peppers simmered in sherry with cream-cheese Dijon mustard; served with Founders' chips

Founders' Wings...$6.75
Jumbo wings tossed in choice of hot or mild sauce; served with bleu-cheese dressing

Coconut Shrimp...$8.50
Large Gulf shrimp breaded with shredded coconut, deep fried; served with mango chutney

Chicken Quesadillas...$7.50
Flour tortillas stuffed with grilled chicken, bell peppers, mangos and Monterey Jack cheese, Served with salsa and sour cream Add guacamole for $1.00

SALADS

Spinach Salad...$7.50
Fresh spinach, oranges, avocado, shaved red onions, toasted walnuts, and julienne red tortilla chips; tossed with lemon chipotle vinaigrette

Santa Fe Chicken Salad...$8.75
Mixed greens tossed with roasted corn, sliced avocado, shredded carrots, diced tomatoes and topped with corn tortilla chips and diced fried chicken tenders

ENTREES

Habanero Grilled Salmon...$16.75
Grilled Atlantic salmon brushed with habanero pepper and honey glaze; served over pineapple and jalapeño pepper polenta and accompanied by the vegetable of the day

Southwestern Chicken Pasta...$13.75
Blackened chicken, sautéed with spicy andouille sausage, diced ham, red peppers and sweet onions; finished with a white-wine and cream sauce and tossed with tri-color penne pasta

Shrimp Scampi...$16.50
Fresh gulf shrimp sautéed with garlic, lemon, basil and white wine, served with angel hair pasta

Vegetable Pasta...$11.50
Portabella mushrooms, bell peppers, artichoke hearts, onions, and broccoli served over angel hair pasta and tossed with a garlic cream sauce

Baked Lasagna...$12.25
Spicy ground beef, lasagna noodles and Monterey jack cheese layered and baked in tomato sauce

Braised Chicken...$14.50
Tender half-chicken braised with sherry wine and baked with fresh vegetables; served over red rice

Panhandle Fajita...$12.75
Bell peppers and onions sautéed in a black iron skillet with either chicken or beef; served with flour tortillas, salsa, and sour cream

Caribbean Pork Chops...$16.75
Grilled center-cut pork chops smothered in rum and molasses BBQ sauce and topped with grilled pineapple salsa; served with bourbon mashed sweet potatoes and the vegetable of the day

Flank Steak Fairfax...$13.75
Grilled flank steak marinated in ginger and honey-teriyaki, served thinly sliced over horseradish mashed potatoes and accompanied by the vegetable of the day

Filet Mignon...$22.50
Filet wrapped in applewood bacon, then grilled and finished with a garlic demi-glaze; served with garlic mashed potatoes and vegetable of the day

N.Y. Strip...$19.75
Grilled N.Y. strip, with a balsamic vinegar reduction paste; served with baked potato and vegetable of the day

Lamb Chops...$18.75
Dijon mustard crusted lamb chops, pan seared and baked; served with butternut squash mashed potatoes and vegetable of the day, finished with a Barboursville

Card No. 19

MEDITERRANEE
LA CUISINE DU SOLEIL

Up To $17.00 Value

Enjoy one complimentary DINNER ENTREE when a second DINNER ENTREE of equal or greater value is purchased.

Dine in only; Prix-fix menu excluded

valid any evening

Friday & Saturday seating before 6:30 p.m. or after 8:30 p.m.

Mediterranee Restaurant is a quaint little French restaurant located just outside Tyson's Corner. We feature French Mediterranean cuisine. Owner/Chef Jacques Imperato welcomes you with his innovating cooking style. Mediterranee Restaurant is a neighborhood place where good food & a friendly atmosphere will meet you whenever you venture inside. Bon Appetit.

10123 Colvin Run Rd.
Great Falls, VA
(703)757-9300

entertainment.
entertainment.com

Discounts exclude tax,tip and/or alcohol where applicable
Offers not valid holidays and subject to Rules of Use
Tipping should be 15% to 20% of the total bill before discount

00635104

MEDITERRANEE
LA CUISINE DU SOLEIL

Dinner
A la Carte

Soup of the day	***5.95***
Fish soup with garlic bread, parmesan and rouille; aioli with saffron	***6.95***
Escargots sautéed in garlic butter over a Portobello wrapped in puffed pastry dough	***7.95***
Mix of tossed lettuce and salad with Dijon mustard vinaigrette	***5.95***
Country pâté served with apple and celery root remoulade	***7.95***
Roasted goat cheese in brick dough over a warm endive salad with basil, roasted bell pepper, garlic, lemon tarragon dressing	***8.95***

♦♦♦♦

Bouillabaisse; a combination of fish and seafood simmered in a rich broth with saffron, served with garlic bread and rouille; aioli with saffron	***21.95***
Cod fish coated with tapenade, wrapped in brick dough and grilled over a light tomato sauce	***17.95***
Sea scallops with fava bean hummus, sun dried tomatoes and asparagus, served in a white wine sauce	***19.95***
Rockfish grilled over Socca; a chick pea crêpe, stuffed with garlic confit, basil, grilled zucchini, eggplant and tomato salad in a balsamic reduction sauce	***21.95***
Beef tenderloin sautéed over pistachio and shiitake mushroom cake with five peppercorn sauce	***22.95***
Marinated chicken breast in ginger served with roasted garlic sauce	***16.95***

Card No. 1

SERBIAN CROWN

www.serbiancrown.com

Up To $20.00 Value

Enjoy one complimentary DINNER ENTREE when a second DINNER ENTREE of equal or greater value is purchased.

valid any evening

Saturday seating before 6 p.m. & after 8:30 p.m.

The award-winning Serbian Crown serves fine Russian & French cuisine. We feature a Piano Bar on Fri. & Sat. 10 p.m.-2 a.m. Russian Bayan & Balalaika Night every Sun. from 4 p.m.-9 p.m. Lunch served Tues.-Fri. Come help us celebrate our 25th anniversary.

1141 Walker Rd.
Great Falls, VA
(703)759-4150

entertainment.
entertainment.com

Discounts exclude tax,tip and/or alcohol where applicable
Offers not valid holidays and subject to Rules of Use
Tipping should be 15% to 20% of the total bill before discount

00403761

SERBIAN CROWN

Les Poissons
(Seafood)

Broiled Rainbow Trout 'Armenian Style' — 19.95
(Pelchonaya Forel' po Armianski)

Cold Lobster 'Russian Style' (1 ½ pounds) — 29.50
(Kholodny Omar po Russki)

Dover Sole Meunière — 27.95
(Doverski Paltus s Podlivkoi)

Grilled Swordfish w/ Béarnaise Sauce — 23.00
(Mech-Riba na Vertele v Masle)

Grilled Salmon Steak w/ White Butter Sauce — 23.00
(Lososina na Vertele v Masle)

Les Gibiers et Volailles
(Wild Game and Poultry)

Emu w/ Green Peppercorn Sauce — 29.50
(Strouss v Zelenom Perzovom Souse)

Antelope w/ Wild Mushrooms and Port Wine Sauce — 29.50
(Antilopa s Lesnimi Gribami v Portweinom Souse)

Rabbit 'Russian Style', Marinated in Sour Cream — 22.95
(Krolik po Russki Marinovanny v Smetane)

Venison St. Hubert w/ Marsala Sauce — 25.95
(Olenina s Sousom Marsala)

Molard Duck, Braised in Sour Kraut — 25.95

Les Spécialités
(Specialties)

Broiled Loin of Lamb 'Bubreznjak' — 25.50
(Baranie File v Dukhovke)

Half Rack of Lamb 'Prolece' — 29.50
(Sedlo Barashka)

Veal Chop 'Orloff' — 29.50
(Telyachuya Otbivnaya 'Orlov')

Beef Stroganoff — 25.50
(Bef Stroganof)

Veal Cutlets 'Soblianka' w/ Morille Sauce — 25.50
(Eskalop iz Telyatini s Sousom 'Morille')

Card No. 28

Eiffel Tower Cafe

Up To $17.00 Value

www.eiffeltowercafe.com

Enjoy one complimentary DINNER ENTREE when a second DINNER ENTREE of equal or greater value is purchased.

Dining room only

valid any evening

Friday & Saturday seating before 6 p.m. or after 8:30 p.m.; Reservations suggested; Special event nights excluded

This pretty French restaurant sits on the ground floor of one of Leesburg's historical homes & looks like a cross between a Victorian tea room & a private dining room. The kitchen serves a classic French fare, with the menu changing every several months. There is something here to please any taste. Bon Appetit. Closed for dinner Sunday & Monday.

107 Loudoun St., SW
Leesburg, VA
(703)777-5142

entertainment
entertainment.com

Discounts exclude tax,tip and/or alcohol where applicable
Offers not valid holidays and subject to Rules of Use
Tipping should be 15% to 20% of the total bill before discount

00398528

Eiffel Tower Cafe

Evening Menu

Le potage du soir 6.25

The traditional Ceasar salad 9.25

The house terrine with garnish and toasted French baguette 8.25

Sauteed shrimp and sea scallops with a lobster sauce risotto
and sezchouan pepper 24.75

Filet of Red Snaper with Lobster Beurre Blanc 23.95

Roasted Maine Lobster with Cognac Lobster Sauce 29.45

Sauteed Monkfish with red and orange pepper coulis
and seasonal vegetables 22.95

Beef Medaillons with mashed potatoes, vegetables
and sauce Roquefort 28.50

Filet of Venison, sauce Grand Veneur 29.25

Duck aiguillettes marinated in sezchouan pepper 23.50

Pork tenderloin with mustard sauce 22.75

Rack of lamb with garlic cream, rosemary jus,
and tomatoes Provencals 28.75

Card No. 59

PAYA THAI

THAI CUISINE AND WINE BAR

www.payathai.com

Up To $15.00 Value

Enjoy one complimentary DINNER ENTREE when a second DINNER ENTREE of equal or greater value is purchased.

Dine in only

valid any evening

The ultimate in Thai Cuisine, located in Tysons Corner, VA. Paya Thai restaurant serves the finest fresh fish dishes & a complete list of other entrees & appetizers seasoned to your request. Take advantage of free delivery options within the local area for both lunch & dinner. Paya Thai also caters meetings & parties.

8417 Old Courthouse Rd.
(at Rte. 123 in Tysons Corner)
Vienna, VA
(703)883-3881

entertainment.
entertainment.com

Discounts exclude tax,tip and/or alcohol where applicable
Offers not valid holidays and subject to Rules of Use
Tipping should be 15% to 20% of the total bill before discount

00614616

PAYA THAI

THAI CUISINE AND WINE BAR

NOODLES AND RICE

	chicken, beef or pork lunch	chicken, beef or pork dinner	scallop shrimp & squid lunch	scallop shrimp & squid dinner
PAD THAI	6.95	8.95	8.95	11.95

(Sauteed Thai noodles with a choice of chicken or shrimp, dried bean curd, bean sprouts, chive and peanuts)

CRABMEAT FRIED RICE WITH EGG 11.95

ENTRÉES

	chicken, beef or pork lunch	chicken, beef or pork dinner	shrimp lunch	shrimp dinner
PAD PRIK KA-PRAO	7.95	8.95	9.95	11.95
(Your choice of meat, sauteed with fresh chili peppers, basil leaves, and onions in light brown sauce)				
GREEN CURRY OR RED CURRY	8.95	9.95	10.95	12.95
(Your choice of meat, sauteed with green or red curry paste, bamboo shoots, mushrooms, basil leaves, chili peppers and coconut milk)				
BROCCOLI IN GARLIC SAUCE	8.95	9.95	10.95	12.95
(Your choice of meat, sauteed with broccoli in garlic sauce)				

VEGETARIAN ENTREES

	lunch	dinner
MIXED VEGETABLES IN CURRY	7.95	9.95

(Sauteed carrots, broccoli, snow peas, baby corns, bamboo shootsmushrooms and tofu with basil leaves , chili peppers in green curry paste and coconut milk)

CHEF'S SPECIALTIES

HONEY ROASTED DUCK 13.95
(Served with steamed watercress and our chef's special sauce)

SESAME BEEF 13.95
(Sliced, marinated beef with sesame oil and our chef's sauce served on a sizzling plate with steamed string beans and carrots)

RED CURRY SALMON 14.95
(Salmon sauteed with red curry paste, bamboo shoots, mushrooms, basil leaves, chili pepper and coconut milk)

SPICY SEAFOOD 14.95
(Shrimp, squid, scallops and mussels stir-fried with chili sauce, carrots, onion and basil leaves)

STEAMED WHOLE FISH market price
(Whole steamed rockfish in lemon grass seasoning served with house special hot sauce)

FISH IN GINGER SAUCE market price
(Whole deep-fried crispy flounder topped with ginger, mushrooms, celery, onions in ginger sauce)

Card No. 49

Up To $14.00 Value

Sala Thai

RESTAURANT

AUTHENTIC THAI CUISINE

www.salathaidc.com

Enjoy one complimentary LUNCH OR DINNER ENTREE when a second LUNCH OR DINNER ENTREE of equal or greater value is purchased.

valid anytime

Sala Thai is recognized as one of the best Thai kitchens in town. An early pioneer on P Street restaurant row, serving D.C. for over 12 years. "It lifts sophistication of Southeast Asia dining several notches" Phyllis Richman, Washington Post. Received Best Bargain honors by the Post. Visit our newest location in Arlington for contemporary Thai dining.

2016 P St., NW
(Dupont Circle Metro)
Washington, DC
(202)872-1144

3507 Connecticut Ave., NW
(Cleveland Park)
Washington, DC
(202)237-2777

2900 N. 10th St.
Arlington, VA
(703)465-2900

Coming Soon: Sala Thai U St., 1301 U St. N.W., Washington, D.C. 20009

entertainment
entertainment.com

Discounts exclude tax,tip and/or alcohol where applicable
Offers not valid holidays and subject to Rules of Use
Tipping should be 15% to 20% of the total bill before discount

00468208

Sala Thai

RESTAURANT

AUTHENTIC THAI CUISINE

SOUP

TOM YUM GOONG Shrimp and mushrooms in hot and sour lemon grass soup.	3.95

APPETIZERS

SALA THAI DUMPLING Steamed crabmeat, shrimp and minced pork wrapped in wonton skin.	4.95
TOD MUNN Fried curried fish cake, served with cucumber sauce.	4.95
LA-AB GAI Minced chicken mixed with Thai spices and lemon juice.	5.25
YUM TALAY Shrimp, squid and scallops mixed with Thai spices, hot chili and lemon juice.	6.95

ENTREES

PAD THAI P STREET A Thai specialty of noodles sautéed with shrimp, and fresh bean sprout.	7.95
PAD MAH KUA Sautéed eggplant with pork, beef, chicken or shrimp In spicy black bean sauce with basil leave.	8.95
With Shrimp	9.95
SALA THAI CURRY SPECIAL Traditional Thai style curry with your choice of:	
• Red curry roasted duck	9.25
• Red curry chicken or beef	8.50
• Red curry shrimp	9.95
• Green curry with chicken or beef	8.50
• Green curry with shrimp	9.95
• Vegetable curry	8.25
PANANG GAI	8.95
PANANG GOONG Chicken or shrimp in curry peanut sauce.	11.95
NUA KRA TING TONE Spicy beef with onion, garlic, and parsley sauce.	9.95
WILD CHIC Grilled chicken breast sautéed with asparagus in red curry sauce.	9.95
POTTERY SHRIMP Baked shrimp, cellophane noodles with exotic Thai herbs served on the side with chili sauce.	11.95
PU-NIM Crispy soft shell crab with: • Hot chili and garlic • Celery in curry sauce.	Seasonal
CATCH OF THE DAY Grilled, steamed, crispy fried.	Seasonal

entertainment Card No. 15

Tempo

restaurant

www.temporestaurant.com

Up To $14.00 Value

Enjoy one complimentary LUNCH OR DINNER ENTREE when a second LUNCH OR DINNER ENTREE of equal or greater value is purchased.

Dine in only

valid anytime

Friday & Saturday seating before 6 p.m. or after 8 p.m.

Tempo is an elegant but unpretentious setting for the inspired cuisine of husband & wife chefs, Serge & Wendy Albert. For pure dining pleasure in an elegant atmosphere, enjoy Tempo's contemporary cuisine. Complement your meal with a bottle of wine & one of our homemade desserts.

4231 Duke St.
Alexandria, VA
(703)370-7900

entertainment®
entertainment.com

Discounts exclude tax,tip and/or alcohol where applicable
Offers not valid holidays and subject to Rules of Use
Tipping should be 15% to 20% of the total bill before discount

00173046

Tempo

restaurant

Pasta

Conchigliette "Tempo" $12.95
Pasta shells with cured Salmon and cream.

Capelli d'Angelo Napoletana $12.95
Very thin egg pasta with tomato, garlic, and basil.

Cavatelli "Amatriciana" $12.95
Pasta with bacon, tomato, and parmesan cheese.

Tortellini "Tricolore" $12.95
Tri-color cheese Tortellini with ham, mushrooms, and gratine.

Linguine con Broccoli Rabe E Granchio $14.95
Thin pasta with garlic, broccoli rabe and Crabmeat.

Linguine "Frutti di Mare" $16.95
Linguini with Seafood in a light tomato sauce.

Rigatoni Putanesca $12.95
With tomato, capers, olives, and anchovies.

(We can split pasta for two as an appetizer)

Seafood

Fritto Misto $16.95
Crisply fried Calamari, Sole, Scallops, Shrimp, and zucchini.

Coquilles "Anna" $15.95
Sea Scallops with ginger, garlic, and spring onions.

Saumon Pomme d'Amour $15.95
Poached Salmon, tomato, basil, and creamy white wine sauce.

Sanglier de Mer au Four $15.95
Red Snapper with shallots and fresh herbs.

Truite "Sambal" $15.95
Mountain Trout, julienne asparagus, shiitakes, hot and sour sambal sauce.

Poisson du Golfe $15.25
Mahi-mahi with lime juice, garlic, and cilantro.

Sole Amandine $15.95
Filet of Sole with almonds and sun dried tomatoes.

Meat

Scaloppine di Vitello "Rosa" $15.95
Veal Scaloppini with sweet red peppers, garlic, oregano, and tomato.

Scaloppine di Vitello Marsala $15.95
Veal Scaloppini with fresh mushrooms and marsala wine.

Scaloppine di Vitello "Rosemary" $15.95
Veal Scaloppini with fresh rosemary, cream, and dijon mustard.

Medaillon de Boeuf au Roquefort* $17.95
Tenderloin with Roquefort cheese, mustard, and cream.

Steak Diablo* $17.95
New York Strip steak with black pepper and whole mustard seed.

Pollo alla Vesuviana $14.95
Breast of Chicken with eggplant, tomato, and mozzarella.

Poulet "Printemps" $14.95
Breast of Chicken with mushrooms and vegetables.

Chicken Colleene $14.95
Breast of Chicken with feta, dill, and cracked black pepper.

Cotelette d'Agneau aux Herbes* $16.95
Lamb Chops with shallots, fresh herbs, and wine sauce.

Mansion House
RESTAURANT

Card No. 35

Up To $25.00 Value

Enjoy one complimentary DINNER ENTREE when a second DINNER ENTREE of equal or greater value is purchased.

Dining room only

valid any evening

The Mansion House Restaurant, located inside the Holiday Inn at historic Carradoc Hall, offers an experience like no other. Set on eight picturesque acres with grand old trees and natural springs, the focal point is a beautiful 18th century mansion. The historic mansion provides a wonderful, warm atmosphere for dining, an experience not to be missed.

1500 E. Market St.
Leesburg, VA
(703)771-9200

entertainment
entertainment.com

00400137

Mansion House

RESTAURANT

SOUPS

Country Tomato & Basil - $4.00
Slow simmered vegetables and tomatoes scented with basil.

Roasted Sweet Corn Chowder - $5.00
Topped with fresh crab meat and chives

WILD GREENS

Simple Tossed Greens - $4.00
Mixed wild greens tossed in herb vinaigrette.

Caesar - $5.00
Crispy romaine hearts, croutons and Parmesan in a creamy Caesar dressing.

Spinach - $7.00
Baby spinach tossed with toasted pecans, sweet onions and oranges in a light poppy seed vinaigrette

Many Layered - $8.00
Baby spinach, wild greens, romaine, tomatoes, crispy bacon, sweet onions, Parmesan and Bleu cheese tossed in red wine vinaigrette

MAIN ENTREES

Portobello Wellington - $14.00
Roasted Portobello mushroom stuffed with sauteed spinach and goat cheese, wrapped in a flaky pastry dough with a sweet pepper sauce

Chicken Scaloppini - $16.00
Scaloppini of chicken sauteed with button mushrooms, garlic and Parmesan cream. Served with Fettuccini and asparagus

Salmon with Wilted Spinach - $21.00
Fire roasted salmon filet on a bed of wilted spinach, drizzled with a lemon cream sauce. Served with whipped potatoes.

Fettuccini with Lobster - $21.00
Medallions of lobster sauteed with wild mushrooms, garlic and herbs tossed with Fettuccini and served with asparagus

Stuffed Lobster - $28.00
Split lobster tail stuffed with jumbo lump crab, oven roasted and topped with Béarnaise sauce. Served with almond chive rice and asparagus.

Veal Oscar - $25.00
Medallions of veal sauteed in garlic and olive oil topped with fresh crab meat and Béarnaise sauce. Served with almond chive rice and asparagus

SIDES

Vegetable of the Day
Sautéed Asparagus with Béarnaise
Almond Chive Rice
Garlic Whipped Potatoes

SIMPLY GRILLED

All grilled items come with whipped potatoes and vegetables

Grilled Roasted Chicken - $17.00
Semi-boneless half chicken.

New York Club Steak - $23.00
Prepared on the bone to insure great flavor and richness

Char-Grilled Snapper - $21.00
Lightly seasoned and roasted

Grilled Prawns - $24.00
Garlic marinated and grilled.

Filet Mignon - $24.00
The most tender of all steaks

Cowboy Steak - $27.00
Fire roasted 14 ounce bone in rib eye.

Menu Sampler - Prices and offerings subject to change.

Card No. 60

John Mandis'

Market Inn

Restaurant

www.marketinndc.com

Up To $23 00 Value

Enjoy one complimentary DINNER ENTREE when a second DINNER ENTREE of equal or greater value is purchased.

Dining room only

valid any evening

Holidays excluded; Reservations recommended

The Market Inn has been a landmark in Southwest Washington since 1959, with the family ownership. We strive to serve seafood at its best and have 85 seafood and beef entrees. Featuring a "pick your own lobster" tank. Free valet parking in our lot next to restaurant serving dinner daily from 4:30 p.m. Visit our website for more information www.marketinndc.com.

200 E Street SW
(2nd & E St., SW)
Washington, DC
(202)554-2100

entertainment
entertainment.com

Discounts exclude tax,tip and/or alcohol where applicable
Offers not valid holidays and subject to Rules of Use
Tipping should be 15% to 20% of the total bill before discount

00152081

John Mandis'

Market Inn

Restaurant

Appetizers

Oysters Rockefeller, New Orleans (6)……7.95
Jumbo Shrimp Cocktail (6)……………8.50

Cold Hors D'Oeuvres for Two……
***Jumbo Shrimp, Oysters, & Clams, on the Half Shell (4 each)*……………………………14.95**

Try Our Soup Sampler…Pick Three of Our Famous Soups……..6.95

***She Crap Soup,** *Charleston Style,* **Snapper Turtle Soup, Crab Gumbo,** *New Orleans Style*
New England **Clam Chowder, or ****Maine* **Lobster Bisque**

Entrees

Baked Imperial Crab
with Fresh Lump Crab Meat
24.95

Baked Jumbo Shrimp
Stuffed with Imperial Crab
25.95

Jumbo Soft Shell Crabs (2) *Sauteed in Butter, or Deep Fried*………………….**22.95**
Our Famous Crab Cake Platter *Fried or Baked*…………………………………**21.95**

Jumbo Cajun Style Shrimp *with Cajun Herb Rice….Spicy*……………………….**21.95**
Shrimp Creole *New Orleans Style with Rice*…………………………………….**20.95**

Blackened Redfish
Seared Cajun Style
20.95

Fresh Swordfish or Tuna Steak,
Grilled or Broiled,
with Dill or Hollandaise Sauce
***Your choice* 22.95**

Fresh Fillet of Salmon *served with Dill Sauce*……………………………….**20.95**

Mariners' Platter, ***Fried Shrimp, Sea Scallops, Filet of Flounder, Crab Cake, & Oysters*……………………………………………………………24.95**
3-Way Seafood Combination, ***Lump Crabmeat, Lobster, & Shrimp,*** *Sauteed, Norfolk, Newburg or Au Gratin*…………………………………………………**23.95**
New England Lobster Bake, ***Half Maine Lobster, Oysters, Clams, Shrimp, & Corn on the Cob…*** *Steamed Together*…………………………………………**24.95**
Broiled Neptune Delight, ***Sea Scallops, Shrimp, Fillet of Orange Roughy, & Crab Cake*……………………………………………………………23.95**

Broiled Jumbo Filet Mignon *(10 oz)*……**24.95**
Broiled Extra Thick Pork Chops *(2)*…….**16.95**
Fresh Prime Ribs of Beef *(1 Pound Cut)*..**24.95**
Fresh Prime Ribs of Beef *(12 oz)*………..**21.95**

Shrimp & Sea Scallops *over Linguini, with a Light Basil Cream Sauce*………………….**20.95**
Fresh Poached Salmon *Flaked over Fusilli, with a Light Dill Sauce*…………………………..**20.95**
Old Fashioned Pork Spare Ribs *Served with Our Own Spicy Bar-B-Q Sauce*…………….**19.95**

Ship or Take Home our Famous She Crab Soup,
Lobster Bisque, and Crab Cakes
Call Toll-Free 866-288-CRAB or visit our website,
www.marketinndc.com
Makes a Great Gift for a Special Occasion!

Menu Sampler - Prices and offerings subject to change.

Card No. 36

Casablanca

Fine Moroccan Cuisine

Up To $22.00 Value

Enjoy one complimentary COMPLETE DINNER when a second COMPLETE DINNER of equal or greater value is purchased.

valid any evening

Reservations required

Taste the specialties of Morocco in an authentic Moroccan atmosphere. Dine with us at Casablanca and let us take you to exotic Morocco. Our romantic decor, costumed waiters and elegant belly dancer will take you there. Enjoy soft, relaxing music while you feast on any one of our delicacies. We're open daily. Reservations required.

1504 King St.
Alexandria, VA
(703)549-6464

entertainment.
entertainment.com

Discounts exclude tax,tip and/or alcohol where applicable
Offers not valid holidays and subject to Rules of Use
Tipping should be 15% to 20% of the total bill before discount

00075416

Casablanca

Fine Moroccan Cuisine

DINNER MENU

As dinner is served family style,
Please make your selection per table. Sorry, no sharing.

Petite Feast

Five Courses

$19.95 per person

Harira soup or salads ~ Bastilla appetizer ~ One entree
Homemade bread ~ Mint tea ~ Pastry

Kasbah Feast

Six Courses

$22.95 per person

Harira soup or salads ~ Bastilla appetizer ~ Two entree choices
Homemade bread ~ Mint tea ~ Pastry

Casablanca Feast

Seven Courses

$24.95 per person

Harira soup ~ salads ~ Bastilla appetizer ~ Two entree choices
Homemade bread ~ Mint tea ~ Pastry

ENTREE CHOICES

Chicken (Tagines)

Chicken with lemon and olives
Chicken with harissa sauce (spicy)
Chicken with onions and raisins
Chicken with sweet peas and carrots
Chicken with string beans
Chicken with onions and chic peas

Kabobs

(Served over rice with vegetables)

Beef kabob
Chicken kabob
Kefta kabob

Lamb (Tagines)

Lamb with honey and almonds
Lamb with onions and chic peas
Lamb with prunes and sesame seeds
Lamb with harrisa sauce (spicy)
Lamb with onions and raisins

Fish (Tagines)

Salmon with sharmoula sauce
Salmon with onions and raisins

Le Canard

www.lecanardrestaurant.com

Card No. 7

Up To $21.00 Value

Enjoy one complimentary LUNCH OR DINNER ENTREE when a second LUNCH OR DINNER ENTREE of equal or greater value is purchased.

valid anytime

Reservations recommended; FOR YOUR CONVENIENCE, WE ARE OPEN SUNDAY - 7 DAYS A WEEK

Le Canard is a French restaurant that has been awarded 3 stars by the prestigious Mobil Travel Guide. Enjoy a moderately priced menu featuring traditional veal, lamb, poultry, beef & pasta favorites. Le Canard has been voted one of the best French restaurants in the Washington metro area - Washingtonian 100 Best. Enjoy the quaint piano bar. Open daily.

132 Branch Rd.
(Donor Plaza)
Vienna, VA
(703)281-0070

Discounts exclude tax,tip and/or alcohol where applicable
Offers not valid holidays and subject to Rules of Use
Tipping should be 15% to 20% of the total bill before discount

00009483

Le Canard

Les Canards

Le Canard à l'Orange
Roasted half duck flambeed with orange Brandy $20.95

Le Suprême de Canard Bigarade
Breast of duck roasted with honey, brandy and Grand-Marnier $20.95

Le Canard Montmorency
Roasted half duck served with cherries, flambeed with Cherry Brandy $20.95

Le Suprême de Canard au Calvados
Breast of duck served with apples, glazed with Calvados $20.95

Le Canard aux Marrons
Roasted half duck accompanied with chestnut stuffing in a natural sauce $20.95

Les Viandes

L'Escalope de Veau Francaise
Medallions of veal sauteed with a citrus butter $20.95

L'Escalope de Veau a la "Meisinger"
A cut of traditional Schnitzel, lightly breaded, served with capers and lemon $20.95

L'Escalope de Veau au Marsala
Medallions of veal sauteed with mushrooms and Marsala Wine $20.95

L'Escalope de Veau a Normande
Medallions of veal sauteed with apples and Calvados $20.95

Assiette Vegetariane
$15.95

Le Chateaubriand (for 2)
A large cut of tenderloin of beef with Bordelaise and Bearnaise $54.50

Le Filet Grillé
Grilled filet mignon with Bearnaise sauce $24.95

Le Filet au Poivre
Filet mignon in crust of cracked black peppercorn served with a Cognac cream sauce $25.50

Paillard Marsala
Grilled breast of chicken in a Marsala sauce $18.95

Le Carré d'Agneau (for 2 or for 1)
Roasted rack of lamb carved at the table accompanied with a natural jus flavored with rosemary $54.50 (for 2) $27.25 (for 1)

Le Foie de Veau Lyonnaise
Fine slice of calf liver sauteed with onions $17.95

Paillard de Volaille
Grilled breast of chicken in a lemon and cracked black pepper crust $17.95

Les Cheveux d'Ange a la Sauce
Capellini with tomato and basil sauce $15.95

Les Poissons

Le Saumon Grillé Bárnaise
Grilled Norwegian Salmon with Bearnaise sauce $21.95

La Truite Belle Meunière
Fresh brook trout sauteed with lemon butter and mushrooms $17.95

Les Crevettes et Coquilles aux pâtes "Penne"
Shrimps and sea scallops tossed with Penne Pasta with herbs of Provence $18.95

Menu Sampler - Prices and offerings subject to change.

The Vantage Point
VP
Windows On Washington

Card No. 89

Up To $20.00 Value

Enjoy one complimentary DINNER ENTREE when a second DINNER ENTREE of equal or greater value is purchased or when dining alone - one DINNER ENTREE at 50% off the regular price - maximum discount $10.00.

valid any evening

For holidays-see Rules of Use

This rooftop restaurant overlooks Georgetown, the Potomac River & Washington D.C. Serving Amercian Continental cuisine, we use the freshest fish, pork, beef & chicken. Dinner is served daily from 5:30 p.m. until 11 p.m. Located one block from Rosslyn Metro. Complimentary indoor parking. Reservations recommended.

1900 Ft. Meyer Dr.
(Holiday Inn Rosslyn)
Arlington, VA
(703)807-2000

entertainment.
entertainment.com

Discounts exclude tax,tip and/or alcohol where applicable
Offers not valid holidays and subject to Rules of Use
Tipping should be 15% to 20% of the total bill before discount

00026292

The Vantage Point

VP

Windows On Washington

MAIN ENTREES

ALL ENTREES SERVED WITH HOUSE SALAD, YOUR CHOICE OF DRESSING, RICE OR BAKED POTATO, VEGETABLE DU JOUR, ROLLS & BUTTER

SALMON IN PARCHMENT $17.25
STEAMED WITH HERBS AND WINE IN PARCHMENT

SHRIMP SCAMPI $17.50
SAUTÉED IN GARLIC, BUTTER, WHITE WINE AND LEMON

SCALLOPS GRATINEE $18.25
SAUTÉED IN HERB BUTTER & SHERRY, SPRINKLED WITH PARMESAN CHEESE & LIGHTLY BROILED

SEAFOOD NORFOLK $19.95
A COMBINATION OF SHRIMP, SCALLOPS, AND CRABMEAT SAUTÉED IN BUTTER, WHITE WINE, AND LEMON

SEAFOOD COMBINATION $17.95
FRIED SHRIMP, CLAMS, SCALLOPS & OYSTER WITH COCKTAIL SAUCE

MARYLAND CRABCAKES $18.25
BACKFIN CRABMEAT PREPARED IMPERIAL STYLE AND PAN FRIED

FLOUNDER ALMANDINE $13.50
IN EGG BATTER, SAUTÉED WITH WHITE WINE & LEMON, TOPPED WITH ROASTED ALMONDS

CHICKEN STIR FRY $13.25
TENDERLOIN STRIPS OF CHICKEN WITH VEGETABLES OVER RICE

CHICKEN VERONIQUE $13.25
SAUTÉED WITH WHITE WINE AND WHITE GRAPE SAUCE

PEANUT ROASTED PORK TENDERLOIN $17.25
ROLLED IN MUSTARD AND PEANUTS

NEW YORK SIRLOIN $18.50
AGED BEEF, CHARBROILED TO YOUR LIKING

PRIME RIB OF BEEF $16.50
A SLOW ROASTED VANTAGE POINT TRADITION

FILET OF BEEF $18.75
MOST TENDER OF CUTS, ACCOMPANIED BY BÉARNAISE

STEAK AU POIVRE $19.95
CRACKED PEPPERCORNS AND BRANDY CREAM SAUCE

VANTAGE POINT STEAK $15.75
½" CUT OF OUR PETITE SIRLOIN, GRILLED MEDIUM~ WELL TO WELL ~DONE

CHOPPED SIRLOIN OF BEEF $12.95
SERVED WITH MUSHROOM SAUCE OR SAUTEED ONIONS

Card No. 10

Bistro Europa

www.bistro-europa.com

Up To $19.00 Value

Enjoy one complimentary LUNCH OR DINNER ENTREE when a second LUNCH OR DINNER ENTREE of equal or greater value is purchased.

Dine in only

valid anytime

Bistro Europa is located in the heart of Old Town Alexandria. Our first floor dining room is reminiscent of a classic European bistro. We feature live jazz Tuesday thru Thursday & Saturday evenings, & live piano on Saturday. The cuisine is Pan European - Italian, French & German with a modern twist. Chef/ Owner Klaus Keckeisen welcomes you.

715 King St.
Alexandria, VA
(703)549-0533

entertainment.
entertainment.com

Discounts exclude tax,tip and/or alcohol where applicable
Offers not valid holidays and subject to Rules of Use
Tipping should be 15% to 20% of the total bill before discount

00582120

Bistro Europa

Pasta Specials

Lasagna
Layers of wide pasta filled with meat & ricotta cheese, topped with melted mozzarella cheese & a light tomato sauce delightfully enhanced with garlic & fresh herbs
13.75

Cannelloni
Homemade pasta rolled with ground veal, spinach, ricotta cheese & fresh herbs, topped with melted mozzarella, light tomato sauce & fresh garlic and wild mushrooms
$14.75

European Specialties

Eggplant Parmigiana
Layers of thinly sliced eggplant and Parmigiano Reggiano
14.00

Veal Marsala
Fresh veal scallopine sautéed in marsala wine, fresh herbs & mushroom cream sauce
18.50

Jaeger Schnitzel
Lightly breaded pork loin served with a wild mushroom sauce
Spaetzle and red cabbage
$ 17.75

Filet de Sole al Limone
Fresh filet of sole sautéed in light lemon & white wine sauce with capers, accompanied by sautéed vegetables
17.50

Saumon aux Champagne
Fresh filet of salmon poached to perfection in champagne, accompanied by medley of fresh julienne steamed vegetables
18.75

Chicken Cordon Bleu
Chicken breast layered with ham & fontina cheese, rolled, lightly breaded, served on a light tomato sauce with fresh vegetables
17.00

New York Strip Steak
Grilled to order served with fresh roasted rosemary–garlic potatoes & vegetables
19.50

Risotto di mare
Shrimp, scallops and clams sautéed in olive oil, garlic and basil
Over Parmesan Risotto
$21.75

Filet Of Beef Gorgonzola
Filet of beef cooked to perfection topped with melted Gorgonzola Cheese
Roasted Red potatoes
$ 24.00

Card No. 31

Laporta's RESTAURANT

www.laportas.com

Up To $19.00 Value

Enjoy one complimentary DINNER ENTREE when a second DINNER ENTREE of equal or greater value is purchased or when dining alone - one DINNER ENTREE at 50% off the regular price - maximum discount $9.00.

DINING ROOM ONLY

valid any evening

This family owned restaurant takes pride in preparing delicious American & Continental cuisine. The Washington Times rates it three stars. Laporta's specializes in fresh seafood & creative pastas. Reservations recommended. LIVE JAZZ NIGHTLY. FREE PARKING.

1600 Duke St.
Alexandria, VA
(703)683-6313

entertainment.
entertainment.com

Discounts exclude tax,tip and/or alcohol where applicable
Offers not valid holidays and subject to Rules of Use
Tipping should be 15% to 20% of the total bill before discount

00012879

Laporta's RESTAURANT

PASTAS

Pasta Laporta 15.99
Penne pasta with Italian sausage in a lightly spiced tomato sauce with red and green peppers and fennel seed

Chicken Fettuccinc 16.99
Julienned chicken tossed in olive oil with pine nuts and Parmesan cheese

Tutta Mare 19.99
Jumbo shrimp and fresh clams, sautéed with a white wine butter over a nest of linguine with a pinch of crushed red pepper

Salmon Fettuccine 17.99
Fresh salmon over fettuccini noodles with a dill infused cream

Wild Mushroom Pasta 15.99
Shiitake, Cremini and Button mushrooms tossed in olive oil with pimento and spinach over penne

ENTREES

Maryland Crab Cakes 24.99
Jumbo lump crabmeat plated with a sesame seed mustard cream

Swordfish Steak 20.99
Pan seared, center-cut swordfish with whole roasted garlic and fresh rosemary
and a white wine reduction

Chicken Envoltine 17.99
Boneless chicken breast
stuffed with feta cheese, spinach and roasted red bell pepper
wrapped with apple wood smoked bacon
roasted and finished with a fresh thyme reduction

Sesame Encrusted Salmon 20.99
North Atlantic salmon rolled in sesame seeds, seared and glazed with honey and Dijon mustard

Port Wine Shrimp 21.99
Plump shrimp over a bed of sautéed, buttered spinach
with a black port wine reduction and topped with Cajun onions

Braised Mushrooms and Potato Crisp 16.99
Assorted wild mushrooms with stewed tomatoes
and sautéed spinach over potato bread crisps

Filet Mignon 24.99
8 ounce tenderloin cut, served with cracked black peppercorn demi-glace and homemade shoestring potatoes*

Veal and Shrimp 24.99
Scaloppini of veal tenderloin topped with jumbo shrimp
sautéed with lemon, butter, and fresh garlic

Roasted Pork Tenderloin 20.99
Pan seared sliced tenderloin medallions served pink with a Marsalla wine sauce*

HOUNDSTOOTH GRILL

Card No. 33

Up To $24.00 Value

Enjoy one complimentary LUNCH OR DINNER ENTREE when a second LUNCH OR DINNER ENTREE of equal or greater value is purchased.

Dine in only

valid anytime

At last, something to sink your teeth into. We serve grilled steak and seafood fit for a king in an atmosphere that's down-home friendly. We are located in the elegant Hyatt Fair Lakes and are open daily. Cocktails, beer and wine are available. Reservations recommended.

12777 Fair Lakes Circle
Fairfax, VA
(703)818-1234

entertainment
entertainment.com

Discounts exclude tax,tip and/or alcohol where applicable
Offers not valid holidays and subject to Rules of Use
Tipping should be 15% to 20% of the total bill before discount

00496116

HOUNDSTOOTH GRILL

APPETIZERS & STARTERS

Pan Seared Potstickers
Oriental Vegetable Dumplings, Tossed with Soy Chili Garlic
6.95

Crab and Artichoke Dip
A Creamy Blend of Crab, Artichoke Hearts, Mozzarella, and Parmesan Cheese Served with Grilled Bread.
6.95

Hoisin Duck Pancakes
With Spicy Asian Slaw
10.95

Chicken Quesadilla
Sautéed Chicken, Peppers, Mushrooms, Jack Cheese, Pico de Gallo, and Sour Cream
7.95

Home Style Chicken Soup 5.00
(Available Daily)

Soup of the Day
5.00

Monday-Beef Minestrone
Tuesday- Roasted Chicken Tortilla
Wednesday- Cream of Asparagus
Thursday- Clam Chowder
Friday- Lobster Bisque
Saturday-Seafood Chowder
Sunday- Roasted Tomato

SALADS

Wedge Salad
Iceberg Lettuce with Red Onion, Bacon, Pear Tomatoes and Gorgonzola Cheese and Choice of Dressing
5.50

Fair Lakes Salad
A Variety of Selection Seasonal Greens in a Parmesan Cheese Basket Served with Cherry Tomatoes, Toasted Pine-nuts and Balsamic Vinaigrette
5.25

ENTREES

Chicken Artichoke
Chicken Breast Medallions Sautéed in Shallots, Hearts of Artichoke, Feta Cheese, Herbs and Lemon Artichoke Cream Sauce
16.95
(Santa Margherita, Pino Grigio)

Shrimp Abruzzi
Jumbo Shrimps Sautéed in White Wine and Garlic, Tossed in Penne Pasta with a Light Cream Sauce
18.95
(RH Phillips, Sauvignon Blanc)

Filet & Shrimp Scampi
Filet Mignon and Jumbo Shrimps Scampi
24.95
(Sterling, Merlot)

Grilled New York Steak
Served with Maple Porter Beer Demi-Glace and Fried Crispy Leeks
23.95
(Seghesio, Zinfandel)

Grilled Salmon
Sautéed Leeks and Tomatoes, Served with Vegetable Ravioli in a Saffron Cream Sauce
21.95
(Kendall- Jackson, Chardonnay)

Card No. 160

Up To $17.00 Value

CAFÉ SOLEIL

Enjoy one complimentary DINNER ENTREE when a second DINNER ENTREE of equal or greater value is purchased.

valid any evening

Reservations recommended

Visit the South of France just 2 blocks from the White House. By day Cafe' Soleil is bustling & cheerful, by night quaint & romantic. Menu ranges from steak to escargot, with an emphasis on fish & fruits du mer. Entrees freshly prepared with superb care, with the choicest ingredients. Wine list accommodates all palates & most budgets.

839 17th St., NW
(two blocks from the White House - Farragut West Metro Station)
Washington, DC
(202)974-4260

entertainment
entertainment.com

Discounts exclude tax,tip and/or alcohol where applicable
Offers not valid holidays and subject to Rules of Use
Tipping should be 15% to 20% of the total bill before discount

00477777

CAFÉ SOLEIL

ESCARGOT
"Petit Gris" escargot sautéed with garlic, shiitake mushrooms, tomato, butter and fresh herbs served in pate au choux
7

ONION AND GORGANZOLA TART
Gorganzola cheese and caramelized onions in pastry with field greens.
7

GRILLED ASPARAGUS EN PHYLLO
Grilled baby asparagus wrapped in phyllo pastry and served with lemon cream sauce.
7

SCALLOP STUFFED SHRIMP
Jumbo shrimp stuffed with sea scallop, pan roasted and topped with an extra lemon butter.
9

ROASTED EGGPLANT SOUP
Tender young eggplant roasted and pureed with chicken stock and herbs.
6

WARM CRUMPET SALAD
Served atop mesculin greens with walnuts and goat cheese.
7

ROASTED CHICKEN
Half a free range chicken slow roasted in it own juices, served with garlic mashed potatoes, spinach and eggplant crisps.
16

GINGERED JUMBO SHRIMP
Ginger marinated jumbo shrimp sautéed with lemon, garlic and julienne vegetables served with basmati rice and asparagus.
19

LOBSTER RAVIOLI
Homemade ravioli stuffed with lobster meat, cheese and fresh herbs, topped with chardonnay sauce and vegetable julienne.
17

PARMESAN CRUSTED SEABASS
Chilean seabass crusted with parmesan and fresh herbs, pan seared and served with mashed potato and spinach.
18

TOURNEDOS MERCHANT
Beef tenderloin pan seared to your specifications, finished with sauce Merchant and served with au gratin potatoes and seasonal vegetables.
19

TUNA AU POIVRE
Center cut tuna loin pepper crusted and pan seared to perfection, drizzled with a balsamic reduction and served with mashed potatoes and vegetables.
19

CHICKEN FETTUCCINI
Sliced grilled chicken breast, wild mushrooms and fresh asparagus tips tossed with fettuccini in Alfredo sauce.
14

SPRING VEGETABLE PAELLA
Tender roasted spring vegetables with Arborio rice and saffron
13

Card No. 6

The Front Page

VOL. 1★ RESTAURANT & GRILLE ★ EST. 1987

www.frontpagerestaurant.com

Up To $17.00 Value

Enjoy one complimentary LUNCH OR DINNER ENTREE when a second LUNCH OR DINNER ENTREE of equal or greater value is purchased.

Dine in only

valid anytime

The Front Page is now open in Arlington. The original location, open in 1987, has offered a perfect place for a business lunch or dinner with friends. A collection of front pages from history adorn the walls & make great topics of conversation. We serve delicious American fare such as steaks, pastas, seafood & sandwiches at great prices. Outdoor patio dining avail.

4201 Wilson Blvd.
(located across from
Ballston Commons Mall)
Arlington, VA
(703)248-9990

entertainment.
entertainment.com

Discounts exclude tax,tip and/or alcohol where applicable
Offers not valid holidays and subject to Rules of Use
Tipping should be 15% to 20% of the total bill before discount

00579705

The Front Page

VOL. 1★ RESTAURANT & GRILLE ★ EST. 1987

Appetizers

Tequila Fried Calamari
With marinara sauce $6.50

Artichoke and Crab Dip
With sliced French Bread $7.25

Salads

Spinach Salad
Baby spinach, cherry tomatoes, chopped walnuts, chopped egg, red onion and sliced apples with a hot applewood bacon dressing $8.95

Grilled Vegetable Salad
Fresh portabellas, zucchini, red peppers, onion and tomatoes marinated, grilled and served on wild field greens with feta cheese and balsamic vinaigrette $8.50

Sandwiches

Front Page Club
Roasted pit ham and turkey breast on a toasted baguette with cheddar, bacon, lettuce, and tomato $8.50

Page One Burger
The Front Page Burger has been famous for our 8-oz fresh ground beef grilled to order, topped with sautéed onions, melted Swiss, coleslaw and Russian dressing $6.50

From the Grill

Black Angus New York Strip Steak
14-oz steak of Black Angus Beef grilled to your order and topped with Maui onions $18.95

Baby Rack Ribs
Danish baby back pork ribs in our bbq spices, slow-roasted until they're tender and finished on the grill. ½ rack $9.95 full $16.95

Chicken Teriyaki
Boneless chicken breast grilled with a shitake mushroom and teriyaki glaze $12.95

Fresh Seafood

Crab cakes
Two 4 oz. patties of jumbo lump crabmeat mixed with Dijon mustard and our own blend of herbs pan-fried then served with coleslaw and seasoned fries. Priced Daily

Trout Provencal
Farm-raised rainbow trout sautéed then topped with a fresh Provencal sauce then served w/ today's vegetable and rice. $14.95

Pasta

Pasta Dupont
Gulf Shrimp sautéed in olive oil, garlic, herbs, tomatoes and spinach tossed with linguine and feta cheese $16.95

Blackened Chicken Fettuccine
Julienne strips of blackened chicken breast and Andouille sausage tossed in a Cajun cream sauce over egg fettuccine $13.95

Menu Sampler - Prices and offerings subject to change.

The Green Tree

Up To $17.00 Value

Enjoy one complimentary DINNER ENTREE when a second DINNER ENTREE of equal or greater value is purchased.

valid any evening

Holidays excluded

This three star Mobil-rated restaurant will take you back in time, back to the 18th Century. Months were spent at the Library of Congress to research these authentic recipes. The Green Tree is enchanted with the 18th Century - a time when art & architecture, music and food, all reached a certain glorious peak.

15 S. King St.
Leesburg, VA
(703)777-7246

The Green Tree

Roasted Chicken Anyone can cook chicken, but no one does it quite the way our skilled chefs do. We take a plump half-a-chicken and roast it until it's toasted and serve it nestled on a bed of rice. 10.75

Perch Baked with Sour Cream and Dill There is a level beyond which Cooking becomes an art. For example, try this delicious dish, you're going to thoroughly enjoy an 18th Century food. First the Perch is Poached in White Wine, then baked with cream and fresh dill. The result is golden, flaky and delicious. 9.25

Jefferson's Delight In the 18th Century liver was soaked in milk, sweet herbs and spices for 2 days before it met the stove. We are very persinckety about our liver. You are going to be delighted with it. Served with sauteed onions and vegetables 10.95

Broiled Brook Trout There is much to be said for the delicacy of brook Trout, gently broiled & served on a bed of rice with a sauce of Butter, Tarragon and white wine. 12.95

Rabbit Fricassee A skilled 18th Century Chef could produce a rare delicacy from a Rabbit, a Red Wine sauce and Egg Noodles. And so can we. 14.95

The Talbott House Feast If your appetite is Healthy, you're going to thoroughly enjoy an 18th Century Feast. All on one platter, you'll be presented with a Lamb Chop, Grilled Chicken, a Choice Filet of Beef, the Liver that we do marinate in milk & sweet herbs, crisp Bacon & broiled Tomato. Large enough for two healthy Ladies. 19.95

Curried Chicken A great and authentic Indian Curry is not easy to find. Once found, it is memorable. We use no curry powder at all at The Green Tree. Rather, we begin with ginger root and build our curry as it was made in Bombay two hundred years ago. Our British cousins would have called it "four-boy curry" for we serve it with four side dishes, each of which ought to be carried to your table by a small Indian boy. But we aren't all that authentic. 12.95

N.Y. Sirloin Beefsteak If you order a steak at The Green Tree, you know it will be superb. We begin with the best possible sirloin and, if left to our choice, we'd serve it sizzling and crusty on the outside and pink in the middle. Served with Ore-Ida baked potatoes or Yorkshire pudding. 16.95

Skewered Lamb Shish-Kabobs Over brown rice pilaf. There is a general tendency among many people of many nations to regard the most important food as the essential source of nourishment and all others considered secondary. Maize for Indian; rice for the Orientalist; Yams for the Pacific area residents. In the Middle East area it is Shish-Kabobs. According to some historians, this dish and recipe dates back to 8000 B.C. 14.95

Roast Duckling Our Duckling is literally toasted in a sauce of Brandy & Red Wine. By taking the time to do this, we can offer you Duckling with an exquisite flavor that permeates the meat. Garnished with pickled watermelon. 15.95

Hampton Crab Our recipe was written down in 1789. The directions began, "Send William out for 24 Prime Crab." We skip that part because we don't have anyone named William to send out. But, save for the lack of a William, the recipe is exactly as it was: a blend of superb Crab, Cream, Fresh Mushrooms, good Bourbon and Cream Sherry, served in a pastry shell. 16.95

Roast Prime Rib of Beef with Yorkshire Pudding Our Recipe is ancient, but our prime ribs are Choice. And a great Yorkshire Pudding isn't all that easy to find these days. 16.95

Card No. 23

M&M Seafood Kitchen

Up To $17.00 Value

Enjoy one complimentary DINNER ENTREE when a second DINNER ENTREE of equal or greater value is purchased.

Dine in only

valid any evening

This popular & authentic creole-cajun restaurant is housed in an office building in Courthouse Plaza, but has all the charm of a New Orleans cafe on Bourbon Street. Enjoy the fun upbeat ambience that features Zydeco, blues & traditional New Orleans music while you dine on their exciting seafood dishes. Meals served daily. Reservations recommended but not mandatory.

2300 Clarendon Blvd.
Arlington, VA
(703)841-0100

entertainment.
entertainment.com

Discounts exclude tax,tip and/or alcohol where applicable
Offers not valid holidays and subject to Rules of Use
Tipping should be 15% to 20% of the total bill before discount

00593364

M & M Seafood Kitchen

Seafood

Southern Fried Catfish *Farm Raised Catfish Lightly Breaded in Corn Flour*	12.95
"Smothered" Catfish *Topped with Crawfish Etouffée*	15.95
All Lump Crabcakes *Broiled or Pan Sauteed with French Fries & Tartar Sauce*	18.95
Oysters "Bayou Têche" *Fried Oysters Topped with Tasso Ham & Crab Etouffée*	16.95
Maryland Fried Oysters *Served with French Fries & Tartar Sauce*	16.95
Seafood Au Gratin *Shrimp, Scallops, Crawfish & Lump Crab*	16.95
Shrimp Norman *Fried Gulf Shrimp Topped with Lump Crab Etouffée*	16.95
Shrimp Diane *Sauteed with Spring Onions, Mushrooms & Garlic*	15.95
Grilled Shrimp & Andouille Sausage *Served on a Bed of Rice with Bell Peppers & Red Beans ~ Topped with a Creole Mustard Sauce*	13.95
Shrimp Etouffée *Florida Rock Shrimp "Smothered" Cajun Style*	14.95
Crawfish Etouffée *Sauteed Crawfish "Smothered" Cajun Style*	14.95
Spicy Crawfish, Andouille, Red Beans & Rice *Sauteed with Garlic, Spring Onions & Cajun Spices*	13.95

Meats & Poultry

Spicy Pecan Crusted Chicken *Topped with Sauteed Crawfish & a Creole Mustard Sauce*	14.95
Grilled T-Bone Steak *16 oz steak with Garlic Mashed Potatoes & Cajun Onion Straw*	24.95
Grilled Pork Chops *Two 8 oz. Chops with Smothered Cabbage & Garlic Mashed Potatoes*	16.95

Pasta

Pasta Jambalaya *Gulf Shrimp, Roast Chicken & Andouille Sausage Tossed with Tomatoes, Sweet Peppers, Onion & Penne Pasta*	14.95
Shellfish & Fettuccine *Shrimp, Scallops & Crawfish Sauteed with Garlic, Shallots & Parmesan Cream*	15.95

Menu Sampler - Prices and offerings subject to change.

Card No. 76

CAFE BERLIN ON CAPITOL HILL

Up To $16.00 Value

Enjoy one complimentary LUNCH OR DINNER ENTREE when a second LUNCH OR DINNER ENTREE of equal or greater value is purchased.

valid anytime

Located on Capitol Hill, Cafe Berlin serves authentic German specialties such as weiner schnitzel. Homemade pastries are the glory of the Cafe Berlin kitchen. Also try grilled salmon steak, smoked loin of pork & sauerbraten. Sidewalk cafe dining available. Reservations accepted.

322 Massachusetts Ave. NE
Washington, DC
(202)543-7656

Discounts exclude tax,tip and/or alcohol where applicable
Offers not valid holidays and subject to Rules of Use
Tipping should be 15% to 20% of the total bill before discount

00005567

CAFE BERLIN
ON CAPITOL HILL

Entrees and German Specialties

Wiener Schnitzel 17.95
Tender breaded cut of veal, sauteed and accompanied by lemon-anchovy garnish. Served with home fries and daily vegetable selection.

Jägerschnitzel "Cafe Berlin Art" 16.95
Tender pork steak, sauteed and topped with spicy bacon and assorted mushroom sauce. Served with spätzle and house salad.

Zwiebelrostbraten 18.95
Grilled, sirloin steak topped with crisp onions. Served with au gratin potatoes and house salad.

Sauerbraten 16.95
Marinated slices of beef served with potato dumplings and red cabbage.

Kassler Rippchen 15.95
Smoked loin of pork served with Cafe Berlin's famous sauerkraut and home fried potatoes.

Deutsche Wurstplatte 15.95
Mixed sausage platter (bratwurst and weisswurst), served with sauerkraut and home fried potatoes.

Chicken "Cordon Bleu" 15.95
Boneless breast of chicken filled with ham and cheese, lightly breaded and sauteed on an orange cream sauce. Served with rice and house salad.

Grilled Salmon Filet 16.95
Topped with cafe de paris butter
Served with thyme potatoes and fresh spinach.

Roasted Half Duck 19.95
on an orange sauce served with potato dumpling and red cabbage.

Card No. 39

Up To $16.00 Value

Jaipur

Royal Indian Cuisine

Enjoy one complimentary DINNER ENTREE when a second DINNER ENTREE of equal or greater value is purchased.

Dining room only

valid any evening

We invite you to join us at Fairfax's newest Indian Restaurant - Jaipur. You will enjoy a taste of Royal Indian Cuisine. The ambiance is cozy, the cuisine is delicious & the staff is warm & friendly. We are open daily.

9401 Lee Hwy
(at Circle Towers)
Fairfax, VA
(703)766-1111

entertainment.
entertainment.com

Discounts exclude tax,tip and/or alcohol where applicable
Offers not valid holidays and subject to Rules of Use
Tipping should be 15% to 20% of the total bill before discount

00506093

Jaipur

Royal Indian Cuisine

Hamare Tandoor Se - From Tandoor

Tandoori Murg .... *Half $11.95 Full $16.95*
Chicken marinated overnight in yogurt and spices; barbecued in a traditional clay oven.

Jheenga Tandoori *$15.95*
Barbecued Shrimps with a subtle taste of Indian spices.

Pink City Machli *$14.95*
Fresh Salmon Fish, lightly marinated, cooked masterfully on skewer over charcoal.

Ghosht Ka Mazaa - Lamb Dishes

Ghosht Saagwala *$11.95*
Lamb masterfully cooked with spinach and a touch of cream curry sauce.

Rogan Josh *$12.95*
Fresh chunks of Lamb cooked in homemade creamy sauce.

Malabari Ghosht *$12.95*
Lamb, cooked in a special sauce with a touch of coconut cream.

Shaan-e Murg - Chicken Specialties

Murg Tikka Makhani *$12.95*
Chicken kababs cooked in a herb and tomato sauce with a buttery taste. A specialty of the house.

Murg Saagwala *11.95*
Boneless Chicken and spinach cooked with a touch of creamy curry sauce.

Chicken Tikka Masala *$12.95*
Boneless white meat Chicken marinated and cooked in Tandoor and then cooked with our special blend of Masalas.

Samunder Se - From the Sea

Jheenga Malabari *$13.95*
Shrimps, cooked in a special sauce with a touch of coconut cream.

Crab Masala *14.95*
Crab meat simmered in a blend of traditional Indian Masala.

Lobster Masala *$16.95*
Pieces of Lobster meat prepared in a blend of traditional Indian Masala.

Subzi Ki Mandi Se - Vegetarian Dishes

Bahaar-E-Subz Jaipuri *8.95*
Assorted vegetables cooked with a blend of traditional spices in Kadai.

Malai Kofta *$8.95*
Cheese and vegetables dumplings cooked in a cream and almond sauce.

Mutter Paneer *$8.95*
Homemade cheese and garden peas cooked in a creamy curry sauce.

Card No. 8

Up To $16.00 Value

Polo Grill

RESTAURANT & TAP ROOM

Enjoy one complimentary DINNER ENTREE when a second DINNER ENTREE of equal or greater value is purchased.

Dining room only

valid any evening

In the tradition of RT's & the Warehouse Bar & Grill in Alexandria, enjoy this American Steak & Seafood Restaurant. Creole & Cajun dishes, unique pastries, specialty salads & sandwiches are available anytime. Join us for Sunday brunch. Banquet room available. We are open daily.

7784 Gunston Plaza Dr.
Lorton, VA
(703)550-0002

entertainment
entertainment.com

Discounts exclude tax,tip and/or alcohol where applicable
Offers not valid holidays and subject to Rules of Use
Tipping should be 15% to 20% of the total bill before discount

00155993

Polo Grill

RESTAURANT & TAP ROOM

PASTAS

SEAFOOD CANNELLONI 12.95
Italian-Style Crepes Stuffed with Shrimp, Scallops and Lump Crab and Topped with Two Sauces

PASTA JAMBALAYA 16.95
Gulf Shrimp, Roast Chicken and Andouille Sausage Tossed with Tomatoes, Sweet Peppers, Onions and Penne Pasta

LINGUINI WITH SHRIMP & SCALLOPS 16.95
Sauteed with Garlic, Shallots, Tomato, Cream and Parmesan Cheese

GRILLED CHICKEN, ASPARAGUS & PENNE PASTA 13.95
With Garlic, Sun-Dried Tomatoes and Parmesan Cheese

DINNER ENTREES

SOUTHERN FRIED CATFISH 13.95
Farm-Raised Fillets Lightly Dusted in Corn Flour

MARYLAND SELECT OYSTERS 16.95
Lightly Dusted in Corn Flour and Deep Fried

CRAWFISH & SHRIMP ETOUFFÉE 16.95
Sauteed Crawfish Tails and Florida Rock Shrimp "Smothered" Cajun Style

ALL LUMP CRABCAKES 18.95
Two Crispy Southern-Style Cakes - Our Specialty

STUFFED CHESAPEAKE FLOUNDER 18.95
With Crawfish-Crab Imperial and Topped with Crab Butter Cream

GRILLED "FLAT IRON" STEAK 17.95
With Corn Maque Choux

BLACKENED RIBEYE STEAK 22.95
A 12 ounce Steak Topped with Cajun Onion Straw and served with our Horseradish Sauce

GRILLED PORK CHOPS 17.95
Two 8 oz. Rib Chops with Country-Fried Apples

SPICY PECAN CRUSTED CHICKEN 16.95
Topped with Sauteed Shrimp and a Creole Mustard Cream Sauce

SAUTEED "NATURE" CALVES LIVER 13.95
Topped with Bacon and Caramelized Onions

Menu Sampler - Prices and offerings subject to change.

Card No. 50

Supper Club OF INDIA

Up To $16.00 Value

Enjoy one complimentary DINNER ENTREE when a second DINNER ENTREE of equal or greater value is purchased.

Dining room only

valid any evening

Enjoy Indian cuisine at its best. All new Supper Club of India invites you to enjoy a wonderful dining experience. Our friendly service & delicious dishes will keep you coming back again & again. Open daily.

13055 Worldgate Dr.
Herndon, VA
(703)736-0466

entertainment
entertainment.com

Discounts exclude tax,tip and/or alcohol where applicable
Offers not valid holidays and subject to Rules of Use
Tipping should be 15% to 20% of the total bill before discount

00520598

SupperClub OF INDIA

TANDOOR

Murg Tandoori $ 13.95
Marinated spring chicken grilled in a Tandoor.

Murg Tikka Kesari $ 13.95
Saffron flavored boneless chicken breast finished in a clay oven.

Murg Malai Tikka $ 13.95
Breast of chicken marinated in yoghurt, cream, cashewnut, green cardamon and cooked on charcoal.

CHICKEN

Murgh Tikka Makhni $ 13.95
Boneless chicken breast grilled in a Tandoor and finished in a rich creamy tomato sauce.

Jehangiri Murg Tikka Masala $ 13.95
Boneless chicken breast grilled in a Tandoor and finished in chef's exotic gravy.

Murg Badami $ 13.95
Chicken breast finished in an almond and cream sauce.

SEAFOOD

Lobster Nizami $ 24.95
Lobster mildly spiced, finished in chef's secret recipe.

Shahjahani Crab $ 19.95
Jumbo lump crab finished in a mild cream and butter sauce.

Jhinga Madras $ 17.95
Prawns cooked with coconut and tempered with mustard seeds.

LAMB

Akbari Lamb Chaamp Masala $ 24.95
Tandoori lamb chops delicately spiced and finished in a rich tomato and brown gravy.

Badshahi Kofta Curry $ 14.95
Minced lamb dumplings finished in an exotic rich sauce.

VEGETABLES

Baingan Lajawab $ 11.95
Baby eggplant stuffed with cottage cheese, dry fruits and finished in brown gravy.

Bhindi Do Piyaza $ 11.95
Okra cooked with onions and mildly spiced.

Menu Sampler - Prices and offerings subject to change.

Card No. 12

★ AMERICA ★
Union Station
www.arkrestaurants.com

Up To $15.00 Value

Enjoy one complimentary LUNCH OR DINNER ENTREE when a second LUNCH OR DINNER ENTREE of equal or greater value is purchased.

valid anytime

An ideal venue for your group to dine is at Washington D.C.'s America Restaurant. Located on Capitol Hill in Union Station's Great Hall, America's menu offers a wide range of American cuisine while enjoying the splendor of Historic Union Station. Join our hospitality M* Card program. Visit our website at www.askrestaurants.com.

50 Massachusetts Ave., NE
(Union Station)
Washington, DC
(202)682-9555

entertainment.
entertainment.com

Discounts exclude tax,tip and/or alcohol where applicable
Offers not valid holidays and subject to Rules of Use
Tipping should be 15% to 20% of the total bill before discount

00407308

★ AMERICA ★
Union Station

APPETIZERS

QUESADILLA *(EAST LA, CA)*
filled with cheese and green chiles, with guacamole, salsa and sour cream 6.50
filled with grilled chicken 7.50

GRILLED PORTOBELLO MUSHROOM QUESADILLA *(EL PASO, TX)*
meaty Portobello mushrooms, fresh tomatoes and Monterey Jack cheese 9.50

CAJUN SPICY "POPCORN" SHRIMP *(BAYOU TECHE, LA)*
crispy, spiced, cornmeal crusted baby shrimp with Creole sauce 7.95

BAKED CLAMS CASINO *(SEASIDE HEIGHTS, NJ)*
fresh clams baked with a bacon, garlic and bread crumb stuffing 8.95

VEGETABLE SPRING ROLL *(HONOLULU, HI)*
stir fried vegetables wrapped in a crisp skin served with a spicy pineapple salsa and soy dipping sauce 5.95

SALADS

VEGETABLE STIR FRY SALAD *(SAN FRANCISCO, CA)*
quickly stir fried fresh vegetables served on mixed greens and crisp cellophane noodles 10.95

SPINACH SALAD *(NAPA, CA)*
spinach leaves tossed with sliced button mushrooms, sliced red onions and balsamic vinaigrette, garnished with crumbled bacon and sliced hard cooked eggs 8.95

GRILLED TUNA SALAD NICOISE *(CAPE HATTERAS, NC)*
grilled Yellowfin Tuna steak atop a salad of mixed greens, poached new potatoes, black olives, green beans, celery, hard cooked eggs, cherry tomatoes and tossed with a light balsamic vinaigrette 14.50

GREEK STYLE SALAD *(ASTORIA, NY)*
romaine lettuce, Feta cheese, grilled chicken, tomatoes, olives and orzo tossed with rosemary and red wine vinaigrette 11.95

PIZZA

SPICY CHICKEN *(TEMPE, AZ)*
smoked chile marinated chicken, avocado, tomato and pico de gallo 9.95

FISH

BLACKENED CATFISH *(LAKE CHARLES, LA)*
dusted with Cajun spices and quickly seared, served over a charred corn succotash, mashed potatoes and a jalapeno butter sauce 15.95

MARYLAND STYLE LUMP CRAB CAKES *(ANNAPOLIS, MD)*
sautéed crab cakes served with grilled vegetables, rice pilaf and tartar sauce 19.95

MIXED SEAFOOD GUMBO *(NEW IBERIA, LA)*
rich stew containing fresh fish and shellfish, vegetables and okra, served with rice 16.95

PASTAS

GRILLED CHICKEN AND PENNE PASTA *(NAPLES, FL)*
grilled, marinated chicken breast, sweet onions, basil and roasted plum tomato sauce 12.95

LINGUINE WITH LITTLE NECK CLAMS *(CAPE MAY, NJ)*
fresh clams poached with white wine, onions, garlic and herbs, served over linguine 12.95

SEARED SCALLOPS AND SPINACH FETTUCCINE *(NORTH BEACH, CA)*
large sea scallops, quickly seared with spinach pasta, herbs and roasted tomato sauce 15.95

MEATS & SPECIALTIES

CHICKEN POT PIE *(NEW YORK CITY)*
tender chicken breast, peas and carrots poached in a rich supreme sauce, served in a flaky pastry shell 14.95

TWO SMOTHERED PORK CHOPS *(WHEELING, WV)*
charcoal grilled and smothered with onion gravy, served with whipped potatoes and seasonal vegetables 14.50

SIZZLING FAJITAS: *(HOUSTON, TX)*
Grilled Chicken, Beef or Portobello Mushrooms
with sautéed peppers and onions, warm flour tortillas, salsa, guacamole and sour cream, served with a side of beans and rice 12.95

RED, WHITE AND BLUE ENCHILADAS *(PHOENIX, AZ)*
tri colored corn tortillas filled with Monterey Jack cheese and stir fried garden vegetables, garnished with black beans, guacamole, sour cream and salsa 14.95

bella luna

RISTORANTE

Card No. 68

Up To $15.00 Value

Enjoy one complimentary LUNCH OR DINNER ENTREE when a second LUNCH OR DINNER ENTREE of equal or greater value is purchased.

valid anytime

Holidays excluded

This Mobil-rated Inn offers the diner the "best of everything." The menu features continental and seafood entrees to entice and embrace the tastebuds. Each entree is skillfully prepared by our award-winning chefs. Enjoy dessert or an after dinner drink on our Garden deck located behind the Bella Luna Ristorante.

19 South King St.
Leesburg, VA
(703)777-5000

entertainment
entertainment.com

Discounts exclude tax,tip and/or alcohol where applicable
Offers not valid holidays and subject to Rules of Use
Tipping should be 15% to 20% of the total bill before discount

00265420

bella luna

RISTORANTE

Continental

First Mate's Stuffed Mushrooms

Mushrooms stuffed full of juicy backfin crabmeat. *6.95*

Baked Brie

Brie glazed with honey and served with fresh fruit and bread. 6.95

Loudoun County Baked Onion Soup

Made as in colonial times with a splash of Spanish sherry. 3.75

17th Century Peanut Soup

Virginia's own. So distinctive it has charmed many a visiting Dignitary.
3.50

Entrees

Mrs. Franklin's Steak

18.95

NY sirloin flamed in cognac with sautéed mushrooms and sauce Béarnaise just as it was served to Ben.

Oak Hill Béarnaise

18.95

A pair of petit Filet Mignons, sautéed and served with mushroom caps and our sauce béarnaise.

The Virginian

15.95

Lightly breaded chicken, sautéed with lemon butter, chives, diced ham and capers.

The Williamsburg

18.95

The best the sea is willing to offer. Scallops, Maryland crab, Filet of flounder and shrimp baked and topped with our sauce mornay.

Jamestown Shrimp Feast

17.95

Bacon wrapped shrimp stuffed with crabmeat. Broiled to perfection and accompanied by lemon hollandaise.

Manzo

Manzo alla Pizzaiola

18.95

A hearty NY strip sautéed with onion, green pepper, mushroom, wine and tomatoes.

Filetto con Vino Madeira

19.95

Butterflied Fillet Mignon sautéed with Madeira wine and mushroom caps.

Pollo

Pollo alla Marsala

16.95

Boneless breast of chicken sautéed with Marsala wine and mushrooms.

Pollo alla Piccata

15.95

Lemon, butter and white wine flavor this dish. Finished with capers for an added "zing"

Pollo alla Fiorentina

16.95

Succulent breast of chicken layered with spinach and mozzarella cheese, topped with cream sauce.

Pollo all'Arrabbiata

15.95

Angry chicken. For those who love some spice in their life. Sautéed in hot pepper and tomatoes.

Pesce

Frutti di Mare

19.95

Scallops, Maryland crab, flounder and shrimp steeped in wine and tomato. Served over pasta.

Gamberi fra Diavola

18.95

Literally from the devil, this spicy dish starts with jumbo shrimp and red pepper in a basil tomato sauce.

Card No. 21

Up To $15.00 Value

CENTER CAFE

www.arkrestaurants.com

Enjoy one complimentary LUNCH OR DINNER ENTREE when a second LUNCH OR DINNER ENTREE of equal or greater value is purchased.

valid anytime

A two story kiosk located in the center of Union Station dominates the activity in the Main Hall. The atmosphere is filled with excitement and grandeur, which typifies Union Station, while the menu offers a delightful choice of favorite entrees. Join our hospitality M* Card program and visit us at www. arkrestaurants.com.

50 Massachusetts Ave., NE
(Union Station)
Washington, DC
(202)682-0143

entertainment.
entertainment.com

Discounts exclude tax,tip and/or alcohol where applicable
Offers not valid holidays and subject to Rules of Use
Tipping should be 15% to 20% of the total bill before discount

00397510

CENTER CAFE

appetizers

oven roasted spicy chicken wings 7.95
marinated with jamaican jerk spices and served with a honey-mango dipping sauce

gulf shrimp cocktail 7.95
with spicy cocktail sauce and coleslaw

spicy chicken quesadilla 7.95
with salsa, guacamole, sour cream, three cheese and spicy grilled chicken

oven roasted maryland crabcake 8.95
served with a classic tartar sauce

entrée salads

crunchy asian chicken salad 11.95
water chestnuts, peppers, snowpeas, pineapple and a sweet plum vinaigrette

teriyaki style salmon salad 12.95
with shiitake mushrooms, mixed greens and rice wine vinaigrette

fresh yellowfin tuna steak salad 14.95
green beans, hard boiled eggs, olives & tomatoes

entrees

roasted half chicken 11.95
marinated with herbs and served with garlic smashed potatoes & roasted vegetables

oven roasted new york sirloin 18.95
wild mushrooms, smashed potatoes & red wine sauce

miso glazed salmon 16.95
served with asian vegetable salad and soba noodles

oven roasted mahi mahi 16.95
served with rice and pineapple salsa

lobster ravioli 18.95
tomato cream sauce topped with baby shrimp

lemon chicken brochette 13.95
two skewers of chicken, peppers, onions & tomatoes served over wild rice with a lemon pepper sauce

Card No. 58

Portabellos

An American Cafe

Up To $15.00 Value

Enjoy one complimentary LUNCH OR DINNER ENTREE when a second LUNCH OR DINNER ENTREE of equal or greater value is purchased.

Dining room only

valid anytime

Friday & Saturday seating before 6:00 p.m. or after 9:00 p.m.

New to the Arlington, Portabellos is a charming neighborhood find. Chef Bill Hamrock & wife Susie will make your dining experience a night to remember. Lunch is served seven days a week, there's brunch on Sunday & dinner is served nightly. Great value, easy parking & food you can't beat is Portabellos winning combination.

2109 N. Pollard St.
Arlington, VA
(703)528-1557

entertainment
entertainment.com

Discounts exclude tax,tip and/or alcohol where applicable
Offers not valid holidays and subject to Rules of Use
Tipping should be 15% to 20% of the total bill before discount

00528532

Portabellos
An American Cafe

Sandwiches & Entrée Salads

The American Burger
Choice of Cheese, Smoked Bacon -Additional .50/each
$8.00

Southwestern Grilled Chicken Tortilla Salad
Chicken Breast, Diced Tomatoes, Corn and Jicama with Cilantro Honey Vinaigrette
$9.00

Chicken Grill & Fried Brie Salad
Grilled Chicken Breast & Fried Brie Cheese over Mixed Greens
with Mango Pepper Dressing
$9.50

Pastas, Pizzas & Vegetarian

Pizza Margherita
With Tomato Sauce, Mozzarella Cheese & Fresh Basil
$8.50

Grilled Portabello & Prosciutto Pizza
Portabello Mushrooms, Prosciutto Ham, Broccoli Raab, Tomato Sauce & Mozzarella Cheese
$11.50

Vegetable Risotto with Goat Cheese
Turnips, Carrots & Shiitake Mushrooms with Creamy Italian Rice
$12.50

Main Courses

Marinated & Grilled Chicken Breast
Over Angel Hair Pasta with Roasted Onions, Sundried Tomatoes,
Parmesan Cheese & Lemon Thyme Chardonnay Sauce
$13.95

Citrus Marinated Salmon Fillet
With Basmati Rice, Mango Salsa, Grilled Asparagus & Pomegranate Molasses
$16.50

Pecan Crusted Rainbow Trout
Served with Crispy Polenta, Creamed Spinach, Brown Butter & Bacon Sauce
$15.95

Sautéed Shrimp Provencal
Shrimp Sautéed with Garlic, Tomatoes, Artichokes, Basil & White Wine Over Basmati Rice
$15.95

Pan Seared Sea Scallops
With Crispy Potato Cake, Julienne Vegetables & Dijon Cream Sauce
$16.50

Pan-Fried Pork Chop with Carolina Bbq Glaze
Pan-Fried Pork Chop with Creamed Spinach & Whipped Potatoes
$15.95

Jumbo Lump Crab Cakes
Two Jumbo Lump Crab Cakes with Jicama Slaw & Old Bay Remoulade
$18.95

Grilled Filet Mignon
With Whipped Potatoes, Creamed Spinach, Glazed Carrots & Chianti Sauce
$20.95

Menu Sampler - Prices and offerings subject to change.

Card No. 118

TEMEL
EURO-MEDITERRANEAN RESTAURANT

Up To $14.00 Value

Enjoy one complimentary LUNCH OR DINNER ENTREE when a second LUNCH OR DINNER ENTREE of equal or greater value is purchased.

Dining room only

valid anytime

At last, a wonderful, cozy restaurant has opened in Fairfax City, meet Temel. We serve Euro Mediterranean Cuisine. Owner, Alex Gungor, invites you to sample the delicious menu. Complement your meal with a nice bottle of wine & don't forget to save room for dessert.

3232 Old Pickett Rd.
Fairfax, VA
(703)352-5477

entertainment.
entertainment.com

Discounts exclude tax,tip and/or alcohol where applicable
Offers not valid holidays and subject to Rules of Use
Tipping should be 15% to 20% of the total bill before discount

00364064

TEMEL

EURO-MEDITERRANEAN RESTAURANT

ENTREES FROM THE GRILL

Shish Kebab $12.95
Two grilled skewers of loin of lamb marinated in olive oil, paprika, garlic and pepper.

Adana Kebab $10.95
Skewer of ground lamb marinated with paprika and peppers served on flat bread.

Spring Kebab (Spicy) $12.95
Skewer of ground lamb with parsley, garlic, and peppers, served on flat bread.

Kofte Kebab $9.95
Grilled ground beef with seasonings, served with caçik sauce.

Lamb Chops $13.95
Grilled lamb cutlets marinated in olive oil and oregano.

SEAFOOD ENTREES

Salmon Filet $13.25
Grilled salmon filet, served with a side of seasoned vegetables.

Swordfish Brochette $14.50
Marinated grilled swordfish with a brown butter sauce.

Baked Turkish Salmon $13.50
Baked layers of salmon, sauteed with butter, spinach and potatoes, finished with a white wine sauce.

TURKISH PIZZA
Baked "Pizza Boats" made in our oven

Lahmacun $4.95
This is the only round pizza. Thin and crispy, with chopped lamb and vegetables, garnish with onions, tomato, and lemon.

Kaser Pizza $5.95
Turkish kaser cheese, tomatoes, green peppers, olives and seasonings.

Spinach Pizza $7.50
Spinach and garlic on a base of kaser cheese with onions, garlic, tomatoes and peppers.

Sucuk Pizza $8.00
Spicy Turkish sausage and mild peppers on a base of kaser cheese with green and red peppers.

TEMEL"S PASTAS

Beef Pasticio $8.50
Baked layers of noodles, ground beef, marinara sauce, ricotta and parmesan.

Shrimp Pasticio $9.25
Baked layers of noodles, shrimp, and green beans, carrot in wine sauce.

Vegatable Pasticio $8.00
Baked layers of noodles, green beans, carrots, broccoli, and marinara sauce.

ENTREES

Musakka $7.95
Eggplant baked with ground beef, baked potato, béchamel , tomato sauce ricotta cheese.

Chicken Guvec $7.95
Stew of mixed vegetables and chicken, served with rice.

Spinach Pie $7.25
Spinach and feta cheese baked in phyllo, served with cacik sauce.

Card No. 29

Attila's Restaurant

Up To $14.00 Value

Enjoy one complimentary LUNCH OR DINNER ENTREE when a second LUNCH OR DINNER ENTREE of equal or greater value is purchased.

Dine in only

valid anytime

Enjoy the flavor of Arlington's famous Attila's Restaurant. For over 20 years, Attila's has brought you the most outstanding culinary delights. Our traditional Turkish menu is designed to please the entire family. Choose from our selection of appetizers, traditional dishes, or our famous Kebabs. Don't forget to save room for dessert.

2705 Columbia Pike
Arlington, VA
(703)920-8100

entertainment.
entertainment.com

Discounts exclude tax,tip and/or alcohol where applicable
Offers not valid holidays and subject to Rules of Use
Tipping should be 15% to 20% of the total bill before discount

00499469

Attila's Restaurant

TRADITIONAL DISHES

MUSAKKA
Lean minced meat, layers of eggplant, potatoes topped with Bechamel sauce and Kashari cheese, served with rice pilaf. $10.95

LAMB SHANK
Cooked slowly with eggplants and spinach, served with rice pilaf. $10.95

COBAN KAVURMA
Sliced pieces of tender beef sauteed with tomatoes, green-pepper, onion, herbs, served with rice pilaf. $11.95

TURLU
Lamb stew cooked with vegetables ,served with rice pilaf. $9.50

KEBAB ENTREES

ADANA KEBAB
Marinated spicy minced lean lamb & beef skewered, served over pita bread, relish onion and rice pilaf. $10.95

YOGURTLU ADANA
Marinated spicy minced lean lamb & beef skewered, served over pita bread with yogurt and fresh tomato sauce. $11.95

ATILLA'S KOFTE KEBAB
Spicy ground beef and lamb, grilled to perfection, served with relish onion and rice pilaf. $9.95

ISLIM KEBAB
Lean chunks of leg of lamb cooked with onion and celery, served with roasted eggplant with yogurt sauce & rice pilaf. $10.95

BEEF SHISH KEBAB
Chunks of filletmignon skewered with onion, tomato, green pepper, served with rice pilaf. $15.95

LAMB SHISH KEBAB
Marinated spicy lamb skewered, served with rice pilaf. $11.95

CHICKEN BURSA
Grilled chicken breast over sauteed pita bread with yogurt and fresh tomato sauce $9.95.

CHICKEN SHIS KEBAB
Marinated chicken skewered, served with rice pilaf. $10.50

COMBINATION ENTREES

ADANA KEBAB & CHICKEN SHISH KEBAB $10.95

LAMB & CHICKEN SHISH KEBAB $10.95

KOFTE & CHICKEN SHISH KEBAB $10.95

ISTANBUL MIXED GRILL
Combination of beef, lamb, chicken shish and Adana Kebab served with rice pilaf. $13.95

FRESH DONER KEBAB - *Friday and Saturday Only*

DONER
Mixture of lamb, beef, and veal charbroiled on a vertical rotisserie, thin, tender slices served over pita bread or rice pilaf. $11.95

ISKENDER
Famous chef Iskender's style from Bursa region doner served over sauteed pita bread with yogurt and tomato sauce. $12.95

Card No. 30

BANJARA
INDIAN CUISINE

www.banjaracuisine.com

Up To $14.00 Value

Enjoy one complimentary DINNER ENTREE when a second DINNER ENTREE of equal or greater value is purchased.

Dine in only

valid any evening

Banjara Indian cuisine located in the heart of Ashburn offers delicious Indian cuisine presented with unforgettable taste & tradition. Our vision is to offer authentic Indian cuisine in a contemporary environment, served by knowledgeable caring staff. Planning a party? We cater for all occasions. Open daily.

44050 Ashburn Shopping Plaza
Ashburn, VA
(703)723-0040

entertainment
entertainment.com

Discounts exclude tax,tip and/or alcohol where applicable
Offers not valid holidays and subject to Rules of Use
Tipping should be 15% to 20% of the total bill before discount

00499517

BANJARA
INDIAN CUISINE

B

Tandoor Entrees

Paneer Tikka — *11.95*
Home made cheese marinated overnight in fresh spices, and yogurt.

Tandoori Chicken — *11.95*
Chicken marinated in a yogurt sauce with fresh ginger, garlic, and spices.

Lamb Boti Kabob — *13.95*
Chunks of Lamb cubes marinated with ginger & garlic in yogurt sauce.

Banjara Curries

Vegetarian

Dal Curry — *9.95*
Mildly spiced lentil curry

Dal Makhani — *9.95*
An assortment of lentils cooked with fresh onions, garlic, ginger and butter.

Malai Kofta — *10.95*
Vegetarian dumplings simmered in a creamy sauce, consisting
of cinamon, nutmeg, mild spices and malai (cream).

Channa Masala — *9.95*
Chickpeas cooked in an onion, tomato and garlic sauce.

Lamb Entrees

Rogan Josh — *12.95*
Classic lamb curry cooked with freshly ground spices.

Lamb Saag — *13.95*
Tender chunks of lamb cooked with fresh spinach.

Lamb Khurma — *13.95*
Lamb in creamy onion sauce cooked with onions, saffron, and almonds.

Seafood Specialities

Goan Fish Curry — *13.95*
Chilli hot konkan fish curry.

Fish Vindaloo — *14.95*
Fish and potatoes cooked in spicy tangy sauce with dash of lemon.

Kovalam Shrimp — *15.95*
Classsic shrimp curry cooked with coconut, red chilli, onion and tomatoes.

Shrimp Lababdar — *16.95*
Jumbo shrimp simmered in creamy tomato sauce with sauteed onions, gentle
Touch of spices and fenugreek.

Biryani Specials

Vegetable Biryani — *11.95*
World famous Basmati rice cooked with fresh vegetables and spices.

Chicken Biryani — *12.95*
Hyderabad's favorite. Basmati rice cooked with marinated chicken, herbs and spices.

Lamb Biryani — *13.95*
Moghul Delight. Basmati rice cooked with marinated lamb, herbs and spices.

Card No. 11

Up To $14.00 Value

Bilbo Baggins
wine cafe & restaurant

www.bilbobaggins.net

Enjoy one complimentary LUNCH OR DINNER ENTREE when a second LUNCH OR DINNER ENTREE of equal or greater value is purchased.

Dining room only

valid anytime

We hope you will find our restaurant to be different. We want to be known as a cozy, local gathering place with tasty food, unusual wines & friendly service - the kind of place Bilbo Baggins & his hobbit companions frequent. Owners Michael & Linda welcome you to one of Old Town's favorite places to wine & dine. Reservations recommended.

208 Queen St.
Alexandria, VA
(703)683-0300

entertainment
entertainment.com

Discounts exclude tax,tip and/or alcohol where applicable
Offers not valid holidays and subject to Rules of Use
Tipping should be 15% to 20% of the total bill before discount

00277972

Bilbo Baggins
wine cafe & restaurant

Pasta Plates

Tortellini Chardonnay ***housemade pasta filled with salmon, crab meat and fresh dill; served in a light apple ginger Chardonnay cream sauce...$13.95 w/ steamed Lobster claw...$14.95***

Smoked Duck & Vegetable Lo Mein ***an aromatic soy, ginger and sesame broth with snow peas, carrots, red peppers and mung beans tossed with Asian noodles...$14.95***

Giardiniera Chicken Penne ***penne pasta tossed with fresh vegetables in a sundried tomato sauce topped with a dollop of sundried tomato pesto and shaved romano cheese...$13.95***

Linguine Frutti Di Mare ***shrimp, calamari, mussels ,scallops and crab meat in a light basil marinara sauce...$17.95***

Crawfish and Andouille Ravioli ***served in a light Lobster cream sauce...$16.95***

Gnocchi Pasta ***potato dumplings with your choice of sauces; Alfredo, Bolognaise, Napolitano or Pomodoro...$12.95***

Main Plates

Wasabi Salmon Filet ***with fresh asparagus and wild mushroom ragout, sesame sticky rice cake seasoned with Forikake; served in a pool of savory miso broth...$16.95***

Veal Scallopini Piccata w/ Crab Meat ***served on a bed of garlic mashed potatoes and grilled asparagus spears with a lemon caper sauce...$16.95***

Cinnamon Porkloin w/ Winter Fruit Chutney ***served with fluffly mashed potatoes, roasted butternut squash puree w/ cranberry, fig, pear, apple and crystallized ginger chutney...$15.95***

Seared Yellowfin Tuna ***with roasted garlic & kalamata olive crust, Yukon gold mashed potatoes, and grilled asparagus with a sundried tomato tapenade....$16.95***

Grilled Lamb Chops ***served with yukon gold mashed potatoes, grilled asparagus spears, roasted butternut squash,citronella rosemary emulsion and roasted chestnut garlic cream.....$19.95***

Wild Mushroom Beef Filet ***served on Stilton blue cheese mashed potatoes, garlic infused wilted spinach, ragout of wild mushrooms, yukon gold potatoes chips and a balsamic demi-glace...Market***

Filet Of Beef Stroganoff ***sauteed with wild mushrooms, fresh garden vegetables, garlic and shallots in a paprika sour cream sauce over rice....$16.95***

Tilapia Filet ***Sweet, lowfat white filet served with a dollop of basil and sundried tomato pesto, sesame sticky rice cake and steamed vegetables....$16.95***

Andouille Chicken Breast ***stuffed with andouille sausage and jalapeno jack cheese, encrusted with walnuts and pecans; served with black bean mango salsa and chilpotles sour cream....$14.95***

Grilled Portabello Chicken ***served on a bed of wild mushroom polenta, topped with a grilled portabello mushroom cap and sundried tomato tapenade...$14.95***

Emu Fan Filets ***Neapolitan of Emu filets with black mission figs, grilled asparagus , apple and Camembert quesadilla, fluffy mashed potatoes and wild mushrooms in a pool of thyme demi-glace...$19.95***

Bilbo Baggins Global Restaurant *Michael Armellino Chef/Owner* *WWW.Bilbobaggins.net*

Gratuity of 18% added with use of coupon

Card No. 16

Up To $14.00 Value

Domani Ristorante

Southern Italian Cuisine

www.domaniristorante.com

Enjoy one complimentary LUNCH OR DINNER ENTREE when a second LUNCH OR DINNER ENTREE of equal or greater value is purchased.

Dine in only

valid anytime

Domani Ristorante, family owned with over 23 years experience in the restaurant business, serves authentic Italian cuisine in a casual pleasant atmosphere. We serve only freshly prepared food. Join us to celebrate a special occasion or anytime you go out to dine. We always make the occasion feel special.

44110 Ashburn Village Blvd.
Ashburn, VA
(703)723-5360

entertainment.
entertainment.com

Discounts exclude tax,tip and/or alcohol where applicable
Offers not valid holidays and subject to Rules of Use
Tipping should be 15% to 20% of the total bill before discount

00520527

Domani Ristorante

Southern Italian Cuisine

PASTA AUTHENTICO

CHICKEN PARMIGIANA . . . . $7.95 . $8.95
Fresh chicken breast breaded and sauteed with tomato sauce. topped with mozzarella cheese and served with pasta.

EGGPLANT PARMIGIANA $6.95. $8.95
Fresh and lightly egg battered, sauteed, topped with tomato sauce & mozzarella cheese, served with pasta.

STEAK & MORE

FILET MIGNON GORGONZOLA $15.95
8 oz. Aungus beef tenderloin grilled to perfection topped with gorgonzola cheese sauce.

NY STEAK TUSCANY $12.95
Marinated in Italian herbs & olive oil. Grilled to perfection.

STUFFED FLOUNDER W/ CRAB MEAT $13.95
With white cream sauce.

ENTREES

SALTIMBOCCA DI POLLO $12.95
Grilled chicken & prosciutto topped with savory mushrooms sauce & provolone cheese oven baked.

CHICKEN ALLA PICCATA $9.95
Fresh chicken breast sauteed with caper, white wine garlic, lemon butter sauce.

VEAL SCALLOPINE ALLA PICCATA $12.95
Fresh veal scallopine with white wine, garlic, lemon butter caper sauce.

SCAMPI ALLA ROMANO $12.95
Sauteed shrimp in olive oil, garlic, lemon and white wine with a touch of tomato over pasta.

CALAMARI AND MUSSELS $10.95
Sauteed fresh mussels and calamari with choice of red or white sauce.

VEAL SCALLOPINE ALLA MARSALA $12.95
Fresh veal scallopine sauteed w/ sweet wine & mushrooms.

SALMON JUVANI $12.95
Sliced salmon sauteed w/ mushrooms, spinach and flamed red peppers over linguine.

Card No. 45

Minerva
Indian Cuisine
www.minervacuisine.com

Up To $14.00 Value

Enjoy one complimentary A LA CARTE DINNER ENTREE when a second A LA CARTE DINNER ENTREE of equal or greater value is purchased.

Dining room only

valid any evening

The first Indian restaurant to serve the Deccan cuisine, with various regional delights. We offer South Indian cuisine from all the Southern states and North Indian cuisine mainly from Punjab & neighboring regions, famous for their Tandoori style of cooking. It's our pleasure to introduce the real flavors of Indian cuisine to the people of this area.

10364 Lee Hwy.
Fairfax, VA
(703)383-9200

2443-G1 Centreville Rd.
(Village Ctr. at Dulles)
Herndon, VA
(703)793-3223

entertainment.
entertainment.com

00095497

Minerva
Indian Cuisine

FROM OUR CLAY OVEN -
"Tandoor Saugaat"

Tandoor is a traditional char coiled fried Clay Oven shaped like a dome. The meats and breads are cooked at very high temperature often reaching 600 F. This locks all the flavors and the juices baking it to perfection – a gourmet delight.

Tandoori Chicken 9.95
Chicken marinated in yogurt, fresh spices & lemon juices then barbecued in Tandoor

Pudhina Paneer 10.95
Cottage cheese with fresh mint, coriander and herbal masala then grilled in tandoor

VEGETARIAN ENTREES -
"Shaka-Hari Bhojan"

Mutter Paneer.......................... 8.95
A true Moghulai delight, lightly sweet & spicy with flavor of cardamoms

Dal Makhani 8.95
Lentils cooked in low heat & tossed with ginger, garlic, onions, tomatoes & spices

Paneer Makhni......................... 8.95
Cottage cheese cubes lightly fried and cooked in home made special sauce

Tadka Dal 8.95
Mildly spiced lentil curry

CHICKEN ENTRÉES

Butter Chicken......................... 9.95
Chicken cooked with spices, herbs & butter sauce

Chicken Masala........................ 9.95
Chicken cooked with hearty blend of tangy tomato sauce & spices

Chicken Shahi Korma 9.95
A true Moghulai delight, lightly sweet & spicy with flavor of cardamoms

Chicken Vindaloo 9.95
For a true adventurer, who has a passion for spicy food. Tangy & spicy Curry

LAMB ENTRÉES

Lakhnavi Methi Kheema........... 11.95
Fresh ground lamb cooked with fresh fenugreek leaves on slow heat with herbs & spices

Khandari Lamb Kofta Curry 12.95
Minced lamb skewed & grilled in tandoor then sautéed with special sauce

SEAFOOD SPECIALTIES

Ginger Shrimp 11.95
Jumbo shrimp marinated with ginger and cooked with herbs & spices

Shrimp Maharaja..................... 11.95
Jumbo shrimp marinated in yogurt & cooked with tomato and mild cream sauce

RICE SPECIALTIES -
"Hyderabadi Biryani"

Biryani is a synonym with Hyderabad (Deccan). Tender meats are marinated in exotic spices and then stir fried with Onion, Ginger, Green peppers and Spices. These meats are added to Basmati Rice and steamed together to spread the flavour into every morsel.

Lamb Biryani 13.95
Chicken Biryani 12.95
Shrimp Biryani 13.95
Vegetable Biryani 11.95

Card No. 40

Up To $14.00 Value

www.old-europe.com

Enjoy one complimentary LUNCH OR DINNER ENTREE when a second LUNCH OR DINNER ENTREE of equal or greater value is purchased.

valid anytime

Reservations recommended

Since opening its doors in 1948, Old Europe has become a true landmark in Washington, DC, enjoying the reputation for being one of the finest restaurants in our nation's capital. Our food is tasty, beautifully presented & authentically German. We have been recognized with many epicurean honors & recommended by Zagat Guide & Washingtonian Magazine. Open daily.

2434 Wisconsin Ave. NW
(Upper Georgetown)
Washington, DC
(202)333-7600

entertainment
entertainment.com

Discounts exclude tax,tip and/or alcohol where applicable
Offers not valid holidays and subject to Rules of Use
Tipping should be 15% to 20% of the total bill before discount

00372649

Old Europe

DEUS NOBIS LUCULLUS

Vorspeisen, Salate und Suppe
(Appetizers, Salads and Soups)

Schmalzhering "Hausfrauen Art" $5.85
Marinated herring in sour cream with sliced apples and onions

Steak "Tatar" $6.65
Beef Steak "Tatar" freshly ground to order with onions, capers and egg

Kartoffelpuffer mit Apfelmus $4.45
Golden brown potato pancakes with apple sauce

Gulasch Suppe $4.25
A spicy, chunky beef soup with paprika and onions

Entrees

Wiener Schnitzel $16.85
Prime veal steak, breaded, sautéed and garnished with a lemon wheel
Presented with home fried potatoes and house salad

Traditioneller Sauerbraten $15.65
Traditionally marinated slices of roast beef served with potato dumplings and red cabbage

Kassler Rippenspeer mit Sauerkraut und Knödel $13.85
Smoked loin of pork presented with sauerkraut and pototo dumplings

Schweinshaxe "Bayerische Art" mit Kartoffelknödel $16.75
Bavarian style, roasted and honey-glazed pork hocks
served with sauerkraut and potato dumplings

Ungarisches Gulasch mit Spätzle $13.55
Hungarian style beef stew served with homemade German noodles

Hähnchen "Schwarzwälder Art" $12.35
Boneless breast of chicken blanketed with mushrooms and sour cherries in a cream sauce
Served with Spätzle and fresh steamed broccoli

Lachsfilet (gebraten oder pochiert) $15.75
Filet of salmon, broiled or poached, with herb butter
Served with Julienne vegetables and parsley potatoes

Für den Gemüsefreund

Bunter Gemüseteller mit Reibekuchen $9.95
Vegetable platter of sauerkraut, broccoli, mushrooms, cauliflower,
grilled tomato and a potato pancake

Card No. 56

Pars Restaurant

Authentic Persian Cousin

www.parsrestaurant.com

Up To $14.00 Value

Enjoy one complimentary LUNCH OR DINNER ENTREE when a second LUNCH OR DINNER ENTREE of equal or greater value is purchased or when dining alone - one LUNCH OR DINNER ENTREE at 50% off the regular price - maximum discount $7.00.

Lunch buffet and specials excluded

valid anytime

Pars Famous Kabob & Steak offers succulent food, friendly service & attractive surroundings at an affordable price. Voted Washingtonian 100 Best Restaurants since 1998. We serve only the finest selection of kabobs, expertly prepared including chicken, beef, lamb & fresh seafood. Enjoy our Persian specialties at their finest. We are closed Monday.

10801 Lee Hwy.
Fairfax, VA
(703)273-3508

entertainment
entertainment.com

Discounts exclude tax,tip and/or alcohol where applicable
Offers not valid holidays and subject to Rules of Use
Tipping should be 15% to 20% of the total bill before discount

00205156

Pars Restaurant

Authentic Persian Cuisine

Appetizers

Halim Bademjan $4.99
A traditional Persian recipe of beef, eggplant, and beans

Combination Mesas 1 (For two) $11.99
A combination platter of, halim(#1), mirsa(#3), and dolmeh(#5)

Combination Mesas 2 (For two) $11.99
A combination platter of, halim(#1), kuku(#2), and dolmeh(#5)

Special Persian Rice with Meat

Baghali Polo $11.99
Basmati rice mixed with dill weed and lima beans, served with fresh seasoned boiled lamb shank or chicken

Zereshk Polo $10.99
Basmati rice mixed with barberries and saffron served with boiled chicken

Adas Polo $10.99
Basmati rice mixed with raisins, lentils, dates and saffron served with boiled chicken

Chicken

Boneless Chicken Kabob $9.99
Delicious marinated charbroiled, boneless breast

Chicken Kabob (with Bones) $10.99
Delicious marinated charbroiled, Cornish hen

Chicken Shish Kabob $11.99
Thick chunks of Charbroiled chicken breast, marinated in our special sauce with bell peppers, onions and tomato

Chicken & Lamb combination $15.99
Combination of boneless chicken and lamb chunks, marinated & charbroiled

Seafood

Salmon & Scallop Combination $17.99
Marinated large cuts of Salmon and jumbo scallops, with bell pepper, onion

Scallop & Shrimp Combo $17.99
Tender pieces of jumbo scallops, bell peppers, and onions

Scallops Linguini with Alfredo Sauce $18.99
Jumbo scallops, charbroiled and served with linguini mixed with diced tomatoes

Beef

Shish Kabob $13.99
Marinated top sirloin marinated, skewered with bell peppers, and onions

Chelo Kabob Soltani $13.99
A combination of Koobideh and Barg

Kabob Naderi $18.99
The most delicious and juicy chunks of center cut filet mignon, marinated in our special sauce

Steaks

Filet Mignon $21.99
10 Oz Charbroiled to perfection, served with rice and vegetables

New York Steak $19.99
12 Oz New York Strip served with rice and vegetables

Lamb

Lamb Kabob
Our finest cut of charbroiled boneless baby spring lamb chunks marinated in special sauce $12.99

Shishlique(Lamb Chop)
Exotic tender spring lamb rack, marinated and charbroiled to perfection $16.99

Menu Sampler - Prices and offerings subject to change.

Card No. 107

Up To $14.00 Value

Squire Rockwells

www.squirerockwells.com

Enjoy one complimentary DINNER ENTREE when a second DINNER ENTREE of equal or greater value is purchased or when dining alone - one DINNER ENTREE at 50% off the regular price - maximum discount $7.00.

Promotional specials excluded

valid any evening

A cozy, English Country Inn style restaurant featuring aged, never frozen, prime rib, delicious steaks & fresh seafood. Squire Rockwells provides good, friendly, caring service in a relaxed, comfortable atmosphere so you may enjoy your visit with us to the fullest. Piano Bar available Tuesday thru Friday & dancing Fridays & Saturdays. Reservations recommended.

8700 Little River Tpk.
Annandale, VA
(703)560-3600

entertainment
entertainment.com

Discounts exclude tax,tip and/or alcohol where applicable
Offers not valid holidays and subject to Rules of Use
Tipping should be 15% to 20% of the total bill before discount

00152545

Squire Rockwells

HERB ROASTED PRIME RIB

- Petite Cut - 8 ounces $12.95
- Hearty Cut - 12 ounces $14.95
- He-Man Cut - 16 ounces $17.95

STEAKS, RIBS AND CHOPS

London Broil $13.95
Sliced flank steak, marinated in Rockwell's special sauce, grilled and topped with fresh sautéed mushroom gravy, and served with garlic basil mashed red potatoes

Filet Mignon $15.95
Grilled 8oz. of aged and hand cut corn-fed beef bacon wrapped, and served with baked potato

Tudor New York Strip Steak $15.95
Grilled 12oz. of aged and hand cut sirloin strip with herb seasoning, and served with baked potato

Hickory BBQ Baby Back Ribs $15.95
Whole rack of tender, hickory smoked and fire grilled pork ribs glazed with hickory BBQ sauce with coleslaw and french fries

Grilled Herb Pork Chops $15.95
Two, 8oz. grilled center cut chops, sprinkled with fresh rosemary, garlic and cracked pepper, glazed with Pernod sauce, and served with garlic basil mashed red potatoes

SEAFOOD

Sea Scallops Au Gratin $15.95
Fresh Maine Sea Scallops broiled in Sherry Chardonnay sauce, then baked with Monterey jack and cheddar cheeses, and served with rice

Shrimp and Scallops Fradiablo $14.95
Scallops, shrimp, chopped clams with garlic and basil, sautéed in spicy marinara sauce over fresh linguini pasta

VEAL AND CHICKEN

Veal Marsala $15.95
Scaloppini of veal with fresh mushrooms sautéed in marsala wine sauce with herbs over linguini pasta

Blackened Cajun Chicken $13.95
Boneless breasts of chicken, grilled with Cajun seasoning over rice

Card No. 121

thunder grill

AT UNION STATION

www.arkrestaurants.com

Up To $14.00 Value

Enjoy one complimentary LUNCH OR DINNER ENTREE when a second LUNCH OR DINNER ENTREE of equal or greater value is purchased.

valid anytime

Located in Union Station, Thunder Grill is Ark Restaurants' newest property. Earth tones, hand painted tables, hardwood floors & southwestern artwork accentuate the ground level. This restaurant is a visual & culinary celebration of the American Southwest. Join our hospitality M* Card program & visit us at www.arkrestaurants.com.

50 Massachusetts Ave.
(at Union Station)
Washington, DC
(202)898-0051

entertainment
entertainment.com

Discounts exclude tax,tip and/or alcohol where applicable
Offers not valid holidays and subject to Rules of Use
Tipping should be 15% to 20% of the total bill before discount

00397574

thunder grill

AT UNION STATION

entrée salads

grilled yellow fin tuna salad 13.95
with beans, avocado, tomato, olives and citrus vinaigrette- potato

honey chipotle duck salad 12.95
with oranges, jicama, peppers, grilled corn, tosted pumpkin seeds and orange vinaigrette

chicken and avocado tostada 12.95
flour tortilla shell filled with shredded chicken, lettuce, cheese, pico de gallo & guacamole

sandwiches

grilled bison burger 10.95
with lettuce, tomato, sliced onions, thunder fries, coleslaw and ancho mayo

shaved smoked turkey in chipotle wrapper 8.95
with grilled onions, sweet peppers and jalapeno

texas barbeque beef brisket sandwich 8.95
lettuce, tomato and jicama slaw

seafood entrees

honey chili glazed salmon steak 17.95
with corn mashed potatoes and sautéed spinach

blue cornmeal crusted catfish 14.95
with potato and okra hash & a spicy corn salsa

chesapeake blue crab cake 19.95
with jicama slaw and tartar

meat entrees

pan seared cowboy steak 19.95
served with chili buttermilk onion rings and pico de gallo

texas style pork ribs 16.95
served with a texas style potato salad, coleslaw and corn on the cob topped with a smoked barbeque sauce

roasted marinated chicken 14.95
served with sautéed seasonal vegetables and mashed sweet potatoes

Card No. 70

Up To $14.00 Value

the white tiger

fine indian cuisine

www.whitetigerdc.com

Enjoy one complimentary DINNER ENTREE when a second DINNER ENTREE of equal or greater value is purchased.

special promotions excluded

valid anytime

Reservations recommended

"Finally an upscale Indian restaurant that we have been waiting for" - "4 STARS" - The Hill. "Nothing at White Tiger gives us anything but pure pleasure. I wouldn't change a thing" - City Paper. Come & enjoy our exotic Indian cuisine with a delicate blend of exquisite spices. Seasonal patio dining is available. Private Party Room & Catering available.

301 Massachusetts Ave., NE
Washington, DC
(202)546-5900

entertainment
entertainment.com

Discounts exclude tax,tip and/or alcohol where applicable
Offers not valid holidays and subject to Rules of Use
Tipping should be 15% to 20% of the total bill before discount

00509174

the white tiger

fine indian cuisine.

Dilli Ke Namkeen
(Appetizers)

Sabzi Ke Pakore
($3.95)
Golden fried fresh vegetable fritters dipped in spiced chickpea flour batter.

Indian Crabettes
($6.95)
Mildly spiced Indian style crab cakes.

Gosht Seekh Kabob
($5.95)
Lamb ground with a combination of herbs and spices and cooked in the tandoor.

Spiced Calamaris
($5.95)
Sautéed tender squids, delicately flavored with aromatic spices and served with crispy flour chips.

Tandoori
(The Great Indian Barbeque)

Chicken, seafood, lamb or beef marinated subtly in varying mixtures of creamy yogurt and spices, then charbroiled fresh daily in our authentic Tandoori ovens.

Murg (Chicken)

Chicken Tikka
($12.95)
Boneless and tangy morsels of chicken marinated in yogurt, ginger and a blend of spices.

Tandoori Chicken
($12.95) half ($17.95) whole
A Kings Feast Succulent whole chicken, blended aromatically and cooked in the tandoor.

Gosht (Lamb)

Gosht Chaamp
($16.95)
Colorfully skewered lamb chops marinated in yogurt, cardamom and garlic.

Beef

Tandoori Tenderloain Beef
($21.95)
The White Tiger's magnificent signature dish, succulent tenderloin beef sprinkled with aromatic spices and herbs and cooked in the tandoor.

Seafood

Tandoori Lobster Tail
(Market Price)
Succulent lobster tails delicately blended with yogurt and freshly ground spices and cooked in the tandoor.

Kababi

A Kabab Lovers Feast
($24.95)
A sumptuous array of different kababs including chicken, lamb, fish and shrimp.

White Tiger Specialties

Murg (Chicken)

Murg Makhani
($13.50)
A house special made with juliennes of tandoor roasted chicken, and sautéed in a tomato based sauce, prepared in garlic butter and flavored with fenugreek and a blend of spices.

Rajma Turkey Keema
($12.50)
Lean ground turkey delicately cooked with a combination of spices and kidney beans; an Indian style chili.

Gosht (Lamb) and Beef

Jordaloo Boti
($15.95)
Tender lamb chops cooked to perfection with aromatic spices and apricots.

Sabzi-Bhaji
(Vegetarian Specialties)

Bhuna Bharta
($9.95)
Tandoor roasted eggplant, sautéed with onions and tomatoes and a blend of spices.

Bhendi Masala
($9.95)
Tender okra combined with onions, herbs and spices.

Card No. 38

SPIRIT OF WASHINGTON

www.spiritcruises.com

Up To $62.00 Value

Enjoy one complimentary LUNCH OR DINNER CRUISE when a second LUNCH OR DINNER CRUISE of equal or greater value is purchased.

valid anytime

Dinner cruise not valid Friday or Saturday; Limit 3 cards per reservation; At time of reservation, please identify yourself as an Entertainment/DOUC member; Offer May not be combined with any other discount; Other restrictions May apply; Sorry, no refunds or exchanges

The Spirit of Washington offers delightful food, spectacular sightseeing, a high energy show & dancing. On every cruise you will feast on wonderful buffets with delicious salads, entrees, side dishes & tempting desserts. What a fabulous way to experience Washington, Virginia and Maryland. Reservations required. Visit our web site www.spiritcruises.com.

Pier 4
(6th & Water Sts., SW)
Washington, DC
(202)554-8000

entertainment.
entertainment.com

Discounts exclude tax, tip and/or alcohol where applicable.
Offers not valid holidays and subject to Rules of Use
Tipping should be 15% to 20% of the total bill before discount

00033011

SPIRIT
OF WASHINGTON

CLASSIC DINNER BUFFET ENHANCED MENU DESCRIPTIONS

SALAD
Gardener's Delight
Festive mix of Tender Young Greens and Freshly Chopped Vegetables tossed in exquisitely aged Balsamic Vinaigrette and served family-style

CARVING STATIONS
Cob Smoked Ham
Lean Ham slow-cured over roasted corn cobs for a distinctively rich, smoky flavor, enhanced with Caramelized Apples and a tangy Honey-Mustard Sauce

Rosemary Round Roast
Tender Top Round of Beef lavishly sprinkled with Rosemary and slowly braised in its own juices, presented with a richly-favored Demi-Glace and classic chilled Horseradish

ENTREES
Stuffed Sole Chesapeake
Tender Fillet of Sole stuffed with Chesapeake Bay Crabmeat and baked in a full-flavored White Wine Infusion

Sesame Stir-Fry Chicken Teriyaki
Marinated Chicken Strips and Fresh, Chopped Vegetables stir-fried in a simmering Teriyaki Sauce and sprinkled with lightly Toasted Sesame Seeds

Roasted Vegetable Lasagna
Layer upon layer of Pasta, Mozzerella, Parmesan and fire-roasted Vegetables, all baked to a flavorful finish

Chicken Marsala
Tender pan-seared Breast of Chicken simmered and served in a sweet Marsala Wine Sauce

Smoked Andouille Sausage
Savory slices of slow-smoked Andouille Sausage pan seared with an abundance of Peppers and Onions

Lemon-Garlic Shellfish
Freshly gathered Mussels steamed and served in a distinctive Lemon-Garlic Broth

DESSERT

Creme Brulee Cheesecake
Incredibly creamy Cheesecake capped with a thin layer of Vanilla Bean Custard and a tantalizing Toffee Shell of Caramelized Sugar

entertainment

Card No. 64

Up To $14.00 Value

DAKS Grill

www.daksgrill.com

Enjoy one complimentary LUNCH OR DINNER ENTREE when a second LUNCH OR DINNER ENTREE of equal or greater value is purchased.

Dine in only

valid anytime

7629 Richmond Hwy., Alexandria, VA (703)765-0400

13641 Minnieville Rd., Dale City, VA (703)583-1997

5838 Columbia Pike, Falls Church, VA (703)820-3333

00006251

Enjoy casual, friendly, neighborhood dining at DAKS Grill. Specialties include hand-cut steaks, a variety of seafood, chicken & delicious homemade soups. If you're interested in a late night snack or cocktail, come & visit our lounge. DAKS is open daily until 2 a.m. Reservations accepted.

Offers not valid holidays and subject to Rules of Use. Tipping should be 15% to 20% of the total bill before discount.

Homestyle Favorites

Beef Burgundy
Tender chunks of sirloin beef simmered in a rich burgundy wine sauce with onions and mushrooms ladled around our skin-on mashed potatoes. Topped with chives. And you don't even have to leave the good ole' USA to sample this French classic. 8.95

Jambalaya
Hot and spicy! Straight out of bayou country. You'll go crazy over this blend of spicy chicken, ham, HUGE shrimp and low country vegetables. All this goodness ladled around steaming long grain and wild rice and garnished with savory slices of green onion. 9.95

Seafood

Grilled Shrimp ala DAKS
We've made the shrimp larger, peeled and skewered them then basted them with Italian herbs and spices while they are slowly charbroiled to perfection. Sooo...good! 13.95

Salmon Your Way
Plump fillet of salmon prepared as you choose; baked, charbroiled or blackened. A hard decision for a great choice. 11.95

Ahi Tuna
Served blackened or grilled, this yellow-fin beauty will melt in your mouth. We think it's best served rare to medium rare, but you decide. 11.95

Chicken

DAKS Marinated Chicken
Our plumpest breasts specially marinated in our secret blend of tropical fruit juices herbs and spices. Flavor plus!
Two breasts 10.95
One breast 8.95

Dirty Chicken and Linguine
Looks so bad...tastes so good. Thin slices of spicy chicken breast over linguine in a cream sauce any Cajun would be proud of... Topped with diced tomatoes, green onions and a side of garlic bread. 9.95

Steaks

Delmonico
We think we've found one of the tastiest, most juicy steaks ever. But, no one could decide what size it should be, so you just tell us the size and we'll cut it to order. Ten ounce minimum. 1.30 per ounce.

Filet Mignon
A gastronomic celebration! An 8 ounce cut of the most tender steak that you have ever put in your mouth. Our bet is that you won't even need to use your knife. 16.95

Pork

Cajun Grilled Pork Chops
Two juicy pork medallions coated with Cajun spices and grilled to perfection. Hot and flavorful.· 9.95

Menu Sampler - Prices and menu subject to change.
Discounts exclude tax, tip and/or alcohol, where applicable.

Card No. 2

THE CLUBHOUSE GRILL

Up To $17.00 Value

Enjoy one complimentary LUNCH OR DINNER ENTREE when a second LUNCH OR DINNER ENTREE of equal or greater value is purchased.

Dine in only

valid anytime

46950 Community Plaza (located in Clock Tower Shpg. Ctr.), **Sterling, VA (703)444-8675**

00611993

The Clubhouse Grill offers diners a taste of favorite American fare at moderate prices. The setting is casual, relaxed & family friendly complete with a kid's menu. The menu features choices in appetizers, soups, salads, sandwiches, pastas & entrees. Bring in the whole gang to catch the game on one of the many large TV's. Full service bar available.

Offers not valid holidays and subject to Rules of Use. Tipping should be 15% to 20% of the total bill before discount.

Entrees

Stuffed Pork Chop $14.95
Thick cut pork stuffed with herb bread stuffing, smothered with sausage gravy and served with mashed potatoes and vegetables.

Chopped Steak $8.95
Seasoned ground beef smothered with caramelized onions and mushroom sauce. Served with mashed potatoes and vegetables.

BBQ Pork Chop $14.95
Double thick cut pork chop glazed with smoky BBQ sauce, garnished with crispy smoked ham, sweet potato fritters and coleslaw.

Yankee Pot-roast $14.95
Fork tender beef braised in rich beef stock with herbs and root vegetables. Served with crusty bread.

Chicken Pot Pie $11.95
Tender pieces of chicken cooked with vegetables and creamy chicken broth and topped with buttery pastry.

Caramelized Salmon $14.95
Fillet of Atlantic Salmon seared golden and served on a bed of vegetables with corn salsa and red pepper vinaigrette.

Blackened Rib Eye $16.95
Smothered with cayenne onions and served with sweet potato fritters and Creole sauce.

Grilled Rib Eye $16.95
Cooked to order and served with mashed potatoes and vegetables.

Pork Schnitzel $13.95
Jumbo pork cutlet sautéed golden, smothered with capers and lemon butter sauce. Served with fries.

Fish and Chips $11.95
Batter fried catfish served with coleslaw, fries and malt vinegar.

Seafood Platter $17.95
Fried platter of scallops, shrimp, crab cake and catfish served with coleslaw, fries and lemon aioli.

Fried Shrimp $13.95
Large fried shrimp served with coleslaw fries and chili aioli.

Menu Sampler - Prices and menu subject to change.
Discounts exclude tax, tip and/or alcohol, where applicable.

www.villageilporto.com

Card No. 65

Up To $14.00 Value

Located in the heart of Del Ray - Village Il Porto Ristorante offers the most authentic Italian food you have ever eaten. Let our professional staff take care of your every need. Choose from our large wine list to make your Italian food more enjoyable.

Offers not valid holidays and subject to Rules of Use. Tipping should be 15% to 20% of the total bill before discount.

Enjoy one complimentary LUNCH OR DINNER ENTREE when a second LUNCH OR DINNER ENTREE of equal or greater value is purchased.

valid anytime

3110 Mt. Vernon Ave., Alexandria, VA (703)837-0666

00528126

Pasta della Casa ~ Homemade Pasta

Pasta alla Veneziana	lobster, shrimp, scallops & fish sautèed in herbed butter, tossed with pasta & fresh broccoli flowerettes in a cream sauce	13.95
Pasta Primavera con Aragosta	lobster, shrimp, scallops, chopped clams & fresh julienne cut vegetables in a light cream sauce tossed with pasta	13.95

Pollo ~ Chicken *Served with side Spaghetti*

Petto di Pollo Angelica	boneless breast of chicken sautèed with fresh mushrooms in a cream sauce	12.95
Pollo alla Primavera	boneless breast of chicken sautèed in a white wine sauce with fresh julienne style vegetables	12.95

Pesce ~ Seafood *Served with side Spaghetti*

Frutti di Mare	shrimp, scallops, chopped clams & fish seasoned with wine & herbs in a red sauce	13.95
Gamberi alla Marinara	shrimp and chopped clams sautèed in oil, garlic, parsley & wine (white or red sauce)	13.95
Filetto di Pesce	filet of fish sautèed with chopped clams, lemon & champagne sauce	11.95

Vitello ~ Veal *Served with side Spaghetti*

Vitello alla Romano	veal medallions topped with ham & mozzarella cheese in a white wine sauce	13.95
Scaloppine alla Picatta	veal scallopine with capers sautèed in a white wine & butter lemon sauce	13.95
Scaloppine alla Angelica	veal scallopine sautèed with fresh mushrooms in a cream sauce	13.95
Vitello alla Parmigiana	veal scallopine lightly fried and topped with mozarella cheese & tomato sauce	13.95

Menu Sampler - Prices and menu subject to change.
Discounts exclude tax, tip and/or alcohol, where applicable.

Card No. 53

Aldo's
Italian Steakhouse

www.urbanbites.com

Up To $20.00 Value

Enjoy one complimentary LUNCH OR DINNER ENTREE when a second LUNCH OR DINNER ENTREE of equal or greater value is purchased.

Dine in only

valid anytime

7630 Lee Hwy., Falls Church, VA (703)560-1210

00525514

Longtime Washington D.C. restaurateur Al Frye's neighborhood establishment has perfected the combination of a classic Italian eatery & a traditional American steak house. The Italian side of the menu offers five kinds of pasta & nine different sauces. On the steak side, the filet mignon is cooked to perfection. Suitable for a business engagement, or an evening out.

Offers not valid holidays and subject to Rules of Use. Tipping should be 15% to 20% of the total bill before discount.

Italian Specialities

CREATE YOUR OWN PASTA $9.95

Pasta

Buccatini **Fettuccine** **Linguine** **Capellini** **Penne**

Sauces

Pomodoro
A classic tomato sauce with basil

Carbonara
A rich Italian bacon, mushroom cream sauce

Alfredo
A classic creamy Parmesan cheese sauce

Basil Pesto
A house made pesto sauce with sun-dried tomatoes and roasted peppers

Vongole Sauce
An Italian white or red clam sauce

Puttanesca
A spicy tomato sauce with kalamata olives, capers and anchovies

Steakhouse Entrees

Filet Mignon $19.95
8 oz. filet topped with roasted peppers, sautéed spinach, and a marsala wine sauce, served with vegetables and roasted potatoes

Pork Chop $15.95
16 oz. Porterhouse Cut Chop smothered with rich au poivre sauce, served with garlic mashed potatoes and Julienne vegetables

Veal Marsala $16.95
Scaloppine of veal smothered in a delicious mushroom marsala wine sauce, served with roasted potatoes and Julienne vegetables

Seafood

Frutti di Mare $17.95
Shrimp, calamari, mussels, clams, and lobster meat in lobster brandy sauce over linguine

Salmon $13.95
Grilled center cut salmon filet topped with cognac Dijon mustard sauce, served with vegetables and rice

Menu Sampler - Prices and menu subject to change.
Discounts exclude tax, tip and/or alcohol, where applicable.

Card No. 66

Hunan Royale

Up To $14.00 Value

Enjoy one complimentary DINNER ENTREE when a second DINNER ENTREE of equal or greater value is purchased.

Dining room only; Daily specials & whole lobster dishes excluded

valid any evening

8746 Cooper Rd., Alexandria, VA (703)360-2888

00031247

Our master chefs create exciting and unique entrees in generous portions. Each selection is prepared to order and suited to your taste. We are conveniently located near Mt. Vernon. We are open daily. Reservations not required.

Offers not valid holidays and subject to Rules of Use. Tipping should be 15% to 20% of the total bill before discount.

Chicken	*Lunch*	*Dinner*
★ Hunan Chicken	4.50	7.95
★ Crispy Sesame Chicken	-	7.95
★ Da-Cheng Chicken	4.50	7.95
Chicken with Cashew Nuts	4.50	7.95
Beef		
★ Hunan Beef	4.95	8.25
★ Sichuan Beef	4.95	8.25
★ Hunan Lamb	-	8.25
Peking Beef	-	8.25
Pork		
★ Hunan Pork	4.50	7.95
Sweet and Sour Pork	4.50	7.95
★ Yu-Shion Pork	4.50	7.95
Shredded Pork Peking Style	4.50	7.95
Seafood		
★ Hunan Shrimp	5.50	9.25
Sweet and Sour Shrimp	5.50	9.25
★ Fish Filet Sichuan Style	-	9.25
★ Lobster Sichuan Style	-	18.95

Menu Sampler - Prices and menu subject to change.
Discounts exclude tax, tip and/or alcohol, where applicable.

Card No. 43

JW & FRIENDS

Up To $20.00 Value

Enjoy one complimentary DINNER ENTREE when a second DINNER ENTREE of equal or greater value is purchased.

Dine in only

valid any evening

6531 Backlick Rd., Springfield, VA (703)451-4556

00615581

Next time you're out with that special someone take them to a special place JW & Friends. Come in our front door for a wonderful white tablecloth dining experience or for a more casual neighborhood feel, come on in to our lounge area through our back door. You'll always be treated like family at JW & Friends. Open daily.

Offers not valid holidays and subject to Rules of Use. Tipping should be 15% to 20% of the total bill before discount.

Sandwiches

The Olympic Game's Steak Sandwich: $10.95
Thinly sliced Strip steak, marinated in fresh herbs and grilled. Served in Pita bread with Tzatziki sauce.

Mexican Grilled Chicken Wrap: $9.95
Marinated with fresh herbs and wrapped in Tortilla with roasted peppers and tomatoes. Served with Pico De Gallo guacamole, sour cream and chipotle sauce.

JW's Famous Burger: $9.95
Half pound of Certified Angus beef grilled to perfection. Served with JW's House fries and onion rings with coleslaw on Kaiser Roll.

Fish and Pasta

Fish of the Day: Market Price
Chef choice of preparation. Served with capers, wine and lemon sauce with fresh Capellini pasta.

Pan Seared Jumbo Sea Scallops: $19.95
Served with Shellfish Saffron cream sauce and Saffron Risotto.

Linguine with Mussels and Clams: $17.95
Served with garlic wine sauce and fresh pasta with Imported Italian aged Parmesan cheese.

Fresh Penne Pasta and Grill Vegetable: $10.95
Grilled mixed summer vegetables marinated in Balsamic vinaigrette. Served with fresh buffalo mozzarella cheese.

Chesapeake Bay Crab Cakes: Market Price
Two cakes with jumbo lump crabmeat sauté and served with JW's House fries and spicy remoulade.

Shrimp Scampi: $19.95
Sautéed shrimps in garlic sauce. Served with fresh Capellini pasta.

Grill Salmon: $18.95
Grilled with spices. Served with Béarnaise sauce and garlic mash potatoes.

Island Grill Tuna: $19.95
Grilled chili sauce. Served with Citrus sauce Saffron Risotto.

Menu Sampler - Prices and menu subject to change.
Discounts exclude tax, tip and/or alcohol, where applicable.

Card No. 62

SPICES
FINE INDIAN CUISINE

Up To $14.00 Value

Come experience an evening of Indian in the heart of Manassas. Enjoy wonderful flavors from our extensive menu from Southern India. Our delicious entrees of chicken, lamb, beef, seafood & vegetables are prepared to your order. We look forward to serving you.

Offers not valid holidays and subject to Rules of Use. Tipping should be 15% to 20% of the total bill before discount.

Enjoy one complimentary LUNCH OR DINNER ENTREE when a second LUNCH OR DINNER ENTREE of equal or greater value is purchased.

Dine in only; Buffet excluded

valid anytime

11010 Sudley Manor Dr. (Festival at Bull Run Shpg. Ctr.), **Manassas, VA (703)330-7200**

00665190

SPICE'S CLAY POT

Paneer Tikka 10.95
Cubes of home made cheese marinated with yogurt and spices cooked in clay pot

Tandoori Chicken 11.95
Chicken marinated in special traditional spices and grilled in the tandoori oven to perfection

CHICKEN DELIGHTS

(All main courses served with Rice/Naan)

Butter chicken 11.25
Boneless pieces of chicken cooked with exotic spices, herbs and butter

Chicken curry 9.95
Chicken cooked with delicately flavored curry sauce

Chicken tikka masala 10.25
Boneless pieces of chicken cooked in clay oven with tomato onion base sauce, exotic herbs and spices

LAMB SPECIALITIES

(All main courses served with Rice/Naan)

Lamb vindaloo 12.95
For the one with "True passion for spicy food!", lamb and potatoes are cooked in fiery red chilly and vinegar sauce

Lamb korma 12.95
Succulent pieces of lamb cooked in creamy, sweet & spicy sauce with delicate flavor of cardamoms

SEA FOOD SPECIALITIES

(All main courses served with Rice/Naan)

Shrimp vindaloo 11.95
Shrimp and baby potatoes cooked in onion gravy

Shrimp korma 12.25
Shrimp cooked in rich creamy sauce

Fish tikka masala 11.95
Cubes of mahi mahi fish cooked in a clay pot and mixed with tomato gravy

VEGETARIAN SPECIALITIES

(All main courses served with Rice/Naan)

Paneer labab dar 9.95
Home made cottage cheese cooked with slices of onion, tomato and capsicum

Dal laknow 8.95
Green lentils temperred with onions, tomato, ginger garlic and spices

Stuffed tomato 8.95
Tomatoes stuffed with chef's special vegetables cooked in cashew gravy

BIRYANI SPECIALITIES

Spice's chicken biryani 12.75
A traditionally cooked basmati rice with succulent pieces of chicken and aromatic Spices cooked over a low fire and served with raita

Lamb biryani 12.95
Succulent pieces of lamb cooked with basmati rice and aromatic spices cooked over low fire dum pukht style, served with raita

Menu Sampler - Prices and menu subject to change.
Discounts exclude tax, tip and/or alcohol, where applicable.

Card No. 27

O'FAOLÁIN'S

FOR A REAL TASTE OF IRELAND

IRISH RESTAURANT & PUB

Up To $15.00 Value

Enjoy one complimentary LUNCH OR DINNER ENTREE when a second LUNCH OR DINNER ENTREE of equal or greater value is purchased.

Dine in only

valid anytime

20921 Davenport Dr., Sterling, VA (703)444-9796

00607699

At O'Faolain's you'll feel like you've just stepped into a pub in Ireland. We create mouth watering dishes to satisfy any palate. Make your next dining experience a memorable one!! Bring the whole family by today. Open daily.

Offers not valid holidays and subject to Rules of Use. Tipping should be 15% to 20% of the total bill before discount.

Entrees

All served with your choice of <u>two</u> sides.

Champ, Baked Potato, Mashed Potatoes, Steamed Spinach with Garlic, Vegetable of the Day or Sautéed Mushrooms.

Bushmills Salmon $16
Grilled fresh salmon steak with an Irish whiskey glaze

Gaelic Steak 12oz $20
New York strip topped with Tabasco onions. Served with a Jameson Irish whiskey & field mushroom demi-glaze.

O'Faolain's Chicken $14
Tender breast of chicken filled with sautéed spinach, cheddar & bacon. Topped with a wholegrain mustard cream sauce.

Roasted Pork Loin $15
Bacon wrapped pork-loin with a portabello mushroom & applejack cognac sauce.

Shrimp & Scallops Scampi $17
Jumbo shrimp & sea scallops, sautéed in a lemon garlic & fresh herb butter.

Rib Eye 12oz $18
A delicious cut - grilled to your preference.

Roast Chicken & Bacon $13
Half a chicken, roasted. Served with traditional bread & onion- herb stuffing, gravy & rashers of Irish bacon.

O'Faolain's Favorites

Wicklow Shepherd's Pie $10
Minced beef slowly simmered with herbs, peas & carrots. Then baked in a pie with champ potato topping.

One 'n One $11
Beer batter fried fish filet. Served with French fries & homemade Tartar sauce.

Guinness Casserole $10
A classic recipe. Beef marinated in Guinness, simmered with carrots, onion & fresh thyme. Served with mashed potatoes.

Chicken Potpie $10
Chicken & vegetables baked in a pie with a tarragon cream sauce & topped with flaky pastry.

Traditional Irish Breakfast $13
Delicious anytime! Two eggs, Irish sausages, rashers of Irish bacon, black & white pudding, Irish baked beans & tomato. Served with brown bread.

Bangers & Mash $10
Irish pork sausages grilled & served with mashed potatoes & Irish baked beans.

Corned Beef & Cabbage $13
A traditional dish. Served with Lakeshore Irish mustards.

Menu Sampler - Prices and menu subject to change.
Discounts exclude tax, tip and/or alcohol, where applicable.

Card No. 34

Omia's Grill & Pub

Up To $15.00 Value

Enjoy one complimentary DINNER ENTREE when a second DINNER ENTREE of equal or greater value is purchased.

Dine in only; This location only

valid any evening

1015 Dranesville Rd., Herndon, VA (703)444-6666

00622993

Enjoy fine dining in a casual, comfortable setting at one of Loudoun County's newest restaurant. Serving the finest in American favorites & local fare. There is something on the menu to please everyone. Omia's Grill & Pub is the perfect place to entertain friends & family with their excellent food, friendly service & warm surroundings.

Offers not valid holidays and subject to Rules of Use. Tipping should be 15% to 20% of the total bill before discount.

PASTA

Eggplant Parmigiana 9.99
fried eggplant topped with melted mozzarella cheese served over pasta and your choice of meat of meatless sauce

Rigatoni Al-Fourno 9.99
rigatoni pasta with special sauce

Veal Parmigiana..9.99

POLLO/CHICKEN

Linguini with Chicken 14.99
Tortellini Alfredo with Chicken 14.99
Chicken Marsala...14.99
Sautéed chicken breast, Marsala wine, mushrooms, garlic, herbs and tomatoes over linguine

Chicken Parmigiana 14.99
Parmesan-breaded chicken breast, fried and topped with marinara sauce and melted mozzarella cheese

SURF & TURF

1lb. Lobster Tail 19.99
Fettuccini with Shrimp..15.99
Crab Dinner 11.99
Fried Fish Dinner 10.99
New York Strip 12oz. 13.99
Filet Mignon 12oz. 19.99

Menu Sampler - Prices and menu subject to change.
Discounts exclude tax, tip and/or alcohol, where applicable.

Card No. 18

Up To $14.00 Value

Emerald's American Grill

BREAKFAST • LUNCH • DINNER

www.emeralsamericangrill.com

Emerald's is the newest American Grill Restaurant to the Fredericksburg/Stafford area in Virginia. It opened it's doors to serve & welcome everyone who enjoys good food & a relaxing atmosphere. It's unique setting is made for families, couples & even singles. Our three dining areas will meet everyone's needs.

Offers not valid holidays and subject to Rules of Use. Tipping should be 15% to 20% of the total bill before discount.

Enjoy one complimentary LUNCH OR DINNER ENTREE when a second LUNCH OR DINNER ENTREE of equal or greater value is purchased.

Dine in only

valid anytime

543 Warrenton Rd., Fredericksburg, VA (540)371-4447

00605600

ENTREES

Prime Rib:

Light Cut.................. $13.99

Emerald's Cut............. $16.99

Babyback Ribs:

Half..................... $10.00

Full..................... $15.99

A rack of babyback ribs, rubbed with spices and slathered with hickory-smoked barbecue sauce; served with house slaw and french fries

Pork Chops.................. $14.99

Double cut pork chops seasoned and charbroiled to order; served with seasonal vegetables, along with your choice of baked potato or roasted garlic mashed potatoes

Lamb Chops.................. $15.99

Lamb chops, marinated, seasoned, and charbroiled to order; served with seasonal vegetables, along with your choice of baked potato, rice pilaf, or roasted garlic mashed potatoes

Veal Marsala $14.99

Veal medallions sautéed in a sweet marsala wine and mushroom sauce; served with seasonal vegetables complemented with pasta

CHICKEN AND PASTA

Emerald's Chicken Sauté........ $11.99

Marinated, sautéed chicken breast with sun-dried tomatoes, pine nuts, and mushrooms; served with angel hair pasta

Chicken Parmesan............. $11.99

Lightly breaded chicken breast, delicately sautéed, topped with marinara sauce, mozzarella and parmesan cheeses; served over pasta

Fettuccine Alfredo.............. $9.99

Creamy alfredo sauce served over fettuccine pasta and garnished with parmesan cheese

SEAFOOD

Atlantic Salmon $14.99

Atlantic salmon, carefully seasoned and slowly baked; served with seasonal vegetables and your choice of baked potato, rice pilaf, or roasted garlic mashed potatoes

Crab Cake.................... $14.99

Maryland crabmeat, hand patted and pan fried to perfection; served with tartar sauce, house slaw, and steak fries

Menu Sampler - Prices and menu subject to change.
Discounts exclude tax, tip and/or alcohol, where applicable.

Card No. 32

25% OFF

MYSTERY Dinner Playhouse

www.mysterydinner.com

Alexandria's original murder mystery dinner theatre & Virginia's Leader in murderously mysterious fun! Now in our 13th smash year with theatres in Alexandria, Richmond, Williamsburg & VA Beach. Enjoy a delicious 4-course dinner while solving a comedy murder mystery. Reservations required in advance & must be secured with a VISA®, MasterCard®, AMEX or Discover.

Offers not valid holidays and subject to Rules of Use. Tipping should be 15% to 20% of the total bill before discount.

Enjoy 25% off the regular price of any DINNER SHOW PACKAGE for up to 4 people.

valid anytime

Please mention Entertainment® when booking reservations; On availability basis

4641 Kenmore Ave. (Sheraton Pentagon South - Alexandria), **Alexandria, VA (888)471-4802**

00656699

Mystery Dinner Playhouse started with this unique style of Dinner Theatre 13 years ago, and since then we have entertained thousands of people all over Virginia!

When you arrive, you will be met at the door by one or two of the evening's characters, who will help you find your table, direct you to our cash bar, or get ready for the mystery that is about to unfold!

Between scenes, our cast (always in character) serves you a Delicious 4-course dinner. This gives you a chance to question Each of the suspects about key elements of the murder.

As the evening progresses and the plot thickens, you will open a clue dossier, which contains riddles and puzzles to help you solve the crime. You will also be given bribe money to use to obtain additional clues from the characters.

At the end of the evening, we collect all of the solution sheets From the audience and have a drawing to give a small prize To the person who best solves the mystery. We also give Prizes to the more stup....uh, well...creative answers!

Mystery Dinner Playhouse also hosts private parties, corporate shows & tour groups.

Showtimes

Every Wednesday, Thursday, Friday & Saturday at 7:30 pm
(Doors open at 7 p.m. – Cash Bar)

Menu Sampler - Prices and menu subject to change.
Discounts exclude tax, tip and/or alcohol, where applicable.

Card No. 136

Up To $14.00 Value

Indian Restaurant

We welcome you to Oasis Indian Restaurant- a dining experience that will take you to India. Our menu selections are healthy. We primarily grill & charbroil using only the freshest ingredients. Our staff is happy to serve you; our chef will prepare your meal to suit your palate. Come to Oasis Indian Restaurant for a taste of India. Reservations accepted.

Offers not valid holidays and subject to Rules of Use. Tipping should be 15% to 20% of the total bill before discount.

Enjoy one complimentary LUNCH OR DINNER ENTREE when a second LUNCH OR DINNER ENTREE of equal or greater value is purchased.

Thali and buffet excluded; Dining room only

valid anytime

13971 Metrotech Dr. (Sully Place), **Chantilly, VA**
(703)222-9544

00007099

Entrées

Oasis Platter 14.95
A delightful assortment of tandoori chicken, reshmi kebab, seekh kebab and mughalai kebab.

Tandoori Fish 13.95
Fillet of fish marinated in our blend of masalas and masterfully grilled.

Seafood Kaju 14.95
Shrimp and scallops cooked in a delicate cashew cream sauce.

Goan Shrimp Curry 13.95
Shrimp cooked to perfection in a spicy coconut sauce.

Chilli Chicken 12.95
Tender pieces of chicken breast marinated in Indian-Chinese spices, sautéed with onions and bell peppers.

Lamb Bengal 11.95
Succulent pieces of lamb sautéed with peas & potatoes; simmered in a curry sauce.

Vindaloo 11.95
Choice of chicken, lamb, or beef, cooked with potatoes in a spicy, tangy sauce. A specialty of Goa.

Roganjosh 13.95
Choice of chicken, lamb, or beef cooked in a light yogurt sauce.

Vegetarian Entrées

Birbal Kebab 12.95
Homemade cheese cubes sautéed in a spicy cilantro sauce, served with a bell pepper stuffed with vegetable curry of the day, on a sizzler.

Malai Kofta 10.95
Vegetable dumplings cooked in a delicate tomato cream sauce.

Menu Sampler - Prices and menu subject to change.
Discounts exclude tax, tip and/or alcohol, where applicable.

Card No. 24

Up To $14.00 Value

Preet Palace
INDIAN CUISINE

Enjoy one complimentary DINNER ENTREE when a second DINNER ENTREE of equal or greater value is purchased.

Dining room only

valid any evening

14112 Lee Hwy. (Newgate Shpg. Ctr.), **Centreville, VA**
(703)815-4500

00454811

Experience authentic Indian cuisine in Centreville. We specialize in Tandoori cooking. All of our dishes are prepared to order. We are located in the Newgate Shopping Center at the intersection of Rte. 29 & 28. Voted one of the best places to eat in Centreville / Manassas by The Washingtonian Magazine. We are open daily.

Offers not valid holidays and subject to Rules of Use. Tipping should be 15% to 20% of the total bill before discount.

Tanandoori, Charcoal Babecues & Grilled

Tandoori Chicken *Grill* **10.95**
Half chicken marinated overnight in yogurt ,spice and herbs . Roastedin the clay oven over charcoal.

Murg Tikka Tandoori *Grill* **11.95**
Boneless chunks of Boneless chicken breast marinated in our special recipe , barbecued over flaming charcoal inclayoven

Seekh Kabab Tandoori *Grill* **11.95**
Minced'Lamb rolls , Skewed and grilled over charcoal and clay oven

Lamb shesh Kabab *Mincedlamb rolss, Skewed* **10.95**

Tandoori Salmon *Fresh fillets of salmon marinated in chef's special sauce and charbroiled in the clay oven Grilled* **12.95**

Shrimp Tandoori *shrimp lightly seasoned in a blend of spices and broil in over charcoal in clay oven Grilled* **14.95**

Paneer Kabob *Homemade cheese cubes grilled on skewers with green peppers and onions Grilled* **11.95**

Basmati Rice Specialties

Vegetable Biryani *Basmati rice and fresh green vegetables richly flavored with saffron and cooked with indian herbs on a low heat* **8.95**

Chicken Biryani *Basmatio rice and peices of chicken richly flavored with saffron and cooked with indian herd on a low heat* **9.95**

Lamb Biryani **10.95**
Tender pieces of lamb cooked with rice and indian herbs and spices

Seafood Specialties

Salmon Curry *Salmon fish-fillet Barbecued over flaming charcoal clay oven.simmered in tantalizing sauce* **11.95**

Shrimp Curry *Medium sized shrimp sauteed with ginger , garlic, onions ,green pepers ,and creamysauce* **12.95**

Shrimp Palak **13.95**
Steamed shrimp cooked with spinach in curry sauce over a slow fire

Shrimp Vindaloo **13.95**
A famous spicy dish . Steamed shrimp cooked in our special hot sauce and yogurt with potattoes

Lamb Specialties

Lamb Curry **10.50**
fresh pieces of lamb cooked with garlic and ginger in curry sauce

Lamb vindaloo *A famous spicy Goan dish . Tender pieces of lamb cooked with fresh herbs potatoes and spices* **10.95**

Lamb Palak **10.95**
Chunks of lamb with spinach cooked in delicate spices and herbs

Lamb Do Plaza **10.95**
Lamb cubes in spicy curry granish with onions

Rogan Josh *A specailty from Kashmir . Lean freash chunks of lamb cookked in chefs creamy yogurt curry suace* **12.50**

Menu Sampler - Prices and menu subject to change.
Discounts exclude tax, tip and/or alcohol, where applicable.

Card No. 69

Up To $18.00 Value

Colonial Tavern home to the Irish Brigade

www.irishbrigadetavern.com

The original train station has been restored to a time when the Irish Brigade reigned as one of our premier colonial regiments. The dining room features authentic Irish cuisine & served by our colonial period dressed staff. The Stonewall bar features local & Irish brews on tap. Nightly entertainment. Outdoor seasonal patio dining. Open from 11:30 a.m. daily.

Offers not valid holidays and subject to Rules of Use. Tipping should be 15% to 20% of the total bill before discount.

Enjoy one complimentary LUNCH OR DINNER ENTREE when a second LUNCH OR DINNER ENTREE of equal or greater value is purchased.

valid anytime

Friday seating before 7 p.m.

406 Lafayette Blvd. (in downtown at the corner of Lafayette & Charles), **Fredericksburg, VA (540)373-1313**

00594937

APPETIZERS & PUB FARE

Celtic Nachos
Potato Wedges topped with Cheddar Cheese + rashers bits. Served with sour cream

6

Tavern Beer Battered Fried Mushrooms
Served with Ranch Dressing

5

MAIN FARE
Served from 4:00pm to 9:00pm

Homestead Shepherd's Pie
A Hearty combination of ground sirloin, carrots, peas and onions in a rich savory brown gravy. Smothered with garlic smashed potatoes and topped with cheddar cheese-n-onion topping.

13

Hibernian Stew
Tender Chunky Lamb Medallions slowly simmered with pearl onions, carrots and potatoes in a savory thyme seasoned broth. An Irish Tradition.

16

Blue & Gray Chicken Breast
Grilled chicken breast marinated in lemon and herb sauce. Accompanied by vegetable of the day and choice of potato.

17

General Meagher's Gaelic Steak
A sizzling 10 oz. New York Strip basted with our own Jamesons Irish Whiskey butter sauce and charbroiled to your specification. Accompanied by vegetable of the day and choice of potato.

18

Tavern's Own Potroast
Braised Guinness marinated Chuck roast seasoned and slowly roasted with potatoes, carrots and onions.

15

Irish Brigade Mixed Grill
From the old sod. Grilled rashers, bangers, lamb cutlet with Bachelors Beans, fried egg, with broiled tomato and mushrooms.

17

Fighting Irish Fish-n-Chips
A generous portion of crispy Beer-battered Cod fillets served with homemade remoulade sauce, with Salt-n-Malt Chip Shop fries.

13

Farmer's Market Platter
Salad lovers ultimate combination. Emerald Green Salad topped with ham, turkey, shrimp, bacon, boiled egg, tomato, red onion, scallions, celery, cheddar cheese and croutons with your choice dressing.

12

Menu Sampler - Prices and menu subject to change.
Discounts exclude tax, tip and/or alcohol, where applicable.

Card No. 67

Up To $15.00 Value

CLASSIC CAFE

Enjoy one complimentary LUNCH OR DINNER ENTREE when a second LUNCH OR DINNER ENTREE of equal or greater value is purchased.

Dine in only

valid anytime

8509 Rixlew Lane, Manassas, VA (703)257-1551

00574567

Welcome back to how dining is supposed to be. Our service is warm & friendly & our food is delicious. We offer soups, salads, pastas, steaks, chicken, seafood & over 9 surf & turf items. We can't wait to see you. Open daily.

Offers not valid holidays and subject to Rules of Use. Tipping should be 15% to 20% of the total bill before discount.

STEAK SPECIALTIES

Cajun Teriyaki Rib Eye
16 oz Rib eye marinated with cajun and teriyaki seasoning served sizzling with peppers and onion topped with jalapenos 15.95

Apple Smoked Pork Chops
Twin chops served on the bone for added flavor, grilled over smoked apple chips and topped with onions and peppers. Served with cinnamon apples 12.95

Oriental Sirloin
12 oz sirloin topped with sautéed shrimp and oriental vegetables in garlic bourbon souce 12.95

Royal Sirloin Merlot
12 oz aged New York Sirloin topped with merlot brown sauce with portabella mushrooms 13.95

Prime Rib
Served Friday and Saturday night
Slow roasted aged beef
12 oz 12.95 16 oz 14.95

FROM THE GRILL

Baby Back Ribs
Twice basted with smokey BBQ sauce
Half Rack 9.95 Full Rack 14.95

New York
We call this steak. The Royal Sirloin, The King of all beef
12 oz 11.95 16 oz 14.95

Porterhouse 16 oz
Some say this is the best of all steak, tell us what you think 15.95

Filet Mignon 10 oz
The leanest cut of meat, now on the menu by popular demand 15.95

SEAFOOD

Classic Fried Fish
8 oz fresh haddock hand breaded and fried until golden served with FF, onion rings, and Classic cole slaw 7.95

Fried Haddock and Scallops
Fresh haddock and sea scallops served with FF, onion rings, and Classic cole slaw 10.95

Fried Oysters
Fresh shucked oysters, hand breaded, served with FF, onion rings, and Classic cole slaw 10.95

Baked Haddock
The best white fish available topped with Classic crumbs 8.95

Coconut Shrimp
8 Jumbo Shrimp hand battered with our secret recipe of shredded coconut and herbs, served with FF, onion rings, and Classic cole slaw 12.95

Broiled sea scallops
The freshest scallops available topped with Classic crumbs 11.99

Lobster and Crabmeat Casserole
Fresh lobster and lump crabmeat topped with Classic seafood stuffing 12.95

Menu Sampler - Prices and menu subject to change.
Discounts exclude tax, tip and/or alcohol, where applicable.

Card No. 71

TAJ BAR & GRILL

Up To $14.00 Value

A diversion of colors, spices, taste, flavors, aroma & presentation. Serving India's finest cuisine. Indian & Tandoor dishes, Crab Masala & Bhuna Gosht. Separate banquet facilities on premises. Lunch buffet every day.

Offers not valid holidays and subject to Rules of Use. Tipping should be 15% to 20% of the total bill before discount.

Enjoy one complimentary DINNER ENTREE when a second DINNER ENTREE of equal or greater value is purchased.

Dine in only

valid any evening

3535 Chain Bridge Rd. (Next to the Best Western),
Fairfax, VA (703)246-9090

00579753

Tandoor

(Traditional Indian Clay Oven)

Tandoori Chicken **$10.95**
Charcoal grilled half chicken marinated in yogurt-based sauce

Lamb Boti Kebab **$12.95**
Lamb chunks marinated in a yogurt-based sauce and charbroiled

Seafood Specialties

Crab Masala **$15.95**
Crab meat mildly spiced and cooked in a mild cream and butter sauce

Lobster Korma **$16.95**
Mildly spiced and cooked in a rich cashew-based sauce

Chicken Specialtics

Butter Chicken **$11.95**
Boneless white chicken grilled in the tandoor and cooked in a tomato-based curry sauce with cream

Murg Tikka Masala **$11.95**
Boneless white chicken grilled in the tandoor and finished in onion and tomato-based gravy with fresh fenugreek

Lamb Specialties

Elachi Gosht Korma **$12.95**
A true Mughlai delicacy

Gosht Palak **$11.95**
Lamb cooked in a mild spinach curry sauce

Menu Sampler - Prices and menu subject to change.
Discounts exclude tax, tip and/or alcohol, where applicable.

Card No. 44

The Cafe

Up To $20.00 Value

Enjoy one complimentary DINNER ENTREE when a second DINNER ENTREE of equal or greater value is purchased.

Dining room only

valid any evening

7920 Jones Branch Dr (Located inside the Hilton McLean Tysons Corner), **McLean, VA (703)847-5000**

00504023

Welcome to The Cafe! One of Tysons Corners best kept secrets. We offer a relaxed & casual atmosphere featuring pasta entrees, entrees from the grill & seafood dishes. We are perfect for business or pleasure. Open daily.

Offers not valid holidays and subject to Rules of Use. Tipping should be 15% to 20% of the total bill before discount.

PASTA

Seafood Creole 20.00

Sautéed jumbo shrimp, scallops, calamari and Andouille sausage with fresh garlic, bell pepper, mushrooms and chardonnay, tossed with spicy Creole sauce and Basmati rice

ENTREES

Pork Chop Bella 19.00

Double-cut pork chop, pan seared with roasted garlic, wild mushroom & port wine sauce

Grilled Filet Mignon 28.00

8 oz Certified Angus Beef® with asparagus, Béarnaise sauce and roasted sweet garlic mashed potatoes

Grilled New York Strip 26.00

10 oz Certified Angus Beef® sirloin, bordelaise sauce, with sautéed wild mushrooms and peppers, classic baked potato

Seared Chicken Parisienne 18.00

Marinated in lemon and rosemary, seared and topped with wild mushrooms, sun-dried tomatoes and brandy cream demi served atop mashed potatoes with steamed asparagus

Menu Sampler - Prices and menu subject to change.
Discounts exclude tax, tip and/or alcohol, where applicable.

Card No. 79

Up To $14.00 Value

Toscana Grill

Ristorante Italiano

Enjoy one complimentary DINNER ENTREE when a second DINNER ENTREE of equal or greater value is purchased.

Dine in only

valid any evening

2300 Clarendon Blvd., Arlington, VA (703)465-2100

00557408

Welcome to Toscana Grill. Our friendly staff invites you to relax & enjoy a wonderful dining experience. We feature all your favorite Italian favorites. We are open daily.

Offers not valid holidays and subject to Rules of Use. Tipping should be 15% to 20% of the total bill before discount.

Homemade Pasta

Gnocchi Marinara 7.95
Potato Pasta with Italian herbs & marinara sauce.

Ziti 7.95
Mixed with fresh ground beef & Italian herbs, topped with melted mozzarella cheese.

Fettuccini Primavera 7.95
With fresh Italian vegetables.

Tortellini a la Panna 8.95
Spinach, cheese & pasta in a rich cream sauce.

Chicken

All Chichen dishes are served with linguini and tomato sauce

Chicken Francese 7.95
Chicken dipped in eggs & sauteed in lemon & butter

Chicken Marsala 7.95
Chicken breast sauteed w/mushrooms & marsala wine.

Chicken Parmagiana 7.95
Chicken covered with bread crumbs & baked with mozzorelll cheese.

Chicken Pizzaiola 7.95
Chicken pounded in small pieces cooked in marinara sauce.

Veal

All Veal dishes are served with Linguini & tomato sauce

Veal Milanese 11.95
Fresh veal, breaded and deep fried

Veal Francese 11.95
Fresh veal dipped in eggs, flour & sauteed in lemon & butter.

Veal Scallopini Picata 11.95
Fresh scallopini of veal cooked w/ lemon butter

Seafood

All seafood dishes are served with linguini

Mussels 8.95
Steamed & served w/ your choice of marinara sauce w/ Italian spices or our white sauce of olive oil, garlic, oregano, parsley, basil & red peppers.

Calamari 8.95
Steamed squid w/ Italian spices, served w/ marinara sauce.

Clams 11.95
Steamed w/ your choice of our red or white sauce as described w/ our steamed mussels.

Shrimp Fradiavalo 11.95
Steamed shrimp w/itallan spices served with our marinara sauce.

Menu Sampler - Prices and menu subject to change.
Discounts exclude tax, tip and/or alcohol, where applicable.

Card No. 111

Grapevine Cafe

Up To $14.00 Value

Enjoy one complimentary LUNCH OR DINNER ENTREE when a second LUNCH OR DINNER ENTREE of equal or greater value is purchased.

Daily specials included

valid anytime

622 Kenmore Ave., Fredericksburg, VA (540)371-9300

00378190

Visit one of downtown historic Fredericksburg's local favorite restaurants. Casual, yet elegant atmosphere sets the mood for a relaxing meal. Start off your meal with a delicious appetizer, homemade soups or salads. Entrees include prime rib, chicken, pork & seafood, along with creative pasta dishes. Live music during the week. Open Mon.- Sat. for lunch & dinner.

Offers not valid holidays and subject to Rules of Use. Tipping should be 15% to 20% of the total bill before discount.

Entrees

All Entrees served with Vegetable and Potato of the Day,

Prime Rib.................................. $12.95
12 oz. Cut of Prime Rib which has been seasoned and slowly roasted.

Pollo Con Carcioei $10.95
Chicken breast sauteed with lemon juice, white wine and Artichoke Hearts

Tunno Ala Livornese.................$13.95
Grilled Tuna sauteed in fresh mint and tomatoes.

Crab Cakes....................................$15.95
Two large Crab Cakes sauteed in white wine, lemon juice and butter.

Salmon Ala Grilia.....................................$13.95
Grilled Salmon sauteed in fresh garlic, white wine, lemon juice and fresh Fennel

Pasta

Fettucini Alla Bolognese ....$ 9.95
Pasta with sauce of ground beef and Vegetables.

Spaghetti Mare Monti.................... $12.95
Fresh Shrimp sauteed with mushrooms, tomatoes and fresh basil

Spaghetti Alla Frutti Di Mare $12.95
resh little neck clams fresh mussels, fresh calamari, fresh shrimp sauteed with

Penne Con Salmone E Vodka................... $13.95
Fresh Salmon sauteed with vodka, fresh garlic, cream, Butter, fresh tomatoes and fresh basil.

Ravioli Alla Bolognese................. $9.95
Ravioli stuffed with a blended cheese mix, sauteed with ground beef, tomatoes and fresh basil.

Menu Sampler - Prices and menu subject to change.
Discounts exclude tax, tip and/or alcohol, where applicable.

Card No. 37

Up To $14.00 Value

Classic favorites and continental cuisine make your meal at the Flight Deck a dining experience you won't forget. Bring the entire family and enjoy our casual atmosphere and aviation memorabilia. Our menu features something for everyone. We are open daily.

Offers not valid holidays and subject to Rules of Use. Tipping should be 15% to 20% of the total bill before discount.

Enjoy one complimentary LUNCH OR DINNER ENTREE when a second LUNCH OR DINNER ENTREE of equal or greater value is purchased.

Dining room only

valid anytime

2200 Centreville Rd., Herndon, VA (703)471-6700

00302556

SANWICHES

MARYLAND CRABCAKE SANDWICH $8.95
Lightly seasoned on a Kaiser roll, accompanied with Tartar sauce

GRILLED CHICKEN SANDWICH $7.95
Marinated grilled chicken breast on a Kaiser roll

ENTREES

PAN SEARED SALMON $14.95
Served with creamy garlic sauce, rice pilaf and vegetables in season

TWIN CRAB CAKES $15.95
Back fin crab cakes over a light mustard sauce, roasted potatoes and vegetables in season

SHRIMP SCAMPI $15.95
Jumbo shrimp sautéed with white wine, garlic, lemon and capers. Served over rice and today's vegetable

NEW YORK STRIP STEAK $15.95
12 oz. choice center cut sirloin broiled to your liking, served with roasted potatoes and vegetables in season

FILET MIGNON $16.95
8 oz. choice filet of beef topped with Merlot sauce, roasted potatoes and vegetables in season

RIBEYE STEAK $15.95
Freshly cut, seasoned and broiled to perfection, baked potato and fresh vegetables

CHICKEN PICATA $12.95
Seared with flour seasoning and served in lemon, capers and artichoke sauce, rice pilaf and vegetables

PAN ROASTED CHICKEN BREAST $12.95
Marinated with fresh herbs, served with rice, vegetables and garlic tomato sauce

All Entrees are served with House salad, choice of dressing, bread and butter

Menu Sampler - Prices and menu subject to change.
Discounts exclude tax, tip and/or alcohol, where applicable.

Card No. 17

Up To $14.00 Value

ELFEGN
ETHIOPIAN RESTAURANT

Enjoy one complimentary LUNCH OR DINNER ENTREE when a second LUNCH OR DINNER ENTREE of equal or greater value is purchased.

Dine in only

valid anytime

664 S. Pickett St., Alexandria, VA (703)823-2050

00603836

Soon to be one of Washington's best Ethiopian Restaurants. Experience the atmosphere & excitement of traditional Ethiopian cuisine. The service is warm & friendly & the entire family will surely enjoy their visit. Come visit us soon!

Offers not valid holidays and subject to Rules of Use. Tipping should be 15% to 20% of the total bill before discount.

Entrees

Doro wat (kay) (chicken stew) ዶሮ ወጥ $10.95
Chicken drumsticks or thigh sauteed in seasoned red pepper stew with onions, butter and spices.

Beg wat (kay) (lamb stew) በግ ወጥ $9.95
Pieces of lamb meat sauteed in seasoned red sauce with onion, butter and spices.

Zilbo ዝልበ $11.00
Collard green leaves cooked with pieces of beef & seasoned with garlic, ginger and butter.

Tibs ጥብስ

Yebeg Tibs (lamb) የበግ ጥብስ $10.50
Chopped lamb meat cooked with onion, green peppers, butter, and spices

Lega Tibs (beef) የበሬ ለጋ ጥብስ $9.50
Beef cooked in butter and onion

Goden Tibs ጎድን ጥብስ $11.95
Short ribs cooked with butter, onion and pepper

Vegeterian Entrees የጾም

Misir Wat ምስር ወጥ $9.00
Slightly cooked lentils simmerd in red sauce and spices.

Kik Alicha ክክ አልጫ $9.00
Yellow split peas simmered in mild sauce made with oil, onion and spices.

Yabesha Gomen ያበሻ ጎመን $9.25
Chopped collard greens cooked with oil onion and garlic

Menu Sampler - Prices and menu subject to change.
Discounts exclude tax, tip and/or alcohol, where applicable.

Card No. 132

Up To $16.00 Value

Enjoy one complimentary DINNER ENTREE when a second DINNER ENTREE of equal or greater value is purchased.

Dining room only

valid any evening

100 S. Reynolds St. (Inside Washington Suites Hotel),
Alexandria, VA (703)823-8162

00386198

Welcome to Duke's Cafe, Alexandria's hidden treasure. We feature fine American cuisine in a relaxed & enjoyable setting. Savor any one of our delicious, expertly prepared entrees. Complement your meal with a nice bottle of wine & don't forget to save room for dessert.

Offers not valid holidays and subject to Rules of Use. Tipping should be 15% to 20% of the total bill before discount.

Pastas & Seafood

Fettuccini Alfredo
Fettuccini with Garlic, Cream, Sherry Wine, and Parmesan Cheese **$11.95**

Seared Shrimp
Sautéed Jumbo Shrimp with Garlic, Tomatoes, Fresh Basil, White Wine, and Angel Hair Pasta **$15.95**

Chicken Marsala
Medallions of Chicken sautéed with Mushrooms, Marsala Sauce, Angel Hair & Wilted Spinach **$12.95**

ENTREES

Crab Cakes
Sautéed Jumbo Lump Crab Cakes with Sundried Tomato Hollandaise **$17.95**

Shrimp Scampi
Five Jumbo Shrimp sautéed with Garlic, White Wine, & Butter **$15.95**

Filet Mignon
A 10oz Steak Broiled to Your Liking; the Most Tender of Steaks **$18.95**

Steak a la Duke
12oz Black Angus Steak with Duke's Sauce **$16.95**

Grilled Pork Chops
Twin 8-oz Center Cut Chops with Cajun Seasoning and Chunky Apple Sauce **$14.95**

Chicken Teriyaki
Grilled Chicken Breasts with Teriyaki Sauce **$12.95**

BBQ Baby Back Ribs
Full or Half Rack of Ribs with Onion Strings Half rack **$ 8.95** Whole **$16.95**

Blackened Salmon
Fresh Salmon with Cajun Spices and Fresh Tomato Salsa **$14.95**

Menu Sampler - Prices and menu subject to change.
Discounts exclude tax, tip and/or alcohol, where applicable.

Card No. 130

CHEQUERS

Up To $22.00 Value

Come experience an evening of great American fare right in the heart of Old Town Alexandria. Our delicious entrees of chicken, fish and beef are prepared to order. Complement your meal with a nice bottle of wine. Don't forget to save room for dessert.

Offers not valid holidays and subject to Rules of Use. Tipping should be 15% to 20% of the total bill before discount.

Enjoy one complimentary LUNCH OR DINNER ENTREE when a second LUNCH OR DINNER ENTREE of equal or greater value is purchased.

Dining room only

valid anytime

901 N. Fairfax St., Alexandria, VA (703)683-6000

00394282

Sandwiches

Mediterranean Grilled Vegetable Sandwich
Layers of Eggplant, Bermuda Onions
Roasted Red Peppers, Zucchini and Yellow Squash
Marinated in Pesto with Extra Virgin Olive Oil
Grilled and Served on Italian Ciabatta
with Roasted Garlic Hummus and Vegetable Chips
$8.95

Create Your Own Deli Sandwich
Choice of: Turkey, Ham, Roast Beef, Bacon
Lettuce, Tomato, Onion
Mayonnaise, Mustard, Horseradish
Cheddar, American, Provolone and Swiss
White, Wheat, Rye, Sour Dough or Kaiser Roll
$7.95

Pasta

Fettuccine Alfredo
Whole Egg Fettuccine
Tossed in a Creamy Alfredo Sauce
$9.95

Wild Mushroom Alfredo
Wild Mushroom Tagliatelle
Shiitake Mushrooms and Spinach Tossed in a Creamy Alfredo Sauce
$11.95

Penne Pollo
Julienne Grilled Chicken Breast
Nestled on Quill Pasta
with Sun Dried Tomatoes
and Fresh Mozzarella Cheese
in Pesto Sauce
$13.95

Entrees

(Entrees Available After 5:00 p.m.)

Chicken Napoleon
Layers of Polenta, Roasted Peppers
Pan Seared Chicken and Swiss Cheese
with a Tangy Port Reduction
and Herbed Cream Sauce
$15.95

Seared Atlantic Salmon Fillet
Presented on a Mirror of Tarragon Infused Beurre Blanc
with Garlic Mashed Red Skin Potatoes
and Fresh Seasonal Vegetables
$18.95

Grilled Angus Strip Loin
Grilled 12 ounce Black Angus Strip Loin
Complimented by Garlic Mashed Red Skin Potatoes
Fresh Seasonal Vegetables and Dijon Mustard Sauce
$19.95

Maryland Jumbo Lump Crab Cake
Sautéed and Presented
with Roasted Garlic Mashed Red Skin Potatoes
and Sautéed Medley of Vegetable
$22.95

Menu Sampler - Prices and menu subject to change.
Discounts exclude tax, tip and/or alcohol, where applicable.

Card No. 47

SANGAM INDIAN RESTAURANT

Up To $14.00 Value

Enjoy one complimentary A LA CARTE LUNCH OR DINNER ENTREE when a second A LA CARTE LUNCH OR DINNER ENTREE of equal or greater value is purchased.

Dining room only; Buffet excluded

valid anytime

1211 N. Glebe Rd., Arlington, VA (703)524-2728

00590075

Welcome to Sangam Indian Restaurant where all the flavors of India meet. We feature the very best of Northern & Southern cuisine. We are conveniently located inside the Comfort Inn - Ballston. Planning a party? Let us cater your next event. Open daily.

Offers not valid holidays and subject to Rules of Use. Tipping should be 15% to 20% of the total bill before discount.

Seafood Specialities

Seafood Vindaloo 15.95
Famous Fiery red, assorted seafood curry.

Shrimp Kadai 14.95
King prawns sauteed with fresh vegetables. Delicious!

Fish Malabari Curry 13.95
Fresh fish cooked in coconut milk curry with mustard seeds. Spicy!

Tandoori Specialties

Jumbo Prawns Tandoor 16.95
Large, juicy Prawns marinated and grilled over hot coals. Served with curry sauce.

Char-Broiled Salmon Tikka 13.95
Boneless Salmon cubes, delicately marinated and broiled in the Tandoori Oven.

Chicken Tikka 11.95
Fresh pieces of marinated chicken, grilled in Tandoor.

Lamb Chops Kandahari 14.95
Tender marinated lamb chops, grilled in Tandoor. Served with Soffron rice and curry sauce.

Chicken Specialties

Chicken Tikka Masala 11.95
Barbecued chicken morsels in an aromatic and zesty sauce.

Chicken Korma Kashmiri 10.95
Lightly spiced cooked in almond sauce with dry fruits.

Chicken Kadai 10.95
Chicken lightly cooked with fresh ginger, garlic, cilantro and diced tomatoes in hot spices.

Madras Chicken Curry 10.95
Traditional South Indian spiced curry.

Fresh Lamb Specialities

Lamb Roganjosh 11.95
Lean chunks of lamb cooked in a rich almond sauce with a blend of fragrant spices.

Saag Gosht - Curried lamb cubes cooked with chopped spinach 11.95

Lamb Vindaloo - Lamb cooked in a fiery red hot curry and spices. 11.95

Menu Sampler - Prices and menu subject to change.
Discounts exclude tax, tip and/or alcohol, where applicable.

Card No. 152

Up To $22.00 Value

Welcome to Tradition's Restaurant & Lounge. From our award winning Champagne Sunday Brunch to our Breakfast Buffet to a romantic dinner for two, Tradition's is the place for fine food & drink. Executive Chef Bill Leffler & his culinary staff are proud to prepare the finest regional American Cuisine. Enjoy your dining experience & make it a Tradition!

Offers not valid holidays and subject to Rules of Use. Tipping should be 15% to 20% of the total bill before discount.

Enjoy one complimentary LUNCH OR DINNER ENTREE when a second LUNCH OR DINNER ENTREE of equal or greater value is purchased.

Dining room only

valid anytime

625 First St., Alexandria, VA (703)548-6300

00395054

SANDWICHES

CLASSIC CLUB SANDWICH — $7.95
THINLY SLICED TURKEY AND HAM SERVED DOUBLE DECKER WITH BACON, LETTUCE, TOMATO AND SWISS CHEESE ON GRILLED SOURDOUGH BREAD

GRILLED CHICKEN BARBECUE — $7.95
8-OUNCE BONELESS BREAST OF CHICKEN, GRILLED, BARBECUED AND SMOTHERED WITH SAUTÉED ONIONS AND MELTED PROVOLONE CHEESE. SERVED ON A TOASTED KAISER ROLL WITH LETTUCE, TOMATO AND PICKLE

ENTREES

FILET MIGNON — $23.95
8-OUNCE CENTER CUT ANGUS BEEF TENDERLOIN COOKED TO YOUR LIKING PRESENTED ON A BED OF GARLIC MASHED POTATOES AND HERBED DEMI GLACE

TRADITION'S T-BONE — $20.95
16 OUNCE ANGUS BEEF T-BONE, GRILLED TO YOUR LIKING SERVED WITH ROASTED NEW POTATOES

GRILLED NEW YORK STRIP — $20.95
10 OUNCE ANGUS BEEF NEW YORK STRIP STEAK, GRILLED TO YOUR LIKING ACCOMPANIED BY GARLIC MASHED POTATOES AND ROSEMARY DEMI GLACE

HALF ROASTED CHICKEN — $13.95
LEMON, GARLIC AND ROSEMARY SCENTED SERVED ON A BED OF GARLIC MASHED POTATOES

PAN SEARED SALMON — $15.95
8-OUNCE COLD WATER SALMON FILET, LIGHTLY DUSTED AND PAN SEARED COMPLIMENTED BY ROASTED NEW POTATOES AND A POMMEREY MUSTARD SAUCE

MARYLAND CRAB CAKES — $21.95
FRESH JUMBO LUMP CRAB MEAT, SEASONED AND LIGHTLY SAUTÉED UNTIL GOLDEN BROWN PRESENTED ON A BED OF GRILLED TOMATOES WITH MUSTARD REMOULADE

Menu Sampler - Prices and menu subject to change.
Discounts exclude tax, tip and/or alcohol, where applicable.

Card No. 72

FRIENDLY FARE
DUKE'S
BAR & GRILL
WITH ROYAL FLAIR

Up To $20.00 Value

Enjoy one complimentary DINNER ENTREE when a second DINNER ENTREE of equal or greater value is purchased.

Dine in only

valid any evening

1755 Duke St. (inside Embassy Suites Hotel), **Alexandria, VA (703)838-9600**

00583749

Welcome to Duke's Bar & Grill, located across from the King Street Metro. We feature all your favorite dishes including entree sized salads, pasta, sandwiches & delicious meat, chicken & fresh entrees. Come in & feel like a king at Duke's.

Offers not valid holidays and subject to Rules of Use. Tipping should be 15% to 20% of the total bill before discount.

ARISTOCRATIC ENTREES

NEW YORK STRIP: COOKED TO YOUR SPECIFICATIONS TOPPED WITH ONION STRAWS AND SERVED WITH ASIAGO SCALLOPED POTATOES AND FRESH VEGETABLES ⇒ $19.95

GRILLED SALMON: PEACH GLAZED FRESH FILET OF SALMON GRILLED TO YOUR LIKING SERVED WITH WILD MUSHROOM RISOTTO AND FRESH VEGETABLES ⇒ $16.25

ROCKFISH AND MANGO SALSA: GARNISHED WITH STEAMED CLAMS OVER RICE PILAF WITH JICAMA CONFETTI ⇒ $16.95

MARYLAND CRAB CAKE PLATTER: TWO PAN FRIED CRAB CAKES WITH CAROLINA COLE SLAW, REMOULADE SAUCE AND FRIES ⇒ $17.95

GRILLED CHICKEN BREAST: TOPPED WITH A SUN-DRIED TOMATO AIOLI OVER WILD MUSHROOM RISOTTO AND FRESH ASPARAGUS ⇒ $14.25

PRIME RIB: SLOW ROASTED TO PERFECTION WITH YOUR CHOICE OF POTATOES FRESH VEGETABLES AND AU JUS
⇒ DUCHESS CUT 12 OZ ⇒ $15.95
⇒ DUKE'S CUT 16OZ ⇒ $19.95

FILET MIGNON: OUR MOST TENDER CUT OF BEEF. SERVED WITH BAKED POTATO AND FRESH ASPARAGUS FINISHED WITH OUR MERLOT DEMI GLAZE ⇒ $22.95

GRILLED VEAL CHOP WITH PANCETTA: A TWELVE OUNCE CHOP GRILLED THEN TOPPED WITH PANCETTA, FAVA BEANS AND PEARL ONIONS, SERVED OVER CREAMED SPINACH WITH SCALLOPED POTATOES ⇒ $24.95

TENDERLOIN AND SHRIMP BROCHETTE: TWO SKEWERS OF MARINATED TENDERLOIN OF BEEF AND GARLIC-GRILLED SHRIMP WITH JUMBO ASPARAGUS AND A ROASTED PEPPER MEDLEY OVER RICE PILAF ⇒ $22.95

Menu Sampler - Prices and menu subject to change.
Discounts exclude tax, tip and/or alcohol, where applicable.

Lunch/Brunch Directory

America Union Station
UP TO $12.00 VALUE 87

Enjoy one complimentary BRUNCH ENTREE when a second BRUNCH ENTREE of equal or greater value is purchased. valid any Saturday or Sunday from 11:30 a.m. till 3:30 p.m..

An ideal venue for your group to dine is at Washington D.C.'s America Restaurant. Located on Capitol Hill in Union Station's Great Hall, America's menu offers a wide range of American cuisine while enjoying the splendor of Historic Union Station. Join our hospitality M* Card program. Visit us at www.askrestaurants.com.

50 Massachusetts Ave., NE (Union Station), Washington, DC
(202)682-9555

★ AMERICA ★
Union Station

A73

Classic Cafe
ONE SUNDAY BRUNCH 95

Enjoy one complimentary SUNDAY BRUNCH when one complimentary SUNDAY BRUNCH of equal or greater value is purchased. Dine in only. SUNDAY. Valid any Sunday.

Welcome back to how dining is suppose to be. Our service is warm & friendly & our food is delicious. We offer soups, salads, pastas, steaks, chicken, seafood & over 9 surf & turf items. We can't wait to see you. Open daily.

8509 Rixlew Lane, Manassas, VA
(703)257-1551

CLASSIC CAFE

A74

El Tejano
ONE BRUNCH ENTREE 163

Enjoy one complimentary BRUNCH ENTREE when a second BRUNCH ENTREE of equal or greater value is purchased. valid anytime.

Come experience a fiesta! El Tejano captures the authentic culinary tradition of the Southwest & Mexico, all made fresh to order & with the finest ingredients. Compliment your entree with a El Tejano's famous margarita or a boot filled sangria.

11514 Middlebrook Rd. (Millbrook Shopping Center), Germantown, MD
(301)528-8100

EL TEJANO
-Fine Tex Mex Cuisine-

A75

The Grand Marquis Cafe
UP TO $13.00 VALUE 105

Enjoy one complimentary LUNCH OR SUNDAY BRUNCH BUFFET when a second LUNCH OR SUNDAY BRUNCH BUFFET of equal or greater value is purchased. Valid during lunch & brunch service hours.

Olney's favorite neighborhood gathering place. Chef Kantar prides himself for over 40 yrs. of experience in restaurants around the world. Menu features appetizers, soups, salads, sandwiches, pizza, pasta, steaks, seafood & our popular "blue plate specials. " Open for lunch, dinner & Sunday Brunch. Catering available. Visit our website www.grandmarquis.com.

18101 Town Center Dr. (Olney Town Ctr.), Olney, MD
(301)260-0500 www.grandmarquis.com

GRAND MARQUIS
C•A•F•E
'Serving Olney Since 1991'

A76

The Green Tree Restaurant
UP TO $12.00 VALUE 114

Enjoy one complimentary SUNDAY BRUNCH ENTREE when a second SUNDAY BRUNCH ENTREE of equal or greater value is purchased. valid any Sunday. Holidays excluded.

This three star Mobil-rated restaurant will take you back in time - back to the 18th Century. Months were spent at the Library of Congress to research these authentic recipes. The Green Tree is enchanted with the 18th Century - a time when art & architecture, music & food, all reached a certain glorious peak.

15 S. King St., Leesburg, VA
(703)777-7246

The Green Tree

A77

O'Toole's
UP TO $8.00 VALUE 80

Enjoy one complimentary SUNDAY BRUNCH when a second SUNDAY BRUNCH of equal or greater value is purchased or when dining alone - SUNDAY BRUNCH at 50% off the regular price - maximum discount $4.00. Dine in only. valid during Sunday brunch.

O'Toole's offers a family atmosphere, inviting large groups to partake of the diversified menu. Sample steaks, ribs, Mexican dishes, pasta, sandwiches, not to mention fresh desserts & a kids' menu. We are located less than one mile from I-66. Ninety-five percent of the menu items are under $10. Late-night dancing Thursday through Sunday. Reservations accepted.

5728 Pickwick Rd. (Pickwick Square), Centreville, VA
(703)222-5171

O'TOOLE'S
Restaurant Pub

A78

Lunch/Brunch Directory

Sequoia 101
UP TO $12.00 VALUE

Enjoy one complimentary BRUNCH ENTREE when a second BRUNCH ENTREE of equal or greater value is purchased. valid any Saturday or Sunday 11:30 a.m. till 3:30 p.m..

Overlooking the Potomac River on Georgetown's waterfront in Washington, D.C. Delightful dining in an elegant setting provides unsurpassed views of The John F. Kennedy Center for the performing Arts, The Watergate & the Historic Virginia Skyline. Join our hospitality M* Card program.

3000 K St. (Washington Harbor), Washington, DC
(202)944-4200 www.arkrestaurants.com

A79

Traditions 117
ONE BRUNCH

Enjoy one complimentary BRUNCH ENTREE when a second BRUNCH ENTREE of equal or greater value is purchased. valid any Sunday.

Welcome to Traditions Restaurant & Lounge. Our award winning Champagne Sunday Brunch & Breakfast Buffet & romantic dinners for two makes Traditions a place for fine food and drink. Our executive Chef and his culinary staff are proud to prepare the finest regional American Cuisine. Our service staff is second to none! Make your dining experience a Tradition!

625 First St., Alexandria, VA
(703)548-6300

A80

Thunder Grill 104
UP TO $12.00 VALUE

Enjoy one complimentary BRUNCH ENTREE when a second BRUNCH ENTREE of equal or greater value is purchased. valid any Saturday or Sunday 11:30 a.m. till 3:30 p.m..

Located on the east side of Union Station, Thunder Grill is Ark Restaurants' newest property. Earth tones, individually hand painted tables, hardwood floors & southwestern artwork accentuate the ground level. The upstairs is comprised of unique catwalks, booths & niches. A visual & culinary celebration of American Southwest. Join our hospitality M* Card program.

50 Massachusetts Ave. (at Union Station), Washington, DC
(202)898-0051 www.arkrestaurants.com

A81

Village Park Cafe 157
ONE SUNDAY BRUNCH BUFFET

Enjoy one complimentary SUNDAY BRUNCH BUFFET when a second SUNDAY BRUNCH BUFFET of equal or greater value is purchased. valid during Sunday brunch hours 11 a.m. till 2 p.m..

Enjoy good times & great food in the friendly, casual atmosphere of the Village Park Cafe. Classic American cuisine features a variety of appetizers & entrees. Dinner hours from 5:30 p.m. - 10 p.m. nightly. Private dining room is available. Perfect for business meetings, family gatherings, rehearsal dinners & other special affairs. Customized menus available.

2 Montgomery Village Ave. (corner of Frederick Ave. & Montgomery Village Ave.), Gaithersburg, MD
(301)948-8900

A82

The Wild Orchid 127
UP TO $8.00 VALUE

Enjoy one complimentary SUNDAY BRUNCH ENTREE when a second SUNDAY BRUNCH ENTREE of equal or greater value is purchased. valid any Sunday.

Located in a quaint little house in Eastport, The Wild Orchid Cafe brings a refreshing and artistic dining experience to Annapolis. We offer an intimate atmosphere with an inventive menu that is sure to please.

909 Bay Ridge Ave. (2nd right over Eastport Bridge), Annapolis, MD
(410)268-8009

A83

Dine & Save™

Enjoy dining and saving at the best fine dine and casual restaurants in your area.

*It's easy!**

How to Use Your Entertainment® Membership Card

entertainment®
Membership Card
More savings at entertainment.com
Valid now thru November 1, 2006

For dining offers with a [symbol] symbol (located in the upper right-hand corner of the offer page), present your Entertainment® Membership Card before your bill is totaled to receive your discount. The merchant will remove the card number from the back of your Entertainment® Membership Card to indicate you have used the offer.

How to Use Your Coupons

entertainment.
entertainment.com
FREE
Buy-One-Get-One-Free!
valid for one FREE item when a second item of equal or greater value is purchased.
Valid now thru December 30, 2006
Offer validity is governed by the Rules of Use and excludes defined holidays. Offers are not valid with other discount offers, unless specified. Discounts exclude tax, tip and/or alcohol, where applicable.

For all other dining offers, remove the coupon or certificate from your book and present it to the merchant before your bill is totaled. The merchant will retain the coupon and subtract the discount amount from the bill.

Register at

www.entertainment.com/register

*For complete program details, please refer to the Rules of Use page located in the back of your book. For offer information, please refer to each individual offer.

COPELAND'S®

Famous New Orleans
Restaurant and Bar

www.alcopeland.com

Valid now thru
November 1, 2006

$5.00 Value

COPELAND'S®
Famous New Orleans
Restaurant and Bar

www.alcopeland.com

Enjoy $5 off with a minimum purchase of fifteen dollars (excluding tax, tip and alcoholic beverages).

valid anytime

One offer per party, per visit

See reverse side for details

A85

Valid now thru
November 1, 2006

Up To $8.00 Value

COPELAND'S®
Famous New Orleans
Restaurant and Bar

www.alcopeland.com

Free Appetizer or Dessert with the purchase of 2 entrees.

valid anytime

One offer per party, per visit

See reverse side for details

A86

Valid now thru
November 1, 2006

Up To $8.00 Value

COPELAND'S®
Famous New Orleans
Restaurant and Bar

www.alcopeland.com

Free Appetizer or Dessert with the purchase of 2 entrees.

valid anytime

One offer per party, per visit

See reverse side for details

A87

COPELAND'S®

Famous New Orleans Restaurant and Bar

177 Jennifer Rd., Annapolis, MD
(410)571-0860
10200 Wincopin Circle, Columbia, MD
(410)992-0020
1584 Rockville Pike, Rockville, MD
(301)230-0968
4300 King St., Alexandria, VA
(703)671-7997
13810 Braddock Rd., Centreville, VA
(703)222-0089

00661023

www.alcopeland.com

177 Jennifer Rd., Annapolis, MD
(410)571-0860
10200 Wincopin Circle, Columbia, MD
(410)992-0020
1584 Rockville Pike, Rockville, MD
(301)230-0968
4300 King St., Alexandria, VA
(703)671-7997
13810 Braddock Rd., Centreville, VA
(703)222-0089

00661023

Not valid holidays & subject to Rules of Use. Not valid with other discount offers, unless specified. Coupon VOID if purchased, sold or bartered. Discounts exclude tax, tip and/or alcohol, where applicable.

177 Jennifer Rd., Annapolis, MD
(410)571-0860
10200 Wincopin Circle, Columbia, MD
(410)992-0020
1584 Rockville Pike, Rockville, MD
(301)230-0968
4300 King St., Alexandria, VA
(703)671-7997
13810 Braddock Rd., Centreville, VA
(703)222-0089

00661023

Not valid holidays & subject to Rules of Use. Not valid with other discount offers, unless specified. Coupon VOID if purchased, sold or bartered. Discounts exclude tax, tip and/or alcohol, where applicable.

177 Jennifer Rd., Annapolis, MD
(410)571-0860
10200 Wincopin Circle, Columbia, MD
(410)992-0020
1584 Rockville Pike, Rockville, MD
(301)230-0968
4300 King St., Alexandria, VA
(703)671-7997
13810 Braddock Rd., Centreville, VA
(703)222-0089

00661023

Not valid holidays & subject to Rules of Use. Not valid with other discount offers, unless specified. Coupon VOID if purchased, sold or bartered. Discounts exclude tax, tip and/or alcohol, where applicable.

The Tortilla Factory Restaurant

648 Elden St.
Herndon, VA
(703)471-1156

- We feature Mexican cuisine at its best since 1975
- Start your meal with one of our many fine appetizers
- House specialties include carne asada, chicken chimichangas & flounder sonora
- Catering services available
- Open daily

Bonus Discounts at entertainment.com

entertainment
entertainment.com

Up To $11.00 Value

Enjoy one complimentary LUNCH OR DINNER ENTREE when a second LUNCH OR DINNER ENTREE of equal or greater value is purchased or when dining alone - one LUNCH OR DINNER ENTREE at 50% off the regular price - maximum discount $5.00.

The Tortilla Factory RESTAURANT

www.thetortillafactory.com

valid anytime

A88

Valid now thru November 1, 2006

Not valid holidays & subject to Rules of Use. Not valid with other discount offers, unless specified. Coupon VOID if purchased, sold or bartered. Discounts exclude tax, tip and/or alcohol, where applicable.

King Street Blues

112 N. Saint Asaph St.
Alexandria, VA
(703)836-8800

- Good eats
- This whimsically decorated Southern roadhouse features country-fried chicken, fresh fish, ribs, BBQ, po boy sandwiches & salads
- Little dudes menu
- Winner of best BBQ, Best Burger & Cheap Eats in Alexandria

Bonus Discounts at entertainment.com

entertainment
entertainment.com

Up To $9.00 Value

KING STREET BLUES

Enjoy one complimentary LUNCH OR DINNER ENTREE when a second LUNCH OR DINNER ENTREE of equal or greater value is purchased.

Blue plate specials, rib specials, email coupons or other offers excluded; Dine in only

valid anytime

www.kingstreetblues.com

A89

Valid now thru November 1, 2006

Not valid holidays & subject to Rules of Use. Not valid with other discount offers, unless specified. Coupon VOID if purchased, sold or bartered. Discounts exclude tax, tip and/or alcohol, where applicable.

King Street Blues

See reverse side for locations

- Good eats
- This whimsically decorated Southern roadhouse features country-fried chicken, fresh fish, ribs, BBQ, po boy sandwiches & salads
- Little dudes menu
- Winner of best BBQ, Best Burger & Cheap Eats in Alexandria

Bonus Discounts at entertainment.com

entertainment
entertainment.com

Up To $9.00 Value

KING STREET BLUES

Enjoy one complimentary LUNCH OR DINNER ENTREE when a second LUNCH OR DINNER ENTREE of equal or greater value is purchased.

Dine in only; Not valid on blue plate specials, rib specials, e-mail coupons or other offers

valid anytime

www.kingstreetblues.com

A90

Valid now thru November 1, 2006

Not valid holidays & subject to Rules of Use. Not valid with other discount offers, unless specified. Coupon VOID if purchased, sold or bartered. Discounts exclude tax, tip and/or alcohol, where applicable.

The Tortilla Factory RESTAURANT

648 Elden St.
(The Pines)
Herndon, VA
(703)471-1156

Tipping should be 15% to 20% of TOTAL bill before discount

00012419

entertainment.com

00012419

KING STREET BLUES

112 N. Saint Asaph St.
(Old Town)
Alexandria, VA
(703)836-8800

Tipping should be 15% to 20% of TOTAL bill before discount

00194849

entertainment.com

00194849

KING STREET BLUES

1648 Crystal Square Arcade
Arlington, VA
(703)415-2583

5810 Kingstowne Ctr.
Kingstowne, VA
(703)313-0400

2866 Jefferson Davis Hwy.
Staffad, VA
(540)288-1100

Tipping should be 15% to 20% of TOTAL bill before discount

00259968

entertainment.com

00259968

O'Toole's

5728 Pickwick Rd.
Centreville, VA
(703)222-5171

- Featuring USDA steaks, baby back ribs, seafood & much more
- "Lite lunch" menu with homemade soups, sandwiches & salads galore
- Happy hour Mon.-Fri.
- Major credit cards accepted
- Brunch every Sunday
- Kids' menu - all under $3.00
- Large parties welcome
- Reservations not required

Bonus Discounts at
entertainment.com

entertainment. entertainment.com

Up To $11.00 Value

Enjoy one complimentary LUNCH OR DINNER ENTREE when a second LUNCH OR DINNER ENTREE of equal or greater value is purchased or when dining alone - one LUNCH OR DINNER ENTREE at 50% off the regular price - maximum discount $5.00.

Dine in only

valid anytime

O'TOOLE'S
Restaurant Pub

www.otoolespub.com

A91

Valid now thru November 1, 2006

Not valid holidays & subject to Rules of Use. Not valid with other discount offers, unless specified. Coupon VOID if purchased, sold or bartered. Discounts exclude tax, tip and/or alcohol, where applicable.

Shooter McGee's

5239 Duke St.
Alexandria, VA
(703)751-9266

- Best gourmet 1/2 lb. burgers
- Seasonal patio dining
- Serving full menu 'til 12:30 a.m.
- Affordable dining in a comfortable neighborhood atmosphere
- Daily specials, baby back ribs, choice steaks & pastas

Bonus Discounts at
entertainment.com

entertainment. entertainment.com

Up To $10.00 Value

Enjoy one complimentary LUNCH OR DINNER ENTREE when a second LUNCH OR DINNER ENTREE of equal or greater value is purchased.

Burger specials & nightly specials excluded; Dine in only

valid anytime

Shooter McGee's
"Delectables & Cure-alls"

www.shootermcgees.com

A92

Valid now thru November 1, 2006

Not valid holidays & subject to Rules of Use. Not valid with other discount offers, unless specified. Coupon VOID if purchased, sold or bartered. Discounts exclude tax, tip and/or alcohol, where applicable.

Sign of the Whale

7279 Arlington Blvd.
Falls Church, VA
(703)573-1616

- Best seafood chowder in town
- Award-winning hamburgers
- Fresh fish
- Gratuity of 18% added with use of coupon
- Kids' menu available
- Weekly specials
- Call for a schedule of events

Bonus Discounts at
entertainment.com

entertainment. entertainment.com

Up To $10.00 Value

Enjoy one complimentary LUNCH OR DINNER ENTREE when a second LUNCH OR DINNER ENTREE of equal or greater value is purchased.

Dine in only

valid anytime

Holidays excluded; Subject to rules of use

SIGN of the WHALE

www.signofthewhale.com

A93

Valid now thru November 1, 2006

Not valid holidays & subject to Rules of Use. Not valid with other discount offers, unless specified. Coupon VOID if purchased, sold or bartered. Discounts exclude tax, tip and/or alcohol, where applicable.

O'TOOLE'S
Restaurant Pub

5728 Pickwick Rd.
(Pickwick Square)
Centreville, VA
(703)222-5171

Tipping should be 15% to 20% of TOTAL bill before discount
00008111

entertainment.com
00008111

Shooter McGee's
"Delectables & Cure-alls"

5239 Duke St.
Alexandria, VA
(703)751-9266

Offers not valid holidays and subject to Rules of Use
Tipping should be 15% to 20% of the total bill before discount
00596746

entertainment.com
00596746

SIGN of the WHALE

7279 Arlington Blvd.
(Loehmann's Plaza)
Falls Church, VA
(703)573-1616

Tipping should be 15% to 20% of TOTAL bill before discount
00012391

entertainment.com
00012391

Chadwicks

See reverse side for locations

- Your neighborhood restaurant/bar
- For 30 years, great food at great prices served by the friendliest faces in town
- Kids' menu available
- Open daily until midnight, featuring fresh seafood, steaks, chicken, burgers, specialty salads & sandwiches
- Daily lunch & dinner specials, Sunday brunch

Bonus Discounts at entertainment.com

entertainment® entertainment.com

Up To $11.00 Value

Enjoy one complimentary DINNER ENTREE when a second DINNER ENTREE of equal or greater value is purchased.

Valid for regular priced menu items only; Dine in only

valid any evening

Chadwicks® est. 1967

A94

Valid now thru November 1, 2006

Not valid holidays & subject to Rules of Use. Not valid with other discount offers, unless specified. Coupon VOID if purchased, sold or bartered. Discounts exclude tax, tip and/or alcohol, where applicable.

Armand's Chicago Pizzeria

See reverse side for locations

- 19 yrs. voted Best Pizza - Washingtonian Magazine readers
- Famous deep dish, traditional & gourmet pizza
- Pastas, sandwiches, salads & full bar
- Sidewalk cafe
- Catering available
- Open daily and open late

Bonus Discounts at entertainment.com

entertainment® entertainment.com

great place for kids

Up To $8.00 Value

Enjoy one complimentary LUNCH OR DINNER ENTREE when a second LUNCH OR DINNER ENTREE of equal or greater value is purchased or for those who prefer - any one pizza at 50% off the regular price.

Buffet excluded; Dine in only, sorry, no carry out or delivery; Participating locations only

valid anytime

ARMAND'S® CHICAGO PIZZERIA EST. 1975

www.armandspizza.com

A95

Valid now thru November 1, 2006

Not valid holidays & subject to Rules of Use. Not valid with other discount offers, unless specified. Coupon VOID if purchased, sold or bartered. Discounts exclude tax, tip and/or alcohol, where applicable.

International House of Pancakes

See reverse side for locations

- Enjoy all your favorites, all day long
- Featuring pancakes, waffles & french toast specialties, new omelette feasts, IHOP signature breakfasts, classic egg breakfast, burgers, sandwiches, distinctive dinners, salads & traditional favorites
- Open daily

Bonus Discounts at entertainment.com

entertainment® entertainment.com

great place for kids

Up To $7.00 Value

Enjoy one complimentary ENTREE when a second ENTREE of equal or greater value is purchased.

Dine in only

valid anytime after 3 p.m.

INTERNATIONAL HOUSE OF PANCAKES RESTAURANT®

www.ihop.com

A96

Valid now thru November 1, 2006

Not valid holidays & subject to Rules of Use. Not valid with other discount offers, unless specified. Coupon VOID if purchased, sold or bartered. Discounts exclude tax, tip and/or alcohol, where applicable.

Chadwicks®
est. 1967

3205 K St. NW
(Georgetown)
Washington, DC
(202)333-2565

5247 Wisconsin Ave. NW
(Friendship Heights - independently owned & operated)
Washington, DC
(202)362-8040

203 Strand St.
(Old Town)
Alexandria, VA
(703)836-4442

Tipping should be 15% to 20% of TOTAL bill before discount

00098677

entertainment.com

00098677

ARMAND'S®
CHICAGO PIZZERIA
EST. 1975

4231 Wisconsin Ave. NW
Washington, DC
(202)686-9450

1909 Seminary Rd.
Silver Spring, MD
(301)588-3400

Tipping should be 15% to 20% of TOTAL bill before discount

00078219

entertainment.com

00078219

INTERNATIONAL HOUSE OF PANCAKES
RESTAURANT®

9490 Blake Lane
Fairfax, VA
(703)277-1022

6655 Arlington Blvd.
Falls Church, VA
(703)237-5191

8785 Centreville Rd.
Manassas, VA
(703)257-1937

00257331

entertainment.com

00257331

California Tortilla

See reverse side for locations

- Featuring great food at great prices
- Everything made fresh daily
- Offering over 75 different hot sauces that'll blow your head off!
- We can make almost anything "light"
- Kid's menu available
- Open daily

Bonus Discounts at entertainment.com

entertainment. entertainment.com

great place for kids

Up To $6.00 Value

Enjoy one complimentary MENU ITEM when a second MENU ITEM of equal or greater value is purchased.

valid anytime

CALIFORNIA TORTILLA™

www.californiatortilla.com

A97

Valid now thru November 1, 2006

Not valid holidays & subject to Rules of Use. Not valid with other discount offers, unless specified. Coupon VOID if purchased, sold or bartered. Discounts exclude tax, tip and/or alcohol, where applicable.

Qdoba Mexican Grill

See reverse side for locations

- Not just big burritos - big flavors
- Flavors like you'll find in our signature burritos & nowhere else
- Poblano pesto, chicken mole, grilled vegetable, fajita ranchera, seasoned shredded beef & 3-cheese queso
- All served with one of our five incredible salsas
- You'll find all the spice you want here & a lot more

Bonus Discounts at entertainment.com

entertainment. entertainment.com

great place for kids

Up To $6.00 Value

Enjoy one complimentary LUNCH OR DINNER ENTREE when a second LUNCH OR DINNER ENTREE of equal or greater value is purchased.

valid anytime

Qdoba MEXICAN GRILL

A98

Valid now thru November 1, 2006

Not valid holidays & subject to Rules of Use. Not valid with other discount offers, unless specified. Coupon VOID if purchased, sold or bartered. Discounts exclude tax, tip and/or alcohol, where applicable.

Qdoba Mexican Grill

See reverse side for locations

- Not just big burritos - big flavors
- Flavors like you'll find in our signature burritos & nowhere else
- Poblano pesto, chicken mole, grilled vegetable, fajita ranchera, seasoned shredded beef & 3-cheese queso
- All served with one of our five incredible salsas
- You'll find all the spice you want here & a lot more

Bonus Discounts at entertainment.com

entertainment. entertainment.com

great place for kids

Up To $6.00 Value

Enjoy one complimentary LUNCH OR DINNER ENTREE when a second LUNCH OR DINNER ENTREE of equal or greater value is purchased.

valid anytime

Qdoba MEXICAN GRILL

A99

Valid now thru November 1, 2006

Not valid holidays & subject to Rules of Use. Not valid with other discount offers, unless specified. Coupon VOID if purchased, sold or bartered. Discounts exclude tax, tip and/or alcohol, where applicable.

CALIFORNIA TORTILLA

2057 Wilson Blvd.
Arlington, VA
(703)243-4151

12239 Fair Lakes Pkwy.
Fairfax, VA
(703)278-0007

00622420

entertainment.com

00622420

Qdoba MEXICAN GRILL

223 Burgess Rd.
(Harrisonburg Crossings Shpg. Ctr.)
Harrisonburg, VA
(540)564-1515

13031 Worldgate Dr.
(in the Worldgate Ctr.)
Herndon, VA
(703)796-1101

00624288

entertainment.com

00624288

Qdoba MEXICAN GRILL

223 Burgess Rd.
(Harrisonburg Crossings Shpg. Ctr.)
Harrisonburg, VA
(540)564-1515

13031 Worldgate Dr.
(in the Worldgate Ctr.)
Herndon, VA
(703)796-1101

00624288

entertainment.com

00624288

Esposito's

9917 Lee Hwy.
Fairfax, VA
(703)385-5912

- Acclaimed Southern Italian cuisine
- "Unusual & should not be overlooked" Mobil Travel Guide
- Specialties include Pollo Cardinale, Fettucine Alla Romano & our famous homemade pizza
- Delicious variety of desserts & coffees
- Beer & wine

Bonus Discounts at
entertainment.com

entertainment.
entertainment.com

Up To $11.00 Value

Enjoy one complimentary LUNCH OR DINNER ENTREE when a second LUNCH OR DINNER ENTREE of equal or greater value is purchased.

Dine in only

valid anytime

The Espositos

A100

Valid now thru November 1, 2006

Not valid holidays & subject to Rules of Use. Not valid with other discount offers, unless specified. Coupon VOID if purchased, sold or bartered. Discounts exclude tax, tip and/or alcohol, where applicable.

Great American Steak & Buffet Co.

See reverse side for locations

- All of your American favorites
- Enjoy Southern style fried chicken, oven baked ham, homemade pot roast with garden vegetables & slow roasted beef hand carved for you
- Also featuring a soup & salad bar
- And don't forget to save room for one of our homemade desserts

Bonus Discounts at
entertainment.com

entertainment.
entertainment.com

great place for kids

ONE BUFFET

Enjoy one complimentary BUFFET when a second BUFFET of equal or greater value is purchased.

Dine in only

valid anytime

Present coupon/card before ordering

GREAT AMERICAN STEAK & BUFFET COMPANY

A101

Valid now thru November 1, 2006

Not valid holidays & subject to Rules of Use. Not valid with other discount offers, unless specified. Coupon VOID if purchased, sold or bartered. Discounts exclude tax, tip and/or alcohol, where applicable.

Foster's Grille

See reverse side for locations

- Modern day, family oriented, old-fashioned hamburger eatery
- Char-broiled burgers, hand-cut french fries, chicken sandwiches, jumbo buffalo wings, salads, grilled hot dogs & daily specials
- Kids menu & fresh baked desserts
- Fresh squeezed lemonade & extra thick milkshakes
- Definitely an affordable & delicious alternative to fast food!

Bonus Discounts at
entertainment.com

entertainment.
entertainment.com

Up To $8.00 Value

Enjoy one complimentary ENTREE when a second ENTREE of equal or greater value is purchased.

Chicken Wings excluded

valid anytime

Foster's Grille
Home of the Charburger

A102

Valid now thru November 1, 2006

Not valid holidays & subject to Rules of Use. Not valid with other discount offers, unless specified. Coupon VOID if purchased, sold or bartered. Discounts exclude tax, tip and/or alcohol, where applicable.

The Espositos

9917 Lee Hwy.
Fairfax, VA
(703)385-5912

Tipping should be 15% to 20% of TOTAL bill before discount

00226310

entertainment.com

00226310

GREAT AMERICAN STEAK & BUFFET COMPANY

5902 Richmond Hwy.
Alexandria, VA
(703)329-1555

3490 S. Jefferson St.
Falls Church, VA
(703)379-0108

8365 Sudley Rd.
Manassas, VA
(703)369-6791

3135 Crain Hwy.
Waldorf, VA
(301)638-0181

00574646

entertainment.com

00574646

Foster's Grille
Home of the Charburger

4418 Costello Way
Haymarket, VA
(571)261-5959

7817 Sudley Rd.
Manassas, VA
(703)393-2427

4199-A Winchester St.
Marshall, VA
(540)964-0470

9417 West St.
Old Town Manassas, VA
(703)257-7272

138-A Maple Ave. W.
Vienna, VA
(703)281-2224

20 Broadview Ave.
Warrenton, VA
(540)349-5776

00526439

entertainment.com

00526439

Atlanta Bread Company

See reverse side for locations

- Atlanta Bread Company is a leader in European Style Bakery/Cafe
- Made to order salads, sandwiches & offering a different homemade soup daily
- Expanded menu includes hot breakfast sandwiches & grilled paninis....a great alternative to fast food, subs & pizza
- Gourmet coffees, espresso drinks, muffins & freshly baked pastries

Bonus Discounts at entertainment.com

entertainment. entertainment.com

Up To $6.00 Value

Enjoy one complimentary LUNCH OR DINNER ENTREE when a second LUNCH OR DINNER ENTREE of equal or greater value is purchased.

Dine in only

valid anytime

ATLANTA · BREAD · COMPANY BAKERY CAFE®

A103

Valid now thru November 1, 2006

Not valid holidays & subject to Rules of Use. Not valid with other discount offers, unless specified. Coupon VOID if purchased, sold or bartered. Discounts exclude tax, tip and/or alcohol, where applicable.

Johnny Rockets

3131 M St., NW
Washington, DC
(202)333-7994

- Take a bite out of the good old days from the vintage 40's
- All American fare including hamburgers, classic sandwiches, fries, shakes & malts
- Dine on a bar stool at the u-shaped chrome counter
- Tabletop jukeboxes that play your tune for only a nickel
- Reasonable prices, fresh food & friendly service will bring you back!

Bonus Discounts at entertainment.com

entertainment. entertainment.com

great place for kids

Up To $6.00 Value

Enjoy one complimentary LUNCH OR DINNER ENTREE when a second LUNCH OR DINNER ENTREE of equal or greater value is purchased.

Dine in only

valid anytime

Johnny Rockets THE ORIGINAL HAMBURGER®

www.johnnyrockets.com

A104

Valid now thru November 1, 2006

Not valid holidays & subject to Rules of Use. Not valid with other discount offers, unless specified. Coupon VOID if purchased, sold or bartered. Discounts exclude tax, tip and/or alcohol, where applicable.

Tippy's Taco House

See reverse side for locations

- The best Mexican food specialties you've ever tasted
- Served in a friendly atmosphere

Bonus Discounts at entertainment.com

entertainment. entertainment.com

great place for kids

Up To $6.00 Value

Enjoy one complimentary DINNER ENTREE when a second DINNER ENTREE of equal or greater value is purchased.

Dine-in or carry out; Sorry, no delivery

valid anytime

TIPPY'S TACO HOUSE

A105

Valid now thru November 1, 2006

Not valid holidays & subject to Rules of Use. Not valid with other discount offers, unless specified. Coupon VOID if purchased, sold or bartered. Discounts exclude tax, tip and/or alcohol, where applicable.

1334 Main Chapel Way
Gambrills, MD
(410)451-8973

551 Ritchie Hwy.
Severna Park, MD
(410)315-7887

5506 A Cherrywood Ln.
(Beltway Plaza Mall)
Greenbelt, MD
(301)982-3200

45633 Dulles Eastern Plaza
(Dulles Town Crossing)
Sterling, VA
(703)444-4360

00102792

entertainment.com

00102792

3131 M St., NW
(Georgetown)
Washington, DC
(202)333-7994

Tipping should be 15% to 20% of TOTAL bill before discount

00467247

entertainment.com

00467247

5912 N. Kings Hwy.
Alexandria, VA
(703)960-1431

11210 Lee Hwy.
Kamp Washington, VA
(703)691-0011

7004 Spring Garden Rd.
Springfield, VA
(703)451-4411

14119 St. Germaine Dr.
(Centrewood Plaza)
Centreville, VA
(703)830-1333

8632 Lee Hwy.
Merrifield, VA
(703)560-0511

147 W. Shirley Ave.
Warrenton, VA
(540)349-2330

Tipping should be 15% to 20% of TOTAL bill before discount

00059025

entertainment.com

00059025

Cosi

Valid at All Participating Locations

- Your ultimate place to drink, dine & unwind from wake - up call to last call
- Imagine all this...
- Cosi coffee, Cosi sandwiches, wine, beer & coffee cocktails
- World famous s'mores, Cosi pizza & much more - in one eclectic, relaxing atmosphere

Bonus Discounts at entertainment.com

entertainment. entertainment.com

Up To $10.00 Value

Enjoy any one complimentary PIZZA when a second PIZZA of equal or greater value is purchased.

valid anytime

COSÍ

A106

Valid now thru November 1, 2006

Not valid holidays & subject to Rules of Use. Not valid with other discount offers, unless specified. Coupon VOID if purchased, sold or bartered. Discounts exclude tax, tip and/or alcohol, where applicable.

Cosi

Valid at All Participating Locations

- Your ultimate place to drink, dine & unwind from wake - up call to last call
- Imagine all this...
- Cosi coffee, Cosi sandwiches, wine, beer & coffee cocktails
- World famous s'mores, Cosi pizza & much more - in one eclectic, relaxing atmosphere

Bonus Discounts at entertainment.com

entertainment. entertainment.com

Up To $2.00 Value

Enjoy $2.00 off the purchase of any LUNCH OR DINNER ENTREE.

valid anytime

Entree includes any sandwich, hot melts, salad or pizza

COSÍ

A107

Valid now thru November 1, 2006

Not valid holidays & subject to Rules of Use. Not valid with other discount offers, unless specified. Coupon VOID if purchased, sold or bartered. Discounts exclude tax, tip and/or alcohol, where applicable.

Cosi

Valid at All Participating Locations

- Your ultimate place to drink, dine & unwind from wake - up call to last call
- Imagine all this...
- Cosi coffee, Cosi sandwiches, wine, beer & coffee cocktails
- World famous s'mores, Cosi pizza & much more - in one eclectic, relaxing atmosphere

Bonus Discounts at entertainment.com

entertainment. entertainment.com

FREE S'MORES (FOR 2)

Enjoy free S'MORES (FOR 2) with purchase of any TWO ENTREES.

valid anytime

Entree includes any sandwich, hot melts, salad or pizza

COSÍ

A108

Valid now thru November 1, 2006

Not valid holidays & subject to Rules of Use. Not valid with other discount offers, unless specified. Coupon VOID if purchased, sold or bartered. Discounts exclude tax, tip and/or alcohol, where applicable.

COSÍ®
Valid at All Participating Locations

Tipping should be 15% to 20% of TOTAL bill before discount
00590819

entertainment.com®
00590819

COSÍ®
Valid at All Participating Locations

Tipping should be 15% to 20% of TOTAL bill before discount
00590825

entertainment.com®
00590825

COSÍ®
Valid at All Participating Locations

Tipping should be 15% to 20% of TOTAL bill before discount
00590831

entertainment.com®
00590831

Moe's Southwest Grill

See reverse side for locations

- Great food, great service, great energy!
- Moe's combines fresh & flavorful with fast & friendly
- Scrumptious burritos, tacos, quesadillas, nachos, salads & fajitas
- Kid's menu includes beverage & cookie
- Moe-Ritas frozen margaritas
- Moe's knows catering

Bonus Discounts at
entertainment.com

entertainment® entertainment.com

great place for kids

Up To $7.00 Value

Enjoy one complimentary MENU ITEM when a second MENU ITEM of equal or greater value is purchased.

valid anytime

Must present coupon/card at time of purchase

Moe's™ southwest grill™

A109

Valid now thru November 1, 2006

Not valid holidays & subject to Rules of Use. Not valid with other discount offers, unless specified. Coupon VOID if purchased, sold or bartered. Discounts exclude tax, tip and/or alcohol, where applicable.

Buffalo Wild Wings Grill & Bar

See reverse side for locations

- What's so hot about Buffalo Wild Wings?
- Chicken wings, signature sauces, big screen TV's & trivia challenges
- Tuesday's $.30 wing night & Wednesday's $.50 leg day
- Great family atmosphere & hot spot to spectate sports
- Home of the real wing
- Weekend live entertainment in Fredericksburg

Bonus Discounts at
entertainment.com

entertainment® entertainment.com

Up To $6.00 Value

Enjoy one complimentary LUNCH OR DINNER ENTREE when a second LUNCH OR DINNER ENTREE of equal or greater value is purchased.

Dine in only

valid anytime

BUFFALO WILD WINGS® GRILL & BAR

A110

Valid now thru November 1, 2006

Not valid holidays & subject to Rules of Use. Not valid with other discount offers, unless specified. Coupon VOID if purchased, sold or bartered. Discounts exclude tax, tip and/or alcohol, where applicable.

Buffalo Wings House

**13005 Worldgate Dr.
Herndon, VA
(703)766-0996**

- House of Inferno
- Featuring the BEST wings in town
- Also featuring sandwiches, salads, chili, burgers, pitas & more
- Kids menu available
- Open daily

Bonus Discounts at
entertainment.com

entertainment® entertainment.com

great place for kids

Up To $8.00 Value

Enjoy one complimentary MENU ITEM when a second MENU ITEM of equal or greater value is purchased.

Dine in only

valid anytime

BWH BUFFALO WINGS HOUSE HOUSE OF THE INFERNO

A111

Valid now thru November 1, 2006

Not valid holidays & subject to Rules of Use. Not valid with other discount offers, unless specified. Coupon VOID if purchased, sold or bartered. Discounts exclude tax, tip and/or alcohol, where applicable.

Moe's southwest grill

10015 York Rd.
Cockeysville, MD
(410)667-6637

7313 Baltimore Ave.
(coming soon)
College Park, MD

5855 Leesburg Pike
Falls Church, VA
(703)578-MOES

667 Potomac Station
Leesburg, VA
(703)777-0004

1495 Stafford Market
Place #111
Stafford, VA
(540)657-2442

00103043

entertainment.com

00103043

BUFFALO WILD WINGS GRILL & BAR

1935 Arlington Blvd.
(Barracks Rd. Shpg. Ctr. - behind Old Navy)
Charlottesville, VA
(434)977-1882

1638 Carl D. Silver
Pkwy.
(Central Park)
Fredericksburg, VA
(540)548-8048

1090 Virginia Center
Pkwy.
Glen Allen, VA
(804)553-9998

1501 E. Cary St.
(corner of 15th & Cary)
Richmond, VA
(804)648-8900

7801 W. Broad St.,
Ste. 10
(Olde Towne Shpg. Ctr.)
Richmond, VA
(804)672-8732

00101747

entertainment.com

00101747

BUFFALO WINGS HOUSE
HOUSE OF THE INFERNO

13005 Worldgate Dr.
(Worldgate Shpg. Ctr.)
Herndon, VA
(703)766-0996

00611872

entertainment.com

00611872

Cafe Mozart

1331 H St. NW
Washington, DC
(202)347-5732

- Endless variety of good old-fashioned home-cooked Viennese & German specialties
- Daily lunch & dinner specials
- Visit our 70 yr. Old German Deli & The Tea Room & Bake Shop
- Private room available for meetings & parties
- Open daily for breakfast, lunch & dinner

Bonus Discounts at
entertainment.com

entertainment.
entertainment.com

Up To $21.00 Value

CAFE Mozart
WWW..CAFEMOZARTGERMANDELI.COM

Enjoy one complimentary LUNCH OR DINNER ENTREE when a second LUNCH OR DINNER ENTREE of equal or greater value is purchased.

Dine in only

valid anytime

www.cafemozartgermandeli.com

A112

Valid now thru November 1, 2006

Not valid holidays & subject to Rules of Use. Not valid with other discount offers, unless specified. Coupon VOID if purchased, sold or bartered. Discounts exclude tax, tip and/or alcohol, where applicable.

Murder Upon Request

See reverse side for locations

- Dine with the victim, chat with the murderer, try to solve a mystery with more twists & turns than a labyrinth...if you can stop laughing long enough to catch the murderer.
- Award winning theatre company with locations in DC, MD, and VA

Bonus Discounts at
entertainment.com

entertainment.
entertainment.com

Up To $15.00 Value

Enjoy one DINNER and SHOW at $15.00 off the regular price when a second DINNER and SHOW of equal or greater value is purchased.

Murder UPON REQUEST

valid anytime

Reservations required; Please present coupon when making reservations; On availability basis

A113

Valid now thru November 1, 2006

Not valid holidays & subject to Rules of Use. Not valid with other discount offers, unless specified. Coupon VOID if purchased, sold or bartered. Discounts exclude tax, tip and/or alcohol, where applicable.

Mansion Mysteries

7711 Eastern Ave.
Silver Spring, MD
(301)588-1688

- You'll dine with the victim & chat with the murderer. If you can follow all the twists & turns, as well as stop laughing long enough, you can catch the culprit
- Located in the Historic Blair Mansion Inn

Bonus Discounts at
entertainment.com

entertainment.
entertainment.com

$15.00 Value

Enjoy $15.00 off the regular price of a DINNER & SHOW, when a second DINNER & SHOW of equal or greater value is purchased.

valid anytime

Reservations required; Please mention coupon when making reservations; On availability basis

www.mansionmysteries.com

A114

Valid now thru November 1, 2006

Not valid holidays & subject to Rules of Use. Not valid with other discount offers, unless specified. Coupon VOID if purchased, sold or bartered. Discounts exclude tax, tip and/or alcohol, where applicable.

CAFE Mozart

WWW..CAFEMOZARTGERMANDELI.COM

1331 H St. NW
(between 13th & 14th Sts.)
Washington, DC
(202)347-5732

Tipping should be 15% to 20% of TOTAL bill before discount

00487320

entertainment.com

00487320

Murder UPON REQUEST

Call (703) 379-8108 for Information, Locations and Reservations

For Private Events, Call (703)587-4504

Tipping should be 15% to 20% of TOTAL bill before discount

00032175

entertainment.com

00032175

Mansion Mysteries

7711 Eastern Ave.
(1/2 blk E. of Georgia Ave. & 2 miles S of 495)
Silver Spring, MD
(301)588-1688

Tipping should be 15% to 20% of TOTAL bill before discount

00151443

entertainment.com

00151443

Charlie Horse Grill

5731 Lee Hwy.
Arlington, VA
(703)532-4112

- Ain't no finer diner
- Best breakfast in town
- Yummy entrees
- Children's menu available
- Happy hour 3 p.m.-6 p.m. everyday
- Parking available
- Open daily

Bonus Discounts at entertainment.com

entertainment. entertainment.com

great place for kids

Up To $14.00 Value

Enjoy one complimentary ENTREE when a second ENTREE of equal or greater value is purchased.

Dine in only

valid anytime

The Charley Horse Grill
Ain't No Finer Diner!

A115

Valid now thru November 1, 2006

Not valid holidays & subject to Rules of Use. Not valid with other discount offers, unless specified. Coupon VOID if purchased, sold or bartered. Discounts exclude tax, tip and/or alcohol, where applicable.

China Jade Restaurant

8357 Sudley Rd.
Manassas, VA
(703)361-5764

- We use a unique blend of seasonings & sauces, mixed with a liberal dash of love for our food
- We specialize in Hong Kong-style seafood
- We serve cocktails, beer & wine
- Open daily

Bonus Discounts at entertainment.com

entertainment. entertainment.com

Up To $14.00 Value

Enjoy one complimentary DINNER ENTREE when a second DINNER ENTREE of equal or greater value is purchased.

Dining room only; Buffet excluded

valid any evening

China Jade RESTAURANT

A116

Valid now thru November 1, 2006

Not valid holidays & subject to Rules of Use. Not valid with other discount offers, unless specified. Coupon VOID if purchased, sold or bartered. Discounts exclude tax, tip and/or alcohol, where applicable.

Delhi Club

1135 N. Highland St.
Arlington, VA
(703)527-5666

- Situated on the corner of Highland St. & Clarendon Blvd.
- We are the perfect balance of color, ambiance & service while celebrating the artistic qualities of authentic Indian cuisine
- Open daily

Bonus Discounts at entertainment.com

entertainment. entertainment.com

Up To $14.00 Value

Enjoy one complimentary LUNCH OR DINNER ENTREE when a second LUNCH OR DINNER ENTREE of equal or greater value is purchased.

Dine in only

valid anytime

DELHI CLUB

www.delhiclub.com

A117

Valid now thru November 1, 2006

Not valid holidays & subject to Rules of Use. Not valid with other discount offers, unless specified. Coupon VOID if purchased, sold or bartered. Discounts exclude tax, tip and/or alcohol, where applicable.

The Charley Horse Grill

Ain't No Finer Diner!

5731 Lee Hwy.
Arlington, VA
(703)532-4112

Tipping should be 15% to 20% of TOTAL bill before discount

00585966

entertainment.com

00585966

China Jade Restaurant

8357 Sudley Rd.
(Manaport Plaza)
Manassas, VA
(703)361-5764

00529833

entertainment.com

00529833

Delhi Club

1135 N. Highland St.
(across from Metro)
Arlington, VA
(703)527-5666

00634873

entertainment.com

00634873

San Antonio Bar & Grill

See reverse side for locations

- Family friendly restaurant serving the best Mexican cuisine in a casual atmosphere
- San Antonio Bar & Grill also features a fully stacked saloon for happy hour
- We make you feel as big as Texas
- Come on in today!
- Arlington location closed Sundays

Bonus Discounts at
entertainment.com

entertainment.
entertainment.com

Up To $12.00 Value

Enjoy one complimentary DINNER ENTREE when a second DINNER ENTREE of equal or greater value is purchased.

Dine in only

valid any evening

SAN ANTONIO BAR & GRILL

A118

Valid now thru November 1, 2006

Not valid holidays & subject to Rules of Use. Not valid with other discount offers, unless specified. Coupon VOID if purchased, sold or bartered. Discounts exclude tax, tip and/or alcohol, where applicable.

Generous Georges Positive Pizza & Pasta Place

3006 Duke St.
Alexandria, VA
(703)370-4303

- Casual family dining
- Home of George's signature Pasta Pie, the famous 6lb. Georgie Combo Pizza, the 32oz. Blue Margarita & more!
- Voted best kid friendly restaurant on washingtonpost.com

Bonus Discounts at
entertainment.com

entertainment.
entertainment.com

great place for kids

50% OFF

Enjoy any TRADITIONAL PIZZA at 50% off the regular price.

Dine in only

valid anytime

Generous George's Positive Pizza & Pasta Place
A Dine-O-Mite Experience Since 1977

www.generousgeorges.com

A119

Valid now thru November 1, 2006

Not valid holidays & subject to Rules of Use. Not valid with other discount offers, unless specified. Coupon VOID if purchased, sold or bartered. Discounts exclude tax, tip and/or alcohol, where applicable.

Pancho Villa Mexican Restaurant

See reverse side for locations

- Best Mexican food in town
- Enjoy one of our famous margaritas
- Open daily

Bonus Discounts at
entertainment.com

entertainment.
entertainment.com

Up To $10.00 Value

Enjoy one complimentary LUNCH OR DINNER ENTREE when a second LUNCH OR DINNER ENTREE of equal or greater value is purchased.

Dine in only

valid anytime

PANCHO VILLA
Mexican Restaurant

A120

Valid now thru November 1, 2006

Not valid holidays & subject to Rules of Use. Not valid with other discount offers, unless specified. Coupon VOID if purchased, sold or bartered. Discounts exclude tax, tip and/or alcohol, where applicable.

SAN ANTONIO BAR & GRILL

200 Swamp Fox Rd.
(across from Eisenhower Metro)
Alexandria, VA
(703)329-6400

1664-A Crystal Sq. Arcade
(Crystal City Underground)
Arlington, VA
(703)415-0126

00657344

entertainment.com

00657344

Generous George's Positive Pizza & Pasta Place®

A Dine-O-Mite Experience Since 1977

3006 Duke St.
Alexandria, VA
(703)370-4303

00659197

entertainment.com

00659197

PANCHO VILLA

Mexican Restaurant

910 S. Main St.
Culpepper, VA
(540)825-5268

10500 Spotslyvannia Ave.
Fredericksburg, VA
(540)710-9999

940 Bragg Rd.
Fredericksburg, VA
(540)785-7458

356 Garrisonville Rd.
Stafford, VA
(540)658-9278

00661656

entertainment.com

00661656

Las Brujas de Cachiche

8909 Centreville Rd.
Manassas, VA
(703)393-7070

- Come on in & visit our neighborly restaurant
- Where all our customers are considered friends
- We specialize in Peruvian cuisine made fresh daily
- Please join us for a memorable evening of dining with family & friends

Bonus Discounts at
entertainment.com

entertainment.
entertainment.com

Up To $14.00 Value

Enjoy one complimentary LUNCH OR DINNER ENTREE when a second LUNCH OR DINNER ENTREE of equal or greater value is purchased.

Dine in only

valid anytime

Las Brujas de Cachiche

A121

Valid now thru November 1, 2006

Not valid holidays & subject to Rules of Use. Not valid with other discount offers, unless specified. Coupon VOID if purchased, sold or bartered. Discounts exclude tax, tip and/or alcohol, where applicable.

Pines of Florence

2100 Connecticut
Ave., NW
Washington, DC
(202)332-8233

- Treat yourself to the ultimate in Southern Italian cuisine.
- Come and taste our homemade manicotti, tortellini and fettuccini.
- Accept this invitation to enjoy a dining experience you won't soon forget.
- Be sure to save room for one of our special desserts.
- Buon Appetito!!
- Visit our website at www.
- pinesofflorence.com.

Bonus Discounts at
entertainment.com

entertainment.
entertainment.com

great place for kids

Up To $14.00 Value

Enjoy one complimentary LUNCH OR DINNER ENTREE when a second LUNCH OR DINNER ENTREE of equal or greater value is purchased.

valid anytime

PINES of Florence
Southern Italian Cuisine

www.pinesofflorence.com

A122

Valid now thru November 1, 2006

Not valid holidays & subject to Rules of Use. Not valid with other discount offers, unless specified. Coupon VOID if purchased, sold or bartered. Discounts exclude tax, tip and/or alcohol, where applicable.

Restaurante Abi Azteca Grill & Bar

13760 Smoketown
Rd.
Woodbridge, VA
(703)590-4080

- Welcome to Restaurante Abi, featuring authentic Salvadorian & Mexican cuisine
- Our restaurant is family owned & operated & welcomes everyone
- Come in prepared to enjoy a wonderful authentic dining experience
- Open daily

Bonus Discounts at
entertainment.com

entertainment.
entertainment.com

Up To $14.00 Value

Enjoy one complimentary LUNCH OR DINNER ENTREE when a second LUNCH OR DINNER ENTREE of equal or greater value is purchased.

Dine in only

valid anytime

RESTAURANTE ABI
AZTECA GRILL & BAR
PUPUSAS · TACOS
SINCE 1986

A123

Valid now thru November 1, 2006

Not valid holidays & subject to Rules of Use. Not valid with other discount offers, unless specified. Coupon VOID if purchased, sold or bartered. Discounts exclude tax, tip and/or alcohol, where applicable.

Las Brujas de Cachiche

8909 Centreville Rd.
Manassas, VA
(703)393-7070

00568891

entertainment.com

00568891

PINES
of Florence
Southern Italian Cuisine

2100 Connecticut Ave., NW
Washington, DC
(202)332-8233

00286402

entertainment.com

00286402

RESTAURANTE
ABI'S
AZTECA GRILL & BAR
PUPUSAS · TACOS

13760 Smoketown Rd.
(Smoketown Plaza - next to Lowe's)
Woodbridge, VA
(703)590-4080

00661659

entertainment.com

00661659

Bombay Curry Co.

3110 Mount Vernon Ave.
Alexandria, VA
(703)836-6363

- Come see what everyone is talking about at the Bombay Curry Company
- "Find authentic curry at the Bombay Curry Company" The Alexandria Gazette
- "This is certainly another neighborhood bargain" The Good Neighbor
- "Alexandria's favorite neighborhood restaurant" as voted by Washingtonian readers

Bonus Discounts at entertainment.com

entertainment. entertainment.com

Up To $13.00 Value

Enjoy one complimentary LUNCH OR DINNER ENTREE when a second LUNCH OR DINNER ENTREE of equal or greater value is purchased.

Dine in only

valid anytime

BOMBAY CURRY COMPANY
Traditional Indian & Indian Inspired Cuisine

A124

Valid now thru November 1, 2006

Not valid holidays & subject to Rules of Use. Not valid with other discount offers, unless specified. Coupon VOID if purchased, sold or bartered. Discounts exclude tax, tip and/or alcohol, where applicable.

Castillo's Cafe

6349 Multiplex Dr.
Centreville, VA
(703)266-6707

- Fine Mexican & Salvadorian cuisine
- Lunch & dinner menu available
- Quesadillas, fajitas, soups, salads & seafood
- Kids menu available
- Open daily

Bonus Discounts at entertainment.com

entertainment. entertainment.com

Up To $13.00 Value

Enjoy one complimentary LUNCH OR DINNER ENTREE when a second LUNCH OR DINNER ENTREE of equal or greater value is purchased.

Dine in only

valid anytime

CASTILLO'S Café

A125

Valid now thru November 1, 2006

Not valid holidays & subject to Rules of Use. Not valid with other discount offers, unless specified. Coupon VOID if purchased, sold or bartered. Discounts exclude tax, tip and/or alcohol, where applicable.

Rudy's Restaurant

2201 Arlington Blvd.
Arlington, VA
(703)525-0300

- Welcome to Rudy's where you & your family are always welcome
- Offering light fare & a complete entree menu
- Open daily for breakfast & dinner
- Closed Sunday evening

Bonus Discounts at entertainment.com

entertainment. entertainment.com

Up To $13.00 Value

Enjoy one complimentary DINNER ENTREE when a second DINNER ENTREE of equal or greater value is purchased.

Dine in only

valid any evening

RUDY'S BAR & GRILL

A126

Valid now thru November 1, 2006

Not valid holidays & subject to Rules of Use. Not valid with other discount offers, unless specified. Coupon VOID if purchased, sold or bartered. Discounts exclude tax, tip and/or alcohol, where applicable.

BOMBAY CURRY COMPANY

Traditional Indian & Indian Inspired Cuisine

3110 Mount Vernon Ave.
Alexandria, VA
(703)836-6363

00549342

entertainment.com

00549342

CASTILLO'S

Café

6349 Multiplex Dr.
Centreville, VA
(703)266-6707

00633484

entertainment.com

00633484

RUDY'S

BAR & GRILL

2201 Arlington Blvd.
Arlington, VA
(703)525-0300

Tipping should be 15% to 20% of TOTAL bill before discount

00477846

entertainment.com

00477846

The Regency Cafe

1800 Old Meadow Rd.
McLean, VA
(703)790-1655

- Located inside The Regency Sport & Health Club
- Featuring all your favorite lunch & dinner items
- Breakfast is served Saturday & Sundays from 10 a.m. - 3 p.m.
- Come on in & give us a try

Up To $13.00 Value

Enjoy one complimentary LUNCH OR DINNER ENTREE when a second LUNCH OR DINNER ENTREE of equal or greater value is purchased.

Dine in only

valid anytime

The Regency Café

A127

Valid now thru November 1, 2006

Not valid holidays & subject to Rules of Use. Not valid with other discount offers, unless specified. Coupon VOID if purchased, sold or bartered. Discounts exclude tax, tip and/or alcohol, where applicable.

Ashton Ave. Restaurant

9920 Cockrell Rd.
Manassas, VA
(703)330-5151

- Welcome back to how traditional "dining" should be
- We feature Greek, Italian, American & Tex-Mex cuisine
- Family owned & operated
- Home style cooking
- Open daily

great place for kids

Up To $12.00 Value

Enjoy one complimentary LUNCH OR DINNER ENTREE when a second LUNCH OR DINNER ENTREE of equal or greater value is purchased.

Dine in only

valid anytime

ASHTON AVE FAMILY RESTAURANT

A128

Valid now thru November 1, 2006

Not valid holidays & subject to Rules of Use. Not valid with other discount offers, unless specified. Coupon VOID if purchased, sold or bartered. Discounts exclude tax, tip and/or alcohol, where applicable.

Beacon Street Boston Cafe

13041 Lee Jackson Memorial Hwy.
Fairfax, VA
(703)803-8110

- A new adventure in dining
- A unique touch - Boston in Fairfax County
- Generous portions of ribs, steaks, chicken & fresh fish
- Acclaimed salad bar offering a large variety of fresh fruits, vegetables & seafood
- Featuring Cheers tavern
- Located in Greenbriar Shopping Center

Up To $12.00 Value

Enjoy one complimentary DINNER ENTREE when a second DINNER ENTREE of equal or greater value is purchased.

valid any evening

BEACON STREET BOSTON CAFE

A129

Valid now thru November 1, 2006

Not valid holidays & subject to Rules of Use. Not valid with other discount offers, unless specified. Coupon VOID if purchased, sold or bartered. Discounts exclude tax, tip and/or alcohol, where applicable.

The Regency Café

1800 Old Meadow Rd.
McLean, VA
(703)790-1655

Offers not valid holidays and subject to Rules of Use
Tipping should be 15% to 20% of the total bill before discount
00566647

entertainment.com

00566647

ASHTON AVE FAMILY RESTAURANT

9920 Cockrell Rd.
(Corner of Ashton Ave. & Cockrell Rd.)
Manassas, VA
(703)330-5151

Offers not valid holidays and subject to Rules of Use
Tipping should be 15% to 20% of the total bill before discount
00606673

entertainment.com

00606673

BEACON STREET BOSTON CAFE

13041 Lee Jackson Memorial Hwy.
(Greenbriar Shpg. Ctr.)
Fairfax, VA
(703)803-8110

Tipping should be 15% to 20% of TOTAL bill before discount
00082414

entertainment.com

00082414

Cafe DaVanzo

2312 Plank Rd.
Fredericksburg, VA
(540)372-3335

- Cafe DaVanzo is a casual restaurant specializing in Italian food with American menu items included
- Cafe DaVanzo is a locally owned, original, one of a kind restaurant
- Our atmosphere is warm, bright & friendly
- We can't wait to serve you!

Bonus Discounts at
entertainment.com

entertainment.
entertainment.com

Up To $12.00 Value

Enjoy one complimentary LUNCH OR DINNER ENTREE when a second LUNCH OR DINNER ENTREE of equal or greater value is purchased.

Dine in only

valid anytime

CAFE DaVanzo ITALIAN

A130

Valid now thru November 1, 2006

Not valid holidays & subject to Rules of Use. Not valid with other discount offers, unless specified. Coupon VOID if purchased, sold or bartered. Discounts exclude tax, tip and/or alcohol, where applicable.

Crystal City Sports Pub

529 S. 23rd St.
Arlington, VA
(703)521-8215

- An all season sports bar in Crystal City
- Featuring billiards, darts, large screen TV, satellite TV & an outdoor patio
- Including pre-game warm-ups like wings, chicken fingers & more
- For those bigger appetites, enjoy one of our main events - steaks, chops, fish & more
- Open daily

Bonus Discounts at
entertainment.com

entertainment.
entertainment.com

Up To $12.00 Value

Enjoy one complimentary LUNCH OR DINNER ENTREE when a second LUNCH OR DINNER ENTREE of equal or greater value is purchased or when dining alone - one LUNCH OR DINNER ENTREE at 50% off the regular price - maximum discount $6.00.

Dine in only

valid anytime

CRYSTAL CITY Sports Pub

A131

Valid now thru November 1, 2006

Not valid holidays & subject to Rules of Use. Not valid with other discount offers, unless specified. Coupon VOID if purchased, sold or bartered. Discounts exclude tax, tip and/or alcohol, where applicable.

Eisenhower Station Restaurant

2460 Eisenhower Ave.
Alexandria, VA
(703)960-3400

- Located less than 200 yards from Eisenhower Metro Station
- Casual, fun & relaxing
- Sunday brunch available 11 a.m. - 2 p.m.
- Open daily

Bonus Discounts at
entertainment.com

entertainment.
entertainment.com

Up To $12.00 Value

Enjoy one complimentary LUNCH OR DINNER ENTREE when a second LUNCH OR DINNER ENTREE of equal or greater value is purchased.

Dine in only

valid anytime

Eisenhower Station Restaurant

A132

Valid now thru November 1, 2006

Not valid holidays & subject to Rules of Use. Not valid with other discount offers, unless specified. Coupon VOID if purchased, sold or bartered. Discounts exclude tax, tip and/or alcohol, where applicable.

CAFE DaVanzo ITALIAN

2312 Plank Rd.
Fredericksburg, VA
(540)372-3335

00633738

entertainment.com

00633738

CRYSTAL CITY Sports Pub

529 S. 23rd St.
Arlington, VA
(703)521-8215

Tipping should be 15% to 20% of TOTAL bill before discount

00065080

entertainment.com

00065080

Eisenhower Station Restaurant

2460 Eisenhower Ave.
Alexandria, VA
(703)960-3400

Tipping should be 15% to 20% of TOTAL bill before discount

00381681

entertainment.com

00381681

El Pollo Ranchero

6324 Richmond Hwy.
Alexandria, VA
(703)721-2000

- Welcome to El Pollo Ranchero, new to Alexandria
- Serving Rotissori, Peruvian style chicken, ceuicas, tacos, nachos, fajitas, burritos, chimichangas, & more
- Full service bar, including our famous margaritas
- Open daily

entertainment.
entertainment.com

Up To $12.00 Value

El Pollo Ranchero
Tex Mex Cafe

Enjoy one complimentary LUNCH OR DINNER ENTREE when a second LUNCH OR DINNER ENTREE of equal or greater value is purchased.

Dine in only

valid anytime

A133

Valid now thru November 1, 2006

Not valid holidays & subject to Rules of Use. Not valid with other discount offers, unless specified. Coupon VOID if purchased, sold or bartered. Discounts exclude tax, tip and/or alcohol, where applicable.

Izalco Bar & Restaurant

8403 E&F Richmond Hwy.
Alexandria, VA
(703)704-9220

- Featuring Mexican & Salvadorean cuisine
- Dine in & enjoy a wonderful dining experience
- Open daily

entertainment.
entertainment.com

Up To $12.00 Value

IZALCO
Bar & Restaurant
COMIDA MEXICANA Y SALVADOREÑA

Enjoy one complimentary LUNCH OR DINNER ENTREE when a second LUNCH OR DINNER ENTREE of equal or greater value is purchased.

Dine in only

valid anytime

A134

Valid now thru November 1, 2006

Not valid holidays & subject to Rules of Use. Not valid with other discount offers, unless specified. Coupon VOID if purchased, sold or bartered. Discounts exclude tax, tip and/or alcohol, where applicable.

Kirkpatricks

44050 Ashburn Shpg. Plaza
Ashburn, VA
(703)724-9801

- Irish pub, sports bar & family grille
- Come in & enjoy good old Irish fare
- Check out our schedule of events listed on our web site
- We can't wait to serve you
- Open daily

entertainment.
entertainment.com

Up To $12.00 Value

Enjoy one complimentary LUNCH OR DINNER ENTREE when a second LUNCH OR DINNER ENTREE of equal or greater value is purchased.

Dine in only

valid anytime

kirkpatrick's

www.kirkpatricks.tv

A135

Valid now thru November 1, 2006

Not valid holidays & subject to Rules of Use. Not valid with other discount offers, unless specified. Coupon VOID if purchased, sold or bartered. Discounts exclude tax, tip and/or alcohol, where applicable.

El Pollo Ranchero
Tex Mex Cafe

6324 Richmond Hwy.
Alexandria, VA
(703)721-2000

Tipping should be 15% to 20% of TOTAL bill before discount

00446438

entertainment.com

00446438

IZALCO
Bar & Restaurant
COMIDA MEXICANA Y SALVADOREÑA

8403 E&F Richmond Hwy.
Alexandria, VA
(703)704-9220

00496075

entertainment.com

00496075

kirkpatrick's

44050 Ashburn Shpg. Plaza
(Ashburn Village Ctr.)
Ashburn, VA
(703)724-9801

Tipping should be 15% to 20% of TOTAL bill before discount

00528122

entertainment.com

00528122

Brittany's Restaurant & Sports Bar

12449 Dillingham Sq.
Woodbridge, VA
(703)730-0728

- Featuring dining in a friendly, relaxed atmosphere
- Daily specials
- Wing night every Wed.
- Live music or DJ every weekend
- Carry out & catering services available
- Open daily

Bonus Discounts at
entertainment.com

entertainment.
entertainment.com

Up To $11.00 Value

BRITTANY'S
Restaurant & Sports Bar

Enjoy one complimentary LUNCH OR DINNER ENTREE when a second LUNCH OR DINNER ENTREE of equal or greater value is purchased or when dining alone - one LUNCH OR DINNER ENTREE at 50% off the regular price - maximum discount $5.00.

valid anytime

A136

Valid now thru November 1, 2006

Not valid holidays & subject to Rules of Use. Not valid with other discount offers, unless specified. Coupon VOID if purchased, sold or bartered. Discounts exclude tax, tip and/or alcohol, where applicable.

DaVinci Family Restaurant

6347 Columbia Pike
Falls Church, VA
(703)916-1147

- Welcome to DaVinci Family Restaurant
- Serving all your favorite Italian specials
- We offer catering & a private room for parties
- Open Mon. - Sat. 11-10 p.m. & Sun. 12-9 p.m.

Bonus Discounts at
entertainment.com

entertainment.
entertainment.com

Up To $11.00 Value

Enjoy one complimentary LUNCH OR DINNER ENTREE when a second LUNCH OR DINNER ENTREE of equal or greater value is purchased.

Dine in only; Specials excluded

valid anytime

A137

Valid now thru November 1, 2006

Not valid holidays & subject to Rules of Use. Not valid with other discount offers, unless specified. Coupon VOID if purchased, sold or bartered. Discounts exclude tax, tip and/or alcohol, where applicable.

Delia's Family Restaurant & Pizzeria

6715 Backlick Rd.
Springfield, VA
(703)451-0242

- Award winning, best tasting low cholesterol pizza in the entire metropolitan area
- Others may imitate, but never duplicate the taste & quality of Delia's
- Open Monday thru Saturday

Bonus Discounts at
entertainment.com

entertainment.
entertainment.com

Up To $11.00 Value

DELIA'S
FAMILY RESTAURANT & PIZZERIA

Enjoy one complimentary DINNER ENTREE when a second DINNER ENTREE of equal or greater value is purchased or for those who prefer - any one pizza at 50% off the regular price.

Dine in only; Specials included at regular price

valid any evening

not valid on Tumi Peruvian menu

A138

Valid now thru November 1, 2006

Not valid holidays & subject to Rules of Use. Not valid with other discount offers, unless specified. Coupon VOID if purchased, sold or bartered. Discounts exclude tax, tip and/or alcohol, where applicable.

BRITTANY'S
Restaurant & Sports Bar

12449 Dillingham Sq.
(Festival at Old Bridge)
Woodbridge, VA
(703)730-0728

Tipping should be 15% to 20% of TOTAL bill before discount

00021875

entertainment.com

00021875

DaVinci Family Restaurant

6347 Columbia Pike
(Barcroft Shpg. Ctr.)
Falls Church, VA
(703)916-1147

Tipping should be 15% to 20% of TOTAL bill before discount

00445986

entertainment.com

00445986

DELIA'S
FAMILY RESTAURANT
& PIZZERIA

6715 Backlick Rd.
Springfield, VA
(703)451-0242

Tipping should be 15% to 20% of TOTAL bill before discount

00201023

entertainment.com

00201023

Las Delicias Restaurant

733 Elden St.
Herndon, VA
(703)464-7922

- Featuring traditional South American cuisine
- Everything made to order
- Bring the whole family & relax & enjoy
- Closed Mon.

Bonus Discounts at
entertainment.com

entertainment.
entertainment.com

Up To $11.00 Value

Enjoy one complimentary LUNCH OR DINNER ENTREE when a second LUNCH OR DINNER ENTREE of equal or greater value is purchased.

Dine in only

valid anytime

Las Delicias Restaurant

A139

Valid now thru November 1, 2006

Not valid holidays & subject to Rules of Use. Not valid with other discount offers, unless specified. Coupon VOID if purchased, sold or bartered. Discounts exclude tax, tip and/or alcohol, where applicable.

Oasis on the Occoquan

13188 Marina Way
Woodbridge, VA
(703)494-5000

- Cool casual cuisine
- Hot Caribbean atmosphere
- Everyday is just another day at the harbor

Bonus Discounts at
entertainment.com

entertainment.
entertainment.com

Up To $11.00 Value

Enjoy one complimentary LUNCH OR DINNER ENTREE when a second LUNCH OR DINNER ENTREE of equal or greater value is purchased.

Dine in only

valid anytime

Oasis on the Occoquan

www.oasisontheoccoquan.com

A140

Valid now thru November 1, 2006

Not valid holidays & subject to Rules of Use. Not valid with other discount offers, unless specified. Coupon VOID if purchased, sold or bartered. Discounts exclude tax, tip and/or alcohol, where applicable.

Pasta Pizza

6410 Lansdowne Centre Dr.
Alexandria, VA
(571)642-0202

- Fast food with style
- Offering dine-in, carry-out or delivery
- Pasta & pizza sauces prepared fresh daily
- We love to cater call us today
- Open daily

Bonus Discounts at
entertainment.com

entertainment.
entertainment.com

Up To $11.00 Value

Enjoy one complimentary DINNER ENTREE when a second DINNER ENTREE of equal or greater value is purchased or for those who prefer - any one pizza at 50% off the regular price - maximum discount $11.00.

Dine in only

valid any evening

PASTA PIZZA

A141

Valid now thru November 1, 2006

Not valid holidays & subject to Rules of Use. Not valid with other discount offers, unless specified. Coupon VOID if purchased, sold or bartered. Discounts exclude tax, tip and/or alcohol, where applicable.

Las Delicias Restaurant

733 Elden St.
Herndon, VA
(703)464-7922

00608557

entertainment.com

00608557

Oasis

on the Occoquan

13188 Marina Way
Woodbridge, VA
(703)494-5000

00542853

entertainment.com

00542853

PASTA
PIZZA

6410 Lansdowne Centre Dr.
(Lansdowne Centre)
Alexandria, VA
(571)642-0202

00569045

entertainment.com

00569045

Philadelphia Tavern

9413 Main St.
Manassas, VA
(703)393-1776

- Specializing in authentic Philadelphia fare
- Antique bar serving a full line of drinks
- Prime Angus steaks
- Philly Cheesesteaks & Hoagies on Amoroso rolls & much more
- Open daily

Up To $11.00 Value

Enjoy one complimentary LUNCH OR DINNER ENTREE when a second LUNCH OR DINNER ENTREE of equal or greater value is purchased.

Dine in only

valid anytime

PHILADELPHIA TAVERN

A142

Valid now thru November 1, 2006

Not valid holidays & subject to Rules of Use. Not valid with other discount offers, unless specified. Coupon VOID if purchased, sold or bartered. Discounts exclude tax, tip and/or alcohol, where applicable.

Quarter Deck

See reverse side for locations

- Family owned & operated
- Casual neighborhood restaurant/crabhouse
- Daily fresh fish specials
- Hot steamed crabs & spiced shrimp
- Seafood platters
- We also have subs, sandwiches & pizza
- Patio dining
- Cocktails, beer & wine
- Open daily

Up To $11.00 Value

QUARTER DECK

"THE DECK"

Enjoy one complimentary LUNCH OR DINNER ENTREE when a second LUNCH OR DINNER ENTREE of equal or greater value is purchased.

STEAMED CRABS EXCLUDED; Dine in only

valid anytime

A143

Valid now thru November 1, 2006

Not valid holidays & subject to Rules of Use. Not valid with other discount offers, unless specified. Coupon VOID if purchased, sold or bartered. Discounts exclude tax, tip and/or alcohol, where applicable.

South Riding Inn

43090 Peacock Market Sq., Ste. 110
South Riding, VA
(703)327-8055

- Featuring home style American cooking
- A definite locals favorite
- Located off Route 50 in South Riding
- Open daily at 11 a.m.

Up To $11.00 Value

Enjoy one complimentary LUNCH OR DINNER ENTREE when a second LUNCH OR DINNER ENTREE of equal or greater value is purchased.

Dine in only

valid anytime

www.southridinginn.com

A144

Valid now thru November 1, 2006

Not valid holidays & subject to Rules of Use. Not valid with other discount offers, unless specified. Coupon VOID if purchased, sold or bartered. Discounts exclude tax, tip and/or alcohol, where applicable.

PHILADELPHIA TAVERN

9413 Main St.
Manassas, VA
(703)393-1776

00503798

entertainment.com

00503798

QUARTER DECK

"THE DECK"

Follow Ft. Myer Dr. thru Rosslyn, across Rte. 50 and take first turn (Arlington Blvd.). Turn again at second left (Ft. Myer Dr.) and go to the top of the hill.

1200 N. Fort Myer Dr.,
Arlington, VA

(703)528-2722

Tipping should be 15% to 20% of TOTAL bill before discount

00043830

entertainment.com

00043830

South Riding Inn

43090 Peacock Market Sq., Ste. 110
South Riding, VA
(703)327-8055

00496017

entertainment.com

00496017

Southside 815

815 S. Washington St.
Alexandria, VA
(703)836-6222

- Alexandria's favorite Southern restaurant
- Featuring amazing appetizers, salads, selections from the grill, sandwiches & our very own Southern classic dishes
- Enjoy patio dining
- Watch any one of your favorite sporting events on our bar-side TV's
- Open daily

Bonus Discounts at entertainment.com

entertainment® entertainment.com

Up To $11.00 Value

Enjoy one complimentary LUNCH OR DINNER ENTREE when a second LUNCH OR DINNER ENTREE of equal or greater value is purchased.

Dine in only

valid anytime

SOUTHSIDE 815

www.southside815.com

A145

Valid now thru November 1, 2006

Not valid holidays & subject to Rules of Use. Not valid with other discount offers, unless specified. Coupon VOID if purchased, sold or bartered. Discounts exclude tax, tip and/or alcohol, where applicable.

T.T. Reynolds

10414 Main St.
Fairfax, VA
(703)591-9292

- Specialties that include steak, chicken & shrimp
- Charbroiled burgers & sandwiches
- Homemade chili & soups
- Nightly dinner specials
- Patio dining
- Cocktails, beer & wine
- Open daily

Bonus Discounts at entertainment.com

entertainment® entertainment.com

Up To $11.00 Value

T.T. REYNOLDS

Restaurant & Tavern

Enjoy one complimentary LUNCH OR DINNER ENTREE when a second LUNCH OR DINNER ENTREE of equal or greater value is purchased.

Dine in only

valid anytime

www.ttreynolds.com **A146**

Valid now thru November 1, 2006

Not valid holidays & subject to Rules of Use. Not valid with other discount offers, unless specified. Coupon VOID if purchased, sold or bartered. Discounts exclude tax, tip and/or alcohol, where applicable.

Zuhair's Cafe & Grill

720 Grant St.
Herndon, VA
(703)437-8733

- Serving traditional Iraqi cuisine....
- Offering Shatila products
- Call us for your next catering event
- Located off Elden St. across from Burger King

Bonus Discounts at entertainment.com

entertainment® entertainment.com

Up To $11.00 Value

Enjoy one complimentary LUNCH OR DINNER ENTREE when a second LUNCH OR DINNER ENTREE of equal or greater value is purchased.

Dine in only

valid anytime

ZUHAIR'S GRILL CAFÉ

A147

Valid now thru November 1, 2006

Not valid holidays & subject to Rules of Use. Not valid with other discount offers, unless specified. Coupon VOID if purchased, sold or bartered. Discounts exclude tax, tip and/or alcohol, where applicable.

SOUTHSIDE 815

815 S. Washington St.
Alexandria, VA
(703)836-6222

Offers not valid holidays and subject to Rules of Use
Tipping should be 15% to 20% of the total bill before discount
00213151

entertainment.com

00213151

T.T. REYNOLDS
Restaurant & Tavern

10414 Main St.
Fairfax, VA
(703)591-9292

00608015

entertainment.com

00608015

ZUHAIR'S GRILL CAFÉ

720 Grant St.
Herndon, VA
(703)437-8733

Offers not valid holidays and subject to Rules of Use
Tipping should be 15% to 20% of the total bill before discount
00601735

entertainment.com

00601735

Aabshaar Restaurant

6550 Backlick Rd.
Springfield, VA
(703)866-1155

- Fresh sweets made on the premises daily
- The famous caterer of Indian & Pakistani cuisine
- Quality food & excellent service
- All entrees are served with nan, rice, & salad
- Vegetarian delights
- Ask about our chef's specialties
- Specializing in catering

Bonus Discounts at
entertainment.com

entertainment® entertainment.com

Up To $10.00 Value

Enjoy one complimentary LUNCH OR DINNER ENTREE when a second LUNCH OR DINNER ENTREE of equal or greater value is purchased.

Aabshaar Restaurant

valid anytime

A148

Valid now thru November 1, 2006

Not valid holidays & subject to Rules of Use. Not valid with other discount offers, unless specified. Coupon VOID if purchased, sold or bartered. Discounts exclude tax, tip and/or alcohol, where applicable.

Afghan Kabob Restaurant

6357 Rolling Rd.
Springfield, VA
(703)913-7008

- Family style dining in a friendly & relaxed atmosphere
- Delicious desserts, appetizers, soups & salads
- Specializing in kabobs cooked over hickory charcoal
- Open daily from 11 a.m. - 11 p.m.

Bonus Discounts at
entertainment.com

entertainment® entertainment.com

Up To $10.00 Value

Enjoy one complimentary LUNCH OR DINNER ENTREE when a second LUNCH OR DINNER ENTREE of equal or greater value is purchased.

AFGHAN KABOB RESTAURANT

Dine in only

valid anytime

A149

Valid now thru November 1, 2006

Not valid holidays & subject to Rules of Use. Not valid with other discount offers, unless specified. Coupon VOID if purchased, sold or bartered. Discounts exclude tax, tip and/or alcohol, where applicable.

Ball's Bluff Tavern

2-D Loudoun St. S.W.
Leesburg, VA
(703)777-7757

- Ball's Bluff Tavern is a place where the past & present meet for food & spirits
- The menu features dishes from North & South
- A touch of real Civil War cookery featuring Yankee beef stew to Dixie chicken
- More up to date appetizers & main courses also available

Bonus Discounts at
entertainment.com

entertainment® entertainment.com

Up To $10.00 Value

Enjoy one complimentary LUNCH OR DINNER ENTREE when a second LUNCH OR DINNER ENTREE of equal or greater value is purchased.

BALL'S ★ BLUFF TAVERN

valid anytime

A150

Valid now thru November 1, 2006

Not valid holidays & subject to Rules of Use. Not valid with other discount offers, unless specified. Coupon VOID if purchased, sold or bartered. Discounts exclude tax, tip and/or alcohol, where applicable.

Aabshaar Restaurant

6550 Backlick Rd.
Springfield, VA
(703)866-1155

00527786

entertainment.com

00527786

AFGHAN KABOB RESTAURANT

6357 Rolling Rd.
Springfield, VA
(703)913-7008

Offers not valid holidays and subject to Rules of Use
Tipping should be 15% to 20% of the total bill before discount
00604322

entertainment.com

00604322

BALL'S BLUFF TAVERN

2-D Loudoun St. S.W.
Leesburg, VA
(703)777-7757

Tipping should be 15% to 20% of TOTAL bill before discount
00065859

entertainment.com

00065859

Bristow Manor Grill & Pub

11507 Valley View Dr.
Bristow, VA
(703)368-3558

- Relax & enjoy a lite meal or snack at the Grill & Pub
- Open daily

Bonus Discounts at
entertainment.com

entertainment®
entertainment.com

Up To $10.00 Value

BRISTOW MANOR GRILL & PUB

Enjoy one complimentary LUNCH OR DINNER ENTREE when a second LUNCH OR DINNER ENTREE of equal or greater value is purchased.

valid anytime

www.bristowmanor.com

A151

Valid now thru November 1, 2006

Not valid holidays & subject to Rules of Use. Not valid with other discount offers, unless specified. Coupon VOID if purchased, sold or bartered. Discounts exclude tax, tip and/or alcohol, where applicable.

Bukom Cafe

2442 18th St. NW
Washington, DC
(202)265-4600

- Savor the flavor of West Africa in Adams Morgan
- Accepts reservations for private parties
- Carry out available
- Catering
- Live music Wed.-Sun.
- Credit cards accepted
- Open daily

Bonus Discounts at
entertainment.com

entertainment®
entertainment.com

Up To $10.00 Value

BUKOM CAFE
West African Cuisine

Enjoy one complimentary DINNER ENTREE when a second DINNER ENTREE of equal or greater value is purchased or when dining alone - one DINNER ENTREE at 50% off the regular price - maximum discount $5.00.

valid any evening

A152

Valid now thru November 1, 2006

Not valid holidays & subject to Rules of Use. Not valid with other discount offers, unless specified. Coupon VOID if purchased, sold or bartered. Discounts exclude tax, tip and/or alcohol, where applicable.

Cafe' at Columbia Island Marina

George Washington Memorial Pkwy.
South Arlington, VA
(202)347-0173

- Come check out the lowest prices on the water
- Happy hour starts at 4 p.m. daily
- Planning a party? Let us cater your next event!

Bonus Discounts at
entertainment.com

entertainment®
entertainment.com

Up To $10.00 Value

Columbia Island MARINA

Enjoy one complimentary MENU ITEM when a second MENU ITEM of equal or greater value is purchased.

valid anytime

www.columbiaisland.com/cafe

A153

Valid now thru November 1, 2006

Not valid holidays & subject to Rules of Use. Not valid with other discount offers, unless specified. Coupon VOID if purchased, sold or bartered. Discounts exclude tax, tip and/or alcohol, where applicable.

BRISTOW MANOR GRILL & PUB

11507 Valley View Dr.
Bristow, VA
(703)368-3558

Tipping should be 15% to 20% of TOTAL bill before discount

00455432

entertainment.com

00455432

BUKOM CAFE
West African Cuisine

2442 18th St. NW
(Adams Morgan)
Washington, DC
(202)265-4600

Tipping should be 15% to 20% of TOTAL bill before discount

00026088

entertainment.com

00026088

Columbia Island MARINA

George Washington Memorial Pkwy.
South Arlington, VA
(202)347-0173

Tipping should be 15% to 20% of TOTAL bill before discount

00596266

entertainment.com

00596266

Cantina D'Italia

See reverse side for locations

- We offer Italian cuisine at its best
- Choose from wide selection of fresh seafood, veal, chicken
- Friendly service and quiet atmosphere
- Open daily

Bonus Discounts at entertainment.com

entertainment. entertainment.com

Up To $10.00 Value

Enjoy one complimentary DINNER ENTREE when a second DINNER ENTREE of equal or greater value is purchased.

Cantina D'Italia

valid any evening

Holidays excluded

A154

Valid now thru November 1, 2006

Not valid holidays & subject to Rules of Use. Not valid with other discount offers, unless specified. Coupon VOID if purchased, sold or bartered. Discounts exclude tax, tip and/or alcohol, where applicable.

Canton Cafe

**6396 Springfield Plaza
Springfield, VA
(703)644-0178**

- Serving authentic Cantonese cuisine
- Located in Springfield Plaza next to MARS
- Bring the whole family
- Open daily

Bonus Discounts at entertainment.com

entertainment. entertainment.com

Up To $10.00 Value

Canton Cafe

FINE CANTONESE CUISINE

Enjoy one complimentary LUNCH OR DINNER ENTREE when a second LUNCH OR DINNER ENTREE of equal or greater value is purchased.

Dine in only

valid anytime

lunch specials excluded

A155

Valid now thru November 1, 2006

Not valid holidays & subject to Rules of Use. Not valid with other discount offers, unless specified. Coupon VOID if purchased, sold or bartered. Discounts exclude tax, tip and/or alcohol, where applicable.

Casa Chimayo

**8209 Sudley Rd.
Manassas, VA
(703)369-2523**

- Featuring Sonora-style Mexican food
- Specailties include super tostada & enchilada de Vera Cruz
- Entrees include dinner combinations & specials
- Cocktails, beer & wine
- Open Daily

Bonus Discounts at entertainment.com

entertainment. entertainment.com

great place for kids

Up To $10.00 Value

Enjoy one complimentary LUNCH OR DINNER ENTREE when a second LUNCH OR DINNER ENTREE of equal or greater value is purchased.

Dine in only

valid anytime

Casa Chimayo

A156

Valid now thru November 1, 2006

Not valid holidays & subject to Rules of Use. Not valid with other discount offers, unless specified. Coupon VOID if purchased, sold or bartered. Discounts exclude tax, tip and/or alcohol, where applicable.

Cantina D'Italia

285 Kentlard Blvd.
Gaithersburg, MD
(301)948-8858

13015 Fairlakes Ctr.
Fairfax, VA
(703)631-2752

150-E Elden St.
Herndon, VA
(703)318-7171

00098676

entertainment.com

00098676

Canton Cafe
FINE CANTONESE CUISINE

6396 Springfield Plaza
Springfield, VA
(703)644-0178

00496141

entertainment.com

00496141

Casa Chimayo

8209 Sudley Rd.
Manassas, VA
(703)369-2523

00633480

entertainment.com

00633480

Charlie Chiang's Chinese Restaurant

11832 Sunrise Valley Dr.
Reston, VA
(703)620-9700

- Rated one of the area's best by "D.C. Ethnic Restaurant Guide"
- Specialties include seafood combinations, chicken, duck, beef & pork
- Choose from a variety of hot & cold appetizers
- Catering & party service available
- Open daily

Bonus Discounts at entertainment.com

entertainment. entertainment.com

Up To $10.00 Value

Enjoy one complimentary LUNCH OR DINNER ENTREE when a second LUNCH OR DINNER ENTREE of equal or greater value is purchased or when dining alone - one LUNCH OR DINNER ENTREE at 50% off the regular price - maximum discount $5.00.

Dine in only

valid anytime

Reston location only; For holidays-see Rules of Use

Charlie Chiang's 營園 Chinese Restaurant

A157

Valid now thru November 1, 2006

Not valid holidays & subject to Rules of Use. Not valid with other discount offers, unless specified. Coupon VOID if purchased, sold or bartered. Discounts exclude tax, tip and/or alcohol, where applicable.

Chikzza Fried Chicken & Pizza

6100 Richmond Hwy.
Alexandria, VA
(703)317-9375

- Featuring chicken, pizza & subs
- Chicken cooked in canola oil - 0 fat - 0 cholesterol
- Freshest food around
- Call us for your next catering event
- Halal available
- Open daily

Bonus Discounts at entertainment.com

entertainment. entertainment.com

great place for kids

Up To $10.00 Value

Enjoy one complimentary MENU ITEM when a second MENU ITEM of equal or greater value is purchased or for those who prefer - any one pizza at 50% off the regular price.

Dine-in or carry out

valid anytime

FRIED CHICKEN CHIKZZA'S & PIZZA

www.chikzzas.com

A158

Valid now thru November 1, 2006

Not valid holidays & subject to Rules of Use. Not valid with other discount offers, unless specified. Coupon VOID if purchased, sold or bartered. Discounts exclude tax, tip and/or alcohol, where applicable.

China Delight

4686 King St.
Alexandria, VA
(703)931-3331

- Dedicated to the art of fine Chinese cooking
- Conveniently located in Alexandria, 5 lights off 395-King St. W. exit
- For holidays - see rules of use
- Open daily

Bonus Discounts at entertainment.com

entertainment. entertainment.com

great place for kids

Up To $10.00 Value

Enjoy one complimentary DINNER ENTREE when a second DINNER ENTREE of equal or greater value is purchased.

DINE IN ONLY

valid any evening

CHINA DELIGHT 中食原府 Chinese Restaurant

A159

Valid now thru November 1, 2006

Not valid holidays & subject to Rules of Use. Not valid with other discount offers, unless specified. Coupon VOID if purchased, sold or bartered. Discounts exclude tax, tip and/or alcohol, where applicable.

Charlie Chiang's 蓉園

Chinese Restaurant

11832 Sunrise Valley Dr.
(Reston Int'l Ctr. next to Chili's)
Reston, VA
(703)620-9700

Tipping should be 15% to 20% of TOTAL bill before discount

00011001

entertainment.com

00011001

FRIED CHICKEN CHIKZZA'S & PIZZA

6100 Richmond Hwy.
(inside Days Inn)
Alexandria, VA
(703)317-9375

00608250

entertainment.com

00608250

CHINA DELIGHT 中原食府

Chinese Restaurant

4686 King St.
(Summit Shpg. Ctr.)
Alexandria, VA
(703)931-3331

00637327

entertainment.com

00637327

Georgetown Cafe

21 S. King St.
Leesburg, VA
(703)777-5000

- Featuring salads, sandwiches & burgers for lunch or light dinner
- Our desserts are baked fresh daily in our own bakery
- Join us for tea Monday through Thursday - 2 p.m. to 5 p.m.
- Located next to the Leesburg Colonial Inn on South King St.

Bonus Discounts at entertainment.com

entertainment. entertainment.com

Up To $10.00 Value

GEORGETOWN Cafe

Enjoy one complimentary LUNCH OR DINNER ENTREE when a second LUNCH OR DINNER ENTREE of equal or greater value is purchased or when dining alone - one LUNCH OR DINNER ENTREE at 50% off the regular price - maximum discount $5.00.

valid anytime

A160

Valid now thru November 1, 2006

Not valid holidays & subject to Rules of Use. Not valid with other discount offers, unless specified. Coupon VOID if purchased, sold or bartered. Discounts exclude tax, tip and/or alcohol, where applicable.

Golden Lion

10579 Lee Hwy.
Fairfax, VA
(703)591-8900

- Best Cantonese, Szechuan & Hunan cuisine
- Featuring pork, beef, chicken, seafood & vegetarian specialties
- Catering services available
- Open daily

Bonus Discounts at entertainment.com

entertainment. entertainment.com

Up To $10.00 Value

金獅
Golden Lion
Chinese Restaurant

Enjoy one complimentary DINNER ENTREE when a second DINNER ENTREE of equal or greater value is purchased or when dining alone - one DINNER ENTREE at 50% off the regular price - maximum discount $5.00.

Dine in only

valid any evening

A161

Valid now thru November 1, 2006

Not valid holidays & subject to Rules of Use. Not valid with other discount offers, unless specified. Coupon VOID if purchased, sold or bartered. Discounts exclude tax, tip and/or alcohol, where applicable.

Grevey's

8130 Arlington Blvd.
Falls Church, VA
(703)560-8530

- We serve the finest food with the greatest value
- Entrees include beef, chicken, seafood and pasta specialties
- Hungry hour Mon. - Fri., 5 - 7 p.m.
- Corner of Rte. 50 & Gallows Rd. in the Yorktowne Shopping Center

Bonus Discounts at entertainment.com

entertainment. entertainment.com

Up To $10.00 Value

GREVEY'S
Restaurant & Sports Bar

Enjoy one complimentary DINNER ENTREE when a second DINNER ENTREE of equal or greater value is purchased.

Dine in only

valid any evening after 5 p.m.

www.greveys.com

A162

Valid now thru November 1, 2006

Not valid holidays & subject to Rules of Use. Not valid with other discount offers, unless specified. Coupon VOID if purchased, sold or bartered. Discounts exclude tax, tip and/or alcohol, where applicable.

GEORGETOWN
Café

21 S. King St.
Leesburg, VA
(703)777-5000

Tipping should be 15% to 20% of TOTAL bill before discount

00068870

entertainment.com

00068870

金獅

Golden Lion
Chinese Restaurant

10579 Lee Hwy.
Fairfax, VA
(703)591-8900

Tipping should be 15% to 20% of TOTAL bill before discount

00090506

entertainment.com

00090506

GREVEY'S
Restaurant & Sports Bar

8130 Arlington Blvd.
Falls Church, VA
(703)560-8530

Tipping should be 15% to 20% of TOTAL bill before discount

00095988

entertainment.com

00095988

Joe Theismann's

1800 Diagonal Rd.
Alexandria, VA
(703)739-0777

- Serving large steaks, creative pastas & fresh seafood
- Where locals, celebrities, & tourists gather for good food & a great time
- Patio dining available
- Free garage parking after 5 p.m.
- No holidays please

Bonus Discounts at
entertainment.com

entertainment.
entertainment.com

Up To $10.00 Value

Enjoy one complimentary DINNER ENTREE when a second DINNER ENTREE of equal or greater value is purchased.

valid any evening after 5 p.m.

A163

Valid now thru November 1, 2006

Not valid holidays & subject to Rules of Use. Not valid with other discount offers, unless specified. Coupon VOID if purchased, sold or bartered. Discounts exclude tax, tip and/or alcohol, where applicable.

Keo's Thai Cafe

8733-F Cooper Rd.
Alexandria,, VA
(703)360-8288

- Enjoy amazing Thai food prepared by renowned Washington, DC area chef & owner Suwanna Saenjan
- Bring the entire family for a real treat!
- Open daily

Bonus Discounts at
entertainment.com

entertainment.
entertainment.com

Up To $10.00 Value

Enjoy one complimentary DINNER ENTREE when a second DINNER ENTREE of equal or greater value is purchased.

Dine in only

valid any evening

KEO'S
Thai Café

A164

Valid now thru November 1, 2006

Not valid holidays & subject to Rules of Use. Not valid with other discount offers, unless specified. Coupon VOID if purchased, sold or bartered. Discounts exclude tax, tip and/or alcohol, where applicable.

Kings Court Tavern

2-C Loudoun St. SW
Leesburg, VA
(703)777-7757

- The atmosphere & ambiance of a colonial meeting place
- Good food, good spirits & good conversation
- Fine food & drink served in a comfortable, friendly ale-house setting

Bonus Discounts at
entertainment.com

entertainment.
entertainment.com

Up To $10.00 Value

The King's Court Tavern

Enjoy one complimentary LUNCH OR DINNER ENTREE when a second LUNCH OR DINNER ENTREE of equal or greater value is purchased.

valid anytime

A165

Valid now thru November 1, 2006

Not valid holidays & subject to Rules of Use. Not valid with other discount offers, unless specified. Coupon VOID if purchased, sold or bartered. Discounts exclude tax, tip and/or alcohol, where applicable.

Joe Theismann's
OLD TOWN

1800 Diagonal Rd.
Alexandria, VA
(703)739-0777

Tipping should be 15% to 20% of TOTAL bill before discount

00170860

entertainment.com

00170860

KEO'S
Thai Café

8733-F Cooper Rd.
Alexandria,, VA
(703)360-8288

00608235

entertainment.com

00608235

The King's Court Tavern

2-C Loudoun St. SW
Leesburg, VA
(703)777-7757

00043340

entertainment.com

00043340

La Hacienda

7037 Brookfield Plaza
Springfield, VA
(703)866-0205

- Featuring Salvadorean, Mexican Tex-Mex and Latin cuisine
- Everything is authentic & homemade
- You've tried the rest, now try the best
- Open daily

entertainment. entertainment.com

Up To $10.00 Value

La Hacienda Restaurant

Enjoy one complimentary DINNER ENTREE when a second DINNER ENTREE of equal or greater value is purchased.

Dine in only

valid any evening

A166

Valid now thru November 1, 2006

Not valid holidays & subject to Rules of Use. Not valid with other discount offers, unless specified. Coupon VOID if purchased, sold or bartered. Discounts exclude tax, tip and/or alcohol, where applicable.

La Tolteca

5614 Ox Rd.
Fairfax Station, VA
(703)425-8844

- Authentic Mexican food
- Voted "Best Mexican Restaurant" since 1998 by Connection Newspaper
- We welcome you & hope that you will enjoy yourself
- Open daily

entertainment. entertainment.com

Up To $10.00 Value

LA TOLTECA

Enjoy one complimentary LUNCH OR DINNER ENTREE when a second LUNCH OR DINNER ENTREE of equal or greater value is purchased.

Dine in only

valid anytime

A167

Valid now thru November 1, 2006

Not valid holidays & subject to Rules of Use. Not valid with other discount offers, unless specified. Coupon VOID if purchased, sold or bartered. Discounts exclude tax, tip and/or alcohol, where applicable.

Las Vegas Restaurant & Night Club

6151 Richmond Hwy.
Alexandria, VA
(703)660-8800

- Visit Las Vegas Restaurant & night club
- Featuring authentic Latino American cuisine
- We specialize in corporate parties
- Open daily

entertainment. entertainment.com

Up To $10.00 Value

LAS VEGAS

Enjoy one complimentary LUNCH OR DINNER ENTREE when a second LUNCH OR DINNER ENTREE of equal or greater value is purchased.

Dine in only

valid anytime

A168

Valid now thru November 1, 2006

Not valid holidays & subject to Rules of Use. Not valid with other discount offers, unless specified. Coupon VOID if purchased, sold or bartered. Discounts exclude tax, tip and/or alcohol, where applicable.

La Hacienda Restaurant

7037 Brookfield Plaza
Springfield, VA
(703)866-0205

00499470

entertainment.com

00499470

LA TOLTECA

5614 Ox Rd.
Fairfax Station, VA
(703)425-8844

00495673

entertainment.com

00495673

LAS VEGAS

6151 Richmond Hwy.
Alexandria, VA
(703)660-8800

Tipping should be 15% to 20% of TOTAL bill before discount

00385454

entertainment.com

00385454

Little Viet Garden

3012 Wilson Blvd.
Arlington, VA
(703)522-9686

- Authentic Vietnamese cuisine
- Cocktails & bar - outdoor cafe
- Open daily

Bonus Discounts at
entertainment.com

entertainment.
entertainment.com

Up To $10.00 Value

Little VIET Garden

Enjoy one complimentary DINNER ENTREE when a second DINNER ENTREE of equal or greater value is purchased.

Dine in only

valid any evening

A169

Valid now thru November 1, 2006

Not valid holidays & subject to Rules of Use. Not valid with other discount offers, unless specified. Coupon VOID if purchased, sold or bartered. Discounts exclude tax, tip and/or alcohol, where applicable.

Los Toltecos

50 Pidgeon Hill Dr.
Sterling, VA
(703)421-3380

- Brand new to Sterling
- It's Fiesta Time Amigos
- Serving authentic Mexican food
- Major credit cards accepted
- Open daily

Bonus Discounts at
entertainment.com

entertainment.
entertainment.com

Up To $10.00 Value

LOS TOLTECOS
RESTAURANT
AUTHENTIC MEXICAN FOOD

Enjoy one complimentary LUNCH OR DINNER ENTREE when a second LUNCH OR DINNER ENTREE of equal or greater value is purchased.

Dine in only

valid anytime

A170

Valid now thru November 1, 2006

Not valid holidays & subject to Rules of Use. Not valid with other discount offers, unless specified. Coupon VOID if purchased, sold or bartered. Discounts exclude tax, tip and/or alcohol, where applicable.

Miss Saigon Vietnamese Cuisine

3057 M St., NW
Washington, DC
(202)333-5545

- Serving Washington DC fine Vietnamese cuisine for over 10 years in the heart of Georgetown
- The decor is like a Vietnamese garden terrace adorned with twinkling lights
- The menu is simple, familiar & affordable
- Dinner is served daily starting at 2:30pm

Bonus Discounts at
entertainment.com

entertainment.
entertainment.com

Up To $10.00 Value

Enjoy one complimentary DINNER ENTREE when a second DINNER ENTREE of equal or greater value is purchased.

Dine in only

valid any evening

Reservations recommended

Miss Saigon
VIETNAMESE CUISINE

A171

Valid now thru November 1, 2006

Not valid holidays & subject to Rules of Use. Not valid with other discount offers, unless specified. Coupon VOID if purchased, sold or bartered. Discounts exclude tax, tip and/or alcohol, where applicable.

Little VIET Garden

3012 Wilson Blvd.
Arlington, VA
(703)522-9686

00528048

entertainment.com

00528048

LOS TOLTECOS
RESTAURANT
AUTHENTIC MEXICAN FOOD

50 Pidgeon Hill Dr.
Sterling, VA
(703)421-3380

00495680

entertainment.com

00495680

Miss SAIGON
VIETNAMESE
CUISINE

3057 M St., NW
Washington, DC
(202)333-5545

00496094

entertainment.com

00496094

Old Dominion Brew Pub

44633 Guilford Dr.
Ashburn, VA
(703)724-9100

- Brewing the best beer in the Mid-Atlantic since 1990
- Come sit down in our smoke-free brew pub & enjoy all of our beers & food selections
- Free Brewery tours available Sat. at 2 p.m. & 4 p.m. & Sun. at 2 p.m.
- Open daily

entertainment.
entertainment.com

Up To $10.00 Value

Enjoy one complimentary LUNCH OR DINNER ENTREE when a second LUNCH OR DINNER ENTREE of equal or greater value is purchased.

Dine in only

valid anytime

OLD DOMINION BREWING Co.

www.olddominion.com

A172

Valid now thru November 1, 2006

Not valid holidays & subject to Rules of Use. Not valid with other discount offers, unless specified. Coupon VOID if purchased, sold or bartered. Discounts exclude tax, tip and/or alcohol, where applicable.

Omia's Restaurant

45529 W. Church Rd.
Sterling, VA
(703)444-7800

- Featuring all your favorite dishes including soups, salads, wraps, calzones, stromboli, subs, sandwiches, burgers, dinners & more
- Open for breakfast daily
- A definite locals favorite

entertainment.
entertainment.com

Up To $10.00 Value

Enjoy one complimentary DINNER ENTREE when a second DINNER ENTREE of equal or greater value is purchased.

Dine in only

valid any evening

Omia's
Restaurante

A173

Valid now thru November 1, 2006

Not valid holidays & subject to Rules of Use. Not valid with other discount offers, unless specified. Coupon VOID if purchased, sold or bartered. Discounts exclude tax, tip and/or alcohol, where applicable.

Pleasant Valley Grille

4715 Pleasant Valley Rd.
Chantilly,, VA
(703)631-7904

- Welcome to Pleasant Valley Grille
- Our menu features the best sandwiches, burgers & grilled favorites
- The friendly staff at Pleasant Valley Grille promise to make your next dining experience a pleasant one
- Call for seasonal hours

entertainment.
entertainment.com

great place for kids

Up To $10.00 Value

Enjoy one complimentary MENU ITEM when a second MENU ITEM of equal or greater value is purchased.

Dine in only

valid anytime

PV
Pleasant Valley
Grille

A174

Valid now thru November 1, 2006

Not valid holidays & subject to Rules of Use. Not valid with other discount offers, unless specified. Coupon VOID if purchased, sold or bartered. Discounts exclude tax, tip and/or alcohol, where applicable.

OLD DOMINION BREWING Co.

44633 Guilford Dr.
Ashburn, VA
(703)724-9100

Tipping should be 15% to 20% of TOTAL bill before discount

00542658

entertainment.com

00542658

Omia's
Restaurante

45529 W. Church Rd.
Sterling, VA
(703)444-7800

00622975

entertainment.com

00622975

PV
Pleasant Valley
Grille

4715 Pleasant Valley Rd.
Chantilly,, VA
(703)631-7904

00618502

entertainment.com

00618502

Pulgarcito Grill

1306 Horner Rd.
Woodbridge, VA
(703)490-9800

- Featuring traditional & Salvadoran cuisine
- We offer salads, burgers, fajitas & beef & seafood dishes

Bonus Discounts at
entertainment.com

entertainment.
entertainment.com

Up To $10.00 Value

Enjoy one complimentary LUNCH OR DINNER ENTREE when a second LUNCH OR DINNER ENTREE of equal or greater value is purchased.

PULGARCITO GRILL

Dine in only; Combination dinners excluded

valid anytime

A175

Valid now thru November 1, 2006

Not valid holidays & subject to Rules of Use. Not valid with other discount offers, unless specified. Coupon VOID if purchased, sold or bartered. Discounts exclude tax, tip and/or alcohol, where applicable.

Ribsters

7243 Little River Tpke.
Annandale, VA
(703)750-2751

- Barbecued baby back ribs & chicken
- "Loaves of onion rings"
- Buffalo wings
- Luncheon specials
- VISA & MasterCard accepted
- Open daily

Bonus Discounts at
entertainment.com

entertainment.
entertainment.com

Up To $10.00 Value

Enjoy one complimentary LUNCH OR DINNER ENTREE when a second LUNCH OR DINNER ENTREE of equal or greater value is purchased.

Ribster's
RIBS WITH SPIRIT

All in-house promotions & rib specials excluded; Dining room only

valid anytime

A176

Valid now thru November 1, 2006

Not valid holidays & subject to Rules of Use. Not valid with other discount offers, unless specified. Coupon VOID if purchased, sold or bartered. Discounts exclude tax, tip and/or alcohol, where applicable.

Rubino's Pizza

2415 Centreville Rd.
Herndon, VA
(703)713-0255

- Featuring the best pizza in town
- Family owned & operated
- Open daily

Bonus Discounts at
entertainment.com

entertainment.
entertainment.com

great place for kids

Up To $10.00 Value

Enjoy one complimentary LUNCH OR DINNER ENTREE when a second LUNCH OR DINNER ENTREE of equal or greater value is purchased or for those who prefer - any one pizza at 50% off the regular price.

NEW YORK STYLE
PIZZERIA
RUBINO'S
PIZZA-PASTA-PANINOS

Dine in only

valid anytime

A177

Valid now thru November 1, 2006

Not valid holidays & subject to Rules of Use. Not valid with other discount offers, unless specified. Coupon VOID if purchased, sold or bartered. Discounts exclude tax, tip and/or alcohol, where applicable.

PULGARCITO
GRILL

1306 Horner Rd.
Woodbridge, VA
(703)490-9800

00619433

entertainment.com

00619433

Ribster's
RIBS WITH SPIRIT

7243 Little River Tpke.
Annandale, VA
(703)750-2751

Tipping should be 15% to 20% of TOTAL bill before discount

00030459

entertainment.com

00030459

NEW YORK STYLE
PIZZERIA
RUBINO'S
PIZZA-PASTA-PANINOS

2415 Centreville Rd.
Herndon, VA
(703)713-0255

00633469

entertainment.com

00633469

Sampan Cafe

6116 Franconia Rd.
Alexandria, VA
(703)971-5405

- Come try what authentic Chinese food tastes like
- Impeccable service
- We offer a wide variety of appetizers, soups, fried rice, beef, pork, seafood, poultry & low fat entrees
- Open daily

Bonus Discounts at
entertainment.com

entertainment.
entertainment.com

Up To $10.00 Value

Enjoy one complimentary LUNCH OR DINNER ENTREE when a second LUNCH OR DINNER ENTREE of equal or greater value is purchased.

Dine in only; Combination platters excluded

valid anytime

SAMPAN CAFE
上埗
Chinese Restaurant

A178

Valid now thru November 1, 2006

Not valid holidays & subject to Rules of Use. Not valid with other discount offers, unless specified. Coupon VOID if purchased, sold or bartered. Discounts exclude tax, tip and/or alcohol, where applicable.

Shooters Grill & Bar

445 Jefferson Davis Hwy.
Fredericksburg, VA
(540)371-9100

- 16 Brunswick pool tables & the best billiards in Fredericksburg
- Something special is going on every night!
- Wing night, food specials for lunch & dinner, league night, tournaments & more
- Daily happy hour & 1/2 price pool with lunch Mon. - Sat.
- Birthday parties, sports team & other events available
- Open daily

Bonus Discounts at
entertainment.com

entertainment.
entertainment.com

Up To $10.00 Value

Enjoy one complimentary LUNCH OR DINNER ENTREE when a second LUNCH OR DINNER ENTREE of equal or greater value is purchased.

valid anytime

Billiards
SHOOTERS
Grill & Bar

A179

Valid now thru November 1, 2006

Not valid holidays & subject to Rules of Use. Not valid with other discount offers, unless specified. Coupon VOID if purchased, sold or bartered. Discounts exclude tax, tip and/or alcohol, where applicable.

Skyline Café

3821-A S. George Mason Dr.
Falls Church, VA
(703)820-0240

- The best Ethiopian restaurant in Northern Virginia
- Bring the whole family
- Open daily

Bonus Discounts at
entertainment.com

entertainment.
entertainment.com

Up To $10.00 Value

Enjoy one complimentary LUNCH OR DINNER ENTREE when a second LUNCH OR DINNER ENTREE of equal or greater value is purchased.

Dine in only

valid anytime

SKYLINE CAFE

A180

Valid now thru November 1, 2006

Not valid holidays & subject to Rules of Use. Not valid with other discount offers, unless specified. Coupon VOID if purchased, sold or bartered. Discounts exclude tax, tip and/or alcohol, where applicable.

SAMPAN CAFE

Chinese Restaurant

6116 Franconia Rd.
Alexandria, VA
(703)971-5405

00568968

entertainment.com

00568968

Billiards SHOOTERS Grill & Bar

445 Jefferson Davis Hwy.
Fredericksburg, VA
(540)371-9100

Tipping should be 15% to 20% of TOTAL bill before discount

00378205

entertainment.com

00378205

SKYLINE CAFE

3821-A S. George Mason Dr.
Falls Church, VA
(703)820-0240

Tipping should be 15% to 20% of TOTAL bill before discount

00470841

entertainment.com

00470841

Stars & Stripes Restaurant

567 S. 23rd St.
Arlington, VA
(703)979-1872

- Offering classic comfort American cuisine
- Celebrating the great foods of America
- Enjoy our friendly services
- Banquet & catering facilities available
- Come enjoy our weekend brunch

Bonus Discounts at
entertainment.com

entertainment®
entertainment.com

Up To $10.00 Value

Enjoy one complimentary LUNCH OR DINNER ENTREE when a second LUNCH OR DINNER ENTREE of equal or greater value is purchased.

Dine in only

valid anytime

www.starsandstripesrestaurant.com

A181

Valid now thru November 1, 2006

Not valid holidays & subject to Rules of Use. Not valid with other discount offers, unless specified. Coupon VOID if purchased, sold or bartered. Discounts exclude tax, tip and/or alcohol, where applicable.

Tequila Grill

1990 K St. NW
Washington, DC
(202)833-3640

- Located at the corner of 20th & K Sts. in the heart of downtown D.C.
- Southwestern cuisine featuring fresh free range chicken, freshly grilled seafood, enchiladas & fajitas
- Extensive choice of appetizers
- Full service bar serving the best margaritas in town with freshly squeezed lemon & lime juice
- Serving continually 11:30 a.m. to 10 p.m.

Bonus Discounts at
entertainment.com

entertainment®
entertainment.com

Up To $10.00 Value

Enjoy one complimentary DINNER ENTREE when a second DINNER ENTREE of equal or greater value is purchased.

valid any evening

A182

Valid now thru November 1, 2006

Not valid holidays & subject to Rules of Use. Not valid with other discount offers, unless specified. Coupon VOID if purchased, sold or bartered. Discounts exclude tax, tip and/or alcohol, where applicable.

The Flying Buffalo

7305 Arlington Blvd.
Falls Church, VA
(703)876-9671

- Featuring wings with homemade sauces & other foods of unique flavors from around the world
- Pool tables
- TV's
- Family friendly

Bonus Discounts at
entertainment.com

entertainment®
entertainment.com

great place for kids

Up To $10.00 Value

Enjoy one complimentary LUNCH OR DINNER ENTREE when a second LUNCH OR DINNER ENTREE of equal or greater value is purchased.

Dine in only

valid anytime

www.theflyingbuffalo.com

A183

Valid now thru November 1, 2006

Not valid holidays & subject to Rules of Use. Not valid with other discount offers, unless specified. Coupon VOID if purchased, sold or bartered. Discounts exclude tax, tip and/or alcohol, where applicable.

Stars and Stripes

567 S. 23rd St.
Arlington, VA
(703)979-1872

00547768

entertainment.com

00547768

Tequila Grill

1990 K St. NW
Washington, DC
(202)833-3640

00003735

entertainment.com

00003735

The Flying Buffalo

7305 Arlington Blvd.
(Loehmann's Plaza)
Falls Church, VA
(703)876-9671

00576167

entertainment.com

00576167

The Taco House

515 S. 23rd St.
Arlington, VA
(703)979-7033

- Zesty Mexican food specialties to take home or to the office
- Enjoy any one of our house specials including chiles rellenos, chimichangas, flautas, sour cream enchiladas & our sizzling fajitas
- Our ingredients are prepared daily under rigidly controlled conditions to guarantee complete freshness
- Buena Comida!!
- Open daily

Bonus Discounts at entertainment.com

entertainment. entertainment.com

Up To $10.00 Value

TACO HOUSE

Enjoy one complimentary DINNER ENTREE when a second DINNER ENTREE of equal or greater value is purchased or when dining alone - one DINNER ENTREE at 50% off the regular price - maximum discount $5.00.

Dine in only

valid any evening

A184

Valid now thru November 1, 2006

Not valid holidays & subject to Rules of Use. Not valid with other discount offers, unless specified. Coupon VOID if purchased, sold or bartered. Discounts exclude tax, tip and/or alcohol, where applicable.

China Gourmet

9901 Lee Highway
Fairfax, VA
(703)293-9898

- We're here to serve you the finest in Hunan & Szechuan cuisine
- Relax in our "house," atmosphere is pleasing
- Open daily

Bonus Discounts at entertainment.com

entertainment. entertainment.com

$10.00 Value

CHINA GOURMET Restaurant & Lounge

Enjoy one complimentary DINNER ENTREE when a second DINNER ENTREE of equal or greater value is purchased.

Dine in only; Special complete dinners & Sunday brunch excluded

valid any evening

A185

Valid now thru November 1, 2006

Not valid holidays & subject to Rules of Use. Not valid with other discount offers, unless specified. Coupon VOID if purchased, sold or bartered. Discounts exclude tax, tip and/or alcohol, where applicable.

Afghan Restaurant

2700 Jefferson Davis Hwy.
Alexandria, VA
(703)548-0022

- Serving authentic Afghan cuisine
- One mile south of Crystal City
- "The service is passionate," raves Phyllis Richman
- Banquet facilities available
- Plan your next office party here. We can accommodate up to 280 people
- Open daily

Bonus Discounts at entertainment.com

entertainment. entertainment.com

Up To $9.00 Value

AFGHAN RESTAURANT

Enjoy one complimentary LUNCH OR DINNER ENTREE when a second LUNCH OR DINNER ENTREE of equal or greater value is purchased.

Dine in only

valid anytime

A186

Valid now thru November 1, 2006

Not valid holidays & subject to Rules of Use. Not valid with other discount offers, unless specified. Coupon VOID if purchased, sold or bartered. Discounts exclude tax, tip and/or alcohol, where applicable.

TACO HOUSE

515 S. 23rd St.
Arlington, VA
(703)979-7033

Tipping should be 15% to 20% of TOTAL bill before discount

00020298

entertainment.com

00020298

CHINA GOURMET
Restaurant & Lounge

9901 Lee Highway
Fairfax, VA
(703)293-9898

Tipping should be 15% to 20% of TOTAL bill before discount

00151752

entertainment.com

00151752

AFGHAN RESTAURANT

2700 Jefferson Davis Hwy.
Alexandria, VA
(703)548-0022

Tipping should be 15% to 20% of TOTAL bill before discount

00290134

entertainment.com

00290134

Alexandria Diner

5821 Richmond Hwy.
Alexandria, VA
(703)960-1700

- Breakfast anytime
- Ask about our lunch specials
- An Alexandria tradition
- 3 egg combination omelets
- All American burgers
- Located next to the Hampton Inn
- Open Mon. - Thurs. 6:30 a.m. - 10:00 p.m.

Bonus Discounts at
entertainment.com

entertainment.
entertainment.com

Up To $9.00 Value

Enjoy one complimentary LUNCH OR DINNER ENTREE when a second LUNCH OR DINNER ENTREE of equal or greater value is purchased.

valid anytime

A187

Valid now thru November 1, 2006

Not valid holidays & subject to Rules of Use. Not valid with other discount offers, unless specified. Coupon VOID if purchased, sold or bartered. Discounts exclude tax, tip and/or alcohol, where applicable.

Ashburn Pub

44110 Ashburn Village Blvd., Unit 196
Ashburn, VA
(703)724-0755

- "....Puttin' Ashburn on the map"
- Located in the Ashburn Shopping Plaza
- Featuring snacks, appetizers, soups, salads, deli sandwiches & pub entrees
- Watch your favorite team via satellite
- Open daily

Bonus Discounts at
entertainment.com

entertainment.
entertainment.com

Up To $9.00 Value

Enjoy one complimentary LUNCH OR DINNER ENTREE when a second LUNCH OR DINNER ENTREE of equal or greater value is purchased.

Dine in only

valid anytime

A188

Valid now thru November 1, 2006

Not valid holidays & subject to Rules of Use. Not valid with other discount offers, unless specified. Coupon VOID if purchased, sold or bartered. Discounts exclude tax, tip and/or alcohol, where applicable.

Cedar Cafe

6409 Shiplett Blvd.
Burke, VA
(703)455-7080

- Featuring foods of Lebanon
- Experience the delicacies of the Middle East
- Deli & catering

Bonus Discounts at
entertainment.com

entertainment.
entertainment.com

Up To $9.00 Value

Enjoy one complimentary DINNER ENTREE when a second DINNER ENTREE of equal or greater value is purchased.

Dine in only

valid any evening

A Taste Of Lebanon

www.cedarcafe.com

A189

Valid now thru November 1, 2006

Not valid holidays & subject to Rules of Use. Not valid with other discount offers, unless specified. Coupon VOID if purchased, sold or bartered. Discounts exclude tax, tip and/or alcohol, where applicable.

ALEXANDRIA DINER

5821 Richmond Hwy.
Alexandria, VA
(703)960-1700

Offers not valid holidays and subject to Rules of Use
Tipping should be 15% to 20% of the total bill before discount
00524860

entertainment.com

00524860

THE Ashburn PUB

44110 Ashburn Village Blvd., Unit 196
(Ashburn Shopping Plaza)
Ashburn, VA
(703)724-0755

Tipping should be 15% to 20% of TOTAL bill before discount
00240743

entertainment.com

00240743

Cedar café
A Taste Of Lebanon

6409 Shiplett Blvd.
(Rolling Valley Mall)
Burke, VA
(703)455-7080

00574620

entertainment.com

00574620

Champion Billiard & Sports Cafe

See reverse side for locations

- Come to Champion Billiards & enjoy fun for the whole family
- Enjoy your favorite super sandwiches, wraps, 1/2 lb. bugers & pizza after you shoot a game of pool
- Also choose from our chef's specials, NY sirloin steak, pastas & ribs

Bonus Discounts at entertainment.com

entertainment. entertainment.com

Up To $9.00 Value

Enjoy one complimentary LUNCH OR DINNER ENTREE when a second LUNCH OR DINNER ENTREE of equal or greater value is purchased.

valid anytime

Champion Billiards® Sports Cafe

A190

Valid now thru November 1, 2006

Not valid holidays & subject to Rules of Use. Not valid with other discount offers, unless specified. Coupon VOID if purchased, sold or bartered. Discounts exclude tax, tip and/or alcohol, where applicable.

Jerusalem Restaurant

3405 Payne St.
Falls Church, VA
(703)379-4200

- Eat good
- Always fresh
- All natural
- Don't forget to save room for one of our homemade sweets
- Located near Bailey's Crossroads
- Open daily

Bonus Discounts at entertainment.com

entertainment. entertainment.com

Up To $9.00 Value

Enjoy one complimentary LUNCH OR DINNER ENTREE when a second LUNCH OR DINNER ENTREE of equal or greater value is purchased.

Dine in only; Buffet excluded

valid anytime

JERUSALEM RESTAURANT & CATERING

www.jerusalemdining.com

A191

Valid now thru November 1, 2006

Not valid holidays & subject to Rules of Use. Not valid with other discount offers, unless specified. Coupon VOID if purchased, sold or bartered. Discounts exclude tax, tip and/or alcohol, where applicable.

Kate's Irish Pub

6131 Backlick Rd.
Springfield, VA
(703)866-0860

- Come to Kate's and enjoy the best in pub fare
- Our hearty sandwiches, pastas & seafood are all specially prepared
- Live music nightly
- Open daily

Bonus Discounts at entertainment.com

entertainment. entertainment.com

Up To $9.00 Value

Enjoy one complimentary LUNCH OR DINNER ENTREE when a second LUNCH OR DINNER ENTREE of equal or greater value is purchased.

Dine in only

valid anytime

Not valid with any other discount offer

Kate's Irish Pub & Restaurant

www.katesirishpub.com

A192

Valid now thru November 1, 2006

Not valid holidays & subject to Rules of Use. Not valid with other discount offers, unless specified. Coupon VOID if purchased, sold or bartered. Discounts exclude tax, tip and/or alcohol, where applicable.

Champion Billiards®

Sports Cafe

1969 E. Joppa Rd.
Baltimore, MD
(410)665-7500

904 Upper Fairlawn Ave.
Laurel, MD
(301)604-1300

2620 Shirlington Rd.
Shirlington, VA
(703)521-3800

5205 Buckeystown Pike
Frederick, MD
(301)309-8893

1776 E Jefferson St.
Rockville, MD
(301)231-4949

00101428

JERUSALEM

RESTAURANT & CATERING

3405 Payne St.
(Mount of Olives Ctr.)
Falls Church, VA
(703)379-4200

Offers not valid holidays and subject to Rules of Use
Tipping should be 15% to 20% of the total bill before discount
00603562

Kate's

Irish Pub & Restaurant

6131 Backlick Rd.
Springfield, VA
(703)866-0860

Tipping should be 15% to 20% of TOTAL bill before discount
00217351

entertainment.com

00101428

entertainment.com

00603562

entertainment.com

00217351

Kilroy's

See reverse side for locations

- Fun dining in a friendly, relaxed atmosphere
- "Hungry Hour" specials
- Famous for Prime Rib
- Nightly entertainment
- Great place for watching all your favorite sporting events
- Best Raw Bar in Town!!!

Bonus Discounts at entertainment.com

entertainment® entertainment.com

Up To $9.00 Value

Enjoy one complimentary LUNCH OR DINNER ENTREE when a second LUNCH OR DINNER ENTREE of equal or greater value is purchased.

Lobster special excluded; Dine in only

valid anytime

For holidays-see Rules of Use

KILROY'S ONLY IN AMERICA

www.kilroys.com

A193

Valid now thru November 1, 2006

Not valid holidays & subject to Rules of Use. Not valid with other discount offers, unless specified. Coupon VOID if purchased, sold or bartered. Discounts exclude tax, tip and/or alcohol, where applicable.

La Choza Grill

8558 Lee Hwy.
Fairfax, VA
(703)560-1192

- Enjoy Mexican cuisine at its finest
- Select from our wide variety of Quesadillas, Enchiladas, Fajitas & Burrito's
- Also try our chicken, beef & pork entrees
- Open daily

Bonus Discounts at entertainment.com

entertainment® entertainment.com

Up To $9.00 Value

LA CHOZA GRILL

South American & Mexican Food

Enjoy one complimentary DINNER ENTREE when a second DINNER ENTREE of equal or greater value is purchased.

Dine in only

valid any evening

A194

Valid now thru November 1, 2006

Not valid holidays & subject to Rules of Use. Not valid with other discount offers, unless specified. Coupon VOID if purchased, sold or bartered. Discounts exclude tax, tip and/or alcohol, where applicable.

La Villa Roma

305 E. Market St.,
STE. G
Leesburg, VA
(703)777-6223

- Italian delicacies
- Featuring calzones, subs & pizza
- Beer available
- Open daily

Bonus Discounts at entertainment.com

entertainment® entertainment.com

great place for kids

Up To $9.00 Value

Enjoy one complimentary LUNCH OR DINNER ENTREE when a second LUNCH OR DINNER ENTREE of equal or greater value is purchased.

Dine in only

valid anytime

Pizzeria & Restaurant LA VILLA ROMA Leesburg, Virginia

www.lavillaroma.com

A195

Valid now thru November 1, 2006

Not valid holidays & subject to Rules of Use. Not valid with other discount offers, unless specified. Coupon VOID if purchased, sold or bartered. Discounts exclude tax, tip and/or alcohol, where applicable.

KILROY'S
ONLY IN AMERICA

5250 Port Royal Rd.
Springfield, VA
(703)321-7733

14633 Jefferson Davis Hwy.
Woodbridge, VA
(703)494-4800

Tipping should be 15% to 20% of TOTAL bill before discount

00012802

entertainment.com

00012802

LA CHOZA GRILL

South American & Mexican Food

8558 Lee Hwy.
Fairfax, VA
(703)560-1192

Tipping should be 15% to 20% of TOTAL bill before discount

00214208

entertainment.com

00214208

Pizzeria & Restaurant
LA VILLA ROMA
Leesburg, Virginia

305 E. Market St., STE. G
(Tollhouse Shpg. Ctr.)
Leesburg, VA
(703)777-6223

00009954

entertainment.com

00009954

Lalibela Ethiopian Restaurant

3111 Columbia Pk.
Arlington, VA
(703)920-9500

- Enjoy traditional Ethiopian cuisine in a warm & relaxing atmosphere
- Family owned & operated
- Bring the entire family
- A local favorite
- Open daily

Bonus Discounts at
entertainment.com

entertainment.
entertainment.com

Up To $9.00 Value

Enjoy one complimentary LUNCH OR DINNER ENTREE when a second LUNCH OR DINNER ENTREE of equal or greater value is purchased.

Dine in only

valid anytime

ላሊበላ ምግብ ቤት
Lalibela Ethiopian Restaurnat

A196

Valid now thru November 1, 2006

Not valid holidays & subject to Rules of Use. Not valid with other discount offers, unless specified. Coupon VOID if purchased, sold or bartered. Discounts exclude tax, tip and/or alcohol, where applicable.

Little Italy Sports Bar & Grill

6920 J Bradlick
Shpg. Ctr.
Annandale, VA
(703)256-9122

- Enjoy Italian cuisine at its finest
- Choose from a wide variety of entrees including the most delicious pastas & sauces
- Located in Bradlick Shopping Center
- Open daily

Bonus Discounts at
entertainment.com

entertainment.
entertainment.com

Up To $9.00 Value

Little Italy
Restaurant/Sports Bar
Grill

Enjoy one complimentary LUNCH OR DINNER ENTREE when a second LUNCH OR DINNER ENTREE of equal or greater value is purchased or when dining alone - one LUNCH OR DINNER ENTREE at 50% off the regular price - maximum discount $4.00.

Dine in only; Specials excluded

valid anytime

A197

Valid now thru November 1, 2006

Not valid holidays & subject to Rules of Use. Not valid with other discount offers, unless specified. Coupon VOID if purchased, sold or bartered. Discounts exclude tax, tip and/or alcohol, where applicable.

Lulu's Club Mardi Gras

1217 22nd Street, NW
Washington, DC
(202)861-5858

- Washington DC's most popular entertainment & dining emporium
- Hamburgers, crab cake sandwich, fish n' chips
- Caribbean style, southern style, black & blue, Santa Fe style burgers
- Red beans & rice & hot n' spicy chicken wings
- Join us for a fun evening of dancing in multiple rooms

Bonus Discounts at
entertainment.com

entertainment.
entertainment.com

Up To $9.00 Value

Enjoy one complimentary DINNER ENTREE when a second DINNER ENTREE of equal or greater value is purchased.

valid any evening

LULU'S
MARDI
GRAS

A198

Valid now thru November 1, 2006

Not valid holidays & subject to Rules of Use. Not valid with other discount offers, unless specified. Coupon VOID if purchased, sold or bartered. Discounts exclude tax, tip and/or alcohol, where applicable.

ላሊበላ ምግብ ቤት
Lalibela Ethiopian Restaurnat

3111 Columbia Pk.
Arlington, VA
(703)920-9500

00583551

entertainment.com

00583551

Little Italy
Restaurant/Sports Bar
Grill

6920 J Bradlick Shpg. Ctr.
Annandale, VA
(703)256-9122

Tipping should be 15% to 20% of TOTAL bill before discount

00214186

entertainment.com

00214186

LULU'S
MARDI
GRAS

1217 22nd Street, NW
Washington, DC
(202)861-5858

Tipping should be 15% to 20% of TOTAL bill before discount

00406316

entertainment.com

00406316

Malek's Pizza Palace

7118 Old Keene Mill Rd.
Springfield, VA
(703)451-6969

- Formerly Plaza Pizza (same ownership)
- Casual with class
- Open 'til 4 a.m. Friday & Saturday
- Serving Italian favorites, Middle Eastern dishes, Greek specialties & more
- Kids' menu available
- Springfield Plaza, next to McDonald's

Bonus Discounts at
entertainment.com

entertainment. entertainment.com

great place for kids

Up To $9.00 Value

Enjoy one complimentary LUNCH OR DINNER ENTREE when a second LUNCH OR DINNER ENTREE of equal or greater value is purchased or for those who prefer - any one pizza at 50% off the regular price.

DINE IN ONLY

MALEK'S PIZZA PALACE

valid anytime

A199

Valid now thru November 1, 2006

Not valid holidays & subject to Rules of Use. Not valid with other discount offers, unless specified. Coupon VOID if purchased, sold or bartered. Discounts exclude tax, tip and/or alcohol, where applicable.

Marcopolo Restaurant

1901 N. Fort Myer Dr.
Arlington, VA
(703)527-5656

- Featuring authentic Afghan cuisine
- For the best kabob, manto, palau & many more delicious dishes in town
- We do parties, weddings & catering

Bonus Discounts at
entertainment.com

entertainment. entertainment.com

Up To $9.00 Value

Enjoy one complimentary DINNER ENTREE when a second DINNER ENTREE of equal or greater value is purchased.

Dine in only

MARCOPOLO RESTAURANT

valid any evening

A200

Valid now thru November 1, 2006

Not valid holidays & subject to Rules of Use. Not valid with other discount offers, unless specified. Coupon VOID if purchased, sold or bartered. Discounts exclude tax, tip and/or alcohol, where applicable.

Peking Garden

6802 Commerce Street
Springfield, VA
(703)451-9350

- Our chef has over 30 years experience cooking Szechuan, Mandarin & Hunan dishes
- We pledge to bring you the best taste & lowest prices with the best service
- Relax & enjoy one of our exotic Polynesian drinks or a refreshing cocktail
- Open daily

Bonus Discounts at
entertainment.com

entertainment. entertainment.com

Up To $9.00 Value

Enjoy one complimentary LUNCH OR DINNER ENTREE when a second LUNCH OR DINNER ENTREE of equal or greater value is purchased.

Buffet excluded; Dine in only

京園 Peking Garden CHINESE RESTAURANT

valid anytime

A201

Valid now thru November 1, 2006

Not valid holidays & subject to Rules of Use. Not valid with other discount offers, unless specified. Coupon VOID if purchased, sold or bartered. Discounts exclude tax, tip and/or alcohol, where applicable.

MALEK'S
PIZZA
PALACE

7118 Old Keene Mill Rd.
Springfield, VA
(703)451-6969

Tipping should be 15% to 20% of TOTAL bill before discount
00074039

entertainment.com

00074039

MARCOPOLO
RESTAURANT

1901 N. Fort Myer Dr.
(in Rosslyn)
Arlington, VA
(703)527-5656

00573371

entertainment.com

00573371

京園
Peking
Garden
CHINESE RESTAURANT

6802 Commerce Street
Springfield, VA
(703)451-9350

Tipping should be 15% to 20% of TOTAL bill before discount
00155131

entertainment.com

00155131

Pines of Naples

3207 Columbia Pike
Arlington, VA
(703)521-7551

- Featuring all of your favorite dishes including spaghetti carbonara, scallopini marsala, francese & all your favorite homemade pastas
- A local favorite

Bonus Discounts at
entertainment.com

entertainment.
entertainment.com

Up To $9.00 Value

Enjoy one complimentary LUNCH OR DINNER ENTREE when a second LUNCH OR DINNER ENTREE of equal or greater value is purchased.

Dine in only

valid anytime

Pines of Naples

A202

Valid now thru November 1, 2006

Not valid holidays & subject to Rules of Use. Not valid with other discount offers, unless specified. Coupon VOID if purchased, sold or bartered. Discounts exclude tax, tip and/or alcohol, where applicable.

Sphinx Kabob Cafe

137 Spring St.
Herndon, VA
(703)464-0001

- Persian style kabobs
- Where East meets West
- Located at the Sunset Business Park across from Spring Hill suites Marriott

Bonus Discounts at
entertainment.com

entertainment.
entertainment.com

Up To $9.00 Value

Enjoy one complimentary LUNCH OR DINNER ENTREE when a second LUNCH OR DINNER ENTREE of equal or greater value is purchased.

Dine in only

valid anytime

SPHINX
Kabob-Cafe

A203

Valid now thru November 1, 2006

Not valid holidays & subject to Rules of Use. Not valid with other discount offers, unless specified. Coupon VOID if purchased, sold or bartered. Discounts exclude tax, tip and/or alcohol, where applicable.

The Pita House Family Restaurant

407 Cameron St.
Alexandria, VA
(703)684-9194

- Featuring the finest in Lebanese Cuisine
- Lots of vegetarian dishes available including our homemade falafel
- Dinners served at 5 p.m. nightly
- Enjoy our casual atmosphere & friendly service
- Family owned & operated
- Hours Mon. - 11 a.m. - 10 p.m.
- Closed Sunday

Bonus Discounts at
entertainment.com

entertainment.
entertainment.com

great place for kids

Up To $9.00 Value

Enjoy one complimentary DINNER ENTREE when a second DINNER ENTREE of equal or greater value is purchased.

Dine in only; Combination appetizer plate excluded

valid any evening

The Pita House
Family Restaurant

A204

Valid now thru November 1, 2006

Not valid holidays & subject to Rules of Use. Not valid with other discount offers, unless specified. Coupon VOID if purchased, sold or bartered. Discounts exclude tax, tip and/or alcohol, where applicable.

Pines of Naples

3207 Columbia Pike
Arlington, VA
(703)521-7551

Tipping should be 15% to 20% of TOTAL bill before discount
00041772

entertainment.com

00041772

SPHINX
Kabob-Cafe

137 Spring St.
(Sunset Business Park)
Herndon, VA
(703)464-0001

00611837

entertainment.com

00611837

The Pita House
Family Restaurant

407 Cameron St.
Alexandria, VA
(703)684-9194

Tipping should be 15% to 20% of TOTAL bill before discount
00152686

entertainment.com

00152686

Uncle Sam's

1444 Central Park Blvd.
Fredericksburg, VA
(540)785-6669

- Fun dining in a friendly relaxed atmosphere
- Hungry hour specials
- Nightly entertainment
- Great for watching your favorite sporting events
- Area's largest banquet facilities

Bonus Discounts at
entertainment.com

entertainment.
entertainment.com

Up To $9.00 Value

Enjoy one complimentary LUNCH OR DINNER ENTREE when a second LUNCH OR DINNER ENTREE of equal or greater value is purchased.

Dine in only

valid anytime

A205

Valid now thru November 1, 2006

Not valid holidays & subject to Rules of Use. Not valid with other discount offers, unless specified. Coupon VOID if purchased, sold or bartered. Discounts exclude tax, tip and/or alcohol, where applicable.

Bar J Restaurant

13275 Gordon Blvd.
Woodbridge, VA
(703)491-3271

- Texas-style Mexican food
- Featuring Texas & Cincinnati chili
- Nachos, burritos & enchiladas
- Catering available, both large & small
- Full service bar
- Open daily

Bonus Discounts at
entertainment.com

entertainment.
entertainment.com

Up To $8.00 Value

Enjoy one complimentary LUNCH OR DINNER ENTREE when a second LUNCH OR DINNER ENTREE of equal or greater value is purchased or when dining alone - one LUNCH OR DINNER ENTREE at 50% off the regular price - maximum discount $4.00.

valid anytime

Valid at these locations only

A206

Valid now thru November 1, 2006

Not valid holidays & subject to Rules of Use. Not valid with other discount offers, unless specified. Coupon VOID if purchased, sold or bartered. Discounts exclude tax, tip and/or alcohol, where applicable.

Bungalow Billiards & Brew Co.

See reverse side for locations

- Enjoy all your favorite dishes including soups, salads, burgers, sandwiches, dogs, grilled pies & more
- Pool tables available
- Need an event catered, give us a call
- Look for our newest location opening soon in Kingstowne
- Open daily

Bonus Discounts at
entertainment.com

entertainment.
entertainment.com

Up To $8.00 Value

Enjoy one complimentary LUNCH OR DINNER ENTREE when a second LUNCH OR DINNER ENTREE of equal or greater value is purchased.

Dine in only; In-house promotions excluded

valid anytime

A207

Valid now thru November 1, 2006

Not valid holidays & subject to Rules of Use. Not valid with other discount offers, unless specified. Coupon VOID if purchased, sold or bartered. Discounts exclude tax, tip and/or alcohol, where applicable.

UNCLE Sam's

An American Grill

1444 Central Park Blvd.
Fredericksburg, VA
(540)785-6669

00576549

entertainment.com

00576549

BAR J

13275 Gordon Blvd.
Woodbridge, VA
(703)491-3271

Tipping should be 15% to 20% of TOTAL bill before discount

00003462

entertainment.com

00003462

BUNGALOW BILLIARDS & BREW COMPANY

7003c Manchester Blvd.
Alexandria, VA
(703)924-8730

2766 S. Arlington Mill Dr.
Arlington, VA
(703)578-0020

13891 Metrotec Dr.
(Sully Place Shpg. Ctr.)
Chantilly, VA
(703)502-3925

46300 McClellan St.
(Cascades)
Sterling, VA
(703)421-3776

Tipping should be 15% to 20% of TOTAL bill before discount

00244645

entertainment.com

00244645

Joe's Place

See reverse side for locations

- Family owned & operated by the Farruggio's
- Featuring all your Italian favorites - pasta, pizza, calzones, subs & more
- Beer & wine available
- Open daily

Bonus Discounts at entertainment.com

entertainment. entertainment.com

great place for kids

Up To $8.00 Value

Enjoy one complimentary ENTREE when a second ENTREE of equal or greater value is purchased.

Dine in only; Buffet excluded

valid anytime

Joe's Place Pizza & Pasta

A208

Valid now thru November 1, 2006

Not valid holidays & subject to Rules of Use. Not valid with other discount offers, unless specified. Coupon VOID if purchased, sold or bartered. Discounts exclude tax, tip and/or alcohol, where applicable.

Mirage Restaurant

5916 Leesburg Pike
Falls Church, VA
(703)845-1600

- Featuring appetizers, salads, sandwiches & our house specialty - kabobs
- Also serving Mirage Sweets
- Catering is welcome
- Open daily

Bonus Discounts at entertainment.com

entertainment. entertainment.com

Up To $8.00 Value

Enjoy one complimentary LUNCH OR DINNER ENTREE when a second LUNCH OR DINNER ENTREE of equal or greater value is purchased.

Dine in only

valid anytime

Mirage Kabob & Sweets Café

A209

Valid now thru November 1, 2006

Not valid holidays & subject to Rules of Use. Not valid with other discount offers, unless specified. Coupon VOID if purchased, sold or bartered. Discounts exclude tax, tip and/or alcohol, where applicable.

Mom's Pizza Restaurant

3255 Columbia Pike
Arlington, VA
(703)920-7789

- Fine family restaurant serving Italian & Greek cuisine
- Located at the corner of Glebe Rd. & Columbia Pike
- Ask about our catering service
- 40 item salad bar
- Now open for breakfast everyday
- Open daily

Bonus Discounts at entertainment.com

entertainment. entertainment.com

Up To $8.00 Value

Enjoy one complimentary LUNCH OR DINNER ENTREE when a second LUNCH OR DINNER ENTREE of equal or greater value is purchased.

Dine in only

valid anytime

Mom's Pizza Restaurant

A210

Valid now thru November 1, 2006

Not valid holidays & subject to Rules of Use. Not valid with other discount offers, unless specified. Coupon VOID if purchased, sold or bartered. Discounts exclude tax, tip and/or alcohol, where applicable.

Joe's Place
Pizza & Pasta

430 N. Frederick Ave.
Gaithersburg, MD
(301)926-5900

3922 Old Lee Hwy.
Fairfax, VA
(703)691-0222

435 Maple Ave. W
Vienna, VA
(703)281-1111

5555 Lee Hwy.
Arlington, VA
(703)532-0990

5870 Leesburg Pike
Falls Church, VA
(703)820-5181

Tipping should be 15% to 20% of TOTAL bill before discount

00074021

entertainment.com

00074021

Mirage
Kabob & Sweets Café

5916 Leesburg Pike
(Bailey's Crossroads)
Falls Church, VA
(703)845-1600

Offers not valid holidays and subject to Rules of Use
Tipping should be 15% to 20% of the total bill before discount
00603595

entertainment.com

00603595

Mom's Pizza Restaurant

3255 Columbia Pike
Arlington, VA
(703)920-7789

Tipping should be 15% to 20% of TOTAL bill before discount

00092567

entertainment.com

00092567

Bertine's North Restaurant

206 S. Main St.
Madison, VA
(540)948-3463

- You need not travel far to experience the Caribbean
- Having spent 10 years on the island of St. Martin, Bernard & Christine have created a special Caribbean atmosphere & delicious authentic food
- An international menu with new world island favorites, accompanied with Bertine's famous hot sauce will add spice to your life!
- Open for dinner Fri.-Mon. 6 p.m.-closing

Bonus Discounts at
entertainment.com

entertainment®
entertainment.com

Up To $20.00 Value

Bertine's North
New World Caribbean Cuisine
540-948-DINE

Enjoy one complimentary DINNER ENTREE when a second DINNER ENTREE of equal or greater value is purchased.

valid any evening

Reservations recommended

A211

Valid now thru November 1, 2006

Not valid holidays & subject to Rules of Use. Not valid with other discount offers, unless specified. Coupon VOID if purchased, sold or bartered. Discounts exclude tax, tip and/or alcohol, where applicable.

Rice & Noodles Thai Gourmet

6111 Franconia Rd.
Alexandria, VA
(703)313-0330

- Hours: Sun.-Thurs. 11 a.m.-9:30 p.m., Fri.-Sat. 11 a.m.-10 p.m.
- Serving delicious dishes from Thailand
- Offering appetizers, soups, salads, rice dishes, noodle dishes & vegetarian entrees
- You are in for a treat!

Bonus Discounts at
entertainment.com

entertainment®
entertainment.com

Up To $8.00 Value

Enjoy one complimentary LUNCH OR DINNER ENTREE when a second LUNCH OR DINNER ENTREE of equal or greater value is purchased.

Dine in only

valid anytime

Lunch specials excluded

Rice & Noodles
Thai Gourmet

A212

Valid now thru November 1, 2006

Not valid holidays & subject to Rules of Use. Not valid with other discount offers, unless specified. Coupon VOID if purchased, sold or bartered. Discounts exclude tax, tip and/or alcohol, where applicable.

Shahi Kabob House

724 Pine St.
Herndon, VA
(703)796-0110

- Featuring 100% Halal & fresh food at Shahi Kabob
- The BEST kabobs in town
- Located next to Zeffirelli Restaurant
- PAK-INDIA Restaurant

Bonus Discounts at
entertainment.com

entertainment®
entertainment.com

Up To $8.00 Value

Enjoy one complimentary LUNCH OR DINNER ENTREE when a second LUNCH OR DINNER ENTREE of equal or greater value is purchased.

Dine in only; Buffet excluded

valid anytime

SHAHI KABOB HOUSE

A213

Valid now thru November 1, 2006

Not valid holidays & subject to Rules of Use. Not valid with other discount offers, unless specified. Coupon VOID if purchased, sold or bartered. Discounts exclude tax, tip and/or alcohol, where applicable.

Bertine's North

New World Caribbean Cuisine

540-948-DINE

206 S. Main St.
Madison, VA
(540)948-3463

Offers not valid holidays and subject to Rules of Use
Tipping should be 15% to 20% of the total bill before discount
00274139

Rice & Noodles
Thai Gourmet

6111 Franconia Rd.
Alexandria, VA
(703)313-0330

Offers not valid holidays and subject to Rules of Use
Tipping should be 15% to 20% of the total bill before discount
00603617

SHAHI
KABOB
HOUSE

724 Pine St.
Herndon, VA
(703)796-0110

00617908

Victor's Pizza & Pasta

7881 Heritage Dr.
Annandale, VA
(703)941-8368

- Featuring fresh salads, sandwiches, burgers, subs, pasta dishes, Greek specialties, wings & more
- Enjoy a traditional pizza or one of our gourmet specialties
- Beer available
- Open daily

Bonus Discounts at
entertainment.com

entertainment.
entertainment.com

Up To $8.00 Value

Victors

Enjoy one complimentary LUNCH OR DINNER ENTREE when a second LUNCH OR DINNER ENTREE of equal or greater value is purchased or for those who prefer - any one pizza at 50% off the regular price - maximum discount $8.00.

valid anytime

A214

Valid now thru November 1, 2006

Not valid holidays & subject to Rules of Use. Not valid with other discount offers, unless specified. Coupon VOID if purchased, sold or bartered. Discounts exclude tax, tip and/or alcohol, where applicable.

Viva Pizza & Family Restaurant

8212 Gunston Corner Ln.
Lorton, VA
(703)690-4500

- Located at the corner of Lorton Rd and Silverbrook Rd
- Featuring appetizers, hand tossed pizzas, calzones, hot and cold subs and sandwiches, salads and entrees
- Open daily

Bonus Discounts at
entertainment.com

entertainment.
entertainment.com

great place for kids

Up To $8.00 Value

VIVA PIZZA & FAMILY RESTAURANT

Enjoy one complimentary LUNCH OR DINNER ENTREE when a second LUNCH OR DINNER ENTREE of equal or greater value is purchased.

Dine in only

valid anytime

A215

Valid now thru November 1, 2006

Not valid holidays & subject to Rules of Use. Not valid with other discount offers, unless specified. Coupon VOID if purchased, sold or bartered. Discounts exclude tax, tip and/or alcohol, where applicable.

Viva Pizza & Family Restaurant

8212 Gunston Corner Ln.
Lorton, VA
(703)690-4500

- Located at the corner of Lorton Rd and Silverbrook Rd
- Featuring appetizers, hand tossed pizzas, calzones, hot and cold subs and sandwiches, salads and entrees
- Open daily

Bonus Discounts at
entertainment.com

entertainment.
entertainment.com

great place for kids

50% OFF

VIVA PIZZA & FAMILY RESTAURANT

Enjoy any one PIZZA at 50% off the regular price.

Dine in only

valid anytime

A216

Valid now thru November 1, 2006

Not valid holidays & subject to Rules of Use. Not valid with other discount offers, unless specified. Coupon VOID if purchased, sold or bartered. Discounts exclude tax, tip and/or alcohol, where applicable.

Victors

7881 Heritage Dr.
(Heritage Mall)
Annandale, VA
(703)941-8368

00578100

entertainment.com

00578100

VIVA PIZZA & FAMILY RESTAURANT

8212 Gunston Corner Ln.
Lorton, VA
(703)690-4500

00574951

entertainment.com

00574951

VIVA PIZZA & FAMILY RESTAURANT

8212 Gunston Corner Ln.
Lorton, VA
(703)690-4500

00575035

entertainment.com

00575035

Anadolla

650 S. Pickett St.
Alexandria, VA
(703)370-2900

- Featuring kabobs, breads & grilled specialties
- International bakery with various types of breads from around the world
- Open daily

great place for kids

Up To $7.00 Value

Enjoy one complimentary MENU ITEM when a second MENU ITEM of equal or greater value is purchased.

Dine in only

valid anytime

Anadolla

www.anadolla.com

A217

Valid now thru November 1, 2006

Not valid holidays & subject to Rules of Use. Not valid with other discount offers, unless specified. Coupon VOID if purchased, sold or bartered. Discounts exclude tax, tip and/or alcohol, where applicable.

Bubba's Bar-B-Q

7810-F Lee Hwy.
Falls Church, VA
(703)560-8570

- Authentic hickory smoked meats
- Featuring sandwiches, platters, salads & more
- Please call for our complete catering menu & brochure
- Open daily

Bonus Discounts at
entertainment.com

entertainment.
entertainment.com

great place for kids

Up To $7.00 Value

Enjoy one complimentary DINNER ENTREE when a second DINNER ENTREE of equal or greater value is purchased.

Platters excluded

valid any evening after 4 p.m.

BUBBA'S BAR-B-Q & CATERING

An American Delicacy

A218

Valid now thru November 1, 2006

Not valid holidays & subject to Rules of Use. Not valid with other discount offers, unless specified. Coupon VOID if purchased, sold or bartered. Discounts exclude tax, tip and/or alcohol, where applicable.

Burger & Kabab Place

367 Warrenton Rd.
Fredericksburg, VA
(540)370-1878

- Eat in or carry out
- Featuring the best kababs, burgers, chicken & more
- Catering & party hall available for 50 people
- Open daily

Bonus Discounts at
entertainment.com

entertainment.
entertainment.com

Up To $7.00 Value

Enjoy one complimentary LUNCH OR DINNER ENTREE when a second LUNCH OR DINNER ENTREE of equal or greater value is purchased.

valid anytime

BURGER & KABAB PLACE

A219

Valid now thru November 1, 2006

Not valid holidays & subject to Rules of Use. Not valid with other discount offers, unless specified. Coupon VOID if purchased, sold or bartered. Discounts exclude tax, tip and/or alcohol, where applicable.

Anadolla

650 S. Pickett St.
Alexandria, VA
(703)370-2900

00615460

entertainment.com

00615460

BUBBA'S BAR-B-Q
& CATERING

An American Delicacy

7810-F Lee Hwy.
Falls Church, VA
(703)560-8570

Tipping should be 15% to 20% of TOTAL bill before discount

00315180

entertainment.com

00315180

BURGER & KABAB PLACE

367 Warrenton Rd.
(Route 17)
Fredericksburg, VA
(540)370-1878

00606676

entertainment.com

00606676

El Tamarindo

7331 Georgia Ave., NW
Washington, DC
(202)291-0525

- Serving Washington, DC, The Best Mexican & Salvadorean cuisine for over 20 years
- Menu highlights include traditional tamales, pupusa, yucca con chicharron, & more favorites
- Full service bar offering Mexican beers, tequila, margaritas & other specialty beverages
- Families welcome - open 7 days a week

entertainment.com

Up To $7.00 Value

Restaurant El Tamarindo

Enjoy one complimentary LUNCH OR DINNER ENTREE when a second LUNCH OR DINNER ENTREE of equal or greater value is purchased.

Dine in only; appetizers excluded

valid anytime

A220

Valid now thru November 1, 2006

Not valid holidays & subject to Rules of Use. Not valid with other discount offers, unless specified. Coupon VOID if purchased, sold or bartered. Discounts exclude tax, tip and/or alcohol, where applicable.

Linda's Cafe

5050 Lee Highway
Arlington, VA
(703)538-2542

- Quality food at low prices in a friendly neighborhood atmosphere
- We cook your food right in front of you
- Breakfast anytime, lunch, dinner
- Open daily 7 a.m. - 8 p.m.

entertainment.com

great place for kids

Up To $7.00 Value

America's Place to Eat — Linda's Cafe — Breakfast

Enjoy one complimentary ENTREE when a second ENTREE of equal or greater value is purchased.

Dine in only

valid anytime

A221

Valid now thru November 1, 2006

Not valid holidays & subject to Rules of Use. Not valid with other discount offers, unless specified. Coupon VOID if purchased, sold or bartered. Discounts exclude tax, tip and/or alcohol, where applicable.

Linda's Cafe

45665 W. Church Rd.
Sterling, VA
(703)433-5637

- America's place to eat for breakfast, lunch & dinner
- Featuring all your favorites including: French toast, pancakes, breakfast sandwiches, omelettes, subs, burgers, deli sandwiches & more
- Kids menu available

entertainment.com

great place for kids

Up To $7.00 Value

Enjoy one complimentary ENTREE when a second ENTREE of equal or greater value is purchased.

Dine in only

valid anytime

America's Place to Eat — Linda's Cafe — Breakfast

A222

Valid now thru November 1, 2006

Not valid holidays & subject to Rules of Use. Not valid with other discount offers, unless specified. Coupon VOID if purchased, sold or bartered. Discounts exclude tax, tip and/or alcohol, where applicable.

Restaurant EL TAMARINDO

7331 Georgia Ave., NW
(Near Silver Spring & Walter Reed Hospital)
Washington, DC
(202)291-0525

00508617

entertainment.com

00508617

Linda's Cafe

5050 Lee Highway
Arlington, VA
(703)538-2542

Tipping should be 15% to 20% of TOTAL bill before discount

00385434

entertainment.com

00385434

Linda's Cafe

45665 W. Church Rd.
Sterling, VA
(703)433-5637

00566456

entertainment.com

00566456

First Break Cafe

46970 Community Plaza
Sterling, VA
(703)444-2551

- Our menu includes appetizers, pizza, salad, subs, sandwiches & house specialties
- Enjoy ladies night every Monday & lunch specials every day
- Special rates available for parties of 10 or more - plan your next party or office function at First Break Cafe
- Open daily

Bonus Discounts at entertainment.com

entertainment. entertainment.com

Up To $7.00 Value

Enjoy one complimentary LUNCH OR DINNER ENTREE when a second LUNCH OR DINNER ENTREE of equal or greater value is purchased.

valid anytime

FIRST BREAK CAFE
FOOD ★ FUN ★ BILLIARDS

A223

Valid now thru November 1, 2006

Not valid holidays & subject to Rules of Use. Not valid with other discount offers, unless specified. Coupon VOID if purchased, sold or bartered. Discounts exclude tax, tip and/or alcohol, where applicable.

Mike's Diner

8401 Digges Rd.
Manassas, VA
(703)361-5248

- Fresh homemade food served 24 hours a day
- Cold & hot sandwiches
- Homemade soup & cornbread
- Moist & tender freshly cooked turkey, chicken, fish & steak
- Kids' menu
- Desserts

Bonus Discounts at entertainment.com

entertainment. entertainment.com

Up To $7.00 Value

Enjoy one complimentary LUNCH OR DINNER ENTREE when a second LUNCH OR DINNER ENTREE of equal or greater value is purchased or when dining alone - one LUNCH OR DINNER ENTREE at 50% off the regular price - maximum discount $3.00 or for those who prefer - any one pizza at 50% off the regular price.

valid anytime

Mike's DINER

A224

Valid now thru November 1, 2006

Not valid holidays & subject to Rules of Use. Not valid with other discount offers, unless specified. Coupon VOID if purchased, sold or bartered. Discounts exclude tax, tip and/or alcohol, where applicable.

Mr. Pepperoni

9570-N Burke Rd.
Burke, VA
(703)426-4500

- Serving pizza, pasta, subs, burgers, salads, gyros & calzones
- We use Grande mozzarella cheese, best cheese money can buy
- Catering & birthday parties available
- Open daily

Bonus Discounts at entertainment.com

entertainment. entertainment.com

great place for kids

Up To $7.00 Value

Enjoy one complimentary LUNCH OR DINNER ENTREE when a second LUNCH OR DINNER ENTREE of equal or greater value is purchased or for those who prefer - any one pizza at 50% off the regular price.

Dine in only

valid anytime

MR. PEPPERONI!

A225

Valid now thru November 1, 2006

Not valid holidays & subject to Rules of Use. Not valid with other discount offers, unless specified. Coupon VOID if purchased, sold or bartered. Discounts exclude tax, tip and/or alcohol, where applicable.

FIRST BREAK CAFE

FOOD ★ FUN ★ BILLIARDS

46970 Community Plaza
(Plaza Ctr.)
Sterling, VA
(703)444-2551

Tipping should be 15% to 20% of TOTAL bill before discount

00072189

entertainment.com

00072189

Mike's DINER

8401 Digges Rd.
Manassas, VA
(703)361-5248

Tipping should be 15% to 20% of TOTAL bill before discount

00021544

entertainment.com

00021544

MR. PEPPERONI

9570-N Burke Rd.
Burke, VA
(703)426-4500

Tipping should be 15% to 20% of TOTAL bill before discount

00276387

entertainment.com

00276387

Spirits Food & Beverage

816 Caroline St.
Fredericksburg, VA
(540)371-9595

- Fun, casual dining in the heart of Fredericksburg
- Traditional American & Italian fare
- Delicious appetizers, soups, salads, sandwiches, subs & burgers
- Variety of pasta entrees with sauces fresh to order
- Just for kids menu
- Open daily, 11:30 a.m. - 2 a.m.

Up To $7.00 Value

Enjoy one complimentary LUNCH OR DINNER ENTREE when a second LUNCH OR DINNER ENTREE of equal or greater value is purchased.

Spirits Food And Beverage The American Way

valid anytime

A226

Valid now thru November 1, 2006

Not valid holidays & subject to Rules of Use. Not valid with other discount offers, unless specified. Coupon VOID if purchased, sold or bartered. Discounts exclude tax, tip and/or alcohol, where applicable.

Summers Restaurant

1520 N. Courthouse Rd.
Arlington, VA
(703)528-8278

- Featuring fine food & spirits
- Choose from a large variety of sandwiches, Summers specialties & gourmet burgers
- Also serving breakfast
- Full service cocktail bar
- Open daily

Up To $7.00 Value

Summers Restaurant

Enjoy one complimentary LUNCH OR DINNER ENTREE when a second LUNCH OR DINNER ENTREE of equal or greater value is purchased.

Dine in only; Daily specials excluded

valid anytime

A227

Valid now thru November 1, 2006

Not valid holidays & subject to Rules of Use. Not valid with other discount offers, unless specified. Coupon VOID if purchased, sold or bartered. Discounts exclude tax, tip and/or alcohol, where applicable.

Sunset Grille

7250 Columbia Pike
Annandale, VA
(703)658-0928

- "The in-land beach bar"
- Open daily for breakfast, lunch and dinner
- Featuring everything from Tex-Mex to chili to seafood

Up To $7.00 Value

Sunset Grille

Enjoy ONE LUNCH OR DINNER MENU ITEM when a second LUNCH OR DINNER MENU ITEM of equal or greater value is purchased or when dining alone - ONE LUNCH OR DINNER MENU ITEM at 50% off the regular price - maximum discount $3.00.

valid anytime

A228

Valid now thru November 1, 2006

Not valid holidays & subject to Rules of Use. Not valid with other discount offers, unless specified. Coupon VOID if purchased, sold or bartered. Discounts exclude tax, tip and/or alcohol, where applicable.

Spirits
Food And Beverage
The American Way

816 Caroline St.
Fredericksburg, VA
(540)371-9595

Tipping should be 15% to 20% of TOTAL bill before discount
00378202

entertainment.com
00378202

Summers Restaurant

1520 N. Courthouse Rd.
Arlington, VA
(703)528-8278

Tipping should be 15% to 20% of TOTAL bill before discount
00020059

entertainment.com
00020059

Sunset Grille

7250 Columbia Pike
Annandale, VA
(703)658-0928

Tipping should be 15% to 20% of TOTAL bill before discount
00201008

entertainment.com
00201008

Taco Baja Grill

6136-F Arlington Blvd.
Falls Church, VA
(703)534-5434

- Featuring Tacos, Burritos, Pupusas, Fajitas, Enchiladas, Pescado, Cervezas & more
- Open daily

Bonus Discounts at entertainment.com

entertainment. entertainment.com

Up To $7.00 Value

TACO Baja

Enjoy one complimentary LUNCH OR DINNER ENTREE when a second LUNCH OR DINNER ENTREE of equal or greater value is purchased.

Dine in only

valid anytime

A229

Valid now thru November 1, 2006

The Clubhouse

9008 Mathis Ave.
Manassas, VA
(703)331-0998

- Select from our variety of dinner entrees, soups & sandwiches
- Open daily
- Banquets, meetings & parties available

Bonus Discounts at entertainment.com

entertainment. entertainment.com

Up To $7.00 Value

Enjoy one complimentary LUNCH OR DINNER ENTREE when a second LUNCH OR DINNER ENTREE of equal or greater value is purchased or when dining alone - one LUNCH OR DINNER ENTREE at 50% off the regular price - maximum discount $3.00.

valid anytime

A230

Valid now thru November 1, 2006

Ana's Pizza

470 Elden St.
Herndon, VA
(703)464-1295

- Featuring an all-you-can eat buffet, Mon.-Sat.
- A-La-Carte menu items include American favorites & Lebanese specialties
- Open Mon.-Sat.
- Sundays are available for private parties & special occasions

Bonus Discounts at entertainment.com

entertainment. entertainment.com

great place for kids

ONE MENU ITEM

Ana's Pizza

Enjoy one complimentary MENU ITEM when a second MENU ITEM of equal or greater value is purchased or for those who prefer - any one pizza at 50% off the regular price.

Buffet excluded; Dine in only

valid anytime

A231

Valid now thru November 1, 2006

TACO Baja

6136-F Arlington Blvd.
(Willston II Shopping Centre)
Falls Church, VA
(703)534-5434

00495840

THE CLUBHOUSE

RESTAURANT & SPORTS BAR

9008 Mathis Ave.
Manassas, VA
(703)331-0998

Tipping should be 15% to 20% of TOTAL bill before discount

00206920

Ana's Pizza

470 Elden St.
(K-Mart Ctr.)
Herndon, VA
(703)464-1295

00651446

entertainment.com

00495840

entertainment.com

00206920

entertainment.com

00651446

Delhi Dhaba

See reverse side for locations

- The original tandoor cuisine
- Our specialties include seafood, chicken, lamb & vegetarian dishes
- Listed in WASHINGTONIAN MAGAZINE'S 100 best bargain restaurants
- Available for private parties
- Closed Monday

Bonus Discounts at entertainment.com

entertainment. entertainment.com

Up To $6.00 Value

Enjoy one complimentary LUNCH OR DINNER ENTREE when a second LUNCH OR DINNER ENTREE of equal or greater value is purchased.

valid anytime

DELHI DHABA
The Original Tandoor Cuisine

www.delhi-dhaba.com

A232

Valid now thru November 1, 2006

Not valid holidays & subject to Rules of Use. Not valid with other discount offers, unless specified. Coupon VOID if purchased, sold or bartered. Discounts exclude tax, tip and/or alcohol, where applicable.

Pitalicious Lebanese Grill

14396 Chantilly Crossing Ln.
Chantilly, VA
(703)961-0664

- Offering the tastiest Lebanese cuisine
- Featuring sandwiches, platters, vegetarian dishes & a complete low carb menu
- A variety of Messa, Lebanese appetizers, is prepared daily
- Catering available

Bonus Discounts at entertainment.com

entertainment. entertainment.com

great place for kids

Up To $6.00 Value

Enjoy one complimentary MENU ITEM when a second MENU ITEM of equal or greater value is purchased.

valid anytime

PITALICIOUS
LEBANESE GRILL

www.pitalicious.com

A233

Valid now thru November 1, 2006

Not valid holidays & subject to Rules of Use. Not valid with other discount offers, unless specified. Coupon VOID if purchased, sold or bartered. Discounts exclude tax, tip and/or alcohol, where applicable.

Savio's Restaurant

516 S. Van Dorn St.
Alexandria, VA
(703)212-9651

- Voted Best Bargain Restaurant by WASHINGTONIAN MAGAZINE
- "Considering the high quality of food, prices are quite reasonable"- THE ALEXANDRIA JOURNAL voted 3 1/2 stars
- Open daily

Bonus Discounts at entertainment.com

entertainment. entertainment.com

Up To $11.00 Value

Enjoy one complimentary DINNER ENTREE when a second DINNER ENTREE of equal or greater value is purchased or when dining alone - one DINNER ENTREE at 50% off the regular price - maximum discount $5.00.

Dining room only

valid any evening

Savio's
ITALIAN RESTAURANT AND BAR

www.saviosrestaurant.com

A234

Valid now thru November 1, 2006

Not valid holidays & subject to Rules of Use. Not valid with other discount offers, unless specified. Coupon VOID if purchased, sold or bartered. Discounts exclude tax, tip and/or alcohol, where applicable.

DELHI DHABA
The Original Tandoor Cuisine

7236 Woodmont Ave.
Bethesda, MD
(301)718-0008

2424 Wilson Blvd.
Arlington, VA
(703)524-0008

4455 Conn Ave. NW
Washington, VA
(202)537-1008

00085525

entertainment.com

00085525

PITALICIOUS
LEBANESE GRILL

14396 Chantilly Crossing Ln.
(located near Costco)
Chantilly, VA
(703)961-0664

00622416

entertainment.com

00622416

Savio's
ITALIAN RESTAURANT AND BAR

516 S. Van Dorn St.
(Van Dorn Station)
Alexandria, VA
(703)212-9651

Tipping should be 15% to 20% of TOTAL bill before discount

00003014

entertainment.com

00003014

Ringmasters Pub & Deli

8607 Westwood Ctr. Dr.
Vienna, VA
(703)448-4444

- Join us at the deli for homemade food
- Free hors d'oeuvres & popcorn
- World famous salads
- Ringmaster specialties
- Best & biggest sandwiches in town
- Fresh baked bread on the premises
- Great happy hour
- Live music daily
- Open daily

entertainment. entertainment.com

Up To $6.00 Value

Enjoy one complimentary DINNER ENTREE when a second DINNER ENTREE of equal or greater value is purchased.

Dine in only

valid any evening

RINGMASTERS DELI

A235

Shiney's

4231-D Markham St.
Annandale, VA
(703)642-0460

- Sweets & delicacies
- Everything is made fresh daily
- A local favorite for years
- Open daily

entertainment. entertainment.com

Up To $6.00 Value

Enjoy one complimentary LUNCH OR DINNER ENTREE when a second LUNCH OR DINNER ENTREE of equal or greater value is purchased.

Dine in only

valid anytime

SHINEY'S
Sweets & Delicacies

A236

Sukh Sagar Indian Cafe

14830 Build America Dr.
Woodbridge, VA
(703)490-1100

- All natural food cooked to perfection
- Food freshly prepared daily on premises
- No chemicals, additives or preservatives
- Catering available
- Featuring the best authentic Indian food in town with casual dining at it's best

entertainment. entertainment.com

Up To $6.00 Value

Enjoy one complimentary LUNCH OR DINNER ENTREE when a second LUNCH OR DINNER ENTREE of equal or greater value is purchased.

Buffet excluded; Dine in only

valid anytime

Sukh Sagar Indian Cafe

A237

RINGMASTERS
DELI

8607 Westwood Ctr. Dr.
(near American Cafe - Tyson's Corner)
Vienna, VA
(703)448-4444

00043659

entertainment.com

00043659

SHINEY'S
Sweets & Delicacies

4231-D Markham St.
Annandale, VA
(703)642-0460

00496041

entertainment.com

00496041

Sukh Sagar
Indian Cafe

14830 Build America Dr.
(across from Taco Bell on Rte. 1, about 1 mile from Potomac Mills)
Woodbridge, VA
(703)490-1100

00617996

entertainment.com

00617996

Teocalli Tamale

336 Elden St.
Herndon, VA
(703)904-9336

- Always fresh, fast & affordable
- "The Guacamole is one of the BEST in the area...top-notch...delightful fast food & slow cooked. Nearly everything is house made & it shows." Washingtonian Magazine, Feb 2002
- Open daily

Bonus Discounts at
entertainment.com

entertainment.
entertainment.com

great place for kids

Up To $6.00 Value

Enjoy one complimentary MENU ITEM when a second MENU ITEM of equal or greater value is purchased.

valid anytime

A238

Valid now thru November 1, 2006

Not valid holidays & subject to Rules of Use. Not valid with other discount offers, unless specified. Coupon VOID if purchased, sold or bartered. Discounts exclude tax, tip and/or alcohol, where applicable.

The Baja Grille

1133 20th Street NW
Washington, DC
(202)659-4562

- Washington's 1st five star casual dining & take-out
- Baja Grill prepares all of its foods fresh each day
- No preservatives, fillers or additives are used
- We make it all, even our own mayo, nothing is fried
- Our kitchen is open so guests can see preparation
- It's a new dining experience, you will enjoy
- Closed Sundays

Bonus Discounts at
entertainment.com

entertainment.
entertainment.com

Up To $6.00 Value

the BAJA grille

Enjoy one complimentary ENTREE when a second ENTREE of equal or greater value is purchased.

valid anytime

A239

Valid now thru November 1, 2006

Not valid holidays & subject to Rules of Use. Not valid with other discount offers, unless specified. Coupon VOID if purchased, sold or bartered. Discounts exclude tax, tip and/or alcohol, where applicable.

Three Pigs Barbeque

1394 Chain Bridge Rd.
McLean, VA
(703)356-1700

- "Three Pigs produce a knock-out of a North Carolina pork barbecue sandwich," raves Phyllis Richman of the WASHINGTON POST MAGAZINE
- Open Sat.-Thurs. 11 a.m.-8 p.m. & Fri. 11 a.m.-9 p.m.

Bonus Discounts at
entertainment.com

entertainment.
entertainment.com

great place for kids

ONE HALF SLAB RIB PLATTER

THREE PIGS BARBECUE

Enjoy one complimentary HALF SLAB RIB PLATTER when a second HALF SLAB RIB PLATTER of equal or greater value is purchased.

Platters May be substituted

valid anytime

A240

Valid now thru November 1, 2006

Not valid holidays & subject to Rules of Use. Not valid with other discount offers, unless specified. Coupon VOID if purchased, sold or bartered. Discounts exclude tax, tip and/or alcohol, where applicable.

Teocalli Tamale

Fresh Burrito Bar

est. 1997

336 Elden St.
Herndon, VA
(703)904-9336

00497963

entertainment.com

00497963

the BAJA grille

1133 20th Street NW
Washington, DC
(202)659-4562

Tipping should be 15% to 20% of TOTAL bill before discount

00141778

entertainment.com

00141778

THREE PIGS BARBECUE

1394 Chain Bridge Rd.
McLean, VA
(703)356-1700

Tipping should be 15% to 20% of TOTAL bill before discount

00020194

entertainment.com

00020194

East Coast Billiards

13989 Jefferson Davis Hwy.
Woodbridge, VA
(703)490-5504

- 20 pool tables, dart boards, arcade games, 15 ft. TV screen & more
- Pool tables, cues, accessories & juke boxes for sale in attached showroom
- Featuring a variety of dishes including steaks, pasta, subs & sandwiches
- Full service bar

Bonus Discounts at entertainment.com

entertainment. entertainment.com

Up To $16.00 Value

Enjoy one complimentary LUNCH OR DINNER ENTREE when a second LUNCH OR DINNER ENTREE of equal or greater value is purchased or when dining alone - one LUNCH OR DINNER ENTREE at 50% off the regular price - maximum discount $8.00.

Dine in only

valid anytime

East Coast Billiards

A241

Valid now thru November 1, 2006

Not valid holidays & subject to Rules of Use. Not valid with other discount offers, unless specified. Coupon VOID if purchased, sold or bartered. Discounts exclude tax, tip and/or alcohol, where applicable.

Al's Place

7020 Old Keene Mill Rd.
Springfield, VA
(703)866-4045

- Visit Al's Place located in Springfield at the mixing bowl for a relaxing dining experience with guaranteed friendly service & delicious food
- Each meal is prepared daily & nothing but the freshest ingredients are used
- We're open early for breakfast & late night as well

Bonus Discounts at entertainment.com

entertainment. entertainment.com

great place for kids

Up To $20.00 Value

Enjoy one complimentary LUNCH OR DINNER ENTREE when a second LUNCH OR DINNER ENTREE of equal or greater value is purchased.

Buffet excluded; Dine in only

valid anytime

Al's Place The Mixing Bowl

www.wackyals.com

A242

Valid now thru November 1, 2006

Not valid holidays & subject to Rules of Use. Not valid with other discount offers, unless specified. Coupon VOID if purchased, sold or bartered. Discounts exclude tax, tip and/or alcohol, where applicable.

Main Street Grill & Bar

315 Garrison Rd.
Stafford, VA
(540)288-9277

- Welcome to the Main Street Grill & Bar, one of Staffords best kept secrets
- We offer traditional American fare in a fun atmosphere
- Start your meal with a sampling from our famous crab dip
- Live entertainment available Fri. & Sat.

Bonus Discounts at entertainment.com

entertainment. entertainment.com

Up To $15.00 Value

Enjoy one complimentary LUNCH OR DINNER ENTREE when a second LUNCH OR DINNER ENTREE of equal or greater value is purchased.

Dine in only

valid anytime

MAINSTREET

GRILL AND BAR

A243

Valid now thru November 1, 2006

Not valid holidays & subject to Rules of Use. Not valid with other discount offers, unless specified. Coupon VOID if purchased, sold or bartered. Discounts exclude tax, tip and/or alcohol, where applicable.

East Coast Billiards

13989 Jefferson Davis Hwy.
Woodbridge, VA
(703)490-5504

Tipping should be 15% to 20% of TOTAL bill before discount

00030313

entertainment.com

00030313

Al's Place
The Mixing Bowl

7020 Old Keene Mill Rd.
(next to Springfield Plaza)
Springfield, VA
(703)866-4045

00615573

entertainment.com

00615573

MAINSTREET
GRILL AND BAR

315 Garrison Rd.
(Brafferton Ctr.)
Stafford, VA
(540)288-9277

00607408

entertainment.com

00607408

Mexico Lindo

2030 Plank Rd.
Fredericksburg, VA
(540)899-9096

- Authentic Mexican food
- Tex-Mex specialties, burritos, enchiladas, chimichangas & fajitas
- Open 7 days a week for lunch & dinner

Bonus Discounts at
entertainment.com

entertainment.
entertainment.com

Up To $13.00 Value

Enjoy one complimentary DINNER ENTREE when a second DINNER ENTREE of equal or greater value is purchased.

Dine in only

valid any evening

Mexico Lindo
Restaurant

A244

Valid now thru November 1, 2006

Not valid holidays & subject to Rules of Use. Not valid with other discount offers, unless specified. Coupon VOID if purchased, sold or bartered. Discounts exclude tax, tip and/or alcohol, where applicable.

American Bar-B-Que

7230 Lockport Place
Lorton, VA
(703)550-7757

- Serving all your favorite bar-b-que specials
- Call us for your next catering event
- Open daily Mon. - Fri. 6 a.m. - 3 p.m. & Sat. 7:30 a.m. - 3 p.m.
- Closed Sunday

Bonus Discounts at
entertainment.com

entertainment.
entertainment.com

great place for kids

Up To $6.00 Value

Enjoy one complimentary MENU ITEM when a second MENU ITEM of equal or greater value is purchased.

valid anytime

AMERICAN BAR-B-QUE

A245

Valid now thru November 1, 2006

Not valid holidays & subject to Rules of Use. Not valid with other discount offers, unless specified. Coupon VOID if purchased, sold or bartered. Discounts exclude tax, tip and/or alcohol, where applicable.

Medieval Times Dinner & Tournament

See reverse side for locations

- Feast on a four-course meal in an 11th century castle
- Daring knights on horseback competing in tournament games & jousting matches
- Beautiful Andalusian horses
- Truly "A Knight to Remember"
- Call for show times & tickets at 888-WE-JOUST ext. 8

Bonus Discounts at
entertainment.com

entertainment.
entertainment.com

great place for kids

$10.00 Value

Enjoy $10.00 off the regular admission price of ONE DINNER & SHOW when a second DINNER & SHOW is purchased at regular admission price.

valid anytime

Not valid on Saturday performances; Not valid with any other discounts or promotions; Reservations required; Coupon must be mentioned at the time of ticket purchace

10ENT06

Medieval Times
DINNER & TOURNAMENT

www.medievaltimes.com

A246

Valid now thru November 1, 2006

Not valid holidays & subject to Rules of Use. Not valid with other discount offers, unless specified. Coupon VOID if purchased, sold or bartered. Discounts exclude tax, tip and/or alcohol, where applicable.

Mexico Lindo Restaurant

2030 Plank Rd.
(next to Burlington Coat Factory)
Fredericksburg, VA
(540)899-9096

00607392

entertainment.com

00607392

AMERICAN BAR-B-QUE

7230 Lockport Place
Lorton, VA
(703)550-7757

00528014

entertainment.com

00528014

Medieval Times
DINNER & TOURNAMENT

7000 Arundel Mills Circle
(Arundel Mills)
Hanover, MD

Call for show times & tickets at
1-888-WE-JOUST ext. 8

00587348

entertainment.com

00587348

Franconia Pizza

6112 Franconia Rd.
Alexandria, VA
(703)971-4766

- Everything is terrific
- Serving pizza, calzones, hot & cold sandwiches, soup, salads & side orders
- Come relax, bring your family & enjoy a great meal
- Service is super friendly

Bonus Discounts at
entertainment.com

entertainment. entertainment.com

great place for kids

Up To $7.00 Value

Franconia Pizza

Enjoy one complimentary LUNCH OR DINNER ENTREE when a second LUNCH OR DINNER ENTREE of equal or greater value is purchased or when dining alone - one LUNCH OR DINNER ENTREE at 50% off the regular price - maximum discount $3.00 or for those who prefer - any one pizza at 50% off the regular price.

Sorry, no delivery

valid anytime A247

Valid now thru November 1, 2006

Not valid holidays & subject to Rules of Use. Not valid with other discount offers, unless specified. Coupon VOID if purchased, sold or bartered. Discounts exclude tax, tip and/or alcohol, where applicable.

Springfield Restaurant & Pizzaria

6416 Brandon Ave.
Springfield, VA
(703)451-4800

- All homemade soups & specials
- 30 item salad bar, great for a quick lunch
- Lunch buffet available
- Italian & Greek cuisine
- Beer & wine available
- Located in Springfield Tower Shopping Center
- Open daily

Bonus Discounts at
entertainment.com

entertainment. entertainment.com

great place for kids

Up To $8.00 Value

SPRINGFIELD RESTAURANT & PIZZARIA

Enjoy any one PIZZA at 50% off the regular price - maximum discount $8.00.

valid anytime

A248

Valid now thru November 1, 2006

Not valid holidays & subject to Rules of Use. Not valid with other discount offers, unless specified. Coupon VOID if purchased, sold or bartered. Discounts exclude tax, tip and/or alcohol, where applicable.

Yorkshire Restaurant

7537 Centreville Rd.
Manassas, VA
(703)368-4905

- Breakfast, lunch & dinner available
- Featuring salads, soups, Yorkshire special sandwiches, steak, seafood & assorted desserts
- Enjoy a meal with that home-cooked difference

Bonus Discounts at
entertainment.com

entertainment. entertainment.com

great place for kids

Up To $7.00 Value

Yorkshire Restaurant

Enjoy one complimentary BREAKFAST, LUNCH OR DINNER ENTREE when a second BREAKFAST, LUNCH OR DINNER ENTREE of equal or greater value is purchased or when dining alone - one BREAKFAST, LUNCH OR DINNER ENTREE at 50% off the regular price - maximum discount $3.00.

Dine in only

valid anytime A249

Valid now thru November 1, 2006

Not valid holidays & subject to Rules of Use. Not valid with other discount offers, unless specified. Coupon VOID if purchased, sold or bartered. Discounts exclude tax, tip and/or alcohol, where applicable.

Franconia Pizza

6112 Franconia Rd.
(Franconia Shpg. Ctr.)
Alexandria, VA
(703)971-4766

Tipping should be 15% to 20% of TOTAL bill before discount

00008880

entertainment.com

00008880

SPRINGFIELD RESTAURANT & PIZZARIA

6416 Brandon Ave.
Springfield, VA
(703)451-4800

00026010

entertainment.com

00026010

Yorkshire Restaurant

7537 Centreville Rd.
Manassas, VA
(703)368-4905

Tipping should be 15% to 20% of TOTAL bill before discount

00021681

entertainment.com

00021681

Lebanese Village

549 S. 23rd St.
Arlington, VA
(703)271-9194

- Featuring the finest in Lebanese cuisine
- Lots of vegetarian dishes available including our homemade falafel
- Family owned & operated
- Open daily

Bonus Discounts at
entertainment.com

entertainment.
entertainment.com

Up To $9.00 Value

Enjoy one complimentary LUNCH OR DINNER ENTREE when a second LUNCH OR DINNER ENTREE of equal or greater value is purchased.

Dine in only; Lunch Specials excluded

valid anytime

Lebanese Village

www.lebanesevillage.com

A250

Valid now thru November 1, 2006

Not valid holidays & subject to Rules of Use. Not valid with other discount offers, unless specified. Coupon VOID if purchased, sold or bartered. Discounts exclude tax, tip and/or alcohol, where applicable.

Cerro Grande Mexican Grill & Cantina

6705 Springfield Mall
Springfield, VA
(703)924-0856

- Join us for fine Mexican cuisine
- Featured items include house specialties & a variety of burritos, tacos, enchiladas & much more
- Open daily for lunch & dinner, no reservations needed
- Relax & enjoy a beverage from our full bar with your meal

Bonus Discounts at
entertainment.com

entertainment.
entertainment.com

Up To $14.00 Value

Enjoy one complimentary LUNCH OR DINNER ENTREE when a second LUNCH OR DINNER ENTREE of equal or greater value is purchased.

Dine in only

valid anytime

CERRO GRANDE
MEXICAN GRILL & CANTINA

A251

Valid now thru November 1, 2006

Not valid holidays & subject to Rules of Use. Not valid with other discount offers, unless specified. Coupon VOID if purchased, sold or bartered. Discounts exclude tax, tip and/or alcohol, where applicable.

O's Place

6723 Richmond Hwy
Alexandria, VA
(703)765-0932

- Welcome to O's Place, Alexandria'a newest restaurant
- "The old Mustache Cafe"
- Our entrees & side dishes will leave your mouth watering
- Don't forget to save room for dessert
- O's Place is the perfect place for rehearsal dinners, wedding receptions, office parties & all types of reunions

Bonus Discounts at
entertainment.com

entertainment.
entertainment.com

Up To $16.00 Value

Enjoy one complimentary LUNCH OR DINNER ENTREE when a second LUNCH OR DINNER ENTREE of equal or greater value is purchased.

valid anytime

O's Place
HALAL CHINESE CUISINE

A252

Valid now thru November 1, 2006

Not valid holidays & subject to Rules of Use. Not valid with other discount offers, unless specified. Coupon VOID if purchased, sold or bartered. Discounts exclude tax, tip and/or alcohol, where applicable.

Lebanese Village

549 S. 23rd St.
(Crystal City)
Arlington, VA
(703)271-9194

00625600

CERRO GRANDE
MEXICAN GRILL & CANTINA

6705 Springfield Mall
(Across from the DMV)
Springfield, VA
(703)924-0856

Offers not valid holidays and subject to Rules of Use
Tipping should be 15% to 20% of the total bill before discount
00574532

O's Place
HALAL CHINESE CUISINE

6723 Richmond Hwy
Alexandria, VA
(703)765-0932

Offers not valid holidays and subject to Rules of Use
Tipping should be 15% to 20% of the total bill before discount
00549057

Taj Palace

13635 Lee Jackson Memorial Hwy.
Chantilly, VA
(703)222-3711

- Taj Palace invites you to a wonderful dining experience right in the middle of Fairfax County
- Join us with your family, friends & guests to enjoy the exotic dishes of India
- Open daily

Bonus Discounts at
entertainment.com

entertainment.
entertainment.com

Up To $12.00 Value

Taj Palace

Indian Restaurant

Enjoy one complimentary LUNCH OR DINNER ENTREE when a second LUNCH OR DINNER ENTREE of equal or greater value is purchased.

Buffet excluded; Dine in only

valid anytime

A253

Valid now thru November 1, 2006

Not valid holidays & subject to Rules of Use. Not valid with other discount offers, unless specified. Coupon VOID if purchased, sold or bartered. Discounts exclude tax, tip and/or alcohol, where applicable.

National Diner

2650 Jefferson Davis Hwy.
Arlington, VA
(703)684-7200

- Enjoy a blast from the past - the 1950's.
- Try our shakes, malts, burgers & fries, a home-style cooked dinner, or breakfast served all day.
- Whatever your care, you can sure get it here at the National Diner.
- Don't forget about our weekend breakfast buffet served until 2 p.m. every Saturday & Sunday
- We are open daily from 6 a.m. - 11 p.m.

Bonus Discounts at
entertainment.com

entertainment.
entertainment.com

Up To $14.00 Value

Enjoy one complimentary LUNCH OR DINNER ENTREE when a second LUNCH OR DINNER ENTREE of equal or greater value is purchased.

Dining room only

valid anytime

National Diner

the best of America

A254

Valid now thru November 1, 2006

Not valid holidays & subject to Rules of Use. Not valid with other discount offers, unless specified. Coupon VOID if purchased, sold or bartered. Discounts exclude tax, tip and/or alcohol, where applicable.

Fast Eddie's Billiard Cafe

See reverse side for locations

- A classic billiard parlour
- Gourmet deli sandwiches, pizzas, salads & subs
- 17 Brunswick tables-2 Dartboards-70 ft. bar
- 14 drafts
- Ongoing leagues & tournaments

Bonus Discounts at
entertainment.com

entertainment.
entertainment.com

Up To $6.00 Value

FAST EDDIE'S

BILLIARD CAFE

Enjoy one complimentary MENU ITEM when a second MENU ITEM of equal or greater value is purchased.

valid anytime

www.fasteddies.com

A255

Valid now thru November 1, 2006

Not valid holidays & subject to Rules of Use. Not valid with other discount offers, unless specified. Coupon VOID if purchased, sold or bartered. Discounts exclude tax, tip and/or alcohol, where applicable.

Taj Palace

Indian Restaurant

13635 Lee Jackson Memorial Hwy.
(next to Food Lion)
Chantilly, VA
(703)222-3711

00658834

entertainment.com

00658834

National Diner

the best of America

2650 Jefferson Davis Hwy.
Arlington, VA
(703)684-7200

Offers not valid holidays and subject to Rules of Use
Tipping should be 15% to 20% of the total bill before discount
00480130

entertainment.com

00480130

Fast Eddie's

Billiard Cafe

9687 Lee Highway
Fairfax, VA
(703)385-7529

7255 Commerce St.
Springfield, VA
(703)912-7529

00003715

entertainment.com

00003715

Family Restaurants, Informal Dining & Carryout Index

kids **Great Place for Kids!** NEW **New Merchants Added This Year**

Family Restaurants, Informal Dining & Carryout Index

kids **Great Place for Kids!** NEW **New Merchants Added This Year**

Domino's Pizza

Valid at All Participating Greater Washington DC, Maryland & Northern Virginia Area Locations

Bonus Discounts at entertainment.com

entertainment. entertainment.com

great place for kids

ONE LARGE PIZZA

Enjoy one complimentary LARGE PIZZA when a second LARGE PIZZA of equal or greater value is purchased.

Carry out only

valid anytime

Not valid with any other discount offer

Domino's Pizza®

www.dominos.com

B1

Valid now thru November 1, 2006

Not valid holidays & subject to Rules of Use. Not valid with other discount offers, unless specified. Coupon VOID if purchased, sold or bartered. Discounts exclude tax, tip and/or alcohol, where applicable.

Domino's Pizza

Valid at All Participating Greater Washington DC, Maryland & Northern Virginia Area Locations

Bonus Discounts at entertainment.com

entertainment. entertainment.com

great place for kids

ONE LARGE PIZZA

Enjoy one complimentary LARGE PIZZA when a second LARGE PIZZA of equal or greater value is purchased.

Carry out only

valid anytime

Not valid with any other discount offer

Domino's Pizza®

www.dominos.com

B2

Valid now thru November 1, 2006

Not valid holidays & subject to Rules of Use. Not valid with other discount offers, unless specified. Coupon VOID if purchased, sold or bartered. Discounts exclude tax, tip and/or alcohol, where applicable.

Domino's Pizza

Valid at All Participating Greater Washington DC, Maryland & Northern Virginia Area Locations

Bonus Discounts at entertainment.com

entertainment. entertainment.com

great place for kids

ONE LARGE PIZZA

Enjoy one complimentary LARGE PIZZA when a second LARGE PIZZA of equal or greater value is purchased.

Carry out only

valid anytime

Not valid with any other discount offer

Domino's Pizza®

www.dominos.com

B3

Valid now thru November 1, 2006

Not valid holidays & subject to Rules of Use. Not valid with other discount offers, unless specified. Coupon VOID if purchased, sold or bartered. Discounts exclude tax, tip and/or alcohol, where applicable.

Valid at All Participating Greater Washington DC, Maryland & Northern Virginia Area Locations

entertainment.com

00665455

00665455

Valid at All Participating Greater Washington DC, Maryland & Northern Virginia Area Locations

entertainment.com

00665455

00665455

Valid at All Participating Greater Washington DC, Maryland & Northern Virginia Area Locations

entertainment.com

00665455

00665455

KFC
Valid at All Participating Locations

Bonus Discounts at entertainment.com

entertainment. entertainment.com

great place for kids

ONE CHICKEN SANDWICH

Enjoy one complimentary CHICKEN SANDWICH when a second CHICKEN SANDWICH of equal or greater value is purchased.

Tax extra

valid anytime

One coupon per customer per visit; Not valid with special offers; No reproductions accepted

B4

Valid now thru November 1, 2006

Not valid holidays & subject to Rules of Use. Not valid with other discount offers, unless specified. Coupon VOID if purchased, sold or bartered. Discounts exclude tax, tip and/or alcohol, where applicable.

KFC
Valid at All Participating Locations

Bonus Discounts at entertainment.com

entertainment. entertainment.com

great place for kids

ONE CHICKEN SANDWICH

Enjoy one complimentary CHICKEN SANDWICH when a second CHICKEN SANDWICH of equal or greater value is purchased.

Tax extra

valid anytime

One coupon per customer per visit; Not valid with special offers; No reproductions accepted

B5

Valid now thru November 1, 2006

Not valid holidays & subject to Rules of Use. Not valid with other discount offers, unless specified. Coupon VOID if purchased, sold or bartered. Discounts exclude tax, tip and/or alcohol, where applicable.

KFC
Valid at All Participating Locations

Bonus Discounts at entertainment.com

entertainment. entertainment.com

great place for kids

ONE TWISTER

Enjoy one complimentary TWISTER when a second TWISTER of equal or greater value is purchased.

Tax extra

valid anytime

One coupon per customer per visit; Not valid with special offers; No reproductions accepted

B6

Valid now thru November 1, 2006

Not valid holidays & subject to Rules of Use. Not valid with other discount offers, unless specified. Coupon VOID if purchased, sold or bartered. Discounts exclude tax, tip and/or alcohol, where applicable.

Valid at All Participating Locations

00398831

entertainment.com

00398831

Valid at All Participating Locations

00398831

entertainment.com

00398831

Valid at All Participating Locations

00512212

entertainment.com

00512212

Subway

See reverse side for locations

- Try one of our Atkins wraps
- We have made to order fresh salads
- Visit one of our 325 locations in the Washington DC Metro area

Bonus Discounts at entertainment.com

entertainment.
entertainment.com

$1.00 OR $.50

Enjoy $1.00 off any foot long sub or $.50 off any 6-inch sub.

valid anytime

SUBWAY

www.subway.com

B7

Valid now thru November 1, 2006

Not valid holidays & subject to Rules of Use. Not valid with other discount offers, unless specified. Coupon VOID if purchased, sold or bartered. Discounts exclude tax, tip and/or alcohol, where applicable.

Subway

See reverse side for locations

- Try one of our Atkins wraps
- We have made to order fresh salads
- Visit one of our 325 locations in the Washington DC Metro area

Bonus Discounts at entertainment.com

entertainment.
entertainment.com

$1.00 OR $.50

Enjoy $1.00 off any foot long sub or $.50 off any 6-inch sub.

valid anytime

SUBWAY

www.subway.com

B8

Valid now thru November 1, 2006

Not valid holidays & subject to Rules of Use. Not valid with other discount offers, unless specified. Coupon VOID if purchased, sold or bartered. Discounts exclude tax, tip and/or alcohol, where applicable.

Subway

See reverse side for locations

- Try one of our Atkins wraps
- We have made to order fresh salads
- Visit one of our 325 locations in the Washington DC Metro area

Bonus Discounts at entertainment.com

entertainment.
entertainment.com

$1.00 OR $.50

Enjoy $1.00 off any foot long sub or $.50 off any 6-inch sub.

valid anytime

SUBWAY

www.subway.com

B9

Valid now thru November 1, 2006

Not valid holidays & subject to Rules of Use. Not valid with other discount offers, unless specified. Coupon VOID if purchased, sold or bartered. Discounts exclude tax, tip and/or alcohol, where applicable.

SUBWAY

DISTRICT OF COLUMBIA
Washington
1339 14th St. NW

1401 K St., NW

14th & Constitution Ave., NW
(American History Museum)

1666 K St., NW

1957 E St., NW

236 Massachusettes Ave., NE

3950 Minnesota Ave.

514 Rhode Island Ave., NE

MARYLAND
Bowie
4855 Glendale Rd.

Chesapeake Beach
8020 Bayside Rd.

Cresaptown
16018 McMullen Hwy.

Damascus
9870-B Main St.

Frederick
177-C Thomas Johnson Dr.

Frostburg
10701 New Georges Creek Rd., SW,Ste. 13

Gaithersburg
6 Bureau Dr.
(Diamond Sq. Shpg. Ctr.)

701 Russell Ave.

Hyattsville
7539 Landover Rd.

Laurel
9105 All Saints Blvd.

Oxen Hill
5482 St. Barnabas Rd.

Silver Spring
8395 Colesville Rd.

Tacoma Park
7056 Carroll Ave.

Thurmont
224 N. Church St., Unit K

Waldorf
158 Smallwood Village Ctr.

VIRGINIA
Annandale
3920 Bradlick Rd., Ste. K

Arlington
2154 Crystal City Plaza

2424 Wilson Blvd.

Fredericksburg
1511 Central Park Blvd.

Leesburg
653 Potomac Station Dr.

Manassas
8300 Sudley Rd.
(Manassas Mall)

McLean
6216 Old Dominion Dr.

Stafford
488 Garrisonville Rd.
(East Coast Truck Stop)

Sterling
23050 Pacific Blvd.
(Exxon Convenience Store)

Vienna
8377 Leesburg Pike

Winchester
992 Millwood Pike

WEST VIRGINIA
Martinsburg
823 Warm Spring Rd.

Shepherdstown
7670 Martinsburg Pike

Valid at All Participating Locations

00597050

entertainment.com

00597050

SUBWAY

DISTRICT OF COLUMBIA
Washington
1339 14th St. NW

1401 K St., NW

14th & Constitution Ave., NW
(American History Museum)

1666 K St., NW

1957 E St., NW

236 Massachusettes Ave., NE

3950 Minnesota Ave.

514 Rhode Island Ave., NE

MARYLAND
Bowie
4855 Glendale Rd.

Chesapeake Beach
8020 Bayside Rd.

Cresaptown
16018 McMullen Hwy.

Damascus
9870-B Main St.

Frederick
177-C Thomas Johnson Dr.

Frostburg
10701 New Georges Creek Rd., SW,Ste. 13

Gaithersburg
6 Bureau Dr.
(Diamond Sq. Shpg. Ctr.)

701 Russell Ave.

Hyattsville
7539 Landover Rd.

Laurel
9105 All Saints Blvd.

Oxen Hill
5482 St. Barnabas Rd.

Silver Spring
8395 Colesville Rd.

Tacoma Park
7056 Carroll Ave.

Thurmont
224 N. Church St., Unit K

Waldorf
158 Smallwood Village Ctr.

VIRGINIA
Annandale
3920 Bradlick Rd., Ste. K

Arlington
2154 Crystal City Plaza

2424 Wilson Blvd.

Fredericksburg
1511 Central Park Blvd.

Leesburg
653 Potomac Station Dr.

Manassas
8300 Sudley Rd.
(Manassas Mall)

McLean
6216 Old Dominion Dr.

Stafford
488 Garrisonville Rd.
(East Coast Truck Stop)

Sterling
23050 Pacific Blvd.
(Exxon Convenience Store)

Vienna
8377 Leesburg Pike

Winchester
992 Millwood Pike

WEST VIRGINIA
Martinsburg
823 Warm Spring Rd.

Shepherdstown
7670 Martinsburg Pike

Valid at All Participating Locations

00597050

entertainment.com

00597050

SUBWAY

DISTRICT OF COLUMBIA
Washington
1339 14th St. NW

1401 K St., NW

14th & Constitution Ave., NW
(American History Museum)

1666 K St., NW

1957 E St., NW

236 Massachusettes Ave., NE

3950 Minnesota Ave.

514 Rhode Island Ave., NE

MARYLAND
Bowie
4855 Glendale Rd.

Chesapeake Beach
8020 Bayside Rd.

Cresaptown
16018 McMullen Hwy.

Damascus
9870-B Main St.

Frederick
177-C Thomas Johnson Dr.

Frostburg
10701 New Georges Creek Rd., SW,Ste. 13

Gaithersburg
6 Bureau Dr.
(Diamond Sq. Shpg. Ctr.)

701 Russell Ave.

Hyattsville
7539 Landover Rd.

Laurel
9105 All Saints Blvd.

Oxen Hill
5482 St. Barnabas Rd.

Silver Spring
8395 Colesville Rd.

Tacoma Park
7056 Carroll Ave.

Thurmont
224 N. Church St., Unit K

Waldorf
158 Smallwood Village Ctr.

VIRGINIA
Annandale
3920 Bradlick Rd., Ste. K

Arlington
2154 Crystal City Plaza

2424 Wilson Blvd.

Fredericksburg
1511 Central Park Blvd.

Leesburg
653 Potomac Station Dr.

Manassas
8300 Sudley Rd.
(Manassas Mall)

McLean
6216 Old Dominion Dr.

Stafford
488 Garrisonville Rd.
(East Coast Truck Stop)

Sterling
23050 Pacific Blvd.
(Exxon Convenience Store)

Vienna
8377 Leesburg Pike

Winchester
992 Millwood Pike

WEST VIRGINIA
Martinsburg
823 Warm Spring Rd.

Shepherdstown
7670 Martinsburg Pike

Valid at All Participating Locations

00597050

entertainment.com

00597050

Boardwalk Fries

Valid at All Participating Mall Locations

- Delicious fries cooked in 100% peanut oil
- Try a variety of toppings & MCCormick® spices
- Coca Cola® beverages served
- Try our fresh-squeezed lemonade, where available
- Some locations offering hot dogs, hamburgers, buffalo wings, barbecue fish & chicken sandwiches

Bonus Discounts at entertainment.com

entertainment® entertainment.com

ONE REGULAR 12 OZ. ORDER OF BOARDWALK FRIES

Enjoy one complimentary REGULAR 12 OZ. ORDER OF BOARDWALK FRIES when a second REGULAR 12 OZ. ORDER OF BOARDWALK FRIES of equal or greater value is purchased.

valid anytime

BOARDWALK FRIES®

An Ocean Of Taste®

B10

Valid now thru November 1, 2006

Not valid holidays & subject to Rules of Use. Not valid with other discount offers, unless specified. Coupon VOID if purchased, sold or bartered. Discounts exclude tax, tip and/or alcohol, where applicable.

Boardwalk Fries

Valid at All Participating Mall Locations

- Delicious fries cooked in 100% peanut oil
- Try a variety of toppings & MCCormick® spices
- Coca Cola® beverages served
- Try our fresh-squeezed lemonade, where available
- Some locations offering hot dogs, hamburgers, buffalo wings, barbecue fish & chicken sandwiches

Bonus Discounts at entertainment.com

entertainment® entertainment.com

ONE REGULAR 12 OZ. ORDER OF BOARDWALK FRIES

Enjoy one complimentary REGULAR 12 OZ. ORDER OF BOARDWALK FRIES when a second REGULAR 12 OZ. ORDER OF BOARDWALK FRIES of equal or greater value is purchased.

valid anytime

BOARDWALK FRIES®

An Ocean Of Taste®

B11

Valid now thru November 1, 2006

Not valid holidays & subject to Rules of Use. Not valid with other discount offers, unless specified. Coupon VOID if purchased, sold or bartered. Discounts exclude tax, tip and/or alcohol, where applicable.

Boardwalk Fries

Valid at All Participating Mall Locations

- Delicious fries cooked in 100% peanut oil
- Try a variety of toppings & MCCormick® spices
- Coca Cola® beverages served
- Try our fresh-squeezed lemonade, where available
- Some locations offering hot dogs, hamburgers, buffalo wings, barbecue fish & chicken sandwiches

Bonus Discounts at entertainment.com

entertainment® entertainment.com

ONE REGULAR 12 OZ. ORDER OF BOARDWALK FRIES

Enjoy one complimentary REGULAR 12 OZ. ORDER OF BOARDWALK FRIES when a second REGULAR 12 OZ. ORDER OF BOARDWALK FRIES of equal or greater value is purchased.

valid anytime

BOARDWALK FRIES®

An Ocean Of Taste®

B12

Valid now thru November 1, 2006

Not valid holidays & subject to Rules of Use. Not valid with other discount offers, unless specified. Coupon VOID if purchased, sold or bartered. Discounts exclude tax, tip and/or alcohol, where applicable.

BOARDWALK FRIES®

An Ocean Of Taste®

Valid at All Participating Mall Locations

00665643

entertainment.com

00665643

BOARDWALK FRIES®

An Ocean Of Taste®

Valid at All Participating Mall Locations

00665643

entertainment.com

00665643

BOARDWALK FRIES®

An Ocean Of Taste®

Valid at All Participating Mall Locations

00665643

entertainment.com

00665643

Roy Rogers

See reverse side for locations

- Real food
- Real choices

Bonus Discounts at entertainment.com

entertainment® entertainment.com

great place for kids

ONE BREAKFAST ITEM

Enjoy one complimentary BREAKFAST ITEM when a second BREAKFAST ITEM of equal or greater value is purchased.

valid anytime

One coupon/card per customer per visit

B13

Valid now thru November 1, 2006

Not valid holidays & subject to Rules of Use. Not valid with other discount offers, unless specified. Coupon VOID if purchased, sold or bartered. Discounts exclude tax, tip and/or alcohol, where applicable.

Roy Rogers

See reverse side for locations

- Real food
- Real choices

Bonus Discounts at entertainment.com

entertainment® entertainment.com

great place for kids

ONE COMBO

Enjoy one complimentary COMBO when a second COMBO of equal or greater value is purchased.

valid anytime

One coupon/card per customer per visit

B14

Valid now thru November 1, 2006

Not valid holidays & subject to Rules of Use. Not valid with other discount offers, unless specified. Coupon VOID if purchased, sold or bartered. Discounts exclude tax, tip and/or alcohol, where applicable.

Roy Rogers

See reverse side for locations

- Real food
- Real choices

Bonus Discounts at entertainment.com

entertainment® entertainment.com

great place for kids

ONE DESSERT

Enjoy one complimentary DESSERT when a second DESSERT of equal or greater value is purchased.

valid anytime

One coupon/card per customer per visit

B15

Valid now thru November 1, 2006

Not valid holidays & subject to Rules of Use. Not valid with other discount offers, unless specified. Coupon VOID if purchased, sold or bartered. Discounts exclude tax, tip and/or alcohol, where applicable.

Roy Rogers

1506 Belleview Blvd.
Alexandria, VA
(703)660-1264

7013-F Manchester Blvd.
Alexandria, VA
(703)719-5980

8860 Richmond Hwy.
Alexandria, VA
(703)799-0170

451 S. King St.
Leesburg, VA
(703)777-5551

540 E. Market St.
Leesburg, VA
(703)777-6322

8502 Centreville Rd.
Manassas Park, VA
(703)368-3799

00107263

entertainment.com

00107263

Roy Rogers

1506 Belleview Blvd.
Alexandria, VA
(703)660-1264

7013-F Manchester Blvd.
Alexandria, VA
(703)719-5980

8860 Richmond Hwy.
Alexandria, VA
(703)799-0170

451 S. King St.
Leesburg, VA
(703)777-5551

540 E. Market St.
Leesburg, VA
(703)777-6322

8502 Centreville Rd.
Manassas Park, VA
(703)368-3799

00107264

entertainment.com

00107264

Roy Rogers

1506 Belleview Blvd.
Alexandria, VA
(703)660-1264

7013-F Manchester Blvd.
Alexandria, VA
(703)719-5980

8860 Richmond Hwy.
Alexandria, VA
(703)799-0170

451 S. King St.
Leesburg, VA
(703)777-5551

540 E. Market St.
Leesburg, VA
(703)777-6322

8502 Centreville Rd.
Manassas Park, VA
(703)368-3799

00107278

entertainment.com

00107278

Arby's

See reverse side for locations

- Tender roast beef piled high on a bun

Bonus Discounts at entertainment.com

great place for kids

ONE BEEF 'N CHEDDAR SANDWICH®

Enjoy one complimentary BEEF 'N CHEDDAR® SANDWICH when a second BEEF 'N CHEDDAR® SANDWICH of equal or greater value is purchased.

valid anytime

www.arbys.com

B16

Valid now thru November 1, 2006

Not valid holidays & subject to Rules of Use. Not valid with other discount offers, unless specified. Coupon VOID if purchased, sold or bartered. Discounts exclude tax, tip and/or alcohol, where applicable.

Arby's

See reverse side for locations

- Curly or regular fries available to compliment any sandwich

Bonus Discounts at entertainment.com

great place for kids

ONE CHICKEN BREAST FILLET ® SANDWICH

Enjoy one complimentary CHICKEN BREAST FILLET ® SANDWICH when a second CHICKEN BREAST FILLET ® SANDWICH of equal or greater value is purchased.

valid anytime

www.arbys.com

B17

Valid now thru November 1, 2006

Not valid holidays & subject to Rules of Use. Not valid with other discount offers, unless specified. Coupon VOID if purchased, sold or bartered. Discounts exclude tax, tip and/or alcohol, where applicable.

Arby's

See reverse side for locations

- The original

Bonus Discounts at entertainment.com

great place for kids

ONE REGULAR ® ROAST BEEF SANDWICH

Enjoy one complimentary complimentry REGULAR ® ROAST BEEF SANDWICH when a second complimentry REGULAR ® ROAST BEEF SANDWICH is purchased.

valid anytime

B18

Valid now thru November 1, 2006

Not valid holidays & subject to Rules of Use. Not valid with other discount offers, unless specified. Coupon VOID if purchased, sold or bartered. Discounts exclude tax, tip and/or alcohol, where applicable.

DISTRICT OF COLUMBIA
Washington
3222 M St.
(202)338-4751

MARYLAND
Beltsville
10425 Baltimore Ave.
(301)937-0023

Jessup
7410 Assateague Dr.
(301)621-1146

Laurel
225 Gorman Ave.
(301)953-1560

Rockville
11710 Rockville Pike
(301)468-6981

Upper Marlboro
4800 Southeast Crain Hwy.
(301)574-1062

VIRGINIA
Alexandria
4815 Beauregard St.
(703)354-4988

Great Falls
9911 Georgetown Pike
(703)757-8115

Manassas
10831 Promenade Ln.
(703)330-6183

9874 Liberia Ave.
(703)330-6183

Merrifield
8127 Lee Hwy.
(703)961-8500

Springfield
Springfield Mall
(703)971-6808

These Locations Coming Soon 6424 Baltimore National Pike, Catonsville, MD 4400 Chantilly Place Shpg. Ctr. Chantilly, VA

00597971

entertainment.com

00597971

DISTRICT OF COLUMBIA
Washington
3222 M St.
(202)338-4751

MARYLAND
Beltsville
10425 Baltimore Ave.
(301)937-0023

Jessup
7410 Assateague Dr.
(301)621-1146

Laurel
225 Gorman Ave.
(301)953-1560

Rockville
11710 Rockville Pike
(301)468-6981

Upper Marlboro
4800 Southeast Crain Hwy.
(301)574-1062

VIRGINIA
Alexandria
4815 Beauregard St.
(703)354-4988

Great Falls
9911 Georgetown Pike
(703)757-8115

Manassas
10831 Promenade Ln.
(703)330-6183

9874 Liberia Ave.
(703)330-6183

Merrifield
8127 Lee Hwy.
(703)961-8500

Springfield
Springfield Mall
(703)971-6808

These Locations Coming Soon 6424 Baltimore National Pike, Catonsville, MD 4400 Chantilly Place Shpg. Ctr. Chantilly, VA

00597984

entertainment.com

00597984

DISTRICT OF COLUMBIA
Washington
3222 M St.
(202)338-4751

MARYLAND
Beltsville
10425 Baltimore Ave.
(301)937-0023

Jessup
7410 Assateague Dr.
(301)621-1146

Laurel
225 Gorman Ave.
(301)953-1560

Rockville
11710 Rockville Pike
(301)468-6981

Upper Marlboro
4800 Southeast Crain Hwy.
(301)574-1062

VIRGINIA
Alexandria
4815 Beauregard St.
(703)354-4988

Great Falls
9911 Georgetown Pike
(703)757-8115

Manassas
10831 Promenade Ln.
(703)330-6183

9874 Liberia Ave.
(703)330-6183

Merrifield
8127 Lee Hwy.
(703)961-8500

Springfield
Springfield Mall
(703)971-6808

These Locations Coming Soon 6424 Baltimore National Pike, Catonsville, MD 4400 Chantilly Place Shpg. Ctr. Chantilly, VA

00597977

entertainment.com

00597977

Cici's Pizza

See reverse side for locations

- All you can eat buffet only $4.49
- Featuring 16 kinds of pizza, pasta, salad & dessert
- Take a pizza to go
- The best pizza value any where

Bonus Discounts at entertainment.com

entertainment. entertainment.com

ONE PIZZA

Enjoy any one complimentary PIZZA when a second PIZZA of equal or greater value is purchased.

Cici's Pizza

valid anytime

B19

Valid now thru November 1, 2006

Not valid holidays & subject to Rules of Use. Not valid with other discount offers, unless specified. Coupon VOID if purchased, sold or bartered. Discounts exclude tax, tip and/or alcohol, where applicable.

Cici's Pizza

See reverse side for locations

- All you can eat buffet only $4.49
- Featuring 16 kinds of pizza, pasta, salad & dessert
- Take a pizza to go
- The best pizza value any where

Bonus Discounts at entertainment.com

entertainment. entertainment.com

ONE BUFFET

Enjoy one complimentary BUFFET when a second BUFFET of equal or greater value is purchased.

Cici's Pizza

valid anytime

B20

Valid now thru November 1, 2006

Not valid holidays & subject to Rules of Use. Not valid with other discount offers, unless specified. Coupon VOID if purchased, sold or bartered. Discounts exclude tax, tip and/or alcohol, where applicable.

Vocelli Pizza

See reverse side for locations

- To make great tasting pizza, you have to start fresh
- Our pizzas are made with our traditional dough, our signature sauce & covered with 100% real cheese
- Give us a try today
- www.vocellipizza.com

Bonus Discounts at entertainment.com

entertainment. entertainment.com

ONE PIZZA

Enjoy any one complimentary PIZZA when a second PIZZA of equal or greater value is purchased.

Carry out only

VOCELLI™ PIZZA DELIVERING GREAT TASTE

valid anytime

B21

Valid now thru November 1, 2006

Not valid holidays & subject to Rules of Use. Not valid with other discount offers, unless specified. Coupon VOID if purchased, sold or bartered. Discounts exclude tax, tip and/or alcohol, where applicable.

Cici's Pizza

MARYLAND

Gaithersburg
642 Quince Orchard Rd.
(301)869-1006

Glen Burnie
26 Mountain Rd.
(410)760-9200

Oxon Hill
6171 Oxon Hill Rd.
(301)749-4001

Rockville
12111 Rockville Pike
(301)770-4600

VIRGINIA

Chantilly
14400 Chantilly Crossing Ln.
(703)961-9100

Falls Church
3520 S. Jefferson St.
(703)845-4900

Fredericksburg
2005 - A Plank Rd.
(540)310-4151

Stafford
50 Dunn Dr. #123
(540)659-3434

Coming soon to: Dale City, Manassas & Central Park

00107006

entertainment.com

00107006

Cici's Pizza

MARYLAND

Gaithersburg
642 Quince Orchard Rd.
(301)869-1006

Glen Burnie
26 Mountain Rd.
(410)760-9200

Oxon Hill
6171 Oxon Hill Rd.
(301)749-4001

Rockville
12111 Rockville Pike
(301)770-4600

VIRGINIA

Chantilly
14400 Chantilly Crossing Ln.
(703)961-9100

Falls Church
3520 S. Jefferson St.
(703)845-4900

Fredericksburg
2005 - A Plank Rd.
(540)310-4151

Stafford
50 Dunn Dr. #123
(540)659-3434

Coming soon to: Dale City, Manassas & Central Park

00107007

entertainment.com

00107007

Vocelli Pizza

Delivering Great Taste

Alexandria
6126 Rose Hill Dr.
(Rose Hill Shpg. Ctr.)
(703)921-9214

Ashburn
44110 Ashburn Village Blvd. 192
(703)729-2929

Burke
5765 - H. Burke Ctr.Parkway
(703)426-1600

Centreville
5663 Stone Rd.
(Sully Station)
(703)802-0100

Herndon
3065-T Centreville Rd.
(McLearnen Shpg. Ctr.)
(800)707-1111

Manassas
8671 Sudley Rd.
(800)707-1111

Reston
12026 N. Shore Dr.
(Tall Oaks Shpg. Ctr.)
(800)707-1111

Sterling
46005 Regal Plaza
(Countryside)
(703)406-1770

00102959

entertainment.com

00102959

Blimpie Subs & Salads

Valid at All Participating Baltimore-Washington DC Metro Area Locations

- America's best dressed sandwich
- Select from a variety of quality meats, cheeses, garden fresh vegetables & salads
- All our sandwiches are sliced fresh to order & served on delicious fresh baked bread
- 3 foot & 6 foot party subs available
- Come in & freshen up at Blimpie
- Open daily

Bonus Discounts at entertainment.com

entertainment. entertainment.com

great place for kids

ONE 6" SUB

Blimpie SUBS & SALADS

Enjoy one complimentary 6" Sub when a second 6" Sub of equal or greater value is purchased.

valid anytime

One coupon per customer per visit

www.blimpie.com

B22

Valid now thru November 1, 2006

Not valid holidays & subject to Rules of Use. Not valid with other discount offers, unless specified. Coupon VOID if purchased, sold or bartered. Discounts exclude tax, tip and/or alcohol, where applicable.

Blimpie Subs & Salads

Valid at All Participating Baltimore-Washington DC Metro Area Locations

- America's best dressed sandwich
- Select from a variety of quality meats, cheeses, garden fresh vegetables & salads
- All our sandwiches are sliced fresh to order & served on delicious fresh baked bread
- 3 foot & 6 foot party subs available
- Come in & freshen up at Blimpie
- Open daily

Bonus Discounts at entertainment.com

entertainment. entertainment.com

great place for kids

ONE 6" SUB

Blimpie SUBS & SALADS

Enjoy one complimentary 6" Sub when a second 6" Sub of equal or greater value is purchased.

valid anytime

One coupon per customer per visit

www.blimpie.com

B23

Valid now thru November 1, 2006

Not valid holidays & subject to Rules of Use. Not valid with other discount offers, unless specified. Coupon VOID if purchased, sold or bartered. Discounts exclude tax, tip and/or alcohol, where applicable.

Blimpie Subs & Salads

Valid at All Participating Baltimore-Washington DC Metro Area Locations

- America's best dressed sandwich
- Select from a variety of quality meats, cheeses, garden fresh vegetables & salads
- All our sandwiches are sliced fresh to order & served on delicious fresh baked bread
- 3 foot & 6 foot party subs available
- Come in & freshen up at Blimpie
- Open daily

Bonus Discounts at entertainment.com

entertainment. entertainment.com

great place for kids

ONE 6" SUB

Blimpie SUBS & SALADS

Enjoy one complimentary 6" Sub when a second 6" Sub of equal or greater value is purchased.

valid anytime

One coupon per customer per visit

www.blimpie.com

B24

Valid now thru November 1, 2006

Not valid holidays & subject to Rules of Use. Not valid with other discount offers, unless specified. Coupon VOID if purchased, sold or bartered. Discounts exclude tax, tip and/or alcohol, where applicable.

SUBS & SALADS

Valid at All Participating Baltimore-Washington DC Metro Area Locations

00397766

entertainment.com

00397766

SUBS & SALADS

Valid at All Participating Baltimore-Washington DC Metro Area Locations

00397766

entertainment.com

00397766

SUBS & SALADS

Valid at All Participating Baltimore-Washington DC Metro Area Locations

00397766

entertainment.com

00397766

Popeyes Chicken and Biscuits

Valid at all Participating Northern Virginia, Washington, DC & Maryland Area Popeyes

- All dinners served with buttermilk biscuits & your choice of either red beans & rice, Cajun battered french fries, Cajun rice, or mashed potatoes with Cajun gravy or cole slaw

Bonus Discounts at entertainment.com

entertainment® entertainment.com

great place for kids

11 PIECES OF CHICKEN (MIXED)

Enjoy 11 complimentary PIECES OF CHICKEN (MIXED)(MILD OR SPICY) when 11 MIXED PIECES OF CHICKEN are purchased at $15.99 (plus tax).

valid anytime

Present coupon when ordering; One coupon per customer per visit; Void where prohibited; Not valid with any other offer; Good at participating Popeyes only; ©2005 AFC Enterprises®, Inc.

Popeyes®

www.popeyeschicken.com

B25

Valid now thru November 1, 2006

Not valid holidays & subject to Rules of Use. Not valid with other discount offers, unless specified. Coupon VOID if purchased, sold or bartered. Discounts exclude tax, tip and/or alcohol, where applicable.

Popeyes Chicken and Biscuits

Valid at all Participating Northern Virginia, Washington, DC & Maryland Area Popeyes

- All dinners served with buttermilk biscuits & your choice of either red beans & rice, Cajun battered french fries, Cajun rice, or mashed potatoes with Cajun gravy or cole slaw

Bonus Discounts at entertainment.com

entertainment® entertainment.com

great place for kids

11 PIECES OF CHICKEN (MIXED)

Enjoy 11 complimentary PIECES OF CHICKEN (MIXED)(MILD OR SPICY) when 11 MIXED PIECES OF CHICKEN are purchased at $15.99 (plus tax).

valid anytime

Present coupon when ordering; One coupon per customer per visit; Void where prohibited; Not valid with any other offer; Good at participating Popeyes only; ©2005 AFC Enterprises®, Inc.

Popeyes®

www.popeyeschicken.com

B26

Valid now thru November 1, 2006

Not valid holidays & subject to Rules of Use. Not valid with other discount offers, unless specified. Coupon VOID if purchased, sold or bartered. Discounts exclude tax, tip and/or alcohol, where applicable.

Popeyes Chicken and Biscuits

Valid at all Participating Northern Virginia, Washington, DC & Maryland Area Popeyes

- All dinners served with buttermilk biscuits & your choice of either red beans & rice, Cajun battered french fries, Cajun rice, or mashed potatoes with Cajun gravy or cole slaw

Bonus Discounts at entertainment.com

entertainment® entertainment.com

great place for kids

11 PIECES OF CHICKEN (MIXED)

Enjoy 11 complimentary PIECES OF CHICKEN (MIXED)(MILD OR SPICY) when 11 MIXED PIECES OF CHICKEN are purchased at $15.99 (plus tax).

valid anytime

Present coupon when ordering; One coupon per customer per visit; Void where prohibited; Not valid with any other offer; Good at participating Popeyes only; ©2005 AFC Enterprises®, Inc.

Popeyes®

www.popeyeschicken.com

B27

Valid now thru November 1, 2006

Not valid holidays & subject to Rules of Use. Not valid with other discount offers, unless specified. Coupon VOID if purchased, sold or bartered. Discounts exclude tax, tip and/or alcohol, where applicable.

POPEYES®

Valid at all Participating Northern Virginia, Washington, DC & Maryland Area Popeyes

00510579

entertainment.com®

00510579

POPEYES®

Valid at all Participating Northern Virginia, Washington, DC & Maryland Area Popeyes

00510579

entertainment.com®

00510579

POPEYES®

Valid at all Participating Northern Virginia, Washington, DC & Maryland Area Popeyes

00510579

entertainment.com®

00510579

Jerry's Subs & Pizza

Valid at All Participating Locations

- Washington's Best Cheesesteaks
- Washington's #1 Pizza
- Over 100 locations
- See reverse side for participating locations

Bonus Discounts at entertainment.com

entertainment. entertainment.com

great place for kids

ONE SMALL CHEESE PIZZA

Enjoy one complimentary SMALL CHEESE PIZZA when a second SMALL CHEESE PIZZA of equal or greater value is purchased.

Valid at all participating locations

valid anytime

Jerry's Subs • Pizza

www.jerrysusa.com

B28

Valid now thru November 1, 2006

Not valid holidays & subject to Rules of Use. Not valid with other discount offers, unless specified. Coupon VOID if purchased, sold or bartered. Discounts exclude tax, tip and/or alcohol, where applicable.

Jerry's Subs & Pizza

Valid at All Participating Locations

- Washington's Best Cheesesteaks
- Washington's #1 Pizza
- Over 100 locations
- See reverse side for participating locations

Bonus Discounts at entertainment.com

entertainment. entertainment.com

great place for kids

ONE SMALL CHEESE PIZZA

Enjoy one complimentary SMALL CHEESE PIZZA when a second SMALL CHEESE PIZZA of equal or greater value is purchased.

Valid at all participating locations

valid anytime

Jerry's Subs • Pizza

www.jerrysusa.com

B29

Valid now thru November 1, 2006

Not valid holidays & subject to Rules of Use. Not valid with other discount offers, unless specified. Coupon VOID if purchased, sold or bartered. Discounts exclude tax, tip and/or alcohol, where applicable.

Jerry's Subs & Pizza

Valid at All Participating Locations

- Washington's Best Cheesesteak
- Washington's #1 Pizza
- Over 100 locations
- See reverse side for participating locations

Bonus Discounts at entertainment.com

entertainment. entertainment.com

great place for kids

ONE 8" PHILLY CHEESESTEAK

Enjoy one complimentary 8" PHILLY CHEESESTEAK when a second 8" PHILLY CHEESESTEAK of equal or greater value is purchased.

Valid at all participating locations

valid anytime

Jerry's Subs • Pizza

www.jerrysusa.com

B30

Valid now thru November 1, 2006

Not valid holidays & subject to Rules of Use. Not valid with other discount offers, unless specified. Coupon VOID if purchased, sold or bartered. Discounts exclude tax, tip and/or alcohol, where applicable.

Jerry's Subs · Pizza

VIRGINIA

Alexandria
Beacon Hill
Manchester Lakes
Old Town
Pickett St.

Annandale

Arlington Courthouse

Ashburn
Ashbrook Commons
Old Ashburn Square

Burke

Chantilly

Dumfries

Fairfax

Falls Church
Bailey's Crossroads
Broaddale
Idylwood
Seven Corners

Herndon

Manassas Parkridge

Oakton

Reston

Springfield Mall

Stafford

Sterling Plaza

Sully Plaza

Vienna

Warrenton

Woodbridge
Dale City
Lake Ridge
Potomac Mills

MARYLAND

Annapolis

AspenHill

Bel Air

Beltsville
Beltsville
Cherry Hill

Cabin John

Capitol Heights

Clinton

College Park

Damascus

Dunkirk

Eldersburg

Ellicott City

Forestville

Frederick
Frederick
Rose Hill Plaza

Gaithersburg
Flower Hill
Gaithersburg
Kentlands
Shady Grove

Germantown

Golden Ring

Hyattsville

Jessup

Kettering

LaVale

Lanham

Laurel
Fort Meade Rd.
Laurel Pond

Olney

Owen Brown

Patuxent Plaza

Rockville
Fallsgrove
Nicholson Ln.
Rockville

Silver Spring
16th St.
Fenton St.
Four Corners

Sumner Place

Temple Hills

Towson

Upper Marlboro

Waldorf

White Flint Mall

Coming Soon
Virgina:
Gainsville
Patent & TrademarkOffice
Maryland:
Adelphi
Clarksburg
Crofton
LaPlata
Prince Frederick
Randallstown

00046542

entertainment.com

00046542

Jerry's Subs · Pizza

VIRGINIA

Alexandria
Beacon Hill
Manchester Lakes
Old Town
Pickett St.

Annandale

Arlington Courthouse

Ashburn
Ashbrook Commons
Old Ashburn Square

Burke

Chantilly

Dumfries

Fairfax

Falls Church
Bailey's Crossroads
Broaddale
Idylwood
Seven Corners

Herndon

Manassas Parkridge

Oakton

Reston

Springfield Mall

Stafford

Sterling Plaza

Sully Plaza

Vienna

Warrenton

Woodbridge
Dale City
Lake Ridge
Potomac Mills

MARYLAND

Annapolis

AspenHill

Bel Air

Beltsville
Beltsville
Cherry Hill

Cabin John

Capitol Heights

Clinton

College Park

Damascus

Dunkirk

Eldersburg

Ellicott City

Forestville

Frederick
Frederick
Rose Hill Plaza

Gaithersburg
Flower Hill
Gaithersburg
Kentlands
Shady Grove

Germantown

Golden Ring

Hyattsville

Jessup

Kettering

LaVale

Lanham

Laurel
Fort Meade Rd.
Laurel Pond

Olney

Owen Brown

Patuxent Plaza

Rockville
Fallsgrove
Nicholson Ln.
Rockville

Silver Spring
16th St.
Fenton St.
Four Corners

Sumner Place

Temple Hills

Towson

Upper Marlboro

Waldorf

White Flint Mall

Coming Soon
Virgina:
Gainsville
Patent & TrademarkOffice
Maryland:
Adelphi
Clarksburg
Crofton
LaPlata
Prince Frederick
Randallstown

00046542

entertainment.com

00046542

Jerry's Subs · Pizza

VIRGINIA

Alexandria
Beacon Hill
Manchester Lakes
Old Town
Pickett St.

Annandale

Arlington Courthouse

Ashburn
Ashbrook Commons
Old Ashburn Square

Burke

Chantilly

Dumfries

Fairfax

Falls Church
Bailey's Crossroads
Broaddale
Idylwood
Seven Corners

Herndon

Manassas Parkridge

Oakton

Reston

Springfield Mall

Stafford

Sterling Plaza

Sully Plaza

Vienna

Warrenton

Woodbridge
Dale City
Lake Ridge
Potomac Mills

MARYLAND

Annapolis

AspenHill

Bel Air

Beltsville
Beltsville
Cherry Hill

Cabin John

Capitol Heights

Clinton

College Park

Damascus

Dunkirk

Eldersburg

Ellicott City

Forestville

Frederick
Frederick
Rose Hill Plaza

Gaithersburg
Flower Hill
Gaithersburg
Kentlands
Shady Grove

Germantown

Golden Ring

Hyattsville

Jessup

Kettering

LaVale

Lanham

Laurel
Fort Meade Rd.
Laurel Pond

Olney

Owen Brown

Patuxent Plaza

Rockville
Fallsgrove
Nicholson Ln.
Rockville

Silver Spring
16th St.
Fenton St.
Four Corners

Sumner Place

Temple Hills

Towson

Upper Marlboro

Waldorf

White Flint Mall

Coming Soon
Virgina:
Gainsville
Patent & TrademarkOffice
Maryland:
Adelphi
Clarksburg
Crofton
LaPlata
Prince Frederick
Randallstown

00046560

entertainment.com

00046560

entertainment®
entertainment.com

great place for kids

6 DONUTS

Dunkin' Donuts

See reverse side for locations

Enjoy 6 FREE DONUTS when 6 DONUTS of equal or greater value are purchased.

valid anytime

DUNKIN' DONUTS®

www.dunkindonuts.com

B31

Valid now thru November 1, 2006

Not valid holidays & subject to Rules of Use. Not valid with other discount offers, unless specified. Coupon VOID if purchased, sold or bartered. Discounts exclude tax, tip and/or alcohol, where applicable.

Bonus Discounts at entertainment.com

entertainment®
entertainment.com

great place for kids

6 DONUTS

Dunkin' Donuts

See reverse side for locations

Enjoy 6 FREE DONUTS when 6 DONUTS of equal or greater value are purchased.

valid anytime

DUNKIN' DONUTS®

www.dunkindonuts.com

B32

Valid now thru November 1, 2006

Not valid holidays & subject to Rules of Use. Not valid with other discount offers, unless specified. Coupon VOID if purchased, sold or bartered. Discounts exclude tax, tip and/or alcohol, where applicable.

Bonus Discounts at entertainment.com

entertainment®
entertainment.com

great place for kids

$1.00 Value

Dunkin' Donuts

See reverse side for locations

Enjoy $1.00 off your purchase of 50-ct. MUNCHKINS DONUT HOLE TREATS.

valid anytime

DUNKIN' DONUTS®

www.dunkindonuts.com

B33

Valid now thru November 1, 2006

Not valid holidays & subject to Rules of Use. Not valid with other discount offers, unless specified. Coupon VOID if purchased, sold or bartered. Discounts exclude tax, tip and/or alcohol, where applicable.

Bonus Discounts at entertainment.com

DUNKIN' DONUTS®

1084 Braddock Rd.
Fairfax, VA
(703)691-4090

13061 Lee Jackson Memorial Hwy.
Fairfax, VA
(703)631-4503

208 Elden St.
Herndon, VA
(703)925-9621

8985 Centreville Rd.
Manassas, VA
(703)393-0010

00633720

entertainment.com

00633720

DUNKIN' DONUTS®

1084 Braddock Rd.
Fairfax, VA
(703)691-4090

13061 Lee Jackson Memorial Hwy.
Fairfax, VA
(703)631-4503

208 Elden St.
Herndon, VA
(703)925-9621

8985 Centreville Rd.
Manassas, VA
(703)393-0010

00633720

entertainment.com

00633720

DUNKIN' DONUTS®

1084 Braddock Rd.
Fairfax, VA
(703)691-4090

13061 Lee Jackson Memorial Hwy.
Fairfax, VA
(703)631-4503

208 Elden St.
Herndon, VA
(703)925-9621

8985 Centreville Rd.
Manassas, VA
(703)393-0010

00634745

entertainment.com

00634745

Wawa

Valid at All Participating Locations

- Large fresh food selection including Wawa brands
- Built-to-order hoagies in 4 sizes
- Award winning fresh brewed coffee
- Wawa brand juices & teas
- Ready-to-go salads, fresh fruits & produce
- Ongoing commitment to communities through a variety of programs

Bonus Discounts at entertainment.com

entertainment.
entertainment.com

ONE 16 OZ. WAWA COFFEE OR HOT BEVERAGE

Enjoy one complimentary 16 OZ. WAWA COFFEE OR HOT BEVERAGE when a second 16 OZ. WAWA COFFEE OR HOT BEVERAGE of equal or greater value is purchased.

valid anytime

Wawa®

www.wawa.com

B34

Valid now thru November 1, 2006

Not valid holidays & subject to Rules of Use. Not valid with other discount offers, unless specified. Coupon VOID if purchased, sold or bartered. Discounts exclude tax, tip and/or alcohol, where applicable.

Wawa

Valid at All Participating Locations

- Large fresh food selection including Wawa brands
- Built-to-order hoagies in 4 sizes
- Award winning fresh brewed coffee
- Wawa brand juices & teas
- Ready-to-go salads, fresh fruits & produce
- Ongoing commitment to communities through a variety of programs

Bonus Discounts at entertainment.com

entertainment.
entertainment.com

ONE 16 OZ. WAWA ICED TEA OR FRUIT DRINK

Enjoy one complimentary 16 OZ. WAWA ICED TEA OR FRUIT DRINK when a second 16 OZ. WAWA ICED TEA OR FRUIT DRINK of equal or greater value is purchased.

valid anytime

Wawa®

www.wawa.com

B35

Valid now thru November 1, 2006

Not valid holidays & subject to Rules of Use. Not valid with other discount offers, unless specified. Coupon VOID if purchased, sold or bartered. Discounts exclude tax, tip and/or alcohol, where applicable.

Wawa

Valid at All Participating Locations

- Large fresh food selection including Wawa brands
- Built-to-order hoagies in 4 sizes
- Award winning fresh brewed coffee
- Wawa brand juices & teas
- Ready-to-go salads, fresh fruits & produce
- Ongoing commitment to communities through a variety of programs

Bonus Discounts at entertainment.com

entertainment.
entertainment.com

ONE WAWA WRAP

Enjoy one complimentary WAWA WRAP when a second WAWA WRAP of equal or greater value is purchased.

valid anytime

Wawa®

www.wawa.com

B36

Valid now thru November 1, 2006

Not valid holidays & subject to Rules of Use. Not valid with other discount offers, unless specified. Coupon VOID if purchased, sold or bartered. Discounts exclude tax, tip and/or alcohol, where applicable.

4 26191 00499 1

Valid at All Participating Locations

00596069

entertainment.com

00596069

4 26191 00498 4

Valid at All Participating Locations

00596075

entertainment.com

00596075

4 26191 00497 7

Valid at All Participating Locations

00596079

entertainment.com

00596079

Wawa

Valid at All Participating Locations

- Large fresh food selection including Wawa brands
- Built-to-order hoagies in 4 sizes
- Award winning fresh brewed coffee
- Wawa brand juices & teas
- Ready-to-go salads, fresh fruits & produce
- Ongoing commitment to communities through a variety of programs

Bonus Discounts at entertainment.com

entertainment. entertainment.com

ONE WAWA BREAKFAST SIZZLI

Enjoy one complimentary WAWA BREAKFAST SIZZLI when a second WAWA BREAKFAST SIZZLI of equal or greater value is purchased.

valid anytime

Wawa®

www.wawa.com

B37

Valid now thru November 1, 2006

Not valid holidays & subject to Rules of Use. Not valid with other discount offers, unless specified. Coupon VOID if purchased, sold or bartered. Discounts exclude tax, tip and/or alcohol, where applicable.

Wawa

Valid at All Participating Locations

- Large fresh food selection including Wawa brands
- Built-to-order hoagies in 4 sizes
- Award winning fresh brewed coffee
- Wawa brand juices & teas
- Ready-to-go salads, fresh fruits & produce
- Ongoing commitment to communities through a variety of programs

Bonus Discounts at entertainment.com

entertainment. entertainment.com

FREE

Enjoy one complimentary 16 OZ. WAWA ICED TEA OR FRUIT DRINK.

valid anytime

Wawa®

www.wawa.com

B38

Valid now thru November 1, 2006

Not valid holidays & subject to Rules of Use. Not valid with other discount offers, unless specified. Coupon VOID if purchased, sold or bartered. Discounts exclude tax, tip and/or alcohol, where applicable.

Wawa

Valid at All Participating Locations

- Large fresh food selection including Wawa brands
- Built-to-order hoagies in 4 sizes
- Award winning fresh brewed coffee
- Wawa brand juices & teas
- Ready-to-go salads, fresh fruits & produce
- Ongoing commitment to communities through a variety of programs

Bonus Discounts at entertainment.com

entertainment. entertainment.com

FREE

Enjoy one complimentary 16 OZ. WAWA COFFEE OR HOT BEVERAGE.

valid anytime

Wawa®

www.wawa.com

B39

Valid now thru November 1, 2006

Not valid holidays & subject to Rules of Use. Not valid with other discount offers, unless specified. Coupon VOID if purchased, sold or bartered. Discounts exclude tax, tip and/or alcohol, where applicable.

4 26191 00495 3

Valid at All Participating Locations

00596085

entertainment.com

00596085

4 26191 00496 0

Valid at All Participating Locations

00596869

entertainment.com

00596869

4 26191 00494 6

Valid at All Participating Locations

00596872

entertainment.com

00596872

On The Run

Valid at All Participating Locations

- Fast! Fresh! Friendly!
- Warm up with a delicious cup of Bengal Traders® Gourmet Coffee
- Wide range of hot beverages; hot chocolate, steamers, cappuccino & chai tea latte
- Fresh breakfast sandwiches
- Fresh delivered donuts

Bonus Discounts at entertainment.com

entertainment. entertainment.com

FREE

Enjoy one FREE 16 OZ. BENGAL TRADERS® GOURMET COFFEE.

valid anytime

Cash value 1/10 of one cent; Redeemable only at time of purchase; One coupon per purchase; Not valid with any other product or where restricted by law

On the Run

GOURMET BENGAL TRADERS COFFEES

B40

Valid now thru November 1, 2006

Not valid holidays & subject to Rules of Use. Not valid with other discount offers, unless specified. Coupon VOID if purchased, sold or bartered. Discounts exclude tax, tip and/or alcohol, where applicable.

On The Run

Valid at All Participating Locations

- Fast! Fresh! Friendly!
- Warm up with a delicious cup of Bengal Traders® Gourmet Coffee
- Wide range of hot beverages; hot chocolate, steamers, cappuccino & chai tea latte
- Fresh breakfast sandwiches
- Fresh delivered donuts

Bonus Discounts at entertainment.com

entertainment. entertainment.com

FREE

Enjoy one FREE 16 OZ. CAPPUCCINO, HOT CHOCOLATE, STEAMER or CHAI TEA LATTE.

valid anytime

Cash value 1/10 of one cent; Redeemable only at time of purchase; One coupon per purchase; Not valid with any other product or where restricted by law

On the Run

GOURMET BENGAL TRADERS COFFEES

B41

Valid now thru November 1, 2006

Not valid holidays & subject to Rules of Use. Not valid with other discount offers, unless specified. Coupon VOID if purchased, sold or bartered. Discounts exclude tax, tip and/or alcohol, where applicable.

On The Run

Valid at All Participating Locations

- Fast! Fresh! Friendly!
- Warm up with a delicious cup of Bengal Traders® Gourmet Coffee
- Wide range of hot beverages; hot chocolate, steamers, cappuccino & chai tea latte
- Fresh breakfast sandwiches
- Fresh delivered donuts

Bonus Discounts at entertainment.com

entertainment. entertainment.com

ONE 16 OZ. BENGAL TRADERS® GOURMET COFFEE

Enjoy one FREE 16 OZ. BENGAL TRADERS® GOURMET COFFEE with the purchase of any FRESH BREAKFAST SANDWICH.

valid anytime

Cash value 1/10 of one cent; Redeemable only at time of purchase; One coupon per purchase; Not valid with any other product or where restricted by law

On the Run

GOURMET BENGAL TRADERS COFFEES

B42

Valid now thru November 1, 2006

Not valid holidays & subject to Rules of Use. Not valid with other discount offers, unless specified. Coupon VOID if purchased, sold or bartered. Discounts exclude tax, tip and/or alcohol, where applicable.

0 77162 46301 1

Valid at All Participating Locations

00659933

entertainment.com

00659933

0 77162 46302 8

Valid at All Participating Locations

00659957

entertainment.com

00659957

0 77162 46304 2

Valid at All Participating Locations

00659965

entertainment.com

00659965

Sheetz

Valid at all Sheetz locations. For the location nearest you, visit www.sheetz.com

- Did you know that when you eat at Sheetz, you are dining on award winning food?
- Sheetz is the recipient of the IFMA Silver Plate Award
- Sheetz is the place for food - fast & just the way you ordered it
- At Sheetz we have fun & easy-to-use touch-screen ordering
- Just touch the items you want & your made-to-order selection is ready in minutes
- Open 24 hours a day

entertainment®
entertainment.com

ONE BURGERZ®

Enjoy one complimentary BURGERZ® when a second BURGERZ® of equal or greater value is purchased.

valid anytime

Sheetz®

www.sheetz.com

B43

Valid now thru November 1, 2006

Not valid holidays & subject to Rules of Use. Not valid with other discount offers, unless specified. Coupon VOID if purchased, sold or bartered. Discounts exclude tax, tip and/or alcohol, where applicable.

Sheetz

Valid at all Sheetz locations. For the location nearest you, visit www.sheetz.com

- Did you know that when you eat at Sheetz, you are dining on award winning food?
- Sheetz is the recipient of the IFMA Silver Plate Award
- Sheetz is the place for food - fast & just the way you ordered it
- At Sheetz we have fun & easy-to-use touch-screen ordering
- Just touch the items you want & your made-to-order selection is ready in minutes
- Open 24 hours a day

entertainment®
entertainment.com

ONE SALADZ

Enjoy one complimentary SALADZ when a second SALADZ of equal or greater value is purchased.

valid anytime

Sheetz®

www.sheetz.com

B44

Valid now thru November 1, 2006

Not valid holidays & subject to Rules of Use. Not valid with other discount offers, unless specified. Coupon VOID if purchased, sold or bartered. Discounts exclude tax, tip and/or alcohol, where applicable.

Sheetz

Valid at all Sheetz locations. For the location nearest you, visit www.sheetz.com

- Did you know that when you eat at Sheetz, you are dining on award winning food?
- Sheetz is the recipient of the IFMA Silver Plate Award
- Sheetz is the place for food - fast & just the way you ordered it
- At Sheetz we have fun & easy-to-use touch-screen ordering
- Just touch the items you want & your made-to-order selection is ready in minutes
- Open 24 hours a day

entertainment®
entertainment.com

ONE NACHOS GRANDE

Enjoy one complimentary NACHOS GRANDE when a second NACHOS GRANDE of equal or greater value is purchased.

valid anytime

Sheetz®

www.sheetz.com

B45

Valid now thru November 1, 2006

Not valid holidays & subject to Rules of Use. Not valid with other discount offers, unless specified. Coupon VOID if purchased, sold or bartered. Discounts exclude tax, tip and/or alcohol, where applicable.

Sheetz®

Valid at all Sheetz locations. For the location nearest you, visit
www.sheetz.com

00546079

entertainment.com

00546079

Sheetz®

Valid at all Sheetz locations. For the location nearest you, visit
www.sheetz.com

00546082

entertainment.com

00546082

Sheetz®

Valid at all Sheetz locations. For the location nearest you, visit
www.sheetz.com

00546102

entertainment.com

00546102

Checkers Drive-Ins

See reverse side for locations

- Experience the food & fun of the fabulous '50s
- Try our famous burgers, fries & colas
- Featuring fresh-made sandwiches, hot dogs, shakes & kid's meals
- Fast, friendly drive-thru service
- Try us & you'll know why we're famous

Bonus Discounts at entertainment.com

entertainment. entertainment.com

great place for kids

ONE CHAMP BURGER

Enjoy one complimentary CHAMP BURGER when a second CHAMP BURGER is purchased.

valid anytime

Limit one coupon per visit

Checkers BURGERS • FRIES • COLAS

FRESH. BECAUSE WE JUST MADE IT.SM

B46

Valid now thru November 1, 2006

Not valid holidays & subject to Rules of Use. Not valid with other discount offers, unless specified. Coupon VOID if purchased, sold or bartered. Discounts exclude tax, tip and/or alcohol, where applicable.

Checkers Drive-Ins

See reverse side for locations

- Experience the food & fun of the fabulous '50s
- Try our famous burgers, fries & colas
- Featuring fresh-made sandwiches, hot dogs, shakes & kid's meals
- Fast, friendly drive-thru service
- Try us & you'll know why we're famous

Bonus Discounts at entertainment.com

entertainment. entertainment.com

great place for kids

ONE CHAMP BURGER

Enjoy one complimentary CHAMP BURGER when a second CHAMP BURGER is purchased.

valid anytime

Limit one coupon per visit

Checkers BURGERS • FRIES • COLAS

FRESH. BECAUSE WE JUST MADE IT.SM

B47

Valid now thru November 1, 2006

Not valid holidays & subject to Rules of Use. Not valid with other discount offers, unless specified. Coupon VOID if purchased, sold or bartered. Discounts exclude tax, tip and/or alcohol, where applicable.

Checkers Drive-Ins

See reverse side for locations

- Experience the food & fun of the fabulous '50s
- Try our famous burgers, fries & colas
- Featuring fresh-made sandwiches, hot dogs, shakes & kid's meals
- Fast, friendly drive-thru service
- Try us & you'll know why we're famous

Bonus Discounts at entertainment.com

entertainment. entertainment.com

great place for kids

ONE CHAMP BURGER

Enjoy one complimentary CHAMP BURGER when a second CHAMP BURGER is purchased.

valid anytime

Limit one coupon per visit

Checkers BURGERS • FRIES • COLAS

FRESH. BECAUSE WE JUST MADE IT.SM

B48

Valid now thru November 1, 2006

Not valid holidays & subject to Rules of Use. Not valid with other discount offers, unless specified. Coupon VOID if purchased, sold or bartered. Discounts exclude tax, tip and/or alcohol, where applicable.

Checkers
BURGERS • FRIES • COLAS

FRESH. BECAUSE WE JUST MADE IT.℠

1417 N. Crain Hwy.
Glen Burnie, MD
(410)761-3830

6899 Baltimore Annapolis Blvd.
Linthicum, MD
(410)789-5326

8538 Liberty Rd.
Randallstown, MD
(410)521-2850

7550 Broken Branch Lane
Manassas, VA
(703)335-0084

00082513

entertainment.com

00082513

Checkers
BURGERS • FRIES • COLAS

FRESH. BECAUSE WE JUST MADE IT.℠

1417 N. Crain Hwy.
Glen Burnie, MD
(410)761-3830

6899 Baltimore Annapolis Blvd.
Linthicum, MD
(410)789-5326

8538 Liberty Rd.
Randallstown, MD
(410)521-2850

7550 Broken Branch Lane
Manassas, VA
(703)335-0084

00082513

entertainment.com

00082513

Checkers
BURGERS • FRIES • COLAS

FRESH. BECAUSE WE JUST MADE IT.℠

1417 N. Crain Hwy.
Glen Burnie, MD
(410)761-3830

6899 Baltimore Annapolis Blvd.
Linthicum, MD
(410)789-5326

8538 Liberty Rd.
Randallstown, MD
(410)521-2850

7550 Broken Branch Lane
Manassas, VA
(703)335-0084

00082513

entertainment.com

00082513

Pizza Boli's

Valid at All Participating Locations

- Pizza delights
- Pizza Boli's unique
- The vegilicious
- The meatster
- White pizza
- www.pizzabolis.com

Bonus Discounts at entertainment.com

entertainment® entertainment.com

great place for kids

PIZZA DELIGHT

Enjoy one complimentary PIZZA DELIGHT when a second PIZZA DELIGHT of equal or greater value is purchased.

Carry out only

valid anytime

Not valid with any other discounts or promotions; Present coupon/card before ordering

B49

Valid now thru November 1, 2006

Not valid holidays & subject to Rules of Use. Not valid with other discount offers, unless specified. Coupon VOID if purchased, sold or bartered. Discounts exclude tax, tip and/or alcohol, where applicable.

Pizza Boli's

Valid at All Participating Locations

- Pizza delights
- Pizza Boli's unique
- The vegilicious
- The meatster
- White pizza
- www.pizzabolis.com

Bonus Discounts at entertainment.com

entertainment® entertainment.com

great place for kids

PIZZA DELIGHT

Enjoy one complimentary PIZZA DELIGHT when a second PIZZA DELIGHT of equal or greater value is purchased.

Carry out only

valid anytime

Not valid with any other discounts or promotions; Present coupon/card before ordering

B50

Valid now thru November 1, 2006

Not valid holidays & subject to Rules of Use. Not valid with other discount offers, unless specified. Coupon VOID if purchased, sold or bartered. Discounts exclude tax, tip and/or alcohol, where applicable.

Pizza Boli's

Valid at All Participating Locations

- Pizza delights
- Pizza Boli's unique
- The vegilicious
- The meatster
- White pizza
- www.pizzabolis.com

Bonus Discounts at entertainment.com

entertainment® entertainment.com

great place for kids

PIZZA DELIGHT

Enjoy one complimentary PIZZA DELIGHT when a second PIZZA DELIGHT of equal or greater value is purchased.

Carry out only

valid anytime

Not valid with any other discounts or promotions; Present coupon/card before ordering

B51

Valid now thru November 1, 2006

Not valid holidays & subject to Rules of Use. Not valid with other discount offers, unless specified. Coupon VOID if purchased, sold or bartered. Discounts exclude tax, tip and/or alcohol, where applicable.

PIZZA BOLI'S

Valid at All Participating Locations

00548049

entertainment.com

00548049

PIZZA BOLI'S

Valid at All Participating Locations

00548049

entertainment.com

00548049

PIZZA BOLI'S

Valid at All Participating Locations

00548049

entertainment.com

00548049

Manny & Olga's Pizza

See reverse side for locations

- The difference is delicious!
- Wings, subs, salads, gyros, Greek specialties & house Italian specialties
- Call your order in advance to be ready for pick-up
- American Express, Visa & Mastercard accepted
- Open daily

great place for kids

ONE DELUXE PIZZA

Enjoy one complimentary DELUXE PIZZA when a second DELUXE PIZZA of equal or greater value is purchased.

Carry out only

valid anytime

Not valid with any other coupon or offer; Please mention coupon when placing order

Manny & Olga's PIZZA WINGS • SUBS • SALADS • GYROS

B52

Valid now thru November 1, 2006

Not valid holidays & subject to Rules of Use. Not valid with other discount offers, unless specified. Coupon VOID if purchased, sold or bartered. Discounts exclude tax, tip and/or alcohol, where applicable.

Manny & Olga's Pizza

See reverse side for locations

- The difference is delicious!
- Wings, subs, salads, gyros, Greek specialties & house Italian specialties
- Call your order in advance to be ready for pick-up
- American Express, Visa & Mastercard accepted
- Open daily

great place for kids

ONE 8" SUB

Enjoy one complimentary 8" SUB when a second 8" SUB of equal or greater value is purchased.

Carry out only

valid anytime

Not valid with any other coupon or offer; Please mention coupon when placing order

Manny & Olga's PIZZA WINGS • SUBS • SALADS • GYROS

B53

Valid now thru November 1, 2006

Not valid holidays & subject to Rules of Use. Not valid with other discount offers, unless specified. Coupon VOID if purchased, sold or bartered. Discounts exclude tax, tip and/or alcohol, where applicable.

Manny & Olga's Pizza

See reverse side for locations

- The difference is delicious!
- Wings, subs, salads, gyros, Greek specialties & house Italian specialties
- Call your order in advance to be ready for pick-up
- American Express, Visa & Mastercard accepted
- Open daily

great place for kids

ONE HOUSE SPECIALTY ENTREE

Enjoy one complimentary HOUSE SPECIALTY ENTREE when a second HOUSE SPECIALTY ENTREE of equal or greater value is purchased.

Carry out only

valid anytime

Not valid with any other coupon or offer; Please mention coupon when placing order

Manny & Olga's PIZZA WINGS • SUBS • SALADS • GYROS

B54

Valid now thru November 1, 2006

Not valid holidays & subject to Rules of Use. Not valid with other discount offers, unless specified. Coupon VOID if purchased, sold or bartered. Discounts exclude tax, tip and/or alcohol, where applicable.

Manny & Olga's PIZZA
WINGS • SUBS • SALADS • GYROS

1641 Wisconsin Ave., NW
(Georgetown)
Washington, DC
(202)337-1000

1841 14th St. NW
(Adams Morgan)
Washington, DC
(202)387-0025

12220 Rockville Pike
Rockville, MD
(301)230-4500

8107 Fenton St.
Silver Spring, MD
(301)608-8050

12134 Georgia Ave.
Wheaton, MD
(301)942-2299

00468314

entertainment.com

00468314

Manny & Olga's PIZZA
WINGS • SUBS • SALADS • GYROS

1641 Wisconsin Ave., NW
(Georgetown)
Washington, DC
(202)337-1000

1841 14th St. NW
(Adams Morgan)
Washington, DC
(202)387-0025

12220 Rockville Pike
Rockville, MD
(301)230-4500

8107 Fenton St.
Silver Spring, MD
(301)608-8050

12134 Georgia Ave.
Wheaton, MD
(301)942-2299

00468320

entertainment.com

00468320

Manny & Olga's PIZZA
WINGS • SUBS • SALADS • GYROS

1641 Wisconsin Ave., NW
(Georgetown)
Washington, DC
(202)337-1000

1841 14th St. NW
(Adams Morgan)
Washington, DC
(202)387-0025

12220 Rockville Pike
Rockville, MD
(301)230-4500

8107 Fenton St.
Silver Spring, MD
(301)608-8050

12134 Georgia Ave.
Wheaton, MD
(301)942-2299

00468322

entertainment.com

00468322

The Great Steak & Potato Co.

See reverse side for locations

- Featuring Philly style cheese steak sandwiches
- Fresh cut fries
- Gourmet baked potatoes, 6 variations to choose from
- Gourmet chicken & steak salads
- Fresh squeezed lemonade

Bonus Discounts at entertainment.com

entertainment. entertainment.com

great place for kids

ONE GREAT STEAK SANDWICH

Enjoy one complimentary GREAT STEAK SANDWICH when a second GREAT STEAK SANDWICH of equal or greater value is purchased.

valid anytime

The Great Steak & Potato Company®

America's Premier Cheesesteak®

B55

Valid now thru November 1, 2006

Not valid holidays & subject to Rules of Use. Not valid with other discount offers, unless specified. Coupon VOID if purchased, sold or bartered. Discounts exclude tax, tip and/or alcohol, where applicable.

The Great Steak & Potato Co.

See reverse side for locations

- Featuring Philly style cheese steak sandwiches
- Fresh cut fries
- Gourmet baked potatoes, 6 variations to choose from
- Gourmet chicken & steak salads
- Fresh squeezed lemonade

Bonus Discounts at entertainment.com

entertainment. entertainment.com

great place for kids

ONE KING POTATO

Enjoy one complimentary KING POTATO when a second KING POTATO of equal or greater value is purchased.

valid anytime

The Great Steak & Potato Company®

America's Premier Cheesesteak®

B56

Valid now thru November 1, 2006

Not valid holidays & subject to Rules of Use. Not valid with other discount offers, unless specified. Coupon VOID if purchased, sold or bartered. Discounts exclude tax, tip and/or alcohol, where applicable.

The Great Steak & Potato Co.

See reverse side for locations

- Featuring Philly style cheese steak sandwiches
- Fresh cut fries
- Gourmet baked potatoes, 6 variations to choose from
- Gourmet chicken & steak salads
- Fresh squeezed lemonade

Bonus Discounts at entertainment.com

entertainment. entertainment.com

great place for kids

SPECIAL OFFER

Enjoy one COMBO MEAL at 1/2 price with the purchase of a second combo meal of equal or greater value.

valid anytime

The Great Steak & Potato Company®

America's Premier Cheesesteak®

B57

Valid now thru November 1, 2006

Not valid holidays & subject to Rules of Use. Not valid with other discount offers, unless specified. Coupon VOID if purchased, sold or bartered. Discounts exclude tax, tip and/or alcohol, where applicable.

The Great Steak & Potato Company®

America's Premier Cheesesteak®

17301 Valley Mall Rd.
(Valley Mall)
Hagerstown, MD
(301)582-9103

3506 Capital Mall Dr.
(Capital City Mall)
Camp Hill, PA
(717)763-8511

21100 Dulles Town Ctr.
(Dulles Town Ctr.)
Sterling, VA
(703)421-3676

489 Prime Outlet Blvd.
(Prime Outlet)
Hagerstown, MD
(301)745-6652

Rte. 22 & Colonial Rd.
(Colonial Park Mall)
Harrisburg, PA
(717)545-4808

00659581

entertainment.com

00659581

The Great Steak & Potato Company®

America's Premier Cheesesteak®

17301 Valley Mall Rd.
(Valley Mall)
Hagerstown, MD
(301)582-9103

3506 Capital Mall Dr.
(Capital City Mall)
Camp Hill, PA
(717)763-8511

21100 Dulles Town Ctr.
(Dulles Town Ctr.)
Sterling, VA
(703)421-3676

489 Prime Outlet Blvd.
(Prime Outlet)
Hagerstown, MD
(301)745-6652

Rte. 22 & Colonial Rd.
(Colonial Park Mall)
Harrisburg, PA
(717)545-4808

00659592

entertainment.com

00659592

The Great Steak & Potato Company®

America's Premier Cheesesteak®

17301 Valley Mall Rd.
(Valley Mall)
Hagerstown, MD
(301)582-9103

3506 Capital Mall Dr.
(Capital City Mall)
Camp Hill, PA
(717)763-8511

21100 Dulles Town Ctr.
(Dulles Town Ctr.)
Sterling, VA
(703)421-3676

489 Prime Outlet Blvd.
(Prime Outlet)
Hagerstown, MD
(301)745-6652

Rte. 22 & Colonial Rd.
(Colonial Park Mall)
Harrisburg, PA
(717)545-4808

00659593

entertainment.com

00659593

Elie's Deli

12055 Government Center Pkwy.
Fairfax, VA
(703)324-8466

- Place your order online at our website
- "Business Catering Experts"
- Large variety of specialty platters
- Catering all business functions, 2 hr. express catering menu available - hotline # 703-748-0555

Bonus Discounts at entertainment.com

entertainment.
entertainment.com

Up To $5.00 Value

Enjoy one complimentary MENU ITEM when a second MENU ITEM of equal or greater value is purchased.

valid anytime

Elie's Deli
Best Subs in Town

www.eliesdeli.com

B58

Valid now thru November 1, 2006

Not valid holidays & subject to Rules of Use. Not valid with other discount offers, unless specified. Coupon VOID if purchased, sold or bartered. Discounts exclude tax, tip and/or alcohol, where applicable.

Elie's Deli

1950 Old Gallows Rd.
#102
Vienna, VA
(703)761-3777

- Place your order online at our website
- "Business Catering Experts"
- Open 7-4 Mon.-Fri. - try our breakfast burritos or Elie's breakfast melt
- Catering all business functions, 2 hr. express catering menu available - hotline # 703-748-0555
- Large variety of specialty platters

Bonus Discounts at entertainment.com

entertainment.
entertainment.com

Up To $5.00 Value

Enjoy one complimentary MENU ITEM when a second MENU ITEM of equal or greater value is purchased.

valid anytime

Elie's Deli
Best Subs in Town

www.eliesdeli.com

B59

Valid now thru November 1, 2006

Not valid holidays & subject to Rules of Use. Not valid with other discount offers, unless specified. Coupon VOID if purchased, sold or bartered. Discounts exclude tax, tip and/or alcohol, where applicable.

Elie's Deli

10629 Braddock Rd.
Fairfax, VA
(703)691-1777

- Place your order online at our website
- "Business Catering Experts"
- Catering all business functions, 2 hr. express catering menu - hotline # 703-748-0555
- Featuring fabulous sandwiches, subs, salads, soups, homemade specialties
- Party platters, six foot subs, box & bag lunches
- Try our lighter alternative menu

Bonus Discounts at entertainment.com

entertainment.
entertainment.com

Up To $5.00 Value

Enjoy one complimentary MENU ITEM when a second MENU ITEM of equal or greater value is purchased.

valid anytime

Elie's Deli
Best Subs in Town

www.eliesdeli.com

B60

Valid now thru November 1, 2006

Not valid holidays & subject to Rules of Use. Not valid with other discount offers, unless specified. Coupon VOID if purchased, sold or bartered. Discounts exclude tax, tip and/or alcohol, where applicable.

Elie's Deli
Best Subs in Town

12055 Government Center Pkwy.
Fairfax, VA
(703)324-8466

00374939

entertainment.com

00374939

Elie's Deli
Best Subs in Town

1950 Old Gallows Rd. #102
(Tyson's Corner)
Vienna, VA
(703)761-3777

00374968

entertainment.com

00374968

Elie's Deli
Best Subs in Town

10629 Braddock Rd.
(University Mall)
Fairfax, VA
(703)691-1777

00374983

entertainment.com

00374983

Auntie Anne's Hand-Rolled Soft Pretzels

Valid at All Participating Locations

- Homemade soft pretzels made fresh daily
- Enjoy your favorite topping with your pretzel
- Fresh squeezed lemonade
- Special orders available upon request
- Store hours vary, call for information

Bonus Discounts at entertainment.com

entertainment. entertainment.com

ONE PRETZEL DOG & MEDIUM SODA FOUNTAIN DRINK

Enjoy ONE PRETZEL DOG & MEDIUM SODA FOUNTAIN DRINK when a second PRETZEL DOG & MEDIUM SODA FOUNTAIN DRINK of equal or greater value is purchased.

Auntie Anne's

valid anytime

Valid at participating locations; Free items must be of equal or greater value; One coupon per person, one time only; Not good with any other offer; Tax extra where applicable; Not a cash substitute; Duplicated or altered coupons will not be accepted

B61

Valid now thru November 1, 2006

Not valid holidays & subject to Rules of Use. Not valid with other discount offers, unless specified. Coupon VOID if purchased, sold or bartered. Discounts exclude tax, tip and/or alcohol, where applicable.

Auntie Anne's Hand-Rolled Soft Pretzels

Valid at All Participating Locations

- Homemade soft pretzels made fresh daily
- Enjoy your favorite topping with your pretzel
- Fresh squeezed lemonade
- Special orders available upon request
- Store hours vary, call for information

Bonus Discounts at entertainment.com

entertainment. entertainment.com

ONE PRETZEL, MED. SODA FOUNTAIN DRINK & DIP

Enjoy ONE PRETZEL, MEDIUM SODA FOUNTAIN DRINK & DIP when a second PRETZEL, MEDIUM SODA FOUNTAIN DRINK & DIP of equal or greater value is purchased.

Auntie Anne's

valid anytime

Valid at participating locations; Free items must be of equal or greater value; One coupon per person, one time only; Not good with any other offer; Tax extra where applicable; Not a cash substitute; Duplicated or altered coupons will not be accepted

B62

Valid now thru November 1, 2006

Not valid holidays & subject to Rules of Use. Not valid with other discount offers, unless specified. Coupon VOID if purchased, sold or bartered. Discounts exclude tax, tip and/or alcohol, where applicable.

Auntie Anne's Hand-Rolled Soft Pretzels

Valid at All Participating Locations

- Homemade soft pretzels made fresh daily
- Enjoy your favorite topping with your pretzel
- Fresh squeezed lemonade
- Special orders available upon request
- Store hours vary, call for information

Bonus Discounts at entertainment.com

entertainment. entertainment.com

ORDER OF AUNTIE ANNE'S STIX & MEDIUM SODA

Enjoy one complimentary ORDER of AUNTIE ANNE'S STIX & MEDIUM SODA FOUNTAIN DRINK when a second ORDER of AUNTIE ANNE'S STIX & MEDIUM SODA FOUNTAIN DRINK of equal or greater value is purchased.

Auntie Anne's

valid anytime

Valid at participating locations; Free items must be of equal or greater value; One coupon per person, one time only; Not good with any other offer; Tax extra where applicable; Not a cash substitute; Duplicated or altered coupons will not be accepted

B63

Valid now thru November 1, 2006

Not valid holidays & subject to Rules of Use. Not valid with other discount offers, unless specified. Coupon VOID if purchased, sold or bartered. Discounts exclude tax, tip and/or alcohol, where applicable.

Auntie Anne's

Valid at All Participating Locations

00661465

entertainment.com

00661465

Auntie Anne's

Valid at All Participating Locations

00661466

entertainment.com

00661466

Auntie Anne's

Valid at All Participating Locations

00661359

entertainment.com

00661359

Splurge
See reverse side for locations

- Frozen custard
- Italian ice
- Splurginator (custard with mixed candies)
- Splurge-split (banana split)
- Classic float
- Sundaes
- Shakes
- Malts
- Smoothies
- Chilato (frozen custard & Italian ice mixed together)

Bonus Discounts at
entertainment.com

---

entertainment
entertainment.com

great place for kids

ONE REGULAR CONE

Enjoy one complimentary REGULAR CONE when a second REGULAR CONE of equal or greater value is purchased.

valid anytime

B64

Valid now thru November 1, 2006
Not valid holidays & subject to Rules of Use. Not valid with other discount offers, unless specified. Coupon VOID if purchased, sold or bartered. Discounts exclude tax, tip and/or alcohol, where applicable.

Splurge
See reverse side for locations

- Frozen custard
- Italian ice
- Splurginator (custard with mixed candies)
- Splurge-split (banana split)
- Classic float
- Sundaes
- Shakes
- Malts
- Smoothies
- Chilato (frozen custard & Italian ice mixed together)

Bonus Discounts at
entertainment.com

---

entertainment
entertainment.com

great place for kids

ONE SUNDAE

Enjoy one complimentary SUNDAE when a second SUNDAE of equal or greater value is purchased.

valid anytime

B65

Valid now thru November 1, 2006
Not valid holidays & subject to Rules of Use. Not valid with other discount offers, unless specified. Coupon VOID if purchased, sold or bartered. Discounts exclude tax, tip and/or alcohol, where applicable.

Splurge
See reverse side for locations

- Frozen custard
- Italian ice
- Splurginator (custard with mixed candies)
- Splurge-split (banana split)
- Classic float
- Sundaes
- Shakes
- Malts
- Smoothies
- Chilato (frozen custard & Italian ice mixed together)

Bonus Discounts at
entertainment.com

---

entertainment
entertainment.com

great place for kids

ONE SPLURGINATOR

Enjoy one complimentary SPLURGINATOR when a second SPLURGINATOR of equal or greater value is purchased.

valid anytime

B66

Valid now thru November 1, 2006
Not valid holidays & subject to Rules of Use. Not valid with other discount offers, unless specified. Coupon VOID if purchased, sold or bartered. Discounts exclude tax, tip and/or alcohol, where applicable.

MARYLAND
Annapolis
1028 Annapolis Mall
(Westfield Annapolis)
(410)224-4555
Bethesda
7101 Democracy Blvd.
(Westfield Montgomery)
(301)767-9481
Germantown
19828 Century Blvd.
(Germantown Town Ctr.)
(301)540-6340

Glen Burnie
7900 Governor Ritchie Hwy.
(Marley Station)
(410)761-6264
North Bethesda
11301 Rockville Pike
(White Flint Mall)
(301)881-4034
Rockville
827 Hungerford Dr.
(Saah Plaza)
(301)762-4343

VIRGINIA
Fairfax
11703 L Fair Oaks
(Fair Oaks Mall)
(703)591-1334
Sterling
21100 Dulles Town Circle
(Dulles Town Ctr.)
(703)433-1170

00634601

entertainment.com

00634601

MARYLAND
Annapolis
1028 Annapolis Mall
(Westfield Annapolis)
(410)224-4555
Bethesda
7101 Democracy Blvd.
(Westfield Montgomery)
(301)767-9481
Germantown
19828 Century Blvd.
(Germantown Town Ctr.)
(301)540-6340

Glen Burnie
7900 Governor Ritchie Hwy.
(Marley Station)
(410)761-6264
North Bethesda
11301 Rockville Pike
(White Flint Mall)
(301)881-4034
Rockville
827 Hungerford Dr.
(Saah Plaza)
(301)762-4343

VIRGINIA
Fairfax
11703 L Fair Oaks
(Fair Oaks Mall)
(703)591-1334
Sterling
21100 Dulles Town Circle
(Dulles Town Ctr.)
(703)433-1170

00634612

entertainment.com

00634612

MARYLAND
Annapolis
1028 Annapolis Mall
(Westfield Annapolis)
(410)224-4555
Bethesda
7101 Democracy Blvd.
(Westfield Montgomery)
(301)767-9481
Germantown
19828 Century Blvd.
(Germantown Town Ctr.)
(301)540-6340

Glen Burnie
7900 Governor Ritchie Hwy.
(Marley Station)
(410)761-6264
North Bethesda
11301 Rockville Pike
(White Flint Mall)
(301)881-4034
Rockville
827 Hungerford Dr.
(Saah Plaza)
(301)762-4343

VIRGINIA
Fairfax
11703 L Fair Oaks
(Fair Oaks Mall)
(703)591-1334
Sterling
21100 Dulles Town Circle
(Dulles Town Ctr.)
(703)433-1170

00634614

entertainment.com

00634614

Mario's Pizza & Subs

3322 Wilson Blvd.
Arlington, VA
(703)525-0200

- Since 1957
- Washington's best kept pizza secret
- Open late everyday

Bonus Discounts at
entertainment.com

entertainment® entertainment.com

great place for kids

Up To $20.00 Value

Enjoy any one complimentary PIZZA when a second PIZZA of equal or greater value is purchased.

Carry out only

valid anytime

Mario's PIZZA HOUSE

B67

Valid now thru November 1, 2006

Not valid holidays & subject to Rules of Use. Not valid with other discount offers, unless specified. Coupon VOID if purchased, sold or bartered. Discounts exclude tax, tip and/or alcohol, where applicable.

Mario's Pizza & Subs

3322 Wilson Blvd.
Arlington, VA
(703)525-0200

- Since 1957
- Washington's best kept pizza secret
- Open late everyday

Bonus Discounts at
entertainment.com

entertainment® entertainment.com

great place for kids

Up To $7.00 Value

Enjoy one complimentary SUB when a second SUB of equal or greater value is purchased.

Carry out only

valid anytime

Mario's PIZZA HOUSE

B68

Valid now thru November 1, 2006

Not valid holidays & subject to Rules of Use. Not valid with other discount offers, unless specified. Coupon VOID if purchased, sold or bartered. Discounts exclude tax, tip and/or alcohol, where applicable.

Carvel

3322 Wilson Blvd.
Arlington, VA
(703)248-3226

- That's right, we've got more than just ice cream cakes, baby
- Featuring cups & cones, sundaes, fizzlers, novelties, carvelanche, smoothies & ultimate thick shakes
- Open daily

Bonus Discounts at
entertainment.com

entertainment® entertainment.com

great place for kids

ONE MENU ITEM

Enjoy one complimentary MENU ITEM when a second MENU ITEM of equal or greater value is purchased.

Cakes excluded

valid anytime

Carvel®

www.carvel.com

B69

Valid now thru November 1, 2006

Not valid holidays & subject to Rules of Use. Not valid with other discount offers, unless specified. Coupon VOID if purchased, sold or bartered. Discounts exclude tax, tip and/or alcohol, where applicable.

Mario's
PIZZA HOUSE

3322 Wilson Blvd.
Arlington, VA
(703)525-0200

00635049

entertainment.com

00635049

Mario's
PIZZA HOUSE

3322 Wilson Blvd.
Arlington, VA
(703)525-0200

00635050

entertainment.com

00635050

Carvel

3322 Wilson Blvd.
Arlington, VA
(703)248-3226

00635055

entertainment.com

00635055

Baskin-Robbins Ice Cream

Valid at All Participating Locations

- One flavor for every day of the month
- Ice cream cakes for all occasions
- Variety of yogurt items
- May not be combined with other Baskin Robbins offers
- One offer per coupon

Bonus Discounts at entertainment.com

entertainment. entertainment.com

great place for kids

REGULAR TWO SCOOP SUNDAE OR DOUBLE DIP CONE

Baskin 31 Robbins.

Ice Cream & Yogurt

Enjoy one complimentary REGULAR TWO SCOOP SUNDAE OR DOUBLE DIP CONE when a second REGULAR TWO SCOOP SUNDAE OR DOUBLE DIP CONE of equal or greater value is purchased.

valid anytime

One coupon per customer per visit

B70

Valid now thru November 1, 2006

Not valid holidays & subject to Rules of Use. Not valid with other discount offers, unless specified. Coupon VOID if purchased, sold or bartered. Discounts exclude tax, tip and/or alcohol, where applicable.

Ben & Jerry's Ice Cream

See reverse side for locations

- Ben & Jerry's® ice cream is produced in Vermont from 100% pure native Vermont milk & cream
- Many euphoric selections to choose from!
- Ben & Jerry's® is a must - come in & try some of the very best ice cream you have ever tasted
- Home of the Vermonster

Bonus Discounts at entertainment.com

entertainment. entertainment.com

great place for kids

ONE REGULAR SIZE CONE OR DISH

Enjoy one complimentary REGULAR SIZE CONE OR DISH when a second REGULAR SIZE CONE OR DISH of equal or greater value is purchased.

valid anytime

BEN&JERRY'S.

ICE CREAM & FROZEN YOGURT SCOOP SHOP

B71

Valid now thru November 1, 2006

Not valid holidays & subject to Rules of Use. Not valid with other discount offers, unless specified. Coupon VOID if purchased, sold or bartered. Discounts exclude tax, tip and/or alcohol, where applicable.

Milwaukee Frozen Custard

See reverse side for locations

- Custard isn't pudding, yogurt or ice cream, but something like Heaven in your mouth™
- We believe it's better than ice cream™
- Enjoy vanilla, chocolate or our flavor of the day
- Open daily

Bonus Discounts at entertainment.com

entertainment. entertainment.com

great place for kids

ONE SMALL CONE

Enjoy one complimentary SMALL CONE when a second SMALL CONE of equal or greater value is purchased.

valid anytime

Milwaukee Frozen Custard®

The King of Custard®

Ice Cream Will Never Be The Same®

www.milwaukeefrozencustard.com

B72

Valid now thru November 1, 2006

Not valid holidays & subject to Rules of Use. Not valid with other discount offers, unless specified. Coupon VOID if purchased, sold or bartered. Discounts exclude tax, tip and/or alcohol, where applicable.

Baskin 31 Robbins
Ice Cream & Yogurt

Valid at All Participating Locations

00107019

entertainment.com

00107019

BEN&JERRY'S
ICE CREAM & FROZEN YOGURT SCOOP SHOP

3135 M St. NW
Washington, DC
(202)965-2222

4901-B Fairmont Ave.
Bethesda, MD
(301)652-2233

199-F E. Montgomery Ave.
Rockville, MD
(301)610-0560

103 S. Union St.
Alexandria, VA
(703)684-8866

00078083

entertainment.com

00078083

Milwaukee Frozen Custard®
The King of Custard®
Ice Cream Will Never Be The Same®

13934 Lee Jackson Hwy.
Chantilly, VA
(703)263-1920

300-A Elden St.
Herndon, VA
(703)467-0900

8411 Sudley Rd.
Manassas, VA
(703)393-9990

13321 Worth Rd.
Woodbridge, VA
(703)497-5511

00500445

entertainment.com

00500445

TCBY Treats

See reverse side for locations

- All frozen yogurt is not created equal & TCBY is here with a delicious variety of great taste
- TCBY - the country's richest, smoothest, creamiest frozen yogurt, with the great taste of premium ice cream
- Almost half the calories of premium ice cream
- Free samples
- All the pleasure - none of the guilt

Bonus Discounts at entertainment.com

entertainment. entertainment.com

great place for kids

ONE MENU ITEM

"TCBY" Treats™

Enjoy one complimentary MENU ITEM when a second MENU ITEM of equal or greater value is purchased.

Pies, cakes, pints & quarts excluded

valid anytime

One coupon per customer per visit

B73

Valid now thru November 1, 2006

Not valid holidays & subject to Rules of Use. Not valid with other discount offers, unless specified. Coupon VOID if purchased, sold or bartered. Discounts exclude tax, tip and/or alcohol, where applicable.

TCBY Treats

See reverse side for locations

- All frozen yogurt & ice cream are not created equal & TCBY is here with a delicious variety of great tastes
- Free samples
- All the pleasure - none of the quilt

Bonus Discounts at entertainment.com

entertainment. entertainment.com

great place for kids

ONE HAND DIPPED SCOOP OR SMALL CUP

"TCBY" Treats™

Enjoy one complimentary HAND DIPPED SCOOP OR SMALL CUP when a second HAND DIPPED SCOOP OR SMALL CUP of equal or greater value is purchased.

valid anytime

One coupon per customer per visit

B74

Valid now thru November 1, 2006

Not valid holidays & subject to Rules of Use. Not valid with other discount offers, unless specified. Coupon VOID if purchased, sold or bartered. Discounts exclude tax, tip and/or alcohol, where applicable.

TCBY Treats

See reverse side for locations

- All frozen yogurt is not created equal & TCBY is here with a delicious variety of great tastes
- TCBY - the country's richest, smoothest, creamiest frozen yogurt, with the great taste of premium ice cream
- Almost half the calories of premium ice cream
- All the pleasure - none of the guilt

Bonus Discounts at entertainment.com

entertainment. entertainment.com

great place for kids

ONE WAFFLE CONE

"TCBY" Treats™

Enjoy one complimentary WAFFLE CONE when a second WAFFLE CONE of equal or greater value is purchased.

valid anytime

One coupon per customer per visit

B75

Valid now thru November 1, 2006

Not valid holidays & subject to Rules of Use. Not valid with other discount offers, unless specified. Coupon VOID if purchased, sold or bartered. Discounts exclude tax, tip and/or alcohol, where applicable.

"TCBY" Treats

DISTRICT OF COLUMBIA
Washington
2001 L St., NW
(202)296-6468

MARYLAND
College Park
7314 Baltimore Ave.
(301)277-8229

Frederick
1306 W. Patrick St.
(301)695-1031

Greenbelt
6300 Greenbelt Rd.
(301)982-2521

Olney
18229 Olney Village Mart Dr.
(301)774-1165

Wheaton
13521 Connecticut Ave.
(301)460-4866

VIRGINIA
Fairfax
10623 Braddock Rd.
(703)385-3847

13048 Fair Lakes Shpg. Ctr.
(703)502-9430

Falls Church
7505-O Leesburg Pike
(703)790-8472

Leesburg
707-A East Market St.
(703)777-6575

Warrenton
183 Lee Hwy.
(540)349-4803

00239630

entertainment.com

00239630

"TCBY" Treats

DISTRICT OF COLUMBIA
Washington
2001 L St., NW
(202)296-6468

MARYLAND
College Park
7314 Baltimore Ave.
(301)277-8229

Frederick
1306 W. Patrick St.
(301)695-1031

Greenbelt
6300 Greenbelt Rd.
(301)982-2521

Olney
18229 Olney Village Mart Dr.
(301)774-1165

Wheaton
13521 Connecticut Ave.
(301)460-4866

VIRGINIA
Fairfax
10623 Braddock Rd.
(703)385-3847

13048 Fair Lakes Shpg. Ctr.
(703)502-9430

Falls Church
7505-O Leesburg Pike
(703)790-8472

Leesburg
707-A East Market St.
(703)777-6575

Warrenton
183 Lee Hwy.
(540)349-4803

00239855

entertainment.com

00239855

"TCBY" Treats

DISTRICT OF COLUMBIA
Washington
2001 L St., NW
(202)296-6468

MARYLAND
College Park
7314 Baltimore Ave.
(301)277-8229

Frederick
1306 W. Patrick St.
(301)695-1031

Greenbelt
6300 Greenbelt Rd.
(301)982-2521

Olney
18229 Olney Village Mart Dr.
(301)774-1165

Wheaton
13521 Connecticut Ave.
(301)460-4866

VIRGINIA
Fairfax
10623 Braddock Rd.
(703)385-3847

13048 Fair Lakes Shpg. Ctr.
(703)502-9430

Falls Church
7505-O Leesburg Pike
(703)790-8472

Leesburg
707-A East Market St.
(703)777-6575

Warrenton
183 Lee Hwy.
(540)349-4803

00409162

entertainment.com

00409162

2 Sisters Coffee Co.

255 W. Broad St.
Falls Church, VA
(703)237-3111

- Drive thru for convenience
- Custom prepared hot & cold drinks for the whole family
- Locally owned by two sisters
- Located next to the F.C. Post Office
- Open daily

Bonus Discounts at entertainment.com

entertainment. entertainment.com

50% OFF

Enjoy any BEVERAGE ORDER at 50% off the regular price - maximum discount $5.00.

valid anytime

B76

Valid now thru November 1, 2006

Not valid holidays & subject to Rules of Use. Not valid with other discount offers, unless specified. Coupon VOID if purchased, sold or bartered. Discounts exclude tax, tip and/or alcohol, where applicable.

A&W Restaurants

13396 Lee Jackson Hwy.
Chantilly, VA
(703)378-8786

- Celebrating over 85 years of America's favorite root beer
- Bring the whole family & enjoy a frosty mug of our famous root beer float

Bonus Discounts at entertainment.com

entertainment. entertainment.com

great place for kids

ONE A&W ROOT BEER FLOAT

Enjoy one complimentary A&W ROOT BEER FLOAT when a second A&W ROOT BEER FLOAT of equal or greater value is purchased.

valid anytime

ALL AMERICAN FOOD

www.awrestaurants.com

B77

Valid now thru November 1, 2006

Not valid holidays & subject to Rules of Use. Not valid with other discount offers, unless specified. Coupon VOID if purchased, sold or bartered. Discounts exclude tax, tip and/or alcohol, where applicable.

Armands Express

See reverse side for locations

- Famous Chicago-style deep dish pizza
- Try our new Manhattan-style thin crust
- Voted "Best Pizza" by the readers of Washingtonian Magazine

Bonus Discounts at entertainment.com

entertainment. entertainment.com

great place for kids

ONE PIZZA

Enjoy any one complimentary PIZZA when a second PIZZA of equal or greater value is purchased.

Carry out only - sorry, no delivery

valid anytime

B78

Valid now thru November 1, 2006

Not valid holidays & subject to Rules of Use. Not valid with other discount offers, unless specified. Coupon VOID if purchased, sold or bartered. Discounts exclude tax, tip and/or alcohol, where applicable.

255 W. Broad St.
(Located between the Post Office & Burke & Herbert)
Falls Church, VA
(703)237-3111

00578464

entertainment.com

00578464

ALL AMERICAN FOOD

13396 Lee Jackson Hwy.
Chantilly, VA
(703)378-8786

00626027

entertainment.com

00626027

ARMAND'S Express CHICAGO PIZZERIA EST. 1975

2151 Arlington Blvd.
Arlington, VA
(705)526-9800

9526 Burke Rd.
(Burke Village Ctr.)
Burke, VA
(703)426-4300

6206 Multiplex Dr.
Centreville, VA
(703)803-3100

00100711

entertainment.com

00100711

Ashburn Bagel Shop

43930 Farmwell Hunt Plaza
Ashburn, VA
(703)858-5883

- We cater to all your needs
- Featuring bagels, salads, sandwiches & much more
- Open daily

Bonus Discounts at entertainment.com

entertainment. entertainment.com

Up To $6.00 Value

Ashburn Bagel Shop

Enjoy one complimentary MENU ITEM when a second MENU ITEM of equal or greater value is purchased.

valid anytime

B79

Valid now thru November 1, 2006

Not valid holidays & subject to Rules of Use. Not valid with other discount offers, unless specified. Coupon VOID if purchased, sold or bartered. Discounts exclude tax, tip and/or alcohol, where applicable.

The Bad Ass Coffee Co.

10390 Portsmouth Rd.
Manassas, VA
(703)335-8877

- It's coffee with an attitude
- Providing an exciting fun & up beat atmosphere
- Serving only Kona coffee straight from Hawaii
- The Aloha spirit is alive & well at The Bad Ass Coffee Company & we share it with each & every customer in our store

Bonus Discounts at entertainment.com

entertainment. entertainment.com

Up To $5.00 Value

Enjoy one BEVERAGE ORDER at 50% off the regular price.

valid anytime

THE BAD ASS COFFEE CO. MERCANTILE COFFEE

www.badasscoffeeco.com

B80

Valid now thru November 1, 2006

Not valid holidays & subject to Rules of Use. Not valid with other discount offers, unless specified. Coupon VOID if purchased, sold or bartered. Discounts exclude tax, tip and/or alcohol, where applicable.

Bella Bagel Cafe

2852 Jefferson Davis Hwy. #119
Stafford, VA
(540)288-9679

- Offering fresh bagels, sandwiches, espresso, gourmet coffee, frozen custard, soup & desserts
- It's a beautiful thing!
- Ask us about our catering services
- Open daily

Bonus Discounts at entertainment.com

entertainment. entertainment.com

great place for kids

Up To $5.00 Value

Enjoy any FOOD/ BEVERAGE ORDER at 50% off the regular price.

valid anytime

BELLA BAGEL CAFÉ

B81

Valid now thru November 1, 2006

Not valid holidays & subject to Rules of Use. Not valid with other discount offers, unless specified. Coupon VOID if purchased, sold or bartered. Discounts exclude tax, tip and/or alcohol, where applicable.

Ashburn Bagel Shop

43930 Farmwell Hunt Plaza
(Ashburn Town Sq.)
Ashburn, VA
(703)858-5883

00557752

THE BAD ASS COFFEE CO.
MERCANTILE COFFEE

10390 Portsmouth Rd.
(Portsmouth Plaza)
Manassas, VA
(703)335-8877

00528223

BELLA BAGEL CAFÉ

2852 Jefferson Davis Hwy. #119
(Aquia Towne Ctr.)
Stafford, VA
(540)288-9679

00604292

Ben's Chili Bowl

1213 U St., NW.
Washington, DC
(202)667-0909

- Open since 1958
- Bill Cosby's favorite place to eat in Washington, D.C.
- Enjoy Ben's chili dogs, Ben's half smoke, Ben's 1/4 lb. chili burger & much more!
- New! Try our chili fries
- Serving breakfast 6 a.m. - 11 a.m.
- Also, visit Ben's Gourmet
- Open daily

Bonus Discounts at entertainment.com

entertainment® entertainment.com

great place for kids

ONE MENU ITEM

Ben's CHILI BOWL

Enjoy one complimentary MENU ITEM when a second MENU ITEM of equal or greater value is purchased.

valid anytime

B82

Valid now thru November 1, 2006

Not valid holidays & subject to Rules of Use. Not valid with other discount offers, unless specified. Coupon VOID if purchased, sold or bartered. Discounts exclude tax, tip and/or alcohol, where applicable.

Ben's Gourmet

2000 14th St., NW.
Washington, DC
(202)667-2313

- Famous for our stuffed croissant sandwiches
- Located at Reeves Municipal Center
- Open Mon. - Fri. 7:30 a.m. - 4 p.m.

Bonus Discounts at entertainment.com

entertainment® entertainment.com

great place for kids

ONE MENU ITEM

Enjoy one complimentary MENU ITEM when a second MENU ITEM of equal or greater value is purchased.

valid anytime

Ben's Gourmet

B83

Valid now thru November 1, 2006

Not valid holidays & subject to Rules of Use. Not valid with other discount offers, unless specified. Coupon VOID if purchased, sold or bartered. Discounts exclude tax, tip and/or alcohol, where applicable.

Besta Pizza

See reverse side for locations

- Specialty pizza
- Fresh dough, home made sauce
- Huge selection of toppings
- No alcohol served
- Serving lunch & dinner
- Open daily

Bonus Discounts at entertainment.com

entertainment® entertainment.com

ONE PIZZA

Enjoy any one complimentary PIZZA when a second PIZZA of equal or greater value is purchased.

valid anytime

Besta Pizza

B84

Valid now thru November 1, 2006

Not valid holidays & subject to Rules of Use. Not valid with other discount offers, unless specified. Coupon VOID if purchased, sold or bartered. Discounts exclude tax, tip and/or alcohol, where applicable.

Ben's CHILI BOWL

1213 U St., NW.
Washington, DC
(202)667-0909

Tipping should be 15% to 20% of TOTAL bill before discount

00226133

entertainment.com

00226133

Ben's Gourmet

2000 14th St., NW.
Washington, DC
(202)667-2313

Tipping should be 15% to 20% of TOTAL bill before discount

00226146

entertainment.com

00226146

Besta Pizza

5029 Connecticut Ave.
Washington, DC
(202)244-8344

4707 Chase Ave.
Bethesda, MD
(301)657-1114

8453 Tyco Rd. Ste. Q
Vienna, VA
(703)749-1600

00576113

entertainment.com

00576113

Big Bite Chicken & Pizzeria

7125 Columbia Pike
Annandale, VA
(703)941-8991

- All items made fresh daily on the premises
- Choose from a large variety of chicken, pizza, sandwiches, subs, salads & delicious desserts
- We open daily at 11 a.m.

Bonus Discounts at
entertainment.com

entertainment. entertainment.com

great place for kids

Up To $5.00 Value

BIG BITE
Chicken & Pizzeria

Enjoy one complimentary ENTREE when a second ENTREE of equal or greater value is purchased or for those who prefer - any one pizza at 50% off the regular price.

Sorry, no delivery

valid anytime

B85

Valid now thru November 1, 2006

Not valid holidays & subject to Rules of Use. Not valid with other discount offers, unless specified. Coupon VOID if purchased, sold or bartered. Discounts exclude tax, tip and/or alcohol, where applicable.

Bruster's Real Ice Cream

See reverse side for locations

- Our ice cream is made fresh everyday - right inside our stores
- That's why Bruster's Ice Cream always tastes so fresh, rich & creamy
- Featuring over 30 flavors daily
- Ask us about our portable ice-cream cart, fundraising coupons or catering your next event

Bonus Discounts at
entertainment.com

entertainment. entertainment.com

great place for kids

ONE ICE CREAM CONE

Enjoy one complimentary ICE CREAM CONE when a second ICE CREAM CONE of equal or greater value is purchased.

valid anytime

BRUSTER'S real ice cream

www.brustersvirginia.com

B86

Valid now thru November 1, 2006

Not valid holidays & subject to Rules of Use. Not valid with other discount offers, unless specified. Coupon VOID if purchased, sold or bartered. Discounts exclude tax, tip and/or alcohol, where applicable.

Buffalo Philly's

See reverse side for locations

- At Buffalo Philly's we aim to please & you live to eat!
- Featuring certified Angus Sirloin Steak Philly Cheesesteaks
- Our Buffalo Wings are made to order using fresh jumbo wings
- Children's menu available
- Open daily

Bonus Discounts at
entertainment.com

entertainment. entertainment.com

great place for kids

Up To $5.00 Value

Enjoy one complimentary MENU ITEM when a second MENU ITEM of equal or greater value is purchased.

Delivery excluded

valid anytime

BUFFALO PHILLY'S

B87

Valid now thru November 1, 2006

Not valid holidays & subject to Rules of Use. Not valid with other discount offers, unless specified. Coupon VOID if purchased, sold or bartered. Discounts exclude tax, tip and/or alcohol, where applicable.

BIG BITE
Chicken & Pizzeria

7125 Columbia Pike
Annandale, VA
(703)941-8991

00007393

entertainment.com

00007393

BRUSTER'S
real ice cream

10713 Courthouse Rd.
Fredericksburg, VA
(540)710-8888

428 Garrisonville Rd.
Stafford, VA
(540)288-2400

00617953

entertainment.com

00617953

BUFFALO PHILLY'S

6310-B Springfield Plaza I
Springfield, VA
(703)866-5055

2072 Daniel Stuart Sq.
(Opitz Shpg. Ctr.)
Woodbridge, VA
(703)497-8318

00105242

entertainment.com

00105242

Burrito Brothers

See reverse side for locations

- Fresh to the Mex
- All menu items & ingredients are made fresh daily & all meals are prepared to order
- Our beans are vegetarian safe
- Catering & large orders available

ONE BURRITO

Enjoy one complimentary BURRITO when a second BURRITO of equal or greater value is purchased.

valid anytime

B88

Valid now thru November 1, 2006

Cafe Wilson

3033 Wilson Blvd.
Arlington, VA
(703)816-8818

- Piled high sandwiches
- Enjoy yours grilled, in a sub or veggie
- Be original - "make your own"
- Free parking available
- Kids menu available

ONE SANDWICH

Enjoy one complimentary SANDWICH when a second SANDWICH of equal or greater value is purchased.

valid anytime

B89

Valid now thru November 1, 2006

Charley's Steakery

Valid at All Participating Locations

- Irresistibly fresh!
- We use only 95% fat-free sirloin steaks, chicken breasts, oven-baked breads, fresh vegetables & real cheese to bring you the irresistible taste of Philadelphia's South Market

ONE REGULAR SANDWICH

Enjoy one complimentary REGULAR SANDWICH when a second REGULAR SANDWICH of equal or greater value is purchased.

valid anytime

B90

Valid now thru November 1, 2006

BURRITO BROTHERS

205 Pennsylvania Ave. S.E.
(Capitol Hill)
Washington, DC
(202)543-6835

50 Massachusetts Ave. N.E.
(Union Station)
Washington, DC
(202)289-3652

7505 E. Leesburg Pike
(Idylwood Shpg. Ctr.)
Falls Church, VA
(703)356-8226

00106655

00106655

CAFE WILSON

3033 Wilson Blvd.
Arlington, VA
(703)816-8818

00633531

00633531

Charley's™ GRILLED SUBS

Valid at All Participating Locations

00554772

00554772

Cinnabon

See reverse side for locations

- Classic Cinnabon, Minibon & Caramel Fosted Pecanbon
- CinaPacks available in 4, 6, 9 or 15
- Our signature coffee - 100% Arabic beans, medium roast, rich smooth taste
- Chillatas - frozen & blended Double Chocolate, Caramel, Strawberry
- Mochalotta Chill - milk chocolate & a hint of coffee topped with whipcream chocolate
- Cinnabon Stix - cinnamon & sugar danish dough stix

Bonus Discounts at
entertainment.com

entertainment. entertainment.com

great place for kids

ONE CLASSIC ROLL

Enjoy one complimentary CLASSIC ROLL when a second CLASSIC ROLL of equal or greater value is purchased.

valid anytime

Not valid with any other discount offer

CINNABON
WORLD FAMOUS CINNAMON ROLLS

www.cinnabon.com

B91

Valid now thru November 1, 2006

Not valid holidays & subject to Rules of Use. Not valid with other discount offers, unless specified. Coupon VOID if purchased, sold or bartered. Discounts exclude tax, tip and/or alcohol, where applicable.

The Coffee House of Occoquan

202 Commerce St.
Occoquan, VA
(703)492-8976

- Choose from your favorite coffee & tea beverages
- Gift items & gourmet foods
- Lite fare available
- Live music available Fri. & Sat. evenings
- Plan your next tea party here!
- Open daily

Bonus Discounts at
entertainment.com

entertainment. entertainment.com

great place for kids

Up To $5.00 Value

Enjoy any Beverage Order at 50% off the regular price - maximum discount $5.00.

valid anytime

The Coffee House of Occoquan

B92

Valid now thru November 1, 2006

Not valid holidays & subject to Rules of Use. Not valid with other discount offers, unless specified. Coupon VOID if purchased, sold or bartered. Discounts exclude tax, tip and/or alcohol, where applicable.

Coffee Time Gourmet

7499 Somerset Crossing Shpg. Ctr.
Gainesville, VA
(703)753-7111

- More than just a coffee shop!
- Espresso, latte, smoothies, tea & more!
- Plan a party in our tea room

Bonus Discounts at
entertainment.com

entertainment. entertainment.com

great place for kids

Up To $5.00 Value

Enjoy any BEVERAGE ORDER at 50% off the regular price - maximum discount $5.00.

valid anytime

CoffeeTime Gourmet

www.coffeetimegourmet.com

B93

Valid now thru November 1, 2006

Not valid holidays & subject to Rules of Use. Not valid with other discount offers, unless specified. Coupon VOID if purchased, sold or bartered. Discounts exclude tax, tip and/or alcohol, where applicable.

CINNABON
WORLD FAMOUS CINNAMON ROLLS

DISTRICT OF COLUMBIA
Washington
National Hall
(Washington National Airport)
(703)417-1652

DELAWARE
Newark
511 Christiana Mall Rd.
(Christiana Mall)
(302)368-8170

Willmington
4737 Concord Pike
(Concord Mall)
(302)478-7944

MARYLAND
Annapolis
1016 Annapolis Mall Rd.
(Westfield Shpg. Town)
(410)897-8490

Baltimore
8200 Perry Hall Blvd. #2067
(White Marsh Mall)
(301)931-7288

Bethesda
7101 Democracy R, #2124
(Montgomery Mall)
(301)365-3959

Columbia
10300 Little Patuxent Pkwy. #1380
(Columbia Mall)
(410)997-6911

Gaithersburg
701 Russel Ave. #H107
(Lake Forest)

Glen Burnie
7900 Governor Ritchie Hwy. #A113
(Marley Station)
(410)766-7497

Hanover
7000 Arundel Mills Circle #342
(Arundel Mills)

Hyattsville
3500 E. West Hwy. #G
(Prince George Plaza)
(301)559-1202

Waldorf
11110 Mall Circle #J08
(St. Charles Sq.)
(301)396-4245

Wheaton
11160 Veirs Mill Rd. #F-110
(Wheaton Plaza)
(301)933-7790

VIRGINIA
McLean
1961 Chain Bridge Rd. #G3LB
(Tyson Corner)
(703)506-8530

Springfield
6500 Springfield Mall
(Springfield Mall)
(703)971-7881

00653259

entertainment.com

00653259

The Coffee House of Occoquan

202 Commerce St.
(Corner of Commerce & Washington Sts.)
Occoquan, VA
(703)492-8976

00605105

entertainment.com

00605105

CoffeeTime Gourmet

7499 Somerset Crossing Shpg. Ctr.
Gainesville, VA
(703)753-7111

00603850

entertainment.com

00603850

Cold Stone Creamery

See reverse side for locations

- Ice-cream made fresh daily
- Choose from one of our signature creations or create your own

entertainment® entertainment.com — great place for kids

ONE COLD STONE ORIGINAL

COLD STONE CREAMERY

Enjoy one complimentary COLD STONE ORIGINAL when a second COLD STONE ORIGINAL of equal or greater value is purchased.

valid anytime

Valid for "Love It" size

B94

Valid now thru November 1, 2006

Coyote Amigo

**1313 Old Chain Bridge Rd.
McLean, VA
(703)821-3888**

- Family owned
- Mexican cuisine including tacos, burritos, enchiladas & more
- Fresh & wholesome foods for a healthy diet
- American & Italian items also available

entertainment® entertainment.com — great place for kids

Up To $5.00 Value

Enjoy one complimentary MENU ITEM when a second MENU ITEM of equal or greater value is purchased.

Coyote Amigo

valid anytime

Combo platters excluded

B95

Valid now thru November 1, 2006

Daily Grind

**7770 Richmond Hwy.
Alexandria, VA
(703)799-4900**

- Whole beans
- Espresso
- Smoothies
- Catering available

entertainment® entertainment.com — great place for kids

Up To $5.00 Value

DAILY GRIND unwind

Enjoy any BEVERAGE ORDER at 50% off the regular price - maximum discount $5.00.

valid anytime

B96

Valid now thru November 1, 2006

COLD STONE CREAMERY

8113 Sudley Rd.
(Westgate Shpg. Ctr.)
Manassas, VA
(703)330-7722

205 Maple Ave. E.
(Vienna Marketplace)
Vienna, VA
(703)281-1940

00106503

entertainment.com

00106503

Coyote Amigo

1313 Old Chain Bridge Rd.
(McLean Shpg. Ctr. behind Safeway)
McLean, VA
(703)821-3888

00586173

entertainment.com

00586173

DAILY GRIND unwind

7770 Richmond Hwy.
(next to Gold's Gym)
Alexandria, VA
(703)799-4900

00614589

entertainment.com

00614589

Danny's Pizza

See reverse side for locations

- Fast & friendly service
- Pizza's made to order
- Call us today!
- Closed Sunday

entertainment. entertainment.com

ONE PIZZA

DANNY'S PIZZA

Enjoy any one complimentary PIZZA when a second PIZZA of equal or greater value is purchased.

valid anytime

B97

Valid now thru November 1, 2006

Not valid holidays & subject to Rules of Use. Not valid with other discount offers, unless specified. Coupon VOID if purchased, sold or bartered. Discounts exclude tax, tip and/or alcohol, where applicable.

Bonus Discounts at entertainment.com

Deli Depot

8961 Center St.
Manassas, VA
(703)368-0714

- New York-style delicatessen
- Homemade salad & sandwiches
- Featuring Depot garden platters, specialties, breakfast platters
- Professional catering for all occasions fixed any way you like

entertainment. entertainment.com

great place for kids

Up To $5.00 Value

DELI DEPOT

BECKER'S

Enjoy one complimentary SANDWICH when a second SANDWICH of equal or greater value is purchased.

valid anytime

B98

Valid now thru November 1, 2006

Not valid holidays & subject to Rules of Use. Not valid with other discount offers, unless specified. Coupon VOID if purchased, sold or bartered. Discounts exclude tax, tip and/or alcohol, where applicable.

Bonus Discounts at entertainment.com

Cookie Bouquets

See reverse side for locations

- Deliciously different
- A floral-like arrangement of colorfully wrapped chocolate chip cookies on stems
- Perfect for all occasions
- Delivered locally & shipped nationwide

entertainment. entertainment.com

50% OFF

cookie bouquets™

Enjoy one HAPPY DAY™ COOKIE ARRANGEMENT OF ONE DOZEN COOKIES at 50% off the regular price.

valid anytime

Coupon Code: ENTHD

www.cookiebouquets.com

B99

Valid now thru November 1, 2006

Not valid holidays & subject to Rules of Use. Not valid with other discount offers, unless specified. Coupon VOID if purchased, sold or bartered. Discounts exclude tax, tip and/or alcohol, where applicable.

Bonus Discounts at entertainment.com

DANNY'S PIZZA

10657 Spotsylvana Ave.
Fredericksburg, VA
(540)898-5008

1625 Carl D. Silver Pkwy.
Fredericksburg, VA
(540)785-3000

9837 Courthouse Rd.
Spotsylvana, VA
(540)898-7080

00577915

entertainment.com

00577915

DELI DEPOT

8961 Center St.
(Historic Old Town)
Manassas, VA
(703)368-0714

Tipping should be 15% to 20% of TOTAL bill before discount

00007868

entertainment.com

00007868

cookie bouquets

To Order or Request a **Catalog Call**
(800)233-2171 Mon.-Fri. 9 **a.m.**-5 p.m.

www.cookiebouquets.com

00595494

entertainment.com

00595494

Dominic's of New York

1361 Carl D. Silver Pkwy.
Fredericksburg, VA
(540)786-3472

- The Yankees aren't the only champions to come out of New York!
- Three generations of vending & street carts in NY evolved into kiosks at shopping centers
- Famous Italian sausage sandwich, Philly cheesesteak, chicken & veggie sandwiches
- Only the best will do for our customers

Bonus Discounts at
entertainment.com

entertainment.
entertainment.com

ONE ITALIAN SAUSAGE

DOMINIC'S®
OF NEW YORK

Enjoy one complimentary ITALIAN SAUSAGE when a second ITALIAN SAUSAGE of equal or greater value is purchased.

valid anytime

www.domofny.com

B100

Valid now thru November 1, 2006

Not valid holidays & subject to Rules of Use. Not valid with other discount offers, unless specified. Coupon VOID if purchased, sold or bartered. Discounts exclude tax, tip and/or alcohol, where applicable.

Dominic's of New York

1361 Carl D. Silver Pkwy.
Fredericksburg, VA
(540)786-3472

- The Yankees aren't the only champions to come out of New York!
- Three generations of vending & street carts in NY evolved into kiosks at shopping centers
- Famous Italian sausage sandwich, Philly cheesesteak, chicken & veggie sandwiches
- Only the best will do for our customers

Bonus Discounts at
entertainment.com

entertainment.
entertainment.com

ONE PAPA FELICO'S HOT PASTRAMI SANDWICH

DOMINIC'S®
OF NEW YORK

Enjoy one complimentary PAPA FELICO'S HOT PASTRAMI SANDWICH when a second PAPA FELICO'S HOT PASTRAMI SANDWICH of equal or greater value is purchased.

valid anytime

www.domofny.com

B101

Valid now thru November 1, 2006

Not valid holidays & subject to Rules of Use. Not valid with other discount offers, unless specified. Coupon VOID if purchased, sold or bartered. Discounts exclude tax, tip and/or alcohol, where applicable.

Dominic's of New York

1361 Carl D. Silver Pkwy.
Fredericksburg, VA
(540)786-3472

- The Yankees aren't the only champions to come out of New York!
- Three generations of vending & street carts in NY evolved into kiosks at shopping centers
- Famous Italian sausage sandwich, Philly cheesesteak, chicken & veggie sandwiches
- Only the best will do for our customers

Bonus Discounts at
entertainment.com

entertainment.
entertainment.com

ONE PAPA FELICO'S HAM & CHEESE GRILL

DOMINIC'S®
OF NEW YORK

Enjoy one complimentary PAPA FELICO'S HAM & CHEESE GRILL when a second PAPA FELICO'S HAM & CHEESE GRILL of equal or greater value is purchased.

valid anytime

www.domofny.com

B102

Valid now thru November 1, 2006

Not valid holidays & subject to Rules of Use. Not valid with other discount offers, unless specified. Coupon VOID if purchased, sold or bartered. Discounts exclude tax, tip and/or alcohol, where applicable.

DOMINIC'S®
OF NEW YORK

1361 Carl D. Silver Pkwy.
(outside of Lowe's)
Fredericksburg, VA
(540)786-3472

00244388

entertainment.com

00244388

DOMINIC'S®
OF NEW YORK

1361 Carl D. Silver Pkwy.
(outside of Lowe's)
Fredericksburg, VA
(540)786-3472

00244910

entertainment.com

00244910

DOMINIC'S®
OF NEW YORK

1361 Carl D. Silver Pkwy.
(outside of Lowe's)
Fredericksburg, VA
(540)786-3472

00244923

entertainment.com

00244923

Downtown Pastry

1340 Central Park Blvd. #104
Fredericksburg, VA
(540)548-8338

- European bakery from scratch
- Full line of cakes, pastries & Swiss chocolates
- Artisan breads made from scratch
- Located across from Uncle Sam's
- Open 8 a.m. - 6 p.m. Tue. - Fri.; Sat. 8 a.m. - 4:30 p.m.

Bonus Discounts at entertainment.com

entertainment. entertainment.com

50% OFF

Downtown Pastry
Fredericksburg, VA

Enjoy any BAKED GOODS ORDER at 50% off the regular price - maximum discount $5.00.

valid anytime

B103

Valid now thru November 1, 2006

Not valid holidays & subject to Rules of Use. Not valid with other discount offers, unless specified. Coupon VOID if purchased, sold or bartered. Discounts exclude tax, tip and/or alcohol, where applicable.

Dupont Market

18th & S Sts. NW
Washington, DC
(202)797-0222

- Catering available for special events
- Featuring gourmet foods & gift baskets
- Enjoy one of our freshly made sandwiches outside on the patio
- Open daily

Bonus Discounts at entertainment.com

entertainment. entertainment.com

great place for kids

Up To $6.00 Value

Dupont Market at Dupont Corner

Enjoy one complimentary SANDWICH when a second SANDWICH of equal or greater value is purchased.

valid anytime

B104

Valid now thru November 1, 2006

Not valid holidays & subject to Rules of Use. Not valid with other discount offers, unless specified. Coupon VOID if purchased, sold or bartered. Discounts exclude tax, tip and/or alcohol, where applicable.

Food Corner

See reverse side for locations

- Kabobs, chicken & gyros
- Dine in or carry out
- We serve halal meat!
- Catering services available
- Open daily

Bonus Discounts at entertainment.com

entertainment. entertainment.com

Up To $5.00 Value

FOOD CORNER

Enjoy one complimentary MENU ITEM when a second MENU ITEM of equal or greater value is purchased.

valid anytime

B105

Valid now thru November 1, 2006

Not valid holidays & subject to Rules of Use. Not valid with other discount offers, unless specified. Coupon VOID if purchased, sold or bartered. Discounts exclude tax, tip and/or alcohol, where applicable.

Downtown Pastry

Fredericksburg, VA

1340 Central Park Blvd. #104
(located in Uptown Central Park)
Fredericksburg, VA
(540)548-8338

00576280

entertainment.com

00576280

Dupont Market at Dupont Corner

18th & S Sts. NW
Washington, DC
(202)797-0222

00077674

entertainment.com

00077674

FOOD CORNER

7031-A Little River Tpke.
Annandale, VA
(703)750-2185

7031 Brookfield Plaza
Springfield, VA
(703)866-7834

00583396

entertainment.com

00583396

Frank-n-Stein

11719 L Fair Oaks Mall
Fairfax, VA
(703)352-0587

- Serving classic American food favorites since 1986
- Great fast food in a fun atmosphere
- Serving the most delicious hot dogs & sausages along side an ice cold draft beer

Bonus Discounts at entertainment.com

entertainment. entertainment.com

great place for kids

ONE FRANK-N-STEIN HOT DOG

Frank & Stein
DOGS & DRAFTS

Enjoy one complimentary FRANK-N-STEIN HOT DOG when a second FRANK-N-STEIN HOT DOG of equal or greater value is purchased.

Combo meals excluded

valid anytime

www.frankandsteinrestaurants.com

B106

Valid now thru November 1, 2006

Not valid holidays & subject to Rules of Use. Not valid with other discount offers, unless specified. Coupon VOID if purchased, sold or bartered. Discounts exclude tax, tip and/or alcohol, where applicable.

Frozen Dairy Bar

6649 Arlington Blvd.
Falls Church, VA
(703)534-4200

- Serving the community since 1950
- Offering home-made frozen custard
- We have all your favorite flavors plus a "flavor of the day"
- Come on in & bring the entire family!

Bonus Discounts at entertainment.com

entertainment. entertainment.com

great place for kids

Up To $5.00 Value

Enjoy any ICE CREAM ORDER at 50% off the regular price.

valid anytime

Frozen
DAIRY BAR

B107

Valid now thru November 1, 2006

Not valid holidays & subject to Rules of Use. Not valid with other discount offers, unless specified. Coupon VOID if purchased, sold or bartered. Discounts exclude tax, tip and/or alcohol, where applicable.

Full O' Beans

4607 Southpoint Plaza Pkwy.
Fredericksburg, VA
(540)891-0960

- Specializing in serving you the freshest coffee drinks
- Buy our coffee by the pound
- Our store carries great gifts for the coffee lover in your life
- Open daily

Bonus Discounts at entertainment.com

entertainment. entertainment.com

ONE MENU ITEM

Enjoy one complimentary MENU ITEM when a second MENU ITEM of equal or greater value is purchased.

valid anytime

FULL O' BEANS

B108

Valid now thru November 1, 2006

Not valid holidays & subject to Rules of Use. Not valid with other discount offers, unless specified. Coupon VOID if purchased, sold or bartered. Discounts exclude tax, tip and/or alcohol, where applicable.

Frank & Stein
DOGS & DRAFTS

11719 L Fair Oaks Mall
(Fair Oaks Mall)
Fairfax, VA
(703)352-0587

00633497

entertainment.com

00633497

Frozen
DAIRY BAR

6649 Arlington Blvd.
Falls Church, VA
(703)534-4200

00571893

entertainment.com

00571893

FULL O' BEANS

4607 Southpoint Plaza Pkwy.
Fredericksburg, VA
(540)891-0960

00478039

entertainment.com

00478039

Giovanni's New York Pizza

520 E. Market St.
Leesburg, VA
(703)777-8440

- "Best pizza in Loudoun County," the Washingtonian
- Dough & sauce made fresh every day
- Featuring pizza, pasta, hot or cold subs
- Draught & bottled beer available
- Open 7 days Mon.-Thur. 11 a.m.-10 p.m., Fri.-Sat. 11 a.m.-11 p.m., Sun. 12 p.m.-9 p.m.

great place for kids

Up To $5.00 Value

GIOVANNI

New York Style Pizza

Enjoy one complimentary MENU ITEM when a second MENU ITEM of equal or greater value is purchased.

valid anytime

B109

Valid now thru November 1, 2006

Not valid holidays & subject to Rules of Use. Not valid with other discount offers, unless specified. Coupon VOID if purchased, sold or bartered. Discounts exclude tax, tip and/or alcohol, where applicable.

Haagen-Dazs

See reverse side for locations

- Our specialty shakes include exclusive flavors such as Chocolate & Baileys Irish Cream, & Belgian Chocolate
- Our smoothie bar has selections made with fresh vanilla yogurt, Haagen Dazs Sorbet blended with a variety of fruit juices & fresh fruit
- Over two dozen ice cream selections to choose from
- Exclusive dessert items & custom made ice cream cakes

Bonus Discounts at entertainment.com

entertainment. entertainment.com

great place for kids

ONE DOUBLE SCOOP ICE CREAM CONE

Enjoy ONE DOUBLE SCOOP ICE CREAM CONE when a second DOUBLE SCOOP ICE CREAM CONE of equal or greater value is purchased.

valid anytime

Häagen-Dazs®

B110

Valid now thru November 1, 2006

Not valid holidays & subject to Rules of Use. Not valid with other discount offers, unless specified. Coupon VOID if purchased, sold or bartered. Discounts exclude tax, tip and/or alcohol, where applicable.

Heaven, Coffee & More

373 Garrisonville Rd.
Stafford, VA
(540)288-3300

- "On the way to Heaven, enjoy the trip, taking as many with us as want to go"
- Featuring coffee & espresso beverages, bakery items & home made sandwiches
- Catering & conference rooms available
- Closed Sunday

Bonus Discounts at entertainment.com

entertainment. entertainment.com

great place for kids

Up To $5.00 Value

Enjoy any FOOD/ BEVERAGE ORDER at 50% off the regular price.

valid anytime

Heaven Coffee And More...

www.heaven-coffee.com

B111

Valid now thru November 1, 2006

Not valid holidays & subject to Rules of Use. Not valid with other discount offers, unless specified. Coupon VOID if purchased, sold or bartered. Discounts exclude tax, tip and/or alcohol, where applicable.

GIOVANNI

New York Style Pizza

520 E. Market St.
Leesburg, VA
(703)777-8440

00004803

Häagen-Dazs®

3120 M St. NW
(Georgetown)
Washington, DC
(202)333-3443

50 Massachusetts Ave. NE
(Union Station)
Washington, DC
(202)789-0953

703 7th St. NW
(The Gallery Pl.)
Washington, DC
(202)783-4711

71 Democracy Blvd.
(Westfield St.)
Bethesda, MD
(301)469-4767

7305 Woodmont Ave.
Bethesda, MD
(301)652-9394

1101 S. Hayes St.
(Pentagon City)
Arlington, VA
(703)415-5540

00104533

Heaven
Coffee And More...

373 Garrisonville Rd.
Stafford, VA
(540)288-3300

00604297

entertainment.com

00004803

entertainment.com

00104533

entertainment.com

00604297

Heidelberg Pastry Shoppe

**2150 N. Culpeper St.
Arlington, VA
(703)527-8394**

- Many German specialties
- Fresh breads, rolls, cakes, pastries, cookies, donuts, Danish & distinctive wedding cakes
- New menu items include American & European gourmet foods

Bonus Discounts at
entertainment.com

entertainment.
entertainment.com

great place for kids

Up To $5.00 Value

Heidelberg Pastry Shoppe

Enjoy any BAKED GOODS ORDER at 50% off the regular price.

Maximum discount $5.00

valid anytime

www.heidelbergbakery.com

B112

Valid now thru November 1, 2006

Not valid holidays & subject to Rules of Use. Not valid with other discount offers, unless specified. Coupon VOID if purchased, sold or bartered. Discounts exclude tax, tip and/or alcohol, where applicable.

See reverse side for locations

- One of Americas oldest premium ice cream manufacturer
- Featuring all your favorite treats!
- Stop by today!

Bonus Discounts at
entertainment.com

entertainment.
entertainment.com

great place for kids

Up To $5.00 Value

Enjoy one complimentary MENU ITEM when a second MENU ITEM of equal or greater value is purchased.

valid anytime

HERSHEY'S® Ice Cream

B113

Valid now thru November 1, 2006

Not valid holidays & subject to Rules of Use. Not valid with other discount offers, unless specified. Coupon VOID if purchased, sold or bartered. Discounts exclude tax, tip and/or alcohol, where applicable.

Hershey's Ice Cream & More

**14412 Chantilly Crossing Ln.
Chantilly, VA
(703)817-7757**

- Featuring more than just ice cream
- More than 50 flavors available
- Specialty drinks, ice cream cakes & regular cakes
- Come by today

Bonus Discounts at
entertainment.com

entertainment.
entertainment.com

great place for kids

Up To $5.00 Value

Enjoy one complimentary MENU ITEM when a second MENU ITEM of equal or greater value is purchased.

valid anytime

HERSHEY'S® *Ice Cream and More!*

www.hersheys.com

B114

Valid now thru November 1, 2006

Not valid holidays & subject to Rules of Use. Not valid with other discount offers, unless specified. Coupon VOID if purchased, sold or bartered. Discounts exclude tax, tip and/or alcohol, where applicable.

Heidelberg Pastry Shoppe

2150 N. Culpeper St.
(corner of 4900 Lee Hwy.)
Arlington, VA
(703)527-8394

00021077

entertainment.com

00021077

HERSHEY'S® Ice Cream

Hersheys Ice Cream
4333 Junction Plaza #112
Ashburn, VA
(703)723-6566

Hershey's Ice-Cream
2415 Centreville Rd
Herndon, VA
(703)713-6003

Hersheys Ice Cream
10928 Bullock Dr.
Manassas, VA
(703)530-0407

Hershey's Ice-Cream
11790-H Baron Cameron Ave.
Reston, VA
(703)787-9495

00101007

entertainment.com

00101007

HERSHEY'S® *Ice Cream and More!*

14412 Chantilly Crossing Ln.
(Chantilly Crossing Shpg. Ctr.)
Chantilly, VA
(703)817-7757

00607648

entertainment.com

00607648

Italian Deli II - Trattoria Cafe

8500 Leesburg Pike
Vienna, VA
(703)448-1212

- Fine Italian specialties
- We specialize in catering for large or small groups
- Open for lunch & dinner daily

Bonus Discounts at
entertainment.com

entertainment®
entertainment.com

great place for kids

Up To $6.00 Value

Enjoy one complimentary MENU ITEM when a second MENU ITEM of equal or greater value is purchased.

valid anytime

ITALIAN DELI II

B115

Valid now thru November 1, 2006

Not valid holidays & subject to Rules of Use. Not valid with other discount offers, unless specified. Coupon VOID if purchased, sold or bartered. Discounts exclude tax, tip and/or alcohol, where applicable.

Jammin' Java

227 Maple Ave.
Vienna, VA
(703)255-1566

- Music, coffee, community
- "Jammin' Java is certainly the classiest music hall, recording studio, music school & coffee house in the area" raves the Washington Post
- Featuring the finest local regional & nationally tour acts 7 nights a week
- For more info. go to our web site

Bonus Discounts at
entertainment.com

entertainment®
entertainment.com

Up To $5.00 Value

Enjoy any FOOD/ BEVERAGE ORDER at 50% off the regular price.

valid anytime

jammin'java

www.jamminjava.com

B116

Valid now thru November 1, 2006

Not valid holidays & subject to Rules of Use. Not valid with other discount offers, unless specified. Coupon VOID if purchased, sold or bartered. Discounts exclude tax, tip and/or alcohol, where applicable.

Java X-press

10344 Lee Hwy.
Fairfax, VA
(703)273-2450

- Located in the parking lot of the Fairfax Shopping Center (next to Hooters)
- Car side service available
- Open weekdays at 5:30 a.m.

Bonus Discounts at
entertainment.com

entertainment®
entertainment.com

ONE ESPRESSO BEVERAGE

JAVA XPRESS

Enjoy one complimentary ESPRESSO BEVERAGE when a second ESPRESSO BEVERAGE of equal or greater value is purchased.

valid anytime

B117

Valid now thru November 1, 2006

Not valid holidays & subject to Rules of Use. Not valid with other discount offers, unless specified. Coupon VOID if purchased, sold or bartered. Discounts exclude tax, tip and/or alcohol, where applicable.

ITALIAN DELI II

8500 Leesburg Pike
(Tyson's Corner)
Vienna, VA
(703)448-1212

00495669

entertainment.com

00495669

jammin'java

227 Maple Ave.
(Glyndon Plaza Shpg. Ctr.)
Vienna, VA
(703)255-1566

00525415

entertainment.com

00525415

JAVA XPRESS

10344 Lee Hwy.
(Fairfax Shopping Ctr.)
Fairfax, VA
(703)273-2450

00076163

entertainment.com

00076163

Johnny Mac's Barbecue

8526 Richmond Hwy.
Alexandria, VA
(703)360-2200

- Home made barbecue
- Breakfast
- Summer sandwiches
- We sell BBQ by the pound
- Family packs

Bonus Discounts at entertainment.com

entertainment® entertainment.com

great place for kids

Up To $5.00 Value

JOHNNY MAC'S N.C. STYLE BARBECUE CHICKEN & RIBS

Enjoy one complimentary MENU ITEM when a second MENU ITEM of equal or greater value is purchased.

valid anytime

B118

Valid now thru November 1, 2006

Not valid holidays & subject to Rules of Use. Not valid with other discount offers, unless specified. Coupon VOID if purchased, sold or bartered. Discounts exclude tax, tip and/or alcohol, where applicable.

Johnny Mac's Ice Cream

8526 Richmond Hwy.
Alexandria, VA
(703)360-2200

- We have the new flavor burst ice-cream - flavor inside the ice-cream
- Milk shakes
- Banana splits
- A great summer time treat

Bonus Discounts at entertainment.com

entertainment® entertainment.com

great place for kids

50% OFF

JOHNNY MAC'S ICE CREAM

Enjoy any ICE CREAM ORDER at 50% off the regular price.

valid anytime

B119

Valid now thru November 1, 2006

Not valid holidays & subject to Rules of Use. Not valid with other discount offers, unless specified. Coupon VOID if purchased, sold or bartered. Discounts exclude tax, tip and/or alcohol, where applicable.

Kavanova Coffee

14019 Noblewood Plaza
Woodbridge, VA
(703)580-5555

- Jump start your day
- Coffee, lattes, frappe, mocha & smoothies
- Mon.-Sat. 7 a.m.-8 p.m., Sun. 8 a.m.-3 p.m.

Bonus Discounts at entertainment.com

entertainment® entertainment.com

great place for kids

Up To $5.00 Value

KavaNova Coffee

Enjoy any BEVERAGE ORDER at 50% off the regular price.

valid anytime

B120

Valid now thru November 1, 2006

Not valid holidays & subject to Rules of Use. Not valid with other discount offers, unless specified. Coupon VOID if purchased, sold or bartered. Discounts exclude tax, tip and/or alcohol, where applicable.

JOHNNY MAC'S
N.C. STYLE BARBECUE
CHICKEN & RIBS

8526 Richmond Hwy.
Alexandria, VA
(703)360-2200

00525026

entertainment.com

00525026

JOHNNY MAC'S
ICE CREAM

8526 Richmond Hwy.
Alexandria, VA
(703)360-2200

00524884

entertainment.com

00524884

KavaNova
Coffee

14019 Noblewood Plaza
(next to Food Lion)
Woodbridge, VA
(703)580-5555

00659650

entertainment.com

00659650

Lake Anne Coffee House

1612 Washington Plaza
Reston, VA
(703)481-9766

- Located on beautiful Lake Anne
- Offering homemade favorites
- Try our delicious tea & coffee beverages
- Open daily

Bonus Discounts at entertainment.com

entertainment.
entertainment.com

Up To $5.00 Value

LAKE ANNE COFFEE HOUSE

Enjoy one complimentary MENU ITEM when a second MENU ITEM of equal or greater value is purchased or for those who prefer, 50% off the regular price of any beverage order.

valid anytime

B121

Valid now thru November 1, 2006

Not valid holidays & subject to Rules of Use. Not valid with other discount offers, unless specified. Coupon VOID if purchased, sold or bartered. Discounts exclude tax, tip and/or alcohol, where applicable.

Las Delicias Bakery

733 Elden St.
Herndon, VA
(703)464-7922

- We offer delicious homemade pastries, cookies & cakes!
- We specialize in wedding, birthday & special occasion cakes
- Call us today!
- Closed Monday

Bonus Discounts at entertainment.com

entertainment.
entertainment.com

great place for kids

Up To $5.00 Value

Las Delicias Bakery

Enjoy any BAKED GOODS ORDER at 50% off the regular price - maximum discount $5.00.

valid anytime

B122

Valid now thru November 1, 2006

Not valid holidays & subject to Rules of Use. Not valid with other discount offers, unless specified. Coupon VOID if purchased, sold or bartered. Discounts exclude tax, tip and/or alcohol, where applicable.

Lazy Sundae

2925 Wilson Blvd.
Arlington, VA
(703)525-4960

- Arlington's favorite ice cream shop
- We can't wait to serve you
- Bring the whole family

Bonus Discounts at entertainment.com

entertainment.
entertainment.com

great place for kids

Up To $5.00 Value

Enjoy any ICE CREAM ORDER at 50% off the regular price.

valid anytime

B123

Valid now thru November 1, 2006

Not valid holidays & subject to Rules of Use. Not valid with other discount offers, unless specified. Coupon VOID if purchased, sold or bartered. Discounts exclude tax, tip and/or alcohol, where applicable.

LAKE ANNE COFFEE HOUSE

1612 Washington Plaza
Reston, VA
(703)481-9766

00368337

entertainment.com

00368337

Las Delicias Bakery

733 Elden St.
Herndon, VA
(703)464-7922

00608604

entertainment.com

00608604

Lazy Sundae

2925 Wilson Blvd.
Arlington, VA
(703)525-4960

00526378

entertainment.com

00526378

Lee's Homemade Ice Cream

5335 Wisconsin Ave.
Washington, DC
(202)686-3542

- Award-winning homemade ice cream
- Variety of favorite & exotic flavors
- Try our specialty sundaes, fountain treats & low-fat frozen yogurts
- Homemade hot fudge sauce, ice cream cakes & fresh baked cookies
- Open daily

great place for kids

ONE SINGLE OR DOUBLE DIP ICE-CREAM CONE

LEE'S HOMEMADE ICE CREAM

Enjoy one complimentary SINGLE or DOUBLE DIP ICE-CREAM CONE when a second SINGLE or DOUBLE DIP ICE-CREAM CONE of equal or greater value is purchased.

valid anytime

B124

Valid now thru November 1, 2006

Not valid holidays & subject to Rules of Use. Not valid with other discount offers, unless specified. Coupon VOID if purchased, sold or bartered. Discounts exclude tax, tip and/or alcohol, where applicable.

Mama's Gourmet Deli

9715 Lee Hwy.
Fairfax, VA
(703)385-2646

- Mama's prepares every meal from the freshest highest quality ingredients available
- We specialize in Corporate banquets & all kinds of parties
- Catering available
- Open daily

Bonus Discounts at
entertainment.com

entertainment®
entertainment.com

Up To $10.00 Value

Enjoy one complimentary MENU ITEM when a second MENU ITEM of equal or greater value is purchased.

Delivery excluded

valid anytime

Valid in Mama's Deli only

MAMA'S ITALIAN RESTAURANT

MAMA'S GOURMET DELI

www.mamasitalianrestaurant.com

B125

Valid now thru November 1, 2006

Not valid holidays & subject to Rules of Use. Not valid with other discount offers, unless specified. Coupon VOID if purchased, sold or bartered. Discounts exclude tax, tip and/or alcohol, where applicable.

Master Wok

See reverse side for locations

- Fresh food
- Tasty
- Healthy Cooking

Bonus Discounts at
entertainment.com

entertainment®
entertainment.com

Up To $6.00 Value

Enjoy one complimentary MENU ITEM when a second MENU ITEM of equal or greater value is purchased.

valid anytime

MASTER WOK

B126

Valid now thru November 1, 2006

Not valid holidays & subject to Rules of Use. Not valid with other discount offers, unless specified. Coupon VOID if purchased, sold or bartered. Discounts exclude tax, tip and/or alcohol, where applicable.

LEE'S HOMEMADE ICE CREAM

5335 Wisconsin Ave.
(Chevy Chase Pavilion)
Washington, DC
(202)686-3542

00004201

MAMA'S
ITALIAN RESTAURANT

MAMA'S GOURMET DELI

9715 Lee Hwy.
Fairfax, VA
(703)385-2646

00552133

MASTER WOK

CONNECTICUT
Farmington
500 Westfarms Mall
(860)561-8791

Stamford
100 Greyrock Place
(Stamford Town Ctr.)
(230)353-3351

KANSAS
Wichita
7700 E. Kellogg Dr.
(Towne East Sq.)
(316)681-2804

MASSACHUSETTS
Auburn
385 Southbridge St.
(Auburn Mall)
(508)721-0228

Marlborough
Solomond Pond Mall
(508)303-6210

N. Attleborough
Emerald Square Mall
(508)643-3767

Peabody
Rte. 128 & 114
(North Shore Mall)
(978)532-4724

Watertown
485 Arsenal St.
(Arsenal Mall)
(617)926-1216

MICHIGAN
Dearborn
18900 Michigan Ave.
(Fairlane Town Ctr.)
(313)271-6211

NEW HAMPSHIRE
Manchester
1500 S. Willow St.
(Mall of New Hampshire)
(603)627-7593

Salem
99 Rockingham Blvd.
(Rockingham Mall)
(603)870-9294

NEW JERSEY
Freehold
3710 Rte. 9 S. Food Ct.
(Freehold Mall)
(732)294-9477

Lawrenceville
144 Quaker Bridge Mall
(609)799-0308

Livingston
Livingston Mall
(Lower Level)
(973)740-9878

Morrestown
Rte. 38 & Lenoia Rd.
(Morrestown Mall)
(856)234-3381

NEW YORK
Massapequa
1 Sunrise Mall
(516)799-1588

Middletown
1 Galleria Dr.
(845)695-2922

Valley Stream
2034 Green Acres Mall
(516)825-4621

PENNSYLVANIA
Philadelphia
1625 Chestnut St.
(Liberty Place)
(215)568-3822

1934 liacouras Walk
(Temple University)
(215)204-2076

The Gallery at Market E.
(215)627-2333

Saugus
Rte. 1 & Main St.
(Square One Mall)
(617)941-9047

VIRGINIA
Dulles
Dulles Town Ctr.
(703)433-0413

00578793

entertainment.com

00004201

entertainment.com

00552133

entertainment.com

00578793

Mirage Sweets

5916 Leesburg Pike
Falls Church, VA
(703)845-1600

- Here at Mirage, we bring to you centuries of fascination & love for baklawa
- All our sweets are sold by the pound
- Come in for any occasion
- Open daily

Bonus Discounts at
entertainment.com

entertainment. entertainment.com

Up To $5.00 Value

Enjoy any BAKED GOODS ORDER at 50% off the regular price.

valid anytime

Mirage
Kabob & Sweets Café

B127

Valid now thru November 1, 2006

Not valid holidays & subject to Rules of Use. Not valid with other discount offers, unless specified. Coupon VOID if purchased, sold or bartered. Discounts exclude tax, tip and/or alcohol, where applicable.

Mr. Pizza & Subs

4232 Plank Rd.
Fredericksburg, VA
(540)785-8999

- Homemade pizzas made with 100% real cheese
- Enjoy a traditional style pizza or one of our specialty pizzas
- Open daily

Bonus Discounts at
entertainment.com

entertainment. entertainment.com

great place for kids

ONE PIZZA

Enjoy any one complimentary PIZZA when a second PIZZA of equal or greater value is purchased.

valid anytime

Mr. Pizza & Subs

B128

Valid now thru November 1, 2006

Not valid holidays & subject to Rules of Use. Not valid with other discount offers, unless specified. Coupon VOID if purchased, sold or bartered. Discounts exclude tax, tip and/or alcohol, where applicable.

Noble, Romans

707 E. Market St.
Leesburg, VA
(703)777-6575

- We have the best hand tossed, oven baked pizza with the freshest sauce
- Hand baked bread sticks, lasagna, fettuccine alfredo & buffalo wings
- Open daily

Bonus Discounts at
entertainment.com

entertainment. entertainment.com

great place for kids

ONE PIZZA

Enjoy any one complimentary PIZZA when a second PIZZA of equal or greater value is purchased.

Carry out only

valid anytime

Noble Roman's®
THE BETTER PIZZA PEOPLE®

B129

Valid now thru November 1, 2006

Not valid holidays & subject to Rules of Use. Not valid with other discount offers, unless specified. Coupon VOID if purchased, sold or bartered. Discounts exclude tax, tip and/or alcohol, where applicable.

Mirage

Kabob & Sweets Café

5916 Leesburg Pike
(Bailey's Crossroads)
Falls Church, VA
(703)845-1600

00603603

entertainment.com

00603603

Mr. Pizza & Subs

4232 Plank Rd.
Fredericksburg, VA
(540)785-8999

00576310

entertainment.com

00576310

Noble Roman's®

THE BETTER PIZZA PEOPLE®

707 E. Market St.
(in TCBY, next to Blockbuster)
Leesburg, VA
(703)777-6575

00478758

entertainment.com

00478758

Papa Joe's

7810-G Lee Hwy.
Falls Church, VA
(703)205-9155

- We deliver the classic food
- Featuring gourmet pizzas
- Open daily

entertainment.
entertainment.com

ONE PIZZA

Papa Joe's PIZZA

Enjoy any one complimentary PIZZA when a second PIZZA of equal or greater value is purchased.

Carry out only

valid anytime

B130

Valid now thru November 1, 2006

Not valid holidays & subject to Rules of Use. Not valid with other discount offers, unless specified. Coupon VOID if purchased, sold or bartered. Discounts exclude tax, tip and/or alcohol, where applicable.

Pizza Movers

See reverse side for locations

- Rated best tasting in the Washingtonian Magazine
- Get a REAL pizza with FAST delivery
- Also featuring hot wings, salads, subs & more
- Our hours are Sun. - Thurs. 11 a.m. to 1:30 a.m. & Fri. - Sat. 11 a.m. to 2:30 a.m.

entertainment.
entertainment.com

ONE PIZZA

PIZZA MOVERS & CALZONES

Enjoy any one complimentary PIZZA when a second PIZZA of equal or greater value is purchased.

Carry out or delivery

valid anytime

B131

Valid now thru November 1, 2006

Not valid holidays & subject to Rules of Use. Not valid with other discount offers, unless specified. Coupon VOID if purchased, sold or bartered. Discounts exclude tax, tip and/or alcohol, where applicable.

Pizza Pantry

923 S. Walter Reed Dr.
Arlington, VA
(703)920-9110

- Since 1957...good to the last bite!
- Home of the famous 'Fillmore'
- Homemade NY 'Ultra Thin Crust Pizza'
- Where Quality, Cleanliness, & Customer Service go hand-in-hand!

entertainment.
entertainment.com

ONE PIZZA

Pizza Pantry

Enjoy any one PIZZA at 50% off the regular price.

Carry out only

valid anytime

B132

Valid now thru November 1, 2006

Not valid holidays & subject to Rules of Use. Not valid with other discount offers, unless specified. Coupon VOID if purchased, sold or bartered. Discounts exclude tax, tip and/or alcohol, where applicable.

Papa Joe's
PIZZA

7810-G Lee Hwy.
Falls Church, VA
(703)205-9155

00571731

entertainment.com

00571731

PIZZA MOVERS & CALZONES

1618 Wisconsin Ave.
(in Georgetown)
Washington, DC
(202)333-9199

2005 18th St.
(in Adams Morgan between Florida Ave. & Columbia Rd.)
Washington, DC
(202)483-8787

2522 Columbia Pike
Arlington, VA
(703)521-2121

00102208

entertainment.com

00102208

Pizza Pantry

923 S. Walter Reed Dr.
Arlington, VA
(703)920-9110

00571863

entertainment.com

00571863

Pizza Pasta Plus

6653-G Little River Tpke.
Annandale, VA
(703)256-8600

- Enjoy the best pizza around
- Open daily

Bonus Discounts at entertainment.com

entertainment. entertainment.com

great place for kids

ONE PIZZA

PIZZA PASTA PLUS

Enjoy any one complimentary PIZZA when a second PIZZA of equal or greater value is purchased.

Carry out only

valid anytime

B133

Valid now thru November 1, 2006

Pizzarama

7432 Gainesville Village Sq.
Gainesville, VA
(703)753-9009

- Family owned & operated since 1972
- Serving the best New York Style pizza
- All sauces & dough prepared fresh daily
- Closed Sunday

Bonus Discounts at entertainment.com

entertainment. entertainment.com

great place for kids

ONE PIZZA

GAINESVILLE PIZZARAMA

Enjoy any one complimentary PIZZA when a second PIZZA of equal or greater value is purchased.

Dine-in or carry out; Gainesville location only

valid anytime

B134

Valid now thru November 1, 2006

Pumpernickles Deli

5504 Connecticut Ave. NW
Washington, DC
(202)244-9505

- Fresh assorted bagels made on the premises everyday
- Flavored cream cheeses
- Whitefish salad
- Gourmet coffee
- Complete breakfast menu

Bonus Discounts at entertainment.com

entertainment. entertainment.com

great place for kids

50% OFF

BAGELRY Pumpernickels DELICATESSEN

Enjoy ONE DOZEN BAGELS at 50% off the regular price.

valid anytime

B135

Valid now thru November 1, 2006

PIZZA
PASTA
PLUS

6653-G Little River Tpke.
Annandale, VA
(703)256-8600

00586309

entertainment.com

00586309

GAINESVILLE
PIZZARAMA

7432 Gainesville Village Sq.
Gainesville, VA
(703)753-9009

00603676

entertainment.com

00603676

BAGELRY
Pumpernickels
DELICATESSEN

5504 Connecticut Ave. NW
Washington, DC
(202)244-9505

Tipping should be 15% to 20% of TOTAL bill before discount

00045067

entertainment.com

00045067

Rappahannock Coffee

2406 Columbia Pike
Arlington, VA
(703)271-0007

- Coffee * conversation * community
- Specialty coffee roasters
- Featuring all your favorite coffee drinks
- Internet hook-up available

Bonus Discounts at
entertainment.com

entertainment.
entertainment.com

Up To $5.00 Value

Enjoy 50% off the regular price of any BEVERAGE ORDER.

valid anytime

Rappahannock Coffee

Coffee•Conversation•Community

www.rappahannockcoffee.com

B136

Valid now thru November 1, 2006

Not valid holidays & subject to Rules of Use. Not valid with other discount offers, unless specified. Coupon VOID if purchased, sold or bartered. Discounts exclude tax, tip and/or alcohol, where applicable.

Rivera's Restaurant

6552 Backlick Rd.
Springfield, VA
(703)451-5344

- Featuring Polla a la Brasa, Pupusas, Tacos, Ceviche ,Lomo Saltado, Carne Asada, Fajitas Mixta, Chupe de Camarones & Pescadeo Frito
- Traditional Latin American cuisine
- We hope you enjoy your visit

Bonus Discounts at
entertainment.com

entertainment.
entertainment.com

Up To $6.00 Value

Enjoy one complimentary MENU ITEM when a second MENU ITEM of equal or greater value is purchased.

Dine in only

valid anytime

Rivera's
Restaurant
Latin American Cuisine

B137

Valid now thru November 1, 2006

Not valid holidays & subject to Rules of Use. Not valid with other discount offers, unless specified. Coupon VOID if purchased, sold or bartered. Discounts exclude tax, tip and/or alcohol, where applicable.

Scoopers Deli & Bar

110-F South St.
Leesburg, VA
(703)777-3317

- Simply great food, always a great time!
- Featuring all your favorite sandwiches, made to order
- Serving ice-cream too!
- Remember we cater!

Bonus Discounts at
entertainment.com

entertainment.
entertainment.com

Up To $5.00 Value

Enjoy one complimentary MENU ITEM when a second MENU ITEM of equal or greater value is purchased.

valid anytime

SCOOPERS
Deli & Bar

B138

Valid now thru November 1, 2006

Not valid holidays & subject to Rules of Use. Not valid with other discount offers, unless specified. Coupon VOID if purchased, sold or bartered. Discounts exclude tax, tip and/or alcohol, where applicable.

Rappahannock
COFFEE

COFFEE • CONVERSATION • COMMUNITY

2406 Columbia Pike
Arlington, VA
(703)271-0007

00571811

entertainment.com

00571811

Rivera's

Restaurant

Latin American Cuisine

6552 Backlick Rd.
Springfield, VA
(703)451-5344

Tipping should be 15% to 20% of TOTAL bill before discount

00525198

entertainment.com

00525198

SCOOPERS
Deli & Bar

110-F South St.
(Market Station)
Leesburg, VA
(703)777-3317

00529989

entertainment.com

00529989

Shenandoah Brewing Co.

652 S. Pickett St.
Alexandria, VA
(703)823-9508

- Washington area's only brewery, brew pub & brew-on-premise
- 8 taps & many bottled beers
- All beer fresh made in Alexandria
- 6 packs & cases to go
- Featuring meat & vegetarian chili
- Call for hours

Bonus Discounts at entertainment.com

entertainment. entertainment.com

Up To $5.00 Value

Enjoy one complimentary MENU ITEM when a second MENU ITEM of equal or greater value is purchased.

valid anytime

Shenandoah Brewing Company
Established 1994 Alexandria, VA.

www.shenandoahbrewing.com

B139

Valid now thru November 1, 2006

Not valid holidays & subject to Rules of Use. Not valid with other discount offers, unless specified. Coupon VOID if purchased, sold or bartered. Discounts exclude tax, tip and/or alcohol, where applicable.

Smoothie Time

4000 Wisconsin Ave. NW
Washington, DC
(202)363-5988

- Over 25 flavors of fresh fruit smoothies
- Offering complete smoothie catering programs
- Have a smoothie bar at your next function or party
- You choose the flavors, we'll take care of everything else
- Full-line of nutritional supplements, energy bars & more
- Gift cards & franchise opportunities available

Bonus Discounts at entertainment.com

entertainment. entertainment.com

great place for kids

ONE SMOOTHIE

Enjoy one complimentary SMOOTHIE when a second SMOOTHIE of equal or greater value is purchased.

valid anytime

extra charge for additions

smoothie time

www.smoothietime.net

B140

Valid now thru November 1, 2006

Not valid holidays & subject to Rules of Use. Not valid with other discount offers, unless specified. Coupon VOID if purchased, sold or bartered. Discounts exclude tax, tip and/or alcohol, where applicable.

Spring Mill Bread Company

See reverse side for locations

- Spring Mill products are made from high protein Montana wheat, stone ground daily in our bakery
- With few exceptions, our breads contain no oils, no dairy products, no processed sugars, no preservatives & no cholesterol
- Closed Sunday's

Bonus Discounts at entertainment.com

entertainment. entertainment.com

ONE LOAF

Enjoy one complimentary LOAF when a second LOAF of equal or greater value is purchased.

valid anytime

Spring Mill Bread Co.

YOUR NEIGHBORHOOD WHOLE WHEAT BAKERY!

B141

Valid now thru November 1, 2006

Not valid holidays & subject to Rules of Use. Not valid with other discount offers, unless specified. Coupon VOID if purchased, sold or bartered. Discounts exclude tax, tip and/or alcohol, where applicable.

Shenandoah Brewing Company
Established 1994 Alexandria, VA.

652 S. Pickett St.
Alexandria, VA
(703)823-9508

00655893

entertainment.com

00655893

smoothie time

4000 Wisconsin Ave. NW
(Tenley Town)
Washington, DC
(202)363-5988

00508453

entertainment.com

00508453

Spring Mill Bread Co.

YOUR NEIGHBORHOOD WHOLE WHEAT BAKERY!

4961 Elm St.
Bethesda, MD
(301)654-7970

9827 Rhode Island Ave.
College Park, MD
(301)220-1554

Rte. 28 & Quince
Orchard Rd.
(Potsmac Valley Shpg. Ctr.)
Gaithersburg, MD
(301)977-7733

11711B Parklawn Dr.
(Inside Mom's Organic Markets)
Rockville, MD
(301)231-0140

3831 S. Mt. Vernon Ave.
Alexandria, VA
(703)684-8680

00598963

entertainment.com

00598963

St. Elmo's Coffee

2300 Mt. Vernon Ave.
Alexandria, VA
(703)739-9268

- Featuring Seattle's Best Coffee & Daily Roast Coffee Co.
- Republic of Tea, teas
- Internet access
- Live music Wed. - Sat.
- Open seven days a week

Bonus Discounts at
entertainment.com

entertainment.
entertainment.com

50% OFF

St. Elmo's

COFFEE PUB

Enjoy ANY BEVERAGE ORDER at 50% off the regular price.

valid anytime

www.stelmoscoffeepub.com

B142

Valid now thru November 1, 2006

Not valid holidays & subject to Rules of Use. Not valid with other discount offers, unless specified. Coupon VOID if purchased, sold or bartered. Discounts exclude tax, tip and/or alcohol, where applicable.

Steak Escape

See reverse side for locations

- No need to settle for ordinary food - The Steak Escape is your ticket to great, fresh taste made-to-order
- Enjoy our Philadelphia cheese steak sandwich & our hand-cut, cooked in peanut oil, french fries
- Choose your favorite grilled sandwich & enjoy your escape to great, fresh taste made-to-order

Bonus Discounts at
entertainment.com

entertainment.
entertainment.com

great place for kids

ONE MENU ITEM

America's Favorite
STEAK ESCAPE
cheesesteaks

Enjoy one complimentary MENU ITEM when a second MENU ITEM of equal or greater value is purchased.

Combination meals excluded

valid anytime

www.steakescape.com

B143

Valid now thru November 1, 2006

Not valid holidays & subject to Rules of Use. Not valid with other discount offers, unless specified. Coupon VOID if purchased, sold or bartered. Discounts exclude tax, tip and/or alcohol, where applicable.

The Broiler

3601 Columbia Pike
Arlington, VA
(703)920-5944

- Since 1959
- Featuring a variety of hot & cold subs
- Delicious selection of pizza toppings
- Breakfast subs also available
- Open daily

Bonus Discounts at
entertainment.com

entertainment.
entertainment.com

great place for kids

Up To $5.00 Value

THE BROILER

Enjoy one complimentary SANDWICH when a second SANDWICH of equal or greater value is purchased or for those who prefer - any one pizza at 50% off the regular price - maximum discount $5.00.

Dine-in or carry out

valid anytime

B144

Valid now thru November 1, 2006

Not valid holidays & subject to Rules of Use. Not valid with other discount offers, unless specified. Coupon VOID if purchased, sold or bartered. Discounts exclude tax, tip and/or alcohol, where applicable.

St. Elmo's

COFFEE PUB

2300 Mt. Vernon Ave.
Alexandria, VA
(703)739-9268

00532302

entertainment.com

00532302

America's Favorite STEAK ESCAPE cheesesteaks

MARYLAND
Annapolis
Annapolis Mall
(410)721-6066

Bethesda
Montgomery Mall
(301)469-6030

Columbia
Columbia Mall
(301)596-1400

Hyattsville
Prince Georges Plaza
(301)853-3155

Wheaton
Wheaton Plaza
(301)942-6020

VIRGINIA
McLean
Tysons Corner Mall
(703)790-9035

Adelphi H Stamp Union;
University of MD, College Park;
COMING SOON!

00090078

entertainment.com

00090078

THE BROILER

3601 Columbia Pike
Arlington, VA
(703)920-5944

00478761

entertainment.com

00478761

The Burrito Joynt

6113 Franconia Rd.
Alexandria, VA
(703)924-8600

- "Enjoy the newest craze in town"
- We put the joy into burritos
- Offering appetizers, nachos, quesadillas, tacos, fajitas, burritos, chimichangas & more
- www.burritojoynt.com
- Open daily

great place for kids

Up To $5.00 Value

The Burrito Joynt

Enjoy one complimentary MENU ITEM when a second MENU ITEM of equal or greater value is purchased.

valid anytime

www.burritojoynt.com

B145

Valid now thru November 1, 2006

Not valid holidays & subject to Rules of Use. Not valid with other discount offers, unless specified. Coupon VOID if purchased, sold or bartered. Discounts exclude tax, tip and/or alcohol, where applicable.

The Coffee Beanery, Ltd.

Fashion Center at Pentagon City
Arlington, VA
(703)415-3909

- Great HOT or ICED specialty drinks
- Over 70 varieties of coffee beans
- Large selection of teas & collectable tea pots
- Coffee & espresso makers, mugs & accessories also available
- Metro stops at Pentagon City
- Located in the food court next to "up" escalator

Up To $5.00 Value

Enjoy one BEVERAGE ORDER at 50% off the regular price.

valid anytime

the coffee beanery, ltd.®

B146

Valid now thru November 1, 2006

Not valid holidays & subject to Rules of Use. Not valid with other discount offers, unless specified. Coupon VOID if purchased, sold or bartered. Discounts exclude tax, tip and/or alcohol, where applicable.

The Coffee Espress

1250 H St., NW
Washington, DC
(202)637-9334

- Coffee
- Cappuccino
- Espresso
- Latte
- Open daily

Up To $5.00 Value

THE COFFEE ESPRESS

Enjoy one BEVERAGE ORDER at 50% off the regular price - maximum discount $5.00.

valid anytime

B147

Valid now thru November 1, 2006

Not valid holidays & subject to Rules of Use. Not valid with other discount offers, unless specified. Coupon VOID if purchased, sold or bartered. Discounts exclude tax, tip and/or alcohol, where applicable.

The Burrito Joynt

6113 Franconia Rd.
Alexandria, VA
(703)924-8600

00455429

entertainment.com

00455429

the coffee beanery, ltd.

Fashion Center at Pentagon City
Arlington, VA
(703)415-3909

00410045

entertainment.com

00410045

THE
COFFEE ESPRESS

1250 H St., NW
(between 12th & 13th near Natl. Museum of Women in the Arts)
Washington, DC
(202)637-9334

00449602

entertainment.com

00449602

The Italian Deli

6813 Elm St.
McLean, VA
(703)506-1136

- Enjoy one of your favorite Italian cold-cut sandwiches or subs
- Also available - your favorite Italian dinner, including stuffed shells, chicken parmigiana & lasagna
- Carry out & delivery available
- Closed Sunday

entertainment® entertainment.com great place for kids

Up To $6.00 Value

The Italian Deli

Enjoy one complimentary MENU ITEM when a second MENU ITEM of equal or greater value is purchased.

valid anytime

B148

Valid now thru November 1, 2006

The Spaghetti Shop

13812 Metrotech Dr.
Chantilly, VA
(703)817-0115

- A different fast food experience
- The Spaghetti Shop is founded on the premise that Americans should be able to get good, wholesome Italian food fast & inexpensively
- Dinners include spaghetti w/meat sauce, fettuccine alfredo, lasagna, ravioli or pasta primavera

entertainment® entertainment.com great place for kids

Up To $8.00 Value

Enjoy one complimentary ITALIAN DINNER when a second ITALIAN DINNER of equal or greater value is purchased.

valid anytime

The Spaghetti Shop™
Fast, Fresh, Fabulous Italian™

B149

Valid now thru November 1, 2006

Tickers Coffee

2037 Plank Rd.
Fredericksburg, VA
(540)899-5330

- The coffee house that's a little bit different
- Enjoy superb coffee & coffeeless drinks
- Can't wait to "Meet you at Tickers"

entertainment® entertainment.com

50% OFF

Enjoy any BEVERAGE ORDER at 50% off the regular price.

valid anytime

Tickers Coffee

"I'll meet you at Tickers"

B150

Valid now thru November 1, 2006

The Italian Deli

6813 Elm St.
(across from McDonald's)
McLean, VA
(703)506-1136

00031908

entertainment.com

00031908

The Spaghetti Shop™

Fast, Fresh, Fabulous Italian™

13812 Metrotech Dr.
(Sully Place Shpg. Ctr.)
Chantilly, VA
(703)817-0115

00002899

entertainment.com

00002899

Tickers Coffee

"I'll meet you at Tickers"

2037 Plank Rd.
(Westwood Shpg. Ctr.)
Fredericksburg, VA
(540)899-5330

00576994

entertainment.com

00576994

Tivoli Gourmet & Pastry Shop

1700 N. Moore St.
Arlington, VA
(703)524-8902

- Welcome to Tivoli Gourmet & Pastry Shop
- Featuring deli sandwiches, salads, pastries & more
- We cater to all your needs - call us today

Bonus Discounts at
entertainment.com

entertainment.
entertainment.com

Up To $5.00 Value

Enjoy one complimentary MENU ITEM when a second MENU ITEM of equal or greater value is purchased.

Valid at Tivoli Gourmet - Rosslyn

valid anytime

Tivoli

www.tivolirestaurant.net

B151

Valid now thru November 1, 2006

Not valid holidays & subject to Rules of Use. Not valid with other discount offers, unless specified. Coupon VOID if purchased, sold or bartered. Discounts exclude tax, tip and/or alcohol, where applicable.

Tres Joli Catering & Cakes Occasions

5799-H Burke Center Pkwy.
Burke, VA
(703)503-8153

- Beautiful custom wedding, birthday & special occasion cakes
- Creative & delicious catering for large & small corporate, private meetings, parties & intimate in home gatherings
- Let us help you make any occasion a special occasion

Bonus Discounts at
entertainment.com

entertainment.
entertainment.com

Up To $5.00 Value

Enjoy any BAKED GOODS ORDER at 50% off the regular price - maximum discount $5.00.

valid anytime

TRES JOLI CATERING
CAKES FOR ALL OCCASIONS

B152

Valid now thru November 1, 2006

Not valid holidays & subject to Rules of Use. Not valid with other discount offers, unless specified. Coupon VOID if purchased, sold or bartered. Discounts exclude tax, tip and/or alcohol, where applicable.

Tropical Smoothie Cafe'

20921 Davenport Dr.
Unit # 131
Sterling, VA
(703)430-1700

- Offering a full line of Smoothies, gourmet wraps, specialty sandwiches, delicious salads & more
- Each item is made fresh to order insuring the best possible products
- For healthy people on the go

Bonus Discounts at
entertainment.com

entertainment.
entertainment.com

great place for kids

Up To $6.00 Value

Enjoy one complimentary MENU ITEM when a second MENU ITEM of equal or greater value is purchased.

valid anytime

Tropical Smoothie Cafe'

B153

Valid now thru November 1, 2006

Not valid holidays & subject to Rules of Use. Not valid with other discount offers, unless specified. Coupon VOID if purchased, sold or bartered. Discounts exclude tax, tip and/or alcohol, where applicable.

Tivoli

1700 N. Moore St.
(@ Rosslyn METRO Center)
Arlington, VA
(703)524-8902

00557431

entertainment.com

00557431

TRES JOLI CATERING
CAKES FOR ALL OCCASIONS

5799-H Burke Center Pkwy.
Burke, VA
(703)503-8153

00575045

entertainment.com

00575045

Tropical Smoothie Cafe

20921 Davenport Dr. Unit # 131
(Located in Regal Center)
Sterling, VA
(703)430-1700

00590092

entertainment.com

00590092

Tubby's

8723-B Cooper Rd.
Alexandria, VA
(703)360-9880

- The best frozen custard around
- Enjoy a cup or a cone of your favorite old fashion flavor
- Also featuring sundaes, concretes, milkshakes & hot fudge brownies
- Open daily

Bonus Discounts at entertainment.com

entertainment. entertainment.com

great place for kids

Up To $5.00 Value

Enjoy any CUSTARD ORDER at 50% off the regular price.

valid anytime

Tubby's Frozen Custard

B154

Valid now thru November 1, 2006

Not valid holidays & subject to Rules of Use. Not valid with other discount offers, unless specified. Coupon VOID if purchased, sold or bartered. Discounts exclude tax, tip and/or alcohol, where applicable.

Tumi Peruvian Cuisine

6715 Backlick Rd.
Springfield, VA
(703)451-0242

- Peruvian cuisine
- Pollo ala Brasa
- Charcoal chicken
- Family owned & operated

Bonus Discounts at entertainment.com

entertainment. entertainment.com

Up To $6.00 Value

Enjoy one complimentary MENU ITEM when a second MENU ITEM of equal or greater value is purchased.

valid anytime

TUMI
PERUVIAN CUISINE

B155

Valid now thru November 1, 2006

Not valid holidays & subject to Rules of Use. Not valid with other discount offers, unless specified. Coupon VOID if purchased, sold or bartered. Discounts exclude tax, tip and/or alcohol, where applicable.

Twist Again Pretzels

See reverse side for locations

- Hot, fresh hand-rolled soft pretzels
- Select from a large variety of flavors & toppings
- Low fat available

Bonus Discounts at entertainment.com

entertainment. entertainment.com

great place for kids

ONE PRETZEL

Enjoy one complimentary PRETZEL when a second PRETZEL of equal or greater value is purchased.

valid anytime

TWIST AGAIN

B156

Valid now thru November 1, 2006

Not valid holidays & subject to Rules of Use. Not valid with other discount offers, unless specified. Coupon VOID if purchased, sold or bartered. Discounts exclude tax, tip and/or alcohol, where applicable.

Tubby's Frozen Custard

8723-B Cooper Rd.
Alexandria, VA
(703)360-9880

00611924

TUMI

PERUVIAN CUISINE

6715 Backlick Rd.
Springfield, VA
(703)451-0242

00651270

TWIST AGAIN

11301 Rockville Pike
(White Flint)
N. Bethesda, MD
(301)881-4034

11703 L. Fairoaks
(Fair Oaks)
Fairfax, VA
(703)591-1334

00286949

Ukrop's

See reverse side for locations

- Visit us at ukrops.com to find the Ukrop's nearest you & a listing of store features
- Full-service Ukrop's Pharmacy
- First Market Bank
- Photofinishing
- Dry Cleaning
- Full-service Floral Department
- US Mail & UPS services
- Grill & Cafe
- Ukrop's Helpline 1-800-868-2270
- Carryout Catering 1-888-793-3663

Bonus Discounts at entertainment.com

entertainment. entertainment.com

ONE UKROP'S 3-PIECE CHICKEN DINNER

Enjoy one complimentary UKROP'S 3-PIECE CHICKEN DINNER when a second UKROP'S 3-PIECE CHICKEN DINNER of equal or greater value is purchased.

Ukrop's™

valid anytime

To redeem, present coupon with your Valued Customer Card. Valid Anytime. One coupon per customer per visit; Valid at all Ukrop's locations.

PLU #1230

www.ukrops.com

B157

Valid now thru November 1, 2006

Not valid holidays & subject to Rules of Use. Not valid with other discount offers, unless specified. Coupon VOID if purchased, sold or bartered. Discounts exclude tax, tip and/or alcohol, where applicable.

Ukrop's

See reverse side for locations

- Visit us at ukrops.com to find the Ukrop's nearest you & a listing of store features
- Full-service Ukrop's Pharmacy
- First Market Bank
- Photofinishing
- Dry Cleaning
- Full-service Floral Department
- US Mail & UPS services
- Grill & Cafe
- Ukrop's Helpline 1-800-868-2270
- Carryout Catering 1-888-793-3663

Bonus Discounts at entertainment.com

entertainment. entertainment.com

great place for kids

ONE UKROP'S KITCHEN KID'S MEAL

Enjoy one complimentary UKROP'S KITCHEN KID'S MEAL when a UKROP'S KITCHEN ADULT MEAL ($3.99 value or above) is purchased.

Ukrop's™

valid anytime

To redeem, present coupon with your Valued Customer Card. Valid Anytime. One coupon per customer per visit; Valid at all Ukrop's locations.

PLU #1201

www.ukrops.com

B158

Valid now thru November 1, 2006

Not valid holidays & subject to Rules of Use. Not valid with other discount offers, unless specified. Coupon VOID if purchased, sold or bartered. Discounts exclude tax, tip and/or alcohol, where applicable.

Ukrop's

See reverse side for locations

- Visit us at ukrops.com to find the Ukrop's nearest you & a listing of store features
- Full-service Ukrop's Pharmacy
- First Market Bank
- Photofinishing
- Dry Cleaning
- Full-service Floral Department
- US Mail & UPS services
- Grill & Cafe
- Ukrop's Helpline 1-800-868-2270
- Carryout Catering 1-888-793-3663

Bonus Discounts at entertainment.com

entertainment. entertainment.com

ONE 20 LB. BAG OF UKROP'S COMPOST

Enjoy one complimentary 20 LB. BAG OF UKROP'S COMPOST when a second 20 LB. BAG OF UKROP'S COMPOST of equal or greater value is purchased.

Ukrop's™

valid anytime

To redeem, present coupon with your Valued Customer Card. Valid Anytime. One coupon per customer per visit; Valid at all Ukrop's locations.

PLU #1197

www.ukrops.com

B159

Valid now thru November 1, 2006

Not valid holidays & subject to Rules of Use. Not valid with other discount offers, unless specified. Coupon VOID if purchased, sold or bartered. Discounts exclude tax, tip and/or alcohol, where applicable.

Ukrop's

Ashland
253 N. Washington Hwy.

Chester
12601 Jefferson Davis Hwy.

Chesterfield
6401 Centralia Rd.

Colonial Heights
3107-15 Boulevard

Fredericksburg
4250 Plank Rd.

Glen Allen
10150 Brook Rd.
10250 Staples Mill Rd.
9645 W. Broad St.

Mechanicsville
7324 Bell Creek Rd. S.

Midlothian
1220 Sycamore Sq.
13700 Hull Street Rd.

Petersburg
3330 S. Crater Rd.

Richmond
10001 Hull Street Rd.
11361 Midlothian Tpke.
2250 John Rolfe Pkwy.
3000 Stony Point Rd.
3460 Pump Rd.
3522 W. Cary St.
4346 S. Laburnum Ave.
500 N. Harrison St.
5201 Chippenham Crossing Ctr.
5700 Brook Rd.
7035 Three Chopt Rd.
7045 Forest Hill Ave.
7129 Staples Mill Rd.
7803 Midlothian Tpke.
9600 Patterson Ave.
9782 Gayton Rd.

Williamsburg
4660 Monticello Ave.

00506912

entertainment.com

00506912

Ukrop's

Ashland
253 N. Washington Hwy.

Chester
12601 Jefferson Davis Hwy.

Chesterfield
6401 Centralia Rd.

Colonial Heights
3107-15 Boulevard

Fredericksburg
4250 Plank Rd.

Glen Allen
10150 Brook Rd.
10250 Staples Mill Rd.
9645 W. Broad St.

Mechanicsville
7324 Bell Creek Rd. S.

Midlothian
1220 Sycamore Sq.
13700 Hull Street Rd.

Petersburg
3330 S. Crater Rd.

Richmond
10001 Hull Street Rd.
11361 Midlothian Tpke.
2250 John Rolfe Pkwy.
3000 Stony Point Rd.
3460 Pump Rd.
3522 W. Cary St.
4346 S. Laburnum Ave.
500 N. Harrison St.
5201 Chippenham Crossing Ctr.
5700 Brook Rd.
7035 Three Chopt Rd.
7045 Forest Hill Ave.
7129 Staples Mill Rd.
7803 Midlothian Tpke.
9600 Patterson Ave.
9782 Gayton Rd.

Williamsburg
4660 Monticello Ave.

00553824

entertainment.com

00553824

Ukrop's

Ashland
253 N. Washington Hwy.

Chester
12601 Jefferson Davis Hwy.

Chesterfield
6401 Centralia Rd.

Colonial Heights
3107-15 Boulevard

Fredericksburg
4250 Plank Rd.

Glen Allen
10150 Brook Rd.
10250 Staples Mill Rd.
9645 W. Broad St.

Mechanicsville
7324 Bell Creek Rd. S.

Midlothian
1220 Sycamore Sq.
13700 Hull Street Rd.

Petersburg
3330 S. Crater Rd.

Richmond
10001 Hull Street Rd.
11361 Midlothian Tpke.
2250 John Rolfe Pkwy.
3000 Stony Point Rd.
3460 Pump Rd.
3522 W. Cary St.
4346 S. Laburnum Ave.
5201 Chippenham Crossing Ctr.
5700 Brook Rd.
7035 Three Chopt Rd.
7045 Forest Hill Ave.
7129 Staples Mill Rd.
7803 Midlothian Tpke.
9600 Patterson Ave.
9782 Gayton Rd.

Williamsburg
4660 Monticello Ave.

00553828

entertainment.com

00553828

Wing Zone

3817 Mount Vernon Ave.
Alexandria, VA
(703)299-9464

- Home of 25 flavors
- Enjoy jumbo wings, chicken fingers, kid'z menu & more
- Open daily

great place for kids

Up To $5.00 Value

Enjoy one complimentary MENU ITEM when a second MENU ITEM of equal or greater value is purchased.

Carry out only

valid anytime

Wing Zone®

www.wingzone.com

B160

Valid now thru November 1, 2006

Not valid holidays & subject to Rules of Use. Not valid with other discount offers, unless specified. Coupon VOID if purchased, sold or bartered. Discounts exclude tax, tip and/or alcohol, where applicable.

Wings

46839 Maple Leaf Place #187
Sterling, VA
(703)433-0730

- Voted "Best Wings"
- Authentic Buffalo wings
- Deli subs
- Salads & soups
- Cheese steaks
- Sandwiches
- Catering available
- Open daily

great place for kids

Up To $5.00 Value

Enjoy one complimentary MENU ITEM when a second MENU ITEM of equal or greater value is purchased.

Combo meals excluded

valid anytime

WINGS

B161

Valid now thru November 1, 2006

Not valid holidays & subject to Rules of Use. Not valid with other discount offers, unless specified. Coupon VOID if purchased, sold or bartered. Discounts exclude tax, tip and/or alcohol, where applicable.

Wings To Go

See reverse side for locations

- "America's best buffalo style wings"
- Featuring 18 authentic sauces
- Sandwiches & wings available
- Hot & fresh so you can enjoy the best wings on the planet

great place for kids

Up To $5.00 Value

Enjoy one complimentary MENU ITEM when a second MENU ITEM of equal or greater value is purchased.

Combo meals excluded

valid anytime

WINGS W TO GO

B162

Valid now thru November 1, 2006

Not valid holidays & subject to Rules of Use. Not valid with other discount offers, unless specified. Coupon VOID if purchased, sold or bartered. Discounts exclude tax, tip and/or alcohol, where applicable.

Wing Zone®

3817 Mount Vernon Ave.
(Mt. Vernon Village Ctr.)
Alexandria, VA
(703)299-9464

00583504

entertainment.com

00583504

WINGS

46839 Maple Leaf Place #187
(Augusta Ctr. next to Dryclean Depot)
Sterling, VA
(703)433-0730

00611825

entertainment.com

00611825

WINGS TO GO

7678-C Richmond Hwy.
(Mt. Vernon Plaza)
Alexandria, VA
(703)660-8547

432 Garrisonville Rd. #10
(610 Ctr.)
Stafford, VA
(540)659-9600

00103051

entertainment.com

00103051

Fas Mart®

Valid at All Participating Locations

- The Fastest Stop Around!
- For a location nearest you visit www.fasmart.com & www.shorestop.com!

Bonus Discounts at entertainment.com

entertainment. entertainment.com

ONE HOT DOG

Enjoy one complimentary HOT DOG when a second HOT DOG of equal or greater value is purchased.

PDI coupon code #33

valid anytime

Please present coupon/card at time of purchase

FAS·LANE Fas mart Cafe VALERO

www.fasmart.com

B163

Valid now thru November 1, 2006

Not valid holidays & subject to Rules of Use. Not valid with other discount offers, unless specified. Coupon VOID if purchased, sold or bartered. Discounts exclude tax, tip and/or alcohol, where applicable.

Fas Mart®

Valid at All Participating Locations

- The Fastest Stop Around!
- For a location nearest you visit www.fasmart.com & www.shorestop.com!

Bonus Discounts at entertainment.com

entertainment. entertainment.com

ONE BBQ SANDWICH

Enjoy one complimentary BBQ SANDWICH when a second BBQ SANDWICH of equal or greater value is purchased.

PDI coupon code #37

valid anytime

Please present coupon/card at time of purchase

FAS·LANE Fas mart Cafe VALERO

www.fasmart.com

B164

Valid now thru November 1, 2006

Not valid holidays & subject to Rules of Use. Not valid with other discount offers, unless specified. Coupon VOID if purchased, sold or bartered. Discounts exclude tax, tip and/or alcohol, where applicable.

Fas Mart®

Valid at All Participating Locations

- The Fastest Stop Around!
- For a location nearest you visit www.fasmart.com & www.shorestop.com!

Bonus Discounts at entertainment.com

entertainment. entertainment.com

$2.00 Value

Enjoy $2.00 off the regular price of one 8 PIECE CHICKEN SNACK.

PDI coupon code #35

valid anytime

Please present coupon/card at time of purchase

FAS·LANE Fas mart Cafe VALERO

www.fasmart.com

B165

Valid now thru November 1, 2006

Not valid holidays & subject to Rules of Use. Not valid with other discount offers, unless specified. Coupon VOID if purchased, sold or bartered. Discounts exclude tax, tip and/or alcohol, where applicable.

FAS·LANE Fas mart Cafe

VALERO

Valid at All Participating Locations

00621613

entertainment.com

00621613

FAS·LANE Fas mart Cafe

VALERO

Valid at All Participating Locations

00621632

entertainment.com

00621632

FAS·LANE Fas mart Cafe

VALERO

Valid at All Participating Locations

00621641

entertainment.com

00621641

ATTRACTIONS

CONCERTS/PERFORMANCE

kids **Great Place for Kids!** NEW **New Merchants Added This Year**

kids **Great Place for Kids!** NEW **New Merchants Added This Year**

ATTRACTIONS INDEX

SPORTING EVENTS

entertainment. entertainment.com

PURCHASE $6.00 TICKETS AT BOX OFFICE

REGAL ENTERTAINMENT GROUP℠

Present this coupon at the Theatre Box Office to purchase up to two (2) *VIP Super Saver Admission Tickets for only $6.00 each. Upgrade to an "UNRESTRICTED" Premiere Super Saver Admission Ticket for only $1.50 extra per ticket.

C1

Not valid holidays & subject to Rules of Use.
Not valid with other discount offers, unless specified.

great place for kids

Valid now thru November 1, 2006

entertainment. entertainment.com

PURCHASE $6.00 TICKETS AT BOX OFFICE

REGAL ENTERTAINMENT GROUP℠

Present this coupon at the Theatre Box Office to purchase up to two (2) *VIP Super Saver Admission Tickets for only $6.00 each. Upgrade to an "UNRESTRICTED" Premiere Super Saver Admission Ticket for only $1.50 extra per ticket.

C2

Not valid holidays & subject to Rules of Use.
Not valid with other discount offers, unless specified.

great place for kids

Valid now thru November 1, 2006

entertainment. entertainment.com

PURCHASE $6.00 TICKETS AT BOX OFFICE

REGAL ENTERTAINMENT GROUP℠

Present this coupon at the Theatre Box Office to purchase up to two (2) *VIP Super Saver Admission Tickets for only $6.00 each. Upgrade to an "UNRESTRICTED" Premiere Super Saver Admission Ticket for only $1.50 extra per ticket.

C3

Not valid holidays & subject to Rules of Use.
Not valid with other discount offers, unless specified.

great place for kids

Valid now thru November 1, 2006

entertainment. entertainment.com

PURCHASE $6.00 TICKETS AT BOX OFFICE

REGAL ENTERTAINMENT GROUP℠

Present this coupon at the Theatre Box Office to purchase up to two (2) *VIP Super Saver Admission Tickets for only $6.00 each. Upgrade to an "UNRESTRICTED" Premiere Super Saver Admission Ticket for only $1.50 extra per ticket.

C4

Not valid holidays & subject to Rules of Use.
Not valid with other discount offers, unless specified.

great place for kids

Valid now thru November 1, 2006

entertainment. entertainment.com

PURCHASE $6.00 TICKETS AT BOX OFFICE

REGAL ENTERTAINMENT GROUP℠

Present this coupon at the Theatre Box Office to purchase up to two (2) *VIP Super Saver Admission Tickets for only $6.00 each. Upgrade to an "UNRESTRICTED" Premiere Super Saver Admission Ticket for only $1.50 extra per ticket.

C5

Not valid holidays & subject to Rules of Use.
Not valid with other discount offers, unless specified.

great place for kids

Valid now thru November 1, 2006

entertainment. entertainment.com

PURCHASE $6.00 TICKETS AT BOX OFFICE

REGAL ENTERTAINMENT GROUP℠

Present this coupon at the Theatre Box Office to purchase up to two (2) *VIP Super Saver Admission Tickets for only $6.00 each. Upgrade to an "UNRESTRICTED" Premiere Super Saver Admission Ticket for only $1.50 extra per ticket.

C6

Not valid holidays & subject to Rules of Use.
Not valid with other discount offers, unless specified.

great place for kids

Valid now thru November 1, 2006

Coupon VOID if purchased, sold, or bartered.
Discounts exclude tax, tip and/or alcohol, where applicable.

* E C 0000000001 *

Check your local newspaper or visit www.REGMovies.com for showtimes & locations nearest you.

Surcharge may be applied if redeemed at any Manhattan, NY location. Valid at all Regal Entertainment Group locations nationwide.

**VIP Super Saver Admission Ticket is not valid during the first 12 days of selected new release films.*

REGAL ENTERTAINMENT GROUP℠

REGAL CINEMAS · UNITED ARTISTS Theatres · EDWARDS THEATRES

00588257

Coupon VOID if purchased, sold, or bartered.
Discounts exclude tax, tip and/or alcohol, where applicable.

* E C 0000000001 *

Check your local newspaper or visit www.REGMovies.com for showtimes & locations nearest you.

Surcharge may be applied if redeemed at any Manhattan, NY location. Valid at all Regal Entertainment Group locations nationwide.

**VIP Super Saver Admission Ticket is not valid during the first 12 days of selected new release films.*

REGAL ENTERTAINMENT GROUP℠

REGAL CINEMAS · UNITED ARTISTS Theatres · EDWARDS THEATRES

00588257

Coupon VOID if purchased, sold, or bartered.
Discounts exclude tax, tip and/or alcohol, where applicable.

* E C 0000000001 *

Check your local newspaper or visit www.REGMovies.com for showtimes & locations nearest you.

Surcharge may be applied if redeemed at any Manhattan, NY location. Valid at all Regal Entertainment Group locations nationwide.

**VIP Super Saver Admission Ticket is not valid during the first 12 days of selected new release films.*

REGAL ENTERTAINMENT GROUP℠

REGAL CINEMAS · UNITED ARTISTS Theatres · EDWARDS THEATRES

00588257

Coupon VOID if purchased, sold, or bartered.
Discounts exclude tax, tip and/or alcohol, where applicable.

* E C 0000000001 *

Check your local newspaper or visit www.REGMovies.com for showtimes & locations nearest you.

Surcharge may be applied if redeemed at any Manhattan, NY location. Valid at all Regal Entertainment Group locations nationwide.

**VIP Super Saver Admission Ticket is not valid during the first 12 days of selected new release films.*

REGAL ENTERTAINMENT GROUP℠

REGAL CINEMAS · UNITED ARTISTS Theatres · EDWARDS THEATRES

00588257

Coupon VOID if purchased, sold, or bartered.
Discounts exclude tax, tip and/or alcohol, where applicable.

* E C 0000000001 *

Check your local newspaper or visit www.REGMovies.com for showtimes & locations nearest you.

Surcharge may be applied if redeemed at any Manhattan, NY location. Valid at all Regal Entertainment Group locations nationwide.

**VIP Super Saver Admission Ticket is not valid during the first 12 days of selected new release films.*

REGAL ENTERTAINMENT GROUP℠

REGAL CINEMAS · UNITED ARTISTS Theatres · EDWARDS THEATRES

00588257

Coupon VOID if purchased, sold, or bartered.
Discounts exclude tax, tip and/or alcohol, where applicable.

* E C 0000000001 *

Check your local newspaper or visit www.REGMovies.com for showtimes & locations nearest you.

Surcharge may be applied if redeemed at any Manhattan, NY location. Valid at all Regal Entertainment Group locations nationwide.

**VIP Super Saver Admission Ticket is not valid during the first 12 days of selected new release films.*

REGAL ENTERTAINMENT GROUP℠

REGAL CINEMAS · UNITED ARTISTS Theatres · EDWARDS THEATRES

00588257

entertainment.com

PURCHASE $6.00 TICKETS AT BOX OFFICE

REGAL ENTERTAINMENT GROUP℠

REGAL CINEMAS · UNITED ARTISTS Theatres · EDWARDS THEATRES

Present this coupon at the Theatre Box Office to purchase up to two (2) *VIP Super Saver Admission Tickets for only $6.00 each. Upgrade to an "UNRESTRICTED" Premiere Super Saver Admission Ticket for only $1.50 extra per ticket.

C7

Not valid holidays & subject to Rules of Use.
Not valid with other discount offers, unless specified.

great place for kids

Valid now thru November 1, 2006

---

entertainment.com

PURCHASE $6.00 TICKETS AT BOX OFFICE

REGAL ENTERTAINMENT GROUP℠

REGAL CINEMAS · UNITED ARTISTS Theatres · EDWARDS THEATRES

Present this coupon at the Theatre Box Office to purchase up to two (2) *VIP Super Saver Admission Tickets for only $6.00 each. Upgrade to an "UNRESTRICTED" Premiere Super Saver Admission Ticket for only $1.50 extra per ticket.

C8

Not valid holidays & subject to Rules of Use.
Not valid with other discount offers, unless specified.

great place for kids

Valid now thru November 1, 2006

---

entertainment.com

PURCHASE $6.00 TICKETS AT BOX OFFICE

REGAL ENTERTAINMENT GROUP℠

REGAL CINEMAS · UNITED ARTISTS Theatres · EDWARDS THEATRES

Present this coupon at the Theatre Box Office to purchase up to two (2) *VIP Super Saver Admission Tickets for only $6.00 each. Upgrade to an "UNRESTRICTED" Premiere Super Saver Admission Ticket for only $1.50 extra per ticket.

C9

Not valid holidays & subject to Rules of Use.
Not valid with other discount offers, unless specified.

great place for kids

Valid now thru November 1, 2006

---

entertainment.com

PURCHASE $6.00 TICKETS AT BOX OFFICE

REGAL ENTERTAINMENT GROUP℠

REGAL CINEMAS · UNITED ARTISTS Theatres · EDWARDS THEATRES

Present this coupon at the Theatre Box Office to purchase up to two (2) *VIP Super Saver Admission Tickets for only $6.00 each. Upgrade to an "UNRESTRICTED" Premiere Super Saver Admission Ticket for only $1.50 extra per ticket.

C10

Not valid holidays & subject to Rules of Use.
Not valid with other discount offers, unless specified.

great place for kids

Valid now thru November 1, 2006

---

entertainment.com

PURCHASE $6.00 TICKETS AT BOX OFFICE

REGAL ENTERTAINMENT GROUP℠

REGAL CINEMAS · UNITED ARTISTS Theatres · EDWARDS THEATRES

Present this coupon at the Theatre Box Office to purchase up to two (2) *VIP Super Saver Admission Tickets for only $6.00 each. Upgrade to an "UNRESTRICTED" Premiere Super Saver Admission Ticket for only $1.50 extra per ticket.

C11

Not valid holidays & subject to Rules of Use.
Not valid with other discount offers, unless specified.

great place for kids

Valid now thru November 1, 2006

---

entertainment.com

GIVE THE GIFT OF MOVIE TICKETS!

REGAL ENTERTAINMENT GROUP℠

REGAL CINEMAS · UNITED ARTISTS Theatres · EDWARDS THEATRES

PURCHASE DISCOUNT MOVIE TICKETS BY MAIL.
(maximum order of 12 tickets of each type)

Ticket Type	Price	Total
VIP Super Saver______	x $6.00	= $_________
Premiere Super Saver ("unrestricted" ticket)______	x $7.00	= $_________
Ultimate Premiere Movie Pack_____ (2 "unrestricted" tickets and one $10 concession gift certificate)	x $24.00	= $_________

Subtotal $________
Handling $________
Total $________

Tickets do not have an expiration date. This coupon not redeemable at theatre box office. Tickets valid at all Regal Cinemas, United Artists Theatres and Edward Theatres nationwide. Discount tickets may not be resold. VIP Super Saver Ticket is not valid during the first 12 days of selected new release films, special engagements & "No Pass" movies. *See back for details.

C12

Not valid holidays & subject to Rules of Use.
Not valid with other discount offers, unless specified.

great place for kids

Valid now thru November 1, 2006

Coupon VOID if purchased, sold, or bartered.
Discounts exclude tax, tip and/or alcohol, where applicable.

EC
* 0000000001 *

Check your local newspaper or visit www.REGMovies.com for showtimes & locations nearest you.

Surcharge may be applied if redeemed at any Manhattan, NY location. Valid at all Regal Entertainment Group locations nationwide.

**VIP Super Saver Admission Ticket is not valid during the first 12 days of selected new release films.*

REGAL ENTERTAINMENT GROUP℠

REGAL CINEMAS · UNITED ARTISTS Theatres · EDWARDS THEATRES

00588257

Coupon VOID if purchased, sold, or bartered.
Discounts exclude tax, tip and/or alcohol, where applicable.

EC
* 0000000001 *

Check your local newspaper or visit www.REGMovies.com for showtimes & locations nearest you.

Surcharge may be applied if redeemed at any Manhattan, NY location. Valid at all Regal Entertainment Group locations nationwide.

**VIP Super Saver Admission Ticket is not valid during the first 12 days of selected new release films.*

REGAL ENTERTAINMENT GROUP℠

REGAL CINEMAS · UNITED ARTISTS Theatres · EDWARDS THEATRES

00588257

Coupon VOID if purchased, sold, or bartered.
Discounts exclude tax, tip and/or alcohol, where applicable.

REGAL ENTERTAINMENT GROUP℠

REGAL CINEMAS · UNITED ARTISTS Theatres · EDWARDS THEATRES

- Visit www.REGMovies.com for show times and locations nationwide.
- Tickets available by mail order only. You will receive tickets to present at the box office for admission. Please note ticket usage restrictions on coupons.
- Ticket orders fulfilled by availability. Ticket prices are subject to change without notice.
- **All checks or money orders must be made payable to: ENTERTAINMENT PUBLICATIONS. Price per ticket is on the front of this coupon. Check/money order must include total cost of tickets ordered plus shipping and handling of $2.25 for orders valued at $39.99 or less and $5.50 for orders valued at $40.00 or more. Do not send cash. Mail payment and completed coupons to:**

  ENTERTAINMENT PUBLICATIONS, INC.
  c/o TICKETS
  P.O. BOX 539
  DUNCAN, SC 29334-5390;
- Allow three weeks for delivery of tickets. Tickets may not be exchanged or returned for refund.
- Call 1-877-814-5292 only if you have ordered more than three weeks ago and have not received your order.

Number of movie tickets you wish to order with this coupon:__________
Name __________
Address __________
City __________ State __________ Zip __________
Daytime Phone (___) __________
Email address__________

00505562

Coupon VOID if purchased, sold, or bartered.
Discounts exclude tax, tip and/or alcohol, where applicable.

EC
* 0000000001 *

Check your local newspaper or visit www.REGMovies.com for showtimes & locations nearest you.

Surcharge may be applied if redeemed at any Manhattan, NY location. Valid at all Regal Entertainment Group locations nationwide.

**VIP Super Saver Admission Ticket is not valid during the first 12 days of selected new release films.*

REGAL ENTERTAINMENT GROUP℠

REGAL CINEMAS · UNITED ARTISTS Theatres · EDWARDS THEATRES

00588257

Coupon VOID if purchased, sold, or bartered.
Discounts exclude tax, tip and/or alcohol, where applicable.

EC
* 0000000001 *

Check your local newspaper or visit www.REGMovies.com for showtimes & locations nearest you.

Surcharge may be applied if redeemed at any Manhattan, NY location. Valid at all Regal Entertainment Group locations nationwide.

**VIP Super Saver Admission Ticket is not valid during the first 12 days of selected new release films.*

REGAL ENTERTAINMENT GROUP℠

REGAL CINEMAS · UNITED ARTISTS Theatres · EDWARDS THEATRES

00588257

Coupon VOID if purchased, sold, or bartered.
Discounts exclude tax, tip and/or alcohol, where applicable.

EC
* 0000000001 *

Check your local newspaper or visit www.REGMovies.com for showtimes & locations nearest you.

Surcharge may be applied if redeemed at any Manhattan, NY location. Valid at all Regal Entertainment Group locations nationwide.

**VIP Super Saver Admission Ticket is not valid during the first 12 days of selected new release films.*

REGAL ENTERTAINMENT GROUP℠

REGAL CINEMAS · UNITED ARTISTS Theatres · EDWARDS THEATRES

00588257

National Amusements

See Reverse Side for Mail Order Information

- Please note expiration date on movie tickets; dates may vary
- No refunds or exchanges
- Allow 3 weeks for delivery

Bonus Discounts at entertainment.com

entertainment. entertainment.com

great place for kids

MAIL IN MOVIE TICKETS

Valid for up to six TICKETS at $7.00 each.

Some Restrictions Apply

THIS COUPON IS NOT REDEEMABLE AT THEATRE BOX OFFICE; Subject to rules of use; Use may be limited on certain films due to contractual obligations; Not valid with other offers, unless specified; Void if purchased, sold, or bartered for cash; Electronic reproductions of this product are void; Cinema de Lux Director's Hall and IMAX theatres subject to additional surcharge; Subject to seating availability; Mail Order Only see reverse side

SHOWCASE AND MULTIPLEX CINEMAS

cinemas DE LUX

NATIONAL AMUSEMENTS

www.nationalamusements.com

C13

Valid now thru November 1, 2006

Not valid holidays & subject to Rules of Use. Not valid with other discount offers, unless specified. Coupon VOID if purchased, sold or bartered. Discounts exclude tax, tip and/or alcohol, where applicable.

National Amusements

See Reverse Side for Mail Order Information

- Please note expiration date on movie tickets; dates may vary
- No refunds or exchanges
- Allow 3 weeks for delivery

Bonus Discounts at entertainment.com

entertainment. entertainment.com

great place for kids

MAIL IN MOVIE TICKETS

Valid for up to six TICKETS at $7.00 each.

Some Restrictions Apply

THIS COUPON IS NOT REDEEMABLE AT THEATRE BOX OFFICE; Subject to rules of use; Use may be limited on certain films due to contractual obligations; Not valid with other offers, unless specified; Void if purchased, sold, or bartered for cash; Electronic reproductions of this product are void; Cinema de Lux Director's Hall and IMAX theatres subject to additional surcharge; Subject to seating availability; Mail Order Only see reverse side

SHOWCASE AND MULTIPLEX CINEMAS

cinemas DE LUX

NATIONAL AMUSEMENTS

www.nationalamusements.com

C14

Valid now thru November 1, 2006

Not valid holidays & subject to Rules of Use. Not valid with other discount offers, unless specified. Coupon VOID if purchased, sold or bartered. Discounts exclude tax, tip and/or alcohol, where applicable.

National Amusements

See Reverse Side for Mail Order Information

- Please note expiration date on movie tickets; dates may vary
- No refunds or exchanges
- Allow 3 weeks for delivery

Bonus Discounts at entertainment.com

entertainment. entertainment.com

great place for kids

MAIL IN MOVIE TICKETS

Valid for up to six TICKETS at $7.00 each.

Some Restrictions Apply

THIS COUPON IS NOT REDEEMABLE AT THEATRE BOX OFFICE; Subject to rules of use; Use may be limited on certain films due to contractual obligations; Not valid with other offers, unless specified; Void if purchased, sold, or bartered for cash; Electronic reproductions of this product are void; Cinema de Lux Director's Hall and IMAX theatres subject to additional surcharge; Subject to seating availability; Mail Order Only see reverse side

SHOWCASE AND MULTIPLEX CINEMAS

cinemas DE LUX

NATIONAL AMUSEMENTS

www.nationalamusements.com

C15

Valid now thru November 1, 2006

Not valid holidays & subject to Rules of Use. Not valid with other discount offers, unless specified. Coupon VOID if purchased, sold or bartered. Discounts exclude tax, tip and/or alcohol, where applicable.

- Tickets available by mail order only. You will receive tickets to present at the box office for admission. Please note ticket usage restrictions on coupons.
- Ticket orders fulfilled by availability. Ticket prices are subject to change without notice.
- **All checks or money orders must be made payable to: <u>Entertainment Publications</u>. Price per ticket is on the front of this coupon. Check/money order must include *total cost of tickets ordered* <u>plus</u> shipping and handling of $2.25 for orders valued at $39.99 or less and $5.50 for orders valued at $40.00 or more. Do not send cash.**
- **Mail payment and completed coupons to:** **Entertainment Publications, Inc.**
  c/o TICKETS
  P.O. BOX 539
  DUNCAN, SC 29334-5390
- Allow three weeks for delivery of tickets. Note expiration dates on tickets received. They may vary. Tickets may not be exchanged or returned for refund.
- Call 1-877-814-5292 only if you have ordered more than three weeks ago and have not received your order.

Number of movie tickets you wish to order with this coupon:_______ Total due: $ ________________

Name: ______________________________

Address: ______________________________

Daytime Phone: (________) ______________________________

City:____________________State _____ ZIP: ______________________

E-Mail Address: ______________________________

00155893

entertainment.com

00155893

- Tickets available by mail order only. You will receive tickets to present at the box office for admission. Please note ticket usage restrictions on coupons.
- Ticket orders fulfilled by availability. Ticket prices are subject to change without notice.
- **All checks or money orders must be made payable to: <u>Entertainment Publications</u>. Price per ticket is on the front of this coupon. Check/money order must include *total cost of tickets ordered* <u>plus</u> shipping and handling of $2.25 for orders valued at $39.99 or less and $5.50 for orders valued at $40.00 or more. Do not send cash.**
- **Mail payment and completed coupons to:** **Entertainment Publications, Inc.**
  c/o TICKETS
  P.O. BOX 539
  DUNCAN, SC 29334-5390
- Allow three weeks for delivery of tickets. Note expiration dates on tickets received. They may vary. Tickets may not be exchanged or returned for refund.
- Call 1-877-814-5292 only if you have ordered more than three weeks ago and have not received your order.

Number of movie tickets you wish to order with this coupon:_______ Total due: $ ________________

Name: ______________________________

Address: ______________________________

Daytime Phone: (________) ______________________________

City:____________________State _____ ZIP: ______________________

E-Mail Address: ______________________________

00155893

entertainment.com

00155893

- Tickets available by mail order only. You will receive tickets to present at the box office for admission. Please note ticket usage restrictions on coupons.
- Ticket orders fulfilled by availability. Ticket prices are subject to change without notice.
- **All checks or money orders must be made payable to: <u>Entertainment Publications</u>. Price per ticket is on the front of this coupon. Check/money order must include *total cost of tickets ordered* <u>plus</u> shipping and handling of $2.25 for orders valued at $39.99 or less and $5.50 for orders valued at $40.00 or more. Do not send cash.**
- **Mail payment and completed coupons to:** **Entertainment Publications, Inc.**
  c/o TICKETS
  P.O. BOX 539
  DUNCAN, SC 29334-5390
- Allow three weeks for delivery of tickets. Note expiration dates on tickets received. They may vary. Tickets may not be exchanged or returned for refund.
- Call 1-877-814-5292 only if you have ordered more than three weeks ago and have not received your order.

Number of movie tickets you wish to order with this coupon:_______ Total due: $ ________________

Name: ______________________________

Address: ______________________________

Daytime Phone: (________) ______________________________

City:____________________State _____ ZIP: ______________________

E-Mail Address: ______________________________

00155893

entertainment.com

00155893

AMC Theatres

See reverse side for locations

- Please note expiration date on movie tickets; dates may vary
- No refunds or exchanges
- Allow 3 weeks for delivery

Bonus Discounts at entertainment.com

entertainment. entertainment.com

great place for kids

DISCOUNT MOVIE TICKETS

Valid for up to (12) twelve DISCOUNT ADMISSION TICKETS at $6.00 each.

Some restrictions may apply.

THIS COUPON IS NOT REDEEMABLE AT THEATRE BOX OFFICE.; Mail order only - see reverse side. Check local newspapers for theatre locations. Tickets on availability basis. Tickets valid at all present and future AMC locations nationwide. Special engagements and "No Pass" engagements excluded.

AMC® THEATRES

C16

Valid now thru November 1, 2006

Not valid holidays & subject to Rules of Use. Not valid with other discount offers, unless specified. Coupon VOID if purchased, sold or bartered. Discounts exclude tax, tip and/or alcohol, where applicable.

AMC Theatres

See reverse side for locations

- Please note expiration date on movie tickets; dates may vary
- No refunds or exchanges
- Allow 3 weeks for delivery

Bonus Discounts at entertainment.com

entertainment. entertainment.com

great place for kids

DISCOUNT MOVIE TICKETS

Valid for up to (12) twelve DISCOUNT ADMISSION TICKETS at $6.00 each.

Some restrictions may apply.

THIS COUPON IS NOT REDEEMABLE AT THEATRE BOX OFFICE.; Mail order only - see reverse side. Check local newspapers for theatre locations. Tickets on availability basis. Tickets valid at all present and future AMC locations nationwide. Special engagements and "No Pass" engagements excluded.

AMC® THEATRES

C17

Valid now thru November 1, 2006

Not valid holidays & subject to Rules of Use. Not valid with other discount offers, unless specified. Coupon VOID if purchased, sold or bartered. Discounts exclude tax, tip and/or alcohol, where applicable.

AMC Theatres

See reverse side for locations

- Please note expiration date on movie tickets; dates may vary
- No refunds or exchanges
- Allow 3 weeks for delivery

Bonus Discounts at entertainment.com

entertainment. entertainment.com

great place for kids

DISCOUNT MOVIE TICKETS

Valid for up to (12) twelve DISCOUNT ADMISSION TICKETS at $6.00 each.

Some restrictions may apply.

THIS COUPON IS NOT REDEEMABLE AT THEATRE BOX OFFICE.; Mail order only - see reverse side. Check local newspapers for theatre locations. Tickets on availability basis. Tickets valid at all present and future AMC locations nationwide. Special engagements and "No Pass" engagements excluded.

AMC® THEATRES

C18

Valid now thru November 1, 2006

Not valid holidays & subject to Rules of Use. Not valid with other discount offers, unless specified. Coupon VOID if purchased, sold or bartered. Discounts exclude tax, tip and/or alcohol, where applicable.

- Tickets available by mail order only. You will receive tickets to present at the box office for admission. Please note ticket usage restrictions on coupons.
- Ticket orders fulfilled by availability. Ticket prices are subject to change without notice.
- **All checks or money orders must be made payable to: Entertainment Publications, Inc. Price per ticket is on the front of this coupon. Check/money order must include *total cost of tickets ordered* plus shipping and handling of $2.25 for orders valued at $39.99 or less and $5.50 for orders valued at $40.00 or more. Do not send cash.**
- **Mail payment and completed coupons to:** **ENTERTAINMENT PUBLICATIONS, INC.
c/o TICKETS
P.O. BOX 539
DUNCAN, SC 29334-5390**
- Allow three weeks for delivery of tickets. Note expiration dates on tickets received. They may vary. Tickets may not be exchanged or returned for refund.
- Call 1-877-814-5292 only if you have ordered more than three weeks ago and have not received your order.

Number of movie tickets you wish to order with this coupon:_________ Total due: $____________

Name: ____

Address: ____

City: ______________________ State: ____________ ZIP: ________________

E-Mail Address: ____________________________________

00000222

entertainment.com

00000222

- Tickets available by mail order only. You will receive tickets to present at the box office for admission. Please note ticket usage restrictions on coupons.
- Ticket orders fulfilled by availability. Ticket prices are subject to change without notice.
- **All checks or money orders must be made payable to: Entertainment Publications, Inc. Price per ticket is on the front of this coupon. Check/money order must include *total cost of tickets ordered* plus shipping and handling of $2.25 for orders valued at $39.99 or less and $5.50 for orders valued at $40.00 or more. Do not send cash.**
- **Mail payment and completed coupons to:** **ENTERTAINMENT PUBLICATIONS, INC.
c/o TICKETS
P.O. BOX 539
DUNCAN, SC 29334-5390**
- Allow three weeks for delivery of tickets. Note expiration dates on tickets received. They may vary. Tickets may not be exchanged or returned for refund.
- Call 1-877-814-5292 only if you have ordered more than three weeks ago and have not received your order.

Number of movie tickets you wish to order with this coupon:_________ Total due: $____________

Name: ____

Address: ____

City: ______________________ State: ____________ ZIP: ________________

E-Mail Address: ____________________________________

00000222

entertainment.com

00000222

- Tickets available by mail order only. You will receive tickets to present at the box office for admission. Please note ticket usage restrictions on coupons.
- Ticket orders fulfilled by availability. Ticket prices are subject to change without notice.
- **All checks or money orders must be made payable to: Entertainment Publications, Inc. Price per ticket is on the front of this coupon. Check/money order must include *total cost of tickets ordered* plus shipping and handling of $2.25 for orders valued at $39.99 or less and $5.50 for orders valued at $40.00 or more. Do not send cash.**
- **Mail payment and completed coupons to:** **ENTERTAINMENT PUBLICATIONS, INC.
c/o TICKETS
P.O. BOX 539
DUNCAN, SC 29334-5390**
- Allow three weeks for delivery of tickets. Note expiration dates on tickets received. They may vary. Tickets may not be exchanged or returned for refund.
- Call 1-877-814-5292 only if you have ordered more than three weeks ago and have not received your order.

Number of movie tickets you wish to order with this coupon:_________ Total due: $____________

Name: ____

Address: ____

City: ______________________ State: ____________ ZIP: ________________

E-Mail Address: ____________________________________

00000222

entertainment.com

00000222

Loews Cineplex

See Reverse Side for Mail Order Information

- Please note expiration dates on movie tickets; dates may vary
- No refunds or exchanges on purchased tickets
- Allow 3 weeks for delivery

Bonus Discounts at entertainment.com

entertainment. entertainment.com

great place for kids

DISCOUNT MOVIE TICKETS

Valid for up to eighteen (18) **GALAXY TICKETS** at $7.00 each.

valid anytime

Not good for special attractions and motion pictures where prohibited by contractual obligations. THIS COUPON IS NOT REDEEMABLE AT THEATRE BOX OFFICE. Offer valid at Loews, Cineplex Odeon, Star, Magic Johnson and Loews Cineplex Imax Theatres nationwide. Mail order only - see reverse side. Tickets on availability basis.

LOEWS CINEPLEX ENTERTAINMENT

LOEWS THEATRES · CINEPLEX ODEON · MAGIC JOHNSON · LOEWS IMAX THEATRE

C19

Valid now thru November 1, 2006

Not valid holidays & subject to Rules of Use. Not valid with other discount offers, unless specified. Coupon VOID if purchased, sold or bartered. Discounts exclude tax, tip and/or alcohol, where applicable.

Loews Cineplex

See Reverse Side for Mail Order Information

- Please note expiration dates on movie tickets; dates may vary
- No refunds or exchanges on purchased tickets
- Allow 3 weeks for delivery

Bonus Discounts at entertainment.com

entertainment. entertainment.com

great place for kids

DISCOUNT MOVIE TICKETS

Valid for up to eighteen (18) **GALAXY TICKETS** at $7.00 each.

valid anytime

Not good for special attractions and motion pictures where prohibited by contractual obligations. THIS COUPON IS NOT REDEEMABLE AT THEATRE BOX OFFICE. Offer valid at Loews, Cineplex Odeon, Star, Magic Johnson and Loews Cineplex Imax Theatres nationwide. Mail order only - see reverse side. Tickets on availability basis.

LOEWS CINEPLEX ENTERTAINMENT

LOEWS THEATRES · CINEPLEX ODEON · MAGIC JOHNSON · LOEWS IMAX THEATRE

C20

Valid now thru November 1, 2006

Not valid holidays & subject to Rules of Use. Not valid with other discount offers, unless specified. Coupon VOID if purchased, sold or bartered. Discounts exclude tax, tip and/or alcohol, where applicable.

Loews Cineplex

See Reverse Side for Mail Order Information

- Please note expiration dates on movie tickets; dates may vary
- No refunds or exchanges on purchased tickets
- Allow 3 weeks for delivery

Bonus Discounts at entertainment.com

entertainment. entertainment.com

great place for kids

DISCOUNT MOVIE TICKETS

Valid for up to eighteen (18) **GALAXY TICKETS** at $7.00 each.

valid anytime

Not good for special attractions and motion pictures where prohibited by contractual obligations. THIS COUPON IS NOT REDEEMABLE AT THEATRE BOX OFFICE. Offer valid at Loews, Cineplex Odeon, Star, Magic Johnson and Loews Cineplex Imax Theatres nationwide. Mail order only - see reverse side. Tickets on availability basis.

LOEWS CINEPLEX ENTERTAINMENT

LOEWS THEATRES · CINEPLEX ODEON · MAGIC JOHNSON · LOEWS IMAX THEATRE

C21

Valid now thru November 1, 2006

Not valid holidays & subject to Rules of Use. Not valid with other discount offers, unless specified. Coupon VOID if purchased, sold or bartered. Discounts exclude tax, tip and/or alcohol, where applicable.

- Tickets available by mail order only. You will receive tickets to present at the box office for admission. Please note ticket usage restrictions on coupons.
- Ticket orders fulfilled by availability. Ticket prices are subject to change without notice.
- **All checks or money orders must be made payable to: <u>Entertainment Publications.</u> Price per ticket is on the front of this coupon. Check/money order must include *total cost of tickets ordered* <u>plus</u> shipping and handling of $2.25 for orders valued at $39.99 or less and $5.50 for orders valued at $40.00 or more. Do not send cash.**
- **Mail payment and completed coupons to:** **ENTERTAINMENT PUBLICATIONS, INC.**
  c/o TICKETS
  P.O. BOX 539
  DUNCAN, SC 29334-5390

- Allow three weeks for delivery of tickets. Note expiration dates on tickets received. They may vary. Tickets may not be exchanged or returned for refund.
- Call 1-877-814-5292 only if you have ordered more than three weeks ago and have not received your order.
- Discount Movie Tickets will have an expiration date (unless purchased in CA or where prohibited by law).

Number of movie tickets you wish to order with this coupon:______________________

Name: ______________________

Address: ______________________

City:______________ State:__________ ZIP:______________

Daytime Phone: (_____) ______________________

E-Mail Address: ______________________

00000259

entertainment.com

00000259

- Tickets available by mail order only. You will receive tickets to present at the box office for admission. Please note ticket usage restrictions on coupons.
- Ticket orders fulfilled by availability. Ticket prices are subject to change without notice.
- **All checks or money orders must be made payable to: <u>Entertainment Publications.</u> Price per ticket is on the front of this coupon. Check/money order must include *total cost of tickets ordered* <u>plus</u> shipping and handling of $2.25 for orders valued at $39.99 or less and $5.50 for orders valued at $40.00 or more. Do not send cash.**
- **Mail payment and completed coupons to:** **ENTERTAINMENT PUBLICATIONS, INC.**
  c/o TICKETS
  P.O. BOX 539
  DUNCAN, SC 29334-5390

- Allow three weeks for delivery of tickets. Note expiration dates on tickets received. They may vary. Tickets may not be exchanged or returned for refund.
- Call 1-877-814-5292 only if you have ordered more than three weeks ago and have not received your order.
- Discount Movie Tickets will have an expiration date (unless purchased in CA or where prohibited by law).

Number of movie tickets you wish to order with this coupon:______________________

Name: ______________________

Address: ______________________

City:______________ State:__________ ZIP:______________

Daytime Phone: (_____) ______________________

E-Mail Address: ______________________

00000259

entertainment.com

00000259

- Tickets available by mail order only. You will receive tickets to present at the box office for admission. Please note ticket usage restrictions on coupons.
- Ticket orders fulfilled by availability. Ticket prices are subject to change without notice.
- **All checks or money orders must be made payable to: <u>Entertainment Publications.</u> Price per ticket is on the front of this coupon. Check/money order must include *total cost of tickets ordered* <u>plus</u> shipping and handling of $2.25 for orders valued at $39.99 or less and $5.50 for orders valued at $40.00 or more. Do not send cash.**
- **Mail payment and completed coupons to:** **ENTERTAINMENT PUBLICATIONS, INC.**
  c/o TICKETS
  P.O. BOX 539
  DUNCAN, SC 29334-5390

- Allow three weeks for delivery of tickets. Note expiration dates on tickets received. They may vary. Tickets may not be exchanged or returned for refund.
- Call 1-877-814-5292 only if you have ordered more than three weeks ago and have not received your order.
- Discount Movie Tickets will have an expiration date (unless purchased in CA or where prohibited by law).

Number of movie tickets you wish to order with this coupon:______________________

Name: ______________________

Address: ______________________

City:______________ State:__________ ZIP:______________

Daytime Phone: (_____) ______________________

E-Mail Address: ______________________

00000259

entertainment.com

00000259

Washington Capitals

401 9th St., NW
Suite 750
Washington, DC

Bonus Discounts at
entertainment.com

entertainment.
entertainment.com

great place for kids

50% OFF

Valid for up to 8 TICKETS at up to 50% off the regular price.

Limited dates and price ranges available; On availability basis

to order online see reverse side

Mail order & Internet orders only; see reverse side

www.washingtoncaps.com

C22

Valid now thru November 1, 2006

Not valid holidays & subject to Rules of Use. Not valid with other discount offers, unless specified. Coupon VOID if purchased, sold or bartered. Discounts exclude tax, tip and/or alcohol, where applicable.

Washington Capitals

401 9th St., NW
Suite 750
Washington, DC

Bonus Discounts at
entertainment.com

entertainment.
entertainment.com

great place for kids

SPECIAL OFFER

Capitals PUCKS INTO BUCKS fundraising program, $5 from every ticket sold will go to your organization.

10 Ticket Minimum

valid anytime

Call (202)266-2323 for details

www.washingtoncaps.com

C23

Valid now thru November 1, 2006

Not valid holidays & subject to Rules of Use. Not valid with other discount offers, unless specified. Coupon VOID if purchased, sold or bartered. Discounts exclude tax, tip and/or alcohol, where applicable.

Washington Capitals

401 9th St., NW
Suite 750
Washington, DC

- The Family Pack includes:
- a game ticket
- an official Capitals souvenir
- a hot dog
- bag of chips
- small soda

Bonus Discounts at
entertainment.com

entertainment.
entertainment.com

great place for kids

SPECIAL OFFER

Enjoy a SPECIALLY PRICED FAMILY PACK.

to order online see reverse side

www.washingtoncaps.com

C24

Valid now thru November 1, 2006

Not valid holidays & subject to Rules of Use. Not valid with other discount offers, unless specified. Coupon VOID if purchased, sold or bartered. Discounts exclude tax, tip and/or alcohol, where applicable.

Order online @ www.capstickets.com/entertainment.tml
Or Mail this form to: Washington Capital Entertainment 401 9th St. NW, Suite 750 Washington, DC 20004

Please send __________ tickets @ $17 each (gate price $45)

Please send __________ tickets @ $27 each (gate price $55)

Check payable to Washington Capitals. No taxes; $5 service charge per order

Game Date 1st choice ____________________

Name: ______________________________ Day Phone: ____________________

Address: ____

City: ______________________________ ST: ________ Zip: ____________

Email: ____

Credit Card #: ______________________ Exp. Date: ____________________

- All sales are final. No refunds or exchanges
- Orders will be mailed to you. Please enclose S.A.S.E
- Orders received within 10 days of game will be held at the box office for pickup on game night. Photo ID required. Name for pickup____________________

00665233

entertainment.com

00665233

WASHINGTON CAPITALS ™

401 9th St., NW Suite 750
Washington, DC

00665238

entertainment.com

00665238

WASHINGTON CAPITALS ™

401 9th St., NW Suite 750
Washington, DC

Order online @ www.capstickets.com/entertainment.html
202-266-2323
groupsales@washcaps.com

00665242

entertainment.com

00665242

Ringling Bros. and Barnum & Bailey Circus

Visit entertainment.com/hotline for additional details such as dates, times, locations and prices.

Bonus Discounts at
entertainment.com

entertainment
entertainment.com

great place for kids

BUY ONE TICKET, GET ONE FREE

Enjoy one complimentary FULL PRICE TICKET when a second FULL PRICE TICKET of equal or greater value is purchased.

Additional adjacent seating may be purchased at regular prices at time of redemption

valid for scheduled performances Monday thru Thursday matinee and evening, and Friday matinee

Limit one free ticket per coupon; Not valid on Front Row & VIP seating; No double discounts; Redeemable only at the arena box office; Tour schedules subject to change

RINGLING BROS. AND BARNUM & BAILEY — THE GREATEST SHOW ON EARTH

www.Ringling.com

C25

Valid now thru November 1, 2006

Not valid holidays & subject to Rules of Use. Not valid with other discount offers, unless specified. Coupon VOID if purchased, sold or bartered. Discounts exclude tax, tip and/or alcohol, where applicable.

Disney On Ice

Visit entertainment.com/hotline for additional details such as dates, times, locations and prices.

- Visit us at www.disneyonice.com

Bonus Discounts at
entertainment.com

entertainment
entertainment.com

great place for kids

BUY ONE TICKET, GET ONE FREE

Enjoy one complimentary FULL PRICE TICKET when a second FULL PRICE TICKET of equal or greater value is purchased. .

Additional adjacent seating may be purchased at regular prices at time of redemption

valid for scheduled performances Monday thru Thursday matinee and evening, and Friday matinee

Limit one free ticket per coupon; Not valid on Front Row & VIP seating; No double discounts; Redeemable only at the arena box office; Tour schedules subject to change

DISNEY ON ICE
PRODUCED BY FELD ENTERTAINMENT

www.disneyonice.com

C26

Valid now thru November 1, 2006

Not valid holidays & subject to Rules of Use. Not valid with other discount offers, unless specified. Coupon VOID if purchased, sold or bartered. Discounts exclude tax, tip and/or alcohol, where applicable.

Big Apple Circus

Dulles Town Center
Dulles, VA
(877)407-8497

- A one-ring circus under an intimate Big Top where your family sits less than 50 feet away!(SM)
- Committed to kids & their families, not for profit
- Call 1-877-407-8497 AFTER August 1 for exact dates & times

Bonus Discounts at
entertainment.com

entertainment
entertainment.com

great place for kids

50% OFF

Enjoy UP TO EIGHT GRANDSTAND TICKETS at 50% off the regular price.

All shows are at 7 p.m.

valid Tuesday, Wednesday & Thursday nights

Offer valid at Big Apple Circus Box Office only; The Circus Box Office will open mid September; Not valid weekends or Columbus Day & Subject to Rules of Use; Tickets are subject to availability & not refundable; Not combinable with any other offer

GHALF

BIG APPLE CIRCUS

C27

Valid now thru November 1, 2006

Not valid holidays & subject to Rules of Use. Not valid with other discount offers, unless specified. Coupon VOID if purchased, sold or bartered. Discounts exclude tax, tip and/or alcohol, where applicable.

Please join our Preferred Mailing list

Name: ____________________

Address: ____________________

City: ____________________ State: ________ ZIP: ____________

Phone: ____________________

E-mail address: ____________________

TICKET SELLER:
Attach upper portion of reserved seat ticket complete with adult stub and retain for audit.

Total Number of Tickets:____

00306345

entertainment.com

00306345

Please join our Preferred Mailing list

Name: ____________________

Address: ____________________

City: ____________________ State: ________ ZIP: ____________

Phone: ____________________

E-mail address: ____________________

TICKET SELLER:
Attach upper portion of reserved seat ticket complete with adult stub and retain for audit.

Total Number of Tickets:______

00545256

entertainment.com

00545256

BIG APPLE CIRCUS

Dulles Town Center
(Under the Big Top Tent)
Dulles, VA
(877)407-8497

00406710

entertainment.com

00406710

Arlington Cinema 'n' Drafthouse

2903 Columbia Pike
Arlington, VA
(703)486-2345

entertainment.
entertainment.com

great place for kids

ONE ADMISSION

Enjoy one complimentary ADMISSION when a second ADMISSION of equal or greater value is purchased.

valid Sunday thru Thursday

Box Office Only

ARLINGTON CINEMA 'N' DRAFTHOUSE.

C28

Valid now thru November 1, 2006

Not valid holidays & subject to Rules of Use. Not valid with other discount offers, unless specified. Coupon VOID if purchased, sold or bartered. Discounts exclude tax, tip and/or alcohol, where applicable.

Riverside Center

95 Riverside Pkwy.
Fredericksburg, VA
(540)370-4300

- Fredericksburg, VA's premier dinner theater
- Broadway musicals presented by professional cast, together with superb cuisine & an elegant ambiance Web-Sat (evenings) & Sun. (matinee)
- Year-round Sat. matinee Children's Theater lunch & shows
- Reservations & information: 540-370-4300 or toll free 888-999-8527
- Conference facility is available for weddings & meetings

entertainment.
entertainment.com

Up To $20.00 Value

Enjoy up to 4 ADULT DINNER-&-SHOW TICKETS at $5.00 off the regular price of each.

valid anytime

One performance only; Not valid with any special offer, discount ticket price or Children's Theatre shows; Must be mentioned at time of reservations & must be presented at the door; Up to 4 tickets per coupon

RIVERSIDE CENTER
DINNER THEATER
CONFERENCE FACILITY

www.riversidedt.com

C29

Valid now thru November 1, 2006

Not valid holidays & subject to Rules of Use. Not valid with other discount offers, unless specified. Coupon VOID if purchased, sold or bartered. Discounts exclude tax, tip and/or alcohol, where applicable.

Shear Madness

2700 F. St. NW
Washington, DC
(202)467-4600

- Washington's hilarious whodunit where the audience gets to solve the crime
- Performances at the Kennedy Center Sun. at 3:30 p.m. & 7 p.m.,Tues. - Thurs. at 8 p.m.

entertainment.
entertainment.com

ONE TICKET

Enjoy one complimentary TICKET when a second TICKET of equal or greater value is purchased.

valid Tuesday, Wednesday, Thursday & Sunday

Must be redeemed in person at the box office no earlier than one week in advance; no phone orders accepted; The following dates are excluded 3/27/05, 5/8/05, 5/29/05, 6/19/05, 7/3/05, 9/4/05 11/22/05 - 11/27/05, 12/19/05 - 12/31/05, 1/15/06, 2/13/06 - 2/20/06, 3/17/06, 4/16/06, 5/07/06, 5/28/06, 6/18/06, 7/03/06, 9/03/06; Other restrictions may apply; limited availability

SHEAR MADNESS
a comedy whodunit

www.shearmadness.com

C30

Valid now thru November 1, 2006

Not valid holidays & subject to Rules of Use. Not valid with other discount offers, unless specified. Coupon VOID if purchased, sold or bartered. Discounts exclude tax, tip and/or alcohol, where applicable.

ARLINGTON CINEMA 'N' DRAFTHOUSE.

SAY GOODBYE TO STIFF NECKS, JAMMED ELBOWS & SORE SEATS AT THE MOVIES...DRINK...AND ESCAPE FROM THE TRADITIONAL MOVIE EXPERIENCE.

Enjoy top box office movies for only $4.50 while waitstaff serves you premium & microbrewed beer, wine, fresh dough pizza, sandwiches and light fare in theater restaurant atmosphere complete with tables and comfortable chairs. Two shows nightly on our SupraMax screen with Dolby Surround Sound. Special weekend matinees and midnight shows. Must be 21 or with a parent to enter.

2903 Columbia Pike
(1/4 mile East of Glebe Rd.)
Arlington, VA
(703)486-2345

00047631

entertainment.com

00047631

RIVERSIDE CENTER
DINNER THEATER
CONFERENCE FACILITY

95 Riverside Pkwy.
Fredericksburg, VA
(540)370-4300

00622984

entertainment.com

00622984

SHEAR MADNESS
a comedy whodunit

2700 F. St. NW
(The John F. Kennedy Center for the Performing Arts)
Washington, DC
(202)467-4600

00046183

entertainment.com

00046183

Harlem Globetrotters

MCI Center 601 F St., NW Washington, DC

- Performances also at the Patriot Center at George Mason University in Fairfax, Virginia

Bonus Discounts at entertainment.com

entertainment. entertainment.com

50% OFF

HARLEM GLOBETROTTERS®

Enjoy UP TO EIGHT TICKETS at 50% off the regular price.

check the Entertainment® Hotline @ www.entertainment.com after Nov. 1, 2005 for available dates & times

Mail Order Only see reverse side; On availability basis

C31

Valid now thru November 1, 2006

Not valid holidays & subject to Rules of Use. Not valid with other discount offers, unless specified. Coupon VOID if purchased, sold or bartered. Discounts exclude tax, tip and/or alcohol, where applicable.

Sesame Street Live

Patriot Center Fairfax, VA

- 90 minutes of singing, dancing & fun

Bonus Discounts at entertainment.com

entertainment. entertainment.com

50% OFF

Enjoy UP TO EIGHT TICKETS at 50% off the regular price.

check the Entertainment® Hotline @ www.entertainment.com after Sept. 1, 2005 for available dates & times

Mail Order or Patriot Center Box Office only; See reverse side; On availability basis; Not valid on premium seats

123 SESAME STREET LIVE®

A VEE Corporation Production

C32

Valid now thru November 1, 2006

Not valid holidays & subject to Rules of Use. Not valid with other discount offers, unless specified. Coupon VOID if purchased, sold or bartered. Discounts exclude tax, tip and/or alcohol, where applicable.

Smuckers Stars on Ice

Visit the Entertainment® hotline at www.entertainment.com or call (800) 608-8299 for show date, performance time & location

- Don't miss Olympic Gold Medalist Alexei Yagudin, Olympic Pairs Gold Medalists Jamie Salé & David Pelletier & Elena Berezhnaya & Anton Sikharulidze, World Champion & six time US National Champion Todd Eldredge, & more of skating's biggest & brightest stars when Smuckers Stars on Ice appears for one performance only!

Bonus Discounts at entertainment.com

entertainment. entertainment.com

great place for kids

50% OFF

Enjoy UP TO FOUR RESERVED TICKETS at 50% off the regular price.

Valid for all tickets $50 or under

valid for performances January 1, 2006 thru April 30, 2006 only

Redeem at Box Office or to redeem on-line, use redemption code EPS; No refunds or exchanges; Date, time & cast subject to change; Tickets subject to availability

SMUCKER'S® STARS on ICE®

www.starsonice.com

C33

Valid now thru November 1, 2006

Not valid holidays & subject to Rules of Use. Not valid with other discount offers, unless specified. Coupon VOID if purchased, sold or bartered. Discounts exclude tax, tip and/or alcohol, where applicable.

TO: HARLEM GLOBETROTTER ENTERTAINMENT
MCI Center/Group Sales
601 F Street, NW
Washington, DC 20004

or

Patriot Center Box Office
4400 University Dr.
Fairfax, VA 22030

Please send ❑2 ❑4 ❑6 ❑8 tickets at 50% off the regular price for MCI Center or Patriot Center

Enclosed is my check payable to ❑MCI Center (for MCI Center game) or ❑Patriot Center (for Patriot Center game)

$______________________ (includes $5.00 handling charge)

NAME: ______________________

ADDRESS: ______________________

DAY PHONE: ______________________

CITY: ______________________ STATE: ______ ZIP: ______

- ORDER WILL NOT BE FILLED WITHOUT SELF-ADDRESSED, STAMPED ENVELOPE
- All sales are final. No refunds or exchanges
- Please allow 10 days for processing
- Orders received within 10 days of event will be held at the box office for pick up by NAME______________________
- Tickets on availability basis

00266203

entertainment.com

00266203

Entertainment® Order Back
Please enclose separate check for this attraction

TO: SESAME STREET LIVE
ENTERTAINMENT®
c/o Patriot Center - Attn: Group Sales
George Mason University
4400 University Dr.
Fairfax, VA 22030

Please send ________ no. tickets at 50% off the regular price
Enclosed is my check payable to Patriot Center for $ ______________________
(includes $5.00 handling fee)

Name: ______________________

Address: ______________________

Phone: ______________________

City: ______________________ State: ______ ZIP: ______

- ORDER WILL NOT BE FILLED WITHOUT SELF-ADDRESSED, STAMPED ENVELOPE
- All sales are final. No refunds or exchanges
- Please allow 10 days for processing
- Orders received within 10 days of event will be held at the box office for pick up by NAME______________________
- Tickets on availability basis

00215402

entertainment.com

00215402

SMUCKER'S STARS on ICE®

Visit the Entertainment® hotline at www.entertainment.com or call (800) 608-8299 for show date, performance time & location

00476661

entertainment.com

00476661

Six Flags America

I-95 Exit 15A
Largo, MD
(301)249-1500

- Over 100 rides, shows & attractions
- Hurricane Harbor Waterpark
- Children's area with 12 pint-sized rides
- For more information & operating schedule call 301-249-1500

Bonus Discounts at
entertainment.com

entertainment®
entertainment.com

great place for kids

$10.00 Value

Enjoy $10 off a purchase of ONE MAIN GATE GENERAL USE ADMISSION.

valid for any regularly scheduled operating day in the 2006 season

Redeem at Six Flags America Box office only; Present coupon prior to purchasing tickets; One coupon good for up to 6 guests; Valid holidays; Offer valid local & this location only; SIX FLAGS and all related indicia are trademarks of Six Flags Theme Parks Inc.®, TM, and © 2005

41051

SixFlags®
AMERICA
BALTIMORE/WASHINGTON, DC

www.sixflags.com

C34

Valid now thru November 1, 2006

Not valid holidays & subject to Rules of Use. Not valid with other discount offers, unless specified. Coupon VOID if purchased, sold or bartered. Discounts exclude tax, tip and/or alcohol, where applicable.

Six Flags America Fright Fest

I-95 Exit 15A
Largo, MD
(301)249-1500

- Haunted train ride & high tech haunted house
- Trick or treat trail for kids, scary shows, & much more
- All of the theme park rides PLUS Halloween attractions
- Call Six Flags America for event dates

Bonus Discounts at
entertainment.com

entertainment®
entertainment.com

great place for kids

$10.00 Value

Enjoy $10 off a purchase of ONE MAIN GATE GENERAL USE ADMISSION.

valid October 2006 for any regular Fright Fest operating day

Redeem at Six Flags America Box office only; Present coupon prior to purchasing tickets; One coupon good for up to 6 guests; Valid holidays; Offer valid local & this location only; SIX FLAGS and all related indicia are trademarks of Six Flags Theme Parks Inc.®, TM, and © 2005

41052

SixFlags®
AMERICA
BALTIMORE/WASHINGTON, DC

www.sixflags.com

C35

Valid now thru November 1, 2006

Not valid holidays & subject to Rules of Use. Not valid with other discount offers, unless specified. Coupon VOID if purchased, sold or bartered. Discounts exclude tax, tip and/or alcohol, where applicable.

The Flying Circus

Located near Bealeton, VA, 22 miles N. of Fredericksburg, 14 miles S. of Warrenton, For info. call (540)439-8661

- Open Sun., May thru Oct. - show time 2:30 p.m.
- Featuring family air shows for the entire family: hayrides, aerobatic rides, open cockpit rides, free parking & picnic area
- Check out our web page for show details, updates & driving directions

Bonus Discounts at
entertainment.com

entertainment®
entertainment.com

great place for kids

ONE ADMISSION

Enjoy one complimentary ADMISSION when a second ADMISSION of equal or greater value is purchased.

valid anytime

The Flying Circus

www.flyingcircusairshow.com

C36

Valid now thru November 1, 2006

Not valid holidays & subject to Rules of Use. Not valid with other discount offers, unless specified. Coupon VOID if purchased, sold or bartered. Discounts exclude tax, tip and/or alcohol, where applicable.

Six Flags
AMERICA
BALTIMORE/WASHINGTON, DC

I-95 Exit 15A
Largo, MD
(301)249-1500

00548633

entertainment.com

00548633

Six Flags
AMERICA
BALTIMORE/WASHINGTON, DC

I-95 Exit 15A
Largo, MD
(301)249-1500

00404106

entertainment.com

00404106

The Flying Circus

Located near Bealeton, VA, 22 miles N. of Fredericksburg, 14 miles S. of Warrenton, For info. call (540)439-8661

00549258

entertainment.com

00549258

Wise Acres Comedy Club

See reverse side for locations

- Eat, drink & be merrily entertained
- Shows Fri. at 9 p.m. & Sat. at 8 p.m. & 10:30 p.m.
- $10 admission charge & 2-item minimum per person
- Menu features gourmet pizza, big juicy burgers, super salads & cheesy nachos
- For a complete list of upcoming events, visit our website

Bonus Discounts at
entertainment.com

entertainment.
entertainment.com

50% OFF

WISEACRES
comedy club & lounge

Enjoy UP TO 10 ADMISSIONS at 50% off the regular price.

valid anytime

Reservations required; On availability basis; Not valid during SPECIAL EVENTS

www.wiseacrescomedyclub.com

C37

Valid now thru November 1, 2006

Not valid holidays & subject to Rules of Use. Not valid with other discount offers, unless specified. Coupon VOID if purchased, sold or bartered. Discounts exclude tax, tip and/or alcohol, where applicable.

Improvisation

1140 Connecticut Ave. NW
Washington, DC
(202)296-7008

- America's original comedy showcase
- Dinner served every night - call for reservations
- Featuring the nation's top comedians who regularly appear on "The Tonight Show" & "David Letterman"
- Showtimes may vary
- Two item minimum
- You must be 21

Bonus Discounts at
entertainment.com

entertainment.
entertainment.com

UP TO TWO ADMISSIONS

IMPROVISATION
America's Original Comedy Showcase & Restaurant

Valid for up to two ADMISSIONS when an identical number of ADMISSIONS of equal or greater value are purchased.

Special events excluded

valid any Sunday thru Thursday or Friday second show only

www.dcimprov.com

C38

Valid now thru November 1, 2006

Not valid holidays & subject to Rules of Use. Not valid with other discount offers, unless specified. Coupon VOID if purchased, sold or bartered. Di$counts exclude tax, tip and/or alcohol, where applicable.

Blues Alley

1069 Rear Wisconsin Ave.
Washington, DC
(202)337-4141

- The finest in jazz
- Specializing in New Orleans Creole-style steaks & seafood dishes
- Reservations required
- Dinner at 6 p.m., showtimes at 8 p.m. & 10 p.m.

Bonus Discounts at
entertainment.com

entertainment.
entertainment.com

ONE COVER CHARGE

Blues Alley

Enjoy one complimentary COVER CHARGE when a second COVER CHARGE of equal or greater value is purchased.

valid evenings Sunday thru Thursday

Please call ahead for information; Certain performances May be excluded; Reservations required

C39

Valid now thru November 1, 2006

Not valid holidays & subject to Rules of Use. Not valid with other discount offers, unless specified. Coupon VOID if purchased, sold or bartered. Discounts exclude tax, tip and/or alcohol, where applicable.

WISEACRES
comedy club & lounge

8401 Westpark Dr.
(inside the Best Western Tysons Westpark Hotel)
McLean, VA
(703)734-2800

Toll-Free 1-877-947-3227

00400162

entertainment.com

00400162

IMPROVISATION
America's Original Comedy Showcase & Restaurant

1140 Connecticut Ave. NW
Washington, DC
(202)296-7008

00020777

entertainment.com

00020777

Blues Alley

1069 Rear Wisconsin Ave.
(below M St., Georgetown)
Washington, DC
(202)337-4141

00030035

entertainment.com

00030035

DC United

Games Played at RFK Staduim in Washington D.C.
2400 E. Capitol St. SE
Washington, DC
(703)478-6600

- Please see web site at www.dcunited.com for ticket pricing

Bonus Discounts at entertainment.com

entertainment. entertainment.com

50% OFF

Enjoy UP TO EIGHT TICKETS at 50% off the regular price.

valid for selected regular season DC United home games

Good on premium tickets only; Mail Order Only see reverse side; On availability basis; Game selection may be limited; U.S., Intl., double headers & play offs excluded

D.C. UNITED

www.dcunited.com

C40

Valid now thru November 1, 2006

Not valid holidays & subject to Rules of Use. Not valid with other discount offers, unless specified. Coupon VOID if purchased, sold or bartered. Discounts exclude tax, tip and/or alcohol, where applicable.

George Mason Patriots

Patriot Center
Fairfax, VA
(703)993-3270

- Call for game times
- Tickets on availability basis
- All sales final
- All seats are reserved
- Call (703) 993-3270 for ticket information
- www.gmusports.com

Bonus Discounts at entertainment.com

entertainment. entertainment.com

50% OFF

Enjoy UP TO FOUR ADULT TICKETS at 50% off the regular price.

valid any 2005- 2006 regular season men's or women's basketball home game

Redeem tickets at Patriot Center Box Office - must be redeemed in advance, not valid day of game; On availability basis; No phone orders please with coupon; Must be redeemed in advance, not valid day of game

George Mason University

www.gmusports.com

C41

Valid now thru November 1, 2006

Not valid holidays & subject to Rules of Use. Not valid with other discount offers, unless specified. Coupon VOID if purchased, sold or bartered. Discounts exclude tax, tip and/or alcohol, where applicable.

George Mason Patriots

GMU Stadium
Fairfax, VA
(703)993-3270

- Enjoy college soccer at its best
- Men's & women's competition
- Tickets on availability basis
- Adults - $5
- Youth (18 & under) - $2
- Senior (62 & over) - $2
- www.gmusports.com

Bonus Discounts at entertainment.com

entertainment. entertainment.com

ONE ADULT TICKET

Enjoy ONE ADULT TICKET when a second ADULT TICKET of equal or greater value is purchased.

valid any 2006 regular season men's or women's soccer home game

Redeem at GMU Stadium day of game only; On availability basis

George Mason University

www.gmusports.com

C42

Valid now thru November 1, 2006

Not valid holidays & subject to Rules of Use. Not valid with other discount offers, unless specified. Coupon VOID if purchased, sold or bartered. Discounts exclude tax, tip and/or alcohol, where applicable.

Entertainment® Order Back

TO: DC United
RFK Stadium 4th floor
2400 East Capital St. S.E.
Washington, DC 20003

Please send ❑2 ❑4 ❑6❑8 tickets at 50 % off the regular price for:

Date (first choice) ______ Date (second choice) ______ Date (third choice) ______

Enclosed is my check payable to ENTERTAINMENT PUBLICATIONS for $______.

NAME: ______

ADDRESS: ______ DAY PHONE ______

CITY: ______ STATE: ______ ZIP ______

E-MAIL: ______

- ORDER WILL NOT BE FILLED WITHOUT SELF-ADDRESSED STAMPED ENVELOPE
- All sales are final. No refunds or exchanges
- Please allow 10 days for processing
- Orders received within 10 days of the game date will be held at the D.C. United Will Call at RFK stadium for pick up by Name: ______

00469600

entertainment.com

00469600

George Mason University

Patriot Center
Fairfax, VA
(703)993-3270

00081976

entertainment.com

00081976

George Mason University

GMU Stadium
Fairfax, VA
(703)993-3270

00082267

entertainment.com

00082267

Georgetown Hoyas

MCI Center 601 F Street, NW
Washington, DC

entertainment. entertainment.com

50% OFF

Georgetown Basketball

Enjoy UP TO EIGHT TICKETS at 50% off the regular price.

check the Entertainment® Hotline @ www.entertainment.com after Sept. 1, 2005 for available dates & times

Mail Order Only see reverse side; On availability basis

C43

Valid now thru November 1, 2006

Not valid holidays & subject to Rules of Use. Not valid with other discount offers, unless specified. Coupon VOID if purchased, sold or bartered. Discounts exclude tax, tip and/or alcohol, where applicable.

Potomac Nationals

See reverse side for locations

- Conveniently located in Northern VA off I-95
- Carolina League Affiliate of the Washington Nationals
- See back of coupon for directions

entertainment. entertainment.com

great place for kids

ONE GRANDSTAND TICKET

Enjoy one complimentary GRANDSTAND TICKET when a second GRANDSTAND TICKET of equal or greater value is purchased.

Valid for Monday-Friday games only during the 2006 regular season

All tickets must be for the same date; Tickets must be purchased at the Pfitzner Stadium Box Office to receive this offer; Tickets may be purchased in advance or on game date; Not valid for July 4th or playoff games; May not be combined with any other offer or discount; One coupon per customer per visit; Based on availability

POTOMAC NATIONALS™

www.potomacnationals.com

C44

Valid now thru November 1, 2006

Not valid holidays & subject to Rules of Use. Not valid with other discount offers, unless specified. Coupon VOID if purchased, sold or bartered. Discounts exclude tax, tip and/or alcohol, where applicable.

Legg Mason Tennis Classic

William H. G. FitzGerald Ctr.
Washington, DC
(202)721-9500

- Call Tournament Hotline at (202)721-9500 for specific dates, locations and ticket prices.

entertainment. entertainment.com

ONE RESERVED SEAT TICKET

Enjoy one complimentary RESERVED SEAT TICKET when a second RESERVED SEAT TICKET is purchased.

valid for sessions 1 thru 4 for the 2006 event

Must be redeemed at box office only on day of event; On availability basis

LEGG MASON TENNIS CLASSIC
PRESENTED BY GEICO

www.leggmasontennisclassic.com

C45

Valid now thru November 1, 2006

Not valid holidays & subject to Rules of Use. Not valid with other discount offers, unless specified. Coupon VOID if purchased, sold or bartered. Discounts exclude tax, tip and/or alcohol, where applicable.

TO: GEORGETOWN BASKETBALL ENTERTAINMENT
c/o MCI Center/Group Sales
601 F Street, NW
Washington, DC 20004

Please send ❑2 ❑4 ❑6 ❑8 tickets at 50% off the regular price for

____

Date(first choice) Date(second choice) Date(third choice)

Enclosed is my check payable to GEORGETOWN BASKETBALL
for $____________________(includes $5.00 handling fee)
or charge my :

NAME: ______________________________

ADDRESS: ______________________________

DAY PHONE: ______________________________

CITY: ______________ STATE: ______ ZIP: ______________

- ORDER WILL NOT BE FILLED WITHOUT SELF-ADDRESSED, STAMPED ENVELOPE
- All sales are final. No refunds or exchanges
- Please allow 10 days for processing
- Orders received within 10 days of event will be held at the box office for pick up by NAME______________
- Tickets on availability basis

00215403

entertainment.com

00215403

POTOMAC NATIONALS™

7 County Complex Ct.
(Prince William County Stadium Complex)
Woodbridge, VA
(703)590-2311

FROM I-66: Take Rte. 28 S. to Manassas. Turn left onto Liberia Ave. Proceed 1.5 miles then turn right, left onto Prince William Pkwy. E. Proceed 7 miles then turn left onto County Complex Ct.

FROM I-95: Take exit 158B for Prince William Pkwy/Manassas. Proceed 5 miles then turn right onto County Complex Ct.

00655968

entertainment.com

00655968

LEGG MASON TENNIS CLASSIC
PRESENTED BY GEICO.

William H. G. FitzGerald Ctr.
(16th & Kennedy Sts. NW)
Washington, DC
(202)721-9500

00158399

entertainment.com

00158399

Broad Run Golf and Practice Facility

10201 Golf Academy Dr.
Bristow, VA
(703)365-2443

- "Best kept secret in Northern Virginia"
- 18 Hole Miniature Golf - Play all day for $5.50
- All the fun in half the time & great price
- Open daily

entertainment.
entertainment.com

ONE ROUND OF MINIATURE GOLF

Enjoy one complimentary ROUND OF MINIATURE GOLF when a second ROUND OF MINIATURE GOLF of equal or greater value is purchased.

valid anytime

BROAD RUN
GOLF & PRACTICE FACILITY

C46

Valid now thru November 1, 2006

Not valid holidays & subject to Rules of Use. Not valid with other discount offers, unless specified. Coupon VOID if purchased, sold or bartered. Discounts exclude tax, tip and/or alcohol, where applicable.

Broad Run Golf and Practice Facility

10201 Golf Academy Dr.
Bristow, VA
(703)365-2443

- "Best kept secret in Northern Virginia"
- 1 Token = 45 Balls
- Check with us for Birthday party packages
- Open daily

entertainment.
entertainment.com

TOKEN

Enjoy one complimentary TOKEN when a second TOKEN of equal or greater value is purchased.

valid anytime

BROAD RUN
GOLF & PRACTICE FACILITY

C47

Valid now thru November 1, 2006

Not valid holidays & subject to Rules of Use. Not valid with other discount offers, unless specified. Coupon VOID if purchased, sold or bartered. Discounts exclude tax, tip and/or alcohol, where applicable.

Broad Run Golf and Practice Facility

10201 Golf Academy Dr.
Bristow, VA
(703)365-2443

- Broad Run features a full-length championship course designed by ward winning architect Rick Jacobson
- Broad Run also boasts one of the best practice facilities in the country
- Rated in the "Top 100 Gold Ranges in America" by the Golf Range Assoc. in America
- Golf clinic & Golf schools available
- Open daily

entertainment.
entertainment.com

9 HOLE ROUND OF GOLF

Enjoy one complimentary 9 HOLE ROUND OF GOLF when a second 9 HOLE ROUND OF GOLF of equal or greater value is purchased.

Valid Mon. - Fri. (9 hole offer only); Golf cart excluded

valid anytime

BROAD RUN
GOLF & PRACTICE FACILITY

C48

Valid now thru November 1, 2006

Not valid holidays & subject to Rules of Use. Not valid with other discount offers, unless specified. Coupon VOID if purchased, sold or bartered. Discounts exclude tax, tip and/or alcohol, where applicable.

BROAD RUN

GOLF & PRACTICE FACILITY

10201 Golf Academy Dr.
Bristow, VA
(703)365-2443

00566614

00566614

BROAD RUN

GOLF & PRACTICE FACILITY

10201 Golf Academy Dr.
Bristow, VA
(703)365-2443

00566637

00566637

BROAD RUN

GOLF & PRACTICE FACILITY

10201 Golf Academy Dr.
Bristow, VA
(703)365-2443

00566645

00566645

Centreville Mini Golf & Games

6205 Multiplex Dr.
Centreville, VA
(703)502-7888

- We have it all: top-of-the-line redemption, video & simulator games, laser storm miniature golf, a great snack bar & more
- The perfect place for your next birthday party - call for details
- Open daily

Bonus Discounts at entertainment.com

entertainment. entertainment.com

great place for kids

ONE ROUND OF MINIATURE GOLF

Enjoy one complimentary ROUND OF MINIATURE GOLF when a second ROUND OF MINIATURE GOLF of equal or greater value is purchased.

valid anytime

One coupon/card per customer per visit; Free day must be used on same day

CENTREVILLE MINI GOLF & GAMES®

C49

Valid now thru November 1, 2006

Not valid holidays & subject to Rules of Use. Not valid with other discount offers, unless specified. Coupon VOID if purchased, sold or bartered. Discounts exclude tax, tip and/or alcohol, where applicable.

Centreville Mini Golf & Games

6205 Multiplex Dr.
Centreville, VA
(703)502-7888

- We have it all: top-of-the-line redemption, video & simulator games, laser storm miniature golf, a great snack bar & more
- The perfect place for your next birthday party - call for details
- Open daily

Bonus Discounts at entertainment.com

entertainment. entertainment.com

great place for kids

ONE CUBES & TUBES ADMISSION

Enjoy one complimentary CUBES & TUBES ADMISSION when a second CUBES & TUBES ADMISSION of equal or greater value is purchased.

valid anytime

One coupon/card per customer per visit; Free day must be used on same day

CENTREVILLE MINI GOLF & GAMES®

C50

Valid now thru November 1, 2006

Not valid holidays & subject to Rules of Use. Not valid with other discount offers, unless specified. Coupon VOID if purchased, sold or bartered. Discounts exclude tax, tip and/or alcohol, where applicable.

Fairfax County Parks

See reverse side for locations

- New 18-hole mini golf
- Snacks & drinks available
- Memorial Day-Labor Day, daily 10 a.m. to dusk
- April, May, September & October, call for hours

Bonus Discounts at entertainment.com

entertainment. entertainment.com

great place for kids

ONE ROUND OF MINIATURE GOLF

Enjoy one complimentary ROUND OF MINIATURE GOLF when a second ROUND OF MINIATURE GOLF of equal or greater value is purchased.

valid anytime

ENT-1

Fairfax County Park Authority

www.fairfaxcounty.gov/parks

C51

Valid now thru November 1, 2006

Not valid holidays & subject to Rules of Use. Not valid with other discount offers, unless specified. Coupon VOID if purchased, sold or bartered. Discounts exclude tax, tip and/or alcohol, where applicable.

CENTREVILLE MINI GOLF & GAMES®

6205 Multiplex Dr.
(Behind Multiplex Cinemas)
Centreville, VA
(703)502-7888

00591855

entertainment.com

00591855

CENTREVILLE MINI GOLF & GAMES®

6205 Multiplex Dr.
(Behind Multiplex Cinemas)
Centreville, VA
(703)502-7888

00591888

entertainment.com

00591888

Fairfax County Park Authority

Burke Lake Miniature Golf Course
7315 Ox Rd.
Fairfax Station, VA
(703)323-6600

Jefferson Falls Mini Golf Course
7900 Lee Hwy.
Falls Church, VA
(703)573-0444

Oak Marr Miniature Golf Course (3200
Jermantown Rd.)
Oakton, VA
(703)281-6501

Lucky Duck Miniature Golf Course
7500 Accotink Park Rd.
Springfield, VA
(703)569-0285

00313097

entertainment.com

00313097

Dulles Golf Center & Sports Park

21593 Jesse Ct.
Sterling, VA
(703)404-8800

- Premium golf range
- Lighted, heated, covered tees
- Batting cages (fast & slow pitch)
- 18 hole miniature golf course
- Open daily all year

Bonus Discounts at
entertainment.com

entertainment.
entertainment.com

TWO BATTING CAGE TOKENS

Enjoy up to TWO complimentary BATTING CAGE TOKENS when TWO BATTING CAGE TOKENS are purchased.

valid anytime

Not valid with any other discount offer

Dulles GOLF CENTER & SPORTS PARK

www.dullesgolfcenter.com

C52

Valid now thru November 1, 2006

Not valid holidays & subject to Rules of Use. Not valid with other discount offers, unless specified. Coupon VOID if purchased, sold or bartered. Discounts exclude tax, tip and/or alcohol, where applicable.

Dulles Golf Center & Sports Park

21593 Jesse Ct.
Sterling, VA
(703)404-8800

- Premium golf range
- Lighted, heated, covered tees
- Batting cages (fast & slow pitch)
- 18 hole miniature golf course
- Open daily all year

Bonus Discounts at
entertainment.com

entertainment.
entertainment.com

50% OFF

Enjoy one complimentary ROUND OF MINIATURE GOLF when a second ROUND OF MINIATURE GOLF of equal or greater value is purchased.

valid anytime

Not valid with any other discount offer

Dulles GOLF CENTER & SPORTS PARK

www.dullesgolfcenter.com

C53

Valid now thru November 1, 2006

Not valid holidays & subject to Rules of Use. Not valid with other discount offers, unless specified. Coupon VOID if purchased, sold or bartered. Discounts exclude tax, tip and/or alcohol, where applicable.

Dulles Golf Center & Sports Park

21593 Jesse Ct.
Sterling, VA
(703)404-8800

- Premium golf range
- Lighted, heated, covered tees
- Batting cages (fast & slow pitch)
- 18 hole miniature golf course
- Open daily all year

Bonus Discounts at
entertainment.com

entertainment.
entertainment.com

ONE SMALL BUCKET OF BALLS

Enjoy one complimentary SMALL BUCKET OF BALLS when a second SMALL BUCKET OF BALLS of equal or greater value is purchased.

valid anytime

Not valid with any other discount offer

Dulles GOLF CENTER & SPORTS PARK

www.dullesgolfcenter.com

C54

Valid now thru November 1, 2006

Not valid holidays & subject to Rules of Use. Not valid with other discount offers, unless specified. Coupon VOID if purchased, sold or bartered. Discounts exclude tax, tip and/or alcohol, where applicable.

Dulles GOLF CENTER & SPORTS PARK

21593 Jesse Ct.
Sterling, VA
(703)404-8800

00249513

entertainment.com

00249513

Dulles GOLF CENTER & SPORTS PARK

21593 Jesse Ct.
Sterling, VA
(703)404-8800

00249524

entertainment.com

00249524

Dulles GOLF CENTER & SPORTS PARK

21593 Jesse Ct.
Sterling, VA
(703)404-8800

00249536

entertainment.com

00249536

Bristow Manor Golf

11507 Valley View Dr.
Bristow, VA
(703)368-3558

- Located just 30 minutes from the Capitol Beltway
- Rated one of the top 15 new courses in 1995
- Offering public golfers all the services & amenities of a private country club
- Treat yourself to a truly extraordinary experience

Bonus Discounts at entertainment.com

entertainment. entertainment.com

ONE GREEN FEE

Enjoy one complimentary GREEN FEE when a second GREEN FEE of equal or greater value is purchased.

valid anytime

Saturday, Sunday & holidays after 2 p.m.; Golf carts required for all players

BRISTOW MANOR GOLF CLUB

www.bristowmanor.com

C55

Valid now thru November 1, 2006

Not valid holidays & subject to Rules of Use. Not valid with other discount offers, unless specified. Coupon VOID if purchased, sold or bartered. Discounts exclude tax, tip and/or alcohol, where applicable.

Fairfax National Golf Club

16850 Sudley Rd.
Centreville, VA
(703)631-9226

- "The best 27-hole facility in Virginia"
- Spacious driving range & fully stocked pro shop available
- Located just 15 minutes from the Capital Beltway - call ahead for directions
- Outing packages available

Bonus Discounts at entertainment.com

entertainment. entertainment.com

ONE GREENS FEE

FAIRFAX NATIONAL GOLF CLUB

Enjoy one complimentary GREENS FEE when a second GREENS FEE of equal or greater value is purchased.

valid anytime

Saturdays, Sundays & holidays after 2 p.m.; Golf carts not included; On availability basis

www.gothamgolf.com

C56

Valid now thru November 1, 2006

Not valid holidays & subject to Rules of Use. Not valid with other discount offers, unless specified. Coupon VOID if purchased, sold or bartered. Discounts exclude tax, tip and/or alcohol, where applicable.

The Gauntlet Golf Club

18 Fairway Dr.
Fredericksburg, VA
(888)755-7888

- Hailed as one of the "Top 10 New Golf Courses in the US & Canada" by Golf Digest in 1996
- Spectacular P.B. Dye design
- Full service club house
- Comprehensive practice facility
- Four sets of tees on each hole

Bonus Discounts at entertainment.com

entertainment. entertainment.com

great place for kids

ONE GREEN FEE

Enjoy one complimentary GREEN FEE when a second GREEN FEE of equal or greater value is purchased.

Cart fee included

valid Monday thru Friday

The G Gauntlet GOLF CLUB

www.golfgauntlet.com

C57

Valid now thru November 1, 2006

Not valid holidays & subject to Rules of Use. Not valid with other discount offers, unless specified. Coupon VOID if purchased, sold or bartered. Discounts exclude tax, tip and/or alcohol, where applicable.

BRISTOW MANOR GOLF CLUB

11507 Valley View Dr.
Bristow, VA
(703)368-3558

00455426

entertainment.com

00455426

FAIRFAX NATIONAL GOLF CLUB

16850 Sudley Rd.
Centreville, VA
(703)631-9226

00288878

entertainment.com

00288878

The Gauntlet GOLF CLUB

18 Fairway Dr.
(located in Curtis Memorial Park)
Fredericksburg, VA
(888)755-7888

00619969

entertainment.com

00619969

South Riding Golfers' Club

43237 Golf View Dr.
South Riding, VA
(703)327-6660

- Voted one of the best new courses in 1998 by Golf Digest
- Located minutes from Washington Dulles Airport
- Offering public golfers a private golf club experience

Bonus Discounts at
entertainment.com

entertainment®
entertainment.com

ONE GREEN FEE

Enjoy one complimentary GREEN FEE when a second GREEN FEE of equal or greater value is purchased.

Valid Monday thru Friday

Not valid on twilight rates; Golf cart required

SOUTH RIDING

www.southridinggc.com

C58

Valid now thru November 1, 2006

Not valid holidays & subject to Rules of Use. Not valid with other discount offers, unless specified. Coupon VOID if purchased, sold or bartered. Discounts exclude tax, tip and/or alcohol, where applicable.

Virginia Oaks Golf Club

7950 Virginia Oaks Dr.
Gainesville, VA
(703)754-4200

- Set amidst the stunning backdrop of Lake Manassas, Virginia Oaks offers 18 holes of challenging golf amid the serenity of long fairways lined by stately oaks
- The perfect combination of extraordinary design & personal attention await you at Virginia Oaks Golf Club

Bonus Discounts at
entertainment.com

entertainment®
entertainment.com

ONE GREEN FEE

Enjoy one complimentary GREEN FEE when a second GREEN FEE of equal or greater value is purchased.

valid Mon. - Fri. before Twilight; valid Sat., Sun. & course holidays after 1 p.m. & before Twilight

Cart rental required

VIRGINIA OAKS

www.americangolf.com

C59

Valid now thru November 1, 2006

Not valid holidays & subject to Rules of Use. Not valid with other discount offers, unless specified. Coupon VOID if purchased, sold or bartered. Discounts exclude tax, tip and/or alcohol, where applicable.

Pleasant Valley Golfers' Club

4715 Pleasant Valley Rd
Chantilly, VA
(703)631-7904

- Championship course designed by Tom Clark of Ault, Clark and Assoc.
- Located just 45 minutes west of Washington DC
- Join us for a memorable golfing experience

Bonus Discounts at
entertainment.com

entertainment®
entertainment.com

ONE GREEN FEE

Enjoy one complimentary GREEN FEE when a second GREEN FEE of equal or greater value is purchased.

valid Monday thru Friday

Not valid on twilight rates; Golf cart required

PV
PLEASANT VALLEY

www.pleasantvalleygc.com

C60

Valid now thru November 1, 2006

Not valid holidays & subject to Rules of Use. Not valid with other discount offers, unless specified. Coupon VOID if purchased, sold or bartered. Discounts exclude tax, tip and/or alcohol, where applicable.

SOUTH RIDING

43237 Golf View Dr.
South Riding, VA
(703)327-6660

00496052

entertainment.com

00496052

VIRGINIA OAKS

7950 Virginia Oaks Dr.
Gainesville, VA
(703)754-4200

00455235

entertainment.com

00455235

PLEASANT VALLEY

4715 Pleasant Valley Rd
Chantilly, VA
(703)631-7904

00495986

entertainment.com

00495986

Meadows Farms Golf Course

4300 Flat Run Rd.
Locust Grove, VA
(540)854-9890

- Home of the longest hole in the U.S. - 841 yards - par 6
- A unique experience
- "Top 65 golfiest places to play" by Golf Magazine
- 45 minutes from DC & Richmond Beltways off Rte. 3 West of Fredericksburg

Bonus Discounts at
entertainment.com

entertainment. entertainment.com

ONE GREEN FEE

MEADOWS FARMS GOLF COURSE

Enjoy one complimentary GREEN FEE when a second GREEN FEE of equal or greater value is purchased.

valid anytime

Saturday, Sunday & holidays after 2 p.m.; Carts & tee times required

www.meadowsfarms.com

C61

Valid now thru November 1, 2006

Not valid holidays & subject to Rules of Use. Not valid with other discount offers, unless specified. Coupon VOID if purchased, sold or bartered. Discounts exclude tax, tip and/or alcohol, where applicable.

Quinton Oaks

262 Quinton Oaks Lane
Callao, VA
(804)529-5367

- Player friendly golf course for all skill levels
- Just 20 minutes East of Tappahannock
- Instruction from PGA professionals
- Top quality practice facility
- Memberships available
- Corporate and group outings welcome

Bonus Discounts at
entertainment.com

entertainment. entertainment.com

ONE GREEN FEE

Enjoy one complimentary GREEN FEE when a second GREEN FEE of equal or greater value is purchased.

valid Monday through Friday

Saturday, Sunday & holidays after 1 p.m.; Golf cart required; Tee times recommended; Offer not valid with twilight & senior rates

Quinton Oaks Golf Course

www.quintonoaks.com

C62

Valid now thru November 1, 2006

Not valid holidays & subject to Rules of Use. Not valid with other discount offers, unless specified. Coupon VOID if purchased, sold or bartered. Discounts exclude tax, tip and/or alcohol, where applicable.

Virginia National Golf Club

1400 Parker Lane
Bluemont, VA
(888)283-4653

- With the Blue Ridge Mountains on one side & the Shenandoah river on the other, Virginia National's vistas go unrivaled
- Instruction available
- Call today to schedule a tee time

Bonus Discounts at
entertainment.com

entertainment. entertainment.com

ONE GREEN FEE

Enjoy one complimentary GREEN FEE when a second GREEN FEE of equal or greater value is purchased.

Golf cart excluded

Valid Monday thru Thursday

VIRGINIA GOLF CLUB NATIONAL
AT THE BATTLEGROUND OF COOL SPRING

www.virginianational.com

C63

Valid now thru November 1, 2006

Not valid holidays & subject to Rules of Use. Not valid with other discount offers, unless specified. Coupon VOID if purchased, sold or bartered. Discounts exclude tax, tip and/or alcohol, where applicable.

MEADOWS FARMS GOLF COURSE

4300 Flat Run Rd.
(16 miles west of Fredericksburg)
Locust Grove, VA
(540)854-9890

00362990

00362990

Quinton Oaks Golf Course

262 Quinton Oaks Lane
(20 minutes East of Tappahannock)
Callao, VA
(804)529-5367

00520419

00520419

VIRGINIA NATIONAL GOLF CLUB
AT THE BATTLEGROUND OF COOL SPRING

1400 Parker Lane
Bluemont, VA
(888)283-4653

00496510

00496510

Pohick Bay Golf Course

10301 Gunston Rd.
Lorton, VA
(703)339-8585

- Picturesque, 18 hole, par 72 Challenging layout
- Practice facilities include chipping, putting & driving range
- Clubhouse, pro shop & snack bar
- Located just 25 minutes south of DC off Rte. 1
- Rental clubs available

entertainment.
entertainment.com

ONE GREEN FEE

Enjoy one complimentary GREEN FEE when a second GREEN FEE of equal or greater value is purchased.

valid anytime Mon.-Thurs. and after 2:00 p.m. on Friday

Golf cart required

Pohick Bay
GOLF COURSE

www.nvrpa.org

C64

Valid now thru November 1, 2006

Not valid holidays & subject to Rules of Use. Not valid with other discount offers, unless specified. Coupon VOID if purchased, sold or bartered. Discounts exclude tax, tip and/or alcohol, where applicable.

Pohick Bay Golf Course

10301 Gunston Rd.
Lorton, VA
(703)339-8585

- 12 stall driving range - plus 2 practice bunker stalls
- 4 covered tees
- Private & group golf instruction available
- Beginner & junior clinics available
- Playing lessons available

entertainment.
entertainment.com

ONE BUCKET OF BALLS

Enjoy one complimentary BUCKET OF BALLS when a second BUCKET OF BALLS of equal or greater value is purchased.

valid anytime

Pohick Bay
GOLF COURSE

www.nvrpa.org

C65

Valid now thru November 1, 2006

Not valid holidays & subject to Rules of Use. Not valid with other discount offers, unless specified. Coupon VOID if purchased, sold or bartered. Discounts exclude tax, tip and/or alcohol, where applicable.

Powerline Golf

15005 Neabsco Mills Rd.
Woodbridge, VA
(703)680-6767

- Professional lessons available
- Full service pro shop
- Repair & custom clubs
- Lighted driving range
- STUB BONUS: 10% off any pro shop purchase up to a $10.00 value

entertainment.
entertainment.com

ONE #3 BUCKET OF BALLS

Enjoy one complimentary #3 BUCKET OF BALLS when a second #3 BUCKET OF BALLS of equal or greater value is purchased.

valid anytime

POWERLINE
GOLF
INC.

www.powerlinegolf.com

C66

Valid now thru November 1, 2006

Not valid holidays & subject to Rules of Use. Not valid with other discount offers, unless specified. Coupon VOID if purchased, sold or bartered. Discounts exclude tax, tip and/or alcohol, where applicable.

Pohick Bay
GOLF COURSE

10301 Gunston Rd.
Lorton, VA
(703)339-8585

00547028

entertainment.com

00547028

Pohick Bay
GOLF COURSE

10301 Gunston Rd.
Lorton, VA
(703)339-8585

00547053

entertainment.com

00547053

POWERLINE GOLF INC.

15005 Neabsco Mills Rd.
Woodbridge, VA
(703)680-6767

00045838

entertainment.com

00045838

Hilltop Golf Club

7900 Telegraph Rd.
Alexandria, VA
(703)719-6504

- 40 stall driving range - 20 of which are covered and heated for year round enjoyment
- $5.00 for regular bucket - 45 balls
- Private lessons available with on staff professionals
- Open daily

Bonus Discounts at entertainment.com

entertainment. entertainment.com

ONE BUCKET OF BALLS

HILLTOP GOLF CLUB

Enjoy one complimentary BUCKET OF BALLS when a second BUCKET OF BALLS of equal or greater value is purchased.

valid anytime

www.hilltopgolfclub.com

C67

Valid now thru November 1, 2006

Not valid holidays & subject to Rules of Use. Not valid with other discount offers, unless specified. Coupon VOID if purchased, sold or bartered. Discounts exclude tax, tip and/or alcohol, where applicable.

Islands in the Park

13241 Braddock Rd.
Clifton, VA
(703)818-8929

- Resort style 18 hole mini golf course
- Breathtaking 3-sided waterfall
- 2 island holes
- Stream
- Challenging for all
- Great for groups
- Call for our seasonal hours

Bonus Discounts at entertainment.com

entertainment. entertainment.com

great place for kids

ONE ROUND OF MINIATURE GOLF

Islands In The Park

Enjoy one complimentary ROUND OF MINIATURE GOLF when a second ROUND OF MINIATURE GOLF of equal or greater value is purchased.

valid anytime

C68

Valid now thru November 1, 2006

Not valid holidays & subject to Rules of Use. Not valid with other discount offers, unless specified. Coupon VOID if purchased, sold or bartered. Discounts exclude tax, tip and/or alcohol, where applicable.

The Dug Out

13241 Braddock Rd.
Clifton, VA
(703)818-3331

- Baseball & softball batting range
- Team rental specials available
- Call for our seasonal hours
- Located in Braddock Park

Bonus Discounts at entertainment.com

entertainment. entertainment.com

great place for kids

TWO BATTING CAGE TOKENS

Enjoy two complimentary BATTING CAGE TOKENS when two BATTING CAGE TOKENS of equal or greater value is purchased.

The Dug Out

valid anytime

C69

Valid now thru November 1, 2006

Not valid holidays & subject to Rules of Use. Not valid with other discount offers, unless specified. Coupon VOID if purchased, sold or bartered. Discounts exclude tax, tip and/or alcohol, where applicable.

HILLTOP
GOLF CLUB

H

7900 Telegraph Rd.
Alexandria, VA
(703)719-6504

00238268

entertainment.com

00238268

Islands In The Park

13241 Braddock Rd.
(between Clifton & Union Mill Rds.)
Clifton, VA
(703)818-8929

00615554

entertainment.com

00615554

The Dug Out

13241 Braddock Rd.
(between Clifton & Union Mill Rds.)
Clifton, VA
(703)818-3331

00615549

entertainment.com

00615549

Northern Virginia Regional Park Authority

See reverse side for locations

- Come to Northern Virginia Regional Parks for the wilderness...for the wildlife...for the fun!
- Northern Virginia Regional Park Authority provides more than a million citizens with some of the finest recreational facilities
- Enjoy miniature golf at 6 locations
- Entrance fees applicable at some parks

Bonus Discounts at entertainment.com

entertainment. entertainment.com

ONE ROUND OF MINIATURE GOLF

Enjoy one complimentary ROUND OF MINIATURE GOLF when a second ROUND OF MINIATURE GOLF of equal or greater value is purchased.

valid anytime

Northern Virginia Regional Park Authority

www.NVRPA.org

C70

Valid now thru November 1, 2006

Not valid holidays & subject to Rules of Use. Not valid with other discount offers, unless specified. Coupon VOID if purchased, sold or bartered. Discounts exclude tax, tip and/or alcohol, where applicable.

Northern Virginia Regional Park Authority

See reverse side for locations

- Come to Northern Virginia Regional Parks for the wilderness...for the wildlife...for the fun!
- Northern Virginia Regional Park Authority provides more than a million citizens with some of the finest recreational facilities
- Enjoy batting at three locations
- Entrance fees applicable at some parks

Bonus Discounts at entertainment.com

entertainment. entertainment.com

ONE ROUND AT BATTING CAGE

Enjoy one complimentary ROUND AT BATTING CAGE when a second ROUND AT BATTING CAGE of equal or greater value is purchased.

valid anytime

Northern Virginia Regional Park Authority

www.NVRPA.org

C71

Valid now thru November 1, 2006

Not valid holidays & subject to Rules of Use. Not valid with other discount offers, unless specified. Coupon VOID if purchased, sold or bartered. Discounts exclude tax, tip and/or alcohol, where applicable.

Northern Virginia Regional Park Authority

See reverse side for locations

- Come surf & sun or splash the day away at the one of the largest pools on the East Coast
- There's a Northern Virginia Regional Park that is just right for you
- Entrance fees applicable at some parks

Bonus Discounts at entertainment.com

entertainment. entertainment.com

great place for kids

ONE ADMISSION TO OUTDOOR SWIMMING POOL

Enjoy one complimentary ADMISSION TO OUTDOOR SWIMMING POOL at Pohick Bay Regional Park when a second ADMISSION TO OUTDOOR SWIMMING POOL at Pohick Bay Regional Park of equal or greater value is purchased.

valid anytime

Northern Virginia Regional Park Authority

www.NVRPA.org

C72

Valid now thru November 1, 2006

Not valid holidays & subject to Rules of Use. Not valid with other discount offers, unless specified. Coupon VOID if purchased, sold or bartered. Discounts exclude tax, tip and/or alcohol, where applicable.

Northern Virginia
Regional Park Authority

Cameron Run Regional Park
(4001 Eisenhower Ave.)
Alexandria, VA
(703)960-8719

Upton Hill Regional Park
(6060 Wilson Blvd.)
Arlington, VA
(703)534-3437

Bull Run Regional Park
(7700 Bull Run Dr.)
Centreville, VA
(703)631-0550

Fountainhead Regional Park
(10875 Hampton Rd.)
Fairfax Station, VA
(703)250-9124

Pohick Bay Regional Park
(6501 Pohick Bay Dr. on Mason Neck Peninsula)
Lorton, VA
(703)339-6104

Algonkian Regional Park
(47001 Fairway Dr.)
Sterling, VA
(703)450-4655

00077505

entertainment.com

00077505

Northern Virginia
Regional Park Authority

Cameron Run Regional Park
(4001 Eisenhower Ave.)
Alexandria, VA
(703)960-8719

Upton Hill Regional Park
(6060 Wilson Blvd.)
Arlington, VA
(703)534-3437

Occoquan Regional Park
(9751 Ox Rd.)
Lorton, VA
(703)690-2121

00077540

entertainment.com

00077540

Northern Virginia
Regional Park Authority

Bull Run Regional Park
(7700 Bull Run Dr.)
Centreville, VA
(703)631-0550

Pohick Bay Regional Park
(6501 Pohick Bay Dr. on Mason Neck Peninsula)
Lorton, VA
(703)339-6104

00033692

entertainment.com

00033692

Prince William Co. Parks Authority

Locust Shade Park
Triangle, VA
(703)221-8579

- Wide choice of family recreational activities in a beautiful & natural wooded setting
- Perfect for group gatherings, family cookouts & company picnics
- Lighted mini-golf course
- Lighted golf driving range
- Batting cage with slow/fast pitch softball & moderate/fast speed baseball
- Call for hours

Bonus Discounts at entertainment.com

entertainment. entertainment.com

great place for kids

ONE MEDIUM BUCKET OF BALLS

Locust Shade Park

Prince William County PARK AUTHORITY

Enjoy one complimentary MEDIUM BUCKET OF BALLS when a second MEDIUM BUCKET OF BALLS of equal or greater value is purchased.

valid anytime

C73

Valid now thru November 1, 2006

Not valid holidays & subject to Rules of Use. Not valid with other discount offers, unless specified. Coupon VOID if purchased, sold or bartered. Discounts exclude tax, tip and/or alcohol, where applicable.

Prince William Co. Parks Authority

See reverse side for locations

- Wide choice of family recreational activities in a beautiful & natural wooded setting
- Perfect for group gatherings, family cookouts & company picnics
- Lighted mini-golf course
- Lighted golf driving range
- Batting cage with slow/fast pitch softball & moderate/fast speed baseball
- Call for hours

Bonus Discounts at entertainment.com

entertainment. entertainment.com

great place for kids

ONE ROUND OF MINIATURE GOLF

Locust Shade Park

Prince William County PARK AUTHORITY

Enjoy one complimentary ROUND OF MINIATURE GOLF when a second ROUND OF MINIATURE GOLF of equal or greater value is purchased.

valid anytime

C74

Valid now thru November 1, 2006

Not valid holidays & subject to Rules of Use. Not valid with other discount offers, unless specified. Coupon VOID if purchased, sold or bartered. Discounts exclude tax, tip and/or alcohol, where applicable.

Prince William Co. Parks Authority

Locust Shade Park
Triangle, VA
(703)221-8579

- Wide choice of family recreational activities in a beautiful & natural wooded setting
- Perfect for group gatherings, family cookouts & company picnics
- Lighted mini-golf course
- Lighted golf driving range
- Batting cage with slow/fast pitch softball & moderate/fast speed baseball
- Call for hours

Bonus Discounts at entertainment.com

entertainment. entertainment.com

great place for kids

TWO BATTING CAGE TOKENS

Locust Shade Park

Prince William County PARK AUTHORITY

Enjoy one complimentary TWO BATTING CAGE TOKENS when a second TWO BATTING CAGE TOKENS is purchased.

valid anytime

C75

Valid now thru November 1, 2006

Not valid holidays & subject to Rules of Use. Not valid with other discount offers, unless specified. Coupon VOID if purchased, sold or bartered. Discounts exclude tax, tip and/or alcohol, where applicable.

Locust Shade Park

Prince William County
PARK AUTHORITY

Locust Shade Park
(4701 Locust Shade Dr.)
Triangle, VA
(703)221-8579

00322978

entertainment.com

00322978

Locust Shade Park

Prince William County
PARK AUTHORITY

Locust Shade Park
(4701 Locust Shade Dr.)
Triangle, VA
(703)221-8579

Lake Ridge Park
(12350 Cotton Mill Dr.)
Woodbridge, VA
(703)494-5564

00322985

entertainment.com

00322985

Locust Shade Park

Prince William County
PARK AUTHORITY

Locust Shade Park
(4701 Locust Shade Dr.)
Triangle, VA
(703)221-8579

00322986

entertainment.com

00322986

Prince William Co. Parks Authority

Waterworks Waterpark
Dale City, VA
(703)680-7137

- Located within Andrew Leitch Park
- Featuring a spacious pool, two slides, climbing hippo, 3 jungle walks, beach volleyball, concessions & certified safety staff
- Open Memorial Day thru Labor Day
- One of NOVA's most popular & innovative aquatic playgrounds for kids

Bonus Discounts at
entertainment.com

entertainment®
entertainment.com

great place for kids

ONE ADMISSION

Enjoy one complimentary ADMISSION when a second ADMISSION of equal or greater value is purchased.

valid anytime before 5 p.m.

Waterworks
WATERPARK

C76

Valid now thru November 1, 2006

Not valid holidays & subject to Rules of Use. Not valid with other discount offers, unless specified. Coupon VOID if purchased, sold or bartered. Discounts exclude tax, tip and/or alcohol, where applicable.

Bull Run Regional Park

7700 Bull Run Dr.
Centreville, VA
(703)631-0552

- New for 2004 - Two 30' tall water slides - 400' of new slides
- Wading pool
- Main pool
- Eight water slides
- Umbrella for shade
- Snack bar

Bonus Discounts at
entertainment.com

entertainment®
entertainment.com

ONE ADMISSION TO OUTDOOR SWIMMING POOL

Enjoy ONE ADMISSION TO OUTDOOR SWIMMING POOL when a second ADMISSION TO OUTDOOR SWIMMING POOL of equal or greater value is purchased.

valid anytime

Northern Virginia
Regional Park Authority

www.nvrpa.org

C77

Valid now thru November 1, 2006

Not valid holidays & subject to Rules of Use. Not valid with other discount offers, unless specified. Coupon VOID if purchased, sold or bartered. Discounts exclude tax, tip and/or alcohol, where applicable.

Loudoun County Parks & Recreation

See reverse side for locations

- Call for hours of operation

Bonus Discounts at
entertainment.com

entertainment®
entertainment.com

great place for kids

ONE ADMISSION TO OUTDOOR SWIMMING POOL

Enjoy one complimentary ADMISSION TO OUTDOOR SWIMMING POOL when a second ADMISSION TO OUTDOOR SWIMMING POOL of equal or greater value is purchased.

valid anytime Memorial Day thru Labor Day

PRCS
COUNTY OF LOUDOUN

C78

Valid now thru November 1, 2006

Not valid holidays & subject to Rules of Use. Not valid with other discount offers, unless specified. Coupon VOID if purchased, sold or bartered. Discounts exclude tax, tip and/or alcohol, where applicable.

Waterworks Waterpark
(5301 Dale Blvd.)
Dale City, VA
(703)680-7137

00322977

entertainment.com

00322977

Northern Virginia
Regional Park Authority

7700 Bull Run Dr.
Centreville, VA
(703)631-0552

00588216

entertainment.com

00588216

PRCS
COUNTY OF LOUDOUN

Lovettsville Community Center Pool
Lovettsville, VA
(540)822-5284

Franklin Park
Purcellville, VA
(540)338-7492

00281451

entertainment.com

00281451

The Water Mine Family Swimmin' Hole

Lake Fairfax Park
Reston, VA
(703)471-5415

- FLOAT in your tube along Rattlesnake River
- ZIP down Big Pete & Little Pete Slides
- LEAP the logs at Box Canyon Crossing
- SPLASH through the bubblers, flumes & geysers
- RIDE the floating rattlesnake
- Great for families with young children!
- Open Memorial Day - Labor Day

entertainment. entertainment.com

great place for kids

ONE ONE-DAY ADMISSION

Enjoy ONE-DAY ADMISSION when a second ONE-DAY ADMISSION of equal or greater value is purchased.

valid anytime

ENT-5

THE WATER MINE
FAMILY SWIMMIN' HOLE

www.fairfaxcounty.gov/parks

C79

Valid now thru November 1, 2006

Not valid holidays & subject to Rules of Use. Not valid with other discount offers, unless specified. Coupon VOID if purchased, sold or bartered. Discounts exclude tax, tip and/or alcohol, where applicable.

Downpour Water Playground

47001 Fairway Dr.
Sterling, VA
(703)450-4655

- 600 - gallon bucket pours every 3 minutes
- Water cannons
- Shipwreck slide
- Foam floating creatures
- 2 huge flume slides
- Free-form pool

entertainment. entertainment.com

great place for kids

ONE ADMISSION

Enjoy one complimentary ADMISSION when a second ADMISSION of equal or greater value is purchased.

valid Monday - Friday

Downpour
Algonkian Regional Park
Water Playground!

www.nvrpa.org

C80

Valid now thru November 1, 2006

Not valid holidays & subject to Rules of Use. Not valid with other discount offers, unless specified. Coupon VOID if purchased, sold or bartered. Discounts exclude tax, tip and/or alcohol, where applicable.

Great Waves

4001 Eisenhower Ave.
Alexandria, VA
(703)960-0767

- There's fun for everyone at Great Waves
- Wave pool
- Water slides
- Water playground
- Snack bar
- Call for our operation hours

entertainment. entertainment.com

great place for kids

ONE ADMISSION

Enjoy one complimentary ADMISSION when a second ADMISSION of equal or greater value is purchased.

valid anytime Monday thru Friday

Great Waves
at Cameron
Run Regional Park

www.NVRPA.org

C81

Valid now thru November 1, 2006

Not valid holidays & subject to Rules of Use. Not valid with other discount offers, unless specified. Coupon VOID if purchased, sold or bartered. Discounts exclude tax, tip and/or alcohol, where applicable.

THE WATER MINE
FAMILY SWIMMIN' HOLE

Lake Fairfax Park
(1400 Lake Fairfax Dr.)
Reston, VA
(703)471-5415

00263441

entertainment.com

00263441

Downpour
Algonkian Regional Park
Water Playground!

47001 Fairway Dr.
(Algonkian Regional Park)
Sterling, VA
(703)450-4655

00546865

entertainment.com

00546865

Great Waves
at Cameron
Run Regional Park

4001 Eisenhower Ave.
(Cameron Run Regional Park)
Alexandria, VA
(703)960-0767

00307025

entertainment.com

00307025

Stafford Cty. Parks & Recreation

2 Northhampton Blvd.
Stafford, VA
(540)658-4241

- Year round swimming
- Summer 2006 splashpad!
- Great family fun!
- Call for operational hours

Bonus Discounts at entertainment.com

entertainment. entertainment.com

great place for kids

ONE GENERAL ADMISSION

Enjoy one complimentary GENERAL ADMISSION when a second GENERAL ADMISSION of equal or greater value is purchased.

valid anytime

Woodlands Pool & Splashpad

www.staffordparks.com

C82

Valid now thru November 1, 2006

Not valid holidays & subject to Rules of Use. Not valid with other discount offers, unless specified. Coupon VOID if purchased, sold or bartered. Discounts exclude tax, tip and/or alcohol, where applicable.

Herndon Community Center

814 Ferndale Ave.
Herndon, VA
(703)435-6868

- The place for family fun
- Fully-equipped fitness room
- Racquetball courts
- 25 yard indoor pool
- Full size gym
- 6 lighted tennis courts
- Park & playground
- Classes & programs

Bonus Discounts at entertainment.com

entertainment. entertainment.com

great place for kids

ONE DAILY ADMISSION

Enjoy one complimentary DAILY ADMISSION when a second DAILY ADMISSION of equal or greater value is purchased.

valid anytime

HERNDON COMMUNITY CENTER

www.herndon-va.gov

C83

Valid now thru November 1, 2006

Not valid holidays & subject to Rules of Use. Not valid with other discount offers, unless specified. Coupon VOID if purchased, sold or bartered. Discounts exclude tax, tip and/or alcohol, where applicable.

Explore & Moore-Children's Discovery Museum

12904 Occoquan Rd.
Woodbridge, VA
(703)492-2222

- A hands-on, interactive environment
- A family place where the young & young at heart can explore
- Open Daily
- Admission is $5.00 - under 2 free
- Private birthday party room available
- Bring the whole family by today!

Bonus Discounts at entertainment.com

entertainment. entertainment.com

great place for kids

ONE ADMISSION

Enjoy one complimentary ADMISSION when a second ADMISSION of equal or greater value is purchased.

valid anytime

Explore & Moore-Discovery Museum

www.exploreandmoore.com

C84

Valid now thru November 1, 2006

Not valid holidays & subject to Rules of Use. Not valid with other discount offers, unless specified. Coupon VOID if purchased, sold or bartered. Discounts exclude tax, tip and/or alcohol, where applicable.

Woodlands Pool & Splashpad

2 Northhampton Blvd.
(off Garrisonville Rd.)
Stafford, VA
(540)658-4241

00621481

entertainment.com

00621481

HERNDON
COMMUNITY
CENTER

814 Ferndale Ave.
Herndon, VA
(703)435-6868

00611942

entertainment.com

00611942

**Explore & Moore-
Discovery Museum**

12904 Occoquan Rd.
Woodbridge, VA
(703)492-2222

00635097

entertainment.com

00635097

Fairfax County Parks

See reverse side for locations

- George Washington, Lee District, Mt. Vernon, Oak Marr, Providence, South Run, Spring Hill, Audrey Moore RECenter
- Fitness room with Nautilus circuit, stationary bikes, stairstepper, tread mill & free weights
- Indoor swimming pool
- Spa & sauna

Bonus Discounts at entertainment.com

entertainment. entertainment.com

great place for kids

FREE

Fairfax County Park Authority

Enjoy one FAMILY ADMISSION FREE.

valid anytime

Valid at any Fairfax County Park Authority RECenter

ENT-2

www.fairfaxcounty.gov/parks

C85

Valid now thru November 1, 2006

Not valid holidays & subject to Rules of Use. Not valid with other discount offers, unless specified. Coupon VOID if purchased, sold or bartered. Discounts exclude tax, tip and/or alcohol, where applicable.

Fairfax County Parks

See reverse side for locations

- Camp in beautiful park settings

Bonus Discounts at entertainment.com

entertainment. entertainment.com

great place for kids

FREE

Fairfax County Park Authority

Enjoy one NIGHT OF CAMP SITE RENTAL FREE.

valid anytime

ENT-4

www.fairfaxcounty.gov/parks

C86

Valid now thru November 1, 2006

Not valid holidays & subject to Rules of Use. Not valid with other discount offers, unless specified. Coupon VOID if purchased, sold or bartered. Discounts exclude tax, tip and/or alcohol, where applicable.

Fairfax County Parks

Mt. Vernon RECenter and Ice Arena
Alexandria, VA
(703)768-3224

- The metro area's best ice!
- Refurbished & improved ice arena
- Individual & group lessons
- Off-ice conditioning programs
- Figure skating & hockey

Bonus Discounts at entertainment.com

entertainment. entertainment.com

great place for kids

ONE PUBLIC SKATING ADMISSION

Fairfax County Park Authority

Enjoy one complimentary PUBLIC SKATING ADMISSION when a second PUBLIC SKATING ADMISSION of equal or greater value is purchased.

valid anytime

Valid at Mt. Vernon RECenter and Ice Arena

ENT-6

www.fairfaxcounty.gov/parks

C87

Valid now thru November 1, 2006

Not valid holidays & subject to Rules of Use. Not valid with other discount offers, unless specified. Coupon VOID if purchased, sold or bartered. Discounts exclude tax, tip and/or alcohol, where applicable.

Alexandria
George Washington Community RECenter
(8426 Old Mount Vernon Rd.)
(703)780-8894

Mt. Vernon RECenter and Ice Arena
(2017 Belle View Blvd.)
(703)768-3224

Annandale
Audrey Moore RECenter
(8100 Braddock Rd.)
(703)321-7081

Chantilly
4630 Stonecroft Blvd.
(Cub Run RECenter)
(703)817-9407

Falls Church
Providence RECenter
(7525 Marc Dr.)
(703)698-1351

Franconia
Lee District Park and RECenter
(6601 Telegraph Rd.)
(703)922-9841

McLean
Spring Hill RECenter
(1239 Spring Hill Rd.)
(703)827-0989

Oakton
Oak Marr RECenter & Golf Complex (3200 Jermantown Rd.)
(703)281-6501

Springfield
South Run RECenter
(7550 Reservation Dr.)
(703)866-0566

00260878

00260878

Burke Lake Park (7315 Ox Rd.)
Fairfax, VA
(703)323-6600

Lake Fairfax Park
(1400 Lake Fairfax Dr.)
Reston, VA
(703)471-5414

00263439

00263439

Mt. Vernon RECenter and Ice Arena
(2017 Belle View Blvd.)
Alexandria, VA
(703)768-3224

00263443

00263443

Planet Play

6789 Springfield Mall
Springfield, VA
(703)313-6770

- Family entertainment center
- Enjoy our video, simulator & redemption games
- WIN EXCITING PRIZES
- Depending on location enjoy: bumper cars, carousel, Laserstorm, Play Stations, games & more

Bonus Discounts at
entertainment.com

entertainment. entertainment.com — great place for kids

ONE INDIVIDUAL ACTIVITY

Enjoy one complimentary INDIVIDUAL ACTIVITY when a second INDIVIDUAL ACTIVITY of equal or greater value is purchased.

valid anytime

One coupon per customer per visit; Free day must be used on same day

www.planetplay.com

C88

Valid now thru November 1, 2006

Not valid holidays & subject to Rules of Use. Not valid with other discount offers, unless specified. Coupon VOID if purchased, sold or bartered. Discounts exclude tax, tip and/or alcohol, where applicable.

Planet Splash & Play

4600 Brookfield Corp. Dr.
Chantilly, VA
(703)378-6600

- Family entertainment & game center
- Including In line/roller skating, go-karts & plenty of games
- Two-acre space theme water park featuring the Master Blaster water coaster, wave pool, lazy river, assorted water rides for all ages, fountains & space toys
- Call for daily hours of operation

Bonus Discounts at
entertainment.com

entertainment. entertainment.com — great place for kids

ONE INDIVIDUAL ACTIVITY

Enjoy one complimentary INDIVIDUAL ACTIVITY when a second INDIVIDUAL ACTIVITY of equal or greater value is purchased.

valid anytime

One coupon per customer per visit; Free day must be used on same day; Waterpark not included

www.planetplay.com

C89

Valid now thru November 1, 2006

Not valid holidays & subject to Rules of Use. Not valid with other discount offers, unless specified. Coupon VOID if purchased, sold or bartered. Discounts exclude tax, tip and/or alcohol, where applicable.

Gymboree

See reverse side for locations

- Through music, art & play, children tell us who they are
- Ages 0 to 5 years
- Make your childs birthday extra special, call us today!
- 4 convienent locations

Bonus Discounts at
entertainment.com

entertainment. entertainment.com — great place for kids

50% OFF

Enjoy up to 3 TRIAL CLASSES at 50% off the regular price.

valid anytime

Reservations required; New families only

www.gymboree.com

C90

Valid now thru November 1, 2006

Not valid holidays & subject to Rules of Use. Not valid with other discount offers, unless specified. Coupon VOID if purchased, sold or bartered. Discounts exclude tax, tip and/or alcohol, where applicable.

PLANET PLAY™

6789 Springfield Mall
Springfield, VA
(703)313-6770

00356946

entertainment.com

00356946

PLANET SPLASH & PLAY™

4600 Brookfield Corp. Dr.
Chantilly, VA
(703)378-6600

00357038

entertainment.com

00357038

GYMBOREE PLAY & MUSIC

318 S. Pickett St.
Alexandria, VA
(703)836-2277

14155 Sully Field Circle # I
Chantilly, VA
(703)836-2277

10635 Braddock Rd.
Fairfax, VA
(703)836-2277

6303 Springfield Mall
Springfield, VA
(703)836-2277

00656581

entertainment.com

00656581

AMF Bowling Centers

For the AMF Bowling Center nearest you, visit us on the web at www.amfcenters.com

- Fun for all ages
- Bumper bowling for kids
- Automatic scoring
- Birthday parties
- Xtreme bowling
- Great food
- Adult & youth bowling leagues

Bonus Discounts at entertainment.com

entertainment. entertainment.com

great place for kids

ONE ADULT GAME OF BOWLING

Enjoy one complimentary ADULT GAME OF BOWLING when a second ADULT GAME OF BOWLING is purchased.

Offer good for up to 6 games; Shoe rental not included

valid anytime

One coupon/card per customer per visit; Not valid during Xtreme or league bowling

AMF

Need fun? Add bowling.

amfcenters.com

www.amfcenters.com

C91

Valid now thru November 1, 2006

Not valid holidays & subject to Rules of Use. Not valid with other discount offers, unless specified. Coupon VOID if purchased, sold or bartered. Discounts exclude tax, tip and/or alcohol, where applicable.

AMF Bowling Centers

For the AMF Bowling Center nearest you, visit us on the web at www.amfcenters.com

- Fun for all ages
- Bumper bowling for kids
- Automatic scoring
- Birthday parties
- Xtreme bowling
- Great food
- Adult & youth bowling leagues

Bonus Discounts at entertainment.com

entertainment. entertainment.com

great place for kids

ONE CHILD'S GAME OF BOWLING

Enjoy one complimentary CHILD'S GAME OF BOWLING with the purchase of an adult game of bowling.

Offer good for up to 4 child's games; Shoe rental not included

valid anytime

One coupon/card per customer per visit; Not valid during Xtreme or league bowling

AMF

Need fun? Add bowling.

amfcenters.com

www.amfcenters.com

C92

Valid now thru November 1, 2006

Not valid holidays & subject to Rules of Use. Not valid with other discount offers, unless specified. Coupon VOID if purchased, sold or bartered. Discounts exclude tax, tip and/or alcohol, where applicable.

AMF Bowling Centers

For the AMF Bowling Center nearest you, visit us on the web at www.amfcenters.com

- Fun for all ages
- Bumper bowling for kids
- Automatic scoring
- Birthday parties
- Xtreme bowling
- Great food
- Adult & youth bowling leagues

Bonus Discounts at entertainment.com

entertainment. entertainment.com

great place for kids

$5.00 Value

Enjoy $5.00 off the regular price of any AMF FUN PACK.

Includes 2 hours of bowling, rental shoes, 1 large popcorn & 1 pitcher of soda; Good for up to 4 people on 1 lane

valid anytime

One coupon/card per customer per visit; Not valid during Xtreme bowling

AMF

Need fun? Add bowling.

amfcenters.com

www.amfcenters.com

C93

Valid now thru November 1, 2006

Not valid holidays & subject to Rules of Use. Not valid with other discount offers, unless specified. Coupon VOID if purchased, sold or bartered. Discounts exclude tax, tip and/or alcohol, where applicable.

%N05004013

For the AMF Bowling Center nearest you, visit us on the web at
www.amfcenters.com

00656164

entertainment.com

00656164

%N05004015

For the AMF Bowling Center nearest you, visit us on the web at
www.amfcenters.com

00656400

entertainment.com

00656400

%N05004014

For the AMF Bowling Center nearest you, visit us on the web at
www.amfcenters.com

00656413

entertainment.com

00656413

Central Park Fun Land

See reverse side for locations

- Virginia's largest indoor/outdoor family entertainment center
- Bunky's play park for kids, rock climb wall, 2 flight & roller coaster simulators
- Grand prix, bumper boats, miniature golf, batting cages
- Private party room for office, group or birthday parties

Bonus Discounts at entertainment.com

entertainment. entertainment.com

great place for kids

UP TO 20 TOKENS

Enjoy UP TO 20 TOKENS at 50% off the regular price or or for those who prefer - any OFFICE, GROUP OR BIRTHDAY PARTY at 10% off the regular price (10 person minimum).

valid anytime

Not valid with any other discount offer

www.CPFunLand.com

C94

Valid now thru November 1, 2006

Not valid holidays & subject to Rules of Use. Not valid with other discount offers, unless specified. Coupon VOID if purchased, sold or bartered. Discounts exclude tax, tip and/or alcohol, where applicable.

Central Park Fun Land

See reverse side for locations

- Open 364 days a year
- Experience laser extreme, the ultimate in laser tag
- Grand prix, go karts & naskart tracks for all ages & abilities
- Activities for all ages from toddler to grandparent

Bonus Discounts at entertainment.com

entertainment. entertainment.com

great place for kids

ONE LASER TAG GAME OR GO KART RIDE

Enjoy one complimentary LASER TAG GAME OR GO KART RIDE when a second LASER TAG GAME OR GO KART RIDE of equal or greater value is purchased.

valid anytime

Not valid with any other discount offer

www.CPFunLand.com

C95

Valid now thru November 1, 2006

Not valid holidays & subject to Rules of Use. Not valid with other discount offers, unless specified. Coupon VOID if purchased, sold or bartered. Discounts exclude tax, tip and/or alcohol, where applicable.

The Little Gym

8056 Rolling Rd.
Springfield, VA
(703)455-4410

- Parent-child classes, 4 months to 3 years
- Pre-school & grade school gymnastics, 3-12 years
- Great place to have your next birthday party
- Call for upcoming class schedule

Bonus Discounts at entertainment.com

entertainment. entertainment.com

great place for kids

50% OFF

Enjoy one ANNUAL MEMBERSHIP FEE at 50% off the regular price.

valid anytime

www.thelittlegym.com

C96

Valid now thru November 1, 2006

Not valid holidays & subject to Rules of Use. Not valid with other discount offers, unless specified. Coupon VOID if purchased, sold or bartered. Discounts exclude tax, tip and/or alcohol, where applicable.

CENTRAL FUN•LAND PARK

1351 Central Park Blvd.
(next to Zany Brainy)
Fredericksburg, VA
(540)785-6700

1-888-FUN-2FUN

00284450

entertainment.com

00284450

CENTRAL FUN•LAND PARK

1351 Central Park Blvd.
(next to Zany Brainy)
Fredericksburg, VA
(540)785-6700

1-888-FUN-2FUN

00284460

entertainment.com

00284460

THE Little gym®

8056 Rolling Rd.
(at Saratoga Shpg. Ctr.)
Springfield, VA
(703)455-4410

00665461

entertainment.com

00665461

Ashburn Ice House

21595 Smiths Switch Rd.
Ashburn, VA
(703)858-0300

- A great place to skate
- Programs include: daily public skating sessions, birthday parties, figure skating school, learn to skate school, youth hockey camps, adult hockey leagues, pick-up hockey & more
- Come give us a try!

great place for kids

ONE ADMISSION

Enjoy one complimentary ADMISSION when a second ADMISSION of equal or greater value is purchased.

Skate rental excluded

valid anytime during public skate session

Ashburn ICe House

www.ashburnice.com

C97

Valid now thru November 1, 2006

Not valid holidays & subject to Rules of Use. Not valid with other discount offers, unless specified. Coupon VOID if purchased, sold or bartered. Discounts exclude tax, tip and/or alcohol, where applicable.

Fairfax Ice Arena

3779 Pickett Rd.
Fairfax, VA
(703)323-1132

- PUBLIC ICE SKATING SESSIONS DAILY!
- Open all year round
- Pro Shop
- Repairs, rentals & lessons
- Disc jockey
- Lessons for all ages & abilities
- Skate rentals not included
- For ice skating times call 703-323-1132

great place for kids

UP TO TWO ADMISSIONS

Enjoy up to TWO complimentary ADMISSIONS when up to TWO ADMISSIONS of equal or greater value are purchased.

valid during public skating sessions

Fairfax Ice Arena

www.fairfaxicearena.com

C98

Valid now thru November 1, 2006

Not valid holidays & subject to Rules of Use. Not valid with other discount offers, unless specified. Coupon VOID if purchased, sold or bartered. Discounts exclude tax, tip and/or alcohol, where applicable.

Fairfax Ice Arena

3779 Pickett Rd.
Fairfax, VA
(703)323-1132

- Introductory lessons includes:
- One 30-minute lesson
- One practice session
- FREE skate rental
- Lessons for adults, teens, children & tots 4-6

great place for kids

50% OFF

Enjoy any INTRODUCTORY ICE SKATING LESSONS at 50% off the regular price.

Inquire at lesson office, for schedule times call Fairfax Ice Arena 703-323-1132

valid anytime

Fairfax Ice Arena

www.fairfaxicearena.com

C99

Valid now thru November 1, 2006

Not valid holidays & subject to Rules of Use. Not valid with other discount offers, unless specified. Coupon VOID if purchased, sold or bartered. Discounts exclude tax, tip and/or alcohol, where applicable.

Ashburn ICe House

21595 Smiths Switch Rd.
Ashburn, VA
(703)858-0300

00457977

entertainment.com

00457977

Fairfax Ice Arena

3779 Pickett Rd.
Fairfax, VA
(703)323-1132

00059861

entertainment.com

00059861

Fairfax Ice Arena

3779 Pickett Rd.
Fairfax, VA
(703)323-1132

00658983

entertainment.com

00658983

Skate Quest

See reverse side for locations

- Public skating sesions offered daily
- Group & private ice-skating lessons available
- Youth & adult hockey leagues & instruction
- Host your next birthday party with private party rooms
- Open all year

entertainment. entertainment.com

great place for kids

ONE ADMISSION

SKATEQUEST

Enjoy one complimentary ADMISSION when a second ADMISSION of equal or greater value is purchased.

valid anytime during public skate session

Skate rental excluded

www.SkateQuest.com

C100

Valid now thru November 1, 2006

Not valid holidays & subject to Rules of Use. Not valid with other discount offers, unless specified. Coupon VOID if purchased, sold or bartered. Discounts exclude tax, tip and/or alcohol, where applicable.

Skate-N-Fun Zone

**7878 Sudley Rd.
Manassas, VA
(703)361-7465**

- We have birthday party plans available
- Class lessons & private lessons available
- Pro shop on premises for all your skating needs
- Call Skate-N-Fun for rates & hours

entertainment. entertainment.com

great place for kids

ONE ADMISSION

SKATE -N- FUN ZONE

Enjoy one complimentary ADMISSION when a second ADMISSION of equal or greater value is purchased.

valid during public sessions

www.skatenfunzone.com

C101

Valid now thru November 1, 2006

Not valid holidays & subject to Rules of Use. Not valid with other discount offers, unless specified. Coupon VOID if purchased, sold or bartered. Discounts exclude tax, tip and/or alcohol, where applicable.

Cavalier Family Skating Centers USA

**1924 Jefferson Davis Hwy.
Stafford, VA
(540)657-0758**

- A great place for the entire family
- Call for available dates & times for open skate
- Planning a birthday party, call us today

entertainment. entertainment.com

great place for kids

ONE ADMISSION

Cavalier Family Skating Centers USA, Inc.

Enjoy one complimentary ADMISSION when a second ADMISSION of equal or greater value is purchased.

valid anytime

Saturday night and special sessions excluded; Skate rental excluded

C102

Valid now thru November 1, 2006

Not valid holidays & subject to Rules of Use. Not valid with other discount offers, unless specified. Coupon VOID if purchased, sold or bartered. Discounts exclude tax, tip and/or alcohol, where applicable.

SKATEQUEST

5180 Dale Blvd.
Dale City, VA
(703)730-8423

1800 Michael Faraday Ct.
Reston, VA
(703)709-1010

00496480

SKATE-N-FUN ZONE

7878 Sudley Rd.
Manassas, VA
(703)361-7465

00013056

Cavalier Family Skating Centers USA, Inc.

1924 Jefferson Davis Hwy.
Stafford, VA
(540)657-0758

00460380

Sport Rock

See reverse side for locations

- Indoor rock climbing gym
- Parties, classes, memberships, teams, clinics, competitions & summer camp
- 3 locations
- Good for fitness, destressing & excitement
- Open 7 days a week
- Call or visit our website for more information
- Waivers are required for all climbers

Bonus Discounts at entertainment.com

entertainment. entertainment.com

great place for kids

4 OPEN BELAY

Sport Rock

Enjoy up to 4 OPEN BELAY at 50% off the regular price.

valid anytime

C103

Valid now thru November 1, 2006

Not valid holidays & subject to Rules of Use. Not valid with other discount offers, unless specified. Coupon VOID if purchased, sold or bartered. Discounts exclude tax, tip and/or alcohol, where applicable.

Hogback Mountain Sports Club

20261 Hogback Mountain Rd.
Leesburg, VA
(703)777-0057

- Paintball...is the thrilling adult version of capture the flag & is played by men & women of all ages
- Hogback Mountain Sports Club has a beautiful Leesburg location
- Specializing in groups of all sizes
- Call for information regarding our offers

Bonus Discounts at entertainment.com

entertainment. entertainment.com

great place for kids

ONE SEMI PACKAGE

HOGBACK MOUNTAIN SPORTS CLUB

Enjoy one complimentary SEMI PACKAGE when a second SEMI PACKAGE of equal or greater value is purchased.

valid anytime

During walk on play

www.hogback.net

C104

Valid now thru November 1, 2006

Not valid holidays & subject to Rules of Use. Not valid with other discount offers, unless specified. Coupon VOID if purchased, sold or bartered. Discounts exclude tax, tip and/or alcohol, where applicable.

Check It Paint Ball Supplies

See reverse side for locations

- New, used & rental guns
- Paintballs
- CO2 & N2 bottle fills
- Air soft guns
- Group field reservations
- Certified techs

Bonus Discounts at entertainment.com

entertainment. entertainment.com

great place for kids

50% OFF

Check It PaintBall Supplies

Enjoy up to 4 AIR FILLS at 50% off the regular price.

valid anytime

C105

Valid now thru November 1, 2006

Not valid holidays & subject to Rules of Use. Not valid with other discount offers, unless specified. Coupon VOID if purchased, sold or bartered. Discounts exclude tax, tip and/or alcohol, where applicable.

Sport Rock

14708 Southlawn Lane
Rockville, MD
(703)212-7625

5308 Eisenhower Ave.
Alexandria, VA
(703)212-7625

45935 Maries Road
Sterling, VA
(703)212-7625

00533302

entertainment.com

00533302

HOGBACK MOUNTAIN SPORTS CLUB

20261 Hogback Mountain Rd.
Leesburg, VA
(703)777-0057

00302399

entertainment.com

00302399

Check It PaintBall Supplies

14511-F Lee Jackson Hwy.
Chantilly, VA
(703)378-1150

9931 Main St.
Fairfax, VA
(703)591-4511

00616303

entertainment.com

00616303

Wildwater Expeditions

P.O. Box 155
Lansing, WV
(304)658-4007

- The experience of a lifetime!
- The Upper New River is perfect for a quiet day on the river without the big rapids
- The Lower New offers 14 major class IV-V rapids through the heart of the New River gorge
- Call for more information on our selection of adventures & reservations

Bonus Discounts at entertainment.com

entertainment® entertainment.com — great place for kids

ONE ONE-DAY UPPER NEW OR LOWER NEW

WILDWATER EXPEDITIONS

Enjoy any ONE-DAY UPPER NEW or LOWER NEW WHITEWATER RAFTING TRIP when a second identical trip is purchased.

valid anytime

Reservations, advance payment & coupon required, see reverse side; Lower New trip valid Tuesday, Wednesday & Thursday only; On availability basis

www.wvaraft.com

C106

Valid now thru November 1, 2006

Not valid holidays & subject to Rules of Use. Not valid with other discount offers, unless specified. Coupon VOID if purchased, sold or bartered. Discounts exclude tax, tip and/or alcohol, where applicable.

My Gym - Children's Fitness Center

Valid at All Participating U.S. Locations

- Age appropriate programs for children 3 months - 13 yrs.
- Gymnastics, games, sports, song, dance & more
- Mommy & Me classes
- Award winning birthday parties
- Over 135 locations nationwide
- 20+ Years of experience
- Unparalleled 5 - 1 student to teacher ratio
- State of the art facility
- New & unique program & gym set-up each week
- For gym nearest you, visit: www.my-gym.com

Bonus Discounts at entertainment.com

entertainment® entertainment.com — great place for kids

Up To $20.00 Value

Enjoy one FREE CLASS.

valid anytime

New members only; Not valid with any other discounts or promotions

MY GYM CHILDREN'S FITNESS CENTER®

www.my-gym.com

C107

Valid now thru November 1, 2006

Not valid holidays & subject to Rules of Use. Not valid with other discount offers, unless specified. Coupon VOID if purchased, sold or bartered. Discounts exclude tax, tip and/or alcohol, where applicable.

My Gym - Children's Fitness Center

Valid at All Participating U.S. Locations

- Age appropriate programs for children 3 months - 13 yrs.
- Gymnastics, games, sports, song, dance & more
- Mommy & Me classes
- Award winning birthday parties
- Over 135 locations nationwide
- 20+ Years of experience
- Unparalleled 5 - 1 student to teacher ratio
- State of the art facility
- New & unique program & gym set-up each week
- For gym nearest you, visit: www.my-gym.com

Bonus Discounts at entertainment.com

entertainment® entertainment.com — great place for kids

Up To $25.00 Value

Enjoy one MEMBERSHIP at 50% off the regular price.

valid anytime

New members only; Not valid with any other discounts or promotions

MY GYM CHILDREN'S FITNESS CENTER®

www.my-gym.com

C108

Valid now thru November 1, 2006

Not valid holidays & subject to Rules of Use. Not valid with other discount offers, unless specified. Coupon VOID if purchased, sold or bartered. Discounts exclude tax, tip and/or alcohol, where applicable.

WILDWATER EXPEDITIONS

P.O. Box 155
Lansing, WV
(304)658-4007

00014256

00014256

MY GYM CHILDREN'S FITNESS CENTER®

Valid at All Participating U.S. Locations

00619332

entertainment.com

00619332

MY GYM CHILDREN'S FITNESS CENTER®

Valid at All Participating U.S. Locations

00619328

entertainment.com

00619328

Laser Quest

14517 Potomac Mills Rd.
Woodbridge, VA
(703)490-4180

- Live action laser tag, the most immersive laser-zapping adventure game!
- Staff parties, sports clubs, social & church groups, agency/client events, office parties
- Call today to play
- Open daily

great place for kids

ONE GAME OF LASER TAG

Enjoy one complimentary GAME OF LASER TAG when a second GAME OF LASER TAG is purchased.

valid anytime

LASER QUEST

LIVE ACTION LASER TAG AT ITS BEST!

www.laserquest.com

C109

Valid now thru November 1, 2006

Not valid holidays & subject to Rules of Use. Not valid with other discount offers, unless specified. Coupon VOID if purchased, sold or bartered. Discounts exclude tax, tip and/or alcohol, where applicable.

Ultrazone

See reverse side for locations

- The Ultimate Laser Adventure
- Between reality & fantasy lies a zone where you can experience live action laser adventure
- Call us to plan your next birthday party

great place for kids

ONE ADMISSION

Enjoy one complimentary ADMISSION when a second ADMISSION of equal or greater value is purchased.

Offer valid for up to 10 admissions; Unlimited plays excluded

valid anytime

ULTRAZONE

www.ultrazone-nova.com

C110

Valid now thru November 1, 2006

Not valid holidays & subject to Rules of Use. Not valid with other discount offers, unless specified. Coupon VOID if purchased, sold or bartered. Discounts exclude tax, tip and/or alcohol, where applicable.

Shadowland Laser Adventures

See reverse side for locations

- Strap on a suit, enter the 6000 sq. ft. arena & prepare yourself for the adventure of a lifetime!
- Master it's mysteries

www.shadowlandadventures.com

great place for kids

ONE LASER TAG ADVENTURE

Enjoy one complimentary LASER TAG ADVENTURE when a second LASER TAG ADVENTURE of equal or greater value is purchased.

valid anytime

Call ahead for open play; On availability basis

ShadowLand
LASER ADVENTURES

www.shadowlandadventures.com

C111

Valid now thru November 1, 2006

Not valid holidays & subject to Rules of Use. Not valid with other discount offers, unless specified. Coupon VOID if purchased, sold or bartered. Discounts exclude tax, tip and/or alcohol, where applicable.

LASER QUEST

LIVE ACTION LASER TAG AT ITS BEST!

14517 Potomac Mills Rd.
Woodbridge, VA
(703)490-4180

00285308

entertainment.com

00285308

ULTRAZONE

7825 Eastpoint Mall Dr.
(Eastpoint Mall)
Baltimore, MD
(410)288-0880

3447 Carlin Springs Rd.
(Bailey's Crossroads)
Falls Church, VA
(703)578-6000

421 S. Sterling Blvd.
(Sterling Park)
Sterling, VA
(703)450-2333

00617855

entertainment.com

00617855

ShadowLand

LASER ADVENTURES

4300 Chantilly Shopping Center Dr.
Chantilly, MD
(703)263-1004

9179 Red Branch Rd.
Columbia, MD
(410)740-9100

624 Quince Orchard Rd.
(Quince Orchard Shpg. Plaza)
Gaithersburg, MD
(301)330-5546

00455594

entertainment.com

00455594

Canaan Valley Ski Resort

HC70 Box 330
Davis, WV
(800)622-4121

- 850 foot vertical drop from a 4,280 foot elevation
- 37 beginner to advanced slopes
- 85% snow making
- Downhill & cross country skiing, tubing park & ice skating rink
- 250 lodge rooms & 23 private cabins available

entertainment. entertainment.com

great place for kids

ONE LIFT TICKET OR TUBE PARK SESSION

Enjoy one complimentary LIFT TICKET OR TUBE PARK SESSION when a second LIFT TICKET OR TUBE PARK SESSION of equal or greater value is purchased.

valid during the 2005-2006 ski season

Please note the following date restrictions:; Weekends 12/25/05 thru 3/26/06 excluded; Ski area holidays 12/25/05 thru 01/02/06 exlcuded; Martin Luther King & President's Day excluded

Canaan Valley
RESORT & CONFERENCE CENTER
A West Virginia State Park

www.canaanresort.com

C112

Valid now thru November 1, 2006

Not valid holidays & subject to Rules of Use. Not valid with other discount offers, unless specified. Coupon VOID if purchased, sold or bartered. Discounts exclude tax, tip and/or alcohol, where applicable.

Village Skis & Bikes

12383 Dillingham Sq.
Lake Ridge, VA
(703)690-4756

- Rental by the day, weekend or week
- Reservations suggested
- Complete service department - tune-ups, major repairs, etc.
- Ski packages include skis, boots & poles
- Call for info. on Fall ski swap & used bike flea markets
- Open year 'round

entertainment. entertainment.com

great place for kids

ONE BICYCLE RENTAL OR DOWNHILL SKI PACKAGE

Enjoy one complimentary BICYCLE RENTAL or DOWNHILL SKI RENTAL PACKAGE when a second BICYCLE RENTAL or DOWNHILL SKI RENTAL PACKAGE of equal or greater value is purchased.

valid anytime

Maximum 2 day limit

VILLAGE SKIS & BIKES

C113

Valid now thru November 1, 2006

Not valid holidays & subject to Rules of Use. Not valid with other discount offers, unless specified. Coupon VOID if purchased, sold or bartered. Discounts exclude tax, tip and/or alcohol, where applicable.

Jow Ga Shaolin Institute

600-D Carlisle Dr.
Herndon, VA
(703)742-7800

- Learn authentic Chinese Martial Arts for body, mind & spirit
- Classes in Jow Ga Kung Fu, Mizong style Shaolin & Yang & Chen style Tai chi
- Training tailored toward each student's abilities & interests
- Programs for kids, teens & adults

entertainment. entertainment.com

great place for kids

50% OFF

Enjoy ONE MONTH LESSONS at 50% off the regular price.

valid anytime

Not valid with any other discount offer

JOW GA SHAOLIN INSTITUTE

www.jowgashaolin.com

C114

Valid now thru November 1, 2006

Not valid holidays & subject to Rules of Use. Not valid with other discount offers, unless specified. Coupon VOID if purchased, sold or bartered. Discounts exclude tax, tip and/or alcohol, where applicable.

Canaan Valley
RESORT & CONFERENCE CENTER
A West Virginia State Park

HC70 Box 330
Davis, WV
(800)622-4121

00467166

entertainment.com

00467166

VILLAGE SKIS & BIKES

12383 Dillingham Sq.
(Festival at Old Bridge)
Lake Ridge, VA
(703)690-4756

00033471

entertainment.com

00033471

JOW GA SHAOLIN INSTITUTE
周家少林堂

600-D Carlisle Dr.
(behind Cardinal Bank near the intersection of Fairfax County Pkwy. & Elden St.)
Herndon, VA
(703)742-7800

00633474

entertainment.com

00633474

Laurel Park

Rte. 198 & Racetrack Rd.
Laurel, MD
(301)725-0400

- Featuring live thoroughbred racing Wednesday through Sunday, with holiday exceptions
- Please call for racing dates & times
- Also offering year-round simulcast racing from top tracks across the country

Bonus Discounts at entertainment.com

entertainment. entertainment.com

50% OFF

LAUREL PARK

Enjoy UP TO FOUR ADMISSIONS at 50% off the regular price.

Preakness Day & Maryland Million Day excluded

valid for any day of live thoroughbred racing

www.marylandracing.com

C115

Valid now thru November 1, 2006

Not valid holidays & subject to Rules of Use. Not valid with other discount offers, unless specified. Coupon VOID if purchased, sold or bartered. Discounts exclude tax, tip and/or alcohol, where applicable.

Colonial Downs Racetrack

10515 Colonial Downs Pkwy.
New Kent, VA
(804)966-7223

- Horse racing, Virginia style, means fun for the whole family!©
- Racing season: Thoroughbreds: Summer dates, Harness: Fall (Fri.-Tues.)
- Enjoy dining in our climate controlled Jockey Club
- Call 1-888-4VA-TRACK for information on post times
- Visit our web site www.colonialdowns.com for upcoming racing & special events
- Children 12 & under FREE!

Bonus Discounts at entertainment.com

entertainment. entertainment.com

SIX GENERAL ADMISSION

Enjoy up to SIX GENERAL ADMISSIONS at 50% off the regular price.

valid anytime

Virginia Derby Day excluded

COLONIAL DOWNS

C116

Valid now thru November 1, 2006

Not valid holidays & subject to Rules of Use. Not valid with other discount offers, unless specified. Coupon VOID if purchased, sold or bartered. Discounts exclude tax, tip and/or alcohol, where applicable.

Pohick Bay Regional Park

6501 Pohick Bay Dr.
Lorton, VA
(703)339-6104

- Boat rentals available per hour or per day
- Come enjoy the sites along the beautiful Pohick Bay
- Great for the entire family

Bonus Discounts at entertainment.com

entertainment. entertainment.com

great place for kids

ONE HOUR RENTAL

Enjoy ONE HOUR RENTAL when a second HOUR RENTAL of equal or greater value is purchased.

valid anytime

Valid on rental of canoes & sea kayaks only

Northern Virginia Regional Park Authority

www.nvrpa.org

C117

Valid now thru November 1, 2006

Not valid holidays & subject to Rules of Use. Not valid with other discount offers, unless specified. Coupon VOID if purchased, sold or bartered. Discounts exclude tax, tip and/or alcohol, where applicable.

LAUREL PARK

Rte. 198 & Racetrack Rd.
Laurel, MD
(301)725-0400

00408194

COLONIAL DOWNS

10515 Colonial Downs Pkwy.
(exit 214 off I-64)
New Kent, VA
(804)966-7223

00282185

Northern Virginia
Regional Park Authority

6501 Pohick Bay Dr.
Lorton, VA
(703)339-6104

00547118

YMCA of Metropolitan Washington

See reverse side for locations

- YMCA of Metropolitan is the 17th largest YMCA in North America
- The association operates more than 20 branches & program centers in MD, VA & DC
- In addition, the YMCA of Metropolitan Washington is the largest nonprofit provider of child care in the region
- The organization is open to people of all ages, faiths, races & cultural backgrounds

Bonus Discounts at entertainment.com

entertainment® entertainment.com

$200.00

Bring this coupon to any YMCA of Metropolitan Washington branch and receive NO JOINER FEE when you sign up for a membership.

valid anytime

Cannot be combined with any other offer

YMCA OF METROPOLITAN WASHINGTON

www.ymcawashdc.org

C118

Valid now thru November 1, 2006

Not valid holidays & subject to Rules of Use. Not valid with other discount offers, unless specified. Coupon VOID if purchased, sold or bartered. Discounts exclude tax, tip and/or alcohol, where applicable.

Arthur Murray Dance Studio

See reverse side for locations

- Offer includes: 2 private, 2 group, 2 variety & 2 practice sessions
- Have fun, meet new people & develop self-confidence.
- Dancing develops muscle tone & balance
- All teachers are certified by Arthur Murray, Inc. Dance Board
- Lessons are transferable
- VISA, MasterCard, Discover, AMEX & personal checks accepted
- Call for information & location nearest you

Bonus Discounts at entertainment.com

entertainment® entertainment.com

50% OFF

Arthur Murray

Enjoy One 8 LESSON INTRODUCTORY OFFER at 50% off the regular price.

valid anytime

Reservations required

www.arthurmurraydc.com

C119

Valid now thru November 1, 2006

Not valid holidays & subject to Rules of Use. Not valid with other discount offers, unless specified. Coupon VOID if purchased, sold or bartered. Discounts exclude tax, tip and/or alcohol, where applicable.

Gold's Gym

See reverse side for locations

Bonus Discounts at entertainment.com

entertainment® entertainment.com

Up To $99.00 Value

GOLD'S GYM®

Valid for any one ENROLLMENT FEE at 50% off the regular price - maximum discount $99.00.

valid anytime

www.goldsgym.com

C120

Valid now thru November 1, 2006

Not valid holidays & subject to Rules of Use. Not valid with other discount offers, unless specified. Coupon VOID if purchased, sold or bartered. Discounts exclude tax, tip and/or alcohol, where applicable.

YMCA OF METROPOLITAN WASHINGTON

DISTRICT OF COLUMBIA
Washington
1711 Rhode Island Ave., NW
(202)862-9622

MARYLAND
Bethesda
9401 Old Georgetown Rd.
(301)530-3725

Montgomery Village
10011 Stedwick Rd.
(301)948-9622

Silver Spring
9800 Hastings Dr.
(301)585-2120

VIRGINIA
Alexandria
420 E. Monroe Ave.
(703)838-8085

Arlington
3422 N. 13th St.
(703)525-5420

Reston
12196 Sunset Hills Rd.
(703)742-8800

00550103

entertainment.com

00550103

Arthur Murray

8227 Woodmont Ave.
Bethesda, MD
(301)657-2700

1 West Deer Park Dr.
Gaithersburg, MD
(301)590-0387

Colewood Centre
Silver Spring, MD
(301)681-4466

6489 Little River Tnpk.
Alexandria, VA
(703)751-4336

8603 Westwood Ctr. Dr.
#205
Vienna, VA
(703)556-0088

00003857

entertainment.com

00003857

GOLD'S GYM.

DISTRICT OF COLUMBIA
Washington
408 4th St., SW
(202)554-4653

4310 Connecticut Ave., NW
(202)364-4653

MARYLAND
Belair
802 Bel Air Rd.
(410)638-9394

Crofton
1641 Crofton Ctr.
(410)451-4653

Frederick
5620 Buckeystown Pike
(301)698-4653

Glen Burnie
6324 Ritchie Hwy.
(410)789-4653

Greenbelt
6222 Greenbelt Rd.
(301)982-6700

Owings Mills
10221 S. Dolfield Rd.
(410)654-4653

Waldorf
3317 Plaza Way
(301)932-4653

VIRGINIA
Alexandria
2960 Southgate Dr.
(703)768-6800

Annandale
6940-A Bradlick Shpg. Ctr.
(703)941-4653

Arlington
1830 Nash St.
(703)528-4653

2900 Clarenden Blvd.
(703)527-4653

Bailey's Crossroads
3505 Carlin Springs Rd.
(703)820-4653

Chantilly
14290-D Sullyfield Cir.,
Suite D
(703)378-4653

Fairfax
10201 Main St.
(703)352-4653

Herndon
490 Eldon St.
(703)467-0500

Manassas
8260 Shoppers Sq.
(703)369-4950

Sterling
21620 Ridgetop Cir.
(703)406-1622

Vienna
8371 Leesburg Pike
(703)893-4653

Winchester
1109 Berryville Ave.
(540)667-4653

Woodbridge
12550 Dillingham Sq.
(703)680-7000

00480175

entertainment.com

00480175

Burke Racquet & Swim Club

6001 Burke Commons Rd.
Burke, VA
(703)250-1299

- We make fitness fun for everyone
- Swim, participate in aerobics class or try our cardiovascular room
- Call for information or to reserve court time
- STUB BONUS: Present this stub & receive one free visit to the cardiovascular room, aerobics class or swimming

Bonus Discounts at entertainment.com

entertainment. entertainment.com

50% OFF

Burke Racquet & Swim Club ©

Enjoy ONE HOUR OF COURT TIME at 50% off the regular price.

valid during "non-prime" time

Reservations required; Maximum of 2 persons per coupon; Non-members only; On availability basis; Credit card required at time of scheduling

C121

Valid now thru November 1, 2006

Not valid holidays & subject to Rules of Use. Not valid with other discount offers, unless specified. Coupon VOID if purchased, sold or bartered. Discounts exclude tax, tip and/or alcohol, where applicable.

Jewish Community Center of N. Virginia

8900 Little River Tpke.
Fairfax, VA
(703)323-0880

- Everyone welcome
- 25 meter indoor pool, cardio fitness room with treadmills, stair climbers, bikes, Cybex & free weights, full court gym & aerobics
- Personal training
- Morning babysitting
- Tours available
- Annual, 3 or 6 month memberships

Bonus Discounts at entertainment.com

entertainment. entertainment.com

FREE

jcc nv Jewish Community Center of Northern Virginia

Enjoy one WEEK GUEST PASS (INDIVIDUAL OR FAMILY) FREE, no purchase necessary.

Includes aerobics, jazzercise & water aerobics classes during the same week; For prospective new members only

valid anytime

Must be 16 yrs. old or accompanied by an adult; One coupon per person please

www.jccnv.org

C122

Valid now thru November 1, 2006

Not valid holidays & subject to Rules of Use. Not valid with other discount offers, unless specified. Coupon VOID if purchased, sold or bartered. Discounts exclude tax, tip and/or alcohol, where applicable.

Jazzercise

For more information on class schedules, locations & pricing call: in Maryland, Washington, DC & No. Virginia 1-800-FIT-IS-IT

- Cardio, strength & stretch
- Fresh moves, new music, pure motivation
- All fitness levels welcome, no experience required
- Register monthly, start anytime, no contracts/ membership fees
- Childcare available at some locations
- For class locations, 1-800-fit-is-it

Bonus Discounts at entertainment.com

entertainment. entertainment.com

50% OFF

jazzercise® it shows.

Enjoy 8 WEEKS OF UNLIMITED CLASSES at 50% off the regular price.

valid anytime

Valid for new customers only who have not attend Jazzercise for 6 months or longer; Not valid with any other discount offer; One coupon per customer per year; Valid at participating locations; Membership card or coupon provided in Entertainment book required to obtain discount

www.jazzercise.com

C123

Valid now thru November 1, 2006

Not valid holidays & subject to Rules of Use. Not valid with other discount offers, unless specified. Coupon VOID if purchased, sold or bartered. Discounts exclude tax, tip and/or alcohol, where applicable.

Burke Racquet & Swim Club

6001 Burke Commons Rd.
Burke, VA
(703)250-1299

00030196

entertainment.com

00030196

Jewish Community Center of Northern Virginia

8900 Little River Tpke.
Fairfax, VA
(703)323-0880

00276404

entertainment.com

00276404

jazzercise® it shows.

For more information on class schedules, locations & pricing call: in Maryland, Washington, DC & No. Virginia 1-800-FIT-IS-IT

00322759

entertainment.com

00322759

Tourmobile Sightseeing

See reverse side for locations

- Visit over 40 historic sights
- Hours: 9:30 a.m. - 4:30 p.m. year round
- Board at any stop on the National Mall or Arlington Cemetery

entertainment.
entertainment.com

great place for kids

ONE ADULT ADMISSION

Enjoy one complimentary ADULT ADMISSION when a second ADULT ADMISSION is purchased.

Washington-Arlington Cemetery one day tour only

valid anytime

Purchase tickets from drivers or available Tourmobile ticket booths

Tourmobile® Sightseeing

www.tourmobile.com

C124

Valid now thru November 1, 2006

Not valid holidays & subject to Rules of Use. Not valid with other discount offers, unless specified. Coupon VOID if purchased, sold or bartered. Discounts exclude tax, tip and/or alcohol, where applicable.

Trolley Tours of Fredericksburg

See reverse side for locations

- Embark on a 75 minute tour of "America's Most Historical City"
- Trolley departs from the Fredericksburg Visitors Center
- Call for schedule of times
- Tour visits 35 monuments/markets & attractions including the Fredericksburg Battlefield

entertainment.
entertainment.com

great place for kids

ONE ADMISSION

Enjoy one complimentary ADMISSION when a second ADMISSION of equal or greater value is purchased.

valid anytime April thru November

"The Original"
Trolley Tours of Fredericksburg

C125

Valid now thru November 1, 2006

Not valid holidays & subject to Rules of Use. Not valid with other discount offers, unless specified. Coupon VOID if purchased, sold or bartered. Discounts exclude tax, tip and/or alcohol, where applicable.

Port Discovery

35 Market Place
Baltimore, MD
(410)727-8120

- Interactive, educational fun for the whole family
- Ever changing activities & programs
- Exhibits designed in collaboration with Walt Disney Imagineering
- Birthday parties, group visits, overnight adventures & catering events
- Open daily Memorial Day thru Labor Day - hours vary during school year

entertainment.
entertainment.com

great place for kids

ONE CHILD ADMISSION

Enjoy one complimentary CHILD ADMISSION when a second CHILD ADMISSION of equal or greater value is purchased.

Special events excluded

valid anytime

One coupon per customer per visit; Not valid with any other discount offer

Port Discovery
The Kid-Powered Museum

www.portdiscovery.org

C126

Valid now thru November 1, 2006

Not valid holidays & subject to Rules of Use. Not valid with other discount offers, unless specified. Coupon VOID if purchased, sold or bartered. Discounts exclude tax, tip and/or alcohol, where applicable.

Tourmobile® Sightseeing

1000 Ohio Dr. SW

Washington, D.C.

Tour Information (202) 554-7950

00032853

entertainment.com

00032853

"The Original"

Trolley Tours of Fredericksburg

706 Caroline St.
Fredericksburg, VA
(540)898-0737

Tickets Must Be Purchased at the Fredericksburg Visitors Center

00459799

entertainment.com

00459799

Port Discovery

The Kid-Powered Museum

35 Market Place
Baltimore, MD
(410)727-8120

00401710

entertainment.com

00401710

National Aquarium

14th St. between Pennsylvania and Constitution Ave., NW
Washington, DC
(202)482-2825

- Wet & Wild for over 125 years
- "Up close & personal" type of experience
- Take a self-guided tour
- 250 different species of fish, invertebrates, reptiles & amphibians
- Lecture & feed shows daily

great place for kids

ONE ADMISSION

Enjoy one complimentary ADMISSION when a second ADMISSION of equal or greater value is purchased.

valid anytime

THE NATIONAL AQUARIUM • WASHINGTON, DC •

C127

Valid now thru November 1, 2006

Not valid holidays & subject to Rules of Use. Not valid with other discount offers, unless specified. Coupon VOID if purchased, sold or bartered. Discounts exclude tax, tip and/or alcohol, where applicable.

Capitol River Cruises

End of 31st & K Street
Washington, DC
(301)460-7447

- Relaxing 50 minute cruise of Washington's monuments
- Narrated tour
- Located at Washington Harbour, Georgetown, end of 31st street
- Group rates available
- Call for information about our private charters and crab feasts
- Call for cruise schedule

great place for kids

ONE ADMISSION

Enjoy one complimentary ADMISSION when a second ADMISSION of equal or greater value is purchased.

valid during operating season April thru October

Tickets are purchased onboard the boat

CAPITOL RIVER CRUISES

www.capitolrivercruises.com

C128

Valid now thru November 1, 2006

Not valid holidays & subject to Rules of Use. Not valid with other discount offers, unless specified. Coupon VOID if purchased, sold or bartered. Discounts exclude tax, tip and/or alcohol, where applicable.

Potomac River Boat Co.

Alexandria City Marina
Alexandria, VA
(703)548-9000

- 90 minute cruise of Washington's majestic monuments
- 40 minute cruise of Alexandria's historic waterfront
- Located in Old Town Alexandria
- Cruises run Apr. - Oct.
- Group rates available
- Ask about our private parties

great place for kids

ONE TICKET

Enjoy one complimentary TICKET when a second TICKET of equal or greater value is purchased.

Cruise to Mt. Vernon excluded

valid May thru September, Tuesday thru Friday

Not valid with any other discounts or promotions; Please present to ticket seller prior to boarding

Potomac Riverboat Company

www.potomacriverboatco.com

C129

Valid now thru November 1, 2006

Not valid holidays & subject to Rules of Use. Not valid with other discount offers, unless specified. Coupon VOID if purchased, sold or bartered. Discounts exclude tax, tip and/or alcohol, where applicable.

THE NATIONAL AQUARIUM
WASHINGTON, DC

14th St. between Pennsylvania and Constitution Ave., NW
(U.S. Department of Commerce Building)
Washington, DC
(202)482-2825

00399307

CAPITOL
RIVER CRUISES

End of 31st & K Street
(on the dock at Washington Harbour in Georgetown)
Washington, DC
(301)460-7447

00397328

entertainment.com

Potomac Riverboat Company

Alexandria City Marina
Alexandria, VA
(703)548-9000

00319293

entertainment.com

Tidal Basin Boathouse

1501 Maine Ave. S.W.
Washington, DC
(202)479-2426

- Offering an unique view of the Tidal Basin
- Boathouse open from mid-March through mid-October
- A beautiful way to view the springtime cherry blossoms

entertainment® entertainment.com

Up To $16.00 Value

Enjoy one complimentary HOUR RENTAL when a second HOUR RENTAL of equal or greater value is purchased.

2 or 4 seat boat rental

valid Monday thru Friday

Holidays excluded

TIDAL BASIN Peddle Boats

C130

Valid now thru November 1, 2006

Not valid holidays & subject to Rules of Use. Not valid with other discount offers, unless specified. Coupon VOID if purchased, sold or bartered. Discounts exclude tax, tip and/or alcohol, where applicable.

Bike The Sites

1100 Pennsylvania Ave, NW
Washington, DC
(202)842-2453

- Guided bike tours
- Bike rentals
- Stroller rentals
- Deluxe padi-cab rides
- Fitness ride
- Located at the Old Post Office Pavilion

entertainment® entertainment.com

great place for kids

ONE GUIDED TOUR

Enjoy ONE GUIDED TOUR when a second GUIDED TOUR of equal or greater value is purchased.

valid anytime

Reservations required; Please present coupon/card at time of purchase; On availability basis

BIKE THE SITES INC

www.bikethesites.com

C131

Valid now thru November 1, 2006

Not valid holidays & subject to Rules of Use. Not valid with other discount offers, unless specified. Coupon VOID if purchased, sold or bartered. Discounts exclude tax, tip and/or alcohol, where applicable.

Maryland Zoo

Madison Ave. & Druid Park Lake Dr.
Baltimore, MD
(410)366-LION

- Home to over 2,200 exotic animals
- Beautiful 180-acre park just 4 miles from the Inner Harbor
- Visit America's #1 rated Children's Zoo
- Celebrating over 125 years!
- Travel to the African Savannah
- Polar bear watch
- Free parking

entertainment® entertainment.com

great place for kids

ONE ADMISSION

Enjoy one complimentary ADMISSION when a second ADMISSION of equal or greater value is purchased.

valid anytime

THE MARYLAND ZOO IN BALTIMORE

www.marylandzoo.org

C132

Valid now thru November 1, 2006

Not valid holidays & subject to Rules of Use. Not valid with other discount offers, unless specified. Coupon VOID if purchased, sold or bartered. Discounts exclude tax, tip and/or alcohol, where applicable.

TIDAL BASIN
Peddle Boats

1501 Maine Ave. S.W.
Washington, DC
(202)479-2426

00659071

entertainment.com

00659071

BIKE THE SITES INC

1100 Pennsylvania Ave, NW
(Outside Federal Triangle Metro Elevator Exit)
Washington, DC
(202)842-2453

00548079

entertainment.com

00548079

THE MARYLAND ZOO
IN BALTIMORE

Madison Ave. & Druid Park Lake Dr.
Baltimore, MD
(410)366-LION

00664610

entertainment.com

00664610

Carlyle House Historic Park

121 N. Fairfax St.
Alexandria, VA
(703)549-2997

- Built in 1751, this building was the home of John Carlyle
- Fully restored in 1976, the house & gardens are open to the public as a museum
- Available for private rental for weddings, parties & corporate events
- Closed Mondays

Bonus Discounts at
entertainment.com

entertainment.
entertainment.com

great place for kids

ONE ADULT TOUR

CARLYLE HOUSE

Enjoy one complimentary ADULT TOUR when a second ADULT TOUR of equal or greater value is purchased.

valid anytime

Special events excluded

www.carlylehouse.org

C133

Valid now thru November 1, 2006

Not valid holidays & subject to Rules of Use. Not valid with other discount offers, unless specified. Coupon VOID if purchased, sold or bartered. Discounts exclude tax, tip and/or alcohol, where applicable.

Gadsby's Tavern Museum

134 North Royal St.
Alexandria, VA
(703)838-4242

- Gadsby's Tavern Museum consists of two tavern buildings, a 1770 Georgian tavern & the 1792 City Tavern & Hotel
- The buildings are named for Englishman John Gadsby who operated them from 1796 to 1808
- Today, vistors are welcomed to tour the historic rooms of both buildings, restored to their 18th-century appearance

Bonus Discounts at
entertainment.com

entertainment.
entertainment.com

ONE ADULT TOUR

GADSBY'S TAVERN MUSEUM

Enjoy one complimentary ADULT TOUR when a second ADULT TOUR is purchased.

valid anytime

Not valid for special events

www.gadsbystavern.org

C134

Valid now thru November 1, 2006

Not valid holidays & subject to Rules of Use. Not valid with other discount offers, unless specified. Coupon VOID if purchased, sold or bartered. Discounts exclude tax, tip and/or alcohol, where applicable.

Lee-Fendall House Museum

614 Oronoco St.
Alexandria, VA
(703)548-1789

- An interpretation of the Lee family home from the period of 1850-1870
- Featuring a splendid collection of Lee family heirlooms
- The house is complemented by it's beautifully restored, award winning garden
- Call for tour hours

Bonus Discounts at
entertainment.com

entertainment.
entertainment.com

great place for kids

ONE ADMISSION

LEE-FENDALL HOUSE MUSEUM

Enjoy one complimentary ADMISSION when a second ADMISSION of equal or greater value is purchased.

valid anytime

Valid for up to 4 admissions

www.leefendallhouse.org

C135

Valid now thru November 1, 2006

Not valid holidays & subject to Rules of Use. Not valid with other discount offers, unless specified. Coupon VOID if purchased, sold or bartered. Discounts exclude tax, tip and/or alcohol, where applicable.

Carlyle House

121 N. Fairfax St.
Alexandria, VA
(703)549-2997

00290015

entertainment.com

00290015

GADSBY'S TAVERN MUSEUM

134 North Royal St.
Alexandria, VA
(703)838-4242

00217433

entertainment.com

00217433

Lee-Fendall House Museum

614 Oronoco St.
Alexandria, VA
(703)548-1789

00617840

entertainment.com

00617840

Loudoun Heritage Farm Museum

21668 Heritage Farm Ln.
Sterling, VA
(703)421-5322

- Experience 300 years of agriculture history thru hands-on activities & special events
- Exhibit hall features a hands-on children's play area, re-created general store & post office & a permanent exhibit on 300 years of farming history in Loudoun County
- Open Tues.-Sat.

Bonus Discounts at
entertainment.com

entertainment.
entertainment.com

great place for kids

ONE ADMISSION

Enjoy one complimentary ADMISSION when a second ADMISSION of equal or greater value is purchased.

valid anytime

Loudoun Heritage Farm Museum

www.loudounfarmmuseum.org

C136

Valid now thru November 1, 2006

Not valid holidays & subject to Rules of Use. Not valid with other discount offers, unless specified. Coupon VOID if purchased, sold or bartered. Discounts exclude tax, tip and/or alcohol, where applicable.

Loudoun Museum

16 Loudoun St.
Leesburg, VA
(703)777-7427

- Explore a special place that evokes images of the past
- Let Loudoun's rich past capture your imagination & curiosity
- Visit our gift shop offering a variety of walking & driving tours
- Open daily

Bonus Discounts at
entertainment.com

entertainment.
entertainment.com

great place for kids

ONE ADULT ADMISSION

Enjoy one complimentary ADULT ADMISSION when a second ADULT ADMISSION of equal or greater value is purchased.

valid anytime

LM Loudoun Museum

www.loudounmuseum.org

C137

Valid now thru November 1, 2006

Not valid holidays & subject to Rules of Use. Not valid with other discount offers, unless specified. Coupon VOID if purchased, sold or bartered. Discounts exclude tax, tip and/or alcohol, where applicable.

Gunston Hall

10709 Gunston Rd.
Mason Neck, VA
(703)550-9220

- Home of George Mason, author of America's first Bill of Rights
- Find out what life was like on an 18th century plantation
- Museum shops available
- Great for the entire family!

Bonus Discounts at
entertainment.com

entertainment.
entertainment.com

great place for kids

ONE ADULT ADMISSION

Enjoy one complimentary ADULT ADMISSION when a second ADULT ADMISSION of equal or greater value is purchased.

valid anytime

GUNSTON HALL

www.gunstonhall.org

C138

Valid now thru November 1, 2006

Not valid holidays & subject to Rules of Use. Not valid with other discount offers, unless specified. Coupon VOID if purchased, sold or bartered. Discounts exclude tax, tip and/or alcohol, where applicable.

Loudoun
HERITAGE FARM
MUSEUM

21668 Heritage Farm Ln.
(located in Claude Moore Park)
Sterling, VA
(703)421-5322

00611853

00611853

Loudoun Museum

16 Loudoun St.
Leesburg, VA
(703)777-7427

00530668

00530668

GUNSTON HALL

10709 Gunston Rd.
Mason Neck, VA
(703)550-9220

00625095

00625095

George Washington's Ferry Farm

268 Kings Hwy.
Fredericksburg, VA
(540)370-0732

- George Washington's boyhood home preserved as an archaeological & environmental site
- Self-guided tours available
- Group & school tours available (call ahead to arrange)
- Seasonal hours call or visit our website

entertainment. entertainment.com

great place for kids

UP TO TWO ADMISSIONS

George Washington's Ferry Farm

Enjoy UP TO TWO COMPLIMENTARY ADMISSIONS with the purchase of UP TO TWO ADMISSIONS of equal or greater value.

valid anytime

Limit two free admissions per coupon

www.kenmore.org

C139

Valid now thru November 1, 2006

Not valid holidays & subject to Rules of Use. Not valid with other discount offers, unless specified. Coupon VOID if purchased, sold or bartered. Discounts exclude tax, tip and/or alcohol, where applicable.

Kenmore Plantation & Gardens

1201 Washington Ave.
Fredericksburg, VA
(540)373-3381

- In the heart of historic Fredericksburg
- Museum offers daily tours & changing exhibits
- Guided tours
- Group & school tours available (call ahead to arrange)
- Seasonal hours, call or visit our website

entertainment. entertainment.com

great place for kids

UP TO TWO ADMISSIONS

Kenmore Plantation & Gardens

Enjoy UP TO TWO COMPLIMETARY ADMISSIONS with the purchase of UP TO TWO ADMISSIONS of equal or greater value.

valid anytime

Limit two admissions per coupon

www.kenmore.org

C140

Valid now thru November 1, 2006

Not valid holidays & subject to Rules of Use. Not valid with other discount offers, unless specified. Coupon VOID if purchased, sold or bartered. Discounts exclude tax, tip and/or alcohol, where applicable.

Morven Park

P.O. Box 6228
Leesburg, VA
(703)777-2414

- Once the home of Thomas Swann, Governor of Maryland & Westmoreland Davis, Governor of Virginia (1918-1922)
- A guided tour of the home includes a history of its former occupants as well as information on the many antiques & artifacts throughout the home
- Also included in the tour: The Museum of Hounds & Hunting and the Winmill Carriage Collection

entertainment. entertainment.com

great place for kids

ONE TOUR ADMISSION

MORVEN PARK

Enjoy one complimentary TOUR ADMISSION when a second TOUR ADMISSION of equal or greater value is purchased.

valid April through December

www.morvenpark.org

C141

Valid now thru November 1, 2006

Not valid holidays & subject to Rules of Use. Not valid with other discount offers, unless specified. Coupon VOID if purchased, sold or bartered. Discounts exclude tax, tip and/or alcohol, where applicable.

George Washington's Ferry Farm

268 Kings Hwy.
(Rte. 3 East)
Fredericksburg, VA
(540)370-0732

00359832

entertainment.com

00359832

Kenmore Plantation & Gardens

1201 Washington Ave.
Fredericksburg, VA
(540)373-3381

00356048

entertainment.com

00356048

MORVEN PARK

P.O. Box 6228
Leesburg, VA
(703)777-2414

00096041

entertainment.com

00096041

Belmont, Gari Melchers Estate & Mem. Gallery

224 Washington St.
Fredericksburg, VA
(540)654-1015

- Former home of the American figure painter Gari Melchers featuring his home, studio & gardens
- Great for the whole family
- Open daily
- Museum shop available

entertainment.
entertainment.com

great place for kids

ONE ADULT ADMISSION

Enjoy one complimentary ADULT ADMISSION when a second ADULT ADMISSION of equal or greater value is purchased.

valid anytime

BELMONT
THE GARI MELCHERS ESTATE AND MEMORIAL GALLERY

www.garimelchers.org

C142

Valid now thru November 1, 2006

Not valid holidays & subject to Rules of Use. Not valid with other discount offers, unless specified. Coupon VOID if purchased, sold or bartered. Discounts exclude tax, tip and/or alcohol, where applicable.

Civil War Life Museum

4712 Southpoint Pkwy.
Fredericksburg, VA
(540)834-1859

- See & experience the areas most extensive collection of original civil war weapons, equipment, life size dioramas & more
- A child friendly museum
- While you are here, shop the Homefront, the areas largest museum store with the greatest selection of gifts, books, toys & much more

entertainment.
entertainment.com

great place for kids

50% OFF

Enjoy up to 4 ADMISSIONS at 50% off the regular price.

valid anytime

Civil War Life - The Soldiers Museum

www.civilwar-life.com

C143

Valid now thru November 1, 2006

Not valid holidays & subject to Rules of Use. Not valid with other discount offers, unless specified. Coupon VOID if purchased, sold or bartered. Discounts exclude tax, tip and/or alcohol, where applicable.

White Oak Civil War Museum

985 White Oak Rd.
Falmouth, VA
(540)371-4234

- Over 120k soldiers camped in Stafford between 1862-1863
- Tens of thousands of artifacts left behind
- Replica winter camp huts
- Self-guided tours
- Group & school tours available
- Special events with reenactors

entertainment.
entertainment.com

great place for kids

50% OFF

Enjoy up to 4 ADMISSIONS at 50% off the regular price.

valid anytime

WHITE OAK CIVIL WAR MUSEUM

http://mywebpage.netscape.com/whiteoakmuseum/

C144

Valid now thru November 1, 2006

Not valid holidays & subject to Rules of Use. Not valid with other discount offers, unless specified. Coupon VOID if purchased, sold or bartered. Discounts exclude tax, tip and/or alcohol, where applicable.

BELMONT
THE GARI MELCHERS ESTATE
AND MEMORIAL GALLERY

224 Washington St.
Fredericksburg, VA
(540)654-1015

00622976

entertainment.com

00622976

Civil War Life - The Soldiers Museum

4712 Southpoint Pkwy.
(next to the Spotsylvania Co. Visitor's Ctr.)
Fredericksburg, VA
(540)834-1859

00607479

entertainment.com

00607479

WHITE OAK
CIVIL WAR
MUSEUM

985 White Oak Rd.
Falmouth, VA
(540)371-4234

00619450

entertainment.com

00619450

Meadowlark Botanical Garden

9750 Meadowlark Garden Ct.
Vienna, VA
(703)255-3631

- A living museum of plant life
- Visitor Center, gift shop, library & educational exhibit available
- Located between Rte. 7 & Rte. 123 off of Beulah Rd.

entertainment. entertainment.com

ONE ADMISSION

Enjoy one complimentary ADMISSION when a second ADMISSION of equal or greater value is purchased.

valid Monday - Friday

Meadowlark Botanical Gardens™

www.nvrpa.org

C145

Valid now thru November 1, 2006

Not valid holidays & subject to Rules of Use. Not valid with other discount offers, unless specified. Coupon VOID if purchased, sold or bartered. Discounts exclude tax, tip and/or alcohol, where applicable.

Colvin Run Mill Historic Site

10017 Colvin Run Rd.
Great Falls, VA
(703)759-2771

- Discover history at Colvin Run Mill Historic Site
- See old-fashioned technology at work as the grist mill turns & the mill stone grinds
- Shop for old-fashioned treasures at the General Store
- Tours on the hour, 11 a.m. to 4 p.m., Wed. - Mon.

entertainment. entertainment.com

great place for kids

ONE TOUR

Enjoy one complimentary TOUR when a second TOUR of equal or greater value is purchased.

valid Wednesday thru Monday

ENT -3

www.fairfaxcounty.gov/parks

C146

Valid now thru November 1, 2006

Not valid holidays & subject to Rules of Use. Not valid with other discount offers, unless specified. Coupon VOID if purchased, sold or bartered. Discounts exclude tax, tip and/or alcohol, where applicable.

Sully Historic Site

3601 Sully Rd.
Chantilly, VA
(703)437-1794

- Discover history at Sully Historic Site
- Learn what life was like for the gentry & the enslaved populations of a Virginia plantation
- Shop for momentos of your visit at the school house store
- Tours on the hour 11-4 p.m.

entertainment. entertainment.com

great place for kids

ONE TOUR

Enjoy one complimentary TOUR when a second TOUR of equal or greater value is purchased.

valid Wednesday thru Monday

ENT-7

www.fairfaxcounty.gov/parks

C147

Valid now thru November 1, 2006

Not valid holidays & subject to Rules of Use. Not valid with other discount offers, unless specified. Coupon VOID if purchased, sold or bartered. Discounts exclude tax, tip and/or alcohol, where applicable.

Meadowlark
Botanical Gardens™

9750 Meadowlark Garden Ct.
Vienna, VA
(703)255-3631

00547226

00547226

COLVIN RUN MILL
Great Falls, Virginia
FLOUR

10017 Colvin Run Rd.
Great Falls, VA
(703)759-2771

00313098

00313098

SULLY

3601 Sully Rd.
Chantilly, VA
(703)437-1794

00401807

00401807

Alexandria Harmonizers

Garwood Whaley Auditorium Bishop Ireton High School 201 Cambridge Rd. Alexandria, VA

- Concert site & date subject to change
- For information call: (703)922-5992

Bonus Discounts at entertainment.com

entertainment. entertainment.com

ONE $22.00 ADMISSION

Enjoy one complimentary $22.00 ADMISSION when a second $22.00 ADMISSION of equal or greater value is purchased.

valid December 2, 2005 for 8 p.m. evening show

Mail Order Only see reverse side; On availability basis

Alexandria Harmonizers

Barbershop Harmony Chorus

C148

Valid now thru November 1, 2006

Not valid holidays & subject to Rules of Use. Not valid with other discount offers, unless specified. Coupon VOID if purchased, sold or bartered. Discounts exclude tax, tip and/or alcohol, where applicable.

Alexandria Harmonizers

Garwood Whaley Auditorium Bishop Ireton High School 201 Cambridge Rd. Alexandria, VA

- Concert site & date subject to change
- For Information call: (703)922-5992

Bonus Discounts at entertainment.com

entertainment. entertainment.com

ONE $22.00 ADMISSION

Enjoy one complimentary $22.00 ADMISSION when a second $22.00 ADMISSION is purchased.

valid April 21, 2006 for 8 p.m. evening show

Mail Order Only see reverse side; On availability basis

Alexandria Harmonizers

Barbershop Harmony Chorus

C149

Valid now thru November 1, 2006

Not valid holidays & subject to Rules of Use. Not valid with other discount offers, unless specified. Coupon VOID if purchased, sold or bartered. Discounts exclude tax, tip and/or alcohol, where applicable.

The Alexandria Singers

PO Box 6151 Alexandria, VA (703)941-SING

- For exact date & time of performance & ticket prices, call (703) 941-SING or log onto the website

Bonus Discounts at entertainment.com

entertainment. entertainment.com

ONE GENERAL ADMISSION TICKET

Enjoy one complimentary GENERAL ADMISSION TICKET when a second GENERAL ADMISSION TICKET of equal or greater value is purchased.

valid for June 2006 Extravaganza

Redeem at box office no later than 45 minutes before performance; Subject to availability

The Alexandria Singers

www.alexandriasingers.com

C150

Valid now thru November 1, 2006

Not valid holidays & subject to Rules of Use. Not valid with other discount offers, unless specified. Coupon VOID if purchased, sold or bartered. Discounts exclude tax, tip and/or alcohol, where applicable.

TO: Alexandria Harmonizers Box Office
P.O. Box 30632
Alexandria, VA 22310-9998

Please send two (2) $22 orchestra seat tickets at 50% off the regular price for:

Friday Evening 8 p.m. Dec. 2nd, 2005

Enclosed is my check payable to Alexandria Harmonizers for $22.00

Name: ____________________

Address: ____________________

Phone: ____________________

City: ____________________

State: __________ ZIP: __________

- Order will not be filled without self-addressed stamped envelope
- Tickets on availability basis

00047296

entertainment.com

00047296

TO: Alexandria Harmonizers Box Office
P.O. Box 30632
Alexandria, VA 22310-9998

Please send two (2) $22 orchestra seat tickets at 50% off the regular price for:

Friday Evening 8 p.m. April 21st, 2006

Enclosed is my check payable to Alexandria Harmonizers for $22.00

Name: ____________________

Address: ____________________

Phone: ____________________

City: ____________________

State: __________ ZIP: __________

- Order will not be filled without self-addressed stamped envelope
- Tickets on availability basis

00085454

entertainment.com

00085454

The Alexandria Singers

PO Box 6151
Alexandria, VA
(703)941-SING

00256490

entertainment.com

00256490

The Arlington Symphony

Schlesinger Center NVCC Alexandria Campus 3001 N. Beauregard St. Alexandria, VA (703)528-1817

- Celebrating over 60 years of artistic excellence
- All concerts begin at 8 p.m.
- Pre-Concert lecture with WGMS, 103.5 FM at 7 p.m.
- Visit www.arlingtonsymphony.org or call (703)528-1817 for the lastest concert information

Bonus Discounts at entertainment.com

entertainment. entertainment.com

Up To $42.00 Value

Enjoy one complimentary ORCHESTRA SEAT when a second ORCHESTRA SEAT is purchased.

Valid now through May 6, 2006

Mail Order or Purchase Tickets at the door 1/2 hour prior to concert; On availability basis; All programs subject to change without notice; ASO concerts are performed at 8:00 p.m. at the Schlesinger Concert Hall, 3001 N. Beauregard St., on the Alexandria campus of Northern Virginia Community College; All sales final; Not valid for special events, pops, or family concerts

ARLINGTON Symphony

www.arlingtonsymphony.org

C151

Valid now thru November 1, 2006

Not valid holidays & subject to Rules of Use. Not valid with other discount offers, unless specified. Coupon VOID if purchased, sold or bartered. Discounts exclude tax, tip and/or alcohol, where applicable.

Center for the Arts - George Mason University

Center for the Arts Ticket Office MS 2F5, 4400 University Drive George Mason University Fairfax, VA 22030-4444 (703) 993-8888

Bonus Discounts at entertainment.com

entertainment. entertainment.com

Up To $42.00 Value

Enjoy one complimentary TICKET when a second TICKET is purchased at full price - maximum discount $42.00.

valid for specific performance only

On availability basis; See reverse side for valid performances; Redeemable only at the Ticket Office located in the lobby of the Concert Hall on the George Mason University Fairfax campus

GEORGE MASON UNIVERSITY

Center for the Arts

C152

Valid now thru November 1, 2006

Not valid holidays & subject to Rules of Use. Not valid with other discount offers, unless specified. Coupon VOID if purchased, sold or bartered. Discounts exclude tax, tip and/or alcohol, where applicable.

The Choral Arts Society

5225 Wisconsin Ave., Ste. 603, NW Washington, DC (202)244-3669

- Norman Scribner, Artistic Director
- 200 member chorus with live orchestra
- Call for repertoire & ticket prices
- Free pre-concert lecture

Bonus Discounts at entertainment.com

entertainment. entertainment.com

ONE MID-ORCHESTRA SEAT

Enjoy one complimentary MID-ORCHESTRA SEAT when a second MID-ORCHESTRA SEAT is purchased.

valid for concert series performances

Not valid for Christmas performances; Subject to availability; All sales final

The Choral Arts Society of Washington

www.choralarts.org

C153

Valid now thru November 1, 2006

Not valid holidays & subject to Rules of Use. Not valid with other discount offers, unless specified. Coupon VOID if purchased, sold or bartered. Discounts exclude tax, tip and/or alcohol, where applicable.

Entertainment Order Back®
Please enclose separate check for this attraction

TO: Arlington Symphony
4238 Wilson Blvd. Suite 3064
Arlington, VA 22203-1823

Please send_________orchestra reserved tickets (buy one get one complimentary) for the performance on ______________________(date).

Enclosed is my check for $______________________payable to Arlington Symphony

Name:______________________________ Email__________________________

Address ____________________________ Day Phone ______________________

City________________________________ State_____________ Zip __________

Please include a self-addressed stamped envelope in order to havetickets mailed. Orders without return envelopes or those received fewer than the days before the concert will be held at the will-call table for pick-up the night of the concert. All sales are final; no refunds or exchanges. Call (703)528-1817

00047254

00047254

GEORGE MASON UNIVERSITY

Center for the Arts

Theater of the First Amendment
Three Hotels
Thurs. Sep. 22 or 29, 2005 at 8 pm
Sun., Sep. 18, 25, or Oct. 2, 2005 at 2 pm

Keyboard Conversations® with Jeffrey Siegel
Sun., Sep. 25, 2005 at 7pm

Keyboard Conversations® with Jeffrey Siegel
Sun., Oct. 30, 2005 at 7 pm

Theater of the First Amendment
Lift: Icarus and Me
Thurs. Jan. 26 or Feb. 2, 2006 at 8 pm
Sun., Jan. 22, 29, or Feb. 5, 2006 at 2pm

Keyboard Conversations® with Jeffrey Siegel
Sun., Jan. 29, 2006 at 7 pm

Mark Morris Dance Group
Fri., Feb. 10, 2006 at 8 pm

Meredith Monk & Vocal Ensemble
The Impermanence Project
Sat., Feb. 25, 2006 at 8 pm

Metropolitan Jazz Orchestra
Sat., Mar. 11, 2006 at 8 pm

The Actors' Gang
The Exonerated
Fri., Mar. 24, 2006 at 8 pm

Doug Varone and Dancers
Fri., Apr. 14, 2006 at 7 pm

Keyboard Conversations® with Jeffrey Siegel
Sun., Apr. 23, 2006 at 7 pm

Marc Bamuthi Joseph
Scourge
Wed., Apr. 26, 2006 at 8 pm

*Dates, programs, and artists are subject to change.

00158126

00158126

The Choral Arts Society of Washington

5225 Wisconsin Ave., Ste. 603, NW
Washington, DC
(202)244-3669

00047177

00047177

entertainment.com

entertainment.com

entertainment.com

Eclipse Chamber Orchestra

For details, call (703) 256-2956

- "An entire evening of sumptuous sound & intricate detail, of breathtaking soloism & unblemished ensemble- outright extraordinary!" Washington Post

entertainment. entertainment.com

ONE $20 GENERAL ADMISSION TICKET

Enjoy one complimentary $20 GENERAL ADMISSION TICKET when a second $20 GENERAL ADMISSION TICKET is purchased.

valid for Eclipse Chamber Orchestra Series and Eclipse Chamber Music Series only

Redeem at Box Office on the day of performance; Call for performance dates & locations

ECLIPSE Chamber Orchestra

C154

Valid now thru November 1, 2006

The McLean Orchestra

P.O. Box 760
McLean, VA
(703)893-8646

- Performances held at Oakerest School, 850 Balls Hill Rd. McLean, VA 22101
- Concert dates are - Oct. 29, 2005 - Dec. 12, 2005 - Feb. 18, 2006 - March 11, 2006 - May 6, 2006
- Program & artists subject to change
- Please call for information (703)893-8646

entertainment. entertainment.com

ONE TICKET

2005-2006 Season (October - May)
Enjoy one complimentary TICKET when a second TICKET of equal or greater value is purchased.

valid for any concert except holiday concert (December)

General admission : $23 - Senior/ Student: $20 - Youth : $5; Mail order on reverse side or redeem in person at the box office no later than 7:15 p.m. the night of performance; Subject to availability; Valid now thru July 1, 2006

MCLEAN ORCHESTRA
SYLVIA ALIMENA
Music Director & Conductor

www.mclean-orchestra.org

C155

Valid now thru November 1, 2006

Pied Piper Theatre

See reverse side for locations

- Holds open auditions for young people ages 8-18, providing them with an opportunity to be involved in all aspects of musical theater. A backstage apprenticeship program offers an opportunity to work behind the scenes learning technical theater. To receive advance notice of next year's auditions, summer theater camps, & year round classes, call the Center fo

entertainment. entertainment.com

ONE GENERAL ADMISSION

Enjoy one complimentary GENERAL ADMISSION when a second GENERAL ADMISSION of equal or greater value is purchased.

valid for the 2005-2006 season

Performances subject to change; Redeem at the box office; On availability basis; For performance dates, call 703-330-ARTS

CENTER FOR THE ARTS PIED PIPER THEATRE

www.center-for-the-arts.com

C156

Valid now thru November 1, 2006

ECLIPSE

Chamber
Orchestra

For details, call (703) 256-2956

00040331

entertainment.com

00040331

Entertainment® Order Back
PLEASE ENCLOSE SEPARATE CHECK FOR THIS ATTRACTION

TO: The McLean Orchestra
P.O. Box 760
McLean, VA 22101

Please send one complimentary ticket with order of at least one ticket of equal or greater value (indicate number of each)

General Admission (GA) $23
Senior/Student (S/S) $20
Youth (under 12 years) (Y) $5

Plus one (1) complimentary ticket GA__________S/S__________Y__________
Enclosed is my check for $______________ made payable to McLean Orchestra
(please enclose self-addressed, stamped envelope

Name: ____

Address: ______________________ City: ______________________

State/ZIP: ______________________ DAY PHONE: ______________________

Email: mcleanorchestra@hotmail.com

- Orders received less than 7 days prior to show will be held at box office
- Purchase subject to availability

00047450

entertainment.com

00047450

CENTER FOR THE ARTS
PIED PIPER THEATRE

Center for the Arts, Manassas/
Woodbridge, VA

Pied Piper Theatre

(703)330-ARTS

www.pwcweb.com/arts

00260500

entertainment.com

00260500

National Symphony Orchestra

Kennedy Center Concert Hall
Washington, DC
(202)467-4600

- Heidi Grant Murphy - Soprano
- Nathaniel Webster - Baritone
- The Choral Arts Society of Washington
- Sierra - Missa Latina

entertainment.
entertainment.com

Up To $75.00 Value

National Symphony Orchestra

Leonard Slatkin, Music Director

Enjoy one complimentary ORCHESTRA SEAT when a second ORCHESTRA SEAT of equal or greater value is purchased.

Leonard Slatkin, conductor

valid Friday, February 3, 2006 at 8:00 p.m.

Valid only for performance listed above; Coupon must be redeemed in person at box office; Not applicable to previously purchased tickets; Programs & artists subject to change; On availability basis; Not valid with any other discount offer; Discount available starting Dec. 9, 2005

Source Code 9717

C157

Valid now thru November 1, 2006

National Symphony Orchestra

Kennedy Center Concert Hall
Washington, DC
(202)467-4600

- Stravinsky - Symphonies of Wind Instruments
- Mendelssohn - Octet in E flat arranged for string orchestra
- Chavez - Toccata for Percussion Instruments
- Bartok - Suite from The Miraculous Mandarin

Bonus Discounts at
entertainment.com

entertainment.
entertainment.com

Up To $75.00 Value

National Symphony Orchestra

Leonard Slatkin, Music Director

Enjoy one complimentary ORCHESTRA SEAT when a second ORCHESTRA SEAT of equal or greater value is purchased.

Leonard Slatkin, Conductor

valid Friday, May 12, 2006 at 8:00 p.m.

Valid only for performance listed above; Coupon must be redeemed in person at box office; Not applicable to previously purchased tickets; Programs & artists subject to change; On availability basis; Not valid with any other discount offer; Discounts available starting Feb. 9, 2006

Source Code 9717

C158

Valid now thru November 1, 2006

Not valid holidays & subject to Rules of Use. Not valid with other discount offers, unless specified. Coupon VOID if purchased, sold or bartered. Discounts exclude tax, tip and/or alcohol, where applicable.

Prince William Symphony

(703)580-8562

- Carl Long, Music Director
- Call for performance dates, times & locations

Bonus Discounts at
entertainment.com

entertainment.
entertainment.com

ONE $21.00 GENERAL ADMISSION TICKET

Enjoy one complimentary $21.00 GENERAL ADMISSION TICKET when a second $21.00 GENERAL ADMISSION TICKET is purchased.

Valid for the 2005 - 2006 Season

Redeem at Box Office; On availability basis

PRINCE WILLIAM
Symphony Orchestra
www.pwso.org

C159

Valid now thru November 1, 2006

Not valid holidays & subject to Rules of Use. Not valid with other discount offers, unless specified. Coupon VOID if purchased, sold or bartered. Discounts exclude tax, tip and/or alcohol, where applicable.

National Symphony Orchestra

Leonard Slatkin, Music Director

Kennedy Center Concert Hall
Washington, DC
(202)467-4600

00047095

entertainment.com

00047095

National Symphony Orchestra

Leonard Slatkin, Music Director

Kennedy Center Concert Hall
Washington, DC
(202)467-4600

00072575

entertainment.com

00072575

PRINCE WILLIAM
Symphony Orchestra
(703)580-8562

00047070

entertainment.com

00047070

The Shakespeare Theatre

450 7th Street NW
Washington, DC
(202)547-1122

- Located two blocks from the Archives/Navy Memorial Metro
- Indoor garage parking available - Enter on 8th St.
- Not valid on Fri. & Sat. evenings or Sat. & Sun. matinees
- Not valid on previously ordered tickets, other specials or discounts
- Orders must be made in person or by mail - no phone orders

Bonus Discounts at entertainment.com

entertainment. entertainment.com

ONE RESERVED SEAT

Valid for one complimentary RESERVED SEAT when a second RESERVED SEAT is purchased at full price.

valid Sunday, Tuesday, Wednesday & Thursday evenings & Wednesday matinees

Coupon May not be used until 2 weeks prior to performance date; The Shakespeare Theatre Box Office or Mail Order see reverse side; Subject to availability; No Phone Orders

THE SHAKESPEARE THEATRE
In the Nation's Capital

www.shakespearetheatre.org

C160

Valid now thru November 1, 2006

Not valid holidays & subject to Rules of Use. Not valid with other discount offers, unless specified. Coupon VOID if purchased, sold or bartered. Discounts exclude tax, tip and/or alcohol, where applicable.

Source Theatre Company

1835 14th Street NW
Washington, DC
(202)462-1073

- Air-conditioned
- Washington's most productive theatre - more shows than anyone!
- Presenting a season of continuous plays, classic & new works
- 2 blocks from U Street-Cordozo Metro Station (Green Line)
- Call for show information

Bonus Discounts at entertainment.com

entertainment. entertainment.com

ONE ADMISSION

SOURCE Theatre Company

Enjoy one complimentary ADMISSION when a second ADMISSION of equal or greater value is purchased.

valid Wednesday, Thursday & Sunday performances

Reservations required, indicate coupon use when making reservations; Regular season only; On availability basis

www.sourcetheatre.org

C161

Valid now thru November 1, 2006

Not valid holidays & subject to Rules of Use. Not valid with other discount offers, unless specified. Coupon VOID if purchased, sold or bartered. Discounts exclude tax, tip and/or alcohol, where applicable.

The Studio Theatre

1333 P St. NW
Washington, DC
(202)332-3300

- Located at 1333 P St. NW, six blocks from Dupont Circle
- Consult newspaper for prices & performance times
- Ask about parking
- Call (202) 332-3300 for theatre dates, performances & ticket prices

Bonus Discounts at entertainment.com

entertainment. entertainment.com

ONE ADMISSION

the**Studio**theatre

Enjoy one complimentary ADMISSION when a second ADMISSION of equal or greater value is purchased.

valid any Wednesday, Thursday or Sunday evening, Saturday or Sunday matinee

Mail Order Only see reverse side; Secondstage performances excluded; On space available basis only

www.studiotheatre.org

C162

Valid now thru November 1, 2006

Not valid holidays & subject to Rules of Use. Not valid with other discount offers, unless specified. Coupon VOID if purchased, sold or bartered. Discounts exclude tax, tip and/or alcohol, where applicable.

Entertainment® Order Back

TO: The Shakespeare Theatre Box Office
450 7th Street NW
Washington, DC 20004
(202)547-1122

Please send 2 tickets at the full price of one Reserved Seat
Enclosed is my check payable to The Shakespeare Theatre Box Office
or charge my:

❑VISA ❑Master Card ❑American Express ❑Discover

Credit Card Number: ______________________ Expiration Date: __________

Signature: ____

(Please include $5.00 handling fee for mail order)

Name: ____

Address: ____

Phone: ____

City: ____

State: ____________________ ZIP: ____________________

Misc: ____

00013085

entertainment.com

00013085

SOURCE Theatre Company

1835 14th Street NW
Washington, DC
(202)462-1073

00033110

entertainment.com

00033110

Entertainment® Order Back

THE STUDIO THEATER
1333 P. St. NW
Washington, DC 20005
(202)3332-3300

Please hold two (2) tickets, buy one get one free

Date __________________ Show __________________ Time __________________

Enclosed is my check for ______________ made payable to THE STUDIO ART THEATRE box office for ticket price:

NAME: ____

ADDRESS: ______________________ DAY PHONE: ______________________

CITY: ______________________ ZIP: ______________________

- Orders will beh eld at box office
- Sales are final SORRY NO EXCHANGES
- Tickets on space availability only
- Mail order only

00034158

entertainment.com

00034158

The Washington Ballet

The Warner Theatre Washington, DC

- Don't miss this new holiday favorite!
- Artistic director Septime Webre presents this timeless holiday classic as only he can
- Set in 1882 in Washington, D.C., Webre's Nutcracker is perfumed with references to the nation's capital as well as America's rich history

entertainment. entertainment.com

ONE ADMISSION

thewashingtonballet

Mary Day, founder / Septime Webre, artistic director

New Nutcracker
The Warner Theatre
Thursday December 1, at 7:00 p.m., Saturday December 3 at 2:00 p.m. & 7:00 p.m.
Sunday December 4, at 1:00 p.m., Friday December 9, at 7:00 p.m.
Saturday December 10, at 2:00 p.m. & 7:00 p.m., Sunday December 11, at 5:00 p.m.

Enjoy one complimentary ADMISSION when a second ADMISSION of equal or greater value is purchased.

valid for above performances only

Redeemable only by mail after October 1, 2005; Purchase subject to availability and not applicable to previously purchased tickets

C163

Valid now thru November 1, 2006

The Washington Ballet

The Warner Theatre Washington, DC

- Genius worlds collide as classical master (Bach) meets 1960's mania (The Beatles) in a unique new project choreographed by Septime Webre & Trey McIntyre

entertainment. entertainment.com

ONE ADMISSION

thewashingtonballet

Mary Day, founder / Septime Webre, artistic director

The Bach/Beatles Project
The Kennedy Center
Wednesday, February 1, 2006 at 8:00pm

Enjoy one complimentary ADMISSION when a second ADMISSION of equal or greater value is purchased.

valid for above performances only

Redeemable only in person at The Kennedy Center Box Office after December 1, 2005; Purchase subject to availability, & not applicable to previously purchased tickets; All programs subject to change

www.washingtonballet.org

C164

Valid now thru November 1, 2006

The Washington Ballet

3515 Wisconsin Avenue NW Washington, DC

- The San Francisco Chronicle deems Lar Lubovitch's Othello "A major new chapter in American ballet as well as a spectacular addition to the international repertory"
- The Washington Ballet performs Lubovitch's gripping interpretation of Shakespeare's tragic tale of deceit, ambition & jealousy

entertainment. entertainment.com

ONE ADMISSION

thewashingtonballet

Mary Day, founder / Septime Webre, artistic director

Othello
The Kennedy Center
Wednesday, May 10, 2006 at 8:00 p.m.

Enjoy one complimentary ADMISSION when a second ADMISSION of equal or greater value is purchased.

valid for above performance only

Redeemable only in person at The Kennedy Center Box Office after March 10, 2006; Purchase subject to availability, and not applicable to previously purchased tickets; All programs subject to change

www.washingtonballet.org

C165

Valid now thru November 1, 2006

Entertainment® Order Back

TO: The Washington Ballet, The Nutcracker
3515 Wisconsin Ave, NW
Washington, DC 20016

Please redeem for two $72 tickets at 50% off the full price for:

Thursday December 1, at 7:00 p.m., Saturday December 3 at 2:00 p.m. & 7:00 p.m.
Sunday December 4, at 1:00 p.m., Friday December 9, at 7:00 p.m.
Saturday December 10, at 2:00 p.m. & 7:00 p.m., Sunday December 11, at 5:00 p.m.

Name: ______________________________

Address: ______________________________

Phone: ______________________________

City: ______________________________

State: ______________ ZIP: ______________

Valid for two orchestra tickets at 50% off ($36.00 per ticket). Redeemable only by mail. Orders require a 21 day advance purchase and a self-addressed, stamped envelope. Tickets will be held at will call window for orders received within 21 days of performance date, or without a self-addressed, stamped envelope. Purchase subject to availability and not applicable to previously purchased tickets. For advanced show information, call (202) 362-3606 x119

00073500

entertainment.com

00073500

Entertainment® Order Back

TO: The Kennedy Center Box Office
Washington, DC

Please redeem for two $41 tickets at 50% off the full price for:

Wednesday, February 1, 2006 at 8:00pm

Name: ______________________________

Address: ______________________________

Phone: ______________________________

City: ______________________________

State: ______________ ZIP: ______________

Valid for two tickets at 50% off ($20.50 each) in the orchestra or front balcony. Redeemable only in person at the Kennedy Center Box Office after December 1, 2005. Purchase subject to availability and not applicable to previously purchased tickets. For advanced information, call (202) 362-3606 X119

00073501

entertainment.com

00073501

Entertainment® Order Back

TO: The Kennedy Center Box Office
Washington, DC

Please redeem for two $41 tickets at 50% off the full price for:

Wednesday, May 10, 2006 at 8:00 p.m.

Name: ______________________________

Address: ______________________________

Phone: ______________________________

City: ______________________________

State: ______________ ZIP: ______________

Valid for two tickets at 50% off ($20.50 each) in the orchestra or front balcony. Redeemable only in person at the Kennedy Center Box Office after March 10, 2006. Purchase subject to availability and not applicable to previously purchased tickets. For advanced information, call (202) 362-3606 x119

00510941

entertainment.com

00510941

Vienna Choral Society

For updated information on the Society, call (703)255-5508 or visit www.viennachoralsociety.org

- Concerts held at Vienna locations
- General Admission - $12.00 in advance
- Seniors/Students - $10.00 in advance
- Schedule subject to change

Bonus Discounts at entertainment.com

entertainment. entertainment.com

ONE TICKET

Vienna Choral Society

Enjoy one complimentary TICKET when a second TICKET of equal or greater value is purchased.

valid for performances listed on reverse

Present at box office or mail order-see reverse side; Check time & location prior to each performance; Venues are subject to change Call (703)255-5508 or visit us on the web

www.viennachoralsociety.org

C166

Valid now thru November 1, 2006

Not valid holidays & subject to Rules of Use. Not valid with other discount offers, unless specified. Coupon VOID if purchased, sold or bartered. Discounts exclude tax, tip and/or alcohol, where applicable.

Potomac Harmony

P.O. Box 7566
Arlington, VA
(703)764-3896

- Visit our website at www.potomacharmony.org or e-mail us for general information or show dates & times at potomacharmony@yahoo.com.

Bonus Discounts at entertainment.com

entertainment. entertainment.com

ONE TICKET

Enjoy one complimentary TICKET when a second TICKET of equal or greater value is purchased.

Call (703)764-3896 for show information starting 9/01/04

valid 9/01/05 thru 12/01/06

Potomac Harmony Chorus

www.potomacharmony.org or e-mail us for general information or show dates &

C167

Valid now thru November 1, 2006

Not valid holidays & subject to Rules of Use. Not valid with other discount offers, unless specified. Coupon VOID if purchased, sold or bartered. Discounts exclude tax, tip and/or alcohol, where applicable.

The Metropolitan Chorus

3700 S. Four Mile Run
Arlington, VA
(703)933-2500

- Celebrating our 39th season!
- Barry S. Hemphill - Artistic Director
- Call The Metropolitan Chorus at (703)933-2500 for ticket information

Bonus Discounts at entertainment.com

entertainment. entertainment.com

ONE ADMISSON

Hummel Mass in E-flat Major - Sat. Oct. 22 2005 8 p.m.

The Many Moods of Christmas - Sat. Dec. 17, 2005 7:30 p.m.

Bacalov Misa Tanqo Sun. April 29, 2006 8 p.m.

Enjoy one complimentary ADMISSION when a second ADMISSION of equal or greater value is purchased.

VALID FOR SELECTED PERFORMANCES ONLY

Advance sales by mail order only; See reverse side

THE METROPOLITAN CHORUS

Barry S. Hemphill • Artistic Director

www.metchorus.org

C168

Valid now thru November 1, 2006

Not valid holidays & subject to Rules of Use. Not valid with other discount offers, unless specified. Coupon VOID if purchased, sold or bartered. Discounts exclude tax, tip and/or alcohol, where applicable.

Entertainment® Order Back

TO: VIENNA CHORAL SOCIETY
374 Maple Ave. East, Suite 300
Vienna, VA 22180

Please send two (2) tickets at 50% off the regular price for:

❑ 10/22/05
❑ 12/10/05
❑ 3/4/06
❑5/6/06

General Admission: ____________ $12 Senior/Student: ____________ $10 (Check only)

Enclosed is my check payable to VIENNA CHORAL SOCIETY for $____________________

Name: ____

Address: ______________________ Phone:______________________

City: ______________________ State:__________ZIP: ____________

- ORDER WILL NOT BE FILLED WITHOUT SELF-ADDRESSED, STAMPED ENVELOPE
- Sales are final
- No cancellations or refunds

00046709

entertainment.com

00046709

Potomac Harmony Chorus

P.O. Box 7566
Arlington, VA
(703)764-3896

00481824

entertainment.com

00481824

Entertainment Order Back

TO: The Metropolitan Chorus
3700 S. Four Mile Run Dr.
Arlington, VA 22206
(703)933-2500

Please send tickets at the regular price of one admission of equal or greater value

❑Sat. 10/22/05 ❑Sat. 12/17/05 ❑Sun. 4/30/06

Enclosed is my check payable to THE METROPOLITAN CHORUS for $____________.

Ticket prices vary by concert. Call The Metropolitan Chorus at 703-933-2500 for ticket information.

Name: ____

Address: ____

Phone: ____

City: ____

State: ______________________ ZIP: ______________________

E-mail: ____

- **ORDERS WILL NOT BE FILLED WITHOUT SELF-ADDRESSED, STAMPED ENVELOPE**

00504679

entertainment.com

00504679

National Values®
brings you great savings on travel, retail & services.

Retail & Services

Travel

Lodging

Take up to $75 off your next qualifying trip on United

Use this promotional coupon to save on one new United Economy® round-trip ticket booked in H, Q, V, W, or S class for travel on United Airlines, Ted℠ or United Express®.

Take **$25** off one round-trip ticket o $150 - $299
Take **$50** off one round-trip ticket of $300 - $474
Take **$75** off one round-trip ticket of $475 or more

You must begin your travel in and fly to a destination within the 50 United States, Puerto Rico, U.S. Virgin Islands, or Canada. Discount does not apply to flights operated by other airlines (such as United-marketed code share and Star Alliance® flights).

Profile Name: PMO/Entertainment 2006
Account Code: EBG25/EBG50/EBG75
Begin Travel: August 1, 2005
Travel Complete: December 31, 2006
Must ticket by: December 31, 2006

To make reservations, call United Airlines at 1-800-241-6522 or your travel professional, and refer to Profile Name: PMO/Entertainment 2006

If Redeeming by Mail:
Passenger last name: ______________
Date of return travel: ______________
Flt # of return travel: ______________

UNITED

1 016 0500 000 447 6

See reverse side for details D1

Take up to $75 off your next qualifying trip on United

Use this promotional coupon to save on one new United Economy® round-trip ticket booked in H, Q, V, W, or S class for travel on United Airlines, Ted℠ or United Express®.

Take **$25** off one round-trip ticket o $150 - $299
Take **$50** off one round-trip ticket of $300 - $474
Take **$75** off one round-trip ticket of $475 or more

You must begin your travel in and fly to a destination within the 50 United States, Puerto Rico, U.S. Virgin Islands, or Canada. Discount does not apply to flights operated by other airlines (such as United-marketed code share and Star Alliance® flights).

Profile Name: PMO/Entertainment 2006
Account Code: EBG25/EBG50/EBG75
Begin Travel: August 1, 2005
Travel Complete: December 31, 2006
Must ticket by: December 31, 2006

To make reservations, call United Airlines at 1-800-241-6522 or your travel professional, and refer to Profile Name: PMO/Entertainment 2006

If Redeeming by Mail:
Passenger last name: ______________
Date of return travel: ______________
Flt # of return travel: ______________

UNITED

1 016 0500 000 447 6

See reverse side for details D2

Take up to $75 off your next qualifying trip on United

Use this promotional coupon to save on one new United Economy® round-trip ticket booked in H, Q, V, W, or S class for travel on United Airlines, Ted℠ or United Express®.

Take **$25** off one round-trip ticket o $150 - $299
Take **$50** off one round-trip ticket of $300 - $474
Take **$75** off one round-trip ticket of $475 or more

You must begin your travel in and fly to a destination within the 50 United States, Puerto Rico, U.S. Virgin Islands, or Canada. Discount does not apply to flights operated by other airlines (such as United-marketed code share and Star Alliance® flights).

Profile Name: PMO/Entertainment 2006
Account Code: EBG25/EBG50/EBG75
Begin Travel: August 1, 2005
Travel Complete: December 31, 2006
Must ticket by: December 31, 2006

To make reservations, call United Airlines at 1-800-241-6522 or your travel professional, and refer to Profile Name: PMO/Entertainment 2006

If Redeeming by Mail:
Passenger last name: ______________
Date of return travel: ______________
Flt # of return travel: ______________

UNITED

1 016 0500 000 447 6

See reverse side for details D3

Terms and Conditions:

1. Valid Carrier: This discount may be applied to United, Ted℠ and United Express® operated flights, but not to flights operated by other airlines (such as United-marketed code share and Star Alliance® flights). Tickets purchased through United reservation offices are $5 per ticket higher and tickets purchased at airport ticket counters are $10 per ticket higher.

2. Valid Routing: To take advantage of this discount you must begin your travel in and fly to a destination within the 50 United States, Puerto Rico, U.S. Virgin Islands or Canada.

3. Allowable Fares: This discount may be used on published United Economy® (H, Q, V, W, S) fares of $150 or more. These qualifying fares are the lower, more restrictive fares for travel in the economy cabin. Since these fares are booked in a special class of service, they might not be available on all flights or on all days of the week when you travel.

4. Restricted Fares: This discount may not be used on the following fare types: United First® (F, A, P), United Business® (C, D), United Economy (Y, B, M, E, U, T), internet-only fares, companion, travel industry G class, contract, bulk, convention, tour conductor, children, family plan, government, group, military, senior citizen, student, youth, infant, tour basing, Visit USA Fares or any non-published fares. This discount does not apply to private fares.

5. Fare Rules: The published fare you qualify for depends on what class of service is available on the days you travel. Some markets may have lower fares available without the discount. Keep in mind, you must travel roundtrip on United (open jaw and circle trips are allowed too). The discount may not be used when you travel one way. Other restrictions may apply.

6. Blackout Dates: This discount is not allowed on the following dates: November 23, 27, 28, 2005; December 22, 23, 26, 29, 30, 31, 2005; January 1, 2, 2006; March 10, 11, 12, 17, 18, 19, 31, 2006; April 1, 2, 7, 8, 9, 14, 15, 16, 17, 2006; November 22, 26, 27, 2006; December 22, 23, 26, 29, 30, 31, 2006.

7. United Mileage Plus® Accrual: The passenger may accrue United Mileage Plus miles, even with this discount.

8. Upgrades: To determine if an upgrade certificate may be used together with this discount, refer to the terms, conditions and booking class restrictions associated with each upgrade.

9. Ticketing: You may redeem this certificate using United's Electronic Ticketing by calling United or your travel professional. You may also ticket by mail (where available) or through a United airport location. Discount only applies when ticket is purchased within the 50 United States, Puerto Rico, the U.S. Virgin Islands, or Canada. All dollar levels are stated in U.S. currency. When using the discount on a ticket purchased in Canada, current conversion rates apply. Certificate must be surrendered at time of initial ticketing and cannot be redeemed via the internet.

10. Changes/Refunds: The rules of the United Economy fare you purchase determine what changes or refunds are allowed. Any refund due is based on the amount actually paid. The certificate discount may not be reapplied toward the purchase of another ticket when exchanging or refunding your original ticket, except when the original ticket qualifies for a reduced fare (guaranteed airfare rule applies). Check with United or your travel professional.

11. Other Important Notes: This discount may only be applied to the purchase of one new ticket and may not be applied to previously ticketed reservations. Certificate has no cash value and may not be altered or duplicated. Lost, stolen, expired or destroyed certificates will not be replaced. Only one discount certificate, discount voucher or discount may be used per ticket. This certificate is transferable, but void if sold or bartered.

Processing Information

Agencies See: S*PMA/Entertainment 2006
UA Representatives See: S*PMO/Entertainment 2006
FastTech: Profile Code: PMO Name: Entertainment 2006

Subject to Rules of Use. Not valid with other discount offers, unless specified. Coupon VOID if purchased, sold or bartered for cash.

Valid for travel from August 1, 2005 through December 31, 2006

Terms and Conditions:

1. Valid Carrier: This discount may be applied to United, Ted℠ and United Express® operated flights, but not to flights operated by other airlines (such as United-marketed code share and Star Alliance® flights). Tickets purchased through United reservation offices are $5 per ticket higher and tickets purchased at airport ticket counters are $10 per ticket higher.

2. Valid Routing: To take advantage of this discount you must begin your travel in and fly to a destination within the 50 United States, Puerto Rico, U.S. Virgin Islands or Canada.

3. Allowable Fares: This discount may be used on published United Economy® (H, Q, V, W, S) fares of $150 or more. These qualifying fares are the lower, more restrictive fares for travel in the economy cabin. Since these fares are booked in a special class of service, they might not be available on all flights or on all days of the week when you travel.

4. Restricted Fares: This discount may not be used on the following fare types: United First® (F, A, P), United Business® (C, D), United Economy (Y, B, M, E, U, T), internet-only fares, companion, travel industry G class, contract, bulk, convention, tour conductor, children, family plan, government, group, military, senior citizen, student, youth, infant, tour basing, Visit USA Fares or any non-published fares. This discount does not apply to private fares.

5. Fare Rules: The published fare you qualify for depends on what class of service is available on the days you travel. Some markets may have lower fares available without the discount. Keep in mind, you must travel roundtrip on United (open jaw and circle trips are allowed too). The discount may not be used when you travel one way. Other restrictions may apply.

6. Blackout Dates: This discount is not allowed on the following dates: November 23, 27, 28, 2005; December 22, 23, 26, 29, 30, 31, 2005; January 1, 2, 2006; March 10, 11, 12, 17, 18, 19, 31, 2006; April 1, 2, 7, 8, 9, 14, 15, 16, 17, 2006; November 22, 26, 27, 2006; December 22, 23, 26, 29, 30, 31, 2006.

7. United Mileage Plus® Accrual: The passenger may accrue United Mileage Plus miles, even with this discount.

8. Upgrades: To determine if an upgrade certificate may be used together with this discount, refer to the terms, conditions and booking class restrictions associated with each upgrade.

9. Ticketing: You may redeem this certificate using United's Electronic Ticketing by calling United or your travel professional. You may also ticket by mail (where available) or through a United airport location. Discount only applies when ticket is purchased within the 50 United States, Puerto Rico, the U.S. Virgin Islands, or Canada. All dollar levels are stated in U.S. currency. When using the discount on a ticket purchased in Canada, current conversion rates apply. Certificate must be surrendered at time of initial ticketing and cannot be redeemed via the internet.

10. Changes/Refunds: The rules of the United Economy fare you purchase determine what changes or refunds are allowed. Any refund due is based on the amount actually paid. The certificate discount may not be reapplied toward the purchase of another ticket when exchanging or refunding your original ticket, except when the original ticket qualifies for a reduced fare (guaranteed airfare rule applies). Check with United or your travel professional.

11. Other Important Notes: This discount may only be applied to the purchase of one new ticket and may not be applied to previously ticketed reservations. Certificate has no cash value and may not be altered or duplicated. Lost, stolen, expired or destroyed certificates will not be replaced. Only one discount certificate, discount voucher or discount may be used per ticket. This certificate is transferable, but void if sold or bartered.

Processing Information

Agencies See: S*PMA/Entertainment 2006
UA Representatives See: S*PMO/Entertainment 2006
FastTech: Profile Code: PMO Name: Entertainment 2006

Subject to Rules of Use. Not valid with other discount offers, unless specified. Coupon VOID if purchased, sold or bartered for cash.

Valid for travel from August 1, 2005 through December 31, 2006

Terms and Conditions:

1. Valid Carrier: This discount may be applied to United, Ted℠ and United Express® operated flights, but not to flights operated by other airlines (such as United-marketed code share and Star Alliance® flights). Tickets purchased through United reservation offices are $5 per ticket higher and tickets purchased at airport ticket counters are $10 per ticket higher.

2. Valid Routing: To take advantage of this discount you must begin your travel in and fly to a destination within the 50 United States, Puerto Rico, U.S. Virgin Islands or Canada.

3. Allowable Fares: This discount may be used on published United Economy® (H, Q, V, W, S) fares of $150 or more. These qualifying fares are the lower, more restrictive fares for travel in the economy cabin. Since these fares are booked in a special class of service, they might not be available on all flights or on all days of the week when you travel.

4. Restricted Fares: This discount may not be used on the following fare types: United First® (F, A, P), United Business® (C, D), United Economy (Y, B, M, E, U, T), internet-only fares, companion, travel industry G class, contract, bulk, convention, tour conductor, children, family plan, government, group, military, senior citizen, student, youth, infant, tour basing, Visit USA Fares or any non-published fares. This discount does not apply to private fares.

5. Fare Rules: The published fare you qualify for depends on what class of service is available on the days you travel. Some markets may have lower fares available without the discount. Keep in mind, you must travel roundtrip on United (open jaw and circle trips are allowed too). The discount may not be used when you travel one way. Other restrictions may apply.

6. Blackout Dates: This discount is not allowed on the following dates: November 23, 27, 28, 2005; December 22, 23, 26, 29, 30, 31, 2005; January 1, 2, 2006; March 10, 11, 12, 17, 18, 19, 31, 2006; April 1, 2, 7, 8, 9, 14, 15, 16, 17, 2006; November 22, 26, 27, 2006; December 22, 23, 26, 29, 30, 31, 2006.

7. United Mileage Plus® Accrual: The passenger may accrue United Mileage Plus miles, even with this discount.

8. Upgrades: To determine if an upgrade certificate may be used together with this discount, refer to the terms, conditions and booking class restrictions associated with each upgrade.

9. Ticketing: You may redeem this certificate using United's Electronic Ticketing by calling United or your travel professional. You may also ticket by mail (where available) or through a United airport location. Discount only applies when ticket is purchased within the 50 United States, Puerto Rico, the U.S. Virgin Islands, or Canada. All dollar levels are stated in U.S. currency. When using the discount on a ticket purchased in Canada, current conversion rates apply. Certificate must be surrendered at time of initial ticketing and cannot be redeemed via the internet.

10. Changes/Refunds: The rules of the United Economy fare you purchase determine what changes or refunds are allowed. Any refund due is based on the amount actually paid. The certificate discount may not be reapplied toward the purchase of another ticket when exchanging or refunding your original ticket, except when the original ticket qualifies for a reduced fare (guaranteed airfare rule applies). Check with United or your travel professional.

11. Other Important Notes: This discount may only be applied to the purchase of one new ticket and may not be applied to previously ticketed reservations. Certificate has no cash value and may not be altered or duplicated. Lost, stolen, expired or destroyed certificates will not be replaced. Only one discount certificate, discount voucher or discount may be used per ticket. This certificate is transferable, but void if sold or bartered.

Processing Information

Agencies See: S*PMA/Entertainment 2006
UA Representatives See: S*PMO/Entertainment 2006
FastTech: Profile Code: PMO Name: Entertainment 2006

Subject to Rules of Use. Not valid with other discount offers, unless specified. Coupon VOID if purchased, sold or bartered for cash.

Valid for travel from August 1, 2005 through December 31, 2006

Take up to $75 off your next qualifying trip on United

Use this promotional coupon to save on one new United Economy® round-trip ticket booked in H, Q, V, W, or S class for travel on United Airlines, Ted℠ or United Express®.

Take **$25** off one round-trip ticket o $150 - $299
Take **$50** off one round-trip ticket of $300 - $474
Take **$75** off one round-trip ticket of $475 or more

You must begin your travel in and fly to a destination within the 50 United States, Puerto Rico, U.S. Virgin Islands, or Canada. Discount does not apply to flights operated by other airlines (such as United-marketed code share and Star Alliance® flights).

Profile Name: PMO/Entertainment 2006
Account Code: EBG25/EBG50/EBG75
Begin Travel: August 1, 2005
Travel Complete: December 31, 2006
Must ticket by: December 31, 2006

To make reservations, call United Airlines at 1-800-241-6522 or your travel professional, and refer to Profile Name: PMO/Entertainment 2006

If Redeeming by Mail:
Passenger last name: ____________
Date of return travel: ____________
Flt # of return travel: ____________

UNITED

1 016 0500 000 447 6

See reverse side for details

D4

Take up to $75 off your next qualifying trip on United

Use this promotional coupon to save on one new United Economy® round-trip ticket booked in H, Q, V, W, or S class for travel on United Airlines, Ted℠ or United Express®.

Take **$25** off one round-trip ticket o $150 - $299
Take **$50** off one round-trip ticket of $300 - $474
Take **$75** off one round-trip ticket of $475 or more

You must begin your travel in and fly to a destination within the 50 United States, Puerto Rico, U.S. Virgin Islands, or Canada. Discount does not apply to flights operated by other airlines (such as United-marketed code share and Star Alliance® flights).

Profile Name: PMO/Entertainment 2006
Account Code: EBG25/EBG50/EBG75
Begin Travel: August 1, 2005
Travel Complete: December 31, 2006
Must ticket by: December 31, 2006

To make reservations, call United Airlines at 1-800-241-6522 or your travel professional, and refer to Profile Name: PMO/Entertainment 2006

If Redeeming by Mail:
Passenger last name: ____________
Date of return travel: ____________
Flt # of return travel: ____________

UNITED

1 016 0500 000 447 6

See reverse side for details

D5

Take up to $75 off your next qualifying trip on United

Use this promotional coupon to save on one new United Economy® round-trip ticket booked in H, Q, V, W, or S class for travel on United Airlines, Ted℠ or United Express®.

Take **$25** off one round-trip ticket o $150 - $299
Take **$50** off one round-trip ticket of $300 - $474
Take **$75** off one round-trip ticket of $475 or more

You must begin your travel in and fly to a destination within the 50 United States, Puerto Rico, U.S. Virgin Islands, or Canada. Discount does not apply to flights operated by other airlines (such as United-marketed code share and Star Alliance® flights).

Profile Name: PMO/Entertainment 2006
Account Code: EBG25/EBG50/EBG75
Begin Travel: August 1, 2005
Travel Complete: December 31, 2006
Must ticket by: December 31, 2006

To make reservations, call United Airlines at 1-800-241-6522 or your travel professional, and refer to Profile Name: PMO/Entertainment 2006

If Redeeming by Mail:
Passenger last name: ____________
Date of return travel: ____________
Flt # of return travel: ____________

UNITED

1 016 0500 000 447 6

See reverse side for details

D6

Terms and Conditions:

1. Valid Carrier: This discount may be applied to United, Ted℠ and United Express® operated flights, but not to flights operated by other airlines (such as United-marketed code share and Star Alliance® flights). Tickets purchased through United reservation offices are $5 per ticket higher and tickets purchased at airport ticket counters are $10 per ticket higher.

2. Valid Routing: To take advantage of this discount you must begin your travel in and fly to a destination within the 50 United States, Puerto Rico, U.S. Virgin Islands or Canada.

3. Allowable Fares: This discount may be used on published United Economy® (H, Q, V, W, S) fares of $150 or more. These qualifying fares are the lower, more restrictive fares for travel in the economy cabin. Since these fares are booked in a special class of service, they might not be available on all flights or on all days of the week when you travel.

4. Restricted Fares: This discount may not be used on the following fare types: United First® (F, A, P), United Business® (C, D), United Economy (Y, B, M, E, U, T), internet-only fares, companion, travel industry G class, contract, bulk, convention, tour conductor, children, family plan, government, group, military, senior citizen, student, youth, infant, tour basing, Visit USA Fares or any non-published fares. This discount does not apply to private fares.

5. Fare Rules: The published fare you qualify for depends on what class of service is available on the days you travel. Some markets may have lower fares available without the discount. Keep in mind, you must travel roundtrip on United (open jaw and circle trips are allowed too). The discount may not be used when you travel one way. Other restrictions may apply.

6. Blackout Dates: This discount is not allowed on the following dates: November 23, 27, 28, 2005; December 22, 23, 26, 29, 30, 31, 2005; January 1, 2, 2006; March 10, 11, 12, 17, 18, 19, 31, 2006; April 1, 2, 7, 8, 9, 14, 15, 16, 17, 2006; November 22, 26, 27, 2006; December 22, 23, 26, 29, 30, 31, 2006.

7. United Mileage Plus® Accrual: The passenger may accrue United Mileage Plus miles, even with this discount.

8. Upgrades: To determine if an upgrade certificate may be used together with this discount, refer to the terms, conditions and booking class restrictions associated with each upgrade.

9. Ticketing: You may redeem this certificate using United's Electronic Ticketing by calling United or your travel professional. You may also ticket by mail (where available) or through a United airport location. Discount only applies when ticket is purchased within the 50 United States, Puerto Rico, the U.S. Virgin Islands, or Canada. All dollar levels are stated in U.S. currency. When using the discount on a ticket purchased in Canada, current conversion rates apply. Certificate must be surrendered at time of initial ticketing and cannot be redeemed via the internet.

10. Changes/Refunds: The rules of the United Economy fare you purchase determine what changes or refunds are allowed. Any refund due is based on the amount actually paid. The certificate discount may not be reapplied toward the purchase of another ticket when exchanging or refunding your original ticket, except when the original ticket qualifies for a reduced fare (guaranteed airfare rule applies). Check with United or your travel professional.

11. Other Important Notes: This discount may only be applied to the purchase of one new ticket and may not be applied to previously ticketed reservations. Certificate has no cash value and may not be altered or duplicated. Lost, stolen, expired or destroyed certificates will not be replaced. Only one discount certificate, discount voucher or discount may be used per ticket. This certificate is transferable, but void if sold or bartered.

Processing Information

Agencies See: S*PMA/Entertainment 2006
UA Representatives See: S*PMO/Entertainment 2006
FastTech: Profile Code: PMO Name: Entertainment 2006

Subject to Rules of Use. Not valid with other discount offers, unless specified. Coupon VOID if purchased, sold or bartered for cash.

Valid for travel from August 1, 2005 through December 31, 2006

Terms and Conditions:

1. Valid Carrier: This discount may be applied to United, Ted℠ and United Express® operated flights, but not to flights operated by other airlines (such as United-marketed code share and Star Alliance® flights). Tickets purchased through United reservation offices are $5 per ticket higher and tickets purchased at airport ticket counters are $10 per ticket higher.

2. Valid Routing: To take advantage of this discount you must begin your travel in and fly to a destination within the 50 United States, Puerto Rico, U.S. Virgin Islands or Canada.

3. Allowable Fares: This discount may be used on published United Economy® (H, Q, V, W, S) fares of $150 or more. These qualifying fares are the lower, more restrictive fares for travel in the economy cabin. Since these fares are booked in a special class of service, they might not be available on all flights or on all days of the week when you travel.

4. Restricted Fares: This discount may not be used on the following fare types: United First® (F, A, P), United Business® (C, D), United Economy (Y, B, M, E, U, T), internet-only fares, companion, travel industry G class, contract, bulk, convention, tour conductor, children, family plan, government, group, military, senior citizen, student, youth, infant, tour basing, Visit USA Fares or any non-published fares. This discount does not apply to private fares.

5. Fare Rules: The published fare you qualify for depends on what class of service is available on the days you travel. Some markets may have lower fares available without the discount. Keep in mind, you must travel roundtrip on United (open jaw and circle trips are allowed too). The discount may not be used when you travel one way. Other restrictions may apply.

6. Blackout Dates: This discount is not allowed on the following dates: November 23, 27, 28, 2005; December 22, 23, 26, 29, 30, 31, 2005; January 1, 2, 2006; March 10, 11, 12, 17, 18, 19, 31, 2006; April 1, 2, 7, 8, 9, 14, 15, 16, 17, 2006; November 22, 26, 27, 2006; December 22, 23, 26, 29, 30, 31, 2006.

7. United Mileage Plus® Accrual: The passenger may accrue United Mileage Plus miles, even with this discount.

8. Upgrades: To determine if an upgrade certificate may be used together with this discount, refer to the terms, conditions and booking class restrictions associated with each upgrade.

9. Ticketing: You may redeem this certificate using United's Electronic Ticketing by calling United or your travel professional. You may also ticket by mail (where available) or through a United airport location. Discount only applies when ticket is purchased within the 50 United States, Puerto Rico, the U.S. Virgin Islands, or Canada. All dollar levels are stated in U.S. currency. When using the discount on a ticket purchased in Canada, current conversion rates apply. Certificate must be surrendered at time of initial ticketing and cannot be redeemed via the internet.

10. Changes/Refunds: The rules of the United Economy fare you purchase determine what changes or refunds are allowed. Any refund due is based on the amount actually paid. The certificate discount may not be reapplied toward the purchase of another ticket when exchanging or refunding your original ticket, except when the original ticket qualifies for a reduced fare (guaranteed airfare rule applies). Check with United or your travel professional.

11. Other Important Notes: This discount may only be applied to the purchase of one new ticket and may not be applied to previously ticketed reservations. Certificate has no cash value and may not be altered or duplicated. Lost, stolen, expired or destroyed certificates will not be replaced. Only one discount certificate, discount voucher or discount may be used per ticket. This certificate is transferable, but void if sold or bartered.

Processing Information

Agencies See: S*PMA/Entertainment 2006
UA Representatives See: S*PMO/Entertainment 2006
FastTech: Profile Code: PMO Name: Entertainment 2006

Subject to Rules of Use. Not valid with other discount offers, unless specified. Coupon VOID if purchased, sold or bartered for cash.

Valid for travel from August 1, 2005 through December 31, 2006

Terms and Conditions:

1. Valid Carrier: This discount may be applied to United, Ted℠ and United Express® operated flights, but not to flights operated by other airlines (such as United-marketed code share and Star Alliance® flights). Tickets purchased through United reservation offices are $5 per ticket higher and tickets purchased at airport ticket counters are $10 per ticket higher.

2. Valid Routing: To take advantage of this discount you must begin your travel in and fly to a destination within the 50 United States, Puerto Rico, U.S. Virgin Islands or Canada.

3. Allowable Fares: This discount may be used on published United Economy® (H, Q, V, W, S) fares of $150 or more. These qualifying fares are the lower, more restrictive fares for travel in the economy cabin. Since these fares are booked in a special class of service, they might not be available on all flights or on all days of the week when you travel.

4. Restricted Fares: This discount may not be used on the following fare types: United First® (F, A, P), United Business® (C, D), United Economy (Y, B, M, E, U, T), internet-only fares, companion, travel industry G class, contract, bulk, convention, tour conductor, children, family plan, government, group, military, senior citizen, student, youth, infant, tour basing, Visit USA Fares or any non-published fares. This discount does not apply to private fares.

5. Fare Rules: The published fare you qualify for depends on what class of service is available on the days you travel. Some markets may have lower fares available without the discount. Keep in mind, you must travel roundtrip on United (open jaw and circle trips are allowed too). The discount may not be used when you travel one way. Other restrictions may apply.

6. Blackout Dates: This discount is not allowed on the following dates: November 23, 27, 28, 2005; December 22, 23, 26, 29, 30, 31, 2005; January 1, 2, 2006; March 10, 11, 12, 17, 18, 19, 31, 2006; April 1, 2, 7, 8, 9, 14, 15, 16, 17, 2006; November 22, 26, 27, 2006; December 22, 23, 26, 29, 30, 31, 2006.

7. United Mileage Plus® Accrual: The passenger may accrue United Mileage Plus miles, even with this discount.

8. Upgrades: To determine if an upgrade certificate may be used together with this discount, refer to the terms, conditions and booking class restrictions associated with each upgrade.

9. Ticketing: You may redeem this certificate using United's Electronic Ticketing by calling United or your travel professional. You may also ticket by mail (where available) or through a United airport location. Discount only applies when ticket is purchased within the 50 United States, Puerto Rico, the U.S. Virgin Islands, or Canada. All dollar levels are stated in U.S. currency. When using the discount on a ticket purchased in Canada, current conversion rates apply. Certificate must be surrendered at time of initial ticketing and cannot be redeemed via the internet.

10. Changes/Refunds: The rules of the United Economy fare you purchase determine what changes or refunds are allowed. Any refund due is based on the amount actually paid. The certificate discount may not be reapplied toward the purchase of another ticket when exchanging or refunding your original ticket, except when the original ticket qualifies for a reduced fare (guaranteed airfare rule applies). Check with United or your travel professional.

11. Other Important Notes: This discount may only be applied to the purchase of one new ticket and may not be applied to previously ticketed reservations. Certificate has no cash value and may not be altered or duplicated. Lost, stolen, expired or destroyed certificates will not be replaced. Only one discount certificate, discount voucher or discount may be used per ticket. This certificate is transferable, but void if sold or bartered.

Processing Information

Agencies See: S*PMA/Entertainment 2006
UA Representatives See: S*PMO/Entertainment 2006
FastTech: Profile Code: PMO Name: Entertainment 2006

Subject to Rules of Use. Not valid with other discount offers, unless specified. Coupon VOID if purchased, sold or bartered for cash.

Valid for travel from August 1, 2005 through December 31, 2006

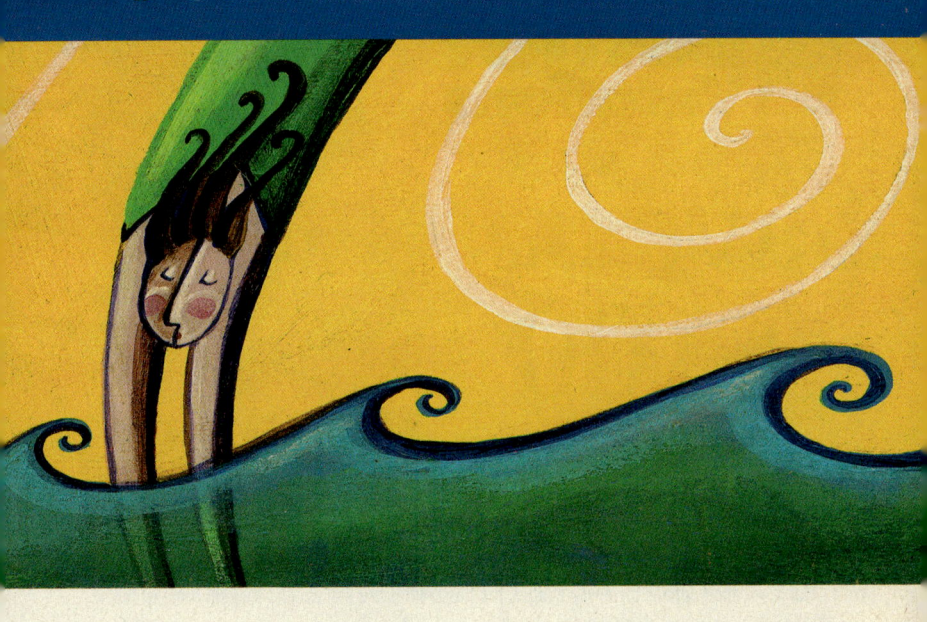

Funjet Vacations®

Photo Courtesy: LVCVA

LAS VEGAS

Save up to $100 on your next Vacation*

when you purchase with your MasterCard®

For over 30 years, Funjet Vacations has provided travelers with what they need to plan the perfect vacation. With flexible vacation options for every budget, the possibilities are endless and they all come at the incredibly reasonable prices that Funjet is so well known for. And now with your Entertainment® Book our deals are even better! Receive $50 off your vacation when you travel to one of our destinations within the U.S. or $100 off International and Hawaii vacations when you purchase with your MasterCard® card. Must reference promotional code: FJ50ENT or FJ100ENT at time of purchase to receive these savings.

Visit your local travel agent or funjet.com to purchase your vacation today.

MasterCard

*Offer is valid on new air and hotel vacations purchased more than 45 days from departure. Vacations must be paid in full with a valid MasterCard® card utilizing promotional code **FJ50ENT** for domestic reservations or **FJ100ENT** for International reservations. Minimum 3 night stay required. Discount might not be combinable with other offers. Maximum savings cannot exceed $100 per reservation. All offers are based on availability and are subject to change without notice. Restrictions and black-out dates may apply. MasterCard and the interlocking circles device are registered trademarks of MasterCard International Incorporated. Offer expires 12/31/06.

We Make Vacations Easy

CARIBBEAN

Photo Courtesy: Visit Mexico

MEXICO

CST#2009218-20 FJV023219.gew

We try harder to make your money go farther.

BOOK BY PHONE OR,
FOR BEST RATES,
BOOK ONLINE AT
entertainment.com/avis

FREE tank of gas

Rent a car for a minimum of five days and you can get a free tank of gas.

For reservations, call
1-800-245-8572
entertainment.com/avis

To save every time you rent, always provide your Avis Worldwide Discount (AWD) # B790069

Be sure to mention the coupon # GUGA024

AVIS We try harder.
avis.com

See reverse side for details. D9

$20 off a weekly rental

Rent a car for a minimum of five days and you can get $20 off. Includes Luxury and Premium vehicles, SUVs, Minivans and Convertibles

For reservations, call
1-800-245-8572
entertainment.com/avis

To save every time you rent, always provide your Avis Worldwide Discount (AWD) # B790069

Be sure to mention the coupon # MUGG904

AVIS We try harder.
avis.com

See reverse side for details. D10

FREE car upgrade

Rent a car and receive a one-time one car group upgrade. An advance reservation with request for upgrade is required.

For reservations, call
1-800-245-8572
entertainment.com/avis

To save every time you rent, always provide your Avis Worldwide Discount (AWD) # B790069

Be sure to mention the coupon # UUGA108

AVIS We try harder.
avis.com

See reverse side for details. D11

FREE weekend day

Rent a car for three or more days and you can get a weekend day free.

For reservations, call
1-800-245-8572
entertainment.com/avis

To save every time you rent, always provide your Avis Worldwide Discount (AWD) # B790069

Be sure to mention the coupon # TUGB269

AVIS We try harder.
avis.com

See reverse side for details. D12

Your choice of savings from Avis!

- A free tank of gas
- $20 off a five-day rental
- A free upgrade
- A free weekend day

And more! See coupons on next page.

AVIS
We try harder.

Terms and Conditions: Coupon valid on Premium (Group G), Luxury (Group H), Convertible (Group K), Sport Utility Vehicle (Group L and W) and Minivan (Group V) cars. Dollars off applies to the daily time and mileage charges only for the entire rental with a minimum of five days that includes a Saturday night stayover. Taxes, concession recovery fees, customer facility charges ($10/contract in CA), optional items and other surcharges may apply and are extra. Coupon must be surrendered at time of rental; one coupon per rental. Offer may not be used in conjunction with any other coupon, promotion or offer, except your Entertainment® discount. **An advance reservation is required.** Coupon valid at participating Avis locations in the contiguous U.S. and Canada. Offer subject to vehicle availability at the time of rental, and may not be available on some rates at some times. Renter must meet Avis age, driver and credit requirements. Minimum age is 25, but may vary by location. **Rental must begin by 06/30/07.**

Rental Sales Agent Instructions

At checkout:

- In AWD, enter **B790069**
- In CPN, enter **MUGG904**
- Complete this information:
  RA #: ______________
  Rental Location: ________
- Attach to COUPON tape

AVIS
We try harder.

COUPON # MUGG904

avis.com

Valid through June 30, 2007

Terms and Conditions: Receive your first tank of gas free when you rent an Intermediate (Group C) through a Full Size four-door (Group E) car for a minimum of five consecutive days at weekly rates, including a Saturday night stayover. **An advance reservation is required.** Coupon must be surrendered at time of rental; one per rental and cannot be used for one-way rentals. May not be used in conjunction with any other coupon, promotion or offer, except your Entertainment® discount. Coupon valid at participating Avis locations in the contiguous U.S. and Canada, excluding the New York Metro area. No credit or refund will apply for unused fuel at time of return. Offer subject to vehicle availability at the time of rental, and may not be available on some rates at some times. Offer may not be available during holiday and other blackout periods. Taxes, concession recovery fees, customer facility charges ($10/contract in CA), optional items and other surcharges may apply and are extra. Renter must meet Avis age, driver and credit requirements. Minimum age is 25, but may vary by location. **Rental must begin by 06/30/07.**

Rental Sales Agent Instructions

At checkout:

- In AWD, enter **B790069**
- In CPN, enter **GUGA024**
- Complete this information:
  RA #: ______________
  Rental Location: ________
- Attach to COUPON tape

AVIS
We try harder.

COUPON # GUGA024

avis.com

Valid through June 30, 2007

Terms and Conditions: Offer of one weekend day free applies to the daily time and mileage charges for the third consecutive day of a minimum three day weekend rental on an Intermediate (Group C) through a Full Size four-door (Group E) car. Taxes, concession recovery fees, customer facility charges ($10/contract in CA), optional items and other surcharges may apply and are extra. Weekend rental period begins Thursday and car must be returned by Monday 11:59 p.m. or a higher rate will apply. Coupon must be surrendered at time of rental; one per rental and cannot be used for one-way rentals. May not be used in conjunction with any other coupon, promotion or offer, except your Entertainment® discount. Coupon valid at participating Avis locations in the contiguous U.S. and Canada, except the New York Metro area. **An advance reservation is required.** Offer may not be available during holiday and other blackout periods. Offer subject to vehicle availability at the time of rental, and may not be available on some rates and at some times. Renter must meet Avis age, driver and credit requirements. Minimum age is 25, but may vary by location. **Rental must begin by 06/30/07.**

Rental Sales Agent Instructions

At checkout:

- In AWD, enter **B790069**
- In CPN, enter **TUGB269**
- Complete this information:
  RA #: ______________
  Rental Location: ________
- Attach to COUPON tape

AVIS
We try harder.

COUPON # TUGB269

avis.com

Valid through June 30, 2007

Terms and Conditions: Coupon valid for a one-time, one-car group upgrade on an Intermediate (Group C) through a Full Size four-door (Group E) car. Maximum upgrade to Premium (Group G). Offer valid on weekend and weekly rates only. Taxes, concession recovery fees, customer facility charges ($10/contract in CA), optional items and other surcharges may apply and are extra. The upgraded car is subject to vehicle availability at the time of rental, and may not be available on some rates and at some times. Coupon valid at participating Avis locations in the contiguous United States and Canada. Coupon must be surrendered at time of rental; one coupon per rental. May not be used in conjunction with any other coupon, promotion or offer, except your Entertainment® discount. **An advance reservation with a request for an upgrade is required.** Renter must meet Avis age, driver and credit requirements. Minimum age is 25, but may vary by location. **Rental must begin by 06/30/07.**

Rental Sales Agent Instructions

At checkout:

- In AWD, enter **B790069**
- Assign customer a car one group higher than car group reserved. Upgrade to no higher than Group G. Charge for car group reserved.
- In CPN, enter **UUGA108**
- Complete this information:
  RA #: ______________
  Rental Location: ________
- Attach to COUPON tape

AVIS
We try harder.

COUPON # UUGA108

avis.com

Valid through June 30, 2007

$20 off a weekly rental

Rent a car for a minimum of five days and you can get $20 off. Includes Luxury and Premium vehicles, SUVs, Minivans and Convertibles

For reservations, call
1-800-245-8572
entertainment.com/avis

To save every time you rent, always provide your Avis Worldwide Discount (AWD) # B790069

Be sure to mention the coupon # MUGG904

AVIS We try harder. avis.com

See reverse side for details. D13

up to $20 off a weekend rental

Rent a car for a minimum of two consecutive weekend days and you can save $5 per day, up to a total of $20 off.

For reservations, call 1-800-245-8572
entertainment.com/avis

To save every time you rent, always provide your Avis Worldwide Discount (AWD) # B790069

Be sure to mention the coupon number of choice below

COUPON #	RENTAL DAYS	$OFF
MUGG905	2	$10
MUGG906	3	$15
MUGG907	4	$20

AVIS We try harder. avis.com

See reverse side for details. D14

FREE weekend day

Rent a car for three or more days and you can get a weekend day free.

For reservations, call
1-800-245-8572
entertainment.com/avis

To save every time you rent, always provide your Avis Worldwide Discount (AWD) # B790069

Be sure to mention the coupon # TUGB269

AVIS We try harder. avis.com

See reverse side for details. D15

FREE car upgrade

Rent a car and receive a one-time one-car group upgrade. An advance reservation with request for upgrade is required.

For reservations, call
1-800-245-8572
entertainment.com/avis

To save every time you rent, always provide your Avis Worldwide Discount (AWD) # B790069

Be sure to mention the coupon # UUGA108

AVIS We try harder. avis.com

See reverse side for details. D16

$15 off a weekly rental

Rent a car for a minimum of five days and you can get $15 off.

For reservations, call
1-800-245-8572
entertainment.com/avis

To save every time you rent, always provide your Avis Worldwide Discount (AWD) # B790069

Be sure to mention the coupon # MUGG908

AVIS We try harder. avis.com

See reverse side for details. D17

$50 off a long-term rental

Rent a car for a minimum of 30 days and receive $50 off.

For reservations, call
1-800-245-8572
entertainment.com/avis

To save every time you rent, always provide your Avis Worldwide Discount (AWD) # B790069

Be sure to mention the coupon # MUGG909

AVIS We try harder. avis.com

See reverse side for details. D18

Terms and Conditions: Coupon valid at participating Avis locations in the contiguous U.S. and Canada on an Intermediate (Group C) through a Full Size four-door (Group E) car. Dollars off applies to the time and mileage charges only for the entire rental with a minimum two-day weekend rental. Taxes, concession recovery fees, customer facility charges ($10/contract in CA), optional items and other surcharges may apply and are extra. Coupon must be surrendered at time of rental; one coupon per rental. May not be used in conjunction with any other coupon, promotion or offer, except your Entertainment® discount. Weekend rental period begins Thursday and car must be returned by Monday 11:59 p.m. or a higher rate may apply. Offer subject to vehicle availability at the time of rental, and may not be available on some rates and at some times. **An advance reservation is required.** Renter must meet Avis age, driver and credit requirements. Minimum age is 25, but may vary by location. **Rental must begin by 06/30/07.**

Rental Sales Agent Instructions

At checkout:

- In AWD, enter **B790069**
- In CPN, enter **MUGG905** for a two-day rental
- In CPN, enter **MUGG906** for a three-day rental
- In CPN, enter **MUGG907** for a four-day rental
- Complete this information:
  RA #: ______________
  Rental Location: __________
- Attach to COUPON tape

AVIS We try harder.

 avis.com

Valid through June 30, 2007

Terms and Conditions: Coupon valid on Premium (Group G), Luxury (Group H), Convertible (Group K), Sport Utility Vehicle (Group L and W) and Minivan (Group V) cars. Dollars off applies to the daily time and mileage charges only for the entire rental with a minimum of five days that includes a Saturday night stayover. Taxes, concession recovery fees, customer facility charges ($10/contract in CA), optional items and other surcharges may apply and are extra. Coupon must be surrendered at time of rental; one coupon per rental. Offer may not be used in conjunction with any other coupon, promotion or offer, except your Entertainment® discount. **An advance reservation is required.** Coupon valid at participating Avis locations in the contiguous U.S. and Canada. Offer subject to vehicle availability at the time of rental, and may not be available on some rates at some times. Renter must meet Avis age, driver and credit requirements. Minimum age is 25, but may vary by location. **Rental must begin by 06/30/07.**

Rental Sales Agent Instructions

At checkout:

- In AWD, enter **B790069**
- In CPN, enter **MUGG904**
- Complete this information:
  RA #: ______________
  Rental Location: __________
- Attach to COUPON tape

COUPON # MUGG904

AVIS We try harder.

 avis.com

Valid through June 30, 2007

Terms and Conditions: Coupon valid for a one-time, one-car group upgrade on an Intermediate (Group C) through a Full Size four-door (Group E) car. Maximum upgrade to Premium (Group G). Offer valid on weekend and weekly rates only. Taxes, concession recovery fees, customer facility charges ($10/contract in CA), optional items and other surcharges may apply and are extra. The upgraded car is subject to vehicle availability at the time of rental, and may not be available on some rates and at some times. Coupon valid at participating Avis locations in the contiguous United States and Canada. Coupon must be surrendered at time of rental; one coupon per rental. May not be used in conjunction with any other coupon, promotion or offer, except your Entertainment® discount. **An advance reservation with a request for an upgrade is required.** Renter must meet Avis age, driver and credit requirements. Minimum age is 25, but may vary by location. **Rental must begin by 06/30/07.**

Rental Sales Agent Instructions

At checkout:

- In AWD, enter **B790069**
- Assign customer a car one group higher than car group reserved. Upgrade to no higher than Group G. Charge for car group reserved.
- In CPN, enter **UUGA108**
- Complete this information:
  RA #: ______________
  Rental Location: __________
- Attach to COUPON tape

COUPON # UUGA108

AVIS We try harder.

 avis.com

Valid through June 30, 2007

Terms and Conditions: Offer of one weekend day free applies to the daily time and mileage charges for the third consecutive day of a minimum three day weekend rental on an Intermediate (Group C) through a Full Size four-door (Group E) car. Taxes, concession recovery fees, customer facility charges ($10/contract in CA), optional items and other surcharges may apply and are extra. Weekend rental period begins Thursday and car must be returned by Monday 11:59 p.m. or a higher rate will apply. Coupon must be surrendered at time of rental; one per rental and cannot be used for one-way rentals. May not be used in conjunction with any other coupon, promotion or offer, except your Entertainment® discount. Coupon valid at participating Avis locations in the contiguous U.S. and Canada, except the New York Metro area. **An advance reservation is required.** Offer may not be available during holiday and other blackout periods. Offer subject to vehicle availability at the time of rental, and may not be available on some rates and at some times. Renter must meet Avis age, driver and credit requirements. Minimum age is 25, but may vary by location. **Rental must begin by 06/30/07.**

Rental Sales Agent Instructions

At checkout:

- In AWD, enter **B790069**
- In CPN, enter **TUGB269**
- Complete this information:
  RA #: ______________
  Rental Location: __________
- Attach to COUPON tape

COUPON # TUGB269

AVIS We try harder.

 avis.com

Valid through June 30, 2007

Terms and Conditions: Coupon valid for $50 off monthly or Mini-Lease rates at participating Avis locations in the contiguous U.S. and Canada. Offer applies to a minimum 30-day rental of an Intermediate (Group C) through a Full Size four-door (Group E) car. Offer of $50 off applies to the cost of the time and mileage charges in the first month of the rental with a minimum of 30 days and a maximum of 330 consecutive days. Taxes, concession recovery fees, customer facility charges ($10/contract in CA), optional items and other surcharges may apply and are extra. Coupon must be surrendered at time of rental; one coupon per rental. **An advance reservation is required.** May not be used in conjunction with any other coupon, promotion or offer, except your Entertainment® discount. Offer subject to vehicle availability at the time of rental, and may not be available on some rates and at some times. Renter must meet Avis age, driver and credit requirements. Minimum age is 25, but may vary by location. **Rental must begin by 06/30/07.**

Rental Sales Agent Instructions

At checkout:

- In AWD, enter **B790069**
- In CPN, enter **MUGG909**
- Complete this information:
  RA #: ______________
  Rental Location: __________
- Attach to COUPON tape

COUPON # MUGG909

AVIS We try harder.

 avis.com

Valid through June 30, 2007

Terms and Conditions: Coupon valid on an Intermediate (Group C) through a Full Size four-door (Group E) car. Dollars off applies to the daily time and mileage charges only for the entire rental with a minimum of five days. Taxes, concession recovery fees, customer facility charges ($10/contract in CA), optional items and other surcharges may apply and are extra. Coupon must be surrendered at time of rental; one coupon per rental. Offer may not be used in conjunction with any other coupon, promotion or offer, except your Entertainment® discount. **An advance reservation is required.** Coupon valid at participating Avis locations in the contiguous U.S. and Canada. Offer subject to vehicle availability at the time of rental, and may not be available on some rates at some times. Renter must meet Avis age, driver and credit requirements. Minimum age is 25, but may vary by location. **Rental must begin by 06/30/07.**

Rental Sales Agent Instructions

At checkout:

- In AWD, enter **B790069**
- In CPN, enter **MUGG908**
- Complete this information:
  RA #: ______________
  Rental Location: __________
- Attach to COUPON tape

COUPON # MUGG908

AVIS We try harder.

 avis.com

Valid through June 30, 2007

Somebody has to give you great rates on cool cars.

We decided it should be us.

Book by phone, or for best rates, book online at entertainment.com/budget

Budget

budget.com

FREE Weekend Day

Get your discount plus a free day when you present this coupon at time of rental.

Offer valid on Compact or higher car class vehicles through 6/30/07.

Mention **BCD # X443024** and **CPN # TUGZ212**

Book online at entertainment.com/budget for the best rates or call Budget at

1-888-724-6212

Budget

Subject to Terms and Conditions on reverse side. D19

Save $15 On A Weekly Rental

Get your discount and take an extra $15 off a weekly rental when you present this coupon at time of rental.

Offer valid on Compact through Full Size cars through 6/30/07.

Mention **BCD # X443024** and **CPN # MUGZ368**

Book online at entertainment.com/budget for the best rates or call Budget at

1-888-724-6212

Budget

Subject to Terms and Conditions on reverse side. D20

Free Double Upgrade

Get your discount plus a double upgrade when you present this coupon at time of rental.

Offer valid when you rent a Compact through Full Size two-door car, which needs to be returned to the same renting location. Subject to vehicle availability through 6/30/07.

Mention **BCD # X443024** and **CPN # UUGZ073**

Book online at entertainment.com/budget for the best rates or call Budget at

1-888-724-6212

Budget

Subject to Terms and Conditions on reverse side. D21

Free Day On A Weekly Rental

Get your discount plus a free day when you present this coupon at time of rental.

Offer valid on Intermediate or Full Size cars through 6/30/07.

Mention **BCD # X443024** and **CPN # TUGZ213**

Book online at entertainment.com/budget for the best rates or call Budget at

1-888-724-6212

Budget

Subject to Terms and Conditions on reverse side. D22

Somebody has to give you great rates on cool cars.

We decided it should be us.

Budget
budget.com

Terms and Conditions: Coupon valid on a Compact two-door (Group Z) through a Full Size four-door (Group E) car. Dollars off applies to the time and mileage charges on a minimum five-day rental. Taxes, concession recovery fees, customer facility charges ($10/contract in CA), optional items and other surcharges may apply and are extra. Coupon must be surrendered at time of rental; one coupon per rental. **A 24-hour advance reservation is required.** May not be used in conjunction with any other coupon, promotion or offer, except your Entertainment® discount. Coupon valid at participating Budget locations in the contiguous U.S. Offer subject to vehicle availability at time of rental and may not be available on some rates at some times. Cars subject to availability. Renter must meet Budget age, driver and credit requirements. Minimum age is 25, but may vary by location. **Rental must begin by 6/30/07.**

For Budget CSR Use Only
- In CPN, enter **MUGZ368**
- In BCD, enter **X443024**
- Attach to COUPON tape

At checkout:
- Complete this information
  RA #: ______________
  Operator ID: ______________
  Rental Location: ______________
  BCD #: ______________

Budget
budget.com

COUPON # MUGZ368

©2005 Budget Rent A Car System, Inc. A global system of corporate and licensee-owned locations. Budget features Ford, Lincoln and Mercury vehicles

Valid through June 30, 2007

Terms and Conditions: Offer of one weekend day free applies to the time and mileage charges only of the third consecutive day of a minimum three day weekend rental on a Compact two-door (Group Z) or higher car class. Taxes, concession recovery fees, customer facility charges ($10/contract in CA), optional items and other surcharges may apply and are extra. Weekend rental period begins Thursday noon and car must be returned by Monday 11:59 p.m. or a higher rate will apply. Coupon must be surrendered at time of rental and cannot be used for one-way rentals; one coupon per rental. Offer may not be used in conjunction with any other coupon, promotion or offer, except your Entertainment® discount. Coupon valid at participating Budget locations in the contiguous U.S., excluding the New York Metro area. **A 24-hour advance reservation is required.** Offer may not be available during holiday and other blackout periods. Offer is subject to vehicle availability at the time of rental and may not be available on some rates at some times. Renter must meet Budget age, driver and credit requirements. Minimum age is 25, but may vary by location. **Rental must begin by 6/30/07.**

For Budget CSR Use Only
- In CPN, enter **TUGZ212**
- In BCD, enter **X443024**
- Attach to COUPON tape

At checkout:
- Complete this information
  RA #: ______________
  Operator ID: ______________
  Rental Location: ______________
  BCD #: ______________

Budget
budget.com

COUPON # TUGZ212

©2005 Budget Rent A Car System, Inc. A global system of corporate and licensee-owned locations. Budget features Ford, Lincoln and Mercury vehicles.

Valid through June 30, 2007

Terms and Conditions: Offer of one day free applies to one day free of the daily time and mileage charges of a minimum five-day consecutive rental at weekly rates on an Intermediate (Group C) through a Full Size four-door (Group E) car. Taxes, concession recovery fees, customer facility charges ($10/contract in CA), optional items and other surcharges may apply and are extra. Coupon must be surrendered at time of rental. One coupon per rental. Offer may not be used in conjunction with any other coupon, promotion or offer, except your Entertainment® discount. Coupon valid at participating Budget locations in the contiguous U.S., excluding the New York Metro area. **A 24-hour advance reservation is required.** Offer may not be available during holiday and other blackout periods. Offer is subject to vehicle availability at the time of rental and may not be available on some rates at some times. Renter must meet Budget age, driver and credit requirements. Minimum age is 25, but may vary by location. **Rental must begin by 6/30/07.**

For Budget CSR Use Only
- In CPN, enter **TUGZ213**
- In BCD, enter **X443024**
- Attach to COUPON tape

At checkout:
- Complete this information
  RA #: ______________
  Operator ID: ______________
  Rental Location: ______________
  BCD #: ______________

Budget
budget.com

COUPON # TUGZ213

©2005 Budget Rent A Car System, Inc. A global system of corporate and licensee-owned locations. Budget features Ford, Lincoln and Mercury vehicles.

Valid through June 30, 2007

Terms and Conditions (return to same location): Coupon valid for a one-time, two-car group upgrade on a Compact two-door (Group Z) through a Full Size two-door (Group D) car. Maximum upgrade to Premium (Group G). Offer valid on weekend and weekly rates. Taxes, concession recovery fees, customer facility charges ($10/contract in CA), optional items and other surcharges may apply and are extra. The upgraded car is subject to vehicle availability at the time of rental and may not be available on some rates at some times. Coupon valid at participating Budget locations in the contiguous U.S. Coupon must be surrendered at time of rental, one per rental, and cannot be used for one-way rentals. **A 24-hour advance reservation with request for a double upgrade is required.** May not be used in conjunction with any other coupon, promotion or offer, except your Entertainment® discount. Renter must meet Budget age, driver and credit requirements. Minimum age is 25, but may vary by location. **Rental must begin by 6/30/07.**

For Budget CSR Use Only
- Assign customer a car two groups higher than car group reserved
- In CPN, enter **UUGZ073**
- In BCD, enter **X443024**
- Attach to COUPON tape

At checkout:
- Complete this information
  RA #: ______________
  Operator ID: ______________
  Rental Location: ______________
  BCD #: ______________

Budget
budget.com

COUPON # UUGZ073

©2005 Budget Rent A Car System, Inc. A global system of corporate and licensee-owned locations. Budget features Ford, Lincoln and Mercury vehicles.

Valid through June 30, 2007

Save Up To 20% On A Weekly Rental

when you present this coupon at time of rental.

Offer valid through 6/30/07.

Mention **BCD # X443025**

Book online at entertainment.com/budget for the best rates or call Budget at

1-888-724-6212

Budget

D23

Subject to Terms and Conditions on reverse side.

FREE Weekend Day

Get your discount plus a free day when you present this coupon at time of rental.

Offer valid on Compact or higher car class vehicles through 6/30/07.

Mention **BCD # X443024** and **CPN # TUGZ212**

Book online at entertainment.com/budget for the best rates or call Budget at

1-888-724-6212

Budget

D24

Subject to Terms and Conditions on reverse side.

Free Double Upgrade

Get your discount plus a double upgrade when you present this coupon at time of rental.

Offer valid on a Compact through Full Size two-door car. Subject to vehicle availability through 6/30/07.

Mention **BCD # X443024** and **CPN # UUGZ072**

Book online at entertainment.com/budget for the best rates or call Budget at

1-888-724-6212

Budget

D25

Subject to Terms and Conditions on reverse side.

Take $50 Off A Long-Term Rental

Get your discount and take an extra $50 off a monthly or Budget By The Month rental when you present this coupon at time of rental.

Offer valid on Compact or higher car class vehicles through 6/30/07.

Mention **BCD # X443024** and **CPN # MUGZ367**

Book online at entertainment.com/budget for the best rates or call Budget at

1-888-724-6212

Budget

D26

Subject to Terms and Conditions on reverse side.

Free Day On A Weekly Rental

Get your discount plus a free day when you present this coupon at time of rental.

Offer valid on Intermediate or Full Size cars through 6/30/07.

Mention **BCD # X443024** and **CPN # TUGZ213**

Book online at entertainment.com/budget for the best rates or call Budget at

1-888-724-6212

Budget

D27

Subject to Terms and Conditions on reverse side.

Save $15 On A Weekly Rental

Get your discount and take an extra $15 off a weekly rental when you present this coupon at time of rental.

Offer valid on Compact through Full Size cars through 6/30/07.

Mention **BCD # X443024** and **CPN # MUGZ368**

Book online at entertainment.com/budget for the best rates or call Budget at

1-888-724-6212

Budget

D28

Subject to Terms and Conditions on reverse side.

Terms and Conditions: Offer of one weekend day free applies to the time and mileage charges only of the third consecutive day of a minimum three day weekend rental on a Compact two-door (Group Z) or higher car class. Taxes, concession recovery fees, customer facility charges ($10/contract in CA), optional items and other surcharges may apply and are extra. Weekend rental period begins Thursday noon and car must be returned by Monday 11:59 p.m. or a higher rate will apply. Coupon must be surrendered at time of rental and cannot be used for one-way rentals; one coupon per rental. Offer may not be used in conjunction with any other coupon, promotion or offer, except your Entertainment® discount. Coupon valid at participating Budget locations in the contiguous U.S., excluding the New York Metro area. **A 24-hour advance reservation is required.** Offer may not be available during holiday and other blackout periods. Offer is subject to vehicle availability at the time of rental and may not be available on some rates at some times. Renter must meet Budget age, driver and credit requirements. Minimum age is 25, but may vary by location. **Rental must begin by 6/30/07.**

For Budget CSR Use Only
- In CPN, enter **TUGZ212**
- In BCD, enter **X443024**
- Attach to COUPON tape

At checkout:
- Complete this information
  RA #: ____________________
  Operator ID: ______________
  Rental Location: ___________
  BCD #: ___________________

COUPON # TUGZ212

Valid through June 30, 2007

Terms and Conditions: The savings of up to 20% applies to Budget leisure weekly rates and is applicable only to the time and mileage charges of the rental. Taxes, concession recovery fees, customer facility charges ($10/contract in CA), optional items and other surcharges may apply and are extra. Mention **BCD # X443025** to take advantage of this offer. Offer is available for U.S. and Canadian residents only for rentals at participating locations in the U.S. Offer may not be used in conjunction with any other BCD number, promotion or offer. Weekly rates require a five-day minimum rental with a 14-day maximum. A Saturday night stayover and an **advance reservation may be required. Discount valid on rentals checked out no later than 6/30/07.** Offer is subject to vehicle availability at the time of rental and may not be available on some rates at some times. Car rental return restrictions may apply. Offer subject to change without notice. Holiday and other blackout periods may apply. Renter must meet Budget age, driver and credit requirements. Minimum age is 25, but may vary by location.

Valid through June 30, 2007

Terms and Conditions: Coupon valid for $50 off monthly or Budget By The Month rentals at participating Budget locations in the contiguous U.S. Offer applies to a minimum 30-day rental of a Compact two-door (Group Z) or higher car class. Offer of $50 off a long-term rental applies to the time and mileage charges of the first month of a minimum 30 days and a maximum of 330 consecutive days rental. Taxes, concession recovery fees, customer facility charges ($10/contract in CA), optional items and other surcharges may apply and are extra. Coupon must be surrendered at time of rental; one coupon per rental period. **A 24-hour advance reservation is required.** Offer is subject to vehicle availability at time of rental and may not be available on some rates at some times. May not be used in conjunction with any other coupon, promotion or offer, except your Entertainment® discount. Renter must meet Budget age, driver and credit requirements. Minimum age is 25, but may vary by location. **Rental must begin by 6/30/07.**

For Budget CSR Use Only
- In CPN, enter **MUGZ367**
- In BCD, enter **X443024**
- Attach to COUPON tape

At checkout:
- Complete this information
  RA #: ____________________
  Operator ID: ______________
  Rental Location: ___________
  BCD #: ___________________

COUPON # MUGZ367

Valid through June 30, 2007

Terms and Conditions: Coupon valid for a one-time, two-car group upgrade on a Compact two-door (Group Z) through a Full Size two-door (Group D) car. Maximum upgrade to Premium (Group G). Offer valid on weekend and weekly rates. Taxes, concession recovery fees, customer facility charges ($10/contract in CA), optional items and other surcharges may apply and are extra. The upgraded car is subject to vehicle availability at the time of rental and may not be available on some rates at some times. Coupon valid at participating Budget locations in the contiguous U.S. Coupon must be surrendered at time of rental; one coupon per rental. **A 24-hour advance reservation with request for a double upgrade is required.** May not be used in conjunction with any other coupon, promotion or offer, except your Entertainment® discount. Renter must meet Budget age, driver and credit requirements. Minimum age is 25, but may vary by location. **Rental must begin by 6/30/07.**

For Budget CSR Use Only
- Assign customer a car two groups higher than car group reserved
- In CPN, enter **UUGZ072**
- In BCD, enter **X443024**
- Attach to COUPON tape

At checkout:
- Complete this information
  RA #: ____________________
  Operator ID: ______________
  Rental Location: ___________
  BCD #: ___________________

COUPON # UUGZ072

Valid through June 30, 2007

Terms and Conditions: Coupon valid on a Compact two-door (Group Z) through a Full Size four-door (Group E) car. Dollars off applies to the time and mileage charges on a minimum five-day rental. Taxes, concession recovery fees, customer facility charges ($10/contract in CA), optional items and other surcharges may apply and are extra. Coupon must be surrendered at time of rental; one coupon per rental. **A 24-hour advance reservation is required.** May not be used in conjunction with any other coupon, promotion or offer, except your Entertainment® discount. Coupon valid at participating Budget locations in the contiguous U.S. Offer subject to vehicle availability at time of rental and may not be available on some rates at some times. Cars subject to availability. Renter must meet Budget age, driver and credit requirements. Minimum age is 25, but may vary by location. **Rental must begin by 6/30/07.**

For Budget CSR Use Only
- In CPN, enter **MUGZ368**
- In BCD, enter **X443024**
- Attach to COUPON tape

At checkout:
- Complete this information
  RA #: ____________________
  Operator ID: ______________
  Rental Location: ___________
  BCD #: ___________________

COUPON # MUGZ368

Valid through June 30, 2007

Terms and Conditions: Offer of one day free applies to one day free of the daily time and mileage charges of a minimum five-day consecutive rental at weekly rates on an Intermediate (Group C) through a Full Size four-door (Group E) car. Taxes, concession recovery fees, customer facility charges ($10/contract in CA), optional items and other surcharges may apply and are extra. Coupon must be surrendered at time of rental. One coupon per rental. Offer may not be used in conjunction with any other coupon, promotion or offer, except your Entertainment® discount. Coupon valid at participating Budget locations in the contiguous U.S., excluding the New York Metro area. **A 24-hour advance reservation is required.** Offer may not be available during holiday and other blackout periods. Offer is subject to vehicle availability at the time of rental and may not be available on some rates at some times. Renter must meet Budget age, driver and credit requirements. Minimum age is 25, but may vary by location. **Rental must begin by 6/30/07.**

For Budget CSR Use Only
- In CPN, enter **TUGZ213**
- In BCD, enter **X443024**
- Attach to COUPON tape

At checkout:
- Complete this information
  RA #: ____________________
  Operator ID: ______________
  Rental Location: ___________
  BCD #: ___________________

COUPON # TUGZ213

Valid through June 30, 2007

DRIVE NATIONAL®
AND SAVE!
Enjoy special offers and
upgrades from National.®
Get the best rates at
entertainment.com/national
or call 1-800-CAR-RENT.®
National.
National features GM vehicles
like this Pontiac G6.

One Car Class Upgrade!

Reserve a compact through a fullsize 2-door car in the United States or Canada.

Request Coupon Code 10009509 and Contract I.D. Number 5000662.

Book online at **entertainment.com/national** or call **1-800-CAR-RENT.**

National.

See reverse side for details

D29

Two Car Class Upgrade!

Reserve a compact through intermediate car in the United States or Canada.

Request Coupon Code 10009510 and Contract I.D. Number 5000662.

Book online at **entertainment.com/national** or call **1-800-CAR-RENT.**

National.

See reverse side for details

D30

$20 Off Weekly Rental

Reserve a compact through fullsize 4-door car for a minimum of 5 days in the United States or Canada.

Request Coupon Code 10009508 and Contract I.D. Number 5000662.

Book online at **entertainment.com/national** or call **1-800-CAR-RENT.**

National.

See reverse side for details

D31

One Free Weekend Day!

Reserve a compact through a fullsize 4-door car for a minimum of 3 days in the United States or Canada.

Request Coupon Code 10009507 and Contract I.D. Number 5000662.

Book online at **entertainment.com/national** or call **1-800-CAR-RENT.**

National.

See reverse side for details

D32

GREAT VALUES FROM NATIONAL.®

Get the best rates at **entertainment.com/national** or call **1-800-CAR-RENT.**®

National.®

National features GM vehicles like this Buick LaCrosse.

Terms and Conditions

- One coupon per National rental; void once redeemed.
- Original coupon must be presented at counter upon arrival.
- **14-Day maximum allowable keep.**
- Renter must meet standard age, driver and credit requirements.
- 24 hour advance reservation required.
- Blackout dates may apply.
- May not be combined with other coupons or certain other discounts or promotions.
- Subject to availability at time of rental pickup.
- **Valid only at participating U.S. and Canadian National locations.**
- **Valid for a free two car class upgrade from the car class reserved.**
- **Not valid in Manhattan, NY, or San Jose, CA.**

National Car Rental™ features GM vehicles.

Subject to Rules of Use. Not valid with other discount offers, unless specified. Coupon VOID if purchased, sold or bartered for cash.

Valid now thru December 31, 2006

Terms and Conditions

- One coupon per National rental; void once redeemed.
- Original coupon must be presented at counter upon arrival.
- **14-Day maximum allowable keep.**
- Renter must meet standard age, driver and credit requirements.
- 24 hour advance reservation required.
- Blackout dates may apply.
- May not be combined with other coupons or certain other discounts or promotions.
- Subject to availability at time of rental pickup.
- **Valid only at participating U.S. and Canadian National locations.**
- **Valid for a free one car class upgrade from the car class reserved.**
- **Not valid in Manhattan, NY, or San Jose, CA.**

National Car Rental™ features GM vehicles.

Subject to Rules of Use. Not valid with other discount offers, unless specified. Coupon VOID if purchased, sold or bartered for cash.

Valid now thru December 31, 2006

Terms and Conditions

- One coupon per National rental; void once redeemed.
- Original coupon must be presented at counter upon arrival.
- Free day is prorated against base rate of entire rental period, which does not include taxes (including GST), governmentally authorized or imposed surcharges, license recoupment/air tax recovery and concession recoupment fees, airport and airport facility fees, fuel, additional driver fee, one-way rental charge or optional items.
- **Weekend rental requires a 3-day minimum (4-day maximum) rental with a Saturday overnight keep.**
- **Vehicle must not be picked up before noon Thursday and must not be returned before the immediately following Sunday.**
- **Vehicles must be returned no later than the immediately following Monday on or before the time the rental began.**
- Renter must meet standard age, driver and credit requirements.
- 24 hour advance reservation required.
- Blackout dates may apply.
- May not be combined with other coupons or certain other discounts or promotions.
- **Subject to availability and valid only at participating National locations.**
- **Not valid in Manhattan, NY, or San Jose, CA.**

National Car Rental™ features GM vehicles.

Subject to Rules of Use. Not valid with other discount offers, unless specified. Coupon VOID if purchased, sold or bartered for cash.

Valid now thru December 31, 2006

Terms and Conditions

- One coupon per National rental; void once redeemed.
- Original coupon must be presented at counter upon arrival.
- Discount applies to base rate only, which does not include taxes (including GST), governmentally authorized or imposed surcharges, license recoupment/air tax recovery and concession recoupment fees, airport and airport facility fees, fuel, additional driver fee, one-way rental charge or optional items.
- **Weekly rental requires a 5-day minimum (14-day maximum) rental.**
- Renter must meet standard age, driver and credit requirements.
- Blackout dates may apply.
- May not be combined with other coupons or certain other discounts or promotions.
- Availability is limited.
- **Valid only at participating U.S. and Canadian National locations.**

National Car Rental™ features GM vehicles.

Subject to Rules of Use. Not valid with other discount offers, unless specified. Coupon VOID if purchased, sold or bartered for cash.

Valid now thru December 31, 2006

Two Car Class Upgrade!

Reserve a compact through intermediate car in the United States or Canada.

Request Coupon Code 10009510 and Contract I.D. Number 5000662.

Book online at **entertainment.com/national** or call **1-800-CAR-RENT.**

National.

See reverse side for details

D33

One Free Weekend Day!

Reserve a compact through a fullsize 4-door car for a minimum of 3 days in the United States or Canada.

Request Coupon Code 10009507 and Contract I.D. Number 5000662.

Book online at **entertainment.com/national** or call **1-800-CAR-RENT.**

National.

See reverse side for details

D34

One Free Weekend Day!

Reserve a compact through a fullsize 4-door car for a minimum of 3 days in the United States or Canada.

Request Coupon Code 10009507 and Contract I.D. Number 5000662.

Book online at **entertainment.com/national** or call **1-800-CAR-RENT.**

National.

See reverse side for details

D35

Two Car Class Upgrade!

Reserve a compact through intermediate car in the United States or Canada.

Request Coupon Code 10009510 and Contract I.D. Number 5000662.

Book online at **entertainment.com/national** or call **1-800-CAR-RENT.**

National.

See reverse side for details

D36

$20 Off Weekly Rental

Reserve a compact through fullsize 4-door car for a minimum of 5 days in the United States or Canada.

Request Coupon Code 10009508 and Contract I.D. Number 5000662.

Book online at **entertainment.com/national** or call **1-800-CAR-RENT.**

National.

See reverse side for details

D37

One Free Weekend Day!

Reserve a compact through a fullsize 4-door car for a minimum of 3 days in the United States or Canada.

Request Coupon Code 10009507 and Contract I.D. Number 5000662.

Book online at **entertainment.com/national** or call **1-800-CAR-RENT.**

National.

See reverse side for details

D38

Terms and Conditions

- One coupon per National rental; void once redeemed.
- Original coupon must be presented at counter upon arrival.
- Free day is prorated against base rate of entire rental period, which does not include taxes (including GST), governmentally authorized or imposed surcharges, license recoupment/air tax recovery and concession recoupment fees, airport and airport facility fees, fuel, additional driver fee, one-way rental charge or optional items.
- **Weekend rental requires a 3-day minimum (4-day maximum) rental with a Saturday overnight keep.**
- **Vehicle must not be picked up before noon Thursday and must not be returned before the immediately following Sunday.**
- **Vehicles must be returned no later than the immediately following Monday on or before the time the rental began.**
- Renter must meet standard age, driver and credit requirements.
- 24 hour advance reservation required.
- Blackout dates may apply.
- May not be combined with other coupons or certain other discounts or promotions.
- **Subject to availability and valid only at participating National locations.**
- **Not valid in Manhattan, NY, or San Jose, CA.**

National Car Rental™ features GM vehicles.

Subject to Rules of Use. Not valid with other discount offers, unless specified. Coupon VOID if purchased, sold or bartered for cash.

Valid now thru December 31, 2006

Terms and Conditions

- One coupon per National rental; void once redeemed.
- Original coupon must be presented at counter upon arrival.
- **14-Day maximum allowable keep.**
- Renter must meet standard age, driver and credit requirements.
- 24 hour advance reservation required.
- Blackout dates may apply.
- May not be combined with other coupons or certain other discounts or promotions.
- Subject to availability at time of rental pickup.
- **Valid only at participating U.S. and Canadian National locations.**
- **Valid for a free two car class upgrade from the car class reserved.**
- **Not valid in Manhattan, NY, or San Jose, CA.**

National Car Rental™ features GM vehicles.

Subject to Rules of Use. Not valid with other discount offers, unless specified. Coupon VOID if purchased, sold or bartered for cash.

Valid now thru December 31, 2006

Terms and Conditions

- One coupon per National rental; void once redeemed.
- Original coupon must be presented at counter upon arrival.
- **14-Day maximum allowable keep.**
- Renter must meet standard age, driver and credit requirements.
- 24 hour advance reservation required.
- Blackout dates may apply.
- May not be combined with other coupons or certain other discounts or promotions.
- Subject to availability at time of rental pickup.
- **Valid only at participating U.S. and Canadian National locations.**
- **Valid for a free two car class upgrade from the car class reserved.**
- **Not valid in Manhattan, NY, or San Jose, CA.**

National Car Rental™ features GM vehicles.

©2005 Vanguard Car Rental USA Inc. All rights reserved.

Subject to Rules of Use. Not valid with other discount offers, unless specified. Coupon VOID if purchased, sold or bartered for cash.

Valid now thru December 31, 2006

Terms and Conditions

- One coupon per National rental; void once redeemed.
- Original coupon must be presented at counter upon arrival.
- Free day is prorated against base rate of entire rental period, which does not include taxes (including GST), governmentally authorized or imposed surcharges, license recoupment/air tax recovery and concession recoupment fees, airport and airport facility fees, fuel, additional driver fee, one-way rental charge or optional items.
- **Weekend rental requires a 3-day minimum (4-day maximum) rental with a Saturday overnight keep.**
- **Vehicle must not be picked up before noon Thursday and must not be returned before the immediately following Sunday.**
- **Vehicles must be returned no later than the immediately following Monday on or before the time the rental began.**
- Renter must meet standard age, driver and credit requirements.
- 24 hour advance reservation required.
- Blackout dates may apply.
- May not be combined with other coupons or certain other discounts or promotions.
- **Subject to availability and valid only at participating National locations.**
- **Not valid in Manhattan, NY, or San Jose, CA.**

National Car Rental™ features GM vehicles.

©2005 Vanguard Car Rental USA Inc. All rights reserved.

Subject to Rules of Use. Not valid with other discount offers, unless specified. Coupon VOID if purchased, sold or bartered for cash.

Valid now thru December 31, 2006

Terms and Conditions

- One coupon per National rental; void once redeemed.
- Original coupon must be presented at counter upon arrival.
- Free day is prorated against base rate of entire rental period, which does not include taxes (including GST), governmentally authorized or imposed surcharges, license recoupment/air tax recovery and concession recoupment fees, airport and airport facility fees, fuel, additional driver fee, one-way rental charge or optional items.
- **Weekend rental requires a 3-day minimum (4-day maximum) rental with a Saturday overnight keep.**
- **Vehicle must not be picked up before noon Thursday and must not be returned before the immediately following Sunday.**
- **Vehicles must be returned no later than the immediately following Monday on or before the time the rental began.**
- Renter must meet standard age, driver and credit requirements.
- 24 hour advance reservation required.
- Blackout dates may apply.
- May not be combined with other coupons or certain other discounts or promotions.
- **Subject to availability and valid only at participating National locations.**
- **Not valid in Manhattan, NY, or San Jose, CA.**

National Car Rental™ features GM vehicles.

©2005 Vanguard Car Rental USA Inc. All rights reserved.

Subject to Rules of Use. Not valid with other discount offers, unless specified. Coupon VOID if purchased, sold or bartered for cash.

Valid now thru December 31, 2006

Terms and Conditions

- One coupon per National rental; void once redeemed.
- Original coupon must be presented at counter upon arrival.
- Discount applies to base rate only, which does not include taxes (including GST), governmentally authorized or imposed surcharges, license recoupment/air tax recovery and concession recoupment fees, airport and airport facility fees, fuel, additional driver fee, one-way rental charge or optional items.
- **Weekly rental requires a 5-day minimum (14-day maximum) rental.**
- Renter must meet standard age, driver and credit requirements.
- Blackout dates may apply.
- May not be combined with other coupons or certain other discounts or promotions.
- Availability is limited.
- **Valid only at participating U.S. and Canadian National locations.**

National Car Rental™ features GM vehicles.

Subject to Rules of Use. Not valid with other discount offers, unless specified. Coupon VOID if purchased, sold or bartered for cash.

Valid now thru December 31, 2006

ALL ROADS LEAD TO
ALAMO COUNTRY℠
Book by phone or, for best rates, book online at entertainment.com/alamo
OFFICIAL RENTAL CAR OF THE AMERICAN VACATION
Alamo

UP TO $20 OFF
PER WEEKEND RENTAL

- Reserve a midsize car-SUV in the United States, Canada, Latin America, or the Caribbean.

Request:

Coupon Code	Days	$ OFF
DY9B	2	$10
DZ2B	3	$15
DZ3B	4	$20

and I.D. Number 7000440

entertainment.com/alamo
1-800 GO ALAMO

Alamo

Book online at entertainment.com/alamo for best rates!

D39

ONE FREE DAY
MINIMUM 5-DAY RENTAL

- Reserve a midsize-fullsize 4-door car in the United States, Canada, Latin America, or the Caribbean.

Request Coupon Code FH1B and I.D. Number 7000440.

entertainment.com/alamo
1-800 GO ALAMO

Alamo

Book online at entertainment.com/alamo for best rates!

D40

ONE FREE UPGRADE

- Reserve a compact-midsize 4-door car in the United States or Canada, or an economy-fullsize car in Europe.

Request Coupon Code U84B and I.D. Number 7000440.

entertainment.com/alamo
1-800 GO ALAMO

Alamo

Book online at entertainment.com/alamo for best rates!

D41

$15 OFF
MINIMUM 3-DAY RENTAL

- Reserve any car, any day in the United States, Canada, Latin America, or the Caribbean.

Request Coupon Code DZ1B and I.D. Number 7000440.

entertainment.com/alamo
1-800 GO ALAMO

Alamo

Book online at entertainment.com/alamo for best rates!

D42

One coupon per Alamo rental and void once redeemed. Original coupon must be presented at counter upon arrival. Free day is prorated against base rate of entire rental period, which does not include taxes (including VAT/GST), governmentally-authorized or imposed surcharges, license recoupment/air tax recovery and concession recoupment fees, or optional items. Offer is subject to standard rental conditions. 24-Hour advance reservation required. Blackout dates may apply. Not valid with any other discount or promotional rate. **Subject to availability and valid only at participating Alamo locations.** Offer not valid in Manhattan, N.Y. or San Jose, Calif. ©2005 Vanguard Car Rental USA Inc. All rights reserved. 1609-AN-205

ALAMO® FEATURES GM VEHICLES.

Subject to Rules of Use. Not valid with other discount offers, unless specified. Coupon VOID if purchased, sold or bartered for cash.
Valid now thru December 31, 2006

One coupon per Alamo rental and void once redeemed. Original coupon must be presented at counter upon arrival. Discount applies to base rate, which does not include taxes (including VAT/GST), governmentally-authorized or imposed surcharges, license recoupment/air tax recovery and concession recoupment fees, or optional items. **2-Day minimum rental required.** Offer is subject to standard rental conditions. 24-Hour advance reservation required. Blackout dates may apply. Not valid with any other discount or promotional rate. **Subject to availability and valid only at participating Alamo locations.** ©2005 Vanguard Car Rental USA Inc. All rights reserved. 1609-AN-205

ALAMO® FEATURES GM VEHICLES.

Subject to Rules of Use. Not valid with other discount offers, unless specified. Coupon VOID if purchased, sold or bartered for cash.
Valid now thru December 31, 2006

One coupon per Alamo rental and void once redeemed. Original coupon must be presented at counter upon arrival. Discount applies to base rate, which does not include taxes (including VAT/GST), governmentally-authorized or imposed surcharges, license recoupment/air tax recovery and concession recoupment fees, or optional items. **3-Day minimum rental required.** Offer is subject to standard rental conditions. **No blackout dates**. Not valid with any other discount or promotional rate. **Subject to availability and good only at participating Alamo locations.** ©2005 Vanguard Car Rental USA Inc. All rights reserved. 1609-AN-205

ALAMO® FEATURES GM VEHICLES.

Subject to Rules of Use. Not valid with other discount offers, unless specified. Coupon VOID if purchased, sold or bartered for cash.
Valid now thru December 31, 2006

One coupon per Alamo rental and void once redeemed. Original coupon must be presented at counter upon arrival. Upgrade is subject to availability at time of rental pickup. Offer is subject to standard rental conditions. Blackout dates may apply. Not valid with any other discount or promotional rate. **Valid only at participating Alamo locations in the United States, Canada, or Europe. Coupon valid for one free upgrade to the next car category.** Not valid in Manhattan, N.Y. or San Jose, Calif. ©2005 Vanguard Car Rental USA Inc. All rights reserved. 1609-AN-205

ALAMO® FEATURES GM VEHICLES.

Subject to Rules of Use. Not valid with other discount offers, unless specified. Coupon VOID if purchased, sold or bartered for cash.
Valid now thru December 31, 2006

UP TO $20 OFF
PER WEEKEND RENTAL

- Reserve a midsize car-SUV in the United States, Canada, Latin America, or the Caribbean.

Request:

Coupon Code	Days	$ OFF
DY9B	2	$10
DZ2B	3	$15
DZ3B	4	$20

and I.D. Number 7000440

entertainment.com/alamo
1-800 GO ALAMO

Book online at entertainment.com/alamo for best rates!

Alamo

D43

ONE FREE DAY
MINIMUM 5-DAY RENTAL

- Reserve a midsize-fullsize 4-door car in the United States, Canada, Latin America, or the Caribbean.

Request Coupon Code FH1B and I.D. Number 7000440.

entertainment.com/alamo
1-800 GO ALAMO

Book online at entertainment.com/alamo for best rates!

Alamo

D44

$15 OFF
MINIMUM 3-DAY RENTAL

- Reserve any car, any day in the United States, Canada, Latin America, or the Caribbean.

Request Coupon Code DZ1B and I.D. Number 7000440.

entertainment.com/alamo
1-800 GO ALAMO

Book online at entertainment.com/alamo for best rates!

Alamo

D45

UP TO $20 OFF
PER WEEKEND RENTAL

- Reserve a midsize car-SUV in the United States, Canada, Latin America, or the Caribbean.

Request:

Coupon Code	Days	$ OFF
DY9B	2	$10
DZ2B	3	$15
DZ3B	4	$20

and I.D. Number 7000440

entertainment.com/alamo
1-800 GO ALAMO

Book online at entertainment.com/alamo for best rates!

Alamo

D46

$25 OFF
MINIMUM 3-DAY RENTAL

- Reserve a convertible, minivan, or SUV in the United States, Canada, Latin America, or the Caribbean, picking up on a Monday, Tuesday or Wednesday.

Request Coupon Code DY8B and I.D. Number 7000440.

entertainment.com/alamo
1-800 GO ALAMO

Book online at entertainment.com/alamo for best rates!

Alamo

D47

$15 OFF
MINIMUM 3-DAY RENTAL

- Reserve any car, any day in the United States, Canada, Latin America, or the Caribbean.

Request Coupon Code DZ1B and I.D. Number 7000440.

entertainment.com/alamo
1-800 GO ALAMO

Book online at entertainment.com/alamo for best rates!

Alamo

D48

One coupon per Alamo rental and void once redeemed. Original coupon must be presented at counter upon arrival. Free day is prorated against base rate of entire rental period, which does not include taxes (including VAT/GST), governmentally-authorized or imposed surcharges, license recoupment/air tax recovery and concession recoupment fees, or optional items. Offer is subject to standard rental conditions. 24-Hour advance reservation required. Blackout dates may apply. Not valid with any other discount or promotional rate. **Subject to availability and valid only at participating Alamo locations.** Offer not valid in Manhattan, N.Y. or San Jose, Calif. ©2005 Vanguard Car Rental USA Inc. All rights reserved. 1609-AN-205

ALAMO® FEATURES GM VEHICLES.

Subject to Rules of Use. Not valid with other discount offers, unless specified. Coupon VOID if purchased, sold or bartered for cash.
Valid now thru December 31, 2006

One coupon per Alamo rental and void once redeemed. Original coupon must be presented at counter upon arrival. Discount applies to base rate, which does not include taxes (including VAT/GST), governmentally-authorized or imposed surcharges, license recoupment/air tax recovery and concession recoupment fees, or optional items. **2-Day minimum rental required.** Offer is subject to standard rental conditions. 24-Hour advance reservation required. Blackout dates may apply. Not valid with any other discount or promotional rate. **Subject to availability and valid only at participating Alamo locations.** ©2005 Vanguard Car Rental USA Inc. All rights reserved. 1609-AN-205

ALAMO® FEATURES GM VEHICLES.

Subject to Rules of Use. Not valid with other discount offers, unless specified. Coupon VOID if purchased, sold or bartered for cash.
Valid now thru December 31, 2006

One coupon per Alamo rental and void once redeemed. Original coupon must be presented at counter upon arrival. Discount applies to base rate, which does not include taxes (including VAT/GST), governmentally-authorized or imposed surcharges, license recoupment/air tax recovery and concession recoupment fees, or optional items. **2-Day minimum rental required.** Offer is subject to standard rental conditions. 24-Hour advance reservation required. Blackout dates may apply. Not valid with any other discount or promotional rate. **Subject to availability and valid only at participating Alamo locations.** ©2005 Vanguard Car Rental USA Inc. All rights reserved. 1609-AN-205

ALAMO® FEATURES GM VEHICLES.

Subject to Rules of Use. Not valid with other discount offers, unless specified. Coupon VOID if purchased, sold or bartered for cash.
Valid now thru December 31, 2006

One coupon per Alamo rental and void once redeemed. Original coupon must be presented at counter upon arrival. Discount applies to base rate, which does not include taxes (including VAT/GST), governmentally-authorized or imposed surcharges, license recoupment/air tax recovery and concession recoupment fees, or optional items. **3-Day minimum rental required.** Offer is subject to standard rental conditions. **No blackout dates.** Not valid with any other discount or promotional rate. **Subject to availability and good only at participating Alamo locations.** ©2005 Vanguard Car Rental USA Inc. All rights reserved. 1609-AN-205

ALAMO® FEATURES GM VEHICLES.

Subject to Rules of Use. Not valid with other discount offers, unless specified. Coupon VOID if purchased, sold or bartered for cash.
Valid now thru December 31, 2006

One coupon per Alamo rental and void once redeemed. Original coupon must be presented at counter upon arrival. Discount applies to base rate, which does not include taxes (including VAT/GST), governmentally-authorized or imposed surcharges, license recoupment/air tax recovery and concession recoupment fees, or optional items. **3-Day minimum rental required.** Offer is subject to standard rental conditions. **No blackout dates.** Not valid with any other discount or promotional rate. **Subject to availability and good only at participating Alamo locations.** ©2005 Vanguard Car Rental USA Inc. All rights reserved. 1609-AN-205

ALAMO® FEATURES GM VEHICLES.

Subject to Rules of Use. Not valid with other discount offers, unless specified. Coupon VOID if purchased, sold or bartered for cash.
Valid now thru December 31, 2006

One coupon per Alamo rental and void once redeemed. Original coupon must be presented at counter upon arrival. Discount applies to base rate, which does not include taxes (including VAT/GST), governmentally-authorized or imposed surcharges, license recoupment/air tax recovery and concession recoupment fees, or optional items. **Vehicle must be picked up on a Monday, Tuesday or Wednesday. 3-Day minimum rental required.** Offer is subject to standard rental conditions. 24-Hour advance reservation required. Blackout dates may apply. Not valid with any other discount or promotional rate. **Subject to availability and valid only at participating Alamo locations.** ©2005 Vanguard Car Rental USA Inc. All rights reserved. 1609-AN-205

ALAMO® FEATURES GM VEHICLES.

Subject to Rules of Use. Not valid with other discount offers, unless specified. Coupon VOID if purchased, sold or bartered for cash.
Valid now thru December 31, 2006

Special Offers Plus Discounts.
Save up to 25%.
Visit entertainment.com/hertz for low web rates too.

$20 Off

A WEEKLY RENTAL

Go to hertz.com for our lowest rates, save $20 and enjoy a discount on the rental too. Mention this offer and your Hertz discount CDP# 205521 when reserving a mid-size/intermediate or higher class vehicle (Class C or higher) for at least five days, including a Saturday night, at Hertz Leisure Weekly Rates. Surrender this coupon at the time of rental.

Visit hertz.com,
call your travel agent or
call Hertz at 1-888-999-7125.

Hertz

See reverse side for details D49

Up to $20 Off

A WEEKEND RENTAL

Go to hertz.com for our lowest rates, save $5 per day (up to $20 off) and receive a discount on the rental too. Mention this offer and your discount Hertz CDP# 205521 when reserving a Premium or Luxury class car, SUV, convertible, minivan, or Hertz Prestige Collection vehicle for at least two days at Hertz Leisure Weekend Rates. Surrender this coupon at the time of rental.

Visit hertz.com,
call your travel agent or
call Hertz at 1-888-999-7125.

Hertz

See reverse side for details D50

2 Free Days

SIRIUS SATELLITE RADIO

Experience more than 120 channels of Satellite Radio, including, news, talk, comedy, sports, and commercial free music. Mention this offer and your Hertz discount CDP# 205521 when reserving and renting a SIRIUS-equipped vehicle for three or more days at Hertz Leisure Rates. You'll receive two days of SIRIUS service free. Surrender this coupon at the time of rental.

Visit hertz.com
call your travel agent or
call Hertz at 1-888-999-7125.

Hertz

See reverse side for details D51

FREE

UPGRADE IN EUROPE

Enjoy a one car class upgrade and a discount too. Mention this offer and your Hertz discount CDP# 205521 when reserving and renting an economy through full-size manual shift vehicle at Hertz Affordable Rates or Time and Kilometer Rates. Surrender this coupon at the time of rental. Upgrades are subject to vehicle availability at the time of rental.

Visit hertz.com
call your travel agent or
call Hertz at 1-888-999-7125.

Hertz

See reverse side for details D52

We're in the neighborhood
Hertz
Local Editic

Mention offer PC# 962850 and CDP# 205521

If there's a Hertz Local Edition® location in your neighborhood, call and ask us to come and get you. Advance reservations are required as blackout periods may apply. Normal weekend restrictions for the renting location apply. This offer is redeemable at participating Hertz locations in the U.S., Canada and Puerto Rico, subject to vehicle availability. Not all makes and models are available at all locations. This coupon has no cash value and may not be used with any other CDP#, coupon, discount, rate or promotion. Hertz standard driver and credit qualifications for the renting location apply and the car must be returned to that location. Minimum rental age is 25 (exceptions apply). Taxes, tax reimbursement, fees and optional service charges are not subject to discount. Discounts apply to time and mileage only. Call for details.

Subject to Rules of Use. Not valid with other discount offers, unless specified. Coupon VOID if purchased, sold or bartered for cash.

Valid through June 30, 2007

Mention offer PC# 962861 and CDP# 205521

If there's a Hertz Local Edition® location in your neighborhood, call and ask us to come and get you. Advance reservations are required as blackout periods may apply. This offer is redeemable at participating Hertz locations in the U.S., Canada, and Puerto Rico, subject to vehicle availability. This coupon has no cash value, must be surrendered on rental and may not be used with any other CDP#, coupon, discount, rate or promotion. Hertz standard driver and credit qualifications for the renting location apply and the car must be returned to that location. Minimum rental age is 25 (exceptions apply). Taxes, tax reimbursement, fees and optional service charges, such as refueling, are not subject to discount. Discounts apply to time and mileage only. Call for details.

Subject to Rules of Use. Not valid with other discount offers, unless specified. Coupon VOID if purchased, sold or bartered for cash.

Valid through June 30, 2007

Mention offer PC# 186583 and CDP# 205521

This offer is available at participating Hertz locations in Europe, subject to availability by country. Reservations must be made in the U.S. at least 24 hours prior to vehicle pickup. Minimum rental period is 3 days. Blackouts may apply in some cities at some times. Upgrade is not guaranteed and is based on availability of a larger car at the time of rental. Not all makes and models are available in each country. This coupon has no cash value, must be surrendered on rental and may not be used with any other CDP#, coupon, discount, Tour Rates, or other rates or promotions. Offer is void where prohibited by law, taxed or otherwise restricted. Renter must meet all Hertz qualifications, standards and requirements, including those relating to age, driving license and credit in effect at the time and place of rental. Car must be returned to renting location.

Subject to Rules of Use. Not valid with other discount offers, unless specified. Coupon VOID if purchased, sold or bartered for cash.

Valid through June 30, 2007

Mention offer PC# 963351 and CDP# 205521

Advance reservations are required as blackout periods may apply. Offer applies to Hertz Standard or Leisure Rates at participating Hertz corporate locations in the United States, and is subject to availability of SIRIUS-equipped vehicles. A minimum rental required for this offer is three days. This offer has no cash value and cannot be combined with any other CDP#, coupon or promotion. Hertz standard driver and credit qualifications for the renting location apply and the car must be returned to that location. Minimum rental age is 25 (exceptions apply). Discounts apply to time and mileage only. Taxes, tax reimbursement, fees and optional service charges, such as refueling, are not subject to discount. Call for details. **This offer cannot be reserved online.**

Subject to Rules of Use. Not valid with other discount offers, unless specified. Coupon VOID if purchased, sold or bartered for cash.

Valid through June 30, 2007

$25 Off

A WEEKLY RENTAL

Go to hertz.com for our lowest rates, save $25 and receive a discount on the rental too. Mention this offer and your Hertz CDP# 205521 when reserving a Hertz Prestige Collection vehicle for at least 5 days, including a Saturday night, at Hertz Leisure Weekly Rates. Surrender this coupon at the time of rental.

Visit hertz.com,
call your travel agent or
call Hertz at 1-888-999-7125.

Hertz®

See reverse side for details

D53

2 Free Days

NEVERLOST

Go to hertz.com for our lowest rates and enjoy two free weekend days of Hertz NeverLost® in-car navigational system when renting a NeverLost-equipped vehicle for at least three days at Hertz Leisure Weekend Rates. Mention this offer and your Hertz discount CDP# 205521 at the time of reservation. Surrender this coupon at the time of rental.

Visit hertz.com,
call your travel agent or
call Hertz at 1-888-999-7125.

Hertz®

See reverse side for details

D54

$50 Off

A MONTHLY RENTAL

Go to hertz.com for our lowest rates, save $50 and enjoy a discount on the rental too. Mention this offer and your Hertz discount CDP# 205521 when reserving and renting a mid-size/intermediate through premium class car or standard SUV for at least twenty-eight days at Hertz Standard or Leisure Monthly Rates. Surrender this coupon at the time of rental.

Visit hertz.com,
call your travel agent or
call Hertz at 1-888-999-7125.

Hertz®

See reverse side for details

D55

FREE

ONE CAR CLASS UPGRADE

Go to hertz.com for our lowest rates, enjoy a one car class upgrade on your daily, weekend or weekly rental and receive a discount too. Mention this offer and your Hertz discount CDP# 205521 when reserving a midsize/intermediate through full-size car. Surrender this coupon at the time of rental. If a car from the next higher class is available, you'll be driving it at the discounted lower car class rate.

Visit hertz.com,
call your travel agent or
call Hertz at 1-888-999-7125.

Hertz®

See reverse side for details

D56

Save $5 a Day

ON A WEEKEND RENTAL

Go to hertz.com for our lowest rates, save $5 per day, up to $15 off and get a discount too. Mention this offer and your Hertz discount CDP# 205521 when reserving and renting a mid-size/intermediate through premium class car, standard SUV, minivan or convertible for at least two days at Hertz Standard or Leisure Weekend Rates. Surrender this coupon at the time of rental.

Visit hertz.com,
call your travel agent or
call Hertz at 1-888-999-7125.

Hertz®

See reverse side for details

D57

$20 Off

A WEEKLY RENTAL

Go to hertz.com for our lowest rates, save $20 and enjoy a discount on the rental too. Mention this offer and your Hertz discount CDP# 205521 when reserving a mid-size/intermediate or higher class vehicle (Class C or higher) for at least five days, including a Saturday night, at Hertz Leisure Weekly Rates. Surrender this coupon at the time of rental.

Visit hertz.com,
call your travel agent or
call Hertz at 1-888-999-7125.

Hertz®

See reverse side for details

D58

Mention offer PC# 963605 and CDP# 205521

If there's a Hertz Local Edition® location in your neighborhood, call and ask us to come and get you. Advance reservations are required as blackout periods may apply. All NeverLost equipped cars are subject to vehicle availability. This offer is redeemable at participating Hertz locations in the U.S. and Canada. This coupon has no cash value, must be surrendered on rental and may not be used with any other CDP#, coupon, discount, rate or promotion. Hertz standard driver and credit qualifications for the renting location apply and the car must be returned to that location. Minimum rental age is 25 (exceptions apply). Discounts apply to time and mileage only. Taxes, tax reimbursement, fees and optional service charges, such as refueling, are not subject to discount. Call for details.

Subject to Rules of Use. Not valid with other discount offers, unless specified. Coupon VOID if purchased, sold or bartered for cash.

Valid through June 30, 2007

Mention offer PC# 962883 and CDP# 205521

If there's a Hertz Local Edition® location in your neighborhood, call and ask us to come and get you. Advance reservations are required as blackout periods may apply. This offer is redeemable at participating Hertz locations in the U.S. and Canada and is subject to vehicle availability. Not all vehicles, vehicle equipment and services are available at all locations. This coupon has no cash value, must be surrendered on rental and may not be used with any other CDP#, coupon, discount, rate or promotion. Hertz standard driver and credit qualifications for the renting location apply and the car must be returned to that location. Minimum rental age is 25 (exceptions apply). Discounts apply to time and mileage only. Taxes, tax reimbursement, fees and optional service charges, such as refueling, are not subject to discount. Call for details.

Subject to Rules of Use. Not valid with other discount offers, unless specified. Coupon VOID if purchased, sold or bartered for cash.

Valid through June 30, 2007

Mention offer PC# 965554 and CDP# 205521

If there's a Hertz Local Edition® location in your neighborhood, call and ask us to come and get you. Advance reservations are required as blackout periods may apply. This offer is redeemable at participating Hertz locations in the U.S. and Canada and is subject to vehicle availability. Highest obtainable upgrade is to a premium class car (Class G). Brand and model are not guaranteed.This coupon has no cash value, must be surrendered on rental and may not be used with any other CDP#, coupon, discount, rate or promotion. Discounts apply to time and mileage only. Hertz standard driver and credit qualifications for the renting location apply and the car must be returned to that location. Minimum rental age is 25 (exceptions apply). Call for details.

Subject to Rules of Use. Not valid with other discount offers, unless specified. Coupon VOID if purchased, sold or bartered for cash.

Valid through June 30, 2007

Mention offer PC# 962975 and CDP# 205521

If there's a Hertz Local Edition® location in your neighborhood, call and ask us to come and get you. Advance reservations are required as blackout periods may apply. This offer is redeemable at participating Hertz locations in the U.S., Canada and Puerto Rico, subject to vehicle availability. This coupon has no cash value, must be surrendered on rental and may not be used with any other CDP#, coupon, discount, rate or promotion. Hertz standard driver and credit qualifications for the renting location apply and the car must be returned to that location. Minimum rental age is 25 (exceptions apply). Taxes, tax reimbursement, fees and optional service charges, such as refueling, are not subject to discount. Discounts apply to time and mileage only. Call for details.

Subject to Rules of Use. Not valid with other discount offers, unless specified. Coupon VOID if purchased, sold or bartered for cash.

Valid through June 30, 2007

Mention offer PC# 962861 and CDP# 205521

If there's a Hertz Local Edition® location in your neighborhood, call and ask us to come and get you. Advance reservations are required as blackout periods may apply. This offer is redeemable at participating Hertz locations in the U.S., Canada and Puerto Rico, subject to vehicle availability. This coupon has no cash value, must be surrendered on rental and may not be used with any other CDP#, coupon, discount, rate or promotion. Hertz standard driver and credit qualifications for the renting location apply and the car must be returned to that location. Minimum rental age is 25 (exceptions apply). Taxes, tax reimbursement, fees and optional service charges, such as refueling, are not subject to discount. Discounts apply to time and mileage only. Call for details.

Subject to Rules of Use. Not valid with other discount offers, unless specified. Coupon VOID if purchased, sold or bartered for cash.

Valid through June 30, 2007

Mention offer PC# 962920 and CDP# 205521

If there's a Hertz Local Edition® location in your neighborhood, call and ask us to come and get you. Advance reservations are required as blackout periods may apply. Normal weekend restrictions for the renting location apply. This offer is redeemable at participating Hertz locations in the U.S., Canada and Puerto Rico and is subject to vehicle availability. This coupon has no cash value and may not be used with any other CDP#, coupon, discount, rate or promotion. Hertz standard driver and credit qualifications for the renting location apply and the car must be returned to that location. Minimum rental age is 25 (exceptions apply). Taxes, tax reimbursement, fees and optional service charges are not subject to discount. Discounts apply to time and mileage only. Call for details.

Subject to Rules of Use. Not valid with other discount offers, unless specified. Coupon VOID if purchased, sold or bartered for cash.

Valid through June 30, 2007

Great Cars, Low Rates, Free Pickup

And Over 5,400 Locations In North America.

Enterprise rent-a-car
Pick Enterprise. We'll pick you up.*

Reserve online at enterprise.com or call 1 888 446-9952.

Up To 20% Off Standard Daily Rates

- To receive this offer, you must log on to **enterprise.com** or call **888 446-9952**.
- You must type in or mention customer **#ETBX6A**.
- No minimum length of rental required!
- Discount will be applied at time of reservation.
- Discount may vary by location and time of rental.
- Coupon must be presented at time of rental.

Enterprise rent-a-car
Pick Enterprise. We'll pick you up.*

See reverse side for details. D59

Up To 20% Off Standard Daily Rates

- To receive this offer, you must log on to **enterprise.com** or call **888 446-9952**.
- You must type in or mention customer **#ETBX6A**.
- No minimum length of rental required!
- Discount will be applied at time of reservation.
- Discount may vary by location and time of rental.
- Coupon must be presented at time of rental.

Enterprise rent-a-car
Pick Enterprise. We'll pick you up.*

See reverse side for details. D60

One Free Weekend Day

- Offer requires a minimum 3-day rental including a Saturday.
- To receive this offer, you must log on to **enterprise.com** or call **888 446-9952**.
- You must type in or mention customer **#ETBX6C**.
- Free day will be applied upon return of vehicle.
- Coupon must be presented at time of rental.

Enterprise rent-a-car
Pick Enterprise. We'll pick you up.*

See reverse side for details. D61

Up To 20% Off Standard Weekly Rates

- Offer requires a minimum 6-day rental.
- To receive this offer, you must log on to **enterprise.com** or call **888 446-9952**.
- You must type in or mention customer **#ETBX6B**.
- Discount will be applied at time of reservation.
- Discount may vary by location and time of rental.
- Coupon must be presented at time of rental.

Enterprise rent-a-car
Pick Enterprise. We'll pick you up.*

See reverse side for details. D62

Up To 20% Off Standard Weekly Rates

- Offer requires a minimum 6-day rental.
- To receive this offer, you must log on to **enterprise.com** or call **888 446-9952**.
- You must type in or mention customer **#ETBX6B**.
- Discount will be applied at time of reservation.
- Discount may vary by location and time of rental.
- Coupon must be presented at time of rental.

Enterprise rent-a-car
Pick Enterprise. We'll pick you up.*

See reverse side for details. D63

Up To 20% Off Standard Weekly Rates

- Offer requires a minimum 6-day rental.
- To receive this offer, you must log on to **enterprise.com** or call **888 446-9952**.
- You must type in or mention customer **#ETBX6B**.
- Discount will be applied at time of reservation.
- Discount may vary by location and time of rental.
- Coupon must be presented at time of rental.

Enterprise rent-a-car
Pick Enterprise. We'll pick you up.*

See reverse side for details. D64

One Free Upgrade

- Valid on Economy through Full-size vehicles.
- To receive this offer, you must log on to **enterprise.com** or call **888 446-9952**.
- You must type in or mention customer **#ETBX6D.**
- Upgrade will be applied at the time of rental.
- Coupon must be presented at time of rental.

Enterprise rent-a-car
Pick Enterprise. We'll pick you up.*

See reverse side for details. D65

Up To 20% Off Standard Daily Rates

- To receive this offer, you must log on to **enterprise.com** or call **888 446-9952**.
- You must type in or mention customer **#ETBX6A**.
- No minimum length of rental required!
- Discount will be applied at time of reservation.
- Discount may vary by location and time of rental.
- Coupon must be presented at time of rental.

Enterprise rent-a-car
Pick Enterprise. We'll pick you up.*

See reverse side for details. D66

One Free Upgrade

- Valid on Economy through Full-size vehicles.
- To receive this offer, you must log on to **enterprise.com** or call **888 446-9952**.
- You must type in or mention customer **#ETBX6D.**
- Upgrade will be applied at the time of rental.
- Coupon must be presented at time of rental.

Enterprise rent-a-car
Pick Enterprise. We'll pick you up.*

See reverse side for details. D67

One Free Weekend Day

- Offer requires a minimum 3-day rental including a Saturday.
- To receive this offer, you must log on to **enterprise.com** or call **888 446-9952**.
- You must type in or mention customer **#ETBX6C**.
- Free day will be applied upon return of vehicle.
- Coupon must be presented at time of rental.

Enterprise rent-a-car
Pick Enterprise. We'll pick you up.*

See reverse side for details. D68

TERMS AND CONDITIONS

Offer applies to vehicles reserved in advance at standard weekly rates for a minimum of 6 days at participating North American locations. All rates are as posted at time of reservation at enterprise.com or by calling 1 888-446-9952. Rental must be 26 days or less and end on or before 6/30/07. Discount may vary by location and time of rental. Discount does not apply to taxes, surcharges, tax reimbursement, airport access and related fees, excess mileage fees, vehicle licensing fees, and optional products and services including, but not limited to damage waiver at $30 or less per day, refueling and additional driver charges. Check your auto policy and/or credit card agreement for rental vehicle coverage. Offer not valid with any other coupon, offer or discounted rate, including weekend special rates. Normal rental qualifications apply. Vehicles are subject to availability. Other restrictions, including holiday and blackout dates may apply. Pickup and drop-off service is subject to geographic and other restrictions. Void where prohibited. Cash value: 1/100¢.

Subject to Rules of Use. Not valid with other discount offers, unless specified. Coupon VOID if purchased, sold or bartered for cash.

Valid now thru June 30, 2007

TERMS AND CONDITIONS

Offer applies to vehicles reserved in advance at standard weekly rates for a minimum of 6 days at participating North American locations. All rates are as posted at time of reservation at enterprise.com or by calling 1 888-446-9952. Rental must be 26 days or less and end on or before 6/30/07. Discount may vary by location and time of rental. Discount does not apply to taxes, surcharges, tax reimbursement, airport access and related fees, excess mileage fees, vehicle licensing fees, and optional products and services including, but not limited to damage waiver at $30 or less per day, refueling and additional driver charges. Check your auto policy and/or credit card agreement for rental vehicle coverage. Offer not valid with any other coupon, offer or discounted rate, including weekend special rates. Normal rental qualifications apply. Vehicles are subject to availability. Other restrictions, including holiday and blackout dates may apply. Pickup and drop-off service is subject to geographic and other restrictions. Void where prohibited. Cash value: 1/100¢.

Subject to Rules of Use. Not valid with other discount offers, unless specified. Coupon VOID if purchased, sold or bartered for cash.

Valid now thru June 30, 2007

TERMS AND CONDITIONS

Offer applies to vehicles reserved in advance at standard daily rates for up to 7 days at participating North American locations. Weekly rates may be available depending on length of rental or for longer rental needs. All rates are as posted at time of reservation at enterprise.com or by calling 1 888-446-9952. Rental must end on or before 6/30/07. **Discount may vary by location and time of rental.** Discount does not apply to taxes, surcharges, tax reimbursement, airport access and related fees, excess mileage fees, vehicle licensing fees, and optional products and services including, but not limited to damage waiver at $30 or less per day, refueling and additional driver charges. Check your auto policy and/or credit card agreement for rental vehicle coverage. Offer not valid with any other coupon, offer or discounted rate, including weekend special rates. Normal rental qualifications apply. Vehicles are subject to availability. Other restrictions, including holiday and blackout dates may apply. Pickup and drop-off service is subject to geographic and other restrictions. Void where prohibited. Cash value: 1/100¢.

Subject to Rules of Use. Not valid with other discount offers, unless specified. Coupon VOID if purchased, sold or bartered for cash.

Valid now thru June 30, 2007

TERMS AND CONDITIONS

Offer valid for an Economy through Full-size vehicle reserved in advance at standard daily or weekly rates at participating North American locations. The upgrade request will be sent to Enterprise along with your reservation of the lower class car. At the time of rental, present this original coupon at the Enterprise counter and if a car in the next higher class is available, you will be upgraded at no extra charge. Rental must be for 30 days or less and end on or before 6/30/07. Coupon may not be used in conjunction with any other coupon, offer or discounted rate. Vehicles are subject to availability. Other restrictions, including holiday and blackout dates, may apply. Normal rental qualifications apply. Pick-up and drop-off service is subject to geographic and other restrictions. Void where prohibited. Cash value: 1/100¢.

Subject to Rules of Use. Not valid with other discount offers, unless specified. Coupon VOID if purchased, sold or bartered for cash.

Valid now thru June 30, 2007

TERMS AND CONDITIONS

Offer valid for one (1) 24-hour day's time charge for a vehicle reserved in advance at standard daily rates for a minimum of three (3) consecutive weekend days, including a Saturday, at participating North American locations. All rates are as posted at time of reservation at enterprise.com or by calling 1 888-446-9952. Rental must end by 6/30/07. Offer does not apply to taxes, surcharges, tax reimbursement, airport access and related fees, excess mileage fees, vehicle licensing fees, and optional products and services, such as refueling, additional drivers, and damage waiver at $30 or less per day. Check your auto policy and/or credit card agreement for rental vehicle coverage. Original coupon must be redeemed at the time of rental and may not be used in conjunction with any other coupon, offer or discounted rate. Normal rental qualifications apply. Vehicles are subject to availability. Other restrictions, including holiday and blackout dates may apply. Pickup and drop-off service is subject to geographic and other restrictions. Void where prohibited. Cash value: 1/100¢. **ERAC Employees: Please RECOMPUTE the Rental Rate, discounting the coupon amount when closing the contract.**

Subject to Rules of Use. Not valid with other discount offers, unless specified. Coupon VOID if purchased, sold or bartered for cash.

Valid now thru June 30, 2007

TERMS AND CONDITIONS

Offer valid for an Economy through Full-size vehicle reserved in advance at standard daily or weekly rates at participating North American locations. The upgrade request will be sent to Enterprise along with your reservation of the lower class car. At the time of rental, present this original coupon at the Enterprise counter and if a car in the next higher class is available, you will be upgraded at no extra charge. Rental must be for 30 days or less and end on or before 6/30/07. Coupon may not be used in conjunction with any other coupon, offer or discounted rate. Vehicles are subject to availability. Other restrictions, including holiday and blackout dates, may apply. Normal rental qualifications apply. Pickup and drop-off service is subject to geographic and other restrictions. Void where prohibited. Cash value: 1/100¢.

Subject to Rules of Use. Not valid with other discount offers, unless specified. Coupon VOID if purchased, sold or bartered for cash.

Valid now thru June 30, 2007

Carnival®
The Fun Ships®
Save an extra $100 per stateroom on a fabulous 7-day Carnival cruise or an extra $50 per stateroom on the newest, largest and most popular 3, 4 and 5 day fleet. This special savings is combinable with our low Super Saver rates...
it's your best vacation value!
SAVE UP TO
$100
See reverse side for details
D69
Carnival®
The Fun Ships®
Save an extra $100 per stateroom on a fabulous 7-day Carnival cruise or an extra $50 per stateroom on the newest, largest and most popular 3, 4 and 5 day fleet. This special savings is combinable with our low Super Saver rates...
it's your best vacation value!
SAVE UP TO
$100
See reverse side for details
D70
Carnival®
The Fun Ships®
Save an extra $100 per stateroom on a fabulous 7-day Carnival cruise or an extra $50 per stateroom on the newest, largest and most popular 3, 4 and 5 day fleet. This special savings is combinable with our low Super Saver rates...
it's your best vacation value!
SAVE UP TO
$100
See reverse side for details
D71

For more details, call your travel agent, call 1-800-CARNIVAL or visit www.carnival.com

Terms and Conditions:

Certificate may be redeemed at any travel agent and is valid on selected 3, 4, 5 and 7 day Carnival cruises departing prior to December 31, 2006.

- Applies to new individual bookings only. Limit one certificate per stateroom.
- Offer is capacity controlled and space may be limited on certain cruises. Certain restrictions apply. Specific cruises may be excluded at any time. Christmas and New Year's cruises will not be available.
- Applies to purchases at the available rates for stateroom categories 6A through 12 (excluding 6E and 9A).
- Offer is combinable with Carnival's Super Saver program.
- Offer is not combinable with any other discount, promotional offer or groups.
- Savings for single occupancy bookings is $50 for 7 day cruises and $25 for 3, 4 and 5 day cruises.
- Only original certificates will be accepted. Reproductions will not be accepted.
- Certificate has no cash value and savings amount is expressed in U.S. dollars.
- Certificate must be submitted with deposit payment. Savings amount may not be deducted from deposit amount.
- Ships registered: Panama and the Bahamas.

TRAVEL AGENT INFORMATION: Request fare code CPEP when making reservations. Please include this completed certificate with deposit. Travel agent commission is based on discounted rate.

Guest Name ______

Booking Number ______

Ship ______ Sailing Date ______

Travel Agency Name ______

Travel Agency Phone Number ______

Subject to Rules of Use. Not valid with other discount offers, unless specified. Coupon VOID if purchased, sold or bartered for cash.

Valid now thru December 31, 2006

ENT1206

For more details, call your travel agent, call 1-800-CARNIVAL or visit www.carnival.com

Terms and Conditions:

Certificate may be redeemed at any travel agent and is valid on selected 3, 4, 5 and 7 day Carnival cruises departing prior to December 31, 2006.

- Applies to new individual bookings only. Limit one certificate per stateroom.
- Offer is capacity controlled and space may be limited on certain cruises. Certain restrictions apply. Specific cruises may be excluded at any time. Christmas and New Year's cruises will not be available.
- Applies to purchases at the available rates for stateroom categories 6A through 12 (excluding 6E and 9A).
- Offer is combinable with Carnival's Super Saver program.
- Offer is not combinable with any other discount, promotional offer or groups.
- Savings for single occupancy bookings is $50 for 7 day cruises and $25 for 3, 4 and 5 day cruises.
- Only original certificates will be accepted. Reproductions will not be accepted.
- Certificate has no cash value and savings amount is expressed in U.S. dollars.
- Certificate must be submitted with deposit payment. Savings amount may not be deducted from deposit amount.
- Ships registered: Panama and the Bahamas.

TRAVEL AGENT INFORMATION: Request fare code CPEP when making reservations. Please include this completed certificate with deposit. Travel agent commission is based on discounted rate.

Guest Name ______

Booking Number ______

Ship ______ Sailing Date ______

Travel Agency Name ______

Travel Agency Phone Number ______

Subject to Rules of Use. Not valid with other discount offers, unless specified. Coupon VOID if purchased, sold or bartered for cash.

Valid now thru December 31, 2006

ENT1206

For more details, call your travel agent, call 1-800-CARNIVAL or visit www.carnival.com

Terms and Conditions:

Certificate may be redeemed at any travel agent and is valid on selected 3, 4, 5 and 7 day Carnival cruises departing prior to December 31, 2006.

- Applies to new individual bookings only. Limit one certificate per stateroom.
- Offer is capacity controlled and space may be limited on certain cruises. Certain restrictions apply. Specific cruises may be excluded at any time. Christmas and New Year's cruises will not be available.
- Applies to purchases at the available rates for stateroom categories 6A through 12 (excluding 6E and 9A).
- Offer is combinable with Carnival's Super Saver program.
- Offer is not combinable with any other discount, promotional offer or groups.
- Savings for single occupancy bookings is $50 for 7 day cruises and $25 for 3, 4 and 5 day cruises.
- Only original certificates will be accepted. Reproductions will not be accepted.
- Certificate has no cash value and savings amount is expressed in U.S. dollars.
- Certificate must be submitted with deposit payment. Savings amount may not be deducted from deposit amount.
- Ships registered: Panama and the Bahamas.

TRAVEL AGENT INFORMATION: Request fare code CPEP when making reservations. Please include this completed certificate with deposit. Travel agent commission is based on discounted rate.

Guest Name ______

Booking Number ______

Ship ______ Sailing Date ______

Travel Agency Name ______

Travel Agency Phone Number ______

Subject to Rules of Use. Not valid with other discount offers, unless specified. Coupon VOID if purchased, sold or bartered for cash.

Valid now thru December 31, 2006

ENT1206

NCL'S
FREESTYLE
CRUISING℠
DIFFERENT THAN
ANYTHING ELSE
ON WATER...
Alaska, Bahamas & Florida, Bermuda, Canada & New England, The Caribbean, Mexican Riviera, Panama Canal & South America
Enjoy savings of:
$200 per stateroom on a cruise of 8 days or longer
or
$100 per stateroom on a 7-day cruise
Save up to $200
NCL
NORWEGIAN CRUISE LINE
FREESTYLE CRUISING
www.ncl.com
See reverse side for details
D72
Alaska, Bahamas & Florida, Bermuda, Canada & New England, The Caribbean, Mexican Riviera, Panama Canal & South America
Enjoy savings of:
$200 per stateroom on a cruise of 8 days or longer
or
$100 per stateroom on a 7-day cruise
Save up to $200
NCL
NORWEGIAN CRUISE LINE
FREESTYLE CRUISING
www.ncl.com
See reverse side for details
D73

TOP FIVE REASONS TO CRUISE WITH NCL

1. FREESTYLE ATTIRE: Wear what you want. Dress according to your mood. It's your vacation. "Resort casual" attire is always appropriate.

2. FREESTYLE DINING: Dine whenever, wherever and with whomever you choose. With up to 10 different restaurants, you'll always find exactly what you're in the mood for.

3. FREESTYLE SERVICE: You're about to be pampered. With almost one crew member per stateroom, you can be assured you'll be very well taken care of when you cruise with us.

4. FREESTYLE ACTIVITIES: Do everything or nothing at all. There's something for everyone: Shore Excursions, Kid's Crew™, art auctions, fitness centers and so much more.

5. FREESTYLE DISEMBARKATION: More guest-friendly. Relax. Linger over coffee. Enjoy every minute of your vacation.

For more details, call your Travel Professional or NCL at 1.800.327.7030

TERMS & CONDITIONS

This coupon may be redeemed at NCL or through your Travel Professional. Savings are per stateroom based on U.S. dollars. Limit one certificate per stateroom. Offer applies to new, individual bookings for Ocean-view, Balcony and Suite staterooms only on select sailings on NCL departing prior to December 31, 2006. Offer does not apply to NCL America cruises. Excludes Christmas and New Year sailings. Excludes Europe and Hawaii sailings. Offer is combinable with Leadership Fares only in Leadership categories. Not combinable with groups, past passenger or promotional fares in non-Leadership categories. Single guests will receive half of coupon value unless paying 200% of applicable fare. Applies to cruise-only and NCL Air/Sea guests. Original coupon must be submitted with final payment. Coupon not applicable retroactively. Do not deduct the coupon value from the deposit amount. Restrictions apply. Ships' Registry: Bahamas. ©2005 NCL Corporation Ltd. All rights reserved.

Travel Agent information: please include coupon with final payment. Agent's commission is based on discounted rate and is not combinable with bonus commission certificates.

Travel Agent Name ____________ Phone ____________

Reservation Number ____________ Booking Date ____________

Ship/Sailing Date ____________ Stateroom Category ____________

Regular Price ____________ Discount ____________ Net Price ____________

Guest Name(s) ____________

Address ____________

City ____________ State/Province ____________

ZIP/Postal Code ____________ Phone ____________

Subject to Rules of Use. Not valid with other discount offers, unless specified. Coupon VOID if purchased, sold or bartered for cash.

Valid now thru December 31, 2006

For more details, call your Travel Professional or NCL at 1.800.327.7030

TERMS & CONDITIONS

This coupon may be redeemed at NCL or through your Travel Professional. Savings are per stateroom based on U.S. dollars. Limit one certificate per stateroom. Offer applies to new, individual bookings for Ocean-view, Balcony and Suite staterooms only on select sailings on NCL departing prior to December 31, 2006. Offer does not apply to NCL America cruises. Excludes Christmas and New Year sailings. Excludes Europe and Hawaii sailings. Offer is combinable with Leadership Fares only in Leadership categories. Not combinable with groups, past passenger or promotional fares in non-Leadership categories. Single guests will receive half of coupon value unless paying 200% of applicable fare. Applies to cruise-only and NCL Air/Sea guests. Original coupon must be submitted with final payment. Coupon not applicable retroactively. Do not deduct the coupon value from the deposit amount. Restrictions apply. Ships' Registry: Bahamas. ©2005 NCL Corporation Ltd. All rights reserved.

Travel Agent information: please include coupon with final payment. Agent's commission is based on discounted rate and is not combinable with bonus commission certificates.

Travel Agent Name ____________ Phone ____________

Reservation Number ____________ Booking Date ____________

Ship/Sailing Date ____________ Stateroom Category ____________

Regular Price ____________ Discount ____________ Net Price ____________

Guest Name(s) ____________

Address ____________

City ____________ State/Province ____________

ZIP/Postal Code ____________ Phone ____________

Subject to Rules of Use. Not valid with other discount offers, unless specified. Coupon VOID if purchased, sold or bartered for cash.

Valid now thru December 31, 2006

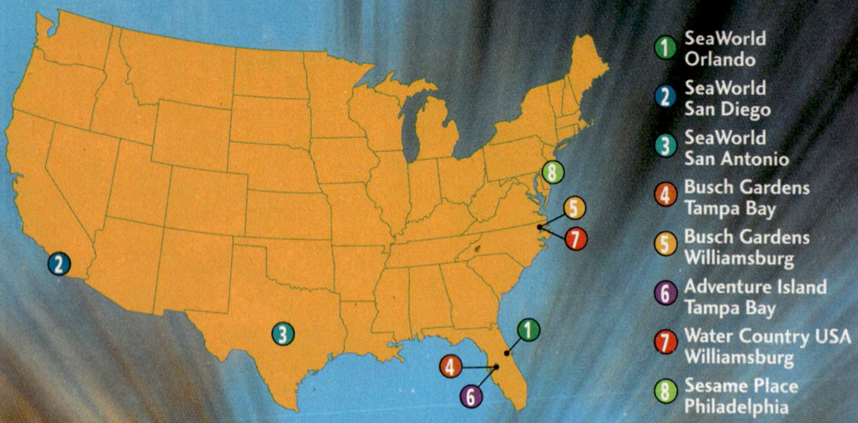

Busch Gardens
WILLIAMSBURG, VA — TAMPA BAY, FL

Not valid with any other discount, special event, special pricing or on purchase of multi-park, multi-day, annual or season passes. NOT FOR SALE. Valid at Busch Gardens in Williamsburg, VA, and Tampa, FL.

A13872 C13871

Subject to Rules of Use. Not valid with other discount offers, unless specified. Coupon VOID if purchased, sold or bartered for cash.

Valid now thru December 31, 2006

SeaWorld.
ADVENTURE PARKS
Orlando, San Antonio, & San Diego

Not valid with any other discount, special event, special pricing or on purchase of multi-park, multi-day, annual or season passes. NOT FOR SALE. Valid at SeaWorld in Orlando, FL, San Antonio, TX, and San Diego, CA.

A13872 C13871

Subject to Rules of Use. Not valid with other discount offers, unless specified. Coupon VOID if purchased, sold or bartered for cash.

Valid now thru December 31, 2006

SESAME PLACE
Philadelphia

Not valid with any other discount, special event, special pricing or on purchase of multi-park, multi-day, annual or season passes. NOT FOR SALE. Valid at Sesame Place in Langhorne, PA.

A13872 C13871

Subject to Rules of Use. Not valid with other discount offers, unless specified. Coupon VOID if purchased, sold or bartered for cash.

Valid now thru December 31, 2006

Adventure Island
TAMPA BAY, FL

WATER COUNTRY USA
Williamsburg, VA

Not valid with any other discount, special event, special pricing or on purchase of multi-park, multi-day, annual or season passes. NOT FOR SALE. Valid at Adventure Island in Tampa, FL, and Water Country USA in Williamsburg, VA.

A13872 C13871

Subject to Rules of Use. Not valid with other discount offers, unless specified. Coupon VOID if purchased, sold or bartered for cash.

Valid now thru December 31, 2006

A VACATION FROM THE ORDINARY®

$7 in Universal Scrip with each 2-Day/2-Park Admission*

Valid for $7 in Universal Scrip with the purchase of each full paid adult 2-Day/2-Park Admission or $5 in Universal Scrip with the purchase of each full paid child (3-9) 2-Day/2-Park Admission.

- Present certificate at front gate at time of purchase.
- Certificate valid for up to (4) people during one park visit.
- Certificate good thru December 31, 2006.

See reverse side for details D78

$10 in Universal Scrip with each 3-Day/2-Park Admission*

Valid for $10 in Universal Scrip with the purchase of each full paid adult 3-Day/2-Park Admission or $7 in Universal Scrip with the purchase of each full paid child (3-9) 3-Day/2-Park Admission.

- Present certificate at front gate at time of purchase.
- Certificate valid for up to (4) people during one park visit.
- Certificate good thru December 31, 2006.

See reverse side for details D79

Meal & Movie Pass

The Meal & Movie Pass entitles one (1) guest to dinner at select Universal CityWalk restaurants. The guest may choose one (1) entrée and one (1) beverage from a select menu. The Meal & Movie Pass also entitles the guest to one (1) movie of guest's choice at the Universal Cineplex located at Universal CityWalk. This pass is valid until used by guest.

This Meal and Movie Pass may be redeemed at any of the following CityWalk Restaurants:

JIMMY BUFFETT'S® MARGARITAVILLE®
HARD ROCK CAFE®
LATIN QUARTER℠
NASCAR CAFE™
NBA CITY
PASTAMORE℠

See reverse side for details D80

EXTRAORDINARY Vacation Offer!

SAVE up to $100 on your next Universal Orlando® Resort Vacation!

Save $50 on any vacation of 4-5 nights or $100 on any vacation of 6 nights or more.* Choose hotel accommodations at one of our 3 magnificently themed on-site resorts or one of the many Orlando area hotels. Your vacation also includes admission to both Universal Orlando theme parks and a CityWalk Party Pass.℠

Use promotional code UNENTBOOK1 to receive $50 savings and promotional code UNENTBOOK2 to receive $100 savings.

Book Online Today at
www.univacations.com/entertainment
or call 877-289-8750

See reverse side for details D81

LOSE YOURSELF...

Give in to your wild side. Scream, shout, laugh and cheer as you experience emotions you'd forgotten you even had. Let loose in the world's TWO most amazing theme parks. Indulge at Orlando's hottest spot for nighttime entertainment. And unwind at one of three magnificently themed on-site hotels. Universal Orlando® Resort is the only place where you can lose yourself – and find yourself – all at the same time.

Universal's Islands of Adventure® Theme Park

Journey through all five Islands of Adventure where you'll defy gravity, escape the jaws of a T-Rex, brave white-water rapids and battle evil high above the city streets.

Universal Studios Florida® Theme Park

At this real working film and TV production studio, an amazing array of rides, shows, movie sets and attractions take you beyond the screen, behind the scenes and into the action and excitement of the movies.

Universal CityWalk® Entertainment Complex

Home to an array of themed nightclubs, restaurants, shops, movie theaters, street performers and more... It's all the excitement of the city neatly wrapped up into one lively package.

UNIVERSAL Orlando RESORT

- Offer not valid with any other discounts, special events, special pricing or on the purchase of Universal CityWalk Party Pass℠, Orlando FlexTicket™ and Annual Passes.
- Not for sale.
- Valid at Universal Studios Florida® or Universal's Islands of Adventure® theme parks.
- Non-transferable.
- No photocopies accepted.

Universal Scrip redeemable toward the purchase of any food or merchandise only at Universal Studios Florida and Universal's Islands of Adventure.

200503001

*Subject to Rules of Use. Not valid with other discount offers, unless specified.
Coupon VOID if purchased, sold or bartered for cash.
Valid now thru December 31, 2006

UNIVERSAL Orlando RESORT

- Offer not valid with any other discounts, special events, special pricing or on the purchase of Universal CityWalk Party Pass℠, Orlando FlexTicket™ and Annual Passes.
- Not for sale.
- Valid at Universal Studios Florida® or Universal's Islands of Adventure® theme parks.
- Non-transferable.
- No photocopies accepted.

Universal Scrip redeemable toward the purchase of any food or merchandise only at Universal Studios Florida and Universal's Islands of Adventure.

200503001

*Subject to Rules of Use. Not valid with other discount offers, unless specified.
Coupon VOID if purchased, sold or bartered for cash.
Valid now thru December 31, 2006

UNIVERSAL Orlando RESORT

*Savings are per reservation and not combinable with any other Universal Orlando® Resort offer. $50 savings is based on 4 or 5 nights minimum hotel and ticket vacation. $100 savings is based on 6 nights minimum hotel and ticket vacation. Travel must be booked by December 17, 2006 and completed by December 22, 2006.

**Not valid for separately ticketed concerts and special events. Some venues may require age 21 or older for admission. Proof of ID required.

Subject to Rules of Use. Not valid with other discount offers, unless specified.
Coupon VOID if purchased, sold or bartered for cash.
Valid now thru December 22, 2006

UNIVERSAL Orlando RESORT

- Offer not valid with any other discounts, special events, special pricing or on the purchase of Universal CityWalk Party Pass℠, Orlando FlexTicket™ and Annual Passes.
- Not for sale.
- Valid at Universal CityWalk only.
- Non-transferable.
- No photocopies accepted.

200501003

Subject to Rules of Use. Not valid with other discount offers, unless specified.
Coupon VOID if purchased, sold or bartered for cash.
Valid now thru December 31, 2006

Hotwire.com[SM]

Save big. Travel big.

Flights
GET $20 OFF ANY DISCOUNTED FARE.
Save even more on our below-published fares!

Hotels
GET $10 OFF ANY ROOM.
Boost the value of 4-star rooms at 2-star prices.

Car Rentals
GET $5 OFF ANY RENTAL.
Our name-brand rentals start at $16.95 a day!

Packages
GET $50 OFF ANY PACKAGE.
Pick your hotel by name and save time planning.

See back for details.

D82

Save Up to $36

LEGO
LEGOLAND® CALIFORNIA

Save $6 on one-day admission to LEGOLAND® California for up to six.

Valid through December 31, 2006

LEGOLAND® California is built for a full day of real family fun with more than 50 rides, shows and attractions. The fun is located in the seaside village of Carlsbad, California, 30 minutes north of San Diego, one hour south of Anaheim. For days and hours of operation call (760) 918-LEGO or visit www.LEGOLAND.com

See reverse side for details

D83

PLANET HOLLYWOOD®

$5 OFF ANY FOOD, BEVERAGE OR MERCHANDISE PURCHASE OF $20 OR MORE

See reverse side for details

D84

PLANET HOLLYWOOD®

$5 OFF ANY FOOD, BEVERAGE OR MERCHANDISE PURCHASE OF $20 OR MORE

See reverse side for details

D85

To redeem your mail-in rebate:*

1. Visit **www.hotwire.com/discount.jsp** You can book your chosen form of travel and find instructions for how to take advantage of your rebate. You must travel between **August 1, 2005** and **December 31, 2006** to qualify for your rebate.

2. Your rebate will appear on your credit card account 6-8 weeks after we receive your request.

Questions? Contact Hotwire Customer Care at 1-866-HOTWIRE.

*Rebate does not apply to cruises or non-Clearance/non-FlexSaver airfare bookings. Mail-in form must be received within 30 days of qualified booking on www.hotwire.com/discount.jsp; no forms accepted after 01/31/07. Rebate open to legal residents of the U.S., age 18 or older at time of entry. Rebates credited to the same credit card used for Hotwire booking. If Hotwire is unable to complete the credit for any reason, Hotwire will not be obligated to fulfill the credit in any other form. Original signed forms only; copies or reproductions will not be accepted. Fraudulent submission could result in federal prosecution under mail fraud statutes. Hotwire is not responsible for lost, late, damaged, misdirected, incomplete, incorrect, illegible or postage due mail. Void where prohibited, taxed or restricted. Hotwire's decision will be final in all matters relating to this rebate. One rebate per Hotwire booking. Offer rights not assignable or transferable. Hotwire reserves the right to verify identification. Offer expires 12/31/06.

LEGO

LEGOLAND

CALIFORNIA

Coupon entitles bearer to $6 off up to six one-day full price admissions. Valid only on the day of purchase at LEGOLAND. Not valid with any other discounts or offers. Children 2 and under are admitted free. Original coupon must be exchanged at the ticket booth at the time of ticket purchase. Restrictions apply. Prices and hours subject to change without notice. **Not for resale. Expires 12/31/2006 NEB**

A-4002 C/S-5002

Subject to Rules of Use. Not valid with other discount offers, unless specified. Coupon VOID if purchased, sold, or bartered for cash.

VALID NOW THROUGH 12/31/2006

PLANET HOLLYWOOD

Not valid with any other offers or discounts. One coupon per table. Excludes alcoholic beverages, tax and gratuity. Valid at participating Planet Hollywood locations.

1 01900 15171 4

Subject to Rules of Use. Not valid with other discount offers, unless specified. Coupon VOID if purchased, sold or bartered for cash.

Valid now thru December 31, 2006

PLANET HOLLYWOOD

Not valid with any other offers or discounts. One coupon per table. Excludes alcoholic beverages, tax and gratuity. Valid at participating Planet Hollywood locations.

1 01900 15171 4

Subject to Rules of Use. Not valid with other discount offers, unless specified. Coupon VOID if purchased, sold or bartered for cash.

Valid now thru December 31, 2006

It's not the places you go,

it's the places you'll come back to

Sunterra offers a variety of spacious and fully-equipped accommodations in some of the most desirable vacation destinations imaginable.

As a special offer for Entertainment® Members, we have discounted vacation packages available to these remarkable destinations...

- Avila Beach, CA
- Sedona, AZ
- Daytona Beach, FL
- St. Maarten, Carib
- Williamsburg, VA
- Branson, MO
- Las Vegas, NV
- South Lake Tahoe, CA
- Orlando, FL
- Scottsdale, AZ
- Gatlinburg, TN

Packages start at just $199 for 4 wonderful days and 3 exciting nights!

That's not per person or per day... that's the entire price of your studio suite accommodations on site at one of our beautiful resorts. Additional packages available for 5-night and 7-night stays ($349 and $499 respectively)!

This is an unbeatable price... and it's all for you, the valued Entertainment® Member.

Call 800.840.5937

M to F, 9-5 PST **Mention code: ZEB**

Visit our website at: **www.sunterravacations.com**
to view our outstanding properties.

This offer is valid through June 30, 2007, and subject to advance reservations and availability.
Prices do not include transportation and no pets are allowed on site at the resorts.

Sunterra®

D86

Guaranteed Best Rate* Hotel Program

Great Hotel Deals Popular Travel Destinations

Go to entertainment.com/hotels or call 1-800-50-HOTEL to check for rates and availability.

Guaranteed Best Rates*

BOOK BY PHONE		BOOK ONLINE
SAVE UP TO* $100 MORE when you book by phone at 1-800-50-HOTEL (1-800-504-6835)	OR	SAVE UP TO* $200 MORE when you book online at entertainment.com/hotels

*See Rebate Rules on page E2 and Program Rules of Use on page E31.

REBATE RULES OF USE

1. You must book and confirm a Guaranteed Best Rate hotel to be eligible for offer. No call-in or faxed rebates will be accepted.

2. The Rebate is only valid for reservations booked and prepaid through this program.

3. Rebate Levels are as follows†:

1-800-50-HOTEL call reservations only:
2 Nights – $10 Rebate
3 or 4 Nights – $20 Rebate
5, 6, or 7 Nights – $30 Rebate
8 or 9 Nights – $50 Rebate, and
10 Nights – $100 Rebate

Online reservation rebates only:
2 Nights – $20 rebate
3 or 4 Nights – $40 Rebate
5, 6, or 7 Nights – $60 Rebate
8 or 9 Nights – $100 Rebate, and
10 Nights – $200 Rebate

4. After Checkout, please cut out and mail this completed form to:
Rebate
807 S. Jackson Road, Suite B
Pharr, TX 78577

5. Not valid with any other offer, including, but not limited to, frequent flyer miles.

6. Form must be mailed in to collect rebates. Rebates will be credited back to your credit card.

7. One rebate per booking number.

8. The envelope must be postmarked within 60 days after your checkout date.

9. "Booking" means a completed stay booked on one calendar day.

10. Our interpretation of the rules of this offer is final.

†All rebates are in U.S. funds.

entertainment®

REBATE CERTIFICATE

Name: ______________________________

Hotel: ______________________________

Date of Stay: ____/____/____ to ____/____/____
(month/day/year) to (month/day/year)

Booking Number: ______________________________

Fill out this rebate form and mail it to: REBATE
807 SOUTH JACKSON ROAD
SUITE B
PHARR, TX 78577

entertainment®

You may print another form from our web site: www.entertainment.com/hotels

Guaranteed Best Rate* Hotel Program

Here's how to save...

1. See "sample" listings on pages E4-E30 or call **1-800-50-HOTEL (800-504-6835)** for savings of up to $100*.

   OR

   Go to **www.entertainment.com/hotels** and book online to save up to $200*.

2. Print your confirmation page or e-mail.

3. Don't forget to mail in your rebate form after your stay.

You do not need to show your Entertainment® card when checking in.

Up To $200 Rebate Available

*See Rebate Rules on page E2 and Program Rules of Use on page E31.

Guaranteed Best Rate*

Book online at **entertainment.com/hotels** for your double rebate.

United States of America

Alabama

Birmingham

ALTA VISTA HOTEL AND SUITES
260 Goodwin Crest Drive, Birmingham.
(800)50-HOTEL.

COMFORT INN BIRMINGHAM EAST
4965 Montevallo Rd., Birmingham.
(800)50-HOTEL.

Gulf Shores

THE BEACH CLUB
925 Beach Club Trail, Gulf Shores.
(800)50-HOTEL.

Alaska

Anchorage

DIMOND CENTER HOTEL
700 East Dimond Blvd., Anchorage.
(800)50-HOTEL.

MILLENNIUM ALASKAN HOTEL
4800 Spenard Rd., Anchorage.
(800)50-HOTEL.

WESTMARK ANCHORAGE HOTEL
720 West 5th Ave., Anchorage.
(800)50-HOTEL.

Arizona

Chandler

COMFORT INN CHANDLER
255 N. Kyrene Rd., Chandler.
(800)50-HOTEL.

RED ROOF INN CHANDLER
7400 West Boston Ave., Chandler.
(800)50-HOTEL.

Flagstaff

AMERISUITES FLAGSTAFF
2455 S. Beulah Blvd., Flagstaff.
(800)50-HOTEL.

BEST WESTERN KINGS HOUSE
1560 East Route 66, Flagstaff.
(800)50-HOTEL.

ECONO LODGE LUCKY LANE
2480 East Lucky Lane, Flagstaff.
(800)50-HOTEL.

FAIRFIELD INN FLAGSTAFF
2005 S. Milton Rd., Flagstaff.
(800)50-HOTEL.

NEW!
Double Your Rebate
By Booking Online!
See page E2

HIGHLAND COUNTRY INN
223 S Milton Rd., Flagstaff.
(800)50-HOTEL.

LA QUINTA INN & STES FLAGSTAFF
2015 South Beulah Blvd., Flagstaff.
(800)50-HOTEL.

QUALITY INN FLAGSTAFF-LUCKY LN
2500 Lucky Lane, Flagstaff.
(800)50-HOTEL.

RADISSON WOODLANDS
1175 West Route 66, Flagstaff.
(800)50-HOTEL.

SUPER 8 MOTEL FLAGSTAFF I-40
3725 N. Kasper Ave., Flagstaff.
(800)50-HOTEL.

Mesa

ARIZONA GOLF RESORT & CONF CTR
425 S Power Rd., Mesa.
(800)50-HOTEL.

BEST WESTERN MESA INN
1625 E. Main St., Mesa.
(800)50-HOTEL.

QUALITY INN PHOENIX MESA
951 West Main, Mesa.
(800)50-HOTEL.

SHERATON EAST HOTEL & CONF CTR
200 North Centennial Way, Mesa.
(800)50-HOTEL.

SLEEP INN MESA
6347 E. Sern Ave., Mesa.
(800)50-HOTEL.

Phoenix

BEST INN
3037 E Van Buren, Phoenix.
(800)50-HOTEL.

BEST WESTERN AIRPORT INN
2425 S 24th St., Phoenix.
(800)50-HOTEL.

BEST WESTERN EXECUTIVE PARK
1100 North Central Ave., Phoenix.
(800)50-HOTEL.

COMFORT INN PHOENIX
5050 N. Black Canyon Hwy., Phoenix.
(800)50-HOTEL.

DOUBLETREE GUEST SUITES
320 N. 44th St., Phoenix.
(800)50-HOTEL.

EMBASSY SUITES
2577 W. Greenway Rd, Phoenix.
(800)50-HOTEL.

EMBASSY SUITES AIRPORT AT 24TH
2333 East Thomas Rd., Phoenix.
(800)50-HOTEL.

EMBASSY SUITES PHX AIRPORT
1515 N. 44th St., Phoenix.
(800)50-HOTEL.

EMBASSY SUITES SCOTTSDALE
4415 E Paradise Village Pkwy S, Phoenix.
(800)50-HOTEL.

HILTON SUITES
10 East Thomas Rd., Phoenix.
(800)50-HOTEL.

HOTEL SAN CARLOS
202 N. Central Ave, Phoenix.
(800)50-HOTEL.

HYATT REGENCY PHOENIX AT CIVIC
122 North 2nd St., Phoenix.
(800)50-HOTEL.

LA QUINTA INN COLISEUM 704
2725 N Black Canyon Highway, Phoenix.
(800)50-HOTEL.

LA QUINTA INN PHX NORTH 908
2510 West Greenway, Phoenix.
(800)50-HOTEL.

QUALITY SUITES CENTRAL
3101 N 32nd St., Phoenix.
(800)50-HOTEL.

RAMADA LIMITED AIRPORT NORTH
4120 E. Van Buren, Phoenix.
(800)50-HOTEL.

SIERRA SUITES METRO CENTER
9455 N. Black Canyon Hwy, Phoenix.
(800)50-HOTEL.

SLEEP INN AIRPORT
2621 S. 47th Place, Phoenix.
(800)50-HOTEL.

SUNSHINE HOTEL AND RESORT
3600 N. Second Ave, Phoenix.
(800)50-HOTEL.

WELLESLEY INN & SUITES MIDTOWN
217 W Osborn Rd, Phoenix.
(800)50-HOTEL.

Prescott

PRESCOTT RESORT & CONF CENTER
1500 Highway 69, Prescott.
(800)50-HOTEL.

Scottsdale

AMERISUITES SCOTTSDALE OLD TWN
7300 East Third Ave, Scottsdale.
(800)50-HOTEL.

BEST WESTERN PAPAGO INN & RST
7017 E Mcdowell Rd, Scottsdale.
(800)50-HOTEL.

CHAPARRAL SUITES RESORT
5001 N. Scottsdale Rd., Scottsdale.
(800)50-HOTEL.

DAYS INN FASHION SQUARE MALL
4710 North Scottsdale Rd., Scottsdale.
(800)50-HOTEL.

DOUBLETREE LA POSADA RESORT
4949 East Lincoln Drive, Scottsdale.
(800)50-HOTEL.

FAIRFIELD INN BY MARRIOTT
5101 N Scottsdale Rd, Scottsdale.
(800)50-HOTEL.

HAMPTON INN OLD TOWN
4415 North Civic Center Plaza, Scottsdale.
(800)50-HOTEL.

RADISSON RESORT & SPA
7171 N. Scottsdale, Scottsdale.
(800)50-HOTEL.

RAMADA LIMITED SCOTTSDALE
6935 5th Ave, Scottsdale.
(800)50-HOTEL.

*See Rebate Rules on page E2 and Program Rules of Use on page E31.

Go to **entertainment.com/hotels** for the entire list of over 15,000 properties.

Guaranteed Best Rate*

Book online at **entertainment.com/hotels** for your double rebate.

SANCTUARY ON CAMELBACK MNT.
5700 E. Mcdonald Dr., Scottsdale.
(800)50-HOTEL.

SUNBURST RESORT
4925 N. Scottsdale Rd., Scottsdale.
(800)50-HOTEL.

THE ORANGE TREE GOLF RESORT
10601 N. 56th St., Scottsdale.
(800)50-HOTEL.

Sedona

LOS ABRIGADOS LODGE
280 North Highway 89-Alt, Sedona.
(800)50-HOTEL.

LOS ABRIGADOS RESORT & SPA
160 Portal Lane, Sedona.
(800)50-HOTEL.

Tempe

AIRPORT QUALITY INN TEMPE/ASU
1375 E. University Dr, Tempe.
(800)50-HOTEL.

AMERISUITES TEMPE MILLS
1520 West Baseline Rd., Tempe.
(800)50-HOTEL.

BEST WESTERN INN OF TEMPE
670 N. Scottsdale Rd., Tempe.
(800)50-HOTEL.

COMFORT SUITES AIRPORT
1625 S 52nd St., Tempe.
(800)50-HOTEL.

MARRIOTT SPRINGHILL SUITES
5211 S Priest Drive, Tempe.
(800)50-HOTEL.

Tucson

ARIZONA INN
2200 East Elm St., Tucson.
(800)50-HOTEL.

COURTYARD TUCSON WILLIAMS CTR
201 S Williams Blvd., Tucson.
(800)50-HOTEL.

QUALITY INN TUCSON AIRPORT
1025 East Benson Highway, Tucson.
(800)50-HOTEL.

RADISSON TUCSON CITY CENTER
181 West Broadway, Tucson.
(800)50-HOTEL.

THE GOLF VILLAS AT ORO VALLEY
10950 N. La Canada, Tucson.
(800)50-HOTEL.

Arkansas

Little Rock

COURTYARD LITTLE ROCK
10900 Financial Center Pkwy, Little Rock.
(800)50-HOTEL.

LA QUINTA INN OTTER CREEK
11701 Interstate 30, Little Rock.
(800)50-HOTEL.

California

Anaheim

ANABELLA HOTEL
1030 W. Katella Ave., Anaheim.
(800)50-HOTEL.

ANAHEIM AT THE PARK TRAVELODGE
1166 W. Katella Ave., Anaheim.
(800)50-HOTEL.

ANAHEIM CARRIAGE INN
2125 S Harbor Blvd, Anaheim.
(800)50-HOTEL.

ANAHEIM PLAZA HOTEL AND SUITES
1700 S. Harbor Blvd., Anaheim.
(800)50-HOTEL.

ANAHEIM RAMADA
1331 E. Katella Ave, Anaheim.
(800)50-HOTEL.

BEST WESTERN ANAHEIM INN
1630 S Harbor Blvd, Anaheim.
(800)50-HOTEL.

BEST WESTERN COURTESY INN
1070 West Ball Rd., Anaheim.
(800)50-HOTEL.

BEST WESTERN PARK PLACE INN
1544 S Harbor Blvd., Anaheim.
(800)50-HOTEL.

BEST WESTERN PAVILIONS
1176 West Katella Ave., Anaheim.
(800)50-HOTEL.

BEST WESTERN RAFFLES INN
2040 S. Harbor Blvd, Anaheim.
(800)50-HOTEL.

BEST WESTERN STOVALL'S INN
1110 West Katella Ave., Anaheim.
(800)50-HOTEL.

CAROUSEL INN AND SUITES
1530 S. Harbor Blvd., Anaheim.
(800)50-HOTEL.

COAST ANAHEIM HOTEL
1855 S Harbor Blvd., Anaheim.
(800)50-HOTEL.

DAYS INN & SUITES
1111 S Harbor Blvd., Anaheim.
(800)50-HOTEL.

DISNEY GRAND CALIFORNIA HOTEL
1600 S Disneyland Drive, Anaheim.
(800)50-HOTEL.

HILTON ANAHEIM
777 Convention Way, Anaheim.
(800)50-HOTEL.

HOLIDAY INN AT THE PARK
1221 S Harbor Blvd., Anaheim.
(800)50-HOTEL.

HOWARD JOHNSON PLAZA
1380 S Harbor Blvd., Anaheim.
(800)50-HOTEL.

JOLLY ROGER
640 W. Katella, Anaheim.
(800)50-HOTEL.

PARK VUE INN
1570 S. Harbor Blvd, Anaheim.
(800)50-HOTEL.

Book Online at www.entertainment.com/hotels or Call 1-800-50-HOTEL (1-800-504-6835)

PORTOFINO INN & SUITES
1831 S. Harbor Blvd., Anaheim.
(800)50-HOTEL.

RADISSON MAINGATE
1850 S Harbor Blvd., Anaheim.
(800)50-HOTEL.

RAMADA INN MAINGATE
1650 S. Harbor Blvd., Anaheim.
(800)50-HOTEL.

RODEWAY INN MAINGATE
1211 West Place, Anaheim.
(800)50-HOTEL.

Bakersfield

BEST WESTERN HILL HOUSE
700 Truxton Ave., Bakersfield.
(800)50-HOTEL.

DAYS INN BAKERSFIELD
4500 Buck Owens Blvd., Bakersfield.
(800)50-HOTEL.

FOUR POINTS SHERATON
5101 California Ave., Bakersfield.
(800)50-HOTEL.

RED LION HOTEL BAKERSFIELD
2400 Camino Del Rio Ct., Bakersfield.
(800)50-HOTEL.

Beverly Hills

BEVERLY HILLS REEVES HOTEL
120 S Reeves Drive, Beverly Hills.
(800)50-HOTEL.

DOUBLETREE LA WESTWOOD
10740 Wilshire Blvd., Los Angeles.
(800)50-HOTEL.

LUXE HOTEL RODEO DRIVE
360 N. Rodeo Dr., Beverly Hills.
(800)50-HOTEL.

ROYAL PALACE WESTWOOD HOTEL
1052 Tiverton Ave., Los Angeles.
(800)50-HOTEL.

Buena Park

EMBASSY SUITES BUENA PARK
7762 Beach Blvd., Buena Park.
(800)50-HOTEL.

HAMPTON INN& SUITES
7828 East Orangethrope Ave., Buena Park.
(800)50-HOTEL.

Burbank

ANABELLE HOTEL
2011 W. Olive Ave, Burbank.
(800)50-HOTEL.

HILTON BURBANK AIRPORT
2500 Hollywood Way, Burbank.
(800)50-HOTEL.

*See Rebate Rules on page E2 and Program Rules of Use on page E31.

Go to **entertainment.com/hotels** for the entire list of over 15,000 properties.

Guaranteed Best Rate*

Book online at **entertainment.com/hotels** for your double rebate.

Carmel/Monterey

DRIFTWOOD MOTEL
2362 Fremont St., Monterey.
(800)50-HOTEL.

HILTON
1000 Aguajito Rd., Monterey.
(800)50-HOTEL.

HOTEL PACIFIC
300 Pacific St., Monterey.
(800)50-HOTEL.

MONTEREY BAY INN
242 Cannery Row, Monterey.
(800)50-HOTEL.

RAMADA LIMITED CARMEL HILL
1182 Cass St., Monterey.
(800)50-HOTEL.

SAND DOLLAR INN
755 Abrego St., Monterey.
(800)50-HOTEL.

SPINDRIFT INN
652 Cannery Row, Monterey.
(800)50-HOTEL.

SUPER 8 MONTEREY/CARMEL
2050 North Fremont St., Monterey.
(800)50-HOTEL.

VICTORIAN INN
487 Foam St., Monterey.
(800)50-HOTEL.

Coronado

EL CORDOVA HOTEL
1351 Orange Ave, Coronado.
(800)50-HOTEL.

HOTEL DEL CORONADO
1500 Orange Ave., Coronado.
(800)50-HOTEL.

LOEWS CORONADO BAY RESORT
4000 Coronado Bay Rd., Coronado.
(800)50-HOTEL.

Costa Mesa

DAYS INN NEWPORT BEACH
2100 Newport Blvd., Costa Mesa.
(800)50-HOTEL.

HILTON COSTA MESA
3050 Bristol St., Costa Mesa.
(800)50-HOTEL.

Fresno

LA QUINTA INN FRESNO 650
2926 Tulare St., Fresno.
(800)50-HOTEL.

RADISSON HOTEL & CONF.CENTER
2233 Ventura St., Fresno.
(800)50-HOTEL.

NEW!
Double Your Rebate
By Booking Online!
See page E2

Garden Grove

EMBASSY SUITES ANAHEIM S
11767 Harbor Blvd, Garden Grove.
(800)50-HOTEL.

HILTON GARDEN INN
11777 Harbor Blvd., Garden Grove.
(800)50-HOTEL.

RESIDENCE INN DISNEYLAND
11931 Harbor Blvd., Garden Grove.
(800)50-HOTEL.

Hollywood

HOLLYWOOD VAGABOND INN
1133 Vine St., Hollywood.
(800)50-HOTEL.

RENAISSANCE HOLLYWOOD HOTEL
1755 North Highland Ave., Hollywood.
(800)50-HOTEL.

Indian Wells

HYATT GRAND CHAMPIONS RESORT
44-600 Indian Wells Lane, Indian Wells.
(800)50-HOTEL.

MIRAMONTE RESORT
45000 Indian Wells Lane, Indian Wells.
(800)50-HOTEL.

Inglewood

BEST WESTERN SUITES HOTEL
5005 W. Century Blvd., Los Angeles.
(800)50-HOTEL.

Long Beach

BEACH PLAZA HOTEL
2010 East Ocean Blvd., Long Beach.
(800)50-HOTEL.

COURTYARD MARRIOTT LONG BEACH
500 East First St., Long Beach.
(800)50-HOTEL.

HYATT REGENCY LONG BEACH
200 S. Pine Ave., Long Beach.
(800)50-HOTEL.

QUEEN MARY HOTEL
1126 Queens Highway, Long Beach.
(800)50-HOTEL.

WESTIN LONG BEACH
333 East Ocean Blvd., Long Beach.
(800)50-HOTEL.

Los Angeles

BEST WESTERN MID-WILSHIRE
603 S. Hampshire Ave., Los Angeles.
(800)50-HOTEL.

CARLYLE INN
1119 S Robertson Blvd., Los Angeles.
(800)50-HOTEL.

CROWNE PLAZA BEVERLY HILLS
1150 S. Beverly Drive, Los Angeles.
(800)50-HOTEL.

FARMERS DAUGHTER
115 S Fairfax, Los Angeles.
(800)50-HOTEL.

HILTON CHECKERS
535 S Grand Ave, Los Angeles.
(800)50-HOTEL.

LE MERIDIEN BEVERLY HILLS
465 S La Cienega Blvd., Los Angeles.
(800)50-HOTEL.

LOEWS BEVERLY HILLS
1224 S Beverwill Drive, Los Angeles.
(800)50-HOTEL.

LUXE HOTEL SUNSET BLVD.
11461 Sunset Blvd, Los Angeles.
(800)50-HOTEL.

MARRIOTT LOS ANGELES DOWNTOWN
333 S Figueroa St., Los Angeles.
(800)50-HOTEL.

MAYFAIR HOTEL
1256 West Seventh St., Los Angeles.
(800)50-HOTEL.

MILLENNIUM BILTMORE
506 S Grand Ave., Los Angeles.
(800)50-HOTEL.

MIYAKO HOTEL LOS ANGELES
328 East 1st St., Los Angeles.
(800)50-HOTEL.

NEW OTANI
120 S Los Angeles, Los Angeles.
(800)50-HOTEL.

RADISSON WILSHIRE PLAZA
3515 Wilshire Blvd., Los Angeles.
(800)50-HOTEL.

SAHARAN MOTOR HOTEL
7212 Sunset Blvd., Hollywood.
(800)50-HOTEL.

SUPER 8 MOTEL HOLLYWOOD
1536 North Western Ave., Hollywood.
(800)50-HOTEL.

WESTIN BONAVENTURE
404 S Figueroa St., Los Angeles.
(800)50-HOTEL.

Los Angeles Int'l Airport

EL SEGUNDO COURTYARD
2000 E. Mariposa, El Segundo.
(800)50-HOTEL.

HILTON LOS ANGELES AIRPORT
5711 West Century Blvd., Los Angeles.
(800)50-HOTEL.

LAX PLAZA HOTEL
6333 Bristol Parkway, Culver City.
(800)50-HOTEL.

LOS ANGELES AIRPORT MARRIOTT
5855 W Century Blvd., Los Angeles.
(800)50-HOTEL.

RADISSON LOS ANGELES WESTSIDE
6161 West Centinella Ave., Culver City.
(800)50-HOTEL.

RAMADA PLAZA LAX NORTH
6333 Bristol Parkway, Culver City.
(800)50-HOTEL.

SUNBURST SPA & SUITES MOTEL
3900 Sepulveda Blvd., Culver City.
(800)50-HOTEL.

TRAVELODGE CULVER CITY
11180 Washington Pl, Culver City.
(800)50-HOTEL.

*See Rebate Rules on page E2 and Program Rules of Use on page E31.

Go to **entertainment.com/hotels** for the entire list of over 15,000 properties.

Guaranteed Best Rate*

Book online at **entertainment.com/hotels** for your double rebate.

TRAVELODGE LAX S
1804 E. Sycamore, El Segundo.
(800)50-HOTEL.

Marina Del Rey

BEST WESTERN JAMAICA BAY INN
4175 Admiralty Way, Marina Del Rey.
(800)50-HOTEL.

MARINA DEL REY HOTEL
13534 Bali Way, Marina Del Rey.
(800)50-HOTEL.

Modesto

RED LION
1612 Sisk Rd., Modesto.
(800)50-HOTEL.

Napa Valley

NAPA RIVER INN
500 Main St., Napa.
(800)50-HOTEL.

Oakland

BEST WESTERN INN AT THE SQUARE
233 BRd.way, Oakland.
(800)50-HOTEL.

COMFORT INN & SUITES
8452 Edes Ave., Oakland.
(800)50-HOTEL.

JACK LONDON INN
444 Embarcadero W, Oakland.
(800)50-HOTEL.

Oceanside

GUEST HOUSE INN OCEANSIDE
1103 North Coast Highway, Oceanside.
(800)50-HOTEL.

RAMADA LIMITED OCEANSIDE
1440 Mission Ave., Oceanside.
(800)50-HOTEL.

Orange

BEST VALUE INN & SUITES
3101 West Chapman Ave., Orange.
(800)50-HOTEL.

COUNTRY INN BY AYRES-ANAHEIM
3737 West Chapman Ave., Orange.
(800)50-HOTEL.

Palm Springs

CALIENTE TROPICS RESORT
411 East Palm Canyon Dr., Palm Springs.
(800)50-HOTEL.

CAMBRIDGE INN
1277 S. Palm Canyon, Palm Springs.
(800)50-HOTEL.

COMFORT INN PALM SPRINGS
390 S. Indian Canyon Dr, Palm Springs.
(800)50-HOTEL.

DESERT LODGE
1177 S. Palm Canyon Dr., Palm Springs.
(800)50-HOTEL.

HOWARD JOHNSON EXPRESS INN
2000 North Palm Canyon Dr., Palm Springs.
(800)50-HOTEL.

MARQUIS VILLAS RESORT
140 S. Calle Encillia, Palm Springs.
(800)50-HOTEL.

PALM COURT INN
1983 N. Palm Canyon Dr., Palm Springs.
(800)50-HOTEL.

PALM MOUNTAIN RESORT & SPA
155 Belardo Rd., Palm Springs.
(800)50-HOTEL.

PALM SPRINGS RIVIERA RESORT
1600 North Indian Canyon Dr., Palm Springs.
(800)50-HOTEL.

PARKER PALM SPRINGS, MERIDIEN
4200 East Palm Canyon, Palm Springs.
(800)50-HOTEL.

SHILO INN PALM SPRINGS
1875 North Palm Canyon Dr., Palm Springs.
(800)50-HOTEL.

Palo Alto

DAYS INN - PALO ALTO
4238 El Camino Real, Palo Alto.
(800)50-HOTEL.

RICKEYS, A HYATT HOTEL
4219 El Camino Real, Palo Alto.
(800)50-HOTEL.

Pismo Beach

COTTAGE INN BY THE SEA
2351 Price St., Pismo Beach.
(800)50-HOTEL.

ROSE GARDEN INN PISMO BEACH
230 Five Cities Drive, Pismo Beach.
(800)50-HOTEL.

SANDCASTLE INN
100 Stimson Ave., Pismo Beach.
(800)50-HOTEL.

Pleasanton

FOUR POINTS PLEASANTON
5115 Hopyard Rd., Pleasanton.
(800)50-HOTEL.

GUESTHOUSE INN & SUITES
2025 Santa Rita Rd., Pleasanton.
(800)50-HOTEL.

Rancho Cordova

HILTON SACRAMENTO ARDEN WEST
2200 Harvard St., Sacramento.
(800)50-HOTEL.

Sacramento

BEST VALUE CAPITAL INN&SUITES
228 Jibboom St., Sacramento.
(800)50-HOTEL.

BEST WESTERN EXPO INN
1413 Howe Ave., Sacramento.
(800)50-HOTEL.

COURTYARD SACRAMENTO
4422 Y St., Sacramento.
(800)50-HOTEL.

Book Online at www.entertainment.com/hotels or Call 1-800-50-HOTEL (1-800-504-6835)

GOOD NITE INN SACRAMENTO
25 Howe Ave., Sacramento.
(800)50-HOTEL.

HAWTHORN SUITES
321 Bercut Drive, Sacramento.
(800)50-HOTEL.

HYATT REGENCY SACRAMENTO
1209 L St., Sacramento.
(800)50-HOTEL.

LA QUINTA INN SACRAMENTO DWTWN
200 Jibboom St., Sacramento.
(800)50-HOTEL.

RADISSON HOTEL SACRAMENTO
500 Leisure Lane, Sacramento.
(800)50-HOTEL.

San Diego

BEST WESTERN MISSION BAY
2575 Clairemont Drive, San Diego.
(800)50-HOTEL.

COMFORT INN & SUITES SEAWORLD
2485 Hotel Circle Place, San Diego.
(800)50-HOTEL.

COMFORT INN MISSION VALLEY
2201 Hotel Circle S, San Diego.
(800)50-HOTEL.

DAYS INN & SUITES SEAWORLD
3350 Rosecrans St, San Diego.
(800)50-HOTEL.

DAYS INN MISSION BAY
4540 Mission Bay Dr., San Diego.
(800)50-HOTEL.

EMPRESS HOTEL
7766 Fay Ave., La Jolla.
(800)50-HOTEL.

GOLDEN TRIANGLE INN
5550 Clairmont Mesa Blvd., San Diego.
(800)50-HOTEL.

GOOD NITE INN QUALCOMM STADIUM
4545 Waring Rd., San Diego
(800)50-HOTEL.

HAMPTON INN DEL MAR
11920 El Camino Real, San Diego.
(800)50-HOTEL.

HARBORVIEW INN
550 West Grape St., San Diego.
(800)50-HOTEL.

HILTON AIRPORT/HARBOR ISLAND
1960 Harbor Island Dr., San Diego.
(800)50-HOTEL.

HILTON GASLAMP QUARTER
401 K St., San Diego.
(800)50-HOTEL.

HILTON LA JOLLA TORREY PINES
10950 North Torrey Pines Rd, La Jolla.
(800)50-HOTEL.

HILTON SAN DIEGO RESORT
1775 East Mission Bay Drive, San Diego.
(800)50-HOTEL.

*See Rebate Rules on page E2 and Program Rules of Use on page E31.

Go to **entertainment.com/hotels** for the entire list of over 15,000 properties.

Guaranteed Best Rate*

Book online at **entertainment.com/hotels** for your double rebate.

HUMPHREY'S HALF MOON & SUITES
2303 Shelter Island Dr., San Diego.
(800)50-HOTEL.

HYATT REGENCY ISLANDIA
1441 Quivira Rd, San Diego.
(800)50-HOTEL.

LA COSTA RESORT AND SPA
2100 Costa Del Mar Rd., Carlsbad.
(800)50-HOTEL.

LA QUINTA RANCHO PENASQUITOS
10185 Paseo Montril, San Diego.
(800)50-HOTEL.

LA VALENCIA HOTEL
1132 Prospect St., La Jolla.
(800)50-HOTEL.

LITTLE ITALY INN
505 West Grape St, San Diego.
(800)50-HOTEL.

MOTEL 6 SAN DIEGO AIRPORT
2353 Pacific Highway, San Diego.
(800)50-HOTEL.

OLD TOWN WESTERN INN & SUITES
3889 Arista St., San Diego.
(800)50-HOTEL.

OLYMPIC RESORT
6111 El Camino Real, Carlsbad.
(800)50-HOTEL.

PACIFIC SHORES INN
4802 Mission Blvd, San Diego.
(800)50-HOTEL.

RADISSON LA JOLLA
3299 Holiday Ct, La Jolla.
(800)50-HOTEL.

RAMADA INN & SUITES CARLSBAD
751 Macadamia Drive, Carlsbad.
(800)50-HOTEL.

SEASIDE INN SAN DIEGO
1315 Morena Blvd., San Diego.
(800)50-HOTEL.

SHERATON SAN DIEGO HOTEL
1433 Camino De Rio S, San Diego.
(800)50-HOTEL.

THE LODGE AT TORREY PINES
11480 North Torrey Pines Rd, La Jolla.
(800)50-HOTEL.

San Francisco

ALAMO SQUARE INN
719 Scott St., San Francisco.
(800)50-HOTEL.

BERESFORD ARMS HOTEL
701 Post St., San Francisco.
(800)50-HOTEL.

BERESFORD HOTEL
635 Sutter St., San Francisco.
(800)50-HOTEL.

BEST INN FISHERMAN'S WHARF
2850 Van Ness Ave., San Francisco.
(800)50-HOTEL.

BRD.WAY MANOR INN
2201 Van Ness Ave., San Francisco.
(800)50-HOTEL.

CASTLE INN
1565 Broadway, San Francisco.
(800)50-HOTEL.

DAYS INN CIVIC CENTER
465 Grove St., San Francisco.
(800)50-HOTEL.

EDWARD II INN & SUITES
3155 Scott St., San Francisco.
(800)50-HOTEL.

GRAND HYATT SAN FRANCISCO
345 Stockton St., San Francisco.
(800)50-HOTEL.

HOTEL DIVA
440 Geary St., San Francisco.
(800)50-HOTEL.

HOTEL DRISCO - JOIE DE VIVRE
2901 Pacific Ave., San Francisco.
(800)50-HOTEL.

LAUREL INN - JOIE DE VIVRE
444 Presidio Ave., San Francisco.
(800)50-HOTEL.

MARINA INN
3110 Octavia St., San Francisco.
(800)50-HOTEL.

NOB HILL MOTOR INN
1630 Pacific Ave., San Francisco.
(800)50-HOTEL.

PACIFIC MOTOR INN
2599 Lombard St., San Francisco.
(800)50-HOTEL.

RED VICTORIAN BED & BREAKFAST
1665 Haight St., San Francisco.
(800)50-HOTEL.

SERRANO HOTEL
405 Taylor St., San Francisco.
(800)50-HOTEL.

THE AMSTERDAM HOTEL
749 Taylor St., San Francisco.
(800)50-HOTEL.

THE HALCYON HOTEL B & B
649 Jones St., San Francisco.
(800)50-HOTEL.

WARWICK REGIS HOTEL
490 Geary St., San Francisco.
(800)50-HOTEL.

WESTIN ST. FRANCIS
335 Powell St., San Francisco.
(800)50-HOTEL.

WHARF INN
2601 Mason St., San Francisco.
(800)50-HOTEL.

San Francisco Int'l Airport

COMFORT INN AIRPORT
1390 El Camino Real, Millbrae.
(800)50-HOTEL.

COMFORT SUITES S
121 East Grand Ave., S San Francisco.
(800)50-HOTEL.

EMBASSY SUITES SFO AIRPORT
150 Anza Blvd., Burlingame.
(800)50-HOTEL.

FOUR POINTS SHERATON AIRPORT
264 S Airport Blvd., S San Francisco.
(800)50-HOTEL.

HYATT REGENCY SFO AIRPORT
1333 Bayshore Highway, Burlingame.
(800)50-HOTEL.

LA QUINTA INN SFO AIRPORT 659
20 Airport Blvd, S San Francisco.
(800)50-HOTEL.

QUALITY SUITES MILLBRAE
250 El Camino Real, Millbrae.
(800)50-HOTEL.

SHERATON GATEWAY
600 Airport Blvd., Burlingame.
(800)50-HOTEL.

TRAVELODGE AIRPORT
326 S Airport Blvd, S San Francisco.
(800)50-HOTEL.

TRAVELODGE AIRPORT S
110 S Elcamino, Millbrae.
(800)50-HOTEL.

WINGATE INN SFO AIRPORT
373 S Airport Blvd., S San Francisco.
(800)50-HOTEL.

San Jose

ADLON HOTEL
1275 North Fourth St., San Jose.
(800)50-HOTEL.

EXECUTIVE INN AIRPORT
1310 N. First St., San Jose.
(800)50-HOTEL.

SANTA CLARA INN SAN JOSE
2188 Alameda, San Jose.
(800)50-HOTEL.

TRAVELODGE CONVENTION CENTER
1415 Monterey Rd., San Jose.
(800)50-HOTEL.

VAGABOND INN SAN JOSE
1488 N. First St., San Jose.
(800)50-HOTEL.

Santa Ana

DOUBLETREE CLUB ORANGE COUNTY
7 Hutton Centre Drive, Santa Ana.
(800)50-HOTEL.

EMBASSY SUITES, SANTA ANA
1325 E. Dyer Rd., Santa Ana.
(800)50-HOTEL.

RAMADA INN ORANGE COUNTY
1600 E. 1st St., Santa Ana.
(800)50-HOTEL.

Santa Barbara

HARBOR HOUSE INN
104 Bath St., Santa Barbara.
(800)50-HOTEL.

MONTECITO INN
1295 Coast Village Rd., Santa Barbara.
(800)50-HOTEL.

RADISSON HOTEL SANTA BARBARA
1111 E. Cabrillo Blvd., Santa Barbara.
(800)50-HOTEL.

*See Rebate Rules on page E2 and Program Rules of Use on page E31.

Go to **entertainment.com/hotels** for the entire list of over 15,000 properties.

Guaranteed Best Rate*

Book online at **entertainment.com/hotels** for your double rebate.

Santa Clara

RAMADA LIMITED SANTA CLARA
1655 El Camino Real, Santa Clara.
(800)50-HOTEL.

TRAVELODGE SANTA CLARA
3477 El Camino Real, Santa Clara.
(800)50-HOTEL.

VAGABOND INN SANTA CLARA
3580 El Camino Real, Santa Clara.
(800)50-HOTEL.

South Lake Tahoe

ECONO LODGE S LAKE TAHOE
3536 Lake Tahoe Blvd, Lake Tahoe.
(800)50-HOTEL.

THE BLOCK
4143 Cedar Avenue, South Lake Tahoe.
(800)50-HOTEL.

Sunnyvale

BEST WESTERN SILICON VALLEY
600 North Mathilda Ave., Sunnyvale.
(800)50-HOTEL.

FOUR POINTS SHERATON
1250 Lakeside Drive, Sunnyvale.
(800)50-HOTEL.

MAPLE TREE INN
711 E. El Camino Real, Sunnyvale.
(800)50-HOTEL.

Colorado

Aspen/Snowmass Area

ASPEN MOUNTAIN LODGE
311 W Main St., Aspen.
(800)50-HOTEL.

Aurora/Denver Int'l Airport

AMERISUITES DENVER AIRPORT
16250 East 40th Ave., Aurora.
(800)50-HOTEL.

HEARTHSIDE SUITES BY VILLAGER
14090 E. Evans Ave., Aurora.
(800)50-HOTEL.

Boulder

BOULDER OUTLOOK HOTEL
800 28th St., Boulder.
(800)50-HOTEL.

Breckenridge

THE LODGE AND SPA BRECKENRIDGE
112 Overlook Drive, Breckenridge.
(800)50-HOTEL.

Colorado Springs

BEST WESTERN PIKES PEAK INN
3010 Chestnut, Colorado Springs.
(800)50-HOTEL.

CHEYENNE MOUNTAIN RESORT
3225 Broadmoor Valley Rd., Colorado Springs.
(800)50-HOTEL.

DAYS INN S COLORADO SPRINGS
2850 South Circle, Colorado Springs.
(800)50-HOTEL.

HILTON GARDEN INN
1810 Briargate Pkwy, Colorado Springs.
(800)50-HOTEL.

LA QUINTA GARDEN OF THE GODS
4385 Sinton Rd., Colorado Springs.
(800)50-HOTEL.

LA QUINTA INN & STES COL SPR
2750 Geyser Dr., Colorado Springs.
(800)50-HOTEL.

LE BARON HOTEL
314 W Bijou St, Colorado Springs.
(800)50-HOTEL.

RESIDENCE INN CENTRAL
3880 North Academy Blvd., Colorado Springs.
(800)50-HOTEL.

SHERATON COLORADO SPRINGS
2886 S. Circle Dr., Colorado Springs.
(800)50-HOTEL.

Denver

BEST WESTERN CENTRAL
200 W. 48th Ave., Denver.
(800)50-HOTEL.

BEST WESTERN STAPLETON HOTEL
3535 Quebec St, Denver.
(800)50-HOTEL.

DOUBLETREE HOTEL DENVER
3203 Quebec St., Denver.
(800)50-HOTEL.

DRURY INN/STES DENVER TECH CTR
9445 East Dry Creek Rd., Englewood.
(800)50-HOTEL.

HYATT REGENCY DENVER
1750 Welton St., Denver.
(800)50-HOTEL.

INVERNESS HOTEL & GOLF CLUB
200 Inverness Drive West, Englewood.
(800)50-HOTEL.

LA QUINTA INN CHERRY CREEK 518
1975 S Colorado Blvd., Denver.
(800)50-HOTEL.

LA QUINTA INN DOWNTOWN 901
3500 Park Ave. West, Denver.
(800)50-HOTEL.

QUALITY SUITES-TECH CENTER
7374 S Clinton St., Englewood.
(800)50-HOTEL.

RADISSON STAPLETON PLAZA
3333 Quebec St., Denver.
(800)50-HOTEL.

RED LION HOTEL
1975 Bryant St., Denver.
(800)50-HOTEL.

THE BURNSLEY ALL SUITE HOTEL
1000 Grant St., Denver.
(800)50-HOTEL.

WARWICK
1776 Grant St., Denver.
(800)50-HOTEL.

Book Online at www.entertainment.com/hotels or Call 1-800-50-HOTEL (1-800-504-6835)

Keystone

ARAPAHOE INN
22859 Highway 6, Keystone.
(800)50-HOTEL.

Steamboat Springs

BEST WESTERN PTARMIGAN
2304 Apres Ski Way, Steamboat Springs.
(800)50-HOTEL.

BUNKHOUSE LODGE
3155 S. Lincoln Ave., Steamboat Springs.
(800)50-HOTEL.

CELEBRITY RESORTS STEAMBOAT
1485 Pine Grove Rd., Steamboat Springs.
(800)50-HOTEL.

SHADOW RUN CONDOMINIUMS
2900 Whistler Rd., Steamboat Springs.
(800)50-HOTEL.

STEAMBOAT GRAND RESORT HOTEL
2300 Mt. Werner Circle, Steamboat Springs.
(800)50-HOTEL.

THUNDERHEAD LODGE
1965 Ski Time Square Dr., Steamboat Springs.
(800)50-HOTEL.

Vail

APEX AT VAIL
2211 North Frontage Rd., Vail.
(800)50-HOTEL.

THE VAIL CASCADE RESORT
1300 Westhaven Drive, Vail.
(800)50-HOTEL.

Connecticut

Hartford

RESIDENCE INN HARTFORD
942 Main St., Hartford.
(800)50-HOTEL.

Mystic

AMERISUITES MYSTIC
224 Greenmanville Ave., Mystic.
(800)50-HOTEL.

New Haven

COURTYARD NEW HAVEN AT YALE
30 Whalley Ave., New Haven.
(800)50-HOTEL.

THE COLONY NEW HAVEN
1157 Chapel St., New Haven.
(800)50-HOTEL.

New London

RADISSON HOTEL NEW LONDON
35 Governor Winthrop Blvd, New London.
(800)50-HOTEL.

*See Rebate Rules on page E2 and Program Rules of Use on page E31.

Go to **entertainment.com/hotels** for the entire list of over 15,000 properties.

Guaranteed Best Rate*

Book online at **entertainment.com/hotels** for your double rebate.

RED ROOF INN NEW LONDON
707 Colman St., New London.
(800)50-HOTEL.

Delaware

For this state's listings go to entertainment.com/hotels

District Of Columbia

Washington D.C.

BEST WESTERN CAPITOL HILL
724 3rd St. NW, Washington.
(800)50-HOTEL.

BEST WESTERN CAPITOL SKYLINE
10 I St. S.W., Washington.
(800)50-HOTEL.

CHANNEL INN
650 Water St., Washington.
(800)50-HOTEL.

CLUB QUARTERS
839 17th St., Washington.
(800)50-HOTEL.

COMFORT INN DOWNTOWN DC
1201 13th St. NW, Washington.
(800)50-HOTEL.

HENLEY PARK
926 Massachusetts Ave., Washington.
(800)50-HOTEL.

HILTON WASHINGTON & TOWERS
1919 Connecticut Ave. Way, Washington.
(800)50-HOTEL.

HOLIDAY INN CAPITOL
550 C S. SW, Washington.
(800)50-HOTEL.

HOTEL LOMBARDY
2019 Penn Ave. NW., Washington.
(800)50-HOTEL.

HYATT REGENCY WASHINGTON
400 New Jersey Ave., NW, Washington.
(800)50-HOTEL.

JURYS NORMANDY INN
2118 Wyoming Ave. N.W., Washington.
(800)50-HOTEL.

KELLOGG CONFERENCE HOTEL
800 Florida Ave., N.E., Washington.
(800)50-HOTEL.

LATHAM GEORGETOWN HOTEL
3000 M St. NW, Washington.
(800)50-HOTEL.

MELROSE HOTEL, WASHINGTON D.C.
2430 Pennsylvania Ave. NW, Washington.
(800)50-HOTEL.

RIVER INN
924 25th St. NW, Washington.
(800)50-HOTEL.

See page E2

SAVOY SUITES
2505 Wisconsin Ave., NW, Washington.
(800)50-HOTEL.

STATE PLAZA HOTEL
2117 E. St. N.W., Washington.
(800)50-HOTEL.

SUPER 8 DOWNTOWN D.C.
501 New York Ave. N.E., Washington.
(800)50-HOTEL.

WASHINGTON SUITES GEORGETOWN
2500 Pennsylvania, Washington.
(800)50-HOTEL.

Florida

Boca Raton

BOCA RATON RESORT & CLUB
501 E. Camino Real, Boca Raton.
(800)50-HOTEL.

FAIRFIELD INN & STES
3400 Airport Rd., Boca Raton.
(800)50-HOTEL.

MARRIOTT BOCA RATON
5150 Town Center Circle, Boca Raton.
(800)50-HOTEL.

Brandon

ASHLEY PLAZA HOTEL
111 W. Fortune St., Tampa.
(800)50-HOTEL.

LA QUINTA INN & SUITES BRANDON
310 Grand Regency Blvd., Tampa.
(800)50-HOTEL.

Clearwater

BELLEVIEW BILTMORE RESORT/SPA
25 Belleview Blvd., Clearwater.
(800)50-HOTEL.

BEST WESTERN SEA WAKE BEACH
691 S. Gulfview Blvd., Clearwater.
(800)50-HOTEL.

DAYS INN ST. PETERSBURG
3910 Ulmerton Rd, Clearwater.
(800)50-HOTEL.

QUALITY HOTEL ON THE BEACH
655 S Gulfview Blvd., Clearwater Beach.
(800)50-HOTEL.

SHEPHARD'S BEACH RESORT
619 S Gulfview, Clearwater Beach.
(800)50-HOTEL.

WINGATE INN
5000 Lake Blvd., Clearwater.
(800)50-HOTEL.

Cocoa Beach

COMFORT INN & SUITES RESORT
3901 N. Atlantic Ave., Cocoa Beach.
(800)50-HOTEL.

HILTON COCOA BEACH OCEANFRONT
1550 North Atlantic Avenue, Cocoa Beach.
(800)50-HOTEL.

LA QUINTA INN COCOA BEACH
1275 North Atlantic Avenue, Cocoa Beach.
(800)50-HOTEL.

WAKULLA SUITES
3550 North Atlantic Avenue, Cocoa Beach.
(800)50-HOTEL.

Daytona Beach

BEACHCOMER RESORT
2000 North Atlantic Ave., Daytona Beach.
(800)50-HOTEL.

BEACHES OCEANFRONT RESORT
1299 S Atlantic Ave., Daytona Beach.
(800)50-HOTEL.

BEST WESTERN MAYAN INN
103 S. Ocean Ave., Daytona Beach.
(800)50-HOTEL.

DAYTONA SURFSIDE INN & SUITES
3125 S. Atlantic Ave, Daytona Beach.
(800)50-HOTEL.

HILTON DAYTONA BEACH
100 N. Atlantic Ave., Daytona Beach.
(800)50-HOTEL.

INN ON THE BEACH
1615 S Atlantic Ave., Daytona Beach.
(800)50-HOTEL.

OCEAN SANDS BEACH RESORT
1024 N. Atlantic Ave., Daytona Beach.
(800)50-HOTEL.

OCEANSIDE INN
1909 S. Atlantic Ave., Daytona Beach.
(800)50-HOTEL.

RAMADA INN SPEEDWAY
1798 West International Speedway Blvd., Daytona Beach.
(800)50-HOTEL.

Deerfield Beach

BEST WESTERN DEERFIELD BEACH
1050 E Newport Center Dr, Deerfield Beach.
(800)50-HOTEL.

COMFORT SUITES DEERFIELD BEACH
1040 East Newport Center Drive, Deerfield Beach.
(800)50-HOTEL.

HOWARD JOHNSON PLZ & CONF CTR
2096 Ne 2nd St., Deerfield Beach.
(800)50-HOTEL.

Destin

COMFORT INN DESTIN
19001 Emerald Coast Pkwy, Destin.
(800)50-HOTEL.

HAMPTON INN DESTIN
1625 Highway 98 East, Destin.
(800)50-HOTEL.

Florida Keys

COMFORT INN KEY WEST
3824 North Roosevelt Blvd., Key West.
(800)50-HOTEL.

DAYS INN KEY WEST
3852 N Roosevelt, Key West.
(800)50-HOTEL.

FAIRFIELD INN KEY WEST
2400 N Roosevelt Blvd., Key West.
(800)50-HOTEL.

*See Rebate Rules on page E2 and Program Rules of Use on page E31.

Go to **entertainment.com/hotels** for the entire list of over 15,000 properties.

Guaranteed Best Rate*

Book online at **entertainment.com/hotels** for your double rebate.

HILTON RESORT & MARINA
245 Front St., Key West.
(800)50-HOTEL.

HOWARD JOHNSON RESORT
Bayside At Mm 102 Overseas Hwy, Key Largo.
(800)50-HOTEL.

MARINA DEL MAR OCEANSIDE
527 Caribbean Drive, Key Largo.
(800)50-HOTEL.

MARRIOTT COURTYARD ON THE GULF
3420 N Roosevelt Blvd, Key West.
(800)50-HOTEL.

QUALITY INN & SUITES
3850 N Roosevelt Blvd., Key West.
(800)50-HOTEL.

RADISSON HOTEL KEY WEST
3820 Roosevelt Rd., Key West.
(800)50-HOTEL.

RAMADA LIMITED KEY LARGO
99751 Overseas Highway, Key Largo.
(800)50-HOTEL.

SHERATON KEY WEST
2001 S Roosevelt Blvd., Key West.
(800)50-HOTEL.

WYNDHAM CASA MARINA
1500 Reynolds St., Key West.
(800)50-HOTEL.

Ft. Lauderdale

BEST WESTERN OAKLAND PARK INN
3001 N. Federal Hwy, Ft. Lauderdale.
(800)50-HOTEL.

DAYS INN OAKLAND PARK
1595 W. Oakland Park Blvd., Oakland Park.
(800)50-HOTEL.

EXECUTIVE AIRPORT INN
1500 West Commerical Blvd, Ft. Lauderdale.
(800)50-HOTEL.

FORT LAUDERDALE BEACH RESORT
4221 N. Ocean Blvd. (A1a), Ft. Lauderdale.
(800)50-HOTEL.

HARBOR BEACH MARRIOTT
3030 Holiday Drive, Ft. Lauderdale.
(800)50-HOTEL.

OCEAN MANOR RESORT HOTEL
4040 Galt Ocean Drive, Ft Lauderdale.
(800)50-HOTEL.

RAMADA PLAZA BEACH RESORT
4060 Galt Ocean Drive, Ft. Lauderdale.
(800)50-HOTEL.

SHERATON YANKEE CLIPPER
1140 Seabreeze Blvd, Ft. Lauderdale.
(800)50-HOTEL.

SHERATON YANKEE TRADER
321 N Ft Lauderdale Beach Blvd, Ft. Lauderdale.
(800)50-HOTEL.

VACATION VILLAGE AT BONAVENTUR
16461 Racquet Club Rd., Ft. Lauderdale.
(800)50-HOTEL.

VILLAS BY THE SEA
4456 El Mar Drive, Lauderdale.
(800)50-HOTEL.

Ft. Myers

COUNTRY INN & SUITES SANIBEL
13901 Shell Point Plaza, Ft. Myers.
(800)50-HOTEL.

Ft. Myers Beach

HAMPTON INN AND SUITES
11281 Summerlin Square Blvd, Ft. Myers Beach.
(800)50-HOTEL.

LANI KAI BEACHFRONT
1400 Estero Blvd., Ft. Myers Beach.
(800)50-HOTEL.

Gainesville

COMFORT INN GAINESVILLE
2435 SW 13th St., Gainesville.
(800)50-HOTEL.

RAMADA UNIVERSITY OF FLORIDA
4021 SW 46th Blvd, Gainesville.
(800)50-HOTEL.

Jacksonville

ADAM'S MARK JACKSONVILLE
225 Coast Line Dr. East, Jacksonville.
(800)50-HOTEL.

BAYMONT INN & STS JACKSONVILLE
3199 Hartley Rd., Jacksonville.
(800)50-HOTEL.

OMNI JACKSONVILLE HOTEL
245 Water St., Jacksonville.
(800)50-HOTEL.

RADISSON RIVERWALK
1515 Prudential Dr., Jacksonville.
(800)50-HOTEL.

THE INN AT MAYO CLINIC
4400 San Pablo Rd., Jacksonville.
(800)50-HOTEL.

Kissimmee

AMERISUITES L.B.V. S
4991 Calypso Cay Way, Kissimmee.
(800)50-HOTEL.

BEST WESTERN EASTGATE
5565 W. Irlo Bronson Memorial, Kissimmee.
(800)50-HOTEL.

CLARION HOTEL MAINGATE
7675 W. Irlo Bronson, Kissimmee.
(800)50-HOTEL.

COUNTRY INN & SUITES KISSIMMEE
5001 Calypso Cay Way, Kissimmee.
(800)50-HOTEL.

DOUBLETREE RESORT VILLAS
4787 W. Irlo Bronson Hwy., Kissimmee.
(800)50-HOTEL.

ECONOLODGE MAINGATE RESORT
7514 W. Irlo Bronson Hwy., Kissimmee.
(800)50-HOTEL.

HOLIDAY INN & SUITES-MAINGATE
5678 Irlo Bronson Hwy, Kissimmee.
(800)50-HOTEL.

HOLIDAY INN MAINGATE WEST
7601 Black Lake Rd., Kissimmee.
(800)50-HOTEL.

Book Online at www.entertainment.com/hotels or Call 1-800-50-HOTEL (1-800-504-6835)

HOWARD JOHNSON MAINGATE EAST
6051 W. Irlo Bronson, Kissimmee.
(800)50-HOTEL.

LA QUINTA INN/STES MAINGATE
3484 Polynesian Isle Blvd., Kissimmee.
(800)50-HOTEL.

RADISSON RESORT PARKWAY
2900 Parkway Blvd., Kissimmee.
(800)50-HOTEL.

RAMADA INN RESORT
2950 Reedy Creek Blvd., Kissimmee.
(800)50-HOTEL.

RAMADA PLAZA & INN GATEWAY
7470 Highway 192 West, Kissimmee.
(800)50-HOTEL.

SUPER 8 AT MAINGATE
7571 W. Irlo Bronson Mem. Hwy., Kissimmee.
(800)50-HOTEL.

TRAVELODGE HOTEL MAINGATE EAST
5711 West Irlo Bronson, Kissimmee.
(800)50-HOTEL.

Lake Buena Vista

BW IN WALT DISNEY WORLD RESORT
2000 Hotel Plaza Blvd. Po Box 22205, Lake Buena Vista.
(800)50-HOTEL.

COURTYARD BY MARRIOTT - DISNEY
1805 Hotel Plaza Blvd., Lake Buena Vista.
(800)50-HOTEL.

DOUBLETREE GUEST SUITES
2305 Hotel Plaza Blvd., Lake Buena Vista.
(800)50-HOTEL.

HILTON WALT DISNEY WORLD
1751 Hotel Plaza Blvd, Lake Buena Vista.
(800)50-HOTEL.

Lakeland

BAYMONT INN & SUITES LAKELAND
4315 Lakeland Park Dr., Lakeland.
(800)50-HOTEL.

Lantana

BEST WESTERN INN OF AMERICA
7051 Seacrest Blvd, Lantana.
(800)50-HOTEL.

Miami

AMERISUITES AIRPORT WEST
3655 NW 82 Ave, Miami.
(800)50-HOTEL.

BAYMONT INN & STES MIA AIRPORT
3501 NW Le Jeune Rd., Miami.
(800)50-HOTEL.

DAYS INN MIAMI AIRPORT NORTH
4767 NW 36 St., Miami.
(800)50-HOTEL.

*See Rebate Rules on page E2 and Program Rules of Use on page E31.

Go to **entertainment.com/hotels** for the entire list of over 15,000 properties.

Guaranteed Best Rate*

Book online at **entertainment.com/hotels** for your double rebate.

DAYS INN MIAMI CIVIC CENTER
1050 N.W. 14th St., Miami.
(800)50-HOTEL.

EMBASSY SUITES AIRPORT
3974 NW S River Drive, Miami.
(800)50-HOTEL.

GOLDEN GLADES INN CONF CENTER
16500 NW 2nd Ave., North Miami.
(800)50-HOTEL.

HILTON MIAMI AIRPORT
5101 Blue Lagoon Drive, Miami.
(800)50-HOTEL.

JW MARRIOTT HOTEL MIAMI
1109 Brickell Ave., Miami.
(800)50-HOTEL.

MICCOSUKEE RESORT
500 SW 177th Ave., Miami.
(800)50-HOTEL.

RED ROOF INN MIAMI
3401 Northwest Lejeune Rd., Miami.
(800)50-HOTEL.

SLEEP INN MIAMI
105 Fairway Drive, Miami.
(800)50-HOTEL.

Miami Beach

BENTLEY BEACH HOTEL
101 Ocean Drive, Miami Beach.
(800)50-HOTEL.

HOTEL NASH
1120 Collins Ave., Miami Beach.
(800)50-HOTEL.

MARCO POLO RAMADA PLAZA
19201 Collins Ave., North Miami Beach.
(800)50-HOTEL.

SOUTH BEACH HOTEL
236 21st St., Miami.
(800)50-HOTEL.

THE ASTOR HOTEL
956 Washington Ave., Miam Beach.
(800)50-HOTEL.

TUDOR HOTEL
1111 Collins Ave., Miami Beach.
(800)50-HOTEL.

Naples

HILTON NAPLES AND TOWERS
5111 Tamiami Trail North, Naples.
(800)50-HOTEL.

HOLIDAY INN NAPLES
1100 9th St. North Us41, Naples.
(800)50-HOTEL.

HOTEL ESCALANTE
290 Fifth Ave. S @ Third St. S, Naples.
(800)50-HOTEL.

NEW!
Double Your Rebate By Booking Online!
See page E2

Orlando

AMERISUITES AIRPORT NORTHEAST
7500 Augusta National Dr, Orlando.
(800)50-HOTEL.

BAYMONT INN & SUITES
2051 Consulate Drive, Orlando.
(800)50-HOTEL.

BEST WESTERN AIRPORT INN
8101 Aircenter Court, Orlando.
(800)50-HOTEL.

COMFORT INN INTERNATIONAL
8134 International Dr., Orlando.
(800)50-HOTEL.

COMFORT SUITES - UNIVERSAL
5617 Major Blvd, Orlando.
(800)50-HOTEL.

COUNTRY INN & SUITES
12191 S Apopka Vineland Rd., Lake Buena Vista.
(800)50-HOTEL.

DAYS INN ORLANDO AIRPORT
2323 Mccoy Rd, Orlando.
(800)50-HOTEL.

FAIRFIELD INN AIRPORT
7100 Augusta National Dr, Orlando.
(800)50-HOTEL.

HAMPTON INN & SUITES INT'L DR
7448 International Drive, Orlando.
(800)50-HOTEL.

HAMPTON INN - UNIVERSAL S
7110 S Kirkman Rd, Orlando.
(800)50-HOTEL.

HAMPTON INN AIRPORT
5767 T.G. Lee Blvd., Orlando.
(800)50-HOTEL.

HILTON GARDEN INN - SEAWORLD
6850 Westwood Blvd., Orlando.
(800)50-HOTEL.

HILTON GARDEN INN UNIVERSAL
6623 Hospitality Way, Orlando.
(800)50-HOTEL.

HOWARD JOHNSON INN INT'L DRIVE
6603 International Drive, Orlando.
(800)50-HOTEL.

LA QUINTA INN AIRPORT WEST 642
7931 Daetwyler Drive, Orlando.
(800)50-HOTEL.

RADISSON PLAZA HOTEL
60 S Ivanhoe Blvd., Orlando.
(800)50-HOTEL.

SLEEP INN - UNIVERSAL
5605 Major Blvd., Orlando.
(800)50-HOTEL.

UNIVERSAL'S ROYAL PACIFIC RSRT
6300 Hollywood Way, Orlando.
(800)50-HOTEL.

Panama City

COMFORT INN & CONFERENCE CNTR
1013 E. 23rd St., Panama City.
(800)50-HOTEL.

LA QUINTA INN/STES PANAMA CITY
1030 E. 23rd St., Panama City.
(800)50-HOTEL.

Panama City Beach

BOARDWALK CONVENTION CENTER
9600 S Thomas Drive, Panama City Beach.
(800)50-HOTEL.

MARRIOTT BAY POINT RESORT
4200 Marriott Drive, Panama City Beach.
(800)50-HOTEL.

Pensacola

HOSPITALITY INN -NAS
4910 Mobile Hwy., Pensacola.
(800)50-HOTEL.

MICROTEL INN AND SUITES
8001 Lavelle Way, Pensacola.
(800)50-HOTEL.

PALM COURT INN AND SUITES
6911 Pensacola Blvd., Pensacola.
(800)50-HOTEL.

RAMADA LIMITED
8060 Lavelle Way, Pensacola.
(800)50-HOTEL.

Pompano Beach

DAYS INN POMPANO
1411 NW 31 St., Pompano Beach.
(800)50-HOTEL.

OCEAN POINTE RESORT
1208 N. Ocean Blvd., Pompano Beach.
(800)50-HOTEL.

PARADISE BEACH INN
1380 S Ocean Blvd, Pompano Beach.
(800)50-HOTEL.

SANDS HARBOR RESORT AND MARINA
125 North Riverside Drive, Pompano Beach.
(800)50-HOTEL.

SPA ATLANTIS RESORT & SPA
1350 N Ocean Blvd, Pompano Beach.
(800)50-HOTEL.

Sarasota

HAMPTON INN SARASOTA BEE RIDGE
5995 Cattleridge Rd., Sarasota.
(800)50-HOTEL.

HELMSLEY SANDCASTLE
1540 Ben Franklin Drive, Sarasota.
(800)50-HOTEL.

St. Augustine

INN AT CAMACHEE HARBOR
201 Yacht Club Drive, St. Augustine.
(800)50-HOTEL.

REGENCY INN & SUITES
331 A1a Beach Blvd, St Augustine Beach.
(800)50-HOTEL.

WORLD GOLF VILLAGE RENAISSANCE
500 S Legacy Trail, St Augustine.
(800)50-HOTEL.

St. Petersburg

HISTORIC COLONIAL INN & SPA
126 2nd Ave., Ne, St. Petersburg.
(800)50-HOTEL.

*See Rebate Rules on page E2 and Program Rules of Use on page E31.

Go to **entertainment.com/hotels** for the entire list of over 15,000 properties.

Guaranteed Best Rate*

Book online at **entertainment.com/hotels** for your double rebate.

HOWARD JOHNSON RESORT HOTEL
6100 Gulf Blvd., St. Pete Beach.
(800)50-HOTEL.

RAMADA INN MIRAGE
5005 34th St. North, St. Petersburg.
(800)50-HOTEL.

THE PIER HOTEL
253 2nd Ave. North, St. Petersburg.
(800)50-HOTEL.

Tallahassee

DOUBLETREE HOTEL
101 South Adams St., Tallahassee.
(800)50-HOTEL.

LA QUINTA INN TALLAHASSEE N
2905 North Monroe, Tallahassee.
(800)50-HOTEL.

LA QUINTA INN TALLAHASSEE S
2850 Apalachee Parkway, Tallahassee.
(800)50-HOTEL.

REGENCY INN TALLAHASSEE
809 Apalachee Parkway, Tallahassee.
(800)50-HOTEL.

Tampa

AMERISUITES BUSCH GARDENS
11408 N. 30Th St., Tampa.
(800)50-HOTEL.

AMERISUITES TAMPA SABAL PARK
10007 Princess Palm Avenue, Tampa.
(800)50-HOTEL.

BEST WESTERN USF BUSCH GARDENS
3001 University Center Dr., Tampa.
(800)50-HOTEL.

BEST WESTERN WESTSHORE
1200 North Westshore Blvd., Tampa.
(800)50-HOTEL.

DOUBLETREE GUEST SUITES
3050 N Rocky Point Dr West, Tampa.
(800)50-HOTEL.

DOUBLETREE HOTEL TAMPA AIRPORT
4500 W. Cypress St., Tampa.
(800)50-HOTEL.

DOUBLETREE SUITES BUSCH GARDNS
11310 North 30Th St., Tampa.
(800)50-HOTEL.

HYATT REGENCY TAMPA
211 N. Tampa St., Tampa.
(800)50-HOTEL.

LA QUINTA INN/STES TAMPA USF
3701 East Fowler, Tampa.
(800)50-HOTEL.

QUALITY INN BUSCH GARDENS
400 E. Bearss Ave., Tampa.
(800)50-HOTEL.

TAMPA RIVERWALK HOTEL
200 North Ashley Dr., Tampa.
(800)50-HOTEL.

TAMPA WESTSHORE MARRIOTT
1001 N Westshore Blvd, Tampa.
(800)50-HOTEL.

Vero Beach

PALM COURT RESORT HOTEL
3244 Ocean Drive, Vero Beach.
(800)50-HOTEL.

THE DRIFTWOOD RESORT
3150 Ocean Drive, Vero Beach.
(800)50-HOTEL.

West Palm Beach

BEST WESTERN PALM BCH LAKE INN
1800 Palm Beach Lakes Blvd., West Palm Beach.
(800)50-HOTEL.

RADISSON SUITE INN AIRPORT
1808 S Australian, West Palm Beach.
(800)50-HOTEL.

WEST PALM BEACH COURTYARD
600 Northpoint Parkway, West Palm Beach.
(800)50-HOTEL.

Georgia

Atlanta

AMERISUITES BUCKHEAD
3242 Peachtree Rd., Atlanta.
(800)50-HOTEL.

AMERISUITES PERIMETER
1005 Crestline Parkway, Atlanta.
(800)50-HOTEL.

ATLANTA DOWNTOWN TRAVELODGE
311 Courtland St. NE, Atlanta.
(800)50-HOTEL.

BAYMONT INN & SUITES ATL LENOX
2535 Chantilly Dr. NE, Atlanta.
(800)50-HOTEL.

COMFORT SUITES GWINNETT MALL
3700 Shackleford Rd NW, Atlanta.
(800)50-HOTEL.

COURTYARD CUMBERLAND CENTER
3000 Cumberland Blvd., Atlanta.
(800)50-HOTEL.

COURTYARD WINDY HILL
2045 South Park Place, Atlanta.
(800)50-HOTEL.

DAYS INN DOWNTOWN ATLANTA
300 Spring St., Atlanta.
(800)50-HOTEL.

DAYS INN EMORY BUCKHEAD
2910 Clairmont Rd., Atlanta.
(800)50-HOTEL.

DOUBLETREE BUCKHEAD
3342 Peachtree Rd. NE., Atlanta.
(800)50-HOTEL.

DOUBLETREE GUEST SUITES GALLERIA
2780 Windy Ridge Parkway, Atlanta.
(800)50-HOTEL.

EMBASSY SUITES CENTENNIAL PARK
267 Marietta St., Atlanta.
(800)50-HOTEL.

EMBASSY SUITES GALLERIA
2815 Akers Mill Rd., Marietta.
(800)50-HOTEL.

FAIRFIELD INN & STES BUCKHEAD
3092 Piedmont Rd., Atlanta.
(800)50-HOTEL.

Book Online at
www.entertainment.com/hotels
or
Call 1-800-50-HOTEL
(1-800-504-6835)

FAIRFIELD INN & SUITES VININGS
2450 Paces Ferry Rd, Atlanta.
(800)50-HOTEL.

HAWTHORN SUITES ATLANTA NW
1500 Parkwood Circle, Atlanta.
(800)50-HOTEL.

HYATT REGENCY ATLANTA
265 Peachtree St. NE, Atlanta.
(800)50-HOTEL.

LA QUINTA INN/STES PACES FERRY
2415 Paces Ferry Rd., Atlanta.
(800)50-HOTEL.

MARRIOTT ATLANTA NORTHWEST
200 Interstate North Parkway, Atlanta.
(800)50-HOTEL.

RAMADA INN SIX FLAGS
4225 Fulton Industrial Blvd., Atlanta.
(800)50-HOTEL.

RESIDENCE INN LENOX PARK
2220 Lake Blvd., Atlanta.
(800)50-HOTEL.

WYNDHAM DOWNTOWN ATLANTA
160 Spring St., Atlanta.
(800)50-HOTEL.

Hartsfield Int'l Airport

DRURY INN & SUITES ATL AIRPORT
1270 Virginia Avenue, Atlanta.
(800)50-HOTEL.

HILTON ATLANTA AIRPORT
1031 Virginia Ave., Atlanta.
(800)50-HOTEL.

RED ROOF ATLANTA AIRPORT NORTH
1200 NE Virginia Ave., Atlanta.
(800)50-HOTEL.

Marietta

COMFORT INN ATLANTA NW
2100 Northwest Pkwy, Marietta.
(800)50-HOTEL.

HYATT REGENCY SUITES PERIMETER
2999 Windy Hill Rd., Marietta.
(800)50-HOTEL.

QUALITY INN ATLANTA MARIETTA
1255 Franklin Rd., Marietta.
(800)50-HOTEL.

Savannah

DAYS INN & SUITES SAVANNAH
201 West Bay St, Savannah.
(800)50-HOTEL.

EAST BAY INN
225 E. Bay St, Savannah.
(800)50-HOTEL.

FAIRFIELD INN SAVANNAH
2 Lee Blvd., Savannah.
(800)50-HOTEL.

*See Rebate Rules on page E2 and Program Rules of Use on page E31.

Go to **entertainment.com/hotels** for the entire list of over 15,000 properties.

Guaranteed Best Rate*

Book online at **entertainment.com/hotels** for your double rebate.

Tucker

RADISSON NORTHLAKE
4156 Lavista Rd., Atlanta.
(800)50-HOTEL.

Hawaii

Big Island

CASTLE HILO HAWAIIAN HOTEL
71 Banyan Drive, Hilo.
(800)50-HOTEL.

HAWAII NANILOA HOTEL
93 Banyan Drive, Hilo.
(800)50-HOTEL.

HILO SEASIDE HOTEL
126 Banyan Drive, Hilo.
(800)50-HOTEL.

KONA SEASIDE HOTEL
75-5646 Palani Rd., Kailua-Kona.
(800)50-HOTEL.

OUTRIGGER KEAUHOU BEACH RESORT
78-6740 Alii Drive, Kailua-Kona.
(800)50-HOTEL.

ROYAL KONA RESORT
75-5852 Alii Drive, Kailua-Kona.
(800)50-HOTEL.

SHERATON KEAUHOU BAY RESORT
78-128 Ehukai St., Kailua-Kona.
(800)50-HOTEL.

UNCLE BILLYS KONA BAY HOTEL
75-5739 Alii Drive, Kailua-Kona.
(800)50-HOTEL.

Kauai

ALOHA BEACH RESORT HOTEL
3-5920 Kuhio Hwy, Kapaa.
(800)50-HOTEL.

CASTLE HALE AWAPUHI
366 Papaloa Rd., Kapaa.
(800)50-HOTEL.

LAE NANI RESORT KAUAI
410 Papaloa Rd., Kapaa.
(800)50-HOTEL.

Maui

GRAND WAILEA RESORT
3850 Wailea Alanui, Wailea.
(800)50-HOTEL.

HYATT REGENCY MAUI
200 Nohea Kai Drive, Lahaina.
(800)50-HOTEL.

KAANAPALI BEACH HOTEL
2525 Kaanapali Parkway, Kaanapali.
(800)50-HOTEL.

KAMAOLE SANDS MAUI CONDO
2695 S Kihei Rd, Kihei.
(800)50-HOTEL.

KIHEI BAY VISTA RESORTQUEST
679 S Kihei Rd., Kihei.
(800)50-HOTEL.

MAUI BEACH HOTEL
170 Kaahumanu Ave., Kahului.
(800)50-HOTEL.

MAUI COAST HOTEL
2259 S Kihei Rd., Kihei.
(800)50-HOTEL.

MAUI ELDORADO
2661 Kekaa Drive, Lahaina.
(800)50-HOTEL.

WAILEA MARRIOTT
3700 Wailea Alanui, Wailea.
(800)50-HOTEL.

WHALER ON KAANAPALI
2481 Kaanapali Parkway, Lahaina.
(800)50-HOTEL.

Oahu

AQUA BAMBOO
2425 Kuhio Ave., Honolulu.
(800)50-HOTEL.

AQUA KUHIO VILLAGE
2463 Kuhio Ave, Honolulu.
(800)50-HOTEL.

AQUA MARINA HOTEL A CONDOTEL
1700 Ala Moana Blvd, Honolulu.
(800)50-HOTEL.

ASTON WAIKIKI BEACH MAUKA TWR
2570 Kalakaua Ave., Honolulu.
(800)50-HOTEL.

ASTON WAIKIKI CIRCLE HOTEL
2464 Kalakaua Ave, Honolulu.
(800)50-HOTEL.

DOUBLETREE ALANA WAIKIKI HOTEL
1956 Ala Moana Blvd., Honolulu.
(800)50-HOTEL.

HAWAII PRINCE HOTEL WAIKIKI
100 Holomoana St., Honolulu.
(800)50-HOTEL.

HILTON HAWAIIAN VILLAGE
2005 Kalia Rd., Honolulu.
(800)50-HOTEL.

HYATT REGENCY WAIKIKI RESORT
2424 Kalakaua Ave, Honolulu.
(800)50-HOTEL.

JW MARRIOTT IHILANI RESORT SPA
92-1001 Olani St., Kapolei.
(800)50-HOTEL.

OCEAN RESORT HOTEL WAIKIKI
175 Paoakalani Ave., Honolulu.
(800)50-HOTEL.

OHANA ROYAL ISLANDER
2164 Kalia Rd, Honolulu.
(800)50-HOTEL.

OUTRIGGER REEF ON THE BEACH
2169 Kalia Rd., Honolulu.
(800)50-HOTEL.

OUTRIGGER WAIKIKI ON THE BEACH
2335 Kalakaua Ave, Honolulu.
(800)50-HOTEL.

PARK SHORE WAIKIKI
2586 Kalakaua Ave., Honolulu.
(800)50-HOTEL.

QUEEN KAPIOLANI HOTEL
150 Kapahulu Ave., Honolulu.
(800)50-HOTEL.

WAIKIKI BEACH MARRIOTT RESORT
2552 Kalakaua Ave., Honolulu.
(800)50-HOTEL.

WAIKIKI GATEWAY HOTEL
2070 Kalakaua Ave., Honolulu.
(800)50-HOTEL.

WAIKIKI RESORT HOTEL
130 Liliuokalani Ave., Honolulu.
(800)50-HOTEL.

WAIKIKI SAND VILLA HOTEL
23475 Ala Wai Blvd., Honolulu.
(800)50-HOTEL.

Idaho

Boise

DOUBLETREE BOISE RIVERSIDE
2900 Chinden Blvd., Boise.
(800)50-HOTEL.

FAIRFIELD INN BOISE
3300 S Shoshone St., Boise.
(800)50-HOTEL.

RED LION HOTEL BOISE DOWNTOWN
1800 Fairview Avenue, Boise.
(800)50-HOTEL.

RED LION PARK CENTER SUITES
424 East Park Centers Suites, Boise.
(800)50-HOTEL.

SHILO INN BOISE AIRPORT
4111 Broadway Avenue, Boise.
(800)50-HOTEL.

SHILO INN RIVERSIDE
3031 Main St., Boise.
(800)50-HOTEL.

THE GROVE HOTEL, A COAST HOTEL
245 South Capitol Blvd., Boise.
(800)50-HOTEL.

Illinois

Arlington Heights

RADISSON ARLINGTON HEIGHTS
75 W Algonquin Rd., Arlington Heights.
(800)50-HOTEL.

Chicago

BELDEN-STRATFORD HOTEL
2300 Lincoln Park West, Chicago.
(800)50-HOTEL.

CONGRESS PLAZA HOTEL
520 S Michigan Ave., Chicago.
(800)50-HOTEL.

DRAKE HOTEL
140 E Walton Place, Chicago.
(800)50-HOTEL.

FAIRFIELD INN & SUITES
216 E.Ontario St, Chicago.
(800)50-HOTEL.

FITZPATRICK CHICAGO HOTEL
166 E. Superior St., Chicago.
(800)50-HOTEL.

NEW!
Double Your Rebate
By Booking Online!
See page E2

*See Rebate Rules on page E2 and Program Rules of Use on page E31.

Go to **entertainment.com/hotels** for the entire list of over 15,000 properties.

Guaranteed Best Rate*

Book online at **entertainment.com/hotels** for your double rebate.

HARD ROCK HOTEL CHICAGO
230 North Michigan Ave., Chicago.
(800)50-HOTEL.

HILTON CHICAGO
720 S. Michigan Ave., Chicago.
(800)50-HOTEL.

HOTEL 71
71 East Wacker Drive, Chicago.
(800)50-HOTEL.

HYATT REGENCY MCCORMICK PLACE
2233 S. Martin L. King Drive, Chicago.
(800)50-HOTEL.

LE MERIDIEN CHICAGO
521 North Rush St., Chicago.
(800)50-HOTEL.

LENOX SUITES HOTEL
616 North Rush St., Chicago.
(800)50-HOTEL.

LOEWS HOUSE OF BLUES
333 N. Dearborn St., Chicago.
(800)50-HOTEL.

MAJESTIC HOTEL
528 West Brompton Ave., Chicago.
(800)50-HOTEL.

MARRIOTT DWNTN AT MEDICAL DIST
625 S Ashland, Chicago.
(800)50-HOTEL.

MILLENNIUM KNICKERBOCKER
163 East Walton Place, Chicago.
(800)50-HOTEL.

SENECA HOTEL & SUITES
200 E. Chestnut, Chicago.
(800)50-HOTEL.

SHERATON CHICAGO
301 E. North Water St., Chicago.
(800)50-HOTEL.

SOFITEL CHICAGO WATER TOWER
20 East Chestnut St., Chicago.
(800)50-HOTEL.

SWISSOTEL CHICAGO
323 E. Wacker Dr., Chicago.
(800)50-HOTEL.

TALBOTT HOTEL
20 E Delaware Pl, Chicago.
(800)50-HOTEL.

THE WILLOWS HOTEL
555 West Surf St., Chicago.
(800)50-HOTEL.

O'Hare Int'l Airport

CLARION BARCELO
5615 N. Cumberland Ave., Chicago.
(800)50-HOTEL.

HILTON O'HARE AIRPORT
Po Box 66414, Chicago.
(800)50-HOTEL.

Rosemont

BEST WESTERN O'HARE
10300 West Higgins Rd., Rosemont.
(800)50-HOTEL.

EMBASSY SUITES HOTEL O'HARE
5500 N. River Rd., Rosemont.
(800)50-HOTEL.

Schaumburg

COMFORT SUITES SCHAUMBURG
1100 East Higgins Rd., Schaumburg.
(800)50-HOTEL.

HAWTHORN SUITES SCHAUMBURG
1251 E. American Lane, Schaumburg.
(800)50-HOTEL.

HYATT REGENCY WOODFIELD-SCHAUM
1800 Golf Rd., Schaumburg.
(800)50-HOTEL.

LA QUINTA INN SCHAUMBURG 562
1730 E Higgins Rd., Schaumburg.
(800)50-HOTEL.

RADISSON SCHAUMBURG
1725 East Algonquin, Schaumburg.
(800)50-HOTEL.

Indiana

Indianapolis

AMERISUITES AIRPORT
5500 Bradbury Ave., Indianapolis.
(800)50-HOTEL.

BAYMONT INN & STES IND AIRPORT
2650 Executive Drive, Indianapolis.
(800)50-HOTEL.

BEST INN INDIANAPOLIS AIRPORT
4585 S Harding St., Indianapolis.
(800)50-HOTEL.

COURTYARD INDIANAPOLIS CAPITOL
320 North Senate Ave., Indianapolis.
(800)50-HOTEL.

ECONO LODGE EAST INDIANAPOLIS
3525 N Shadeland Ave., Indianapolis.
(800)50-HOTEL.

Iowa

Clive

BAYMONT INN & SUITES CLIVE
1390 N.W. 118th St., Clive.
(800)50-HOTEL.

CLIVE HOTEL & SUITES
11040 Hickman Rd, Clive.
(800)50-HOTEL.

Des Moines

DES MOINES COMFORT INN
5231 Fleur Drive, Des Moines.
(800)50-HOTEL.

MARRIOTT WEST DES MOINES
1250 Jordan Creek Parkway, Des Moines.
(800)50-HOTEL.

Kansas

Overland Park

CLUBHOUSE INN & SUITES
10610 Marty, Overland Park.
(800)50-HOTEL.

COMFORT INN AND SUITES
7200 West 107th St., Overland Park.
(800)50-HOTEL.

Book Online at www.entertainment.com/hotels or Call 1-800-50-HOTEL (1-800-504-6835)

DAYS INN OVERLAND PARK
4401 W 107Th St., Overland Park.
(800)50-HOTEL.

DOUBLETREE HOTEL OVERLAND PARK
10100 College Blvd., Overland Park.
(800)50-HOTEL.

EMBASSY SUITES OVERLAND PARK
10601 Metcalf, Overland Park.
(800)50-HOTEL.

PEAR TREE INN K.C. BY DRURY
10951 Metcalf Ave., Overland Park.
(800)50-HOTEL.

Kentucky

Lexington

CONTINENTAL INN OF LEXINGTON
801 New Circle Rd., Lexington.
(800)50-HOTEL.

COUNTRY INN & SUITES
2297 Executive Dr., Lexington.
(800)50-HOTEL.

COURTYARD LEXINGTON NORTH
775 Newtown Court, Lexington.
(800)50-HOTEL.

Louisville

COURTYARD LOUISVILLE EAST
9608 Blairwood Rd., Louisville.
(800)50-HOTEL.

LA QUINTA INN/STES LOUISVILLE
4125 Preston Highway, Louisville.
(800)50-HOTEL.

RED ROOF INN LOUISVILLE EAST
9330 Blairwood Rd, Louisville.
(800)50-HOTEL.

Louisiana

Baton Rouge

BAYMONT INN & STES BATON ROUGE
10555 Rieger Rd., Baton Rouge.
(800)50-HOTEL.

COMFORT SUITES COLLEGE DR.
3045 Valley Creek Rd, Baton Rouge.
(800)50-HOTEL.

EMBASSY SUITES BATON ROUGE
4914 Constitution, Baton Rouge.
(800)50-HOTEL.

LA QUINTA INN BATON ROUGE
2333 South Acadian Thruway, Baton Rouge.
(800)50-HOTEL.

Kenner

BEST WESTERN NEW ORLEANS ARPT
1021 Airline Highway, Kenner.
(800)50-HOTEL.

*See Rebate Rules on page E2 and Program Rules of Use on page E31.

Go to **entertainment.com/hotels** for the entire list of over 15,000 properties.

Guaranteed Best Rate*

Book online at **entertainment.com/hotels** for your double rebate.

LA QUINTA INN AIRPORT 913
2610 Williams Blvd, Kenner.
(800)50-HOTEL.

Metairie

BEST WESTERN LANDMARK HOTEL
2601 Severn Ave., Metairie.
(800)50-HOTEL.

DOUBLETREE HOTEL LAKESIDE
3838 N. Causeway Blvd., Metairie.
(800)50-HOTEL.

SLEEP INN METAIRIE
4601 North I-10 Service Rd., Metairie.
(800)50-HOTEL.

New Orleans

BARONNE PLAZA
201 Baronne St., New Orleans.
(800)50-HOTEL.

CHATEAU SONESTA
800 Iberville St., New Orleans.
(800)50-HOTEL.

COTTON EXCHANGE HOTEL
231 Carondelet St., New Orleans.
(800)50-HOTEL.

DOUBLETREE HOTEL DOWNTOWN
300 Canal St., New Orleans.
(800)50-HOTEL.

EMBASSY SUITES
315 Julia St., New Orleans.
(800)50-HOTEL.

HILTON RIVERSIDE
2 Poydras St., New Orleans.
(800)50-HOTEL.

HOTEL ST. PIERRE
911 Burgundy St., New Orleans.
(800)50-HOTEL.

HYATT REGENCY NEW ORLEANS
500 Poydras Plaza, New Orleans.
(800)50-HOTEL.

INTERNATIONAL HOUSE
221 Camp St., New Orleans.
(800)50-HOTEL.

LA QUINTA INN & SUITES 983
301 West Camp St., New Orleans.
(800)50-HOTEL.

LAFAYETTE HOTEL
600 Saint Charles St., New Orleans.
(800)50-HOTEL.

LE PAVILLON
833 Poydras St., New Orleans.
(800)50-HOTEL.

LOFT 523
523 Gravier St., New Orleans.
(800)50-HOTEL.

MAISON ORLEANS
904 Iberville St., New Orleans.
(800)50-HOTEL.

PARC ST. CHARLES
500 St. Charles Ave., New Orleans.
(800)50-HOTEL.

PONTCHARTRAIN HOTEL
2031 St Charles Av, New Orleans.
(800)50-HOTEL.

QUEEN & CRESCENT HOTEL
344 Camp St., New Orleans.
(800)50-HOTEL.

RENAISSANCE PERE MARQUETTE
817 Common St., New Orleans.
(800)50-HOTEL.

SAINT JAMES HOTEL
330 Magazine St., New Orleans.
(800)50-HOTEL.

SHERATON NEW ORLEANS
500 Canal St., New Orleans.
(800)50-HOTEL.

ST. LOUIS HOTEL
730 Bienville St., New Orleans.
(800)50-HOTEL.

THE RITZ-CARLTON NEW ORLEANS
921 Canal St., New Orleans.
(800)50-HOTEL.

Shreveport

BEST WESTERN RICHMOND SUITES
5101 Monkhouse Dr., Shreveport.
(800)50-HOTEL.

RAMADA INN SHREVEPORT
5116 Monkhouse Drive, Shreveport.
(800)50-HOTEL.

Maine

For this state's listings go to entertainment.com/hotels

Maryland

Baltimore

ADMIRAL FELL INN
888 S BRd.way, Baltimore.
(800)50-HOTEL.

BEST WESTERN HOTEL
5625 O'Donnell St., Baltimore.
(800)50-HOTEL.

FOUR POINTS BY SHERATON
7032 Elm Rd., Baltimore.
(800)50-HOTEL.

HOPKINS INN
3404 St Paul St, Baltimore.
(800)50-HOTEL.

HYATT REGENCY BALTIMORE
300 Light St., Baltimore.
(800)50-HOTEL.

MARRIOTT BALTIMORE WATERFRONT
700 Aliceanna St., Baltimore.
(800)50-HOTEL.

MOUNT VERNON HOTEL
24 West Franklin St., Baltimore.
(800)50-HOTEL.

PIER 5 HOTEL
711 Eastern Ave., Baltimore.
(800)50-HOTEL.

THE HARBOR COURT HOTEL
550 Light St., Baltimore.
(800)50-HOTEL.

Linthicum Heights

EMBASSY SUITES BWI AIRPORT
1300 Concourse Drive, Linthicum.
(800)50-HOTEL.

MICROTEL INN & SUITES BWI
1170 Winterson Rd., Linthicum.
(800)50-HOTEL.

Ocean City

CLARION RESORT FONTAINEBLEAU
10100 Coastal Highway, Ocean City.
(800)50-HOTEL.

COCONUT MALORIE RESORT
200 59th St., Ocean City.
(800)50-HOTEL.

Massachusetts

Boston

BOSTON MILNER HOTEL
78 Charles St. South, Boston.
(800)50-HOTEL.

CHANDLER INN
26 Chandler At Berkeley, Boston.
(800)50-HOTEL.

DOUBLETREE GUEST SUITES BOSTON
400 Soldiers Field Rd., Boston.
(800)50-HOTEL.

EMBASSY SUITES LOGAN AIRPORT
207 Porter St., Boston.
(800)50-HOTEL.

HILTON BACK BAY
40 Dalton St., Boston.
(800)50-HOTEL.

MARRIOTT BOSTON COPLEY PLACE
110 Huntington Ave., Boston.
(800)50-HOTEL.

MARRIOTT BOSTON LONG WHARF
296 State St., Boston.
(800)50-HOTEL.

SHAWMUT INN
280 Friend St., Boston.
(800)50-HOTEL.

THE COLONNADE
120 Huntington Avenue, Boston.
(800)50-HOTEL.

THE ELIOT HOTEL
370 Commonwealth Ave., Boston.
(800)50-HOTEL.

THE NEWBURY GUESTHOUSE B&B
261 Newbury St., Boston.
(800)50-HOTEL.

Cambridge

CAMBRIDGE GATEWAY INN
211 Concord Turnpike, Cambridge.
(800)50-HOTEL.

KENDALL HOTEL
350 Main St., Cambridge.
(800)50-HOTEL.

See page E2

*See Rebate Rules on page E2 and Program Rules of Use on page E31.

Guaranteed Best Rate*

Book online at **entertainment.com/hotels** for your double rebate.

ROYAL SONESTA
5 Cambridge Parkway, Cambridge.
(800)50-HOTEL.

Revere

COURTYARD BY MARRIOTT REVERE
100 Morris St., Revere.
(800)50-HOTEL.

FOUR POINTS SHERATON LOGAN A/P
407 Squire Rd., Revere.
(800)50-HOTEL.

HAMPTON INN LOGAN AIRPORT
230 Lee Burbank Highway, Revere.
(800)50-HOTEL.

Michigan

Detroit

DOUBLETREE METRO AIRPORT
31500 Wick Rd., Romulus.
(800)50-HOTEL.

HOTEL ST. REGIS
3071 West Grand Blvd., Detroit.
(800)50-HOTEL.

Grand Rapids

HILTON GRAND RAPIDS AIRPORT
4747 28th St. Se, Grand Rapids.
(800)50-HOTEL.

RADISSON HOTEL GRAND RAPIDS N.
270 Ann St. NW, Grand Rapids.
(800)50-HOTEL.

Minnesota

Bloomington

FAIRFIELD INN BLOOMINGTON
2401 East 80th St., Bloomington.
(800)50-HOTEL.

HAMPTON INN BLOOMINGTON
4201 West 80th St., Bloomington.
(800)50-HOTEL.

HILTON GARDEN INN
8100 Bridge Rd., Bloomington.
(800)50-HOTEL.

WYNDHAM MINNEAPOLIS AIRPORT
4460 West 78th St. Circle, Bloomington.
(800)50-HOTEL.

Minneapolis

BAYMONT INN/STES BROOKLYN CTR
6415 James Circle North, Brooklyn Center.
(800)50-HOTEL.

COMFORT INN BROOKLYN CENTER
1600 James Circle N, Brooklyn Center.
(800)50-HOTEL.

EMBASSY SUITES DOWNTOWN
425 S 7th St., Minneapolis.
(800)50-HOTEL.

HILTON MINNEAPOLIS NORTH
2200 Freeway Blvd., Minneapolis.
(800)50-HOTEL.

HYATT REGENCY MINNEAPOLIS
1300 Nicollet Mall, Minneapolis.
(800)50-HOTEL.

MILLENNIUM HOTEL
1313 Nicollett Mall, Minneapolis.
(800)50-HOTEL.

RADISSON PLAZA HOTEL
35 S 7th St., Minneapolis.
(800)50-HOTEL.

Minneapolis/St. Paul Int'l Airport

AMERISUITES MALL OF AMERICA
7800 International Drive, Bloomington.
(800)50-HOTEL.

DAYS INN MALL OF AMERICA ARPT
1901 Killebrew Drive, Bloomington.
(800)50-HOTEL.

DOUBLETREE AIRPORT AT THE MALL
7901 24th Ave. S, Bloomington.
(800)50-HOTEL.

HILTON AIRPORT
3800 E. 80th St., Minneapolis.
(800)50-HOTEL.

RADISSON S & PLAZA TOWER
7800 Normandale Blvd., Bloomington.
(800)50-HOTEL.

SOFITEL MINNEAPOLIS
5601 West 78th St., Bloomington.
(800)50-HOTEL.

St. Paul

EMBASSY SUITES ST PAUL
175 East 10th St., St. Paul.
(800)50-HOTEL.

FOUR POINTS SHERATON
400 North Hamline Ave., St. Paul.
(800)50-HOTEL.

Mississippi

Biloxi

BEAU RIVAGE
875 Beach Blvd., Biloxi.
(800)50-HOTEL.

BEST WESTERN SWAN
1726 Beach Blvd., Biloxi.
(800)50-HOTEL.

CASINO MAGIC BILOXI
195 Beach Blvd., Biloxi.
(800)50-HOTEL.

GRAND CASINO BILOXI BAY VIEW
265 Beach Blvd., Biloxi.
(800)50-HOTEL.

GULF BEACH RESORT
2428 Beach Blvd., Biloxi.
(800)50-HOTEL.

Missouri

Branson

ALPENROSE INN
2875 Green Mountain Dr., Branson.
(800)50-HOTEL.

Book Online at
www.entertainment.com/hotels
or
Call 1-800-50-HOTEL
(1-800-504-6835)

AMERIHOST INN & SUITES BRANSON
1000 W Main, Branson.
(800)50-HOTEL.

BEST WESTERN CENTER POINTE INN
3215 W. Highway 76, Branson.
(800)50-HOTEL.

CHATEAU ON THE LAKE RESORT
415 N. State Highway 265, Branson.
(800)50-HOTEL.

HALL OF FAME HOTEL
3005 W Hwy 76, Branson.
(800)50-HOTEL.

POINTE ROYALE
158-A Pointe Royale Dr., Branson.
(800)50-HOTEL.

THOUSAND HILLS GOLF RESORT
245 S Wildwood Dr., Branson.
(800)50-HOTEL.

WELK RESORT
1984 State Highway 165, Branson.
(800)50-HOTEL.

Hazelwood

BAYMONT INN & SUITES HAZELWOOD
318 Taylor Rd., Hazelwood.
(800)50-HOTEL.

LA QUINTA INN ST LOUIS HAZELWD
5781 Campus Court, Hazelwood.
(800)50-HOTEL.

Kansas City

AMERISUITES KANSAS CITY ARPT
7600 Nw 97th Terrace, Kansas City.
(800)50-HOTEL.

BEST WESTERN COUNTRY INN
7100 Ne Parvin Rd., Kansas City.
(800)50-HOTEL.

BEST WESTERN SEVILLE PLAZA
4309 Main St., Kansas City.
(800)50-HOTEL.

DOUBLETREE KANSAS CITY
1301 Wyandotte, Kansas City.
(800)50-HOTEL.

HYATT REGENCY CROWN CENTER
2345 McGee, Kansas City.
(800)50-HOTEL.

RAPHAEL HOTEL
325 Ward Parkway, Kansas City.
(800)50-HOTEL.

THE QUARTERAGE HOTEL
560 Westport Rd., Kansas City.
(800)50-HOTEL.

St. Louis

BEST WESTERN KIRKWOOD INN
1200 S. Kirkwood Rd., St. Louis.
(800)50-HOTEL.

*See Rebate Rules on page E2 and Program Rules of Use on page E31.

Go to **entertainment.com/hotels** for the entire list of over 15,000 properties.

Guaranteed Best Rate*

Book online at **entertainment.com/hotels** for your double rebate.

DRURY INN ST. LOUIS AIRPORT
10490 Natural Bridge Rd., St. Louis.
(800)50-HOTEL.

FOUR POINTS SHERATON WEST
3400 Rider Trail S, St. Louis.
(800)50-HOTEL.

MARYVILLE COURTYARD BY MARRIOT
511 Maryville University Drive, St. Louis.
(800)50-HOTEL.

MILLENNIUM HOTEL ST. LOUIS
200 S 4th St., St. Louis.
(800)50-HOTEL.

Montana

For this state's listings go to entertainment.com/hotels

Nebraska

Omaha

BAYMONT INN & SUITES
10760 M St., Omaha.
(800)50-HOTEL.

DOUBLETREE GUEST SUITES
7270 Cedar St., Omaha.
(800)50-HOTEL.

OMAHA COMFORT INN
10919 J St., Omaha.
(800)50-HOTEL.

Nevada

Henderson

GREEN VALLEY MARRIOTT
2800 N Green Valley Parkway, Henderson.
(800)50-HOTEL.

Las Vegas

ALADDIN RESORT & CASINO
3667 S Las Vegas Blvd., Las Vegas.
(800)50-HOTEL.

ALEXIS RESORT & VILLAS
375 E. Harmon, Las Vegas.
(800)50-HOTEL.

ARIZONA CHARLIES EAST HOTEL
4575 Boulder Highway, Las Vegas.
(800)50-HOTEL.

ATRIUM SUITES
4255 S Paradise Rd., Las Vegas.
(800)50-HOTEL.

BALLYS LAS VEGAS
3645 Las Vegas Blvd, Las Vegas.
(800)50-HOTEL.

BARBARY COAST HOTEL & CASINO
3595 Las Vegas Blvd., Las Vegas.
(800)50-HOTEL.

NEW! Double Your Rebate By Booking Online! See page E2

BELLAGIO
3600 Las Vegas Blvd S, Las Vegas.
(800)50-HOTEL.

BOARDWALK HOTEL & CASINO
3750 Las Vegas Blvd S, Las Vegas.
(800)50-HOTEL.

CAESARS PALACE
3570 Las Vegas Blvd S, Las Vegas.
(800)50-HOTEL.

CIRCUS CIRCUS HOTEL & CASINO
2880 Las Vegas Blvd S Po Box 14967, Las Vegas.
(800)50-HOTEL.

COLORADO BELLE HOTEL & CASINO
2100 S. Casino Dr., Laughlin.
(800)50-HOTEL.

EL CORTEZ HOTEL & CASINO
600 E Fremont St., Las Vegas.
(800)50-HOTEL.

FOUR QUEENS
202 E. Fremont, Las Vegas.
(800)50-HOTEL.

GOLD COAST HOTEL & CASINO
4000 West Flamingo Rd., Las Vegas.
(800)50-HOTEL.

HARRAHS HOTEL & CASINO
3475 Las Vegas Blvd. S, Las Vegas.
(800)50-HOTEL.

HAWTHORN INN & SUITES CASINO
910 S Boulder Highway, Henderson.
(800)50-HOTEL.

HOTEL SAN REMO CASINO RESORT
115 East Tropicana Ave., Las Vegas.
(800)50-HOTEL.

IMPERIAL PALACE HOTEL CASINO
3535 Las Vegas Blvd. S., Las Vegas.
(800)50-HOTEL.

JOCKEY RESORT SUITES
3700 Las Vegas Blvd S, Las Vegas.
(800)50-HOTEL.

MGM GRAND
3799 Las Vegas Blvd. So., Las Vegas.
(800)50-HOTEL.

NEW YORK NEW YORK HTL & CASINO
3790 Las Vegas Blvd So., Las Vegas.
(800)50-HOTEL.

PARIS
3655 Las Vegas Blvd, Las Vegas.
(800)50-HOTEL.

PLAZA HOTEL & CASINO
One S Main St., Las Vegas.
(800)50-HOTEL.

RESIDENCE INN LAS VEGAS S
5875 Industrial Rd., Las Vegas.
(800)50-HOTEL.

RIO SUITES
3700 W Flamingo, Las Vegas.
(800)50-HOTEL.

ROYAL RESORT
99 Convention Center Drive, Las Vegas.
(800)50-HOTEL.

ST TROPEZ ALL SUITE HOTEL
455 East Harmon Ave., Las Vegas.
(800)50-HOTEL.

STRATOSPHERE TOWER
2000 S. Las Vegas Blvd, Las Vegas.
(800)50-HOTEL.

TERRIBLES HOTEL & CASINO
4100 S Paradise Rd, Las Vegas.
(800)50-HOTEL.

THE MIRAGE
3400 Las Vegas Blvd., Las Vegas.
(800)50-HOTEL.

THE PALMS CASINO RESORT
4321 W. Flamingo Rd., Las Vegas.
(800)50-HOTEL.

TREASURE ISLAND AT THE MIRAGE
3300 Las Vegas Blvd S, Las Vegas.
(800)50-HOTEL.

VENETIAN
3355 Las Vegas Blvd S, Las Vegas.
(800)50-HOTEL.

Laughlin

FLAMINGO LAUGHLIN
1900 S. Casino Dr., Laughlin.
(800)50-HOTEL.

GOLDEN NUGGET
2300 S. Casino Dr., Laughlin.
(800)50-HOTEL.

HARRAH'S LAUGHLIN
2900 South Casino Dr, Laughlin.
(800)50-HOTEL.

RIVER PALMS RESORT & CASINO
2700 South Casino Dr., Laughlin.
(800)50-HOTEL.

Reno

ATLANTIS RESORT
3800 S Virginia St, Reno.
(800)50-HOTEL.

CAESARS TAHOE
55 Highway 50, State Line.
(800)50-HOTEL.

CIRCUS CIRCUS RENO
500 N. Sierra St., Reno.
(800)50-HOTEL.

ELDORADO HOTEL CASINO
345 North Virginia St., Reno.
(800)50-HOTEL.

GOLDEN PHOENIX HOTEL & CASINO
255 N Sierra St Po Box 1291, Reno.
(800)50-HOTEL.

HARRAHS RENO
219 N Center Po Box 10, Reno.
(800)50-HOTEL.

HARVEYS RESORT AND CASINO
Highway 50/State Line Ave., State Line.
(800)50-HOTEL.

HOLIDAY INN RENO
1000 E 6th St, Reno.
(800)50-HOTEL.

LA QUINTA INN RENO 545
4001 Market St., Reno.
(800)50-HOTEL.

RENO HILTON
2500 East Second St., Reno.
(800)50-HOTEL.

SANDS REGENCY
345 North Arlington Ave, Reno.
(800)50-HOTEL.

*See Rebate Rules on page E2 and Program Rules of Use on page E31.

Go to **entertainment.com/hotels** for the entire list of over 15,000 properties.

Guaranteed Best Rate*

Book online at **entertainment.com/hotels** for your double rebate.

SHOWBOAT INN
660 North Virginia St., Reno.
(800)50-HOTEL.

SIENA HOTEL SPA & CASINO
One S Lake St., Reno.
(800)50-HOTEL.

SPEAKEASY HOTEL
200 East 6th St., Reno.
(800)50-HOTEL.

SUPER 8 MEADOWWOOD COURTYARD
5851 S Virginia St., Reno.
(800)50-HOTEL.

New Hampshire

For this state's listings go to entertainment.com/hotels

New Jersey

Atlantic City

ATLANTIC PALACE SUITES
1507 Boardwalk, Atlantic City.
(800)50-HOTEL.

BALLYS ATLANTIC CITY
Park Place And Boardwalk, Atlantic City.
(800)50-HOTEL.

CAESARS ATLANTIC CITY
2100 Pacific Ave Arkansas Ave And Boardwalk, Atlantic City.
(800)50-HOTEL.

LA RENAISSANCE SUITES
190 S Kentucky Ave., Atlantic City.
(800)50-HOTEL.

Newark

BEST WESTERN NEWARK AIRPORT W
101 International Way, Newark.
(800)50-HOTEL.

COURTYARD LIBERTY INT'L AIRPRT
600 Route 1 And 9, Newark.
(800)50-HOTEL.

HILTON NEWARK GATEWAY
Gateway Ctr.@ Raymond Blvd, Newark.
(800)50-HOTEL.

HOWARD JOHNSON NEWARK AIRPORT
20 Frontage Rd., Newark.
(800)50-HOTEL.

SPRINGHILL SUITES BY MARRIOTT
652 Route 1 And 9 S, Newark.
(800)50-HOTEL.

New Mexico

Albuquerque

AIRPORT UNIVERSITY INN
1901 University Blvd. Se, Albuquerque.
(800)50-HOTEL.

ALBUQUERQUE MARRIOTT
2101 Louisiana Blvd Ne, Albuquerque.
(800)50-HOTEL.

BEST WESTERN RIO GRANDE INN
1015 Rio Grande Blvd NW, Albuquerque.
(800)50-HOTEL.

CLUBHOUSE INN&STES ALBUQUERQUE
1315 Menaul Blvd. Ne, Albuquerque.
(800)50-HOTEL.

COMFORT INN EAST
13031 Central Ne, Albuquerque.
(800)50-HOTEL.

FAIRFIELD INN ALBUQUERQUE
1760 Menaul Rd. Ne, Albuquerque.
(800)50-HOTEL.

RADISSON HOTEL CONF. CENTER
2500 Carlisle Blvd., Albuquerque.
(800)50-HOTEL.

RESIDENCE INN ALBUQUERQUE
3300 Prospect Ave. Ne, Albuquerque.
(800)50-HOTEL.

Santa Fe

CIELO GRANDE
750 N. St. Francis Dr., Santa Fe.
(800)50-HOTEL.

ELDORADO HOTEL & SPA
309 West San Francisco St., Santa Fe.
(800)50-HOTEL.

HOTEL ST FRANCIS
210 Don Gaspar Ave, Santa Fe.
(800)50-HOTEL.

INN AT LORETTO
211 Old Santa Fe Trail, Santa Fe.
(800)50-HOTEL.

LUXURY INN
3752 Cerrillos Rd., Santa Fe.
(800)50-HOTEL.

New York

Albany

BEST WESTERN SOVEREIGN
1228 Western Ave., Albany.
(800)50-HOTEL.

SUSSE CHALET
44 Wolf Rd., Albany.
(800)50-HOTEL.

JFK Int'l Airport

COMFORT INN BRIARWOOD
87 Van Wyck Expressway, Jamaica.
(800)50-HOTEL.

RADISSON JFK AIRPORT
135-30 140th St., Jamaica.
(800)50-HOTEL.

SUPER 8 MOTEL JAMAICA
139 01 Jamaica Ave., Jamaica.
(800)50-HOTEL.

La Guardia Airport

WYNDHAM LA GUARDIA AIRPORT
100-15 Ditmars Blvd, New York.
(800)50-HOTEL.

New York City/Manhattan

BROADWAY PLAZA
12 East 31St St., New York.
(800)50-HOTEL.

Book Online at www.entertainment.com/hotels or Call 1-800-50-HOTEL (1-800-504-6835)

CARNEGIE SUITES
130 E. 57Th St., New York.
(800)50-HOTEL.

CLARION PARK AVE.NUE
106 West 83Rd St., New York.
(800)50-HOTEL.

COLUMBUS STUDIOS HOSTEL
16 E. 32nd St., New York.
(800)50-HOTEL.

DOUBLETREE METROPOLITAN HOTEL
511 Lexington Ave., New York.
(800)50-HOTEL.

EDISON
2178 Broadway At 77Th St., New York.
(800)50-HOTEL.

HELMSLEY PARK LANE
1155 Broadway, New York.
(800)50-HOTEL.

HOTEL BELLECLAIRE
109 W. 45Th St., New York.
(800)50-HOTEL.

HOTEL CHANDLER, FRM LE MARQUIS
215 West 94Th St., New York.
(800)50-HOTEL.

MILFORD PLAZA
401 7Th Ave., New York.
(800)50-HOTEL.

ON THE AVE. HOTEL
229 West 58Th, New York.
(800)50-HOTEL.

PARK CENTRAL NEW YORK
250 West 77Th, New York.
(800)50-HOTEL.

PENNSYLVANIA
569 Lexington Ave., New York.
(800)50-HOTEL.

QUALITY HOTEL ON BROADWAY
228 West 47Th St., New York.
(800)50-HOTEL.

RADISSON LEXINGTON HOTEL
870 7th Avenue, New York.
(800)50-HOTEL.

RAMADA PLAZA & INN NEW YORKER
36 Central Park South, New York.
(800)50-HOTEL.

ST JAMES TIMES SQUARE
481 8Th Ave., New York.
(800)50-HOTEL.

THE AVALON
130 West 46Th St., New York.
(800)50-HOTEL.

THE MUSE
308 W. 58th St, New York.
(800)50-HOTEL.

WESTPARK
270 West 45Th St., New York.
(800)50-HOTEL.

*See Rebate Rules on page E2 and Program Rules of Use on page E31.

Go to **entertainment.com/hotels** for the entire list of over 15,000 properties.

Guaranteed Best Rate*

Book online at **entertainment.com/hotels** for your double rebate.

Niagara Falls

QUALITY HOTEL AND SUITES
240 Rainbow Blvd., Niagara Falls.
(800)50-HOTEL.

TRAVELODGE HOTEL FALLSVIEW
201 Rainbow Blvd., Niagara Falls.
(800)50-HOTEL.

Rochester

COMFORT INN CENTRAL
395 Buell Rd., Rochester.
(800)50-HOTEL.

HAMPTON INN ROCHESTER SOUTH
717 East Henrietta Rd., Rochester.
(800)50-HOTEL.

HYATT REGENCY ROCHESTER
125 E. Main St., Rochester.
(800)50-HOTEL.

White Plains

SUMMERFIELD SUITES WESTCHESTER
101 Corporate Park Drive, White Plains.
(800)50-HOTEL.

WESTCHESTER RENAISSANCE
80 West Red Oak Lane, White Plains.
(800)50-HOTEL.

North Carolina

Asheville

RAMADA PLAZA HOTEL ASHEVILLE
435 Smoky Park Highway, Asheville.
(800)50-HOTEL.

RENAISSANCE ASHEVILLE HOTEL
One Thomas Wolfe Plaza, Asheville.
(800)50-HOTEL.

RESIDENCE INN ASHEVILLE
701 Biltmore Ave., Asheville.
(800)50-HOTEL.

Charlotte

AMERISUITES CHARLOTTE-ARROWOOD
7900 Forest Point Blvd., Charlotte.
(800)50-HOTEL.

COMFORT INN EXECUTIVE PARK
5822 Westpark Dr, Charlotte.
(800)50-HOTEL.

DRURY INN & SUITES CHARLOTTE
415 West W.T. Harris Blvd., Charlotte.
(800)50-HOTEL.

HILTON EXECUTIVE PARK
5624 Westpark Drive, Charlotte.
(800)50-HOTEL.

NEW!
Double Your Rebate
By Booking Online!
See page E2

Durham

DAYS INN DURHAM
3460 Hillsborough Rd., Durham.
(800)50-HOTEL.

DUKE TOWER RESIDENTIAL SUITES
807 W. Trinity Ave., Durham.
(800)50-HOTEL.

Greensboro

CLARION GREENSBORO AIRPORT
415 Swing Rd., Greensboro.
(800)50-HOTEL.

MARRIOTT GREENSBORO AIRPORT
1 Marriott Drive, Greensboro.
(800)50-HOTEL.

Raleigh

AMERISUITES RALEIGH/WAKE FORST
1105 Navaho Drive, Raleigh.
(800)50-HOTEL.

QUALITY SUITES
4400 Capital Blvd., Raleigh.
(800)50-HOTEL.

North Dakota

For this state's listings go to entertainment.com/hotels

Ohio

Cincinnati

BEST WESTERN
4004 Williams Drive, Cincinnati.
(800)50-HOTEL.

FOUR POINTS SHERATON
8020 Montgomery, Cincinnati.
(800)50-HOTEL.

HOMEWOOD SUITES SHARONVILLE
2670 East Kemper Rd., Sharonville.
(800)50-HOTEL.

MILLENIUM HOTEL
141 West Sixth St., Cincinnati.
(800)50-HOTEL.

Cleveland

BAYMONT INN & SUITES CLE ARPRT
4222 West 150 St., Cleveland.
(800)50-HOTEL.

CLEVELAND AIRPORT MARRIOTT
4277 W. 150th St., Cleveland.
(800)50-HOTEL.

CROSS COUNTRY INN
7233 Engle Rd., Cleveland.
(800)50-HOTEL.

Columbus

COMFORT SUITES COLUMBUS ARPT
4270 Sawyer Rd., Columbus.
(800)50-HOTEL.

THE LOFTS
55 East Natiowide Blvd., Columbus.
(800)50-HOTEL.

WESTIN GREAT SOUTHERN HOTEL
310 South High St., Columbus.
(800)50-HOTEL.

Dublin

AMERISUITES COLUMBUS DUBLIN
6161 Park Center Circle, Columbus.
(800)50-HOTEL.

Oklahoma

Oklahoma City

BRICKTOWN CENTRAL PLAZA HOTEL
2001 East Reno Ave., Oklahoma City.
(800)50-HOTEL.

DAYS INN S
2616 S I-35, Oklahoma City.
(800)50-HOTEL.

LA QUINTA INN S 807
8315 S Interstate 35, Oklahoma City.
(800)50-HOTEL.

Tulsa

RODEWAY INN & SUITES
8181 East 41st St., Tulsa.
(800)50-HOTEL.

TULSA LEXINGTON SUITES
8525 E 41st St., Tulsa.
(800)50-HOTEL.

TULSA MARRIOTT SERN HILLS
1902 E 71st St., Tulsa.
(800)50-HOTEL.

Oregon

Eugene

FRANKLIN INN
1857 Franklin Blvd, Eugene.
(800)50-HOTEL.

RED LION HOTEL EUGENE
205 Coburg Rd., Eugene.
(800)50-HOTEL.

VALLEY RIVER INN, A WESTCOAST
1000 Valley River Way, Eugene.
(800)50-HOTEL.

Hillsboro

RED LION HOTEL HILLSBORO
3500 Ne Corneli Rd., Hillsboro.
(800)50-HOTEL.

WELLESLEY INN & STES HILLSBORO
19311 N.W. Cornell Rd, Hillsboro.
(800)50-HOTEL.

Portland

DAYS INN CITY CENTER
1414 SW Sixth Ave., Portland.
(800)50-HOTEL.

DOUBLETREE HOTEL JANTZEN BEACH
909 North Hayden Island Drive, Portland.
(800)50-HOTEL.

EVERGREEN INN & SUITES
3828 Ne 82nd St., Portland.
(800)50-HOTEL.

*See Rebate Rules on page E2 and Program Rules of Use on page E31.

Go to **entertainment.com/hotels** for the entire list of over 15,000 properties.

Guaranteed Best Rate*

Book online at **entertainment.com/hotels** for your double rebate.

HAWTHORN INN & SUITES
2323 Ne 181st Ave., Portland.
(800)50-HOTEL.

LA QUINTA INN PORTLAND AIRPORT
11207 NE Holman St., Portland.
(800)50-HOTEL.

LA QUINTA PORTLAND CONV CENTER
431 Ne Multnomah, Portland.
(800)50-HOTEL.

RADISSON HOTEL
6233 N.E. 78th Court, Portland.
(800)50-HOTEL.

RED LION & SUITES/AIRPORT
5019 Ne 102nd Ave., Portland.
(800)50-HOTEL.

RED LION HOTEL PORTLAND CONVEN
1021 Ne Grand Ave., Portland.
(800)50-HOTEL.

RIVERPLACE HOTEL
1510 SW Harbor Way, Portland.
(800)50-HOTEL.

SHILO INN SUITES
11707 NE Airport Way, Portland.
(800)50-HOTEL.

THE BENSON, A WESTCOAST HOTEL
309 Swest Broadway, Portland.
(800)50-HOTEL.

Springfield

DOUBLETREE HOTEL EUGENE
3280 Gateway St., Springfield.
(800)50-HOTEL.

SHILO INN EUGENE-SPRINGIELD
3350 Gateway, Springfield.
(800)50-HOTEL.

Pennsylvania

Harrisburg

HOWARD JOHNSON HARRISBURG
473 Eisenhower Blvd, Harrisburg.
(800)50-HOTEL.

RED ROOF INN HARRISBURG S
950 Eisenhower Blvd, Harrisburg.
(800)50-HOTEL.

Lancaster

LANCASTER HOST RESORT
2300 Lincoln Highway East, Lancaster.
(800)50-HOTEL.

THE KING'S COTTAGE B & B INN
1049 East King St., Lancaster.
(800)50-HOTEL.

Philadelphia

CLUB QUARTERS
1628 Chestnut St., Philadelphia.
(800)50-HOTEL.

CONWELL INN
1331 West Berks St., Philadelphia.
(800)50-HOTEL.

COURTYARD PHILADELPHIA AIRPORT
8900 Bartram Ave., Philadelphia.
(800)50-HOTEL.

COURTYARD PHILADELPHIA DOWNTWN
21 North Juniper St., Philadelphia.
(800)50-HOTEL.

FOUR PTS BY SHERATON AIRPORT
4101a Island Ave, Philadelphia.
(800)50-HOTEL.

HILTON GARDEN INN PHILADELPHIA
1100 Arch St., Philadelphia.
(800)50-HOTEL.

MICROTEL INN & SUITES-PHILA AI
8840 Tinicum Blvd., Philadelphia.
(800)50-HOTEL.

SHERATON SOCIETY HILL HOTEL
1 Dock St, Philadelphia.
(800)50-HOTEL.

SPRUCE HILL MANOR
331 S 46th St., Philadelphia.
(800)50-HOTEL.

Pittsburgh

HYATT REGENCY PITTSBURGH
1111 Airport Blvd, Pittsburgh.
(800)50-HOTEL.

MICROTEL INN & SUITES
900 Chauvet Drive, Pittsburgh.
(800)50-HOTEL.

RESIDENCE INN BY MARRIOTT
3896 Bigelow Blvd., Pittsburgh.
(800)50-HOTEL.

Rhode Island

Providence

PROVIDENCE BILTMORE HOTEL
11 Dorrance St, Providence.
(800)50-HOTEL.

RADISSON PROVIDENCE HARBOR
220 India St, Providence.
(800)50-HOTEL.

South Carolina

Charleston

BEST WESTERN SWEETGRASS INN
1540 Savannah Hwy, Charleston.
(800)50-HOTEL.

COMFORT INN RIVERVIEW
144 Bee St., Charleston.
(800)50-HOTEL.

COURTYARD CHARLESTON NORTH
2415 Mall Dr., Charleston.
(800)50-HOTEL.

DAYS INN AIRPORT COLISEUM
2998 W Montague Ave., Charleston.
(800)50-HOTEL.

FRENCH QUARTER INN
166 Church St., Charleston.
(800)50-HOTEL.

HILTON CHARLESTON HARBOR RSRT
20 Patriots Point Rd., Charleston.
(800)50-HOTEL.

HOWARD JOHNSON RIVERFRONT
250 Spring St., Charleston.
(800)50-HOTEL.

Book Online at
www.entertainment.com/hotels
or
Call 1-800-50-HOTEL
(1-800-504-6835)

WENTWORTH MANSION
149 Wentworth St., Charleston.
(800)50-HOTEL.

Columbia

ADAM'S MARK HOTEL COLUMBIA
1200 Hampton St., Columbia.
(800)50-HOTEL.

AMERISUITES COLUMBIA NORTHEAST
7525 Two Notch Rd., Columbia.
(800)50-HOTEL.

CLAUSSEN'S INN
2003 Greene St., Columbia.
(800)50-HOTEL.

Greenville

HAWTHORN SUITES
48 Mcprice Court, Greenville.
(800)50-HOTEL.

HILTON GREENVILLE
45 West Orchard Park Dr., Greenville.
(800)50-HOTEL.

LA QUINTA INN WOODRUFF RD.
31 Old Country Rd., Greenville.
(800)50-HOTEL.

SLEEP INN PALMETTO EXPO CENTER
231 N Pleasantburg Dr, Greenville.
(800)50-HOTEL.

Hilton Head Island

HILTON HEAD PLAZA HOTEL
36 South Forest Beach Dr., Hilton Head.
(800)50-HOTEL.

SHOREWOOD
27-C Coligny Plaza, Hilton Head.
(800)50-HOTEL.

THE SEACREST
27-C Coligny Plaza, Hilton Head.
(800)50-HOTEL.

Myrtle Beach

BEST WESTERN CAROLINIAN RESORT
2506 North Ocean Blvd., Myrtle Beach.
(800)50-HOTEL.

CAMELOT BY THE SEA
1902 North Ocean Blvd., Myrtle Beach.
(800)50-HOTEL.

COMPASS COVE OCEANFRONT RESORT
2311 South Ocean Blvd., Myrtle Beach.
(800)50-HOTEL.

COURT CAPRI
2610 North Ocean Blvd., Myrtle Beach.
(800)50-HOTEL.

COURTYARD MYRTLE BEACH
1000 Commons Blvd., Myrtle Beach.
(800)50-HOTEL.

DUNES VILLAGE RESORT
5200 North Ocean Blvd., Myrtle Beach.
(800)50-HOTEL.

*See Rebate Rules on page E2 and Program Rules of Use on page E31.

Go to **entertainment.com/hotels** for the entire list of over 15,000 properties.

Guaranteed Best Rate*

Book online at **entertainment.com/hotels** for your double rebate.

EL DORADO
2800 S Ocean Blvd, Myrtle Beach.
(800)50-HOTEL.

HILTON MYRTLE BEACH
10000 Beach Club Dr., Myrtle Beach.
(800)50-HOTEL.

OCEAN DUNES RESORT & VILLAS
201 75Th Avenue North, Myrtle Beach.
(800)50-HOTEL.

PATRICIA GRAND RESORT HOTEL
2710 North Ocean Blvd., Myrtle Beach.
(800)50-HOTEL.

RADISSON PLAZA HOTEL
2101 North Oak St., Myrtle Beach.
(800)50-HOTEL.

SANDS BEACH CLUB RESORT
9400 Shore Dr., Myrtle Beach.
(800)50-HOTEL.

SHERATON'S BROADWAY PLANTATION
3301 Robert M. Grissom Parkway, Myrtle Beach.
(800)50-HOTEL.

Spartanburg

SPARTANBURG MARRIOTT
299 North Church St., Spartanburg.
(800)50-HOTEL.

South Dakota

Rapid City

AMERICINN LODGE & SUITES
1632 Rapp St, Rapid City.
(800)50-HOTEL.

RAMADA INN RAPID CITY
1721 Lacrosse St., Rapid City.
(800)50-HOTEL.

Tennessee

Chattanooga

CHATTANOOGA QUALITY INN
5505 Brainerd Rd., Chattanooga.
(800)50-HOTEL.

HILTON GARDEN INN
311 Chestnut St., Chattanooga.
(800)50-HOTEL.

RAMADA LIMITED
30 Birmingham Highway, Chattanooga.
(800)50-HOTEL.

WELLESLEY INN CHATTANOOGA
7620 Hamilton Park Drive, Chattanooga.
(800)50-HOTEL.

Gatlinburg

DEER RIDGE MOUNTAIN RESORT
3710 Weber Rd., Gatlinburg.
(800)50-HOTEL.

MCKAY'S INN DOWNTOWN
903 Parkway, Suite One, Gatlinburg.
(800)50-HOTEL.

PARK VISTA RESORT HOTEL
705 Cherokee Orchard Rd., Gatlinburg.
(800)50-HOTEL.

SIDNEY JAMES MOUNTAIN LODGE
610 Historic Nature Trail, Gatlinburg.
(800)50-HOTEL.

Knoxville

BUDGET INNS OF AMERICA
323 North Cedar Bluff Rd., Knoxville.
(800)50-HOTEL.

HOTEL ST. OLIVER
407 Union Ave., Knoxville.
(800)50-HOTEL.

Memphis

AMERISUITES CORDOVA
7905 Giacosa Place, Memphis.
(800)50-HOTEL.

BAYMONT INN & SUITES AIRPORT
3005 Millbranch, Memphis.
(800)50-HOTEL.

COURTYARD MEMPHIS PARK AVE.
6015 Park Ave., Memphis.
(800)50-HOTEL.

HOMESTEAD STUDIOS EAST MEMPHIS
6500 Poplar Ave, Memphis.
(800)50-HOTEL.

MARRIOTT DOWNTOWN
250 N Main St, Memphis.
(800)50-HOTEL.

Nashville

AMERISUITES OPRYLAND
220 Rudy's Circle, Nashville.
(800)50-HOTEL.

BEST WESTERN DOWNTOWN
1407 Division St., Nashville.
(800)50-HOTEL.

COMFORT INN DOWNTOWN
1501 Demonbreun St., Nashville.
(800)50-HOTEL.

COURTYARD NASHVILLE OPRYLAND
125 Music City Circle, Nashville.
(800)50-HOTEL.

DOUBLETREE NASHVILLE
315 4th Ave. North, Nashville.
(800)50-HOTEL.

FAIRFIELD INN OPRYLAND
211 Music City Circle, Nashville.
(800)50-HOTEL.

HAMPTON INN AND SUITES
2330 Elliston Place, Nashville.
(800)50-HOTEL.

LA QUINTA INN NASHVILLE AIRPRT
2345 Atrium Way, Nashville.
(800)50-HOTEL.

LOEWS VANDERBILT HOTEL
2100 West End Ave., Nashville.
(800)50-HOTEL.

NASHVILLE AIRPORT MARRIOTT
600 Marriott Drive, Nashville.
(800)50-HOTEL.

RADISSON NASHVILLE AIRPORT
733 Briley Parkway, Nashville.
(800)50-HOTEL.

Pigeon Forge

BAYMONT INN & STES PIGEON FRG
2179 Parkway, Pigeon Forge.
(800)50-HOTEL.

COMFORT SUITES PIGEON FORGE
2423 Teaster Lane, Pigeon Forge.
(800)50-HOTEL.

GREEN VALLEY S
4109 Parkway, Pigeon Forge.
(800)50-HOTEL.

MICROTEL INN PIGEON FORGE
202 Emert St., Pigeon Forge.
(800)50-HOTEL.

Texas

Arlington

AMERISUITES ARLINGTON
2380 Rd. To Six Flags, Arlington.
(800)50-HOTEL.

HILTON ARLINGTON
2401 East Lamar Blvd, Arlington.
(800)50-HOTEL.

WINGATE INN ARLINGTON
1024 Brookhollow Plaza Drive, Arlington.
(800)50-HOTEL.

Austin

AMERISUITES AUSTIN AIRPORT
7601 E. Ben White Blvd, Austin.
(800)50-HOTEL.

AUSTIN MARRIOTT AT THE CAPITOL
701 East 11Th St., Austin.
(800)50-HOTEL.

BAYMONT INN & STES ROUND ROCK
150 Parker Dr., Austin.
(800)50-HOTEL.

BEST VALUE INN AUSTIN SOUTH
2525 Ih-35 South, Austin.
(800)50-HOTEL.

BRADFORD HOMESUITES AUSTIN
10001 N Capitol Of Texas Hwy, Austin.
(800)50-HOTEL.

CLARION INN & SUITES
2200 S. I-35, Austin.
(800)50-HOTEL.

DOUBLETREE AUSTIN NORTH
6505 Ih 35 North, Austin.
(800)50-HOTEL.

HYATT REGENCY AUSTIN
208 Barton Springs, Austin.
(800)50-HOTEL.

LAKEWAY INN CONFERENCE RESORT
101 Lakeway Dr., Austin.
(800)50-HOTEL.

OMNI AUSTIN DOWNTOWN
700 San Jacinto, Austin.
(800)50-HOTEL.

NEW!
Double Your Rebate
By Booking Online!
See page E2

*See Rebate Rules on page E2 and Program Rules of Use on page E31.

Go to **entertainment.com/hotels** for the entire list of over 15,000 properties.

Guaranteed Best Rate*

Book online at **entertainment.com/hotels** for your double rebate.

OMNI AUSTIN SOUTHPARK
4140 Governor's Row, Austin.
(800)50-HOTEL.

Corpus Christi

BAYFRONT INN
601 North Shoreline Blvd, Corpus Christi.
(800)50-HOTEL.

BEST WESTERN MARINA GRAND
300 North Shoreline Blvd, Corpus Christi.
(800)50-HOTEL.

OMNI MARINA HOTEL
707 N. Shoreline Blvd., Corpus Christi.
(800)50-HOTEL.

QUALITY INN AND SUITES
3202 Surfside Blvd., Corpus Christi.
(800)50-HOTEL.

RADISSON BEACH HOTEL
3200 Surfside Blvd., Corpus Christi.
(800)50-HOTEL.

Dallas

AMERISUITES PARK CENTRAL
12411 N. Central Expwy, Dallas.
(800)50-HOTEL.

BEST WESTERN MARKET CENTER
2023 Market Center Blvd, Dallas.
(800)50-HOTEL.

HAMPTON INN WEST END
1015 Elm St., Dallas.
(800)50-HOTEL.

HEARTHSIDE STUDIO SUITES NORTH
12301 N Central Expressway, Dallas.
(800)50-HOTEL.

RAMADA PLAZA DOWNTWN CONV.CTR
1011 S. Akard, Dallas.
(800)50-HOTEL.

STERLING HOTEL DALLAS
1055 Regal Row, Dallas.
(800)50-HOTEL.

STONELEIGH
2927 Maple Ave, Dallas.
(800)50-HOTEL.

THE ADOLPHUS
1321 Commerce St., Dallas.
(800)50-HOTEL.

THE MAGNOLIA
1401 Commerce Ave., Dallas.
(800)50-HOTEL.

THE MANSION ON TURTLE CREEK
2821 Turtle Creek Blvd., Dallas.
(800)50-HOTEL.

THE MELROSE HOTEL, DALLAS
3015 Oaklawn Ave., Dallas.
(800)50-HOTEL.

WINGATE INN MARKET CENTER
8650 North Stemmons Freeway, Dallas.
(800)50-HOTEL.

Dallas/Ft. Worth Airport

BEST WESTERN IRVING INN
4110 West Airport Freeway, Irving.
(800)50-HOTEL.

COMFORT SUITES DFW AIRPORT
4700 W. John Carpenter Frwy., Irving.
(800)50-HOTEL.

HAWTHORN SUITES DFW AIRPORT
5000 Plaza Drive, Irving.
(800)50-HOTEL.

RADISSON HOTEL DFW S
4600 W Airport Freeway, Irving.
(800)50-HOTEL.

WYNDHAM GARDEN LAS COLINAS
110 West John Carpenter Frwy, Irving.
(800)50-HOTEL.

El Paso

AMERISUITES EL PASO AIRPORT
6030 Gateway East, El Paso.
(800)50-HOTEL.

BAYMONT INN & STES EL PASO W.
7620 North Mesa, El Paso.
(800)50-HOTEL.

BEST WESTERN SUNLAND PARK
1045 Sunland Park Dr, El Paso.
(800)50-HOTEL.

LA QUINTA INN CIELO VISTA
9125 Gateway West, El Paso.
(800)50-HOTEL.

Ft. Worth

CLARION HOTEL
600 Commerce St., Fort Worth.
(800)50-HOTEL.

PARK CENTRAL HOTEL
1010 Houston St., Fort Worth.
(800)50-HOTEL.

THE DORAL TESORO HOTEL
3300 Championship Parkway, Fort Worth.
(800)50-HOTEL.

Galveston

BEACHCOMBER INN
2825 61st St., Galveston.
(800)50-HOTEL.

HOTEL GALVEZ, A WYNDHAM HOTEL
2024 Seawall Blvd, Galveston.
(800)50-HOTEL.

LA QUINTA INN GALVESTON
1402 Seawall Blvd., Galveston.
(800)50-HOTEL.

Houston

COMFORT INN - HOUSTON NASA
750 W Nasa Rd. 1, Houston.
(800)50-HOTEL.

COMFORT INN DOWNTOWN
5820 Katy Freeway, Houston.
(800)50-HOTEL.

DOUBLETREE HOUSTON DOWNTOWN
400 Dallas St., Houston.
(800)50-HOTEL.

EMBASSY SUITES HOUSTON SW FRWY
9090 Swest Freeway, Houston.
(800)50-HOTEL.

GREAT WESTERN INN
6060 Hooton St., Houston.
(800)50-HOTEL.

Book Online at www.entertainment.com/hotels or Call 1-800-50-HOTEL (1-800-504-6835)

HAMPTON INN HOUSTON GALLERIA
4500 Post Oak Parkway, Houston.
(800)50-HOTEL.

HOUSTON W UNIVERSITY COURTYARD
2929 Westpark Drive, Houston.
(800)50-HOTEL.

LA QUINTA INN HOBBY AIRPORT
9902 Gulf Highway, Houston.
(800)50-HOTEL.

THE WARWICK HOTEL
5701 Main St., Houston.
(800)50-HOTEL.

Houston Intercontinental Airport

AMERISUITES IAH GREENSPOINT
300 Ronan Park Place, Houston.
(800)50-HOTEL.

FAIRFIELD INN I-45 NORTH
17617 North Freeway, Houston.
(800)50-HOTEL.

San Antonio

AMERISUITES RIVERWALK
601 S St. Mary's St., San Antonio.
(800)50-HOTEL.

BEST WESTERN LACKLAND/KELLYUSA
6815 Highway 90 West, San Antonio.
(800)50-HOTEL.

COMFORT INN FIESTA
6755 North Loop 1604 West, San Antonio.
(800)50-HOTEL.

DAYS INN COLISEUM
3443 Pan Am Expressway I35 N., San Antonio.
(800)50-HOTEL.

DRURY INN SAN ANTONIO A/P
95 Ne Loop 410, San Antonio.
(800)50-HOTEL.

ECONO LODGE INGRAM SEA WORLD
6360 N.W. Loop 410, San Antonio.
(800)50-HOTEL.

EMILY MORGAN
705 East Houston St., San Antonio.
(800)50-HOTEL.

HAWTHORN SUITES RIVERWALK
830 N. St. Mary's, San Antonio.
(800)50-HOTEL.

HILTON AIRPORT NORTHSTAR
611 N.W. Loop 410, San Antonio.
(800)50-HOTEL.

KNIGHTS INN AT LACKLAND
6735 Us 90 West, San Antonio.
(800)50-HOTEL.

LA QUINTA INN SEAWORLD
7134 NW Loop 410, San Antonio.
(800)50-HOTEL.

LA QUINTA INN VANCE JACKSON
5922 Northwest Expressway, San Antonio.
(800)50-HOTEL.

*See Rebate Rules on page E2 and Program Rules of Use on page E31.

Go to **entertainment.com/hotels** for the entire list of over 15,000 properties.

Guaranteed Best Rate*

Book online at **entertainment.com/hotels** for your double rebate.

LA QUINTA SAN ANTONIO AIRPORT
850 Halm Blvd., San Antonio.
(800)50-HOTEL.

MENGER HOTEL
204 Alamo Plaza, San Antonio.
(800)50-HOTEL.

RADISSON MARKET SQUARE
502 West Durango Blvd., San Antonio.
(800)50-HOTEL.

RAMADA LIMITED SEAWORLD
7043 Culebra Rd, San Antonio.
(800)50-HOTEL.

RESIDENCE INN SAN ANTONIO NW
4041 Bluemel Rd., San Antonio.
(800)50-HOTEL.

SHERATON GUNTER
205 E. Houston St., San Antonio.
(800)50-HOTEL.

THE CROCKETT HOTEL
320 Bonham, San Antonio.
(800)50-HOTEL.

South Padre Island

HOWARD JOHNSON EXPRESS INN
1709 Padre Blvd, South Padre Island.
(800)50-HOTEL.

RAMADA LTD SOUTH PADRE ISLAND
4109 Padre Blvd, South Padre Island.
(800)50-HOTEL.

William P. Hobby Airport

DRURY INN & SUITES HOBBY ARPT
7902 Mosley Rd, Houston.
(800)50-HOTEL.

Utah

Park City

HAMPTON INN & SUITES PARK CITY
6609 North Landmark Drive, Park City.
(800)50-HOTEL.

Salt Lake City

BEST INN & SUITES SALT LAKE
1009 S Main, Salt Lake City.
(800)50-HOTEL.

COMFORT INN SALT LAKE NORTH
2437 Wildcat Way, Salt Lake City.
(800)50-HOTEL.

FAIRFIELD INN
594 West 4500 S, Salt Lake City.
(800)50-HOTEL.

HAMPTON INN SALT LAKE CITY
2055 S. Redwood Rd., Salt Lake City.
(800)50-HOTEL.

LA QUINTA INN SALT LAKE CITY W
3540 S 2200 West, Salt Lake City.
(800)50-HOTEL.

See page E2

MARRIOTT UNIVERSITY PARK
480 Wakara Way, Salt Lake City.
(800)50-HOTEL.

RAMADA LIMITED
2455 S. State, Salt Lake City.
(800)50-HOTEL.

RED LION HOTEL DOWNTOWN
161 West 600 S, Salt Lake City.
(800)50-HOTEL.

SHERATON CITY CENTRE
150 West 500 S, Salt Lake City.
(800)50-HOTEL.

Vermont

Killington

COMFORT INN KILLINGTON
905 Killington Rd, Killington.
(800)50-HOTEL.

INN OF THE SIX MOUNTAINS
2617 Killington Rd., Killington.
(800)50-HOTEL.

Rutland

TRAVEL INN
125 Woodstock Ave., Rutland.
(800)50-HOTEL.

Virginia

Alexandria

RADISSON OLD TOWN ALEXANDRIA
901 North Fairfax, Alexandria.
(800)50-HOTEL.

SHERATON PENTAGON S HOTEL
4641 Kenmore Ave., Alexandria.
(800)50-HOTEL.

Arlington

COMFORT INN PENTAGON
2480 S Glebe Rd., Arlington.
(800)50-HOTEL.

DAYS INN PENTAGON
3030 Columbia Pike, Arlington.
(800)50-HOTEL.

POTOMAC SUITES ROSSLYN
1730 Arlington Blvd., Arlington.
(800)50-HOTEL.

QUALITY INN IWO JIMA
1501 Arlington Blvd., Arlington.
(800)50-HOTEL.

Ashland

DAYS INN ASHLAND
806 England St., Ashland.
(800)50-HOTEL.

Norfolk

BEST WESTERN HOLIDAY SANDS INN
1330 East Ocean View Ave., Norfolk.
(800)50-HOTEL.

CLARION HOTEL JAMES MADISON
345 Granby St, Norfolk.
(800)50-HOTEL.

Richmond

DAYS INN - WEST BRD.
2100 Dickens Rd., Richmond.
(800)50-HOTEL.

INNS OF VIRGINIA-RICHMOND
5215 West BRd. Rd., Richmond.
(800)50-HOTEL.

QUALITY INN
201 E. Cary St., Richmond.
(800)50-HOTEL.

Virginia Beach

CLARION HOTEL
4453 Bonney Rd, Virginia Beach.
(800)50-HOTEL.

DOUBLETREE VIRGINIA BEACH
1900 Pavilion Drive, Virginia Beach.
(800)50-HOTEL.

LA QUINTA INN VIRGINIA BCH 583
192 Newtown Rd., Virginia Beach.
(800)50-HOTEL.

Williamsburg

LA QUINTA INN WILLIAMSBURG
119 Bypass Rd., Williamsburg.
(800)50-HOTEL.

POWHATAN PLANTATION
3601 Ironbound Rd., Williamsburg.
(800)50-HOTEL.

WILLIAMSBURG TRAVE.L INN
1800 Richmond Rd., Williamsburg.
(800)50-HOTEL.

Washington

Bellevue

COAST BELLEVUE HOTEL
625 116th Ave. Ne, Bellevue.
(800)50-HOTEL.

FAIRFIELD INN BY MARRIOTT
14595 Northeast 29th Place, Bellevue.
(800)50-HOTEL.

HILTON BELLEVUE
100 - 112th Ave. Ne, Bellevue.
(800)50-HOTEL.

HYATT REGENCY BELLEVUE
900 Bellevue Way Ne, Bellevue.
(800)50-HOTEL.

SILVER CLOUD BELLEVUE EASTGATE
14632 Seast Eastgate Way, Bellevue.
(800)50-HOTEL.

Lynnwood

COURTYARD BY MARRIOTT-LYNNWOOD
4220 Alderwood Mall Blvd, Lynnwood.
(800)50-HOTEL.

EMBASSY SUITES SEATTLE NORTH
20610 44th Ave. West, Lynwood.
(800)50-HOTEL.

*See Rebate Rules on page E2 and Program Rules of Use on page E31.

Go to **entertainment.com/hotels** for the entire list of over 15,000 properties.

Guaranteed Best Rate*

Book online at **entertainment.com/hotels** for your double rebate.

Seattle

BEST VALUE SEATTLE INN & SUITE
225 Aurora Ave. North, Seattle.
(800)50-HOTEL.

DAYS INN SEATTLE DOWNTOWN
2205 7th Ave., Seattle.
(800)50-HOTEL.

HOMEWOOD SUITES ELLIOT BAY
206 Western Ave. West, Seattle.
(800)50-HOTEL.

RED LION HOTEL ON 5TH AVE.
1415 5th Ave., Seattle.
(800)50-HOTEL.

ROOSEVELT, A WESTCOAST HOTEL
1531 7th Ave., Seattle.
(800)50-HOTEL.

SILVER CLOUD HOTEL BRD.WAY
1100 Broadway, Seattle.
(800)50-HOTEL.

SILVER CLOUD INN - LAKE UNION
1150 Fairview Ave. North, Seattle.
(800)50-HOTEL.

SIXTH AVE. INN
2000 6th Ave., Seattle.
(800)50-HOTEL.

TRAVELODGE BY THE SPACE NEEDLE
200 6th Ave. North, Seattle.
(800)50-HOTEL.

Seattle/Tacoma Int'l Airport

BEST VALUE AIRPORT INN
20620 International Blvd., Seatac.
(800)50-HOTEL.

BEST WESTERN AIRPORT EXECUTEL
20717 International Blvd., Seattle.
(800)50-HOTEL.

COMFORT INN - SEATAC
19333 Pacific Hwy.,S., Seattle.
(800)50-HOTEL.

CREST MOTOR INN - SEATAC
18845 Pacific Hwy. S, Seatac.
(800)50-HOTEL.

DOUBLETREE HOTEL SEATAC
18740 Pacific Hwy S., Seattle.
(800)50-HOTEL.

HILTON SEATTLE AIRPORT
17620 Pacific Highway S, Seattle.
(800)50-HOTEL.

RADISSON HOTEL SEATTLE AIRPORT
17001 Pacific Highway S, Seattle.
(800)50-HOTEL.

RED LION HOTEL SEATTLE AIRPORT
18220 International Blvd, Seattle.
(800)50-HOTEL.

RED LION HOTEL SEATTLE S
11244 Pacific Hwy S., Seattle.
(800)50-HOTEL.

SCENTER HOTEL ON THE RIVER
15901 West Valley Highway, Seattle.
(800)50-HOTEL.

SEATAC SUPER 8 MOTEL
3100 S 192nd St., Seattle.
(800)50-HOTEL.

SUTTON SUITES & EXTENDED STAYS
3423 S 160th St., Sea Tac.
(800)50-HOTEL.

WESTCOAST GATEWAY HOTEL
18415 Pacific Hwy. S, Seatac.
(800)50-HOTEL.

Silverdale

RED LION SILVERDALE HOTEL
3073 N.W. Bucklin Hill Rd., Silverdale.
(800)50-HOTEL.

Spokane

ECONO LODGE SPOKANE
120 W. 3Rd Avenue, Spokane.
(800)50-HOTEL.

FAIRFIELD INN SPOKANE
311 North Riverpoint Blvd., Spokane.
(800)50-HOTEL.

HOWARD JOHNSON INN SPOKANE
211 South Division, Spokane.
(800)50-HOTEL.

LA QUINTA INN & SUITES SPOKANE
3080 N. Sullivan Rd., Spokane.
(800)50-HOTEL.

QUALITY INN VALLEY SUITES
8923 E. Mission Ave., Spokane.
(800)50-HOTEL.

WESTCOAST RIDPATH HOTEL
515 W. Sprague Ave., Spokane.
(800)50-HOTEL.

West Virginia

For this state's listings go to entertainment.com/hotels

Wisconsin

Green Bay

MARINER MOTEL
2222 Riverside Dr, Green Bay.
(800)50-HOTEL

Madison

HILTON MONONA TERRACE
9 East Wilson St., Madison.
(800)50-HOTEL.

WINGATE INN
3510 Mill Pond Rd, Madison.
(800)50-HOTEL.

WOODFIELD SUITES MADISON
5217 East Terrace Drive, Madison.
(800)50-HOTEL.

Milwaukee

COURTYARD MILWAUKEE DOWNTOWN
300 West Michigan St., Milwaukee.
(800)50-HOTEL.

MANCHESTER EAST HOTEL & SUITES
7065 North Port Washington Rd., Milwaukee.
(800)50-HOTEL.

Book Online at www.entertainment.com/hotels or Call 1-800-50-HOTEL (1-800-504-6835)

RADISSON MILWAUKEE WEST
2303 North Mayfair Rd., Milwaukee.
(800)50-HOTEL.

Wyoming

Jackson Hole

THE ALPINE HOUSE A COUNTRY INN
285 N Glenwood St, Jackson.
(800)50-HOTEL.

Canada

Alberta

Calgary

BEST WESTERN PORT O CALL INN
1935 McKnight Blvd. NE, Calgary.
(800)50-HOTEL.

BEST WESTERN SUITES DOWNTOWN
1330 8Th St. SW, Calgary.
(800)50-HOTEL.

CALGARY MARRIOTT
110 9Th Avenue SE, Calgary.
(800)50-HOTEL.

DELTA BOW VALLEY
209 4Th Avenue SE, Calgary.
(800)50-HOTEL.

FOUR POINTS SHERATON W CALGARY
8220 Bowridge Crescent NW, Calgary.
(800)50-HOTEL.

HOWARD JOHNSON EXPRESS CALGARY
5307 MacLeod Trail South, Calgary.
(800)50-HOTEL.

HYATT REGENCY CALGARY
700 Center St. SE, Calgary.
(800)50-HOTEL.

RADISSON HOTEL CALGARY AIRPORT
2120 16Th Ave. Ne, Calgary.
(800)50-HOTEL.

SANDMAN HOTEL DOWNTOWN CALGARY
888 7Th Ave., Calgary.
(800)50-HOTEL.

TRAVELODGE CALGARY AIRPORT
2750 Sunridge Blvd. NE, Calgary.
(800)50-HOTEL.

Canmore

QUALITY RESORT CHATEAU CANMORE
1720 Bow Valley Trail, Canmore.
(800)50-HOTEL.

RADISSON HOTEL CANMORE
511 Bow Valley Trail, Canmore.
(800)50-HOTEL.

*See Rebate Rules on page E2 and Program Rules of Use on page E31.

Go to **entertainment.com/hotels** for the entire list of over 15,000 properties.

Guaranteed Best Rate*

Book online at **entertainment.com/hotels** for your double rebate.

Edmonton

COAST TERRACE INN - SOUTH
4440 Gateway Blvd., Edmonton.
(800)50-HOTEL.

COMFORT INN & SUITES
10425-100 Avenue, Edmonton.
(800)50-HOTEL.

COMFORT INN EDMONTON
17610 100 Ave., Edmonton.
(800)50-HOTEL.

DAYS INN DOWNTOWN EDMONTON
10041 106Th St., Edmonton.
(800)50-HOTEL.

DELTA EDMONTON CENTRE SUITE
10222 102 St., Edmonton.
(800)50-HOTEL.

DELTA EDMONTON SOUTH
4404 Gateway Blvd., Edmonton.
(800)50-HOTEL.

MAYFIELD INN & SUITES
16615 109 Avenue, Edmonton.
(800)50-HOTEL.

RAMADA HOTEL EDMONTON
11830 Kingsway Ave., Edmonton.
(800)50-HOTEL.

SUTTON PLACE HOTEL EDMONTON
10235 101St St., Edmonton.
(800)50-HOTEL.

TRAVELODGE EDMONTON SOUTH
10320 45Th Avenue, Edmonton.
(800)50-HOTEL.

TRAVELODGE EDMONTON WEST
18320 Stony Plain Rd., Edmonton.
(800)50-HOTEL.

British Columbia

Richmond

DELTA VANCOUVER AIRPORT
3500 Cessna Drive, Richmond.
(800)50-HOTEL.

PARK PLAZA VANCOUVER AIRPORT
10251 St Edwards Dr, Richmond.
(800)50-HOTEL.

RADISSON PRESIDENT
8181 Cambie Rd., Richmond.
(800)50-HOTEL.

TRAVELODGE HOTEL VANCOUVER ARP
3071 St. Edwards Drive, Richmond.
(800)50-HOTEL.

Vancouver

BEST WESTERN DOWNTOWN
718 Drake St., Vancouver.
(800)50-HOTEL.

COMFORT INN DOWNTOWN
654 Nelson St., Vancouver.
(800)50-HOTEL.

CROWNE PLAZA
801 West Georgia St., Vancouver.
(800)50-HOTEL.

DELTA VANCOUVER SUITE HOTEL
550 West Hastings St., Vancouver.
(800)50-HOTEL.

HAMPTON INN & SUITES
111 Robson St., Vancouver.
(800)50-HOTEL.

HILTON VANCOUVER METROTOWN
6083 Mckay Ave., Vancouver.
(800)50-HOTEL.

HYATT REGENCY VANCOUVER
655 Burrard St., Vancouver.
(800)50-HOTEL.

INN AT FALSE CREEK
1335 Howe St., Vancouver.
(800)50-HOTEL.

LANDIS HOTEL & SUITES
1200 Hornby St., Vancouver.
(800)50-HOTEL.

LE SOLEIL HOTEL AND SUITES
567 Hornby St., Vancouver.
(800)50-HOTEL.

LISTEL VANCOUVER
1300 Robson St., Vancouver.
(800)50-HOTEL.

METROPOLITAN HOTEL VANCOUVER
645 Howe St., Vancouver.
(800)50-HOTEL.

PAN PACIFIC VANCOUVER
300-999 Canada Place, Vancouver.
(800)50-HOTEL.

PLAZA 500 HOTEL
500 West 12th Ave., Vancouver.
(800)50-HOTEL.

RAMADA INN & SUITES
1221 Granville St., Vancouver.
(800)50-HOTEL.

RAMADA LIMITED
435 West Pender St., Vancouver.
(800)50-HOTEL.

RAMADA VANCOUVER CENTRE
898 West Boardway, Vancouver.
(800)50-HOTEL.

RIVIERA HOTEL
1431 Robson St., Vancouver.
(800)50-HOTEL.

SUNSET INN & SUITES
1111 Burnaby St., Vancouver.
(800)50-HOTEL.

Victoria

BRENTWOOD BAY LODGE & SPA
2915 Douglas St., Victoria.
(800)50-HOTEL.

CHATEAU VICTORIA HOTEL & STES
427 Belleville St., Victoria.
(800)50-HOTEL.

DELTA VICTORIA OCEAN POINTE RE
45 Songhees Rd., Victoria.
(800)50-HOTEL.

GATSBY MANSION INN
309 Belleville St., Victoria.
(800)50-HOTEL.

HOTEL GRAND PACIFIC
3020 Douglas St., Victoria.
(800)50-HOTEL.

JAMES BAY INN
520 Menzies St., Victoria.
(800)50-HOTEL.

LAUREL POINT INN
680 Montreal St., Victoria.
(800)50-HOTEL.

THE ENGLISH INN RESORT
429 Lampson St., Victoria.
(800)50-HOTEL.

TRAVELLER'S INN- EXTENDED STAY
45 Songhees Rd., Victoria.
(800)50-HOTEL.

Whistler

DELTA WHISTLER VILLAGE SUITES
4308 Main St., Whistler.
(800)50-HOTEL.

LISTEL WHISTLER HOTEL
4121 Village Green, Whistler.
(800)50-HOTEL.

MOUNTAINSIDE LODGE
4417 Sundial Place, Whistler.
(800)50-HOTEL.

PAN PACIFIC WHISTLER MOUNTAIN
4320 Sundial Crescent, Whistler.
(800)50-HOTEL.

RESORTQUEST - THE MARQUISE
4809 Spearhead Dr., Whistler.
(800)50-HOTEL.

RESORTQUEST MARKETPLACE LODGE
4360 Lorimer Rd., Whistler.
(800)50-HOTEL.

RQ STONEY CREEK NORTHSTAR
4355 Northlands Blvd, Whistler.
(800)50-HOTEL.

THE COAST WHISTLER HOTEL
4005 Whistler Way, Whistler.
(800)50-HOTEL.

WHISTLER PINNACLE HOTEL
4319 Main St., Whistler.
(800)50-HOTEL.

Manitoba

Winnipeg

COMFORT INN AIRPORT
1770 Sargent Ave., Winnipeg.
(800)50-HOTEL.

SHERATON WINNIPEG
161 Donald St., Winnipeg.
(800)50-HOTEL.

Ontario

Leamington

COMFORT INN LEAMINGTON
279 Erie St. S, Leamington.
(800)50-HOTEL.

See page E2

*See Rebate Rules on page E2 and Program Rules of Use on page E31.

Go to **entertainment.com/hotels** for the entire list of over 15,000 properties.

Guaranteed Best Rate*

Book online at **entertainment.com/hotels** for your double rebate.

Mississauga

COMFORT INN & SUITES
2085 North Sheridan Way, Mississauga.
(800)50-HOTEL.

NOVOTEL TORONTO MISSISSAUGA
3670 Hurontario St., Mississauga.
(800)50-HOTEL.

SANDALWOOD SUITES
5050 Orbitor Dr, Mississauga.
(800)50-HOTEL.

Niagara Falls

BEST WESTERN FIRESIDE HOTEL
4067 River Rd., Niagara Falls.
(800)50-HOTEL.

CLARION HOTEL BY THE FALLS
6045 Stanley Ave., Niagara Falls.
(800)50-HOTEL.

FOUR POINTS SHERATON NIAGARA
6045 Stanley Ave., Niagara Falls.
(800)50-HOTEL.

HAMPTON INN N. OF THE FALLS
4357 River Rd., Niagara Falls.
(800)50-HOTEL.

NIAGARA FALLS MARRIOTT
6740 Falls View Blvd., Niagara Falls.
(800)50-HOTEL.

RADISSON HOTEL FALLSVIEW
6733 Fallsview Blvd., Niagara Falls.
(800)50-HOTEL.

RAMADA CORAL RESORT
7429 Lundy's Lane, Niagara Falls.
(800)50-HOTEL.

SHERATON ON THE FALLS
5875 Falls Ave., Niagara Falls.
(800)50-HOTEL.

THE PENINSULA INN & RESORT
7373 Niagara Square Drive, Niagara Falls.
(800)50-HOTEL.

Ottawa

NOVOTEL OTTAWA
33 Nicholas St., Ottawa.
(800)50-HOTEL.

QUALITY HOTEL OTTAWA DOWNTOWN
290 Rideau St., Ottawa.
(800)50-HOTEL.

RADISSON OTTAWA PARLIAMENT
402 Queen St., Ottawa.
(800)50-HOTEL.

Toronto

BOND PLACE
65 Dundas St.E., Toronto.
(800)50-HOTEL.

DAYS HOTEL & CONF CTR TORONTO
30 Carlton St., Toronto.
(800)50-HOTEL.

DELTA CHELSEA
33 Gerrard St. West, Toronto.
(800)50-HOTEL.

DOUBLETREE TORONTO AIRPORT
655 Dixon Rd., Toronto.
(800)50-HOTEL.

FOUR POINTS SHERATON LAKESHORE
1926 Lakeshore Blvd West, Toronto.
(800)50-HOTEL.

LE ROYAL MERIDIEN KING EDWARD
37 King St. East, Toronto.
(800)50-HOTEL.

NOVOTEL TORONTO CENTRE
45 The Esplanade, Toronto.
(800)50-HOTEL.

PANTAGES HOTEL SUITES SPA
200 Victoria St., Toronto.
(800)50-HOTEL.

PARK PLAZA TORONTO AIRPORT
33 Carlson Court, Toronto.
(800)50-HOTEL.

QUALITY HOTEL BLOOR ST.
280 Bloor St. W., Toronto.
(800)50-HOTEL.

QUALITY HOTEL DOWNTOWN
111 Lombard St., Toronto.
(800)50-HOTEL.

QUALITY SUITES TORONTO AIRPORT
262 Carlingview Dr., Toronto.
(800)50-HOTEL.

RADISSON HOTEL TORONTO EAST
55 Hallcrown Place, Toronto.
(800)50-HOTEL.

RADISSON SUITE TORONTO AIRPORT
640 Dixon Rd., Toronto.
(800)50-HOTEL.

RAMADA HOTEL & SUITES TORONTO
300 Jarvis St., Toronto.
(800)50-HOTEL.

RENAISSANCE TORONTO AIRPORT
801 Dixon Rd., Toronto.
(800)50-HOTEL.

STRATHCONA
60 York St., Toronto.
(800)50-HOTEL.

THE GRAND HOTEL
225 Jarvis St., Toronto.
(800)50-HOTEL.

THE SUTTON PLACE HOTEL
955 Bay St., Toronto.
(800)50-HOTEL.

VALHALLA INN
1 Valhalla Inn Rd., Toronto.
(800)50-HOTEL.

WYNDHAM BRISTOL PLACE
950 Dixon Rd., Toronto.
(800)50-HOTEL.

Québec

Montreal

BEST WESTERN VILLE-MARIE
3407 Peel St., Montreal.
(800)50-HOTEL.

CHATEAU ROYAL HOTEL & SUITES
1420 Crescent St., Montreal.
(800)50-HOTEL.

CHATEAU VERSAILLES
1659 Sherbrooke West, Montreal.
(800)50-HOTEL.

Book Online at www.entertainment.com/hotels or Call 1-800-50-HOTEL (1-800-504-6835)

DAYS INN MONTREAL METRO CENTRE
1005 Rue Guy, Montreal.
(800)50-HOTEL.

HILTON MONTREAL BONAVENTURE
1 Place Bonaventure, Montreal.
(800)50-HOTEL.

HOTEL PARK AVE.
4544 Ave. Du Park, Montreal.
(800)50-HOTEL.

HOTEL SOFITEL MONTREAL
1155 Sherbrooke St West, Montreal.
(800)50-HOTEL.

HOTEL ST. PAUL
355 Mcgill St., Montreal.
(800)50-HOTEL.

LE MERIDIEN VERSAILLES
1808 Sherbrooke West, Montreal.
(800)50-HOTEL.

LE SAINT SULPICE HOTEL
414 Rue Saint Sulpice, Montreal.
(800)50-HOTEL.

LOEWS HOTEL VOGUE
1425 Rue De La Montagne, Montreal.
(800)50-HOTEL.

QUALITY HOTEL DOWNTOWN
3440 Ave. Du Parc, Montreal.
(800)50-HOTEL.

TRAVELODGE MONTREAL CENTRE
50 Rene-Levesque West, Montreal.
(800)50-HOTEL.

Québec

DELTA QUÉBEC
690 Blvd. Rene Levesque, Québec.
(800)50-HOTEL.

Québec City

HOTEL DES COUTELLIER
253 Rue St. Paul, Quebec City.
(800)50-HOTEL.

Saskatchewan

Saskatoon

HOWARD JOHNSON SASKATOON
610 Idylwyld Drive, Saskatoon.
(800)50-HOTEL.

SASKATOON INN
2002 Airport Drive, Saskatoon.
(800)50-HOTEL.

Mexico

Acapulco

FIESTA AMERICANA CONDESA
Av. Costea Miguel Aleman No 97, Acapulco.
(800)50-HOTEL.

*See Rebate Rules on page E2 and Program Rules of Use on page E31.

Go to **entertainment.com/hotels** for the entire list of over 15,000 properties.

Guaranteed Best Rate*

Book online at **entertainment.com/hotels** for your double rebate.

HYATT REGENCY ACAPULCO
Ave. Costera Miguel Aleman #1 Col. Icacos, Acapulco.
(800)50-HOTEL.

Cancun

CANCUN PALACE
Blvd. Kukulkan Km 14.5 Quintana Roo, Cancun.
(800)50-HOTEL.

FIESTA AMERICANA GRAND CORAL
Blvd. Kukulkan Km 9.5, Cancun.
(800)50-HOTEL.

HYATT REGENCY CANCUN
Blvd. Kukulcan Km 8.5, Cancun.
(800)50-HOTEL.

J W MARRIOTT CANCUN RESORT&SPA
Blvd. Kukulkan Km 14.5 Lote 40-A, Zona Hotelera, Cancun.
(800)50-HOTEL.

Cozumel

CORAL PRINCESS HOTEL & RESORT
Carretera Costera Norte Km 2.5, Cozumel.
(800)50-HOTEL.

FIESTA AMERICANA DIVE RESORT
Carretera A Chankanaab Km 7.5, Cozumel.
(800)50-HOTEL.

Mexico City

FIESTA AMERICAN CHAPULTEPEC
Mariano Escobedo 756 Colonia Anzures, Mexico City.
(800)50-HOTEL.

MISION REFORMA
Morelos #110, Mexico City.
(800)50-HOTEL.

Puerto Vallarta

CANTO DEL SOL PLAZA VALLARTA
Jose Clemente Orozco S/N, Puerto Vallarta.
(800)50-HOTEL.

CLUB EMBARCADERO PACIFICO
Av Paseo La Marina S/N, Puerto Vallarta.
(800)50-HOTEL.

Caribbean

Bahamas

Freeport

BELL CHANNEL INN
Kings Rd., Lucaya P.O. Box F, Freeport.
(800)50-HOTEL.

Lucaya

PELICAN BAY AT LUCAYA
Seahorse Rd. Port Lucaya Marketplace, Lucaya.
(800)50-HOTEL.

Nassau

COMFORT SUITES PARADISE ISLAND
Po Box 6202, Nassau.
(800)50-HOTEL.

NASSAU BEACH HOTEL BAHAMAS
Cable Beach P.O. Box N-7756, Nassau.
(800)50-HOTEL.

WYNDHAM
Cable each Po Box N-8306, Nassau.
(800)50-HOTEL.

Paradise Island

RIU PARADISE ISLAND
6307 Casino Drive P.O. Box Ss, Paradise Island.
(800)50-HOTEL.

Cayman Islands

Grand Cayman

COMFORT SUITES & RESORT
Seven Mile Beach, Grand Cayman.
(800)50-HOTEL.

HYATT REGENCY RESORT & VILLA
Seven Mile Beach, Grand Cayman.
(800)50-HOTEL.

Puerto Rico

San Juan

BEST WESTERN HOTEL PIERRE
105 Dediego Ave., San Juan.
(800)50-HOTEL.

DIAMOND PALACE HOTEL
55 Condado Ave, San Juan.
(800)50-HOTEL.

RADISSON AMBASSADOR PLAZA
1369 Ashford Ave., Condado, San Juan.
(800)50-HOTEL.

Virgin Islands

St. John

THE WESTIN ST JOHN RESORT
Great Cruz Bay, St. John.
(800)50-HOTEL.

St. Thomas

SAPPHIRE BEACH RESORT & MARINA
6270 Smith Bay, St. Thomas.
(800)50-HOTEL.

South America

Argentina

Buenos Aires

HOWARD JOHNSON PLAZA FLORIDA
944 Florida, Buenos Aires.
(800)50-HOTEL.

NH CITY HOTEL BUENOS AIRES
Bolivar 160, Buenos Aires.
(800)50-HOTEL.

Europe

Austria

Bad Gastein

ARCOTEL ELISABETH PARK
Kaiser Franz Josef Str. 5, Bad Gastein.
(800)50-HOTEL.

Anif-Niederalm

HOTEL KAISERHOF
Salzachtal Bundesstrabe 135, Anif-Niederalm.
(800)50-HOTEL.

Czech Republic

Prague

ANNA HOTEL
Budecska 17, Prague.
(800)50-HOTEL.

GOLDEN TULIP DIPLOMAT
Evropská 15, Prague.
(800)50-HOTEL.

Denmark

Copenhagen

COMFORT HOTEL EUROPA
Colbjornsensgade 5-11, Copenhagen.
(800)50-HOTEL.

PALACE HOTEL COPENHAGEN
Raadhuspladsen 57, Copenhagen.
(800)50-HOTEL.

France

Cannes

EXCLUSIVE HOTELS BELLE PLAGE
2, Rue Brougham, Cannes.
(800)50-HOTEL.

HOTEL EDEN
133 Rue D'Antibes, Cannes.
(800)50-HOTEL.

Lille

CITADINES LILLE CENTER
Ave. Willy-Brandt-Euralille, Lille.
(800)50-HOTEL.

NEW! Double Your Rebate By Booking Online!
See page E2

*See Rebate Rules on page E2 and Program Rules of Use on page E31.

Go to **entertainment.com/hotels** for the entire list of over 15,000 properties.

Guaranteed Best Rate*

Book online at **entertainment.com/hotels** for your double rebate.

HOTEL CARLTON
3 Rue De Paris Bp 335, Lille.
(800)50-HOTEL.

Lyon

BEST WESTERN LE CHARLEMAGNE
23, Cours Charlemagne, Lyon.
(800)50-HOTEL.

Nice

BOSCOLO HOTEL PARK
6, Ave. De Suède, Nice.
(800)50-HOTEL.

HOTEL DU CENTRE
2 Rue De Suisse, Nice.
(800)50-HOTEL.

Paris

CITADINES PARIS AUSTERLITZ
27 Rue Esquirol, Paris.
(800)50-HOTEL.

COMFORT HOTEL LAMARCK
147 Rue Marcadet, Paris.
(800)50-HOTEL.

Germany

Berlin

BERLIN MARK HOTEL
Meinekestrasse 18-19, Berlin.
(800)50-HOTEL.

PARK PLAZA HOTEL BERLIN
Storkower Strasse 160/162, Berlin..
(800)50-HOTEL.

Cologne

HOTEL CRISTALL COLOGNE
Ursulaplatz 9-11, Cologne.
(800)50-HOTEL.

RADISSON SAS HOTEL
Messe Kreisel 3, Cologne.
(800)50-HOTEL.

Frankfurt

GOLDEN LEAF HOTEL & RESIDENCE
Launhardtstrasse 2-4, Frankfurt.
(800)50-HOTEL.

HOTEL MIRAMAR
Berliner Strasse 31, Frankfurt.
(800)50-HOTEL.

Hamburg

RADISSON SAS
Marseiller Strasse 2, Hamburg.
(800)50-HOTEL.

RAFFLES HTL VIER JAHRESZEITEN
Neuer Jungfernstieg 9-14, Hamburg.
(800)50-HOTEL.

Munich

GOLDEN LEAF ALTMUENCHEN
Mariahilfplatz 4, Munich.
(800)50-HOTEL.

INTERCITY HOTEL
Bayerstrasse 10, Munich.
(800)50-HOTEL.

Greece

Athens

EMMANTINA HOTEL
33 Possidonos Ave.nue, Athens.
(800)50-HOTEL.

HOTEL RIO ATHENS
13 Odysseos St., Athens.
(800)50-HOTEL.

Hungary

Budapest

BEST WESTERN GRAND HUNGARIA
Rakoczi Ut 90, Budapest.
(800)50-HOTEL.

LE MERIDIEN BUDAPEST
Erzsebet Ter 9-10, Budapest.
(800)50-HOTEL.

Ireland

Dublin

DAVENPORT HOTEL
At Merrion Square, Dublin.
(800)50-HOTEL.

GEORGIAN HOTEL
18-22 Baggot St. Lower, Dublin.
(800)50-HOTEL.

JURYS INN CUSTOM HOUSE
Custom House Quay, Dublin.
(800)50-HOTEL.

Italy

Florence

GRAND HOTEL MEDITERRANEO
Lungarno Del Tempio, 42-44, Florence.
(800)50-HOTEL.

HOTEL LONDRA
Via Jacopo Da Diacetto 16/20, Florence.
(800)50-HOTEL.

Milan

HOTEL MADISON
Via Gasparotto 8, Milan.
(800)50-HOTEL.

JOLLY HOTEL PRESIDENT
Largo Augusto, 10, Milan.
(800)50-HOTEL.

Rome

AURELIA ANTICA SUITES
Via Aurelia Antica 425, Rome.
(800)50-HOTEL.

PRINCESS
Via Andrea Ferrara, 33, Rome.
(800)50-HOTEL.

Book Online at
www.entertainment.com/hotels
or
Call 1-800-50-HOTEL
(1-800-504-6835)

TRILUSSA PALACE HOTEL
Piazza Ippolito Nievo 27, Rome.
(800)50-HOTEL.

Venice

HESPERIA
Cannaregio 459-Calle Riello, Venice.
(800)50-HOTEL.

HOTEL BUON PESCE
Riviera S. Nicolo 50, Venice.
(800)50-HOTEL.

Netherlands

Amsterdam

AMS HOTEL BEETHOVEN
Beethovenstraat 43, Amsterdam.
(800)50-HOTEL.

TULIP INN AMSTERDAM CENTRE
Nassaukade 387/390, Amsterdam.
(800)50-HOTEL.

Norway

Oslo

BEST WESTERN WEST HOTEL
Skovveien 15, Oslo.
(800)50-HOTEL.

RADISSON SAS SCANDINAVIA
Holbersgate 30, Oslo.
(800)50-HOTEL.

Portugal

Lisbon

HOTEL DO CAMPO GRANDE
Campo Grande 7, Lisbon.
(800)50-HOTEL.

HOTEL ROMA
Ave De Roma, 33, Lisbon.
(800)50-HOTEL.

Spain

Barcelona

ICARIA BARCELONA
Av. Icaria, 195, Barcelona.
(800)50-HOTEL.

REY JUAN CARLOS I
Avda.Diagonal 661-671, Barcelona.
(800)50-HOTEL.

Granada

EH SAN ANTON
San Anton S/N, Granada.
(800)50-HOTEL.

*See Rebate Rules on page E2 and Program Rules of Use on page E31.

Go to **entertainment.com/hotels** for the entire list of over 15,000 properties.

Guaranteed Best Rate*

Book online at **entertainment.com/hotels** for your double rebate.

HOTEL ALIXARES
Paseo De La Sabika 27, Granada.
(800)50-HOTEL.

Madrid

EMPERADOR
Gran Vía, 53, Madrid.
(800)50-HOTEL.

HIGH TECH PRIME CLIPER
Chinchilla, 6, Madrid.
(800)50-HOTEL.

Sweden

Gothenburg

ELITE PLAZA
Vastra Hamngatan 3, Gothenburg.
(800)50-HOTEL.

QUALITY HOTEL PANORAMA
Eklandagatan 51-53, Gothenburg.
(800)50-HOTEL.

Stockholm

ELITE HOTEL PLAZA
Birger Jarlsgatan 29 Box 7707, Stockholm.
(800)50-HOTEL.

RADISSON SAS SKYCITY HOTEL
P.O. Box 82 Terminal 5, Stockholm.
(800)50-HOTEL.

Switzerland

Geneva

BRISTOL
10 Rue Du Mont-Blanc, Geneva.
(800)50-HOTEL.

LE WARWICK
14 Rue De Lausanne, Geneva.
(800)50-HOTEL.

Zurich

HOTEL BRISTOL
Stampfenbachstrasse 34, Zurich.
(800)50-HOTEL.

Zurich-Kloten

HOTEL ALLEGRA
Hamelirainstrasse 3, Zurich-Kloten.
(800)50-HOTEL.

Turkey

Istanbul

GERMIR PALAS HOTEL
Cumhuriyet Caddesi No 17, Istanbul.
(800)50-HOTEL.

HOTEL SABA
Sehit Mehmet Pasa Yk No. 8, Istanbul.
(800)50-HOTEL.

United Kingdom

England

London

BEST WESTERN LODGE HOTEL
52-54 Upper Richmond Rd., London.
(800)50-HOTEL.

COMFORT INN EARL'S COURT
11-13 Pennywern Rd., London.
(800)50-HOTEL.

JURYS INN
60 Pentonville Rd., London.
(800)50-HOTEL.

Manchester

BRITANNIA AIRPORT HOTEL
Palatine Rd.,Northenden, Manchester.
(800)50-HOTEL.

RADISSON EDWARDIAN MANCHESTER
Free Trade Hall, Peter St., Manchester.
(800)50-HOTEL.

Scotland

Edinburgh

APEX CITY HOTEL
61 Grassmarket, Edinburgh.
(800)50-HOTEL.

BANK HOTEL
1 S Bridge,, Edinburgh.
(800)50-HOTEL.

Glasgow

CITY INN GLASGOW
Finnieston Quay, Glasgow.
(800)50-HOTEL.

THISTLE GLASGOW
Cambridge St., Glasgow.
(800)50-HOTEL.

Middle East

United Arab Emirates

Dubai

DUBAI GRAND HOTEL
Damascus St., Dubai.
(800)50-HOTEL.

METROPOLITAN DEIRA HOTEL
P.O.Box 33214, Dubai.
(800)50-HOTEL.

Asia

Japan

Tokyo

DAI-ICHI HOTEL TOKYO SEAFORT
2-3-15 Higashi Shinagawa Shinagawa-Ku, Tokyo.
(800)50-HOTEL.

ROYAL PARK HOTEL
2-1-1 Nihonbashi Kakigara-Cho Chuo-Ku, Tokyo.
(800)50-HOTEL.

SHIMBASHI ATAGOYAMA TOKYU INN
1-28-2 Atago Minato-Ku, Tokyo.
(800)50-HOTEL.

Singapore

Singapore

CITY BAYVIEW SINGAPORE
30 Bencoolen St., Singapore.
(800)50-HOTEL.

ORCHARD HOTEL
442 Orchard Rd., Singapore.
(800)50-HOTEL.

Thailand

Bangkok

ASIA HOTEL BANGKOK
296 Phayathai Rd., Rajthavee, Bangkok.
(800)50-HOTEL.

LE MERIDIEN PRESIDENT BANGKOK
971 Ploenchit Rd., Lumpini Pratumwan, Bangkok.
(800)50-HOTEL.

Australia

Melbourne

ASTORIA CITY TRAVEL INN
288 Spencer St., Melbourne.
(800)50-HOTEL.

HOTEL GRAND CHANCELLOR
131 Lonsdale St., Melbourne.
(800)50-HOTEL.

Perth

SULLIVANS HOTEL PERTH
166 Mounts Bay Rd., Perth.
(800)50-HOTEL.

Sydney

ADDISON'S ON ANZAC
147 Anzac Parade, Sydney.
(800)50-HOTEL.

NEW!
Double Your Rebate
By Booking Online!
See page E2

*See Rebate Rules on page E2 and Program Rules of Use on page E31.

Go to **entertainment.com/hotels** for the entire list of over 15,000 properties.

Guaranteed Best Rate* Program

Rules of Use

- Rate is guaranteed at the time of reservation to be the best rate for the room type at the same hotel on the dates booked. If you find a lower rate available for the same dates at the same hotel, within 24 hours of booking the reservation with us, call 1-800-50-HOTEL (800-504-6835) and we will either refund the difference or cancel the reservation without a cancellation fee.

- You will be required to prepay with a major credit card.

- To change or cancel your reservation, call 1-800-50-HOTEL (800-504-6835). A fee will be applied to your credit card for any change or cancellation.

- The cancellation fee as of May 1, 2005, is $25 USD, which is subject to change. In addition, if you do not change or cancel your reservation before the cancellation policy period applicable to the hotel you reserved, which varies by hotel (usually 24 to 72 hours prior to your date of arrival), you will be subject to a charge of one-night's room rate, tax recovery charges, service fees and additional fees that may vary by hotel or property. Please request information on the applicable cancellation fees prior to making your reservation. No refunds will be made for no-shows or early checkouts.

- Some peak dates may not be discounted, and the rate guarantee does not apply to special events such as New Year's Eve and the Super Bowl.

- Guaranteed Best Rate Program hotels are not subject to any additional discounts, except the rebate. See Page E2.

- All rates are quoted and billed in U.S. funds unless otherwise specified.

All information was current at the time of printing and is expected to be in effect through the expiration of the Entertainment® book. However, changes beyond our control may affect the information prior to the expiration. Please note that Entertainment Publications, Inc. cannot guarantee the level of services offered at a property and/or if services are operational at the time of visit. Services may be closed due to seasonality reasons and/or may be closed for renovation.

Chain-Wide Savings

GREAT BRANDS GREAT SAVINGS

UP TO 20% OFF

How to Save:

1. Call the Hotel of Your Choice
2. Give the ID Number
3. Receive Your Savings

Travelodge
800-407-0241
ID# 00007700-50309

Days Inn
800-477-0593
ID# 00007700-928378

Best Western
888-897-8962
ID# 00138130

Wingate Inn
877-371-1564
ID# 00007700-928378

Red Roof Inns (Accor hotels)
888-317-7581
ID# CP501838

Comfort Inn · Comfort Suites · Quality · Sleep Inn · Clarion · MainStay Suites · Econo Lodge · Rodeway Inn

CHOICE HOTELS INTERNATIONAL®

800-533-2100*
ID# 00057187

Chain-Wide Savings

La Quinta Inn / La Quinta Inn & Suites
800-533-6821
ID# ROOMS

Howard Johnson
Where you feel at home.℠
800-769-0951
ID# 00007700-928378

Radisson
800-419-3333*
ID# 80478436

RAMADA WORLDWIDE
800-862-4368
ID# 00007700-928378

InterContinental Hotels & Resorts
888-211-9872*
ID# 100200985

Hotel Indigo
888-211-9872*
ID# 100200985

Crowne Plaza Hotels & Resorts
888-211-9872*
ID# 100200985

Holiday Inn Hotels · Resorts
888-211-9872*
ID# 100200985

Holiday Inn Express
888-211-9872*
ID# 100200985

Staybridge Suites
888-211-9872*
ID# 100200985

Candlewood Suites
888-211-9872*
ID# 100200985

IMPORTANT: Valid only at participating locations. Discount rates apply to regular (rack) non-discounted room rates and are subject to program room availability. Advance reservations required. Some blackout periods may apply. This program cannot be used in conjunction with any other discount promotional room rate. The toll-free numbers listed are valid only for booking the promotional rate that accompanies the ID# listed. Not valid for group travel. Asterisk (*) denotes chains offering savings at participating international locations. **Expires December 31, 2006.**

Direct To Hotel Program

Save 50% *off full-priced rates*
or 10% off the best promotional rate available to the public.

Here's how...

1. Find your city and choose a hotel. See listings on pages E35–E45 or go to www.entertainment.com/directtohotel.

2. Call the hotel directly using the number listed to make advance reservations.
   - Identify yourself as an **Entertainment®** Member.
   - Check if the Entertainment® rate* is available for your travel dates.
   - Receive a confirmation number and retain it for your records.

3. Present your Entertainment® membership card at check-in.

*See the Rules of Use on page E46 for full program details.

Your Key to Savings

$ Indicates the hotel's full-priced (rack) room rate before the discount.

$	=	Up to $60
$$	=	$61–$100
$$$	=	$101–$150
$$$$	=	$151 and Up

R30 Indicates reservations only accepted within 30 days of arrival.

U.S. funds. (Canadian hotels are in Canadian funds.)
(Rates subject to change. Hotel rates may fluctuate throughout the year due to seasonal factors.)

Direct To Hotel

50% off full-priced (rack) room rates or 10% off the best promotional rate–subject to availability.

United States of America

Alabama

For this state's listings go to entertainment.com/directtohotel

Alaska

Anchorage

COAST INTERNATIONAL INN, $$$
3333 International Airport Rd., Anchorage. Valid for any room. Valid September thru May. R30. (907)243-2233, (800)544-0986

DAYS INN DOWNTOWN, $$$$
321 E. 5th Ave., Anchorage. Valid for any room. Valid September thru May. (907)276-7226

Arizona

Scottsdale

RENAISSANCE SCOTTSDALE RESORT, $$$$
6160 N. Scottsdale Rd, Scottsdale. Valid for any room or suite. (480)991-1414

SUMMERFIELD SUITES BY WYNDHAM - SCOTTSDALE, $$$$
4245 North Drinkwater Blvd., Scottsdale. Valid for one suite. (972)915-7070, (800)WYN-DHAM

THE SCOTTSDALE PLAZA RESORT, $$$$
7200 N. Scottsdale Rd., Scottsdale. Valid for any room or suite. R30. (480)948-5000, (800)832-2025

THE WESTIN KIERLAND VILLAS, $$$$
15620 North Clubgate Dr., Scottsdale. Valid for any room. R30. (480)624-1700, (866)837-4273

Tucson

DOUBLETREE HOTEL REID PARK, $$$$
445 S. Alvernon Way, Tucson. Valid for any room. (520)881-4200

OMNI TUCSON NATIONAL GOLF RESORT & SPA, $$$$
2727 W. Club Dr., Tucson. Valid for one deluxe room. Valid April thru December. R30. (520)297-2271, (800)THE-OMNI

RESIDENCE INN - TUCSON, $$$$
6477 E. Speedway Blvd., Tucson. Valid for any room. Valid April 15 thru December 15. R30. (520)721-0991

Arkansas

For this state's listings go to entertainment.com/directtohotel

California

Anaheim

ANAHEIM PLAZA HOTEL & SUITES, $$$
1700 South Harbor Blvd., Anaheim. Valid for any room. (714)772-5900

CARRIAGE INN, $$
2125 S. Harbor Blvd., Anaheim. Valid for any room. (714)740-1440, (800)345-2131

CASTLE INN, $$$
1734 S. Harbor Blvd., Anaheim. Valid for one standard room. Valid September thru May. (714)774-8111, (800)227-8530

DESERT PALMS HOTEL & SUITES, $$$
631 W. Katella Ave., Anaheim. Valid for any room. Valid September thru May. (714)535-1133, (888)521-6420

PORTOFINO INN & SUITES, $$$$
1831 S. Harbor Blvd, Anaheim. Valid for any room. Valid September thru May. Holidays & special events excl. (714)782-7600, (888)368-7971

RAMADA INN MAINGATE, $$$
1650 S. Harbor Blvd., Anaheim. Valid for one standard room. Holidays excl. (714)772-0440, (800)854-6097

SUPER 8 ANAHEIM/DISNEYLAND PARK, $$
415 W. Katella Ave., Anaheim. Valid for any room. Holidays excl. (714)778-6900, (800)777-7123

Beverly Hills

BEST WESTERN BEVERLY PAVILION, $$$$
9360 Wilshire Blvd., Beverly Hills. Valid for any room. Valid Sunday thru Thursday. July, August, special events & holidays excl. R30. (310)273-1400, (800)441-5050

DOUBLETREE HOTEL - LOS ANGELES/ WESTWOOD, $$$$
10740 Wilshire Blvd., Los Angeles. Valid for any room. Special events & New Year's Eve excl. (310)475-8711

LUXE HOTEL RODEO DRIVE, $$$$
360 North Rodeo Drive, Beverly Hills. Valid for any room. (310)273-0300

Carmel/Monterey

THE INN AT PASATIEMPO, $$$$
555 Hwy. 17, Santa Cruz. Valid for any room. Valid Sunday thru Thursday. (831)423-5000, (800)834-2546

WAYSIDE INN, $$$$
Corner of 7th St. & Mission, Carmel. Valid for any room or suite. Valid Sunday thru Thursday. July, Aug, holidays & special events excl. (831)624-5336, (800)433-4732

Los Angeles

HOTEL SOFITEL, $$$$
8555 Beverly Blvd., Los Angeles. Valid for any room. Suites excluded. (310)278-5444, (800)521-7772

NEW OTANI HOTEL & GARDEN, $$$$
120 S. Los Angeles St., Los Angeles. Valid for one deluxe room. (213)629-1200, (800)639-6826

OMNI LOS ANGELES HOTEL AT CALIFORNIA PLAZA, $$$$
251 S. Olive St., Los Angeles. Valid for one deluxe room. (213)617-3300, (800)THE-OMNI

Los Angeles Int'l Airport

SUMMERFIELD SUITES BY WYNDHAM - EL SEGUNDO, $$$$
810 S. Douglas St., El Segundo. Valid for one suite. (972)915-7070, (800)WYN-DHAM

TRAVELODGE HOTEL AT LAX, $$
5547 W. Century Blvd., Los Angeles. Valid for any room. (800)421-3939

Napa Valley

CALISTOGA GOLDEN HAVEN SPA & RESORT, $$$
1713 Lake St., Calistoga. Valid for any room. Economy rooms excl. Valid Sunday thru Thursday October thru June. R30. (707)942-6793

THE CHABLIS INN, $$$
3360 Solano Ave., Napa. Valid for one standard room. Valid Sunday thru Thursday October - June. (707)257-1944, (800)443-3490

Palm Springs

AZURE SKY RESORT, $$
1661 Calle Palo Fierro, Palm Springs. Valid for any room or suite. Holidays excl. R30. (760)325-9109, (800)874-8770

PALM SPRINGS COURTYARD, $$$$
1300 Tahquitz Canyon Way, Palm Springs. Valid for one standard room. (760)322-6100, (800)321-2211

PALM SPRINGS TENNIS CLUB RESORT, $$$$
701 W. Baristo Rd., Palm Springs. Valid for any room or condo. Holidays excluded. (714)777-3700, (800)854-2324

Sacramento

GOVERNORS INN, $$$
210 Richards Blvd., Sacramento. Valid for any room. Valid Friday, Saturday & Sunday. (916)448-7224

HILTON SACRAMENTO ARDEN WEST, $$$$
2200 Harvard St., Sacramento. Valid for any room. (916)922-4700

LA QUINTA INN DOWNTOWN, $$$
200 Jibboom St, Sacramento. Valid for any room. Special events excluded. (210)616-7601, (800)531-5900

San Diego

BEST WESTERN BLUE SEA LODGE, $$$$
707 Pacific Beach Dr., San Diego. Valid for any room. Valid Sunday thru Thursday. July-Aug, special events & holidays excl. (858)488-4700, (800)258-3732

BEST WESTERN ISLAND PALMS HOTEL & MARINA, $$$$
2051 Shelter Island Dr., San Diego. Valid for marina view room or suite. (619)222-0561, (800)345-9995

COMFORT INN & SUITES - HOTEL CIRCLE, $$$$
2201 Hotel Circle S, San Diego. Valid for any room. Valid September thru May. Holidays & special events excl. (619)881-6800, (800)621-1304

HOLIDAY INN RANCHO BERNARDO, $$$$
17065 W. Bernardo Dr., San Diego. Valid for any room. Valid September thru June. Holiday wknds excl. (858)485-6530, (800)777-6055

HOWARD JOHNSON EXPRESS INN - SEAWORLD, $$$
1631 Hotel Circle South, San Diego. Valid for any room. Holidays & special events excl. (619)293-7792, (800)876-8937

PACIFIC TERRACE HOTEL, $$$$
610 Diamond St., San Diego. Valid for any room. Valid Sunday thru Thursday September 15 thru May 31. R30. (858)581-3500, (800)344-3370

SOMMERSET SUITES HOTEL, $$$$
606 Washington St., San Diego. Valid for one suite. Valid Sunday thru Thursday. July thru August, special events & holidays excl. (619)692-5200, (800)962-9665

THE DANA ON MISSION BAY, $$$$
1710 W. Mission Bay Dr., San Diego. Valid for one marina view room. R30. (619)222-6440, (800)345-9995

TOWN & COUNTRY RESORT HOTEL, $$$$
500 Hotel Circle N., San Diego. Valid for any room. Holiday wknds excl. (619)291-7131, (800)772-8527

WYNDHAM EMERALD PLAZA, $$$$
400 W. Broadway, San Diego. Valid for one standard room. (972)915-7070, (800)WYN-DHAM

Direct To Hotel

Contact the hotels directly to get your Entertainment® Membership rate availability.

San Francisco

FRANCISCO BAY INN, $$$
1501 Lombard St., San Francisco. Valid for one deluxe room. (415)474-3030, (800)410-7007

MARK HOPKINS INTER-CONTINENTAL, $$$$
One Nob Hill, San Francisco. Valid for one standard room. R30. (415)392-3434

PAN PACIFIC, $$$$
500 Post St., San Francisco. Valid for any room. (415)771-8600

THE PICKWICK HOTEL, $$$$
85 Fifth St., San Francisco. Valid for any room. (415)421-7500, (800)227-3282

San Francisco Int'l Airport

HYATT REGENCY SAN FRANCISCO AIRPORT, $$$$
1333 Bayshore Hwy., Burlingame. Valid for any room. R30. (650)347-1234, (800)233-1234

STAYBRIDGE SUITES SAN FRANCISCO AIRPORT, $$$$
1350 Huntington Ave., San Bruno. Valid for one suite. (650)588-0770

Santa Barbara

MONTECITO INN, $$$$
1295 Coast Village Rd., Santa Barbara. Valid for any room. Valid Sunday thru Thursday. Holidays excl. July & Aug excl. R30. (805)969-7854, (800)843-2017

RADISSON HOTEL SANTA BARBARA, $$$$
1111 E. Cabrillo Blvd., Santa Barbara. Valid for any room. Valid Sunday thru Thursday. Holidays excluded. (805)963-0744, (800)643-1994

Colorado

Avon/Beaver Creek

SHERATON MOUNTAIN VISTA, $$$$
160 W Beaver Creek Blvd, Avon. Valid for any room. R30. (970)748-6000, (888)627-8098

THE CHARTER AT BEAVER CREEK, $$$$
120 Offerson Road, Beaver Creek. Valid for one unit. R30. (970)949-6660, (800)525-6660

THE SEASONS AT AVON, $$$$
137 Benchmark Road, Avon. Valid for any room. R30. (970)845-5990, (877)930-7669

Colorado Springs

APOLLO PARK EXECUTIVE SUITES, $$$
805 S. Circle Dr. #2-B, Colorado Springs. Valid for one suite. (719)634-0286, (800)279-3620

COLORADO SPRINGS HAMPTON INN, $$$
7245 Commerce Center Dr., Colorado Springs. Valid for any room. Valid September thru May. R30. (719)593-9700

Denver

HAMPTON INN NE, $$
4685 Quebec St., Denver. Valid for any room. R30. (303)388-8100

SUMMERFIELD STES BY WYNDHAM - DENVER TECH CTR, $$$$
9280 E. Costilla Ave., Englewood. Valid for one suite. (972)915-7070, (800)WYN-DHAM

THE BURNSLEY ALL SUITE HOTEL, $$$$
1000 Grant St., Denver. Valid for one suite. (303)830-1000, (800)231-3915

Telluride

WYNDHAM PEAKS RESORT & GOLDEN DOOR SPA, $$$$
136 Country Club Dr., Telluride. Valid for one standard room. (972)915-7070, (800)WYN-DHAM

Connecticut

Danbury

WELLESLEY INN, $$$
116 Newton Rd., Danbury. Valid for any room. Special events excluded. R30. (203)792-3800

Hartford

CROWN PLAZA HARTFORD DOWNTOWN, $$$$
50 Morgan St., (13 miles from Bradley International Airport), Hartford. Valid for one standard room. (860)549-2400

HOLIDAY INN EAST HARTFORD, $$$
363 Roberts St., East Hartford. Valid for any room. Valid Friday, Saturday & Sunday. (860)528-9611

Mystic

COMFORT INN, $$$
48 Whitehall Ave., Mystic. Valid for any room. Valid Sunday thru Thursday October thru June. Special events & holidays excl. (860)572-8531

DAYS INN MYSTIC, $$
55 Whitehall Ave., Mystic. Valid for any room. Valid Sunday thru Thursday November thru June. Special events & holidays excl. (860)572-0574

New Haven

NEW HAVEN HOTEL, $$$
229 George St., New Haven. Valid for any room. (203)498-3100, (800)NHH-OTEL

OMNI NEW HAVEN HOTEL AT YALE, $$$$
155 Temple St., New Haven. Valid for one deluxe room. (203)772-6664, (800)THE-OMNI

Delaware

Wilmington

BRANDYWINE SUITES HOTEL, $$$$
707 North King St., Wilmington. Valid for one suite. (302)656-9300, (800)756-0070

HOLIDAY INN SELECT - WILMINGTON, $$$
630 Naamans Rd., Claymont. Valid for any room. (302)792-2700

WYNDHAM WILMINGTON, $$$$
700 N. King St., Wilmington. Valid for one standard room. (972)915-7070, (800)WYN-DHAM

District Of Columbia

Washington D.C.

BEACON HOTEL & CORPORATE QUARTERS, $$$$
1615 Rhode Island Ave. NW, Washington. Valid for any room or suite. Valid Friday, Saturday, Sunday & holidays. (202)296-2100

GEORGETOWN SUITES, $$$
1000 29th St. NW, Washington. Valid for one suite. April, May & October excluded. (202)298-1600

HOLIDAY INN DOWNTOWN, $$$$
1155 14th Street, NW, Washington. Valid for any room. (202)737-1200

OMNI SHOREHAM HOTEL, $$$$
2500 Calvert St. N.W., Washington. Valid for one deluxe room. (202)234-0700, (800)THE-OMNI

WASHINGTON PLAZA, $$$$
10 Thomas Circle, NW, Washington. Valid for any room. (202)842-1300, (800)424-1140

WYNDHAM WASHINGTON DC, $$$$
1400 M St. NW, Washington. Valid for one standard room. (972)915-7070, (800)WYN-DHAM

Florida

Clearwater

ECONOLODGE INN & SUITES, $$
11333 US Hwy 19 N., Clearwater. Valid for one deluxe or standard room. Valid April thru December. Holidays excl. (727)572-4929

HOLIDAY INN EXPRESS, $$$
13625 ICOT Blvd., Clearwater. Valid for any room. (727)536-7275

RADISSON RESORT ON CLEARWATER BEACH, $$$$
430 S. Gulfview Blvd., Clearwater Beach. Valid for any room. (727)433-5714, (866)707-8924

Florida Keys

SHERATON SUITES KEY WEST, $$$$
2001 Roosevelt Blvd., Key West. Valid for one suite. Fantasy Fest & Dec 23-31 excl. (305)292-9800, (800)45B-EACH

WYNDHAM CASA MARINA RESORT, $$$$
1500 Reynolds St., Key West. Valid for one standard room. (972)915-7070, (800)WYN-DHAM

Ft. Lauderdale

BONAVENTURE RESORT & SPA, $$$$
250 Racquet Club Rd., Ft. Lauderdale. Valid for one standard room. (972)915-7070, (800)996-3426

FT. LAUDERDALE BEACH RESORT, $$$$
909 Breakers Ave., Ft. Lauderdale. Valid for any room or suite. Holidays excl. R30. (954)566-8800, (800)874-8770

SHERATON YANKEE TRADER BEACH HOTEL, $$$$
321 N. Ft. Lauderdale Beach Blvd., Ft. Lauderdale. Valid for any room or suite. (954)467-1111, (888)627-7108

Jacksonville

BEST WESTERN JTB/SOUTHPOINT, $$$$
4660 Sailsbury Rd., Jacksonville. Valid for any room. Special events excl. R30. (904)281-0900, (800)842-1348

LA QUINTA INN AIRPORT/NORTH, $$
812 Dunn Ave, Jacksonville. Valid for any room. Special events excluded. (210)616-7601, (800)531-5900

Kissimmee

CYPRESS PALMS, $$$$
5324 Fairfield Lake Dr., Kissimmee. Valid for any room. R30. (800)438-6493

MASTER'S INN MAINGATE, $$
2945 Entry Point Blvd., Kissimmee. Valid for one standard room. (407)396-7743, (800)633-3434

Discount subject to availability. Please read the **Rules of Use** on page E46.

Remember to identify yourself as an Entertainment® Member

Direct To Hotel

50% off full-priced (rack) room rates or 10% off the best promotional rate–subject to availability.

QUALITY SUITES AT DISNEY'S MAINGATE, $$$$
5876 W. Irlo Bronson Hwy (US 192), Kissimmee. Valid for one 1 or 2 bedroom suites. (407)396-8040, (800)848-4148

WYNDHAM PALMS RESORT & COUNTRY CLUB, $$$$
7900 Palms Pkwy., Kissimmee. Valid for one 1 or 2 bedroom condo. (972)915-7070, (800)WYN-DHAM

Lake Buena Vista

COURTYARD BY MARRIOTT - LAKE BUENA VISTA, $$$
8501 Palm Pkwy., Lake Buena Vista. Valid for any room. (407)239-6900, (800)787-3636

GROSVENOR RESORT, $$$
1850 Hotel Plaza Blvd., Lake Buena Vista. Valid for any room. (407)828-4444, (800)624-4109

WALT DISNEY WORLD SWAN & DOLPHIN, $$$$
1500 Epcot Resorts Blvd., Lake Buena Vista. Valid for any room. Dec 25-Jan 1 excl. (800)227-1500

WYNDHAM PALACE RESORT & SPA, $$$$
1900 Buena Vista Dr., Lake Buena Vista. Valid for one standard room. (972)915-7070, (800)WYN-DHAM

Miami

HOTEL PLACE ST. MICHEL, $$$
162 Alcazar Ave., Coral Gables. Valid for any room. Suites excluded. (305)444-1666, (800)848-4683

OMNI COLONNADE HOTEL, $$$$
180 Aragon Ave., Coral Gables. Valid for one deluxe room. (305)441-2600, (800)THE-OMNI

SUMMERFIELD SUITES BY WYNDHAM - MIAMI AIRPORT, $$$$
5710 Blue Lagoon Dr., Miami. Valid for one suite. (972)915-7070, (800)WYN-DHAM

WYNDHAM GRAND BAY - COCONUT GROVE, $$$$
2669 S. Bayshore Dr., Miami. Valid for one standard room. (972)915-7070, (800)WYN-DHAM

Miami Beach

SOUTH SEAS HOTEL, $$$
1751 Collins Ave., Miami Beach. Valid for any room. Holidays & special events excl. R30. (305)538-1411, (800)345-2678

WYNDHAM MIAMI BEACH RESORT, $$$$
4833 Collins Ave., Miami Beach. Valid for one standard room. (972)915-7070, (800)WYN-DHAM

Orlando

DOUBLETREE CLUB LAKE BUENA VISTA, $$$
12490 Apopka-Vineland, Orlando. Valid for any room. (407)239-4646, (800)521-3297

HOMEWOOD SUITES - ORLANDO, $$$$
8745 International Dr., Orlando. Valid for one suite. R30. (407)248-2232

LA QUINTA INN & SUITES U.C.F., $$
11805 Research Pkwy, Orlando. Valid for any room. Special events excluded. (210)616-7601, (800)531-5900

SHERATON STUDIO CITY HOTEL, $$$$
5905 International Dr., Orlando. Valid for any room. (407)351-2100, (800)327-1366

SHERATON SUITES ORLANDO AIRPORT, $$$$
7550 Augusta National Dr., Orlando. Valid for one suite. (407)240-5555, (888)675-2477

WYNDHAM ORLANDO RESORT, $$$$
8001 International Dr., Orlando. Valid for one standard room. (972)915-7070, (800)WYN-DHAM

Tampa

HAMPTON INN TAMPA AIRPORT, $$$
4817 W. Laurel St., Tampa. Valid for any room. Valid Friday, Saturday & Sunday April thru December. (813)287-0778

LA QUINTA INN & SUITES U.S.F., $$$
3701 E Fowler, Tampa. Valid for any room. Special events excluded. (210)616-7601, (800)531-5900

WYNDHAM HARBOUR ISLAND, $$$$
725 S. Harbour Island Blvd., Tampa. Valid for one standard room. (972)915-7070, (800)WYN-DHAM

Georgia

Atlanta

COURTYARD BY MARRIOTT DOWNTOWN, $$$
175 Piedmont Ave., NE, Atlanta. Valid for any room. Suites excluded. R30. (404)659-2727

SIERRA SUITES-ATLANTA PERIMETER, $$$
6330 Peachtree Dunwoody Rd. N.E., Atlanta. Valid for one suite. (770)379-0111, (800)474-3772

WYNDHAM ATLANTA, $$$$
160 Spring St. NW, Atlanta. Valid for one standard room. (972)915-7070, (800)WYN-DHAM

Savannah

DAYS INN, $$$
201 W. Bay St., Savannah. Valid for any room or suite. (912)236-4440

LA QUINTA INN MIDTOWN, $$
6805 Abercorn St, Savannah. Valid for any room. Special events excluded. (210)616-7601, (800)531-5900

Hawaii

Big Island

KING KAMEHAMEHA'S KONA BEACH HOTEL, $$$$
75-5660 Palani Rd., Kailua-Kona. Valid for one partial oceanview or garden view room. R30. (808)329-2911, (800)367-6060

KONA REEF, $$$$
75-5888 Alii Dr., Kailua-Kona. Valid for one one bedroom suite. 2- & 3-bedroom units excl. Triathlon period excl. R30. (808)545-3510, (800)367-5004

OUTRIGGER KEAUHOU BEACH RESORT, $$$$
78-6740 Alii Dr., Keauhou. Valid for any room. R30. (303)369-7777, (800)462-6262

THE SHORES AT WAIKOLOA, $$$$
69-1035 Keana Place, Waikoloa. Valid for one condo. Dec 23-Jan 3 & Feb 18-21 excl. (403)444-4136, (800)922-7866

Kauai

ASTON ISLANDER ON THE BEACH, $$$$
4-484 Kuhio Hwy., Kapaa. Valid for any room. Dec 23-Jan 3 & Feb 18-21 excl. (403)444-4136, (800)922-7866

LANIKAI RESORT, $$$$
390 Papaloa Rd., Honolulu. Valid for any room. (808)545-3510, (800)367-5004

PALI KE KUA AT PRINCEVILLE, $$$$
5300 Ka Haku Rd., Princeville-Hanalei. Valid for one suite. (808)922-9700, (800)535-0085

RADISSON KAUAI BEACH RESORT, $$$$
4331 Kauai Beach Dr., Lihue. Valid for any room. (808)245-1955, (888)805-3843

Maui

ASTON KAANAPALI SHORES, $$$$
3445 Lower Honoapiilani Rd., Kaanapali. Valid for one one bedroom suite. Dec 23-Jan 3 & Feb 18-21 excl. (403)444-4136, (800)922-7866

ASTON MAHANA AT KAANAPALI, $$$$
110 Kaanapali Shores Place, Kaanapali. Valid for one suite. Min stay 3 nts. Dec 23-Jan 3 & Feb 18-21 excl. (403)444-4136, (800)922-7866

MAUI SEASIDE HOTEL, $$$
100 W. Kaahumanu Ave., Kahului. Valid for any room. Standard rooms excl. (808)877-3311, (800)560-5552

OHANA MAUI ISLANDER HOTEL, $$$
660 Wainee Street, Lahaina. Valid for any room. R30. (303)369-7777, (800)462-6262

Molokai

KALUAKOI VILLAS, $$$$
1131 Kaluakoi Rd., Maunaloa. Valid for any room. Special events excl. (808)545-3510, (800)367-5004

MARC MOLOKAI SHORES, $$$$
Kamehameha Hwy., Star Rte., Kaunakakai. Valid for one suite. (808)922-9700, (800)535-0085

Oahu

ASTON AT THE WAIKIKI BANYAN, $$$$
201 Ohua Ave., Honolulu. Valid for one condo. Dec 23-Jan 3 & Feb 18-21 excl. (403)444-4136, (800)922-7866

ISLAND COLONY - HONOLULU, $$$$
445 Seaside Ave., Honolulu. Valid for any room. (808)545-3510, (800)367-5004

MARC SUITES WAIKIKI, $$$
412 Lewers St., Honolulu. Valid for one suite. (808)922-9700, (800)535-0085

OHANA ISLANDER WAIKIKI, $$$$
270 Lewers St., Honolulu. Valid for select categories of rooms. R30. (303)369-7777, (800)462-6262

Idaho

For this state's listings go to entertainment.com/directtohotel

Illinois

Chicago

DAYS INN GOLD COAST, $$$$
1816 N. Clark, Chicago. Valid for any room. Valid Sunday thru Thursday. Special events & holidays excl. (312)664-3040

OMNI AMBASSADOR EAST, $$$$
1301 North State Pkwy., Chicago. Valid for one deluxe room. (312)787-7200, (800)THE-OMNI

OMNI CHICAGO HOTEL, $$$$
676 N. Michigan Ave., Chicago. Valid for one suite. (312)944-6664, (800)THE-OMNI

RADISSON HOTEL & SUITES CHICAGO, $$$$
160 E. Huron St., Chicago. Valid for any room. (312)787-2900

WESTIN CHICAGO RIVER NORTH, $$$$
320 North Dearborn, Chicago. Valid for any room. Suites excl. R30. (312)744-1900

Direct To Hotel

Contact the hotels directly to get your Entertainment® Membership rate availability.

WYNDHAM CHICAGO, $$$$
633 N. St. Clair St., Chicago. Valid for one standard room. (972)915-7070, (800)WYN-DHAM

Des Plaines

BEST WESTERN DES PLAINES, $$$
1231 Lee, Des Plaines. Valid for any room. (847)297-2100

WYNDHAM O'HARE, $$$$
6810 N. Mannheim Rd., Rosemont. Valid for one standard room. (972)915-7070, (800)WYN-DHAM

Elk Grove

BEST WESTERN CHICAGO WEST, $$$
1600 Oakton St., Elk Grove Village. Valid for any room. (847)981-0010

LA QUINTA INN O'HARE AIRPORT, $$$
1900 E Oakton St, Chicago. Valid for any room. Special events excluded. (210)616-7601, (800)531-5900

Oak Brook

LA QUINTA INN OAKBROOK, $$$
15666 Midwest Rd, Oakbrook Terrace. Valid for any room. Special events excluded. (210)616-7601, (800)531-5900

OAK BROOK HILLS HOTEL & RESORT, $$$
3500 Midwest Rd., Oak Brook. Valid for any room. Suites excluded. (630)850-5555

Schaumburg

HAWTHORN SUITES CHICAGO/ SCHAUMBURG, $$$$
1251 E. American Lane, Schaumburg. Valid for any room. (847)706-9007

WYNDHAM GARDEN - SCHAUMBURG, $$$$
800 National Pkwy., Schaumburg. Valid for one standard room. (972)915-7070, (800)WYN-DHAM

Indiana

Indianapolis

ADAM'S MARK INDIANAPOLIS, $$$$
2544 Executive Dr., Indianapolis. Valid for any room. (317)248-2481

CLARION HOTEL & CONFERENCE CENTER, $$$
2930 Waterfront Pkwy. W., Indianapolis. Valid for any room. Wknds in May, Race wknds & special events excl. (317)299-8400

COMFORT INN & SUITES, $$$$
9090 Wesleyan Rd., Indianapolis. Valid for any room. Valid Sunday thru Thursday. Indy 500 & special events excl. R30. (317)875-7676

MARRIOTT INDIANAPOLIS EAST, $$$$
7202 E. 21st St., Indianapolis. Valid for any room. Advance purchase rates excl. (317)352-1231

MARTEN HOUSE HOTEL & LILLY CONFERENCE CENTER, $$$
1801 W. 86th St., Indianapolis. Valid for any room. Special events excl. (317)872-4111, (800)736-5634

OMNI SEVERIN HOTEL, $$$$
40 W. Jackson Place, Indianapolis. Valid for one deluxe room. (317)634-6664, (800)THE-OMNI

SHERATON INDIANAPOLIS HOTEL & SUITES, $$$$
8787 Keystone Crossing, Indianapolis. Valid for one standard room. Special events excl. R30. (317)846-2700

Iowa

For this state's listings go to entertainment.com/directtohotel

Kansas

For this state's listings go to entertainment.com/directtohotel

Kentucky

For this state's listings go to entertainment.com/directtohotell

Louisiana

New Orleans

LA QUINTA INN CROWDER, $$$$
8400 I-10 Service Rd, New Orleans. Valid for any room. Special events excluded. (210)616-7601, (800)531-5900

OMNI ROYAL CRESCENT HOTEL, $$$$
535 Gravier St., New Orleans. Valid for one deluxe room. Valid Sunday thru Thursday. Dec 31-Jan 3, Mardi Gras & special events excl. (504)527-0006, (800)THE-OMNI

THE PONTCHARTRAIN HOTEL, $$$$
2031 St. Charles Ave., New Orleans. Valid for any room. Mardi Gras and special events excl. (504)524-0581, (800)777-6193

THE PRYTANIA PARK HOTEL, $$$
1525 Prytania St., New Orleans. Valid for any room or suite. (504)524-0427, (800)862-1984

THE WHITNEY - A WYNDHAM HISTORIC HOTEL, $$$$
610 Poydras St., New Orleans. Valid for one standard room. (972)915-7070, (800)WYN-DHAM

Maine

For this state's listings go to entertainment.com/directtohotel

Maryland

Annapolis

BEST WESTERN ANNAPOLIS, $$$
2520 Riva Rd., Annapolis. Valid for any room. (410)224-2800, (800)638-5179

SHERATON HOTEL ANNAPOLIS, $$$$
173 Jennifer Rd., Annapolis. Valid for any room. (410)266-3131

Baltimore

PEABODY COURT-A CLARION HOTEL, $$$$
612 Cathedral St., Baltimore. Valid for any room. May 20 & 21, New Year's Eve & Special events excl. R30. (410)727-7101

RADISSON HOTEL AT CROSS KEYS, $$$$
100 Village Square, Baltimore. Valid for any room. (410)532-6900

WYNDHAM BALTIMORE - INNER HARBOR, $$$$
101 West Fayette St., Baltimore. Valid for one standard room. (972)915-7070, (800)WYN-DHAM

Beltsville

SHERATON COLLEGE PARK HOTEL, $$$$
4095 Powder Mill Rd., College Park. Valid for any room. (301)937-4422

Gaithersburg

COMFORT INN SHADY GROVE, $$$
16216 Frederick Rd., Gaithersburg. Valid for any room. (301)330-0023

COURTYARD BY MARRIOTT GAITHERSBURG, $$$
805 Russell Ave., Gaithersburg. Valid for any room. Valid Thursday thru Sunday. (301)670-0008

Massachusetts

Boston

BEST WESTERN/INN AT LONGWOOD, $$$$
342 Longwood, Boston. Valid for any room. Suites excluded. R30. (617)731-4700, (800)GOT-BEST

COPLEY SQUARE HOTEL, $$$$
47 Huntington Ave., Boston. Valid for any room. (617)536-9000, (800)225-7062

MIDTOWN HOTEL, $$$$
220 Huntington Ave., Boston. Valid for any room. Sept & Oct excl. R30. (617)262-1000, (800)343-1177

OMNI PARKER HOUSE, $$$$
60 School St., Boston. Valid for one deluxe room. (617)227-8600, (800)THE-OMNI

WYNDHAM BOSTON, $$$$
89 Broad St., Boston. Valid for one standard room. (972)915-7070, (800)WYN-DHAM

Cape Cod Area

COVE AT YARMOUTH, $$$
183 Route 28 / 183 Main St., (Rte. 228), West Yarmouth. Valid for any room or suite. Holidays excl. R30. (508)771-3666, (800)874-8770

HOLIDAY INN, $$$$
291 Jones Rd., Falmouth. Valid for any room. R30. (508)540-2000

SEASHORE PARK INN, $$$$
24 Canal Rd., Orleans. Valid for any room. R30. (508)255-2500, (800)772-6453

Rockland

RADISSON HOTEL ROCKLAND, $$$
929 Hingham St., Rockland. Valid for any room. Special events & holidays excl. (781)871-0545

Springfield

BEST WESTERN SOVEREIGN HOTEL, $$$
1080 Riverdale St., W. Springfield. Valid for any room. Valid Sunday thru Thursday. (413)781-8750

SPRINGFIELD MARRIOTT, $$$$
Corner of Boland Way & Columbus St., Springfield. Valid for any room. Valid Friday, Saturday, Sunday & holidays. (413)781-7111

Worcester

CROWNE PLAZA WORCESTER, $$$$
10 Lincoln Square, Worcester. Valid for any room. Suites excl. R30. (508)791-1600

Discount subject to availability. Please read the **Rules of Use** on page E46.

Remember to identify yourself as an Entertainment® Member.

Direct To Hotel

50% off full-priced (rack) room rates or 10% off the best promotional rate–subject to availability.

HOLIDAY INN, $$$$
500 Lincoln St., Worcester. Valid for any room. Suites excluded. R30. (508)852-4000

Michigan

Acme

GRAND TRAVERSE RESORT & SPA, $$$$
100 Grand Traverse Village Blvd., Acme. Valid for any room. Condos excl. June, July & August weekends excl. R30. (231)938-2100, (800)748-0303

Ann Arbor

COURTYARD ANN ARBOR, $$$$
3205 Boardwalk, Ann Arbor. Valid for any room. (734)995-5900

HOLIDAY INN NORTH CAMPUS, $$$
3600 Plymouth Rd., Ann Arbor. Valid for any room or suite. (734)769-9800

Detroit

OMNI DETROIT HOTEL RIVER PLACE, $$$$
1000 River Place Dr., Detroit. Valid for one deluxe room. (313)259-9500, (800)THE-OMNI

THE INN ON FERRY STREET, $$$$
84 E Ferry St., Detroit. Valid for any room. R30. (313)871-6000

Lansing

QUALITY INN, $$$
3121 E. Grand River Rd., Lansing. Valid for any room. (517)351-1440

QUALITY SUITES, $$$
901 Delta Commerce Dr., Lansing. Valid for one suite. New Year's Eve & special events excl. R30. (517)886-0600, (800)456-6431

Mackinac Island

MISSION POINT RESORT, $$$$
1 Lakeshore Dr., Mackinac Island. Valid for any room. (800)833-7711

Mackinaw City

BEST WESTERN DOCKSIDE, $$$
505 S. Huron St., Mackinaw City. Valid for any room. Valid Sunday thru Thursday. July, August, holidays & special events excl. (231)436-5001, (800)774-1794

ECONO LODGE BAYVIEW, $$
712 S. Huron, Mackinaw City. Valid for any room. Open April thru October; valid Sunday thru Thursday. July thru August & holidays excl. (231)436-5777, (800)253-7216

Sterling Heights

BEST WESTERN STERLING INN, $$$$
34911 Van Dyke Ave., Sterling Heights. Valid for one standard room. Valid Sunday thru Friday. Jacuzzi rooms, New Year's Eve, holiday weeks & school breaks excl. (586)979-1400

Traverse City

BEST WESTERN FOUR SEASONS, $$$
305 Munson Ave., Traverse City. Valid for any room. Holidays & special events excl. Valid Sunday thru Thursday September thru May. (231)946-8424

PARK PLACE HOTEL, $$$$
300 E. Front St., Traverse City. Valid for any room. R30. (231)946-5000, (800)748-0133

Troy

HILTON NORTHFIELD, $$$$
5500 Crooks Rd., Troy. Valid for any room. Valid Friday, Saturday & Sunday. R30. (248)879-2100

HOLIDAY INN TROY, $$$
2537 Rochester Ct., Troy. Valid for any room. Jacuzzi rooms excl. (248)689-7500

SOMERSET INN, $$$$
2601 W. Big Beaver, Troy. Valid for any room. (248)643-7800

Wayne County Int'l Airport

CLARION BARCELO' HOTEL, $$$
8600 Merriman Rd., Romulus. Valid for any room or suite. (734)728-7900

HILTON SUITES DETROIT METRO AIRPORT, $$$$
8600 Wickham Rd., Romulus. Valid for one suite. Executive suites excluded. (734)728-9200

Minnesota

Eagan

HOLIDAY INN EXPRESS - EAGAN, $$$
1950 Rahncliff Ct., Eagan. Valid for any room or suite. Valid September thru May. R30. (651)681-9266, (800)681-5290

RESIDENCE INN MINNEAPOLIS/ST. PAUL AIRPORT, $$$$
3040 Eagandale Place, Eagan. Valid for any room. Valid Friday, Saturday & Sunday. R30. (651)688-0363

Minneapolis

DAYS INN-MINNEAPOLIS/UNIVERSITY, $$$
2407 University Ave. S.E, Minneapolis. Valid for any room. (612)623-3999

HILTON GARDEN INN BLOOMINGTON, $$$
8100 Bridge Rd., Bloomington. Valid for any room. Valid September thru May. R30. (952)831-1012, (800)645-2319

HOLIDAY INN METRODOME, $$$$
1500 Washington Ave. S, Minneapolis. Valid for one double room. Max stay 7 nts. (612)333-4646

Prior Lake

MYSTIC LAKE CASINO HOTEL, $$$
2400 Mystic Lake Blvd., Prior Lake. Valid for one standard room. Valid Sunday thru Thursday. (952)445-9000, (800)262-7799

Rochester

HOLIDAY INN CITY CENTER, $$$
220 S. Broadway, Rochester. Valid for any room. Valid Friday & Saturday. R30. (507)288-3231, (800)241-1597

SPRINGHILL SUITES - ROCHESTER, $$$
1125 2nd St. SW, Rochester. Valid for any room. Valid September thru May. R30. (507)281-5455, (800)678-9894

St. Paul

FOUR POINTS SHERATON ST. PAUL CAPITOL, $$$$
400 N. Hamline Ave., St. Paul. Valid for any room. R30. (651)642-1234, (800)535-2339

HAMPTON INN SHOREVIEW, $$$
1000 Gramsie Rd., Shoreview. Valid for any room. Valid September thru May. R30. (651)482-0402, (877)233-3194

HOLIDAY INN RIVER CENTRE, $$$$
175 W. 7th St., St. Paul. Valid for any room. (651)225-1515

RADISSON CITY CENTER HOTEL ST. PAUL, $$$$
411 Minnesota St., St. Paul. Valid for any room. (651)291-8800

Mississippi

For this state's listings go to entertainment.com/directtohotel

Missouri

Branson

BRANSON TOWERS HOTEL, $$$
236 Shepherd of the Hills Expwy., Branson. Valid for any room. Valid February thru December. (417)336-4500, (800)683-1122

HOLIDAY INN EXPRESS HOTEL & SUITES, $$
1970 W. Hwy. 76, Branson. Valid for any room or suite. (417)336-1100

RAMADA LIMITED, $$
2316 Shepherd of the Hills Expy., Branson. Valid for one standard room. Special events & holidays excl. R30. (417)337-5207, (800)856-0730

Kansas City

CHASE SUITE HOTEL BY WOODFIN, $$$
9900 NW Prairie View Rd., Kansas City. Valid for one suite. (816)891-9009, (888)433-6171

HAMPTON INN AT KANSAS CITY INT'L AIRPORT, $$$
11212 N. Newark Circle, Kansas City. Valid for one studio suite. Valid Sunday thru Thursday. R30. (816)464-5454

Lake of the Ozarks

QUAIL'S NEST, $$$
4644 Hwy 54, Osage Beach. Valid for any room. Valid Sunday thru Thursday. July & August excl. (573)348-2834, (800)700-1006

THE LODGE OF FOUR SEASONS, $$$$
Horseshoe Bend Parkway, Lake Ozark. Valid for any room. Condominiums excluded. Valid Sunday thru Thursday. Holidays excluded. R30. (800)843-5253

St. Louis

CLUBHOUSE INN & SUITES, $$$
1970 Craig Rd., St. Louis. Valid for any room. R30. (314)205-8000

ST. LOUIS MARRIOTT WEST, $$$$
660 Maryville Centre Dr., St. Louis. Valid for one standard room. Valid Friday, Saturday & Sunday. (314)878-2747

THE ROBERTS MAYFAIR-A WYNDHAM HISTORIC HOTEL, $$$$
806 St. Charles St., St. Louis. Valid for one standard room. (972)915-7070, (800)WYN-DHAM

Montana

For this state's listings go to entertainment.com/directtohotel

Direct To Hotel

Contact the hotels directly to get your Entertainment® Membership rate availability.

Nebraska

For this state's listings go to entertainment.com/directtohotel

Nevada

For this state's listings go to entertainment.com/directtohotel

New Hampshire

Bartlett

ATTITASH MOUNTAIN VILLAGE, $$$$
Route 302, Bartlett. Valid for any room or suite. Min stay 2 nts. Holidays excluded. (603)374-6500, (800)862-1600

Nashua

HOLIDAY INN NASHUA, $$$
9 Northeastern Blvd., Nashua. Valid for any room. (603)888-1551

SHERATON NASHUA HOTEL, $$$$
11 Tara Blvd., Nashua. Valid for any room. (603)888-9970, (888)627-7183

New Jersey

Atlantic City

QUALITY INN BEACH BLOCK, $$$
South Carolina & Pacific Aves., Atlantic City. Valid for any room. Valid Sunday thru Thursday. Holidays excl. (609)345-7070, (800)356-6044

TROPICANA CASINO AND RESORT, $$$$
2831 Boardwalk at Brighton Ave, Atlantic City. Valid for any room. Valid Sunday thru Thursday. July & August excl. Havana Tower rooms, holidays & special events excl. (609)340-4000, (800)THE-TROP

Elizabeth

HAMPTON INN NEWARK AIRPORT, $$$
1128-38 Spring St., Elizabeth. Valid for any room. Valid Friday, Saturday & Sunday. (908)355-0500

WYNDHAM NEWARK AIRPORT, $$$$
1000 Spring St., Elizabeth. Valid for one standard room. (972)915-7070, (800)WYN-DHAM

Fairfield

WELLESLEY INN, $$$
38 Two Bridges Rd., Fairfield. Valid for any room. Special events excluded. R30. (973)575-1742

Mt. Laurel

SUMMERFIELD SUITES BY WYNDHAM - MOUNT LAUREL, $$$$
3000 Crawford Place, Mt. Laurel. Valid for one suite. (972)915-7070, (800)WYN-DHAM

WYNDHAM MOUNT LAUREL, $$$$
1111 Route 73 North, Mt. Laurel. Valid for one standard room. (972)915-7070, (800)WYN-DHAM

Secaucus

COURTYARD BY MARRIOTT MEADOWLANDS, $$$$
455 Harmon Meadow Blvd., Secaucus. Valid for any room. R30. (201)617-8888

HAMPTON INN SECAUCUS, $$$
250 Harmon Meadow Blvd., Secaucus. Valid for any room. Valid Friday, Saturday & Sunday. (201)867-4400

HOLIDAY INN HARMON MEADOW, $$$$
300 Plaza Dr., Secaucus. Valid for any room. (201)348-2000, (800)222-2676

Tinton Falls

HOLIDAY INN TINTON FALLS, $$$$
700 Hope Rd., Tinton Falls. Valid for any room. (732)544-9300, (800)2JE-RSEY

SHERATON EATONTOWN HOTEL, $$$$
Route 35, Eatontown. Valid for any room. Suites excluded. Valid September thru April. (732)542-6500

Whippany

SUMMERFIELD SUITES BY WYNDHAM - PARSIPPANY, $$$$
1 Ridgedale Ave., Whippany. Valid for one suite. (972)915-7070, (800)WYN-DHAM

WELLESLEY INN, $$$
1255 Rte. 10 E, Whippany. Valid for any room. R30. (973)539-8350

Wildwood

IVANHOE/PANORAMIC MOTELS, $$$
430 E. 21st Ave. & Beach, North Wildwood. Valid for any room. July & Aug excl. Holidays excl. (609)522-5874

New Mexico

Albuquerque

BEST WESTERN RIO GRANDE INN, $$$
1015 Rio Grande Blvd. N.W., Albuquerque. Valid for any room. Balloon Fiesta week excl. (505)843-9500, (800)959-4726

LA QUINTA INN AIRPORT, $$$
2116 Yale Blvd, Albuquerque. Valid for any room. Special events excluded. (210)616-7601, (800)531-5900

WYNDHAM ALBUQUERQUE AT INTERNATIONAL SUNPORT, $$$$
2910 Yale Blvd. SE, Albuquerque. Valid for one standard room. (972)915-7070, (800)WYN-DHAM

Santa Fe

BEST WESTERN LAMPLIGHTER INN, $$
2405 Cerrillos Rd., Santa Fe. Valid for any room. Valid September thru June. Holidays & Indian Market excl. (505)471-8000, (800)767-5267

HOTEL SANTA FE, $$$$
1501 Paseo de Peralta, Santa Fe. Valid for one suite. R30. (505)982-1200

New York

Albany

HAMPTON INN - ALBANY, $$$
10 Ulenski Dr., Albany. Valid for any room. Valid Friday, Saturday & Sunday September thru May. R30. (518)438-2822

HOLIDAY INN TURF ON WOLF ROAD, $$$$
205 Wolf Rd., Albany. Valid for any room. Valid Friday, Saturday, Sunday & holidays September thru June. (518)458-7250

RADISSON HOTEL UTICA CENTRE, $$$
200 Genesee St., Utica. Valid for any room. July, August & special events excl. R30. (315)797-8010

RAMADA INN, $$$
416 Southern Blvd., Albany. Valid for any room. Aug excl. (518)462-6555, (866)465-6736

THE DESMOND HOTEL & CONFERENCE CENTER, $$$$
660 Albany Shaker Rd., Albany. Valid for any room. Valid Friday, Saturday, Sunday & holidays. Track Season, New Year's Eve & Wine Festival excl. (518)869-8100, (800)448-3500

La Guardia Airport

PAN AMERICAN HOTEL, $$$
79-00 Queens Blvd., Elmhurst. Valid for any room. (718)446-7676, (800)937-7374

WYNDHAM GARDEN - LA GUARDIA AIRPORT, $$$$
100-15 Ditmars Blvd., East Elmhurst. Valid for one standard room. (972)915-7070, (800)WYN-DHAM

New York City/Manhattan

AFFINIA DUMONT, $$$$
150 E. 34th Street, New York. Valid for one suite. Valid Friday, Saturday & Sunday. R30. (212)320-8019, (866)AFF-INIA

HOWARD JOHNSON @ PENN STATION, $$$
215 West 34th St, New York. Valid for any room. (212)947-5050, (888)651-6111

LYDEN GARDENS, $$$$
215 E. 64th Street, New York. Valid for one suite. Valid Friday, Saturday & Sunday. R30. (212)320-8022, (866)AFF-INIA

OMNI BERKSHIRE PLACE, $$$$
21 E. 52nd St. & Madison Ave., New York. Valid for one deluxe room. R30. (212)753-5800, (800)THE-OMNI

SOUTHGATE TOWER, $$$$
371 Seventh Avenue, New York. Valid for one suite. Valid Friday, Saturday & Sunday. R30. (212)320-8026, (866)AFF-INIA

THE BENJAMIN, $$$$
125 East 50th Street, New York. Valid for any room. Valid Friday, Saturday & Sunday. R30. (212)320-8002, (888)423-6526

WELLINGTON HOTEL, $$$$
871 Seventh Ave. at 55th St., New York. Valid for any room or suite. R30. (212)247-3900, (800)652-1212

Painted Post

ECONO LODGE, $$
200 Robert Dann Dr., Corning. Valid for any room. (607)962-4444

LODGE ON THE GREEN, $$
3171 Canada Rd., Painted Post. Valid for any room. (607)962-2456

Rochester

HOLIDAY INN ROCHESTER AIRPORT, $$$
911 Brooks Ave., Rochester. Valid for one standard room. (585)328-6000

STRATHALLAN HOTEL, $$$$
550 East Ave., Rochester. Valid for any room. Valid September thru May. (585)461-5010, (800)678-7284

Discount subject to availability. Please read the **Rules of Use** on page E46.

Remember to identify yourself as an Entertainment® Member.

Direct To Hotel

50% off full-priced (rack) room rates or 10% off the best promotional rate–subject to availability.

WELLESLEY INN SOUTH, $$
797 E. Henrietta Rd., Rochester. Valid for any room. Wknds May-July & special events excl. R30. (585)427-0130

Syracuse

WYNDHAM SYRACUSE, $$$$
6301 Rte. 298, East Syracuse. Valid for one standard room. (972)915-7070, (800)WYN-DHAM

North Carolina

Charlotte

LA QUINTA INN AIRPORT, $$
3100 South I-85 Service Rd, Charlotte. Valid for any room. Special events excluded. (210)616-7601, (800)531-5900

SLEEP INN, $$
701 Yorkmont Rd., Charlotte. Valid for any room. Race wknds & special events excl. (704)525-5005

SUMMERFIELD SUITES BY WYNDHAM - CHARLOTTE A/P, $$$$
4920 S. Tryon St., Charlotte. Valid for one suite. (972)915-7070, (800)WYN-DHAM

Raleigh

BEST WESTERN CRABTREE, $$
6619 Glenwood Ave., Raleigh. Valid for any room. Valid Friday, Saturday, Sunday & holidays. R30. (919)782-8650

HAMPTON INN RALEIGH-NORTH, $$
1011 Wake Towne Dr., Raleigh. Valid for any room. (919)828-1813

LA QUINTA INN & SUITES CRABTREE, $$
2211 Summit Park Ln, Raleigh. Valid for any room. Special events excluded. (210)616-7601, (800)531-5900

North Dakota

For this state's listings go to entertainment.com/directtohotel

Ohio

Cincinnati

HAMPSHIRE HOUSE HOTEL, $$$
30 Tri County Pkwy., Cincinnati. Valid for one standard room. Holidays & special events excl. R30. (513)772-5440, (800)543-4211

HILTON CINCINNATI NETHERLAND PLAZA, $$$$
35 W. 5th St., Cincinnati. Valid for any room. Valid Friday, Saturday, Sunday & holidays. R30. (513)421-9100

HOLIDAY INN I-275 NORTH, $$$
3855 Hauck Rd., Cincinnati. Valid for any room. (513)563-8330

Cleveland

WYNDHAM CLEVELAND AT PLAYHOUSE SQUARE, $$$$
1260 Euclid Ave., Cleveland. Valid for one standard room. (972)915-7070, (800)WYN-DHAM

Columbus

BEST WESTERN COLUMBUS NORTH, $$
888 E. Dublin-Granville Rd., Columbus. Valid for any room. Suites excluded. (614)888-8230

DOUBLETREE GUEST SUITES - DOWNTOWN, $$$$
50 S. Front St., Columbus. Valid for one suite. (614)228-4600

HOLIDAY INN EAST AIRPORT AREA, $$$
4560 Hilton Corporate Dr., Columbus. Valid for any room. (614)868-1380

HOWARD JOHNSON PLAZA HOTEL, $$
2124 S. Hamilton Rd., Columbus. Valid for any room. (614)861-7220

THE MIDWEST HOTEL & CONFERENCE CENTER, $$$
4900 Sinclair Rd., Columbus. Valid for one standard room. (614)846-0300, (877)609-6086

Sandusky

COMFORT INN SANDUSKY, $$$
5909 Milan Rd., Sandusky. Valid for one standard room. Valid September 10 thru May 23. (419)621-0200

QUALITY INN GREENTREE, $$
1935 Cleveland Rd., Sandusky. Valid for one standard room. Valid Sunday thru Thursday September thru May. Holidays excl. (419)626-6761

RAMADA INN, $$$
5608 Milan Rd., Sandusky. Valid for any room. Valid September 10 thru May 23. (419)626-9890

Oklahoma

For this state's listings go to entertainment.com/directtohotel

Oregon

For this state's listings go to entertainment.com/directtohotel

Pennsylvania

Allentown

CROWNE PLAZA - ALLENTOWN, $$$$
904 Hamilton St., Allentown. Valid for one king or 2-double bedded room. (610)433-2221

DAYS INN & CONFERENCE CENTER, $$$
1151 Bulldog Dr. Rtes. 22 & 309, Allentown. Valid for any room. Valid Sunday thru Thursday. Special events & holidays excl. (610)395-3731, (888)395-5200

Coraopolis

CROWNE PLAZA HOTEL, $$$$
1160 Thorn Run Rd. Extension, Coraopolis. Valid for any room. R30. (412)262-2400

WYNDHAM PITTSBURGH AIRPORT, $$$$
777 Aten Road, Coraopolis. Valid for one standard room. (972)915-7070, (800)WYN-DHAM

Harrisburg

HILTON HARRISBURG, $$$$
One N. Second St., Harrisburg. Valid for any room. Valid Friday, Saturday, Sunday & holidays. Special events excluded. R30. (717)233-6000

WYNDHAM GARDEN - HARRISBURG, $$$$
765 Eisenhower Blvd., Harrisburg. Valid for one standard room. (972)915-7070, (800)WYN-DHAM

Lancaster

BEST WESTERN EDEN RESORT INN & SUITES, $$$$
222 Eden Rd., Lancaster. Valid for any room. July, Aug & Oct excl. (717)569-6444, (866)890-2339

TRAVELODGE, $$
2101 Columbia Ave., Lancaster. Valid for any room. July-Aug, Oct, holidays & special events excl. (717)397-4201

Philadelphia

CLUB HOTEL BY DOUBLETREE, $$$$
9461 Roosevelt Blvd., Philadelphia. Valid for any room. (215)671-9600

COURTYARD BY MARRIOTT PHILADELPHIA DOWNTOWN, $$$$
21 N. Juniper St., Philadelphia. Valid for any room or suite. (215)496-3200, (888)887-8130

CROWNE PLAZA PHILADELPHIA, $$$$
1800 Market St., Philadelphia. Valid for any room. Valid Friday, Saturday, Sunday & holidays. (215)561-7500

HOLIDAY INN PHILADELPHIA STADIUM, $$$$
900 Packer Ave., Philadelphia. Valid for any room. Special events excluded. (215)755-9500

SHERATON UNIVERSITY CITY HOTEL, $$$$
36th & Chestnut Sts., Philadelphia. Valid for any room. (215)387-8000, (877)459-1146

THE LATHAM HOTEL, $$$$
135 S. 17th St., Philadelphia. Valid for any room. R30. (215)563-7474

WYNDHAM PHILADELPHIA AT FRANKLIN PLAZA, $$$$
17th & Race Street, Philadelphia. Valid for one standard room. (972)915-7070, (800)WYN-DHAM

Pittsburgh

BEST WESTERN - PARKWAY CENTER INN, $$
875 Greentree Road, Pittsburgh. Valid for any room. Max stay 7 nts. Jacuzzi & economy rooms excl. New Year's Eve & special events excl. (412)922-7070, (877)541-8990

HOLIDAY INN GREENTREE, $$$
401 Holiday Dr., Pittsburgh. Valid for any room. R30. (412)922-8100

HOLIDAY INN SELECT - PITTSBURGH SOUTH, $$$$
164 Fort Couch Road, Pittsburgh. Valid for any room. Valid November thru March & Sunday-Thursday April thru October. (412)833-5300, (866)882-5477

OMNI WILLIAM PENN, $$$$
530 William Penn Place, Pittsburgh. Valid for one deluxe room. (412)281-7100, (800)THE-OMNI

WYNDHAM GARDEN - PITTSBURGH UNIVERSITY PLACE, $$$$
3454 Forbes Ave., Pittsburgh. Valid for one standard room. (972)915-7070, (800)WYN-DHAM

Pocono Mountains Area

BEST WESTERN POCONO INN, $$$
700 Main St., Stroudsburg. Valid for any room. Valid Sunday thru Thursday. Holidays excl. (570)421-2200

CHATEAU RESORT & CONFERENCE CENTER, $$$$
300 Camelaback Rd., Tannersville. Valid for any room. Valid Sunday thru Thursday. Holidays excl. R30. (800)245-5900

Direct To Hotel

Contact the hotels directly to get your Entertainment® Membership rate availability.

COMFORT INN - HAMLIN/ NEWFOUNDLAND, $$$
I-84, Exit 17, RR9 Box 9420, Lake Ariel. Valid for any room. Suites excluded. Valid Sunday thru Thursday. (570)689-4148, (800)523-4426

TANGLEWOOD RESORT, $$$
Junction of Rte. 6 & 507, Hawley. Valid for any room or suite. Holidays excluded. R30. (570)226-6161, (800)874-8770

Reading

WELLESLEY INN, $$$
910 Woodland Rd., Reading. Valid for any room. Fri & Sat Aug-Oct & special events excl. R30. (610)374-1500

WYNDHAM READING, $$$$
100 N Fifth St., Reading. Valid for one standard room. (972)915-7070, (800)WYN-DHAM

Rhode Island

Newport

WELLINGTON RESORT, $$$
551 Thames St., Newport. Valid for any room or suite. Holidays excluded. R30. (401)849-1770, (800)874-8770

Warwick

SHERATON PROVIDENCE AIRPORT HOTEL, $$$$
1850 Post Rd., Warwick. Valid for any room. R30. (401)738-4000

Woonsocket

HOLIDAY INN EXPRESS HOTEL & SUITES, $$$
194 Fortin Dr., Woonsocket. Valid for any room or suite. Valid November - March & Sunday - Thursday April - October. (401)769-5000, (866)769-5001

South Carolina

Greenville

GUESTHOUSE SUITES, $$$
48 McPrice Court, Greenville. Valid for one studio suite. Valid Friday, Saturday & Sunday. (864)297-0099

HYATT REGENCY GREENVILLE, $$$$
220 North Main St., Greenville. Valid for any room. (864)235-1234, (800)233-1234

Hilton Head Island

HAMPTON INN HILTON HEAD ISLAND, $$$
1 Dillon Rd., Hilton Head Island. Valid for any room. (843)681-7900

THE BREAKERS, $$
27C Coligny Plaza, Hilton Head Island. Valid for one condo. Min stay 3 nts. (800)845-6802

Myrtle Beach

FAIRFIELD MYRTLE BEACH AT SEAWATCH PLANTATION, $$$$
151 Sea Watch Dr., Myrtle. Valid for any room. R30. (800)438-6493

SHERATON'S BROADWAY PLANTATION, $$$$
3301 Robert M. Grissom Parkway, Myrtle Beach. Valid for any room. R30. (843)916-8855, (866)207-8602

South Dakota

For this state's listings go to entertainment.com/directtohotel

Tennessee

Memphis

FRENCH QUARTER SUITES, $$
2144 Madison Ave., Memphis. Valid for one suite. Valid Sunday thru Thursday. Special events & holidays excl. R30. (901)728-4000, (800)843-0353

WYNDHAM GARDEN - MEMPHIS, $$$$
300 N. Second St., Memphis. Valid for one standard room. (972)915-7070, (800)WYN-DHAM

Nashville

BEST WESTERN, $$
1407 Division St., Nashville. Valid for any room. (615)242-1631

LA QUINTA INN AIRPORT, $$
2345 Atrium Way, Nashville. Valid for any room. Special events excluded. (210)616-7601, (800)531-5900

LOEWS VANDERBILT HOTEL, $$$$
2100 West End Ave., Nashville. Valid for any room. Fan Fair & Vanderbilt University special events excluded. R30. (800)336-3335

UNION STATION - A WYNDHAM HISTORIC HOTEL, $$$$
1001 Broadway, Nashville. Valid for one standard room. (972)915-7070, (800)WYN-DHAM

WINGATE INN, $$$$
800 Royal Pkwy., Nashville. Valid for any room. Special events excl. (615)884-9777

Texas

For this state's listings go to entertainment.com/directtohotel

Utah

For this state's listings go to entertainment.com/directtohotel

Vermont

Burlington

CLARION HOTEL, $$$
1117 Williston Rd., S. Burlington. Valid for one standard room. Valid October 17 thru July 14. Special events & holidays excl. (802)658-0250

HOWARD JOHNSON HOTEL, $$$
1720 Shelburne Rd., South Burlington. Valid for any room. Valid Sunday thru Thursday. Special events & holidays excl. (802)860-6000

SHERATON BURLINGTON HOTEL & CONFERENCE CENTER, $$$$
870 Williston Rd., Burlington. Valid for one deluxe room. Univ of VT graduation & Memorial Day wknds excl. (802)865-6600, (800)677-6576

UNIVERSITY INN AND SUITES, $$$
5 Dorset St. @ Williston Rd., S. Burlington. Valid for any room or suite. (802)863-5541, (800)808-4656

WYNDHAM BURLINGTON, $$$$
60 Battery St., Burlington. Valid for one standard room. (972)915-7070, (800)WYN-DHAM

Stowe/Waterbury

GOLDEN EAGLE RESORT, $$$$
Mountain Rd, Rte 108, PO Box 1090, Stowe. Valid for any room. Valid Sunday thru Thursday. February, July-August & holidays excl. R30. (802)253-4811

GREEN MOUNTAIN INN, $$$
1 Main St., Stowe. Valid for one standard room. Valid Sunday thru Thursday. Sept 22-Oct 14 & holiday periods excl. (802)253-7301, (800)253-7302

STOWEFLAKE MOUNTAIN RESORT & SPA, $$$$
1746 Mountain Rd., Stowe. Valid for any room. Valid Sunday thru Thursday. Holidays excluded. (802)253-7355, (800)253-2232

Virginia

Arlington

RESIDENCE INN BY MARRIOTT, $$$$
550 Army Navy Dr., Arlington. Valid for one studio suite. Valid Friday, Saturday & Sunday. (703)413-6630

THE VIRGINIAN SUITES, $$$$
1500 Arlington Blvd., Arlington. Valid for one suite. (703)522-9600, (800)275-2866

Norfolk

HILTON NORFOLK AIRPORT, $$$$
1500 N. Military Hwy., Norfolk. Valid for any room. Valid Friday, Saturday & Sunday. (757)466-8000

Richmond

LINDEN ROW INN, $$$
100 E. Franklin St., Richmond. Valid for any room. Parlor suites excluded. Holidays & New Year's Eve excluded. (804)783-7000

QUALITY INN, $$$
8008 W. Broad St., Richmond. Valid for any room. Special events excluded. R30. (804)346-0000

Virginia Beach

FOUNDERS INN, $$$$
5641 Indian River Rd., Virginia Beach. Valid for any room. (757)424-5511, (800)926-4466

VIRGINIA BEACH RESORT HOTEL & CONFERENCE CTR., $$$$
2800 Shore Dr., Virginia Beach. Valid for one suite. Holidays, special events & News Year's Eve excl. June thru August wknds excl. R30. (757)481-9000, (800)468-2722

Washington/Dulles Int'l Airport

EMBASSY SUITES DULLES AIRPORT, $$$$
13341 Woodland Park Rd., Herndon. Valid for one suite. Special events excl. (703)464-0200

HOLIDAY INN EXPRESS RESTON/ HERNDON, $$$$
485 Elden St., Herndon. Valid for any room. Valid Thursday thru Sunday & holidays. (703)478-9777

Williamsburg

HAMPTON INN, $$$
201 Bypass Rd., Williamsburg. Valid for any room. Valid Sunday thru Thursday September thru May. (757)220-0880

Discount subject to availability. Please read the **Rules of Use** on page E46.

Direct To Hotel

50% off full-priced (rack) room rates or 10% off the best promotional rate–subject to availability.

HOWARD JOHNSON HOTEL & SUITES, $$
7135 Pocahontas Trail, Williamsburg. Valid for one double room. Valid September thru May. (757)229-6900, (800)841-9100

RAMADA INN 1776, $$$
725 Bypass Rd., Williamsburg. Valid for any room. Valid September thru May. R30. (757)220-1776, (800)446-2848

Washington

For this state's listings go to entertainment.com/directtohotel

West Virginia

For this state's listings go to entertainment.com/directtohotel

Wisconsin

Appleton

BEST WESTERN MIDWAY HOTEL APPLETON, $$$
3033 W. College Ave., Appleton. Valid for executive room. Pool rooms excl. EAA, Packer home games & special events excl. (920)731-4141

HOLIDAY INN NEENAH RIVERWALK, $$$
123 E. Wisconsin Ave., Neenah. Valid for any room. R30. (920)725-8441, (800)725-6348

RADISSON PAPER VALLEY HOTEL, $$$$
333 W. College Ave., Appleton. Valid for one standard room. EAA, Packer home games & special events excl. R30. (920)733-8000, (800)242-3499

Brookfield

RESIDENCE INN BY MARRIOTT, $$$$
950 S. Pinehurst Ct., Brookfield. Valid for one suite. Studio double & one bedroom suites excl. R30. (262)782-5990

SHERATON MILWAUKEE BROOKFIELD HOTEL, $$$$
375 S. Moorland Rd., Brookfield. Valid for any room. (262)364-1100

WYNDHAM GARDEN - BROOKFIELD, $$$
18155 Bluemound Rd., Brookfield. Valid for one standard room. (972)915-7070, (800)WYN-DHAM

Green Bay

DAYS INN LAMBEAU FIELD, $$
1978 Holmgren Way, Green Bay. Valid for one double room. Valid Sunday thru Thursday. July, Aug & Packer events excl. (920)498-8088, (800)329-7466

KRESS INN, $$$
300 Grant St., De Pere. Valid for one suite. (920)403-5100, (800)221-5070

Kenosha

DAYS INN, $$
12121 75th St., Kenosha. Valid for any room. Valid Sunday-Thursday September thru May. (262)857-2311

Madison

CLARION SUITES - CENTRAL MADISON, $$$
2110 Rimrock Rd., Madison. Valid for one studio suite. Special events excluded. (608)284-1234

HILTON, $$$$
9 East Wilson St., (1 block from Capitol Square), Madison. Valid for any room. (608)255-5100, (866)403-8838

Milwaukee

BEST WESTERN INN TOWNE HOTEL, $$$
710 N. Old World Third St., Milwaukee. Valid for any room. (414)224-8400, (877)ITH-OTEL

COURTYARD BY MARRIOTT, $$$$
5200 W. Brown Deer Rd., Brown Deer. Valid for any room. R30. (414)355-7500

HOLIDAY INN EXPRESS MEDICAL CENTER, $$$
11111 W. North Ave., Wauwatosa. Valid for any room. Suites excluded. R30. (414)778-0333

HOLIDAY INN EXPRESS MILWAUKEE MEDICAL CENTER, $$$
11111 W. North Ave., Milwaukee. Valid for any room. Special events excluded. (414)778-0333

HOSPITALITY INN, $$$
4400 S. 27th St., Milwaukee. Valid for one suite. Specialty & whirlpool suites excl. (414)282-8800, (800)825-8466

HYATT REGENCY MILWAUKEE, $$$$
333 W. Kilbourn Ave., Milwaukee. Valid for any room. (414)276-1234

RESIDENCE INN BY MARRIOTT, $$$$
7275 N. Port Washington Rd., Glendale. Valid for one suite. Studio double & one bedroom suites excl. R30. (414)352-0070

WYNDHAM MILWAUKEE CENTER, $$$$
139 E. Kilbourn Ave., Milwaukee. Valid for one standard room. (972)915-7070, (800)WYN-DHAM

Superior

BEST WESTERN BAY WALK INN, $$
1405 Susquehanna, Superior. Valid for any room. Valid Sunday - Thursday September thru May. Holidays excl. (715)392-7600

BEST WESTERN BRIDGEVIEW MOTOR INN, $$
5th St. & Hammond Ave., Superior. Valid for one double room. Valid Sunday thru Thursday. July & Aug excl. (715)392-8174, (800)777-5572

DAYS INN SUPERIOR, $$
110 Harborview Pkwy., Superior. Valid for any room. R30. (715)392-4783, (888)515-5040

HOLIDAY INN EXPRESS, $$
303 Second Ave., Superior. Valid for one standard room. Valid Sunday thru Thursday September thru June. R30. (715)392-3444

Wisconsin Dells

ATLANTIS WATERPARK HOTEL, $$$
1570 Wisconsin Dells Pkwy., Wisconsin Dells. Valid for any room or suite. Valid Sunday thru Friday September thru May. Special events & holiday periods excl. R30. (608)253-6606, (800)800-6179

GREAT WOLF LODGE, $$$$
1400 Great Wolf Dr., P.O. Box 50, Wisconsin Dells. Valid for any room. Valid Sunday thru Thursday. Memorial Day thru Labor Day & holidays excl. R30. (608)253-2222, (800)559-9653

HOWARD JOHNSON HOTEL & CONFERENCE CENTER, $$$
655 Frontage Rd., Wisconsin Dells. Valid for one double queen room. Valid Sunday thru Thursday. June 20 thru August, Memorial & Labor Day wknds & Dec 30-31 excl. (608)254-8306, (800)543-3557

RIVERWALK HOTEL, $$$
1015 River Rd., Wisconsin Dells. Valid for one deluxe room. July-August, Memorial & Labor Day wknds excl. R30. (608)253-1231, (800)659-5395

TREASURE ISLAND WATER & THEME PARK, $$$$
1701 Wisconsin Dells Pkwy., Wisconsin Dells. Valid for any room or suite. Valid Sunday thru Thursday. June 13 - Sept 6 & holidays excluded. R30. (608)254-8560, (800)800-4997

WINTERGREEN RESORT & CONFERENCE CENTER, $$
60 Gasser Rd., Wisconsin Dells. Valid for any room. Valid Sunday thru Thursday September thru May. Holidays excluded. R30. (608)254-2285, (800)648-4765

Wyoming

For this state's listings go to entertainment.com/directtohotell

Canada

Alberta

Banff

BANFF PARK LODGE RESORT & CONFERENCE CENTRE, $$$
222 Lynx St., Banff. Valid for any room. Valid Sunday thru Friday October thru June. Dec 27-Jan 2 excl. (403)762-4433, (800)661-9266

INNS OF BANFF, $$$$
600 Banff Ave., Banff. Valid for any room. Valid October thru May. Holidays excl. (403)762-4581, (800)661-1272

SWISS VILLAGE, $$$$
600 Banff Ave., Banff. Valid for any room. Valid October thru May. Holidays excl. (403)762-4581, (800)661-1272

Calgary

DELTA CALGARY AIRPORT, $$$$
2001 Airport Rd. N.E., Calgary. Valid for any room or suite. (403)291-2600

HOLIDAY INN CALGARY AIRPORT, $$$$
1250 McKinnon Dr. NE, Calgary. Valid for any room. (403)230-1999, (877)519-7113

QUALITY INN AIRPORT, $$
4804 Edmonton Trail, Calgary. Valid for any room. Stampede & special events excl. (403)276-3391

THE FAIRMONT PALLISER, $$$$
133 - 9 Ave. SW, Calgary. Valid for any room. (403)262-1234, (800)441-1414

Edmonton

ALBERTA PLACE SUITE HOTEL, $$$
10049 - 103 St., Edmonton. Valid for one suite. Penthouse suite excluded. (780)423-1565, (800)661-3982

DAYS INN, $$$
10041 - 106 St., Edmonton. Valid for any room. (780)423-1925

DELTA EDMONTON SOUTH HOTEL & CONFERENCE CTR, $$$$
4404 Gateway Blvd., Edmonton. Valid for any room. (780)434-6415, (800)661-1122

RAMADA HOTEL & CONFERENCE CENTRE, $$$$
11834 Kingsway, Edmonton. Valid for any room. Suites excluded. (780)454-5454

Direct To Hotel

Contact the hotels directly to get your Entertainment® Membership rate availability.

British Columbia

Vancouver

PACIFIC PALISADES HOTEL, $$$$
1277 Robson St., Vancouver. Valid for any room or suite. Labor Day weekend excl. (604)688-0461, (800)663-1815

RAMADA LIMITED DOWNTOWN VANCOUVER, $$$$
435 W. Pender St., Vancouver. Valid for any room. Special events excl. (604)488-1088, (888)389-5888

RENAISSANCE VANCOUVER HOTEL HARBOURSIDE, $$$$
1133 West Hastings St., Vancouver. Valid for any room. (604)689-9211, (800)905-8582

SANDMAN HOTEL VANCOUVER DOWNTOWN, $$$$
180 W. Georgia St., Vancouver. Valid for any room. (604)681-2211, (800)726-3626

Whistler

GOLDEN DREAMS ACCOMMODATIONS, $$$$
Whistler Village, Whistler. Valid for valid for one chalet or townhome rental. (604)938-1617

TANTALUS RESORT LODGE, $$$$
4200 Whistler Way, Whistler. Valid for one condo. Valid May thru November & Sunday thru Thursday December thru April. (604)932-4146

Whistler Village

RESORTQUEST WHISTLER, $$$$
105-4360 Lorimer Rd., Whistler Village. Valid for any room. Min stay 2 nts. Valid May thru November & Sunday thru Thursday December thru April. (604)932-6699, (866)512-5273

Manitoba

Winnipeg

CARLTON INN, $$
220 Carlton St., Winnipeg. Valid for any room. (204)942-0881, (877)717-2885

DELTA WINNIPEG, $$$$
350 St. Mary Ave., Winnipeg. Valid for any room. (204)942-0551

HOLIDAY INN WINNIPEG SOUTH, $$$$
1330 Pembina Hwy., Winnipeg. Valid for one standard room. Business Class floors & suites excl. (204)452-4747, (800)423-1337

RAMADA MARLBOROUGH HOTEL, $$$
331 Smith St., Winnipeg. Valid for any room. Special events & holidays excl. (204)942-6411, (800)667-7666

Nova Scotia

Halifax

DELTA BARRINGTON, $$$$
1875 Barrington St., Halifax. Valid for any room. (902)429-7410

LORD NELSON HOTEL & SUITES, $$$$
1515 South Park St., Halifax. Valid for any room. (902)423-6331, (800)565-2020

PRINCE GEORGE HOTEL, $$$$
1725 Market St., Halifax. Valid for any room. R30. (902)425-1986, (800)565-1567

Ontario

Hamilton

HOLIDAY INN EXPRESS HAMILTON - STONEY CREEK, $$$
QEW & Centennial Pkwy. 51 Keefer Court, Hamilton. Valid for one standard room. (905)578-1212

SHERATON HAMILTON, $$$$
116 King St. W., Hamilton. Valid for one traditional or deluxe room. (905)529-5515, (800)514-7101

London

DELTA LONDON ARMOURIES HOTEL, $$$$
325 Dundas St., London. Valid for any room. (519)679-6111, (800)668-9999

RAMADA INN LONDON, $$$
817 Exeter Rd., London. Valid for any room. Valid Sunday thru Thursday. Special events & holidays excl. (519)681-4900, (800)303-3733

Niagara Falls

BEST WESTERN CAIRN CROFT HOTEL, $$$$
6400 Lundy's Lane, Niagara Falls. Valid for any room. Valid October thru June. R30. (905)356-1161, (800)263-2551

DOUBLETREE RESORT LODGE & SPA FALLSVIEW, $$$
6039 Fallsview Blvd., Niagara Falls. Valid for any room. Valid Sunday thru Thursday October 16 thru May. (905)358-3817

OLD STONE INN, $$$$
5425 Robinson St., Niagara Falls. Valid for one standard room. Jacuzzi suites excluded. (905)357-1234, (800)263-6208

RENAISSANCE FALLSVIEW HOTEL, $$$$
6455 Fallsview Blvd., Niagara Falls. Valid for any room. Holidays & Special events excl. (905)357-5200, (800)363-3255

Ottawa

ALBERT AT BAY SUITE HOTEL, $$$$
435 Albert St., Ottawa. Valid for one suite. R30. (613)238-8858, (800)267-6644

DELTA OTTAWA HOTEL & SUITES, $$$$
361 Queen St., Ottawa. Valid for any room or suite. (613)238-6000

LES SUITES HÔTEL - OTTAWA, $$$$
130 Besserer St., Ottawa. Valid for one suite. (613)232-2000

OTTAWA MARRIOTT, $$$$
100 Kent St., Ottawa. Valid for any room. (613)238-1122, (800)853-8463

Toronto

DELTA TORONTO AIRPORT WEST, $$$$
5444 Dixie Rd., Toronto (West). Valid for any room. (905)624-1144, (800)737-3211

DELTA TORONTO EAST HOTEL, $$$$
2035 Kennedy Rd., Toronto (East). Valid for any room. (416)299-1500, (800)663-3386

DOUBLETREE INT'L PLAZA HOTEL TORONTO AIRPORT, $$$$
655 Dixon Rd., Toronto. Valid for any room. (416)244-1711, (800)668-3656

INN ON THE PARK, $$$$
1100 Eglinton Ave. E., Toronto. Valid for any room. (416)444-2561, (877)644-4687

NOVOTEL NORTH YORK, $$$$
3 Park Home Ave., North York. Valid for any room. (416)733-2929

SHERATON GATEWAY HOTEL TORONTO INT'L AIRPORT, $$$$
Box 3000 - Terminal 3, Toronto. Valid for one regular room. (905)672-7000, (800)565-0010

WESTIN HARBOUR CASTLE, $$$$
1 Harbour Square, Toronto. Valid for any room. Suites & executive club floor excluded. (416)869-1600

WESTIN PRINCE HOTEL, $$$$
900 York Mills Rd., Toronto. Valid for any deluxe room or suite. (416)444-2511, (800)937-8461

WYNDHAM BRISTOL PLACE - TORONTO AIRPORT, $$$$
950 Dixon Rd., Toronto. Valid for one standard room. (972)915-7070, (800)WYN-DHAM

Windsor

HOLIDAY INN SELECT WINDSOR, $$$$
1855 Huron Church Rd., Windsor. Valid for any room. R30. (519)966-1200

RAMADA PLAZA HOTEL & SUITES, $$$$
430 Ouellette Ave., Windsor. Valid for any room. (519)256-4656, (877)256-4656

Québec

Montreal

CHÂTEAU ROYAL, $$$$
1420 Crescent St., Montreal. Valid for one suite. (514)848-0999, (800)363-0335

DELTA MONTREAL, $$$$
475 President Kennedy Ave., Montreal. Valid for any room. (514)286-1986

HOLIDAY INN MONTREAL - MIDTOWN, $$$$
420 Sherbrooke St. W., Montreal. Valid for any room. (514)842-6111, (800)387-3042

HOTEL LORD BERRI, $$$$
1199 rue Berri, Montreal. Valid for any room. (514)845-9236, (888)363-0363

HOTEL OMNI MONT-ROYAL, $$$$
1050 Sherbrooke St. W., Montreal. Valid for one deluxe room. (514)284-1110, (800)THE-OMNI

HÔTEL GOUVERNEUR PLACE DUPUIS, $$$
1415 St-Hubert St., Montreal. Valid for any room. Suites excluded. (514)842-4881, (888)910-1111

HÔTEL LE CANTLIE SUITES, $$$$
1110 Sherbrooke St. W., Montreal. Valid for any room. (514)842-2000, (800)567-1110

Québec City

BEST WESTERN CITY CENTRE/ CENTRE-VILLE, $$$$
330 rue de la Couronne, Québec City. Valid for any room. (418)649-1919, (800)667-5345

DELTA QUÉBEC, $$$$
690 Rene Levesque Blvd. E., Québec City. Valid for any room. (418)647-1717

Mexico

Colima

Isla Navidad

GRAND BAY ISLA NAVIDAD WYNDHAM LUXURY RESORT, $$$$
Apartado Postal #20 Barra de Navidad, Isla Navidad. Valid for one standard room. (972)915-7070, (800)WYN-DHAM

Discount subject to availability. Please read the **Rules of Use** on page E46.

Remember to identify yourself as an Entertainment® Member.

Direct To Hotel

50% off full-priced (rack) room rates or 10% off the best promotional rate–subject to availability.

Distrito Federal

Mexico City

CAMINO REAL MEXICO, $$$$
Mariano Escobedo No. 700, Col. Anzures, Mexico City. Valid for one standard room. Valid Friday, Saturday & Sunday. 52-55-5263-8888

MARCO POLO HOTEL, $$$$
Calle Amberes #27, Mexico City. Valid for any room. 52-55-50800063

Guerrero

Acapulco

ACAPULCO MALIBU, $$$
Av. Costera M Aleman #20 Fracc Club Deportivo, Acapulco. Valid for any room. 52-744-4841070

EL TROPICANO, $$
Ave. Costera Miguel Aleman #510, Acapulco. Valid for any room. Valid Jan 5 thru December 19. Holy week excl. 52-744-4841332

PLAYA SUITES ACAPULCO, $$$$
Av. Costera Miguel Aleman #123, Acapulco. Valid for one suite. 52-744-4858050

Jalisco

Puerto Vallarta

LA JOLLA DE MISMALOYA ALL SUITE RESORT, $$$$
Km. 11.5 Zona Hotelera Sur, Puerto Vallarta. Valid for one suite. 52-322-60660, (877)868-6124

SHERATON BUGANVILIAS RESORT & CONV. CENTER, $$$$
Blvd. Fco. Medina Ascencio #999, Puerto Vallarta. Valid for any room. (818)842-6155, (800)433-5451

VALLARTA TORRE, $$$$
Paseo de la Garzas #168, Puerto Vallarta. Valid for one condo. Min stay 2 nts. R30. (888)333-1962

Quintana Roo

Cancun

BEACH PALACE, $$$$
Blvd. Kukulkan KM 11.5, Zona Hotelera, Cancun. Valid for one suite. 52-998-891-4110, (800)635-1836

MOON PALACE GOLF & SPA RESORT, $$$$
KM 340 Carretera Cancun-Chetumal, Cancun. Valid for any room. 52-998-881-6000, (800)635-1836

OMNI CANCUN HOTEL & VILLAS, $$$$
Blvd. Kukulkan, L-48, KM. 16.5, M. 53, Cancun. Valid for one deluxe room. Dec 26 - Jan 2 & Holidays excl. 52-998-881-0600, 800-446-8977

Playa del Carmen

AVENTURA SPA PALACE, $$$$
KM 72 Carretera-Cancun Chetumal, Cancun. Valid for any room. 52-984-875-1100, (800)635-1836

VIVA WYNDHAM AZTECA, $$$$
Paseo Xaman-Ha Mza. No. 8, Lote 1 Fracc. Playacar, Playa del Carmen. Valid for one standard room. (972)915-7070, (800)WYN-DHAM

VIVA WYNDHAM MAYA, $$$$
Paseo Xaman-Ha, Lote Hotelero No. 5 Fracc. Playacar, Playa del Carmen. Valid for one standard room. (972)915-7070, (800)WYN-DHAM

Sinaloa

Mazatlan

HOLIDAY INN SUNSPREE RESORT, $$$
Av. Camaron Sabalo 696 Zona dorada, Mazatlan. Valid for any room. Holy week, Easter week & holidays excl. 52-669-913-2222

TORRES MAZATLAN, $$$$
Av. Sabalo Cerritos Esq Lopez Portillo, Mazatlan. Valid for one condo. Min stay 2 nts. R30. (888)333-1962

Caribbean

Antigua/Barbuda

Mamora Bay

ST. JAMES'S CLUB, $$$$
P.O. Box 63, Mamora Bay. Valid for any room. Christmas, New Year's, President's & Easter Weeks excl. Bonus: 25% off the all-inclusive rate. (268)460-5000, (800)345-0356

Aruba

Aruba

WYNDHAM ARUBA RESORT, SPA & CASINO, $$$$
JE Irausquin Blvd., 77 Palm Beach, Aruba. Valid for one standard room. (972)915-7070, (800)WYN-DHAM

Bahamas

Freeport

VIVA WYNDHAM FORTUNA BEACH, $$$$
Doubloon Rd. & Churchill Dr. P.O. Box F-42398, Freeport. Valid for one standard room. (972)915-7070, (800)WYN-DHAM

Nassau

WYNDHAM NASSAU RESORT & CRYSTAL PALACE CASINO, $$$$
West Bay Road P.O. Box 8306, Nassau. Valid for one standard room. (972)915-7070, (800)WYN-DHAM

Paradise Island

SHERATON GRAND RESORT PARADISE ISLAND, $$$$
Casino Dr., P.O. Box SS-6307, Paradise Island. Valid for any room. Suites excluded. R30. (242)363-3500

Barbados

Christ Church

SEA BREEZE BEACH HOTEL, $$$$
Maxwell Coast Rd., Christ Church. Valid for any room. (246)428-2825

Bermuda

Southampton

WYNDHAM BERMUDA RESORT & SPA, $$$$
Southampton Beach, Southampton. Valid for one standard room. (972)915-7070, (800)WYN-DHAM

Jamaica

Negril

HOME SWEET HOME, $$$
West End Rd., Negril. Valid for any room. R30. (612)377-6336

Puerto Rico

Fajardo

WYNDHAM EL CONQUISTADOR RESORT & COUNTRY CLUB, $$$$
1000 El Conquistador Ave., Fajardo. Valid for one standard room. (972)915-7070, (800)WYN-DHAM

Rio Mar

THE WESTIN RIO MAR BEACH RESORT & GOLF CLUB, $$$$
6000 Rio Mar Blvd, Rio Grande. Valid for any room. Dec 20-Jan 1 & President's week excl. (787)888-6000, (800)4RI-OMAR

San Juan

WYNDHAM CONDADO PLAZA HOTEL & CASINO, $$$$
999 Ashford Avenue, San Juan. Valid for one standard room. (972)915-7070, (800)WYN-DHAM

Saint Maarten/ St. Martin

Cupecoy

SUMMIT RESORT HOTEL, $$$$
42 Jordan Rd., Box 4046, Cupecoy. Valid for one studio suite. (718)518-7470

St. Maarten

WYNDHAM SAPPHIRE BEACH CLUB & RESORT, $$$$
Cupecoy Beach, St. Maarten. Valid for one suite. (972)915-7070, (800)WYN-DHAM

Virgin Islands

St. Thomas

WYNDHAM SUGAR BAY RESORT & SPA, $$$$
6500 Estate Smith Bay, St. Thomas. Valid for any room. (972)915-7070, (800)WYN-DHAM

POINT PLEASANT RESORT, $$$$
6600 Estate Smith Bay #4, St. Thomas. Valid for one suite. Dec 20-Jan 2 excl. (340)775-7200

Discount subject to availability. Please read the **Rules of Use** on page E46.

Direct To Hotel Program

Rules of Use

- The Entertainment® 50% discount applies only to full-priced (rack) room rates, not to any other discount, Internet or daily rate; 10% discount applies only to the promotional rate available to the general public. Rates cannot be used in conjunction with any other discounts, including daily rates or rates found on the Internet.
- Entertainment® rates do not apply to walk-ins, group/convention rates, packages, travel agency bookings, special amenities, taxes/fees, meal plans or Internet rates, and cannot be combined with any other discount rate programs. All rates are subject to availability.
- Availability—Reservations with the Entertainment rate are accepted until the **hotel projects** to be 80% or more occupied. As a result, the discount may not be available for your entire stay because occupancy varies on a daily basis.
- Due to limited availability, hotels offering discounts on "any room" may exclude special rooms such as suites, concierge and premium rooms.
- Only one room can be discounted per Entertainment® membership card and the card is non-transferable.
- Hotels participate in the program on an individual basis. You must call the number listed for the hotel and state that you are an **"Entertainment® Member"** to be eligible for the Entertainment rate, if available.
- Remaining flexible with your travel dates may offer the greatest opportunity for the Entertainment rate. Discounts may not be available for every night of your stay, especially if traveling during peak seasons, holidays, conventions or special events such as Mardi Gras, Race Weekends & New Year's Eve.
- If the Entertainment rate is not available, check alternate dates, call back closer to your travel date, or contact other hotels listed in the area. Be sure to register your Entertainment membership card and view a complete listing of participating hotels on **www.entertainment.com/directtohotel**.
- Be sure to ask for the hotel's policy on deposits, cancellations and late arrival guarantees.
- The Guaranteed Best Rate rebate is not applicable to Direct to Hotel bookings.
- **Advance reservations are required and you must present your Entertainment membership card at check-in to obtain your discount.**

All information was current at the time of printing and is expected to be in effect through the expiration of the Entertainment® book. However, changes beyond our control may affect the information prior to the expiration. Please note that Entertainment Publications, Inc. cannot guarantee the level of services offered at a property and/or if services will be operational at the time of visit. Services may be closed due to seasonality reasons and/or may be closed for renovation.

ENTERTAINMENT PUBLICATIONS DOES NOT CONTROL ANY HOTEL'S MANAGEMENT POLICY.

THE SHARPER IMAGE®

sharperimage.com™

SHARPER IMAGE™

Save up to $50

Save $10 Off Any Purchase of $50 or More
or $50 Off Any Purchase of $250 or More at
The Sharper Image Stores, Catalog and Website

The Sharper Image® shares the fun of discovering innovative products that make life easier and more enjoyable. As America's premier specialty retailer, The Sharper Image is a great place to shop for gifts and products for the home, office and travel.

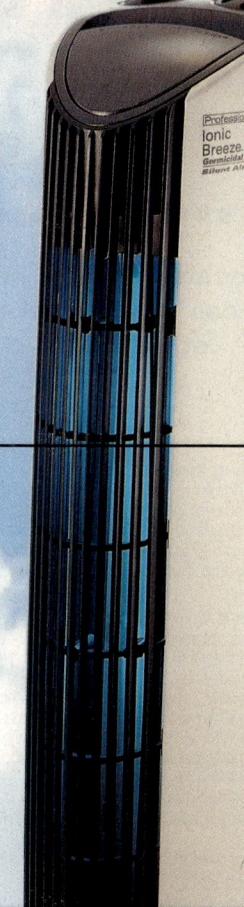

POS CODE: EB6

See reverse side for details.

F1

©2005 by Sharper Image Corporation

SHARPER IMAGE™

Save up to $50

Save $10 Off Any Purchase of $50 or More
or $50 Off Any Purchase of $250 or More at
The Sharper Image Stores, Catalog and Website

The Sharper Image® shares the fun of discovering innovative products that make life easier and more enjoyable. As America's premier specialty retailer, The Sharper Image is a great place to shop for gifts and products for the home, office and travel.

POS CODE: EB6

See reverse side for details.

F2

©2005 by Sharper Image Corporation

THE SHARPER IMAGE®

sharperimage.com™

To locate the store nearest you, call The Sharper Image® at 1-800-344-5555.

Ordering Instructions
1. To redeem online, go to www.sharperimage.com/eb6 to receive your savings.
2. To redeem in store, surrender this coupon at the time of purchase.
3. To redeem by mail order, subtract the discount from the total merchandise amount before calculating tax and shipping and submit this coupon with the mail order form.
4. To locate the store nearest you, call The Sharper Image® at 1-800-344-5555.

Terms & Conditions
1. Offer not valid with phone orders or at any Sharper Image Auction site.
2. The discount is applicable to, and the minimum purchased based on, merchandise prices only and excludes tax, shipping and tax on shipping.
3. Not valid toward previously purchased merchandise or for the purchase of Gift Certificates.
4. The Sharper Image is not required to honor this coupon if any portion of it is printed or posted in error.
5. Not valid with Price Matching Policy, merchandise certificates or other discount/promotional offers.
6. Not all products are eligible for discount. See individual product pages or consult with a Sharper Image associate for details.
7. Limit two purchases per customer per year.
8. Offer expires 12/31/2006.

Subject to Rules of Use. Not valid with other discount offers, unless specified. Coupon VOID if purchased, sold or bartered for cash.

Valid now thru December 31, 2006

Ordering Instructions
1. To redeem online, go to www.sharperimage.com/eb6 to receive your savings.
2. To redeem in store, surrender this coupon at the time of purchase.
3. To redeem by mail order, subtract the discount from the total merchandise amount before calculating tax and shipping and submit this coupon with the mail order form.
4. To locate the store nearest you, call The Sharper Image® at 1-800-344-5555.

Terms & Conditions
1. Offer not valid with phone orders or at any Sharper Image Auction site.
2. The discount is applicable to, and the minimum purchased based on, merchandise prices only and excludes tax, shipping and tax on shipping.
3. Not valid toward previously purchased merchandise or for the purchase of Gift Certificates.
4. The Sharper Image is not required to honor this coupon if any portion of it is printed or posted in error.
5. Not valid with Price Matching Policy, merchandise certificates or other discount/promotional offers.
6. Not all products are eligible for discount. See individual product pages or consult with a Sharper Image associate for details.
7. Limit two purchases per customer per year.
8. Offer expires 12/31/2006.

Subject to Rules of Use. Not valid with other discount offers, unless specified. Coupon VOID if purchased, sold or bartered for cash.

Valid now thru December 31, 2006

TARGET COUPON **EXPIRES 12/31/06**

Limit one offer per coupon. Void if copied, transferred, purchased, sold or where prohibited by law. No cash value.

Cashier: Scan product, then scan coupon.

Subject to Rules of Use. Not valid with other discount offers, unless specified. Coupon VOID if purchased, sold, or bartered for cash.

photo

5 85239 28987 2 (8100) 0 09289

TARGET COUPON **EXPIRES 12/31/06**

Limit one offer per coupon. Void if copied, transferred, purchased, sold or where prohibited by law. No cash value. Maximum retail value $2.50 for combined free offer.

Cashier: Scan 10 prints, then scan coupon.

Subject to Rules of Use. Not valid with other discount offers, unless specified. Coupon VOID if purchased, sold, or bartered for cash.

photo

5 85239 28701 4 (8100) 0 09287

circuit city®
great prices
great brands
Just what I needed.SM
use one, use them all, or use them all at once
coupons good now through Dec. 31, 2006
circuit city®
SAVE $5
on all video game &
PC software titles
39.99 & up
Limit 3 titles per customer.
See reverse side for details
circuit city®
10% OFF
on all TVs
$199 & up
See reverse side for details
circuit city®
10% OFF
any memory card
or memory card
accessory
See reverse side for details
circuit city®
$5 OFF
any CD-R/DVD
blank media
14.99 & up
See reverse side for details
F4

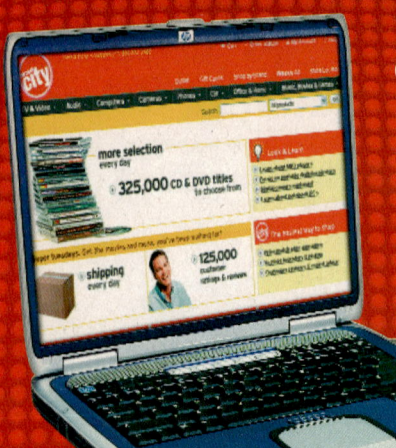

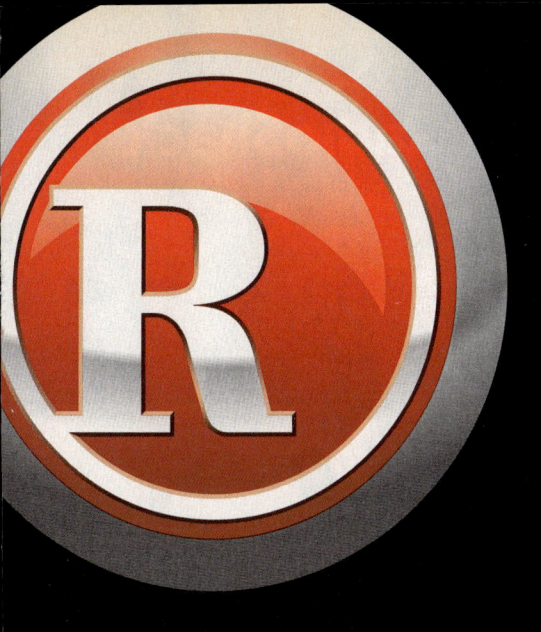

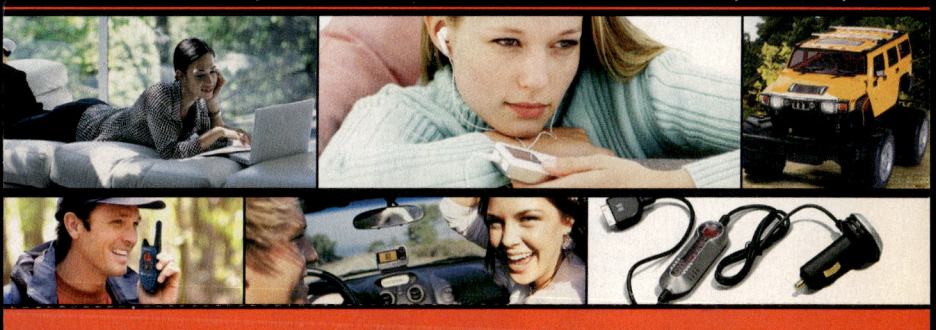

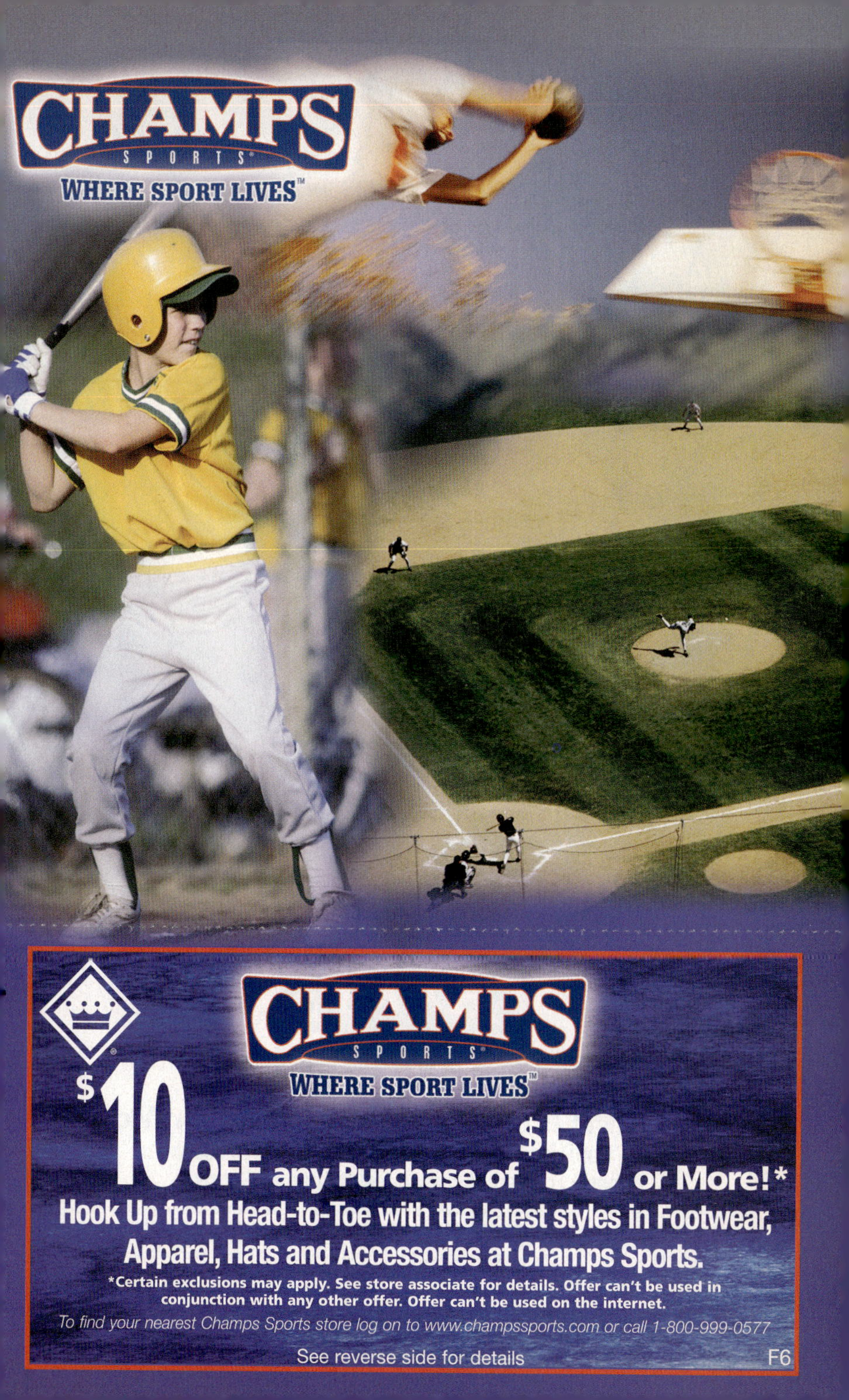

CHAMPS
SPORTS
WHERE SPORT LIVES™
CHAMPS
SPORTS
WHERE SPORT LIVES™
$10 OFF any Purchase of $50 or More!*
Hook Up from Head-to-Toe with the latest styles in Footwear, Apparel, Hats and Accessories at Champs Sports.
*Certain exclusions may apply. See store associate for details. Offer can't be used in conjunction with any other offer. Offer can't be used on the internet.
To find your nearest Champs Sports store log on to www.champssports.com or call 1-800-999-0577
See reverse side for details
F6

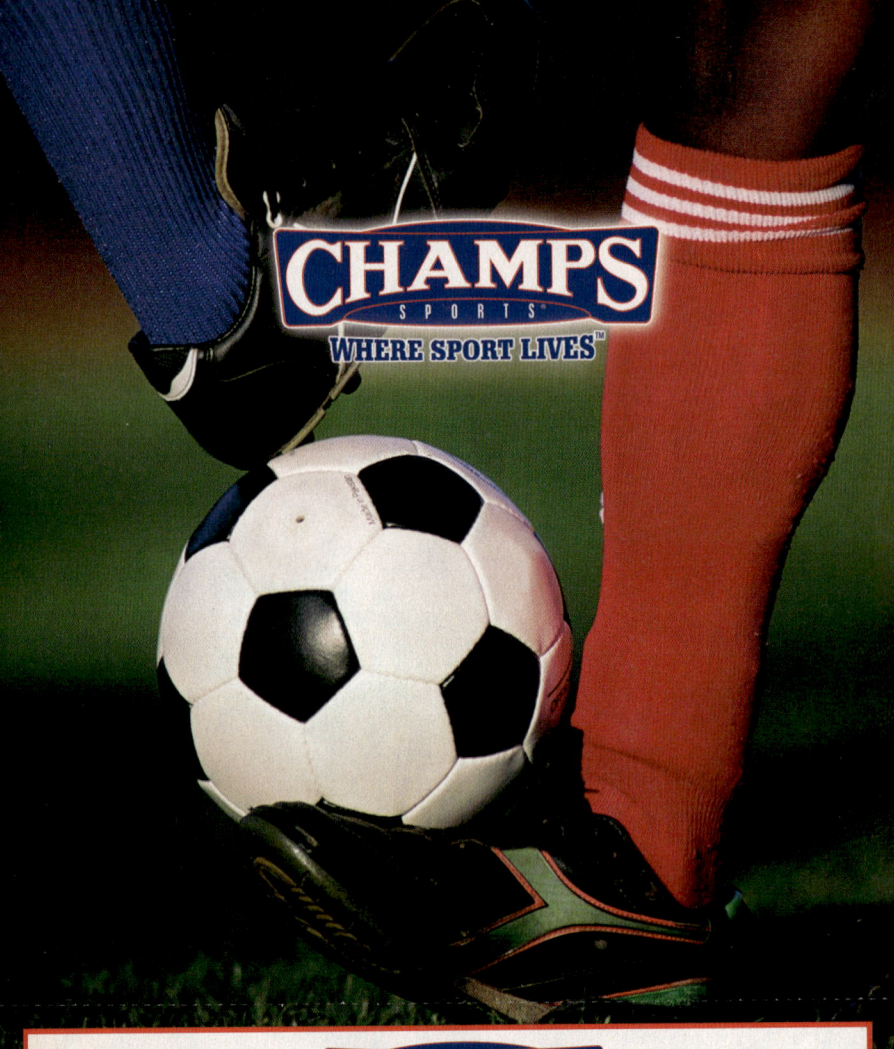

Fashion that goes the distance.

take $25 off

your purchase of $75 or more.

Doubles to $**50** off a purchase of **$150** or more.

NEW YORK & COMPANY

great style. great value. always sexy.

Redeem at any New York & Company store. Expires 12/31/06. See reverse side for details.

F7

take $25 off

your purchase of $75 or more.

Doubles to $**50** off a purchase of **$150** or more.

NEW YORK & COMPANY

great style. great value. always sexy.

Redeem at any New York & Company store. Expires 12/31/06. See reverse side for details.

F8

Fashion that goes the distance.

avenue®
nothing should stop you®

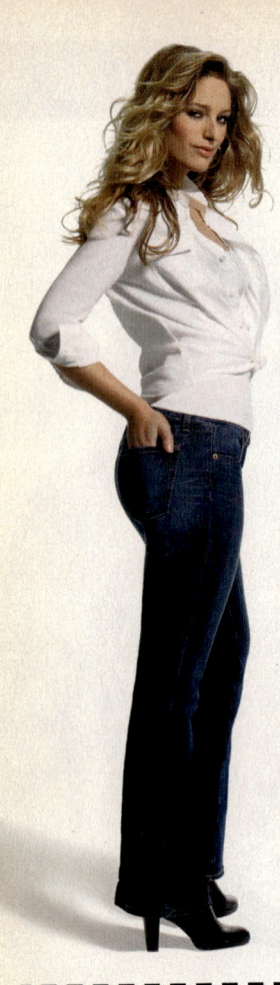

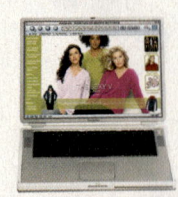

DRAPER'S & DAMON'S
fashion
that fits the time of your life
MISSES • PETITES • WOMEN'S
1.800.843.1174
stores • catalog
drapers.com

ARIZONA

Mesa • Cooper Village
(480) 396-9910

NEW! Mesa • Dana Park Village Square
(480) 539-2921

Phoenix • Biltmore Plaza
(602) 956-0735

Scottsdale • Scottsdale Seville
(480) 951-1331

Sun City • Greenway Terrace
(623) 974-2501

Sun City Outlet • Thunderbird Plaza
(623) 933-0411

Sun City West • Mercado Del Sol
(623) 584-3989

Tucson • Crossroads Festival
(520) 327-5700

Tucson Outlet • 4752 E. Grant Road
(520) 319-2677

CALIFORNIA

Camarillo • Las Posas Plaza
(805) 484-5991

Carlsbad • The Forum
(760) 635-1406

Escondido • 101 E. Grand Avenue
(760) 745-3800

Laguna Hills • Moulton Plaza
(949) 768-6622

Laguna Hills Outlet • Moulton Plaza
(949) 206-1310

La Jolla • 7636 Girard Avenue
(858) 459-3838

Newport Beach • Westcliff Plaza
(949) 646-5521

Palm Desert • 73-930 El Paseo
(760) 346-0559

Pasadena • 396 S. Lake Avenue
(626) 449-4410

Rancho Bernardo • The Plaza
(858) 451-3352

Rancho Mirage
Rancho Las Palmas Center
(760) 568-1165

Sacramento • Loehmann's Plaza
(916) 979-9695

San Marino • 2116 Huntington Drive
(626) 282-4703

San Mateo • Borel Square
(650) 341-8510

Santa Rosa • Montgomery Village
(707) 566-0961

Seal Beach • Rossmoor Center
(562) 596-3306

Stockton • Lincoln Center
(209) 952-1597

Studio City • 12199 Ventura Blvd.
(818) 761-6050

Sunnyvale • Loehmann's Plaza
(408) 524-0667

Torrance • Town & Country Center
(310) 326-5557

Tustin • Larwin Square
(714) 544-5040

Walnut Creek • Rossmoor Center
(925) 937-5512

COLORADO

NEW! Colorado Springs
The Shops at Briargate
(719) 388-8393

FLORIDA

Clearwater • Northwood Plaza
(727) 712-9886

Fort Myers • The Bell Tower Shops
(239) 433-9771

Jacksonville Beach
South Beach Regional Center
(904) 241-0500

Naples • Neapolitan Way Center
(239) 434-5342

North Palm Beach
Winn-Dixie Marketplace
(561) 691-1840

Sarasota • The Landings
(941) 921-3717

Stuart • Ocean East Mall
(772) 781-1610

ILLINOIS

Peoria
The Shoppes at Grand Prairie
(309) 691-1592

IOWA

NEW! West Des Moines
Jordan Creek Town Center
(515) 273-9993

MARYLAND

Bethesda • Shops at Sumner Place
(301) 263-3001

NEBRASKA

Omaha • Village Pointe
(402) 289-0870

TEXAS

Dallas • Inwood Village
(214) 352-7664

Fort Worth • Trinity Commons
(817) 731-3975

Houston • Town & Country Village
(713) 722-7661

Houston • Champion Forest Plaza
(281) 895-6039

San Antonio • Alamo Quarry Market
(210) 804-1755

VIRGINIA

Fairfax • Main Street Marketplace
(703) 691-3660

Visit the store nearest you for a similar selection of the beautiful styles shown in our catalog.
Stores carry Misses and Petites sizes only.
For more information, visit us at drapers.com or call toll-free 1-800-843-1174.

Free Shipping Offer is applicable for "standard shipping" only. Overnight and 2nd day air-freight available for an additional charge. Offer not valid in retail stores. Must surrender, present, or mention Promo Code P1309 at time of order. No store credits given or adjustments made on previous purchases. May not be combined with any other discounts or offers. Limit one coupon per customer. Offer expires 12/31/06.

DRAPER'S & DAMON'S

Subject to Rules of Use. Not valid with other discount offers, unless specified. Coupon VOID if purchased, sold or bartered for cash.

Valid now thru December 31, 2006

$20 or $50 Offer valid in retail stores, online and for catalog orders. Qualifying amount applies to merchandise only. Gift card purchases, taxes and shipping & handling do not count toward the qualifying amount. Not valid for cash redemption. Must surrender, present, or mention Promo Code P1307 or P1308 at time of order. No store credits given or adjustments made on previous purchases. May not be combined with any other discounts or offers. Limit one coupon per customer. Offer expires 12/31/06.

DRAPER'S & DAMON'S

Subject to Rules of Use. Not valid with other discount offers, unless specified. Coupon VOID if purchased, sold or bartered for cash.

Valid now thru December 31, 2006

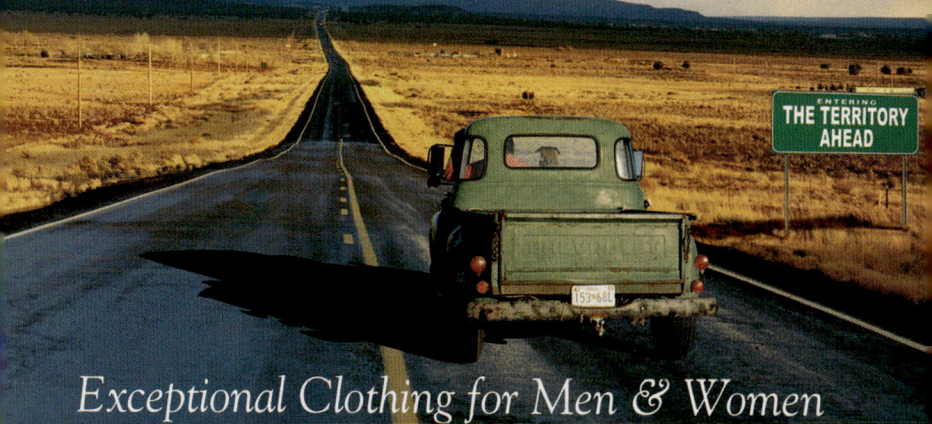

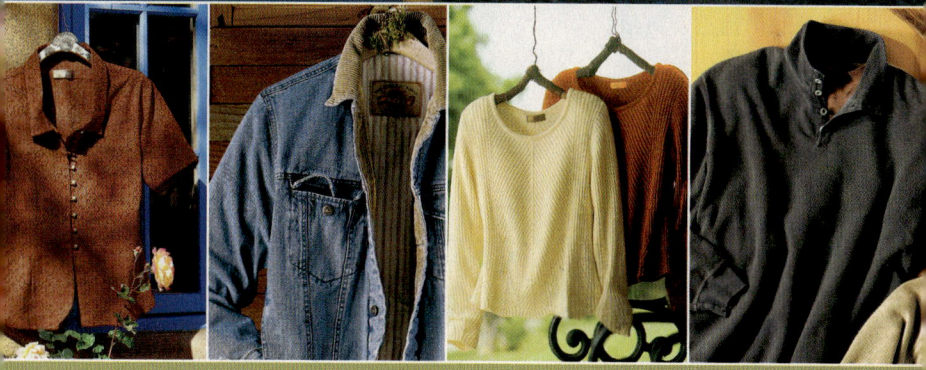

Growing Up with
garnet hill
a spirited collection of designs with kids in mind

Save $10

on any purchase of $50 or more

How to Redeem:

Phone: Request a catalog at garnethill.com or by calling 1-800-622-6216 and mention Promotion Code ENT when ordering.

Web: Visit garnethill.com and enter ENT in Promotion Code box during online checkout.

Growing Up with garnet hill

Terms & Conditions:

This offer valid on purchases from Growing Up with Garnet Hill. It is limited to one time use and cannot be combined with other discount offers. Qualified purchase amounts and discounts are based on merchandise prices only and excludes shipping, handling and taxes. There is no cash value to this offer and it cannot be used towards purchase of gift certificates or be applied to prior purchase. Offer void where prohibited.

Valid now thru December 31, 2006 F14

Save $50

on any purchase of $250 or more

How to Redeem:

Phone: Request a catalog at garnethill.com or by calling 1-800-622-6216 and mention Promotion Code ENT when ordering.

Web: Visit garnethill.com and enter ENT in Promotion Code box during online checkout.

Growing Up with garnet hill

Terms & Conditions:

This offer valid on purchases from Growing Up with Garnet Hill. It is limited to one time use and cannot be combined with other discount offers. Qualified purchase amounts and discounts are based on merchandise prices only and excludes shipping, handling and taxes. There is no cash value to this offer and it cannot be used towards purchase of gift certificates or be applied to prior purchase. Offer void where prohibited.

Valid now thru December 31, 2006 F15

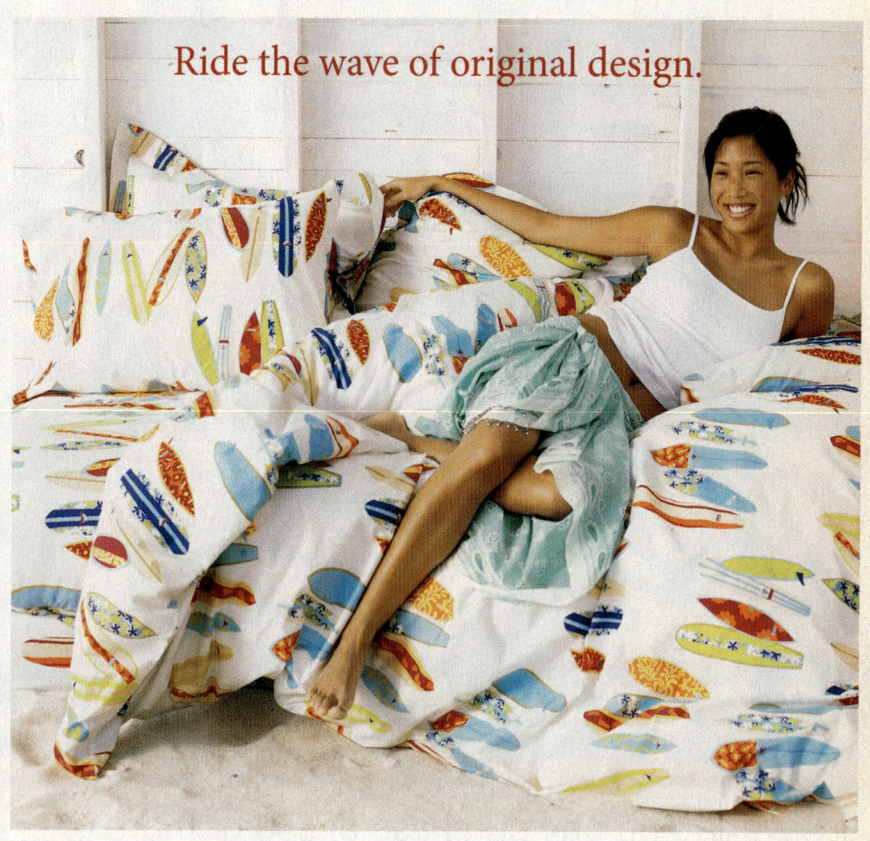

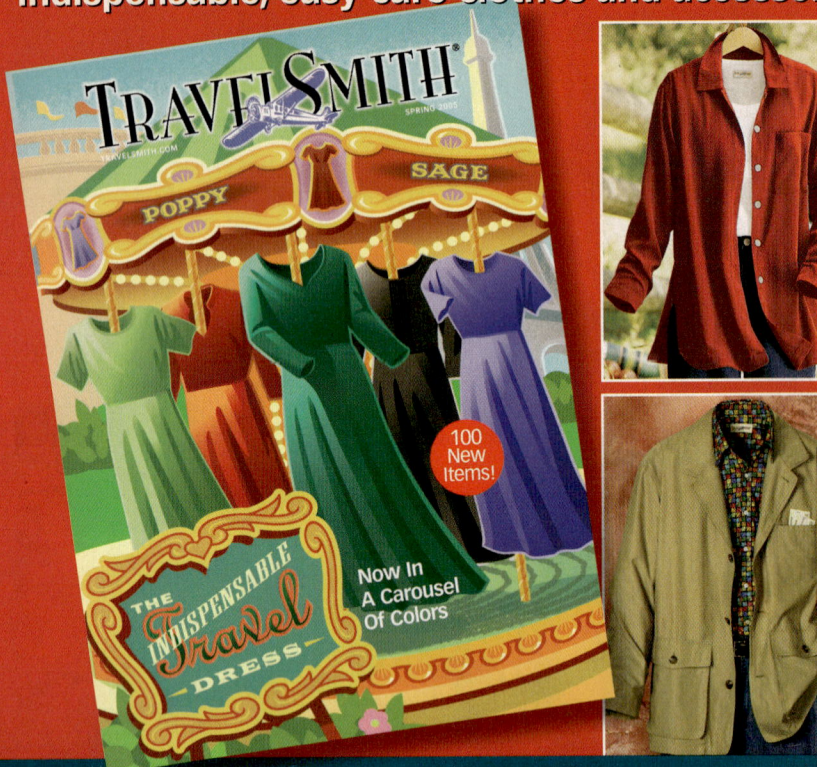

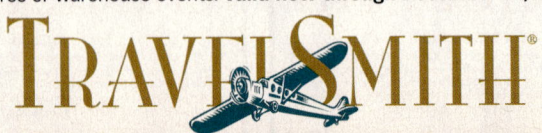

SAVE $10

WHEN YOU MAKE A PURCHASE OF $50 OR MORE.

Redeem in stores, by phone or online. Visit us at *www.isabellabird.com* for online purchases and the store nearest you, or call 888-472-2473.

Isabella Bird
by The Territory Ahead

Please mention Key Code 5G1200 if ordering by phone. If ordering online, enter Key Code at checkout.

See reverse side for details F19

SAVE $20

WHEN YOU MAKE A PURCHASE OF $100 OR MORE.

Redeem in stores, by phone or online. Visit us at *www.isabellabird.com* for online purchases and the store nearest you, or call 888-472-2473.

Isabella Bird
by The Territory Ahead

Please mention Key Code 5G1200 if ordering by phone. If ordering online, enter Key Code at checkout.

See reverse side for details F20

$15 off your $75 order
$20 off your $100 order
$30 off your $150 or more order

Save now at Blair.com!

BLAIR®.com

Quality fashions for women, men and home. Clearance bargains at 40%-75% off. Shop our entire line today and save up to $30 with this exclusive offer.

To take advantage of the savings, go to

www.blair.com/entertainment

See reverse for details. F21

SEE REVERSE FOR DETAILS

$20 OFF

YOUR ORDER OF $80 OR MORE

Over 200 brands of lingerie, sleepwear, swimwear and activewear

FREE SHIPPING & FREE RETURNS

figleaves.com

Go to www.figleaves.com/entertainment F22

Limit one offer per coupon. Reproductions are not accepted. Void where prohibited by law. No cash value. Savings may not be combined with any other promotions, and discount is not valid on gift certificate purchases. May not be applied to previous purchases. Offer good now through December 31, 2006.

Isabella Bird

by The Territory Ahead

Subject to Rules of Use. Not valid with other discount offers, unless specified. Coupon VOID if purchased, sold, or bartered for cash.

VALID NOW THROUGH 12/31/2006

Limit one offer per coupon. Reproductions are not accepted. Void where prohibited by law. No cash value. Savings may not be combined with any other promotions, and discount is not valid on gift certificate purchases. May not be applied to previous purchases. Offer good now through December 31, 2006.

Isabella Bird

by The Territory Ahead

Subject to Rules of Use. Not valid with other discount offers, unless specified. Coupon VOID if purchased, sold, or bartered for cash.

VALID NOW THROUGH 12/31/2006

Shop our entire line with this special offer!

Women's • Men's • Home • Clearance

You must go to www.blair.com/entertainment to receive this special offer. You'll see your **discount** automatically at checkout with your merchandise order of **at least $75 or more**. This offer applies to online orders only and cannot be combined with any other offers. Good through December 31, 2006.

BLAIR®.com

Subject to Rules of Use. Not valid with other discount offers, unless specified. Coupon VOID if purchased, sold, or bartered for cash.

figleaves.com

Go to www.figleaves.com/entertainment and $20 will be automatically deducted from your order when you spend $80 or more. One discount per customer.

Expires 12/31/06

Subject to Rules of Use. Not valid with other discount offers, unless specified. Coupon VOID if purchased, sold, or bartered for cash.

Figleaves.com has the largest online selection of branded lingerie, sleepwear, swimwear, activewear and men's underwear, with over 200 brands, including favorites from DKNY, Calvin Klein, La Perla, and Wacoal... plus hard-to-find fashion forward styles from around the world.

MasterCuts

$4 OFF your next haircut!

Get cool styles at great prices!
Save $4 on your next haircut at MasterCuts.*

Present this coupon at any MasterCuts. To find a MasterCuts near you, call 1-800-888-1117 or visit us at www.mastercuts.com.

Coupon Code: N18

See reverse side for details

F23

TRADE SECRET. BEAUTY EXPRESS.

THE NEWEST SALON PRODUCTS NOW

$10 off any $35 product purchase

Trade Secret/Beauty Express offers exceptional professional salon products at great prices – including 3,000 of the newest salon products on the market.

Present this coupon at any Trade Secret/Beauty Express. To find a Trade Secret/Beauty Express near you, call 1.800.888.1117 or visit us at www.tradesecret.com or www.beautyexpresssalon.com.

Coupon Code: N282

See reverse side for details

F24

REGIS SALON

The Cut & Color Experts

Save $10

on services of $40 or more

or

Save $20

on services of $75 or more

Present this coupon at any Regis Salon. To find a Regis Salon near you, call 1-800-777-4444 or visit us at www.regissalons.com.

Coupon Codes:
N194 ($10 off)
N196 ($20 off)

See reverse side for details

F25

MasterCuts

Terms and conditions

*Cuts from $11.95. Monday – Thursday only. One coupon per customer. Coupon not valid with any other coupon offer. Coupons cannot be retroactive. One-time use only. No double discounts. No cash value. Not for resale. Offer only redeemable in the United States. Void where prohibited, taxed or restricted by law. MasterCuts is a trademark of Regis Corporation or its subsidiaries.

Subject to Rules of Use. Not valid with other discount offers, unless specified. Coupon VOID if purchased, sold or bartered for cash.

Valid now thru December 31, 2006

TRADE SECRET. BEAUTY EXPRESS.

THE NEWEST SALON PRODUCTS NOW

Terms and conditions

Not valid on salon services, Dermalogica products, clearance items or gift cards. One coupon per customer. Coupon not valid with any other coupon offer. Coupons cannot be retroactive. One-time use only. No double discounts. No cash value. Not for resale. Offer only redeemable in the United States. Void where prohibited, taxed or restricted by law. Trade Secret/Beauty Express is a trademark of Regis Corporation or its subsidiaries.

Subject to Rules of Use. Not valid with other discount offers, unless specified. Coupon VOID if purchased, sold or bartered for cash.

Valid now thru December 31, 2006

REGIS SALON

The Cut & Color Experts

Terms and conditions

One coupon per customer. Coupon not valid with any other coupon offer. Coupons cannot be retroactive. One-time use only. No double discounts. No cash value. Not for resale. Offer only redeemable in the United States. Void where prohibited, taxed or restricted by law. Good only for purchases of product or services indicated. Any other use constitutes fraud. Regis Salons is a trademark of Regis Corporation or its subsidiaries.

Subject to Rules of Use. Not valid with other discount offers, unless specified. Coupon VOID if purchased, sold or bartered for cash.

Valid now thru December 31, 2006

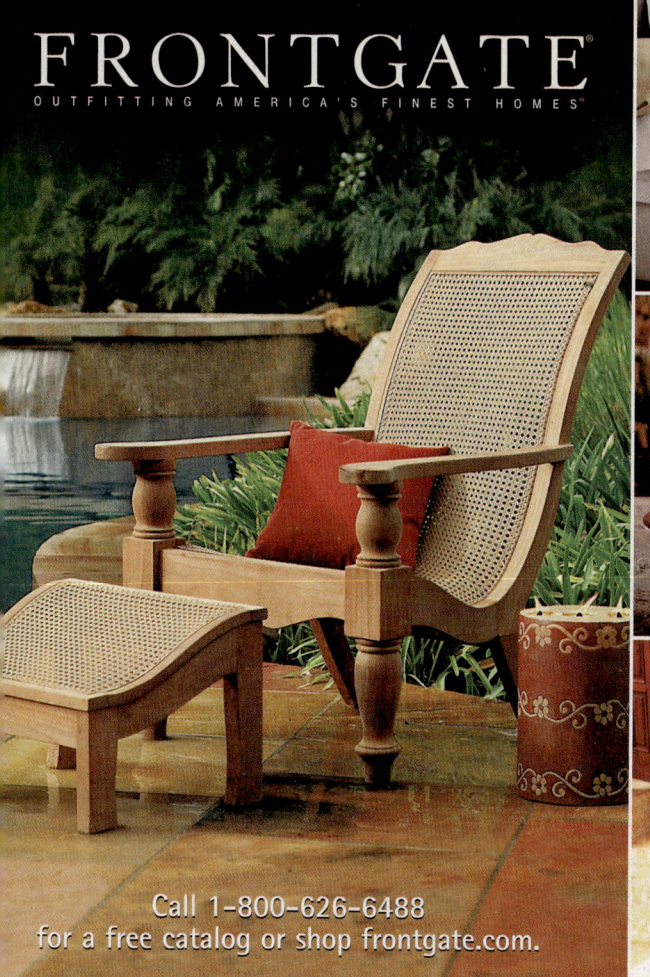

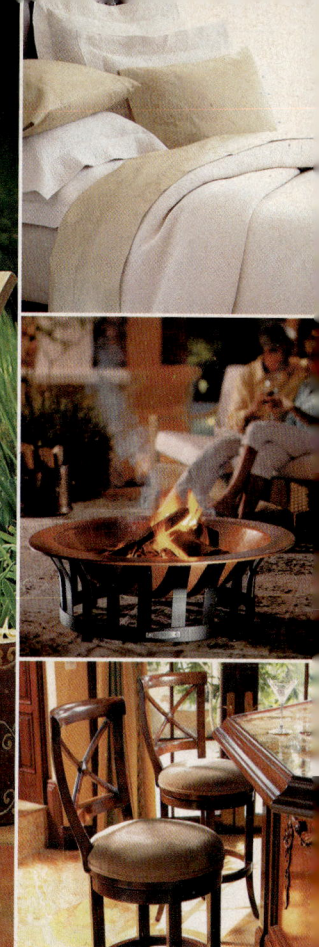

grandinroad®
The catalog of inspired ideas for every home.
Call 1-800-491-5194 for a free catalog —
or shop grandinroad.com for hundreds of affordable
products that are built to thrive in the real world.

BALLARD DESIGNS

Easy to create
Easy to order
Easy to afford
Hard to Ignore
smith+noble®
America's leading resource for window treatments
$150 OFF YOUR PURCHASE OF $600 OR MORE
Or
$100 OFF YOUR PURCHASE OF $500 OR MORE
Or
$50 OFF YOUR PURCHASE OF $300 OR MORE
use offer code SAVE-5TSF when ordering
For a Free Catalog and 10 Free Swatches
Call 1-888-251-7895 or go online smithnoble.com/freeswatches
50517017
F31
Offer expires December 31, 2006

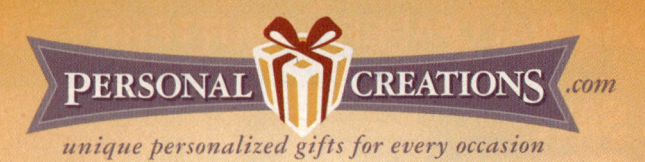

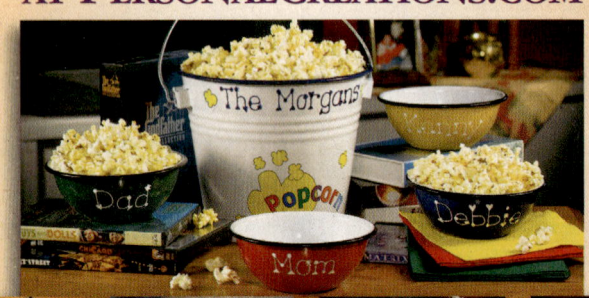

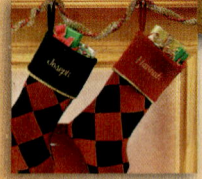

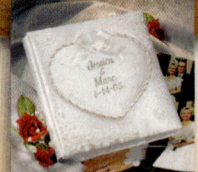

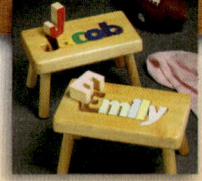

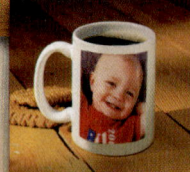

save $15 on your first order

HSN
hsn.com

New customers can save $15 on a single-item purchase of $50 or more on hsn.com or HSN TV. Shop from the comfort of home for jewelry, beauty, fashion, cookware, health & fitness, collectibles, sports, home items and much more. (Offer excludes electronics, clearance and Today's Special.) **To order, call 1.800.284.3100 or visit hsn.com anytime.**

Valid through December 31, 2006. For your $15 savings, please refer to coupon code #701126.

F34

save $10 on house & home

All customers save $10 on a single-item house/home purchase of $50 or more.

Valid through December 31, 2006.
Refer to coupon #903471.

F35

save $10 on fashion

All customers save $10 on a single-item fashion purchase of $50 or more.

Valid through December 31, 2006.
Refer to coupon #921041.

F36

save $10 on cookware

All customers save $10 on a single-item cookware purchase of $50 or more.

Valid through December 31, 2006.
Refer to coupon #502622.

F37

save $10 on jewelry

All customers save $10 on a single-item jewelry purchase of $50 or more.

Valid through December 31, 2006.
Refer to coupon #801036.

F38

Coupon #701126 is valid for $15 off a new customer's first single-item purchase of $50 or more (excluding electronics). Coupon #903471 is for all customers and is valid for $10 off a single-item house/home purchase of $50 or more. Coupon #502622 is for all customers and is valid for $10 off a single-item cookware purchase of $50 or more. Coupon #801036 is for all customers and is valid for $10 off a single-item jewelry purchase of $50 or more. Coupon #921041 is for all customers and is valid for $10 off a single-item fashion purchase of $50 or more. Coupons are non-transferable and each coupon can be used once per customer. Excludes shipping & handling, sales tax, Flex Pay, Today's Special, Clearance Department and sale-priced merchandise. Coupons cannot be applied on extended service plans or combined with other coupons or offers. We reserve the right to cancel orders when unexpected coupon system errors occur. Offers are only valid for HSN TV or hsn.com.

BURBERRY BRIT
EAU DE TOILETTE NATURAL SPRAY VAPORISATEUR
OMEGA
Save an extra 10% on all orders,
plus free shipping on orders over $150 at ashford.com!*
Ashford.com features a wide selection of luxury goods from Prada, Gucci, Fendi, TAG Heuer and more at savings of up to 60%.
Coupon valid through December 31, 2006
Offer redeemable via phone or online
*Terms: This offer is valid only on in-stock merchandise and excludes special order items, loose diamonds, Cartier and Breitling watches, and pre-owned Rolex watches. See below for more terms.
ashford.com™
Online - www.ashford.com/ent Phone - 1-866-274-3673 Phone orders mention: ASENTTNP
DIAMOND.COM™
Design the ring of her dreams with GIA-graded diamonds, plus shop for fine jewelry and brand-name watches, all at incredible values.
Save $100 on all loose diamond orders over $1,000
plus free shipping!*
Coupon valid through December 31, 2006
Offer redeemable via phone or online
*Terms: Promotion applies to orders that include diamonds from our Design-Your-Ring and/or loose diamond inventory. Order subtotal must be $1,000 USD or more. Promotion cannot be applied to special orders or pre-set jewelry. See below for more terms.
Online - www.diamond.com/ent
Phone - 1-888-342-6663
Phone orders mention: DCENT1CD
World of Watches®
Shop WorldofWatches.com and save up to 60% on TAG Heuer, Omega, Movado and more than 40 other top brand-name watches.
Save an extra 10% on all orders of $299 or more
plus free shipping!*
Coupon valid through December 31, 2006
Offer redeemable via phone or online
*Terms: This offer is valid only on in-stock merchandise and excludes special order items, Cartier and Breitling watches, and all pre-owned watches including Rolex. See below for more terms.
Online - www.worldofwatches.com/ent
Phone - 1-888-928-2437
Phone orders mention: WWENT1P2
Terms: Discount will be applied to qualifying items only and will be automatically calculated at checkout. Offer valid through 11:59 pm EST December 31, 2006. Discount is not applicable to canceled orders due to out-of-stock merchandise. Discount cannot be applied to gift certificates. Discount does not apply to taxes, shipping and handling charges, gift wrapping or other similar processing charges. Discount cannot be combined with any other promotional offer nor can it be applied to previous purchases. This offer may be modified or withdrawn at any time without prior notice. See web sites for full terms and conditions.

CRUTCHFIELD®
The Electronics Shopping Alternative
$10 off $50
mention code PA440
$50 off $250
mention code PA440
You must purchase over $50 or $250 in merchandise in order to receive this discount. This discount is not valid towards the purchase of Bose products, Monster Cable products, Polk Audio products, Cambridge Soundworks products, Escort products, Rockford Fosgate products, K & N products, Apple products, HP iPaqs and Tivoli Audio products. All offers are based on availability and are subject to change without notice.
Order online at www.crutchfield.com, by calling 1-800-555-8346 or from the catalog
Not valid with other discounts, coupons or offers. Discount does not include shipping or taxes.
Discount not valid on prior purchases. Coupon VOID is purchased, sold or bartered for cash.
Valid now thru December 31, 2006
F40

Abt
"Best Independent Retailer In The USA"
Awarded By TWICE - Leading Electronics & Appliance Industry Magazine, 2004
Appliances Video Audio Portable Electronics Computers
Enjoy $15 Off
Any Purchase of $100 or More, or Save Up to 5% Off Our Everyday, Low Marked Prices.*
• Free shipping (on most electronics)
• $78 shipping (on most appliances)
• Low Price Guarantee
Vaild now through December 31, 2006
To Receive Your Special Offer Call
800.698.7582
www.abtelectronics.com/entbook
*Not valid toward previously purchased merchandise or other offers.
Some brands are excluded from this offer. See site for complete details.

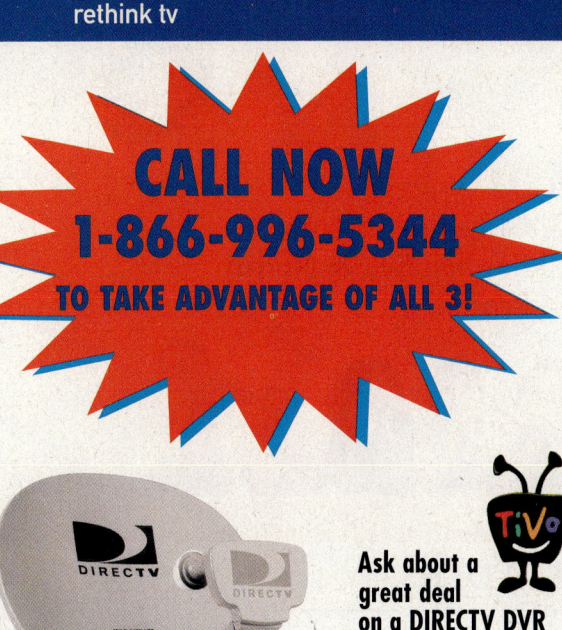

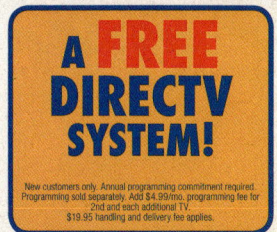

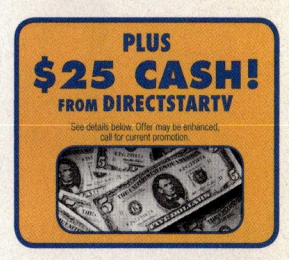

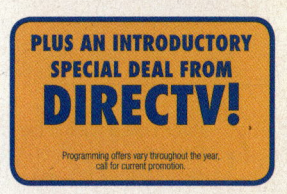

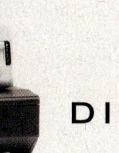

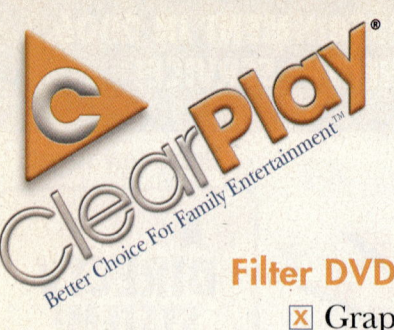

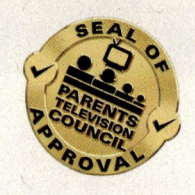

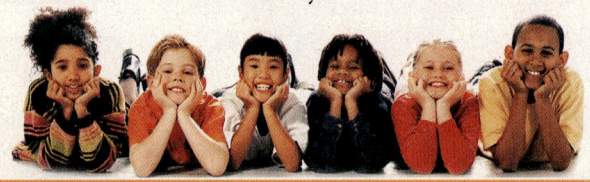

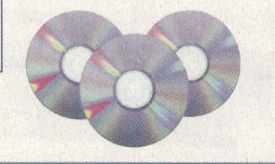

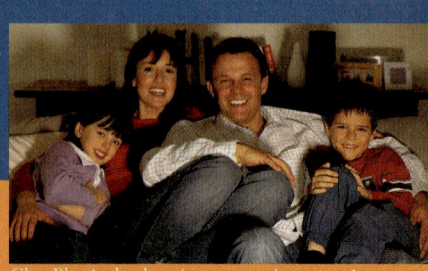

SAVE UP TO $175⁰⁰

Save $175

$49* Standard Installation

Plus call today and receive a

FREE*

2nd keypad installation

CONSUMERS DIGEST BEST BUY
BRINKS HOME SECURITY
Standard & Premium Systems

Call Now! **1-800-531-3985**

BRINKS HOME SECURITY®

F44

Save 20%

on your first purchase of $50 or more!

- To redeem this coupon online at www.improvementscatalog.com and receive your 20% discount, enter the following Source Code when asked for it on the order screen: **ENT2006**
- You may also call toll-free 1-800-642-2112, and mention **"Source Code ENT2006"** to our operator to receive your 20% discount.
- Discount is 20% off any order with a merchandise total of $50 or more.
- Not valid with any other offer.

See reverse side for details

Battery Storage Rack & Tester

Improvements®
Quick & Clever Problem-Solvers!

F45

Save on the Best in Home Lighting

chandeliers | ceiling fans | kitchen & bathroom lighting | outdoor | table & floor lamps

$10 off	$30 off	$75 off
purchase of $50 or more code QP33ENFB7Z	purchase of $200 or more code QP78ENFB7Z	purchase of $500 or more code QP98ENFB7Z

Enter code online at LAMPSPLUS.com or bring coupon to store

LAMPS PLUS®
America's Lighting Superstore

See reverse side for details

F46

BRINKS HOME SECURITY®

Call now to schedule a FREE security system needs analysis!

1-800-531-3985

***Call for information on Brink's® monitoring fees and other terms. REFERENCED CONNECTION FEE AND KEYPAD OFFER REQUIRE BRINK'S EASYPAY™ AUTO PAYMENT. Three-year minimum monitoring agreement required at the Brink's® current rate.** Applicable taxes and permit fees not included. Offer may not be combined with any other discount. Limited time offer, offer subject to change. Home ownership and credit approval required. Home must be located in a Brink's® service area. The Best Buy seal is a registered trademark of Consumers Digest Communications, LLC, used under license. ©2005 Brink's Home Security®, 8880 Esters Blvd., Irving, TX 75063. AL#333, AR#E93-29, AZ#ROC085024, AZ#ROC149890, CA#ACO3843, FL#EF0000921, GA#LVA004165, IL#127-000756, MD#107-319, MI – 11918 Farmington Rd., Livonia, MI 48150, NC#1633-CSA, NY#12000046324 - licensed by the NYS Department of State, OK#587, OR#44421, SC#BA-5249 and #FA-3273, TN Alarm Cert. #C-0053 and #00000234, TX#B04296, UT#325152-6501, VA#11-1964, WV#031960. Market Source: ENTER1

Subject to Rules of Use. Not valid with other discount offers, unless specified. Coupon VOID if purchased, sold, or bartered for cash.

VALID NOW THROUGH 12/31/2006

Improvements®

Quick & Clever Problem-Solvers!

Limit one order per coupon.
Offer cannot be combined with any other discounts or special promotions.

Subject to Rules of Use. Not valid with other discount offers, unless specified. Coupon VOID if purchased, sold or bartered for cash.

Valid now thru December 31, 2006

LAMPSPLUS.com

to browse our complete selection or find a store near you

Finest Selection, Certified Lighting Designers, Competitive Prices–Always!

Terms and Conditions:
Redeemable in stores or online. Minimum purchase requirement excludes shipping and applicable taxes. Offer valid on regular priced, in-stock merchandise only; not valid on special orders or previous orders. In ceiling fan category, only valid on Casa Vieja brand. Offer may not be combined with any other discount. One coupon per customer, one time use only. Offer is non-transferable and not redeemable for cash or gift certificates. Other restrictions may apply, see stores or call 1-800-782-1967 for details. Coupon expires: 12-31-2006

Subject to Rules of Use. Not valid with other discount offers, unless specified. Coupon VOID if purchased, sold, or bartered for cash.

VALID NOW THROUGH 12/31/2006

$15 OFF ORDERS OF $100 OR MORE

Cooking.com™

$15 OFF
orders of $100 or more

Visit www.cooking.com/promos/ent
for complete details

See reverse side for details

F47

Experience the 5-Day Difference!

RENT 2, GET 1 FREE

Valid on all Movies and Games

Valid Now - December 31, 2006.

HOLLYWOOD VIDEO®

See reverse side for details

F48

K·B toys™

$20 off
any toy purchase of $100 or more at K·B Toys, K·B Toy Works and K·B Toy Outlets.

See reverse side for details

F49

K·B toys™

15% off
any toy purchase of $75 or more at K·B Toys, K·B Toy Works and K·B Toy Outlets.

See reverse side for details

F50

Cooking.com™

$15 OFF
orders of $100 or more

Visit www.cooking.com/promos/ent for complete details

Discount applies to the merchandise total per each shipment before tax and shipping. Excludes Merchant Partner products, All-Clad, Breville, Capresso, Emerilware, Henckels, Kershaw, KitchenAid Stand Mixers, Krups, Kuhn Rikon, Musso, Saeco, Seattle's Best Coffee, Starbucks, Torrefazione, Viking, Wusthof, Global, Clearance and gift certificates. Cannot be combined with any other offers or discounts, promotional gift certificates, or 3rd party site offers including but not limited to rebate, miles, or affiliate programs. Cannot be applied to a previous purchase. Terms are subject to change. No rain checks on out of stock items.

Subject to Rules of Use. Not valid with other discount offers, unless specified. Coupon VOID if purchased, sold, or bartered for cash.

VALID NOW THROUGH 12/31/2006

- **Free rental of equal or lesser value.**
- **Membership terms and conditions apply.**
- **Limit one coupon per membership account per visit.**
- **Valid at all Hollywood Video stores, with the exception of Game Crazy.**
- **Customer responsible for all applicable taxes and additional rental period charges; see stores for details.**
- **This coupon must be relinquished at the time of redemption and may not be printed, reproduced, sold or transferred.**

+CNPEBAA

Subject to Rules of Use. Not valid with other discount offers, unless specified. Coupon VOID if purchased, sold, or bartered for cash.

VALID NOW THROUGH 12/31/2006

K·B toys™

Discount cannot be combined with any other coupon or applied to purchase of Gift Cards or video games, systems and accessories. Discount taken off lowest prices at register. Sales tax not valid toward $75 purchase requirement. Limit one coupon per visit. Not valid at K·B Toys at Wisebuys, K·B Toys at Safeway, online or during storewide sale events. Associates: to process 15% savings use discount #1000512 or select "ET Book."

Subject to Rules of Use. Not valid with other discount offers, unless specified. Coupon VOID if purchased, sold or bartered for cash.

Offer valid 9/1/2005-12/31/2006.

K·B toys™

Discount cannot be combined with any other coupon or applied to purchase of Gift Cards or video games, systems and accessories. Discount taken off lowest prices at register. Sales tax not valid toward $100 purchase requirement. Limit one coupon per visit. Not valid at K·B Toys at Wisebuys, K·B Toys at Safeway, online or during storewide sale events. Associates: to process $20 savings use discount #1000843 or select "$20 Entertainment."

Subject to Rules of Use. Not valid with other discount offers, unless specified. Coupon VOID if purchased, sold or bartered for cash.

Offer valid 9/1/2005-12/31/2006.

Save up to $197

12 CDs for the price of 1

with membership

Nothing more to buy, ever!

A shipping and handling charge will be added to each selection.

BMG music service

bmgmusic.com/ent2006

See reverse side for details F51

$3 off

any regularly priced DVD

($9.99 and up)

SUNCOAST[SM]

The store for movie lovers.

See reverse side for details F52

---

sam goody

$3 off

any regularly priced CD or DVD

($9.99 and up)

See reverse side for details F53

SAVE $3

On any regularly priced CD or DVD. Low Price $9.99 or above.

MEDIA PLAY

See reverse side for details F54

SAVE $10

TAKE $10 OFF ON ANY PURCHASE OF $50 OR MORE

As the world's largest online retailer of bags and accessories, we have the perfect bag for every lifestyle. Choose from premium and popular brands including Samsonite, JanSport, Adidas, Kenneth Cole, Eagle Creek, Kipling and hundreds more! From backpacks and handbags to computer cases and luggage, eBags combines the best selection of products with unrivaled services and prices up to 60% below retail. All eBags orders come with a 110% price guarantee and free returns.

eBags what's your bag?

http://www.ebags.com/entertainment2006

See reverse side for details F55

12 CDs for the price of 1

with membership

Nothing more to buy, ever!

A shipping and handling charge will be added to each selection.

14,000 titles to choose from

Modern Rock • Country • Pop • Classical • R&B/Hip-Hop • Latin and more!

BMG music service bmgmusic.com/ent2006

Subject to Rules of Use. Not valid with other discount offers, unless specified. Coupon VOID if purchased, sold or bartered for cash.

VALID NOW THROUGH 12/31/2006

---

sam goody

Limit one item per coupon.

Offer cannot be used in conjunction with any other offer, special order or online purchase.

Markdown Code 411.

Subject to Rules of Use. Not valid with other discount offers, unless specified. Coupon VOID if purchased, sold or bartered for cash.

Valid now thru December 31, 2006

SUNCOAST

The store for movie lovers.

Limit one item per coupon.

Offer cannot be used in conjunction with any other offer, special order or online purchase.

Markdown Code 414.

Subject to Rules of Use. Not valid with other discount offers, unless specified. Coupon VOID if purchased, sold or bartered for cash.

Valid now thru December 31, 2006

---

eBags

what's your bag?

RESTRICTIONS: Discount price applies only to available inventory. Discounts cannot be combined with any other offer, cannot be applied to gift certificate purchases, apply only to your next purchase, and does not apply to select brands. See site for brand restrictions and further details. Offers not valid on eBags Corporate Sales orders. Offer expires 12/31/06.

Go to http://www.ebags.com/entertainment2006 to receive your offer.

SAVE $10

TAKE $10 OFF ON ANY PURCHASE OF $50 OR MORE

http://www.ebags.com/entertainment2006

VALID NOW THROUGH 12/31/2006

Subject to Rules of Use. Not valid with other discount offers, unless specified. Coupon VOID if purchased, sold, or bartered for cash.

MEDIA PLAY

Limit one item per coupon.

Offer cannot be used in conjunction with any other offer, special order or online purchase.

Markdown Code 412.

Subject to Rules of Use. Not valid with other discount offers, unless specified. Coupon VOID if purchased, sold or bartered for cash.

Valid now thru December 31, 2006

it's all inside.
JCPenney
Portraits you will love...
from the family portrait experts
Free 8x10 plus
50% Off
portrait purchase
(with $9.99 sitting fee)
Valid for 50% off entire portrait purchase
including Enhancements and fees
Call 1-800-59-SMILE for the location nearest you or visit jcpenneyportraits.com
See reverse side for details
it's all inside.
JCPenneyportraits
F56

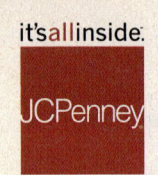

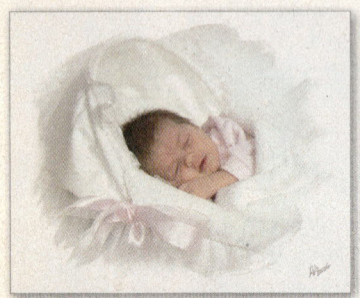

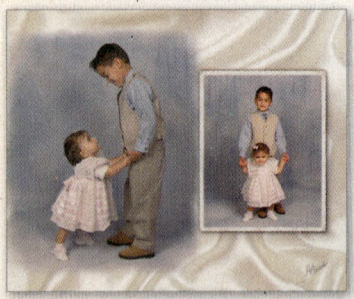

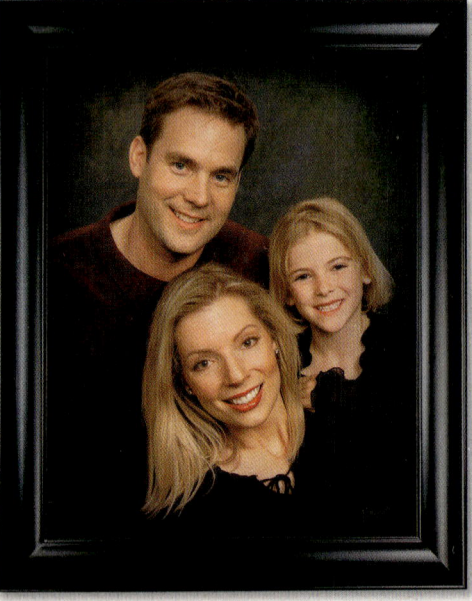

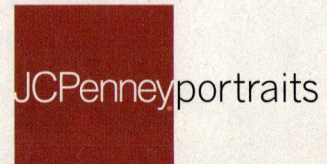

EXTRA $15 OFF all orders of $150 or more!

SmartBargains.com®

Top Brands. Smart Prices.[SM]

Take $15 off all orders of $150 or more.
Save up to 70% on luxury bedding, cutting-edge electronics, the hottest designer accessories, diamond jewelry & more!

To order online, please visit us at:
www.smartbargains.com/ent

See reverse side for details F57

You Gotta Share Those Shots.

Kodak EasyShare Gallery

Do more with your digital photos online.

- Share multiple photos with online slideshows
- Get KODAK prints delivered right to your door
- Make Photo Gifts, including albums and framed pictures

www.kodakgallery.com

SAVE TODAY! See back for details.

Develop & Share Photos Free

Try Snapfish and get

- 30 digital camera prints on Kodak paper
- 1 roll of film developed free
- Unlimited online photo sharing & storage
- Plus 20% off fun photo gifts checkout coupon code: ENTERTAIN

Go to www.snapfish.com/entertainment

snapfish®

See reverse side for details F59

shutterfly®

New Customers get
30 4x6 prints Free

Do more with your digital pictures.

- Get film-quality prints
- Free online sharing
- Create unique Photo Gifts

Get your Free prints now.
Go to **www.shutterfly.com/entertain**
Offer ends December 31, 2006

See reverse side for details. F60

SmartBargains.com® *Top Brands. Smart Prices.*℠

EXTRA $15 OFF all orders of $150 or more!

Up to 70% off luxury bedding, top electronics, designer accessories, jewelry & more

To order online, please visit us at: **www.smartbargains.com/ent**

Discount applies to new customers only, excluding shipping charges and taxes. Not valid on prior purchases, pending orders or with any other discounts, certificates or promotions. This offer expires and is only valid on orders which are placed and confirmed on or before 11:59 PM/EST on December 31, 2006. **Expires 12/31/06.**

Kodak EasyShare Gallery

www.kodakgallery.com

Save 20% on Photo Greeting Cards

Use coupon code ENTCARD20 at checkout to redeem.

Save 20% offer expires 12/31/06. Offer applies to Photo Greeting Cards only. Does not apply to shipping costs, film processing, Kodak Mobile Service subscription or applicable sales tax. One coupon redemption per customer. Cannot be combined with other offers. No substitutions, transfer rights or cash equivalents will be given.

Kodak EasyShare Gallery

www.kodakgallery.com

Save 20% on Photo Books

Use coupon code ENTPHB20 at checkout to redeem.

20% offer expires on 12/31/06. Offer applies to Photo Books only. Does not apply to shipping costs, film processing, Kodak Mobile Service subscription or applicable sales tax. One coupon redemption per customer. Cannot be combined with other offers. No substitutions, transfer rights or cash equivalents will be given.

Kodak EasyShare Gallery

www.kodakgallery.com

Buy one 8"x10" print, and get one 8"x10" print FREE

Use coupon code ENT8X10 at checkout to redeem.

Offer expires on 12/31/06. Offer applies to 8"x10" prints only. Must buy one 8"x10" print to qualify. Does not apply to shipping costs, film processing, Kodak Mobile Service subscription or applicable sales tax. One coupon redemption per customer. Cannot be combined with other offers in same order. No substitutions, transfer rights or cash equivalents will be given.

Get 30 free 4x6 prints when you try Shutterfly!

Go to **www.shutterfly.com/entertain** to sign up. The free prints will automatically be entered into your new account.

Offer ends December 31, 2006. New Customers Only.

shutterfly

---

snapfish®

the best value in film & digital photography

To receive your free film developing (1 roll 35mm or 1 APS) and digital camera prints, you must register at: **www.snapfish.com/entertainment**

Offer available to new Snapfish members only. Valid email address required.

Free Roll and Prints are subject to a shipping and handling charge as listed on snapfish.com.

Subject to Rules of Use. Not valid with other discount offers, unless specified. Coupon VOID if purchased, sold, or bartered for cash.

VALID NOW THROUGH 12/31/2006

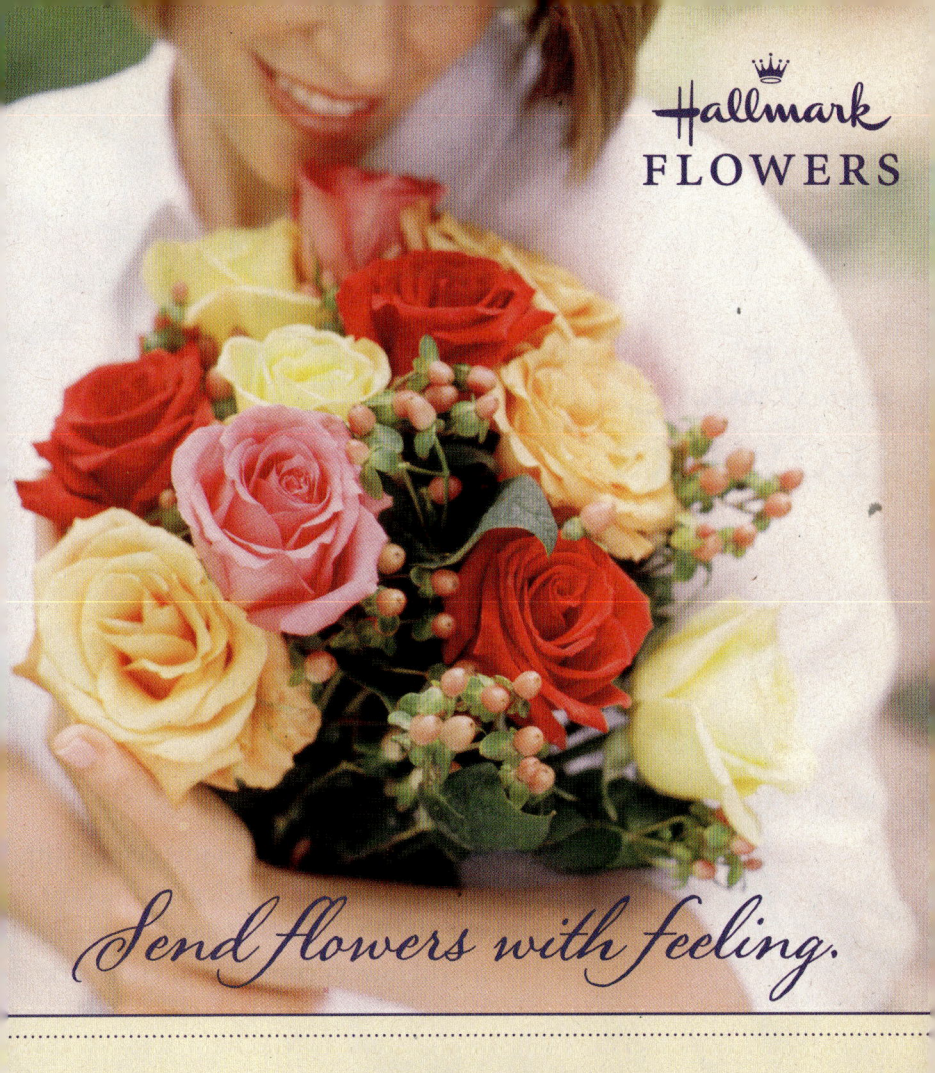

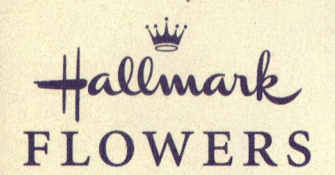

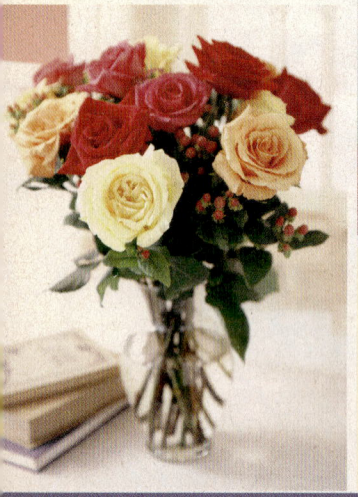

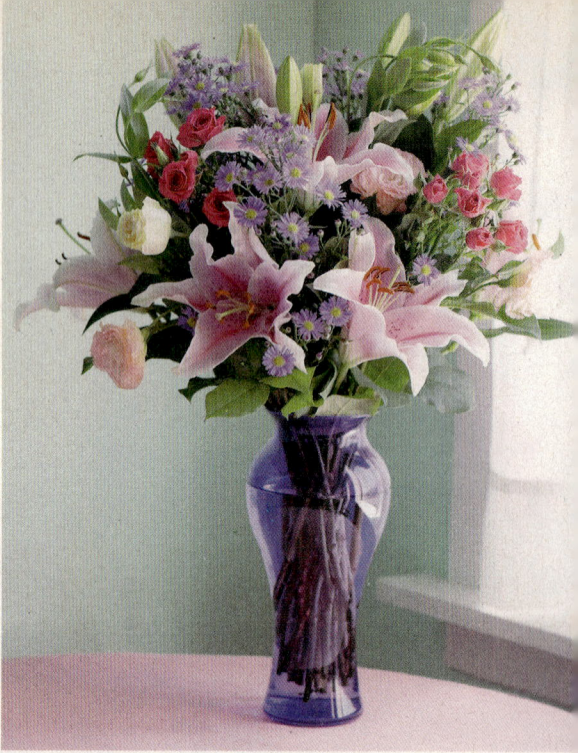

Save $10
FTD.COM
SHOP ONLINE OR DIAL 1-800-SEND-FTD
Same Day Delivery by a quality FTD® Florist.
Save $10 when you order at www.ftd.com/ent2006
or by visiting your participating FTD® Florist.
Save $7.50 when you call 1-800-SEND-FTD
and mention promo code 10541.
SAVE $10 online or at your local FTD® Florist
Save $10
FTD.COM
when you order online at www.ftd.com/ent2006
or by visiting your participating FTD® Florist.
Save $7.50 when you call 1-800-SEND-FTD
and mention promo code 10541.
See reverse side for details
F62

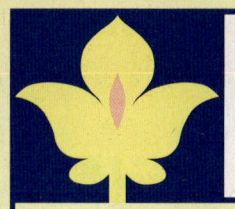

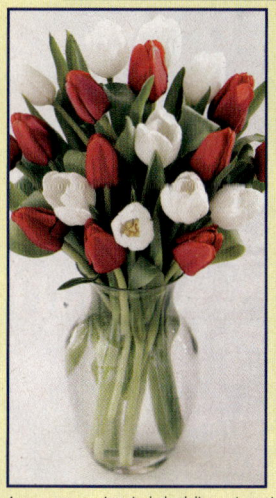

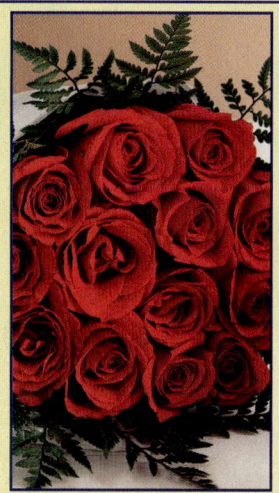

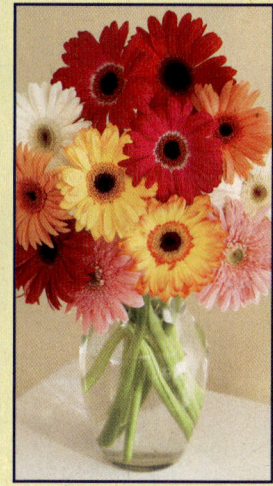

Birthdays • Holidays • Get Well • Baby Arrivals • Anniversaries • Sympathy
Flowers Sent TODAY!
Join Over One Million Satisfied Customers.
Friendly Agents 24/7
NATIONWIDE & LOCAL
SAME DAY DELIVERY GUARANTEED
FLOWERS, ROSES, PLANTS, GIFT BASKETS, FUNERAL DESIGNS AND MANY MORE GIFTS
SERVING ALL U.S. CITIES
Funeral Homes & Hospitals
BloomsUSA
1-800-521-6920
It takes less than 5 minutes to place an order.
Shop Online:
Family Owned & Operated
www.BloomsUSA™.com
Creating Smiles Across America!
Save 25% on Every Order!
Flowers, Roses, And Plants
Hand Delivered By A Local Florist
Same Day Delivery Guarantee (If Ordered By 3pm)
Coupon Code ENB
F64
Save 15% on Every Order!
Fresh Flowers, Roses and Gifts
From our Direct Ship Categories
Starting At $29.99
Coupon Code ENB
F65
Coupons Valid Now Thru December 31, 2006

from you FLOWERS
SAVE $15
say it with color
Product # TF68-3
fromyouflowers.com/ent
1-800-758-9353
mention code ENT
flowers & plants • balloons • gift baskets • chocolates • and much, much more!
Same-Day Delivery Until 3 PM!
Fast, easy ordering online or by phone!
SAVE $15 on a dozen long stem roses!
fromyouflowers.com/ent
1-800-758-9353
mention code ENT
SAVE $10 on all other flowers and gifts!
F66
See reverse side for details

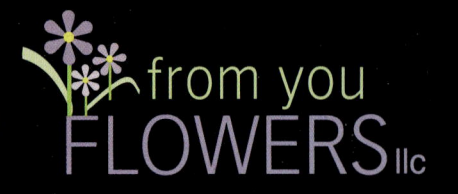

Save 30-50%

Off Florist Prices

Join Over 3 Million People Who Have Found A Better Way To Buy Flowers

Bouquets Starting at: 24^{99} + S/H

ProFlowers®

The Art of Fresher Flowers℠

12 FREE Roses

($20 Savings)

Get 24 Red or Assorted Roses for the price of 12.

(color availability dependent on time of year)

Order at: **www.proflowers.com/ENB**

or call: **1-800-776-3569** Reference Entertainment® Book

ProFlowers®

The Art of Fresher Flowers℠

F67

15% OFF

Any product. Anytime.

Order at: **www.proflowers.com/ENB**

or call: **1-800-776-3569** Reference Entertainment® Book

ProFlowers®

The Art of Fresher Flowers℠

F68

Freshest flowers
for every occasion!
1-800-FLOWERS.COM®, Your Florist of Choice℠ always offers:
• Freshest flowers artistically designed
• Personal service 24/7 for delivery same day, any day
• 100% satisfaction guaranteed
• The finest selection of flowers, plants, gift baskets, plush toys, gourmet foods and more
• Gifts exclusively designed for 1-800-FLOWERS.COM® by leading brands you trust
15% off* all purchases.
Use Promotion Code ENTB2.
Call 1-800-FLOWERS® (1-800-356-9377)
Or Click www.1800flowers.com!
1-800-flowers.com℠
Your florist of choice℠
15% off*
all your purchases!
Use Promotion Code ENTB2 at checkout.
Call 1-800-FLOWERS® (1-800-356-9377)
Or Click www.1800flowers.com!
1-800-flowers.com℠
Your florist of choice℠
*Exclusive of applicable service and shipping charges and taxes. Items may vary and are subject to availability, delivery rules and times. Offers available online and by phone. Offers cannot be combined, are not available on all products and are subject to restrictions and limitations. Offer valid through 12/31/06. Prices and charges are subject to change without notice. Void where prohibited. © 2005 1-800-FLOWERS.COM®, INC.
1-800-FLOWERS.COM® uses Secure Socket Layer (SSL) encryption technology to secure its website.
F69

Save 15%

online at **berries.com**: use code ENT06W
call **1.877.BERRIES**: use code ENT06C

Valid now through December 31, 2006.

Shari's Berries
The unforgettable gift.™

Not valid with other discounts, coupons, or offers. Discount does not include shipping or taxes. Discount not valid on prior purchases. Coupon VOID if purchased, sold, or bartered for cash.

F70

Special Offer – Click or Call!

10% OFF

your first purchase

Order online or by phone. Receive 10% off your first purchase. One time use only. Order online at harryanddavid.com/go/ent2006 or call 800-547-3033 and mention quick service number 26493 and coupon code H65. Cannot be used for stores, corporate sales, gift card, or Same Day Delivery orders, nor in combination with any other offers or discounts. For orders over $2500, please call our Corporate Sales Department at 800-344-1500.

Offer expires 12/31/06

H65

Offer valid for Internet and phone orders only.

F71

Store Coupon

10% OFF

Bring this coupon to any Harry and David Store and receive 10% OFF your purchase.

Harry and David®

See reverse side for details.

F72

Store Coupon

10% OFF

Bring this coupon to any Harry and David Store and receive 10% OFF your purchase.

Harry and David®

See reverse side for details.

F73

Harry and David®
Any Day Can Be a Celebration!℠
• Unique gifts for any occasion
• Delectable gourmet foods
• Quick, easy entertaining ideas
• Holiday and home décor
100% guaranteed to delight.
CHEDDAR CHEESE
To find the Store nearest you:
Call 877-233-1000
or click harryanddavid.com
Valid only in a Harry and David retail store. Cannot be combined with catalog, internet, corporate sales, gift card, We Deliver or Same Day Delivery orders, nor with any other offers or discounts. One coupon per visit. Offer expires 12/31/06.
7 80994 65725 0
Subject to Rules of Use. Not valid with other discount offers, unless specified.
Coupon VOID if purchased, sold or bartered for cash.
Valid now through December 31, 2006
To find the Store nearest you:
Call 877-233-1000
or click harryanddavid.com
Valid only in a Harry and David retail store. Cannot be combined with catalog, internet, corporate sales, gift card, We Deliver or Same Day Delivery orders, nor with any other offers or discounts. One coupon per visit. Offer expires 12/31/06.
7 80994 65725 0
Subject to Rules of Use. Not valid with other discount offers, unless specified.
Coupon VOID if purchased, sold, or bartered for cash.
Valid now through December 31, 2006

The World of Wine **Uncorked!**

Wine.com is the world's largest wine store, offering a vast selection of quality domestic and international wines and champagnes. With more than 14,000 bottles of wine, Wine.com has something for every taste. There's also monthly wine clubs, wine collections, gourmet gift baskets and a great selection of wine accessories, all of which make perfect gifts for any occasion.

wine.com

Free Shipping

on purchases of $100 or more

redeem online by using code: ENT100 upon checkout

F74

wine.com

Save 15%

redeem online by using code: ENT15B upon checkout

F75

Discount not valid on gift certificates, shipping, sales tax or other product specials. Offer void where prohibited. Offer valid through December 31, 2006. Wine can only be sold and delivered to a person who is at least 21 years old. Due to state and local regulations, wine and/or wine discounts may not be available for all areas and states.

Subject to Rules of Use. Not valid with other discount offers, unless specified. Coupon VOID if purchased, sold or bartered for cash. Each coupon is valid for one time use only per customer.

Valid now through December 31, 2006.

redENVELOPE
BE A GREAT GIFT GIVER
cashmere
men's accessories
jewelry
home
flowers
wedding
new baby
because.

GIVE THE GIFT OF SPA
Spa Finder gift certificates are accepted at over 3,000 resort, destination and day spas worldwide
Spafinder.com
Subscribe to LUXURY SPA FINDER MAGAZINE for one year and SAVE 50%
Available on Spafinder.com
Use Promo Code: ENT06
F77
SAVE $10 ON EVERY Spa finder GIFT CERTIFICATE ORDER OF $100 OR MORE
Order online at Spafinder.com or call 1.888.ALL.SPAS
Use Promo Code: ENT06
F78
These discounts cannot be combined with other discounts. See actual gift certificate for full terms & conditions governing its use. Offer expires 12/31/06.

$10 off

Any Vermont Teddy Bear
with purchase of $60 or more

Send the Creative Alternative to Flowers® for any special occasion!

More than 100 Bears to choose from for every occasion. Each Bear is guaranteed for life and sent in a colorful gift box with air hole, along with a free candy treat and personalized gift card.

1-800-829-BEAR
www.VermontTeddyBear.com
Use CODE: VETBK5

Minimum purchase of $60.00 required, excluding taxes and shipping. This offer is valid from 8/1/2005-12/31/2006 and cannot be combined with any other offer. Not valid toward the purchase of gift certificates.

F79

$10 off Any PajamaGram Gift
with purchase of $60 or more

Pajamagram®

Pamper someone with a PajamaGram!

She'll receive the softest, most luxurious pajamas along with a personalized card, lavendar sachet, and "Do Not Disturb" sign, all wrapped in a keepsake hatbox. Over 100 styles to choose from and great gifts for men, too!

1-800-GIVE PJS
www.PajamaGram.com
Use CODE: PETBK5

Minimum purchase of $60.00 required, excluding taxes and shipping. This offer is valid from 8/1/2005-12/31/2006 and cannot be combined with any other offer. Not valid toward the purchase of gift certificates.

F80

SAVE $10 ON EVERY SPAWISH CERTIFICATE ORDER!*

The Best Way To Give a Spa Experience to Anyone, Anywhere!
SpaWish Certificates are welcomed at over 1000 day spas nationwide.

Gift recipients select any spa and any services desired. Order online at **www.SpaWish.com** or call 1-888-SPA-WISH.

SpaWish.com 1-888-SPA-WISH

Refer to Savings Code
ETB6195

F81

THREE COMPLETE MEALS FOR TWO

à la ZING

6535THB The Entertainment Sampler

The Entertainment Sampler includes six servings...

Top Sirloin Suite
Omaha Steaks Top Sirloins
Roasted Garlic Mashed Potatoes
Glazed Julienne Carrots
& A La Zing Natural Seasoning

Roast Chicken Rendezvous
Roasted Chicken Breasts
Red Roasted Potatoes
& Broccoli/Cauliflower

Traditional Lasagna Dinner
Traditional Meat Lasagna
Whole Green Beans
& Tiramisu Cake

Reg. $69.97,
ONLY $39.97
You Save 42%

FREE APPLE COBBLER
Dessert with Purchase

See reverse side for details

F82

Save this coupon and order as often as you wish!

fromyoubaskets.com/ent

Save $10 on all Gift Baskets!

1-800-838-8853
mention code 395

Order 24 hours a day, 7 days a week!
Delivery anywhere in the country!
100% Satisfaction Guaranteed!

fruit & wine
gourmet
champagne
chocolates
spa baskets
cookies
flowers
much more!

See reverse side for details

F83

SpaWish.com
1-888-SPA-WISH

Save $10.00 On SpaWish Certificate Orders Valued $100 Or More. Order As Often As You Wish!

With over 1000 day spas from which to choose, your recipient will delight in selecting any spa & any services desired, like massages, facials, manicures, and more!

Certificates can also be redeemed online at SpaWish.com/redeem for spa-related merchandise.

SpaWish Certificates come elegantly packaged with a nationwide directory of participating day spas, and a gift card with your personalized message. A perfectly pampering way to say "Happy Birthday," "Happy Anniversary" or HAPPY ANYTHING!

*To receive this savings, orders must be placed online at **www.SpaWish.com** or by phone at 1-888-SPA-WISH, savings code **ETB6195** must be used at time of purchase, and the SpaWish order must be valued at $100 or higher before shipping.

To view the entire day spa directory online, visit **SpaWish.com**.

Subject to Rules of Use. Not valid with other discount offers, unless specified. Coupon VOID if purchased, sold or bartered for cash.

VALID NOW THROUGH 12/31/2006

à la ZING

www.alazing.com/promo/ent2006
or call toll-free **1-888-959-9464**
and mention coupon **RY1277**

Limit of two Entertainment Samplers at this special price.
Standard shipping and handling will be applied per address. Offer expires 12/31/06.

Subject to Rules of Use. Not valid with other discount offers, unless specified. Coupon VOID if purchased, sold or bartered for cash.

VALID NOW THROUGH 12/31/2006

fromyoubaskets.com/ent

Save $10 on all Gift Baskets!

1-800-838-8853

mention code 395

Choose from a wide variety of thoughtful gifts for any occasion and every sentiment! Gourmet Baskets, Fruit Baskets, Wine Baskets, Cookie & Chocolate Baskets, Spa Baskets, Custom Gift Baskets and so much more! Fast, easy ordering online or by phone! Order anytime, 24 hours a day, 7 days a week with 100% Satisfaction Guarantee!

Subject to Rules of Use. Not valid with other discount offers, unless specified. Coupon VOID if purchased, sold or bartered for cash.

VALID NOW THROUGH 12/31/2006

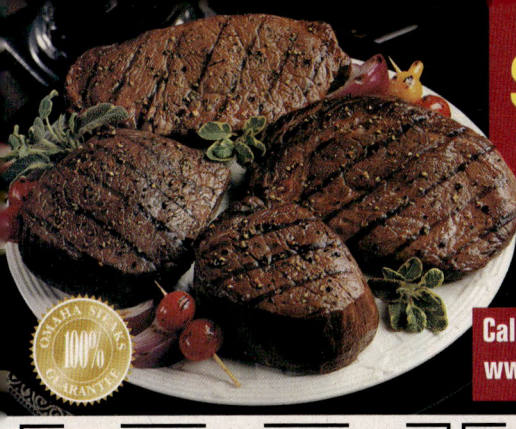

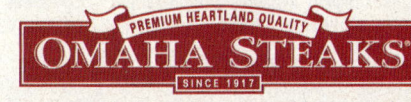

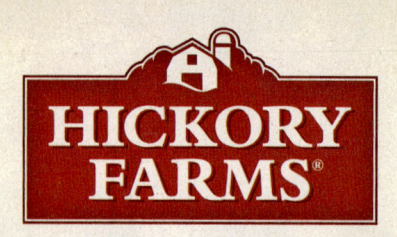

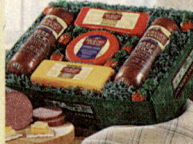

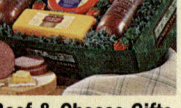

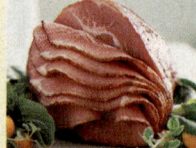

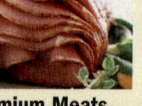

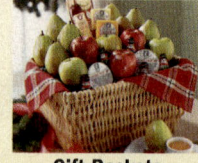

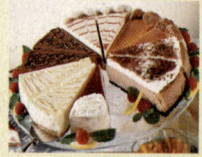

CHERRY MOON FRESHEST QUALITY F·A·R·M·S

SAVE 15%

cherrymoonfarms.com/enb

1.888.378.2758 *Mention: "Entertainment® Book"*

Fruit Baskets & Organic Fruit

Gourmet Snacks & Chocolate Gifts

Delicious Samplers & Monthly Fruit Clubs

Brought to you by the same people who brought you ProFlowers®.

FRESH PACK Two 2 Day GUARANTEE

The freshest quality delivered direct on the day you choose.

Always received within 2 days from when we hand-pack your order.

15% OFF

EVERY ORDER

Order online at
cherrymoonfarms.com/enb
Or call 1.888.FRT.BSKT *(1.888.378.2758)*,
Mention code: "Entertainment® Book"

15% Discount will appear upon checkout. Discount may not be used in conjunction with other special offers, coupons, or discounts. Discount applies to item cost only and does not include discount on shipping and handling charges or taxes. Offer expires December 31, 2006.

F92

FREE CHOCOLATE

WITH ANY ORDER

Order online at
cherrymoonfarms.com/enb1
Or call 1.888.FRT.BSKT *(1.888.378.2758)*,
Mention code: "Entertainment® Book1"

A discount for a FREE Chocolate item will appear upon checkout. Discount may not be used in conjunction with other special offers, coupons, or discounts. Offer expires December 31, 2006, or while supplies last.

F93

Uptown® PRIME
UP TO
$25 OFF
Steakhouse quality cuts including Kobe Beef and USDA Prime. Previously only available in the finest restaurants.
FREE SHIPPING OFFERS ONLINE
Order at: www.uptownprime.com/ENT
or call: 1-877-987-8696 Reference "Entertainment® Book"
FREE Kobe BURGERS (a $15 savings)
With any Kobe Beef purchase. Order required to receive Kobe Burgers. Limit one offer per order. Offer expires Dec. 31, 2006. Offer valid while supplies last. Price savings subject to change.
Uptown® PRIME
Order at: www.uptownprime/ENT
or call: 1-877-987-8696 Reference "Entertainment® Book"
F94
Exclusive Offer: COUPONS CAN BE USED IN COMBINATION
$10 OFF
On Selected Steak & Seafood Products
Visit our web site to see special Entertainment Book Savings. Special Savings will be reflected in product prices. Can be used in conjunction with Free Burger offer, but cannot be combined with other offers or discounts. Offer expires Dec. 31, 2006.
Uptown® PRIME
Order at: www.uptownprime/ENT
or call: 1-877-987-8696 Reference "Entertainment® Book"
F95

PIZZA HUT® MENU

GATHER 'ROUND THE GOOD STUFF!™

PICK YOUR CRUST!	CREATE YOUR OWN!	PICK YOUR RECIPE!	MORE FOR YOUR MEAL!
Pan Pizza, 4 for All, Thin 'n Crispy, Stuffed Crust, Hand-Tossed, Full House XL Pizza	**Toppings:** Pepperoni, Beef Topping, Chicken, Bacon, Italian Sausage, Pork Topping, Ham, Black Olives, Red Onions, Tomatoes, Extra Cheese, Fresh Mushrooms, Green Peppers, Pineapple	Meat Lover's® Pepperoni Lover's® Cheese Lover's Veggie Lover's® Super Supreme Supreme Carb Tracker™ Lower Fat	Breadsticks Buffalo Wings Drinks Baked Cinnamon Sticks
Crust Types May Vary By Location.	Toppings May Vary By Location.	Recipes May Vary By Location.	Side Items May Vary By Location.

For complete nutritional information, contact your local Pizza Hut restaurant or go to www.pizzahut.com. Prices, participation, delivery areas and charges may vary. Credit card availability may vary by location. The Pizza Hut name, logos and related marks are trademarks of Pizza Hut, Inc. © 2005 Pizza Hut, Inc.

Large Any Way You Want It

$9.99 9W 8268
Monday and Tuesday

$10.99 TW 6253
Wednesday through Sunday

Up to 3 toppings. Any Lover's Line® or Supreme. Super Supreme $1 More
Valid on Pan, Thin 'N Crispy® and Hand-Tossed Style Pizza (where available)

Only at participating locations. One coupon per order. Not valid with other offers. No duplication of toppings. Delivery areas and charges may vary. 1/20 cent cash redemption value. ©2005 Pizza Hut, Inc.

Expires 12/31/06.

JA P6Y F96

Family Feeding Frenzy

Buy 2 Medium Pizzas Any Way You Want Them & 10 Breadsticks for

$18.99 1842

and get a FREE Pepsi® 2-Liter

Up to 3 toppings. Any Lover's Line® or Supreme. Super Supreme $1 More
Valid on Pan, Thin 'N Crispy® and Hand-Tossed Style Pizza (where available)
May substitute for 2-Liter

Only at participating locations. One coupon per order. Not valid with other offers. No duplication of toppings. Delivery areas and charges may vary. 2-liter substitutions may occur. 1/20 cent cash redemption value. PEPSI and PEPSI-COLA are registered trademarks of PepsiCo, Inc. ©2005 Pizza Hut, Inc.

Expires 12/31/06.

JB P6Y F97

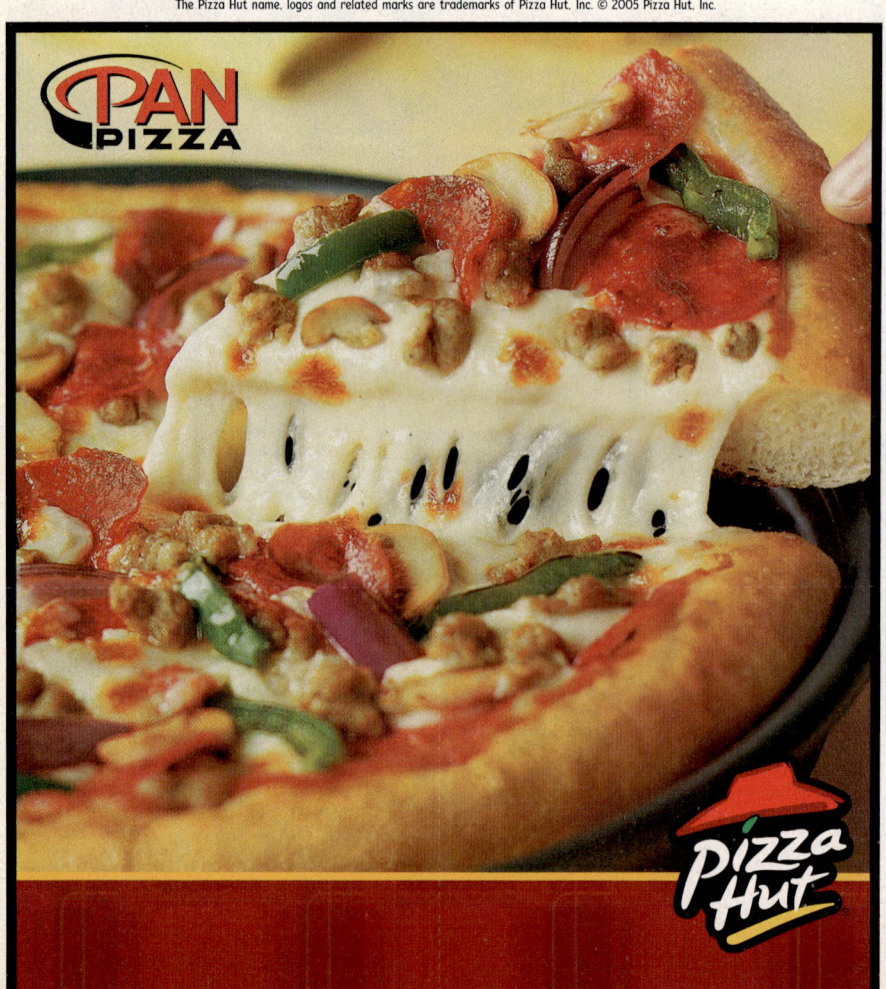

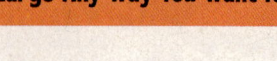

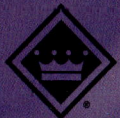

Come see what's in store for you.

- Hundreds of Designer Frames
- Latest Prescription Lens Technology
- Brand Name Contact Lenses available from the Independent Doctors of Optometry

For the Pearle Vision location nearest you, call **1-800-YES-EYES** or visit **www.pearlevision.com**

60 Day Total Satisfaction Guarantee

If after wearing your glasses, they do not meet your expectations, we will adjust, repair, replace or exchange your glasses at no charge to you. Any accidental damage, such as scratches or broken parts, is not covered under this guarantee.

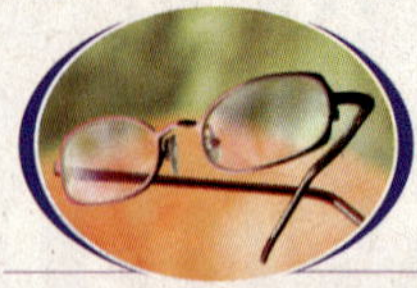

Free eyeglass cleaning and adjustments.

No purchase necessary.

PEARLE VISION®

Nobody cares for eyes more than Pearle®

Complete Pair (frame and lenses) purchase required. Coupon can be used on multiple pairs. Coupon must be presented at time of purchase. Not valid with other coupons, discounts, package offers, sale items, promotional offers, previous purchases, most insurance programs, readers or non-prescription sunglasses. Savings applied to lenses. Valid at participating locations. Eye exam not included.

Subject to Rules of Use. Not valid with other discount offers, unless specified. Coupon VOID if purchased, sold or bartered for cash.

Valid now thru December 31, 2006 PEP1

PEARLE VISION®

Nobody cares for eyes more than Pearle®

Two complete pairs (frame and lenses) purchase required. Coupon must be presented at time of purchase. Not valid with other coupons, discounts, package offers, sale items, promotional offers, previous purchases, most insurance programs, readers or non-prescription sunglasses. Savings applied to lenses. Valid at participating locations. Eye exam not included.

Subject to Rules of Use. Not valid with other discount offers, unless specified. Coupon VOID if purchased, sold or bartered for cash.

Valid now thru December 31, 2006 PEP2

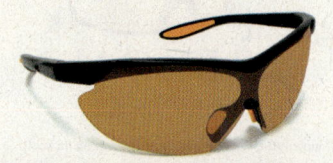

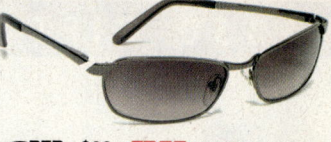

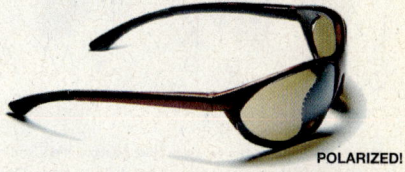

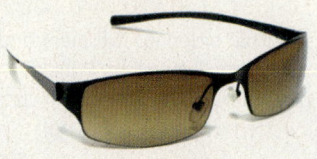

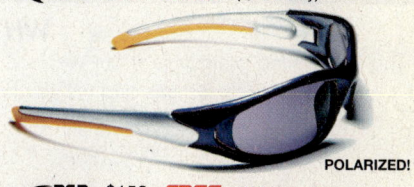

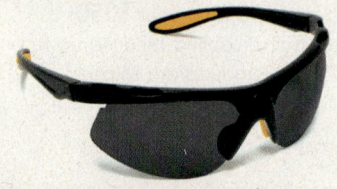

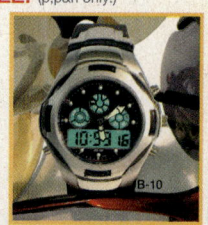

FactoryOutlets.com™
Spend Small, Live Large

$350 GIFT CERTIFICATE

LOOK SHARP LOOK SMART LOOK BEYOND

Authorization # 179336

Subject to Rules of Use. Not valid with other discount offers, unless specified. Coupon VOID if purchased, sold or bartered for cash.

Valid now thru December 31, 2006

WHY?

This is a limited prelaunch of our web site to help test our ordering, fulfillment and customer service systems and we've chosen Entertainment® members to help. IT'S THAT SIMPLE! Use this FREE Gift Certificate to pay for $350 worth of high quality products. They're yours to keep—no charge, we're buying them for you!

NO KIDDING!

Go to www.factoryoutlets.com right now and start spending your $350! If you do not spend all $350, we'll keep track of your remaining balance up to the expiration date of December 31, 2006. Your products are shipped immediately—various shipping methods are available (p,p&h not included).

Thank you for helping us with this test site promotion.

Authorization # 179336
We ship within the United States only. No foreign orders.

Visit www.factoryoutlets.com or call: 1-541-322-7213.

Spend Small, Live Large

FactoryOutlets.com™
Spend Small, Live Large

Expires December 31, 2006.
275 Madison Avenue, 4th Floor, New York, NY 10016

Save up to **50%** off retail on contact lenses

1 800 CONTACTS®

We deliver. You *save*.®

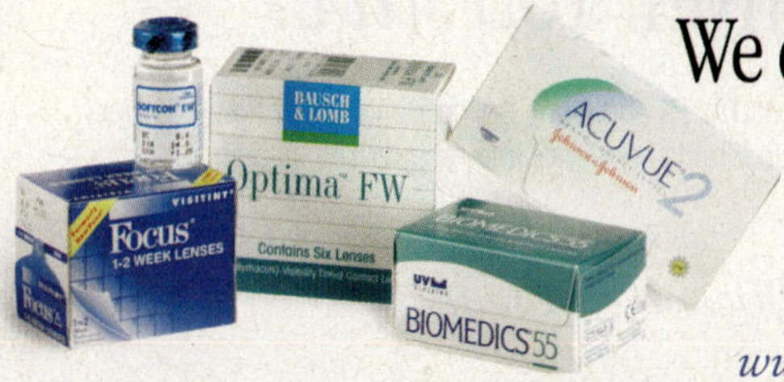

- The World's Largest Contact Lens Store®
- **Easy** and **convenient**
- More than 20 million contacts **in stock**

Free Shipping on all Internet orders (value of $5.95).

www.1800contacts.com/ent3

See reverse side for details

F105

JOIN NOW AND START SAVING

How far can you stretch $12.50?

AARP®

Join now to get the benefits you're entitled to and save long after your last coupon is gone.

Call Now
1.800.319.2342

Log Onto
www.AARP.org/entertainment

K4WAC

See reverse side for details

F106

ALL the news for HALF the price

Subscribe to USA TODAY and SAVE 50% off newsstand prices!

At just 38¢ a day it's like getting half your subscription FREE. Plus, free delivery means America's favorite newspaper is waiting for you bright and early each weekday morning. Act now to get 13 weeks for only $24.38, normally $48.75!*

1-800-USA 0001 Special Offer Code: 560 **www.myusatoday.com/eb**

See reverse side for details

F107

1 800 CONTACTS®

We deliver. You *save*.®

Save on contact lenses at 1-800 CONTACTS and enjoy the convenience of home delivery.
Order online at www.1800contacts.com/ent3 and receive free shipping.

www.1800contacts.com/ent3

Subject to Rules of Use. Not valid with other discount offers, unless specified. Coupon VOID if purchased, sold, or bartered for cash.

VALID NOW THROUGH 12/31/2006

AARP®

Join AARP now and receive ***Taking Charge of Your Health, Grandparenting: The Joys and Challenges*** and ***Future Focus: Financial Planning for Retirement.*** Three information packed guides designed to help you take control of your life.

Call Now
1.800.319.2342

Log Onto
www.AARP.org/entertainment

Subject to Rules of Use. Not valid with other discount offers, unless specified. Coupon VOID if purchased, sold, or bartered for cash.

VALID NOW THROUGH 12/31/2006

Subject to Rules of Use. Not valid with other discount offers, unless specified.
Coupon VOID if purchased, sold or bartered for cash.

VALID NOW THROUGH 12/31/2006

Local sales tax, when applicable, will be added to your order. Savings calculated against the newsstand rate of $0.75 per issue. Carrier delivery in selected areas. Offer void outside USA. Refunds on all undelivered issues. Offer expires 12/31/06.

* Your credit card will automatically be charged upon renewal of your subscription at the renewal rate for the offer you have selected. You will notice a charge on your credit card at the end of every term for your subscription. You may notify us to cancel automatic payments at any time.

Subject to Rules of Use. Not valid with other discount offers, unless specified. Coupon VOID if purchased, sold, or bartered for cash.

VALID NOW THROUGH 12/31/2006

Start Investing Online Today
with ShareBuilder
Buy stocks for just $4*
No investment or account minimums
Special Offer for Entertainment® Members
Get $30 Cash! when you start investing
No inactivity fees
Invest any dollar amount in the stocks you want
100% online service
Free investment advice
Redeem $30 bonus now**
The easy, low-cost way to invest in the stock market
1. Visit www.sharebuilder.com/entertainment
2. Open a new ShareBuilder, Individual, Joint or Custodial Account
3. Enter Promo Code: ENTERTAIN30
* See ShareBuilder website for complete information including full fee schedule. Does not include Real-time trades.
** You must open a new ShareBuilder Individual, Joint or Custodial Account and enter promo code ENTERTAIN30 to receive the $30 bonus offer. Please note the $30 credit will post to your account approximately 4-5 weeks after the first transaction executes. The $30 offer is not valid with IRA or Education Savings Accounts. Not valid with any other offers. ShareBuilder is not affiliated with Entertainment Publications.
©2005 ShareBuilder Corporation. ShareBuilder is offered through ShareBuilder Securities Corporation, a registered broker-dealer and member NASD/SIPC, and a subsidiary of ShareBuilder Corporation.
Please call (800) 215-4679 with any questions about ShareBuilder.
shareBUILDER®
F108
Valid now through December 31, 2006.

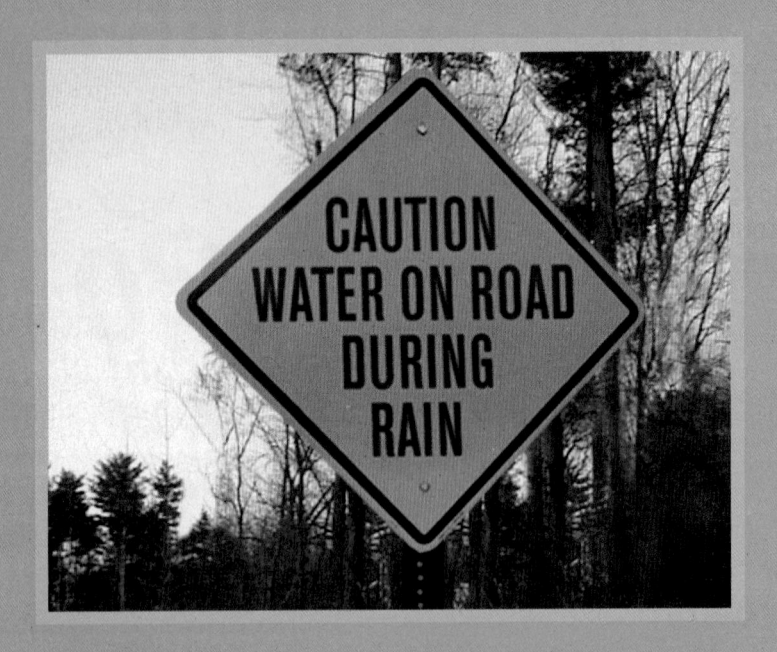

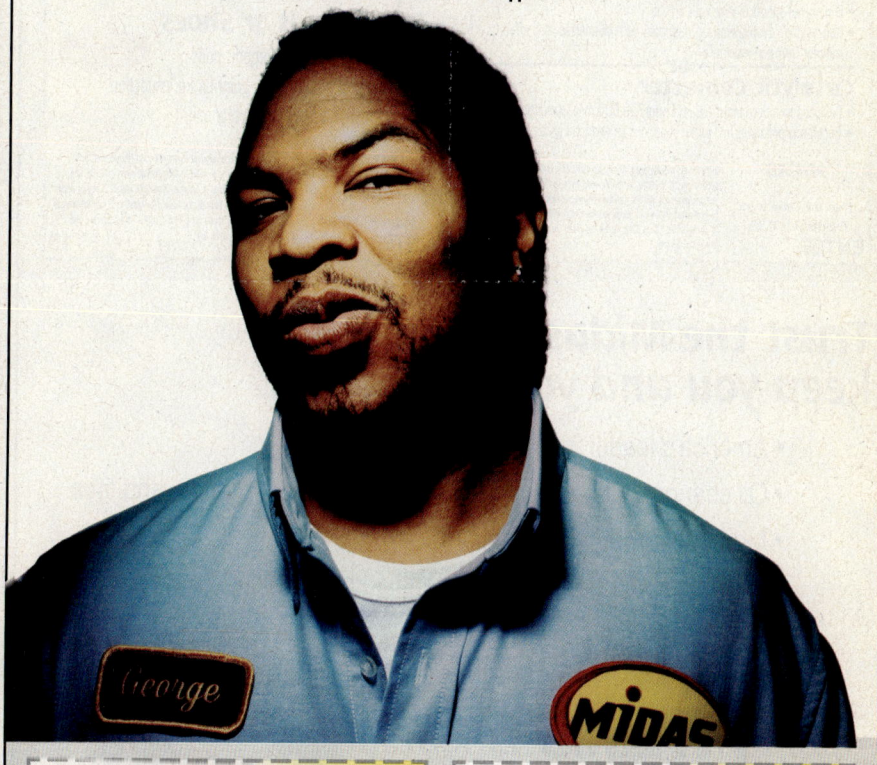

$10.00 off

Midas Lifetime* Guaranteed Muffler

- Engineered specifically for your vehicle
- Heavy-gauge double-wrapped steel body with aluminized shell offers superior corrosion resistance

or

Catalytic Converter

- Designed to reduce emissions
- 5-year/50,000 mile warranty
- Transforms pollutants into water vapor and less-harmful gases

Trust the Midas touch.

Expires 12/31/06

ENT06

Discount off regular price. Many domestic cars and some import car applications. *Lifetime guarantee valid as long as you own your car. See manager for limited guarantee terms and details. Coupon must be presented at time of purchase. Not good with any other offer. At participating shops only. Void if copied or transferred and where prohibited by law.

F112

25% off

Lifetime* Guaranteed Brake Pads or Shoes

LIFETIME GUARANTEE*

- Semi-Metallic or NAO organic pads
- Top off brake fluid
- 45-point brake inspection
- Road test
- Discount off parts only

Trust the Midas touch.

Expires 12/31/06

ENT06

Discount off regular price. Many cars, light trucks and SUVs. *Lifetime guarantee valid as long as you own your car. See manager for limited guarantee terms and details. Coupon must be presented at time of purchase. Not good with any other offer. At participating shops only. Void if copied or transferred and where prohibited by law.

F113

Trust the Midas Touch to help keep you and your car going.

- America's leader in brakes and exhaust
- Oil changes, factory scheduled maintenance, batteries, and tires
- More than 1600 stores nationwide
- Expert service by over 3,000 certified mechanics

MIDAS®

Trust the Midas touch.™

Call **1-800-GO MIDAS** or visit **www.Midas.com** to find a location near you.

Four Tickets to Savings at Walgreens

For the store nearest you,
call 1-800-WALGREENS
(1-800-925-4733)
or visit
www.walgreens.com/findastore

Walgreens Coupon Good thru 12/31/06

Only 20¢ ea.

4x6 in. digital prints!
with the purchase of 50 or more

From Digital Camera Cards only. Submit coupon with order. One coupon per order. Excludes Kodak Perfect Touch, APS and Panoramic Prints.

Limit one coupon per customer. Offer may not be combined with other offers. Customer pays any sales tax. Void if copied or where prohibited.

Walgreens

0 00000 06126 1

F114

Walgreens Coupon Good thru 12/31/06

Save $3

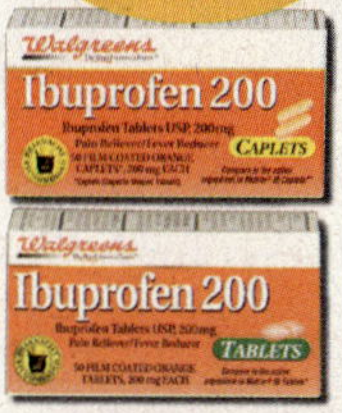

99¢

Walgreens Ibuprofen, 200 mg., 50 pack

Limit one coupon per customer. Offer may not be combined with other offers. Customer pays any sales tax. Void if copied or where prohibited.

Walgreens

0 00000 02848 6

F115

Walgreens Coupon Good thru 12/31/06

79¢

Walgreens Nail Polish Remover, 8 oz.

Limit one coupon per customer. Offer may not be combined with other offers. Customer pays any sales tax. Void if copied or where prohibited.

Walgreens

0 00000 02849 3

F116

Walgreens Coupon Good thru 12/31/06

Half Price!

99¢

Walgreens Lotion, 11 oz.

Limit one coupon per customer. Offer may not be combined with other offers. Customer pays any sales tax. Void if copied or where prohibited.

Walgreens

0 00000 02851 6

F117

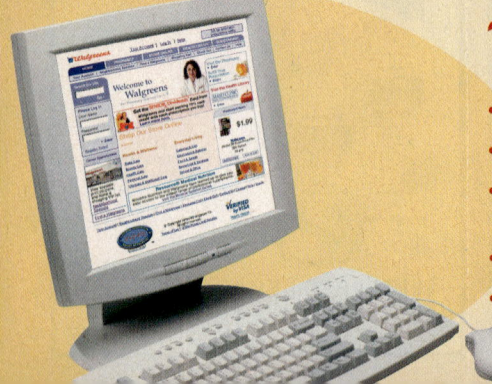

Retail & Services Index

kids Great Place for Kids!

NEW New Merchants Added This Year

kids **Great Place for Kids!**   NEW **New Merchants Added This Year**

auto
insurance

*Promotion code required at time of scheduling/ordering. Offer valid only on Terminix® purchases made through www.servicemaster.com or 1-888-WE SERVE® and valid only with participating providers. Call for locations. Single-family dwelling units only. Offer valid only with the purchase of a new quarterly exterior residential Pest Control Service Plan. This offer must be presented at time of sale to be eligible for discount on a new Pest Control Agreement. This offer cannot be combined with any other offers or discounts. Only one discount is available per household per year. This offer entitles you to a discount on the purchase of Terminix Pest Control Service. Once our representative has provided you with your best price, you should present this coupon to obtain the stated discount. Offer is void if transferred and where prohibited. Any other use may constitute fraud. Cash value 1/100 of 1 cent. Offer expires 12/31/06.

Subject to Rules of Use. Not valid with other discount offers, unless specified. Coupon VOID if purchased, sold or bartered for cash.

Valid now thru December 31, 2006

*Promotion code required at time of scheduling/ordering. Offer valid for new residential customers only. Not valid with other offers, on previous purchases, or existing services. Some restrictions may apply. Good on purchases made through www.servicemaster.com or 1-888-WE SERVE® and valid only with participating TruGreen ChemLawn® providers. Call for locations. Offer applies to lawns up to 5,000 square feet. For lawns over 5,000 square feet, please call for an estimate. Home services that require specialized licensing or certification will be performed by companies appropriately qualified and/or licensed. Offer void if copied or transferred and where prohibited. Any other use may constitute fraud. Cash value 1/100 of 1 cent. Offer expires 12/31/06.

Subject to Rules of Use. Not valid with other discount offers, unless specified. Coupon VOID if purchased, sold or bartered for cash.

Valid now thru December 31, 2006

*Maximum discount of $200. Promotion code required at time of scheduling/ordering. Discount cannot be used toward any trade service call fee. Not valid with any other offers, on prior sales, purchases financed at time of installation, commercial establishments, new construction or on existing services. Good on purchases made through www.servicemaster.com or 1-888-WE SERVE® and valid only with participating ARS Service Express℠ service centers. Call for locations. Service availability varies by market. See contract for additional terms and conditions. Offer is void if copied or transferred and where prohibited. Any other use may constitute fraud. Cash value 1/100 of 1 cent. Offer expires 12/31/06.
The following licenses are held by or on behalf of American Residential Services L.L.C.: AZ (ROC165579, ROC162560, ROC184045); CA - ARS® and affiliates (#804948, #799361, #799365, #795580, #791813, #765155, #610780, #764099, #757505, #791820, #765074, #742039; CO (232122); FL (CAC1813365, CMC1249406 and others); IL (PL17275); IN (H0001066, H0001176, H0000854, H0001146, H0000607); MD (6574, 8022); MO (MCC-X0188); NC (13713, 19719, 19913, 19745); NE (2115, 46399); NV (#46075, 46076, 56196, 56197); NY (081); OH (30016); OK (035525); PA (HV01783); SC (2842); TN (HVAC 48365, #21520); TX (TACLA018810E, TACLA00000283C, TACLA00016853E, TACLB010268E, & others); VA (Class A cont. #2705059347A); WV (#WV034354). Additional American Residential Services L.L.C. license information available upon request. Some services performed by ServiceMaster® affiliates.

Subject to Rules of Use. Not valid with other discount offers, unless specified. Coupon VOID if purchased, sold or bartered for cash.

Valid now thru December 31, 2006

*Maximum discount of $200. Promotion code required at time of scheduling/ordering. Discount cannot be used toward any trade service call fee. Not valid with any other offers, on prior sales, purchases financed at time of installation, commercial establishments, new construction or on existing services. Good on purchases made through www.servicemaster.com or 1-888-WE SERVE® and valid only with participating ARS Service Express℠ service centers. Call for locations. Service availability varies by market. See contract for additional terms and conditions. Offer is void if copied or transferred and where prohibited. Any other use may constitute fraud. Cash value 1/100 of 1 cent. Offer expires 12/31/06.
The following licenses are held by or on behalf of American Residential Services L.L.C.: AZ (ROC131214, ROC131215, ROC185121); CA - ARS and affiliates (744542, 811085, 800846, 799361, 799365, 795545, 795580, 795540, 795556, 791813, 797531, 765155, 791820, 798615); CO (187709); FL (CFCO56938, CFC1426130); GA (MP209315); IN (PC88900192); MD (19074); MO (P7255); NC (13713); NE (49064, 3240); NV (52555, 46075, 56196); OH (11737, 14613); OK (071113); OR (CCB 127325); SC (2842); TN (48365, 21520); TX (MPL18279, MPL36605, MPL10609, MPL17105, MPL17251 & others); UT (353474-5501); VA (2705 059347A); WA (RESCUR*007Q7, ARSSEE*963KG). Additional American Residential Services L.L.C. license information available upon request. Some services performed by ServiceMaster® affiliates.

Subject to Rules of Use. Not valid with other discount offers, unless specified. Coupon VOID if purchased, sold or bartered for cash.

Valid now thru December 31, 2006

*Minimum purchase of $100. Promotion code required at time of scheduling/ordering. Offer valid for new residential customers only. Not valid with any other offer, on previous purchases, or on existing services. Good on purchases made through www.servicemaster.com or 1-888-WE SERVE® and valid only with participating providers. Call for locations. Only one discount per service per address. One free room per order. Rooms over 225 sq. feet are considered two or more rooms. Sensitive fabrics may be an additional cost. All services will be provided by independently owned and operated franchises or corporate-owned offices of ServiceMaster Clean® depending on location. Some restrictions may apply. Offer is void if copied or transferred and where prohibited. Any other use may constitute fraud. Cash value 1/100 of 1 cent. Offer expires 12/31/06.

Subject to Rules of Use. Not valid with other discount offers, unless specified. Coupon VOID if purchased, sold or bartered for cash.

Valid now thru December 31, 2006

*Promotion code required at time of scheduling/ordering. Offer valid for new residential customers only. Not valid with any other offer, on previous purchases, or on existing services. Good on purchases made through www.servicemaster.com or 1-888-WE SERVE® and valid only with participating providers. Call for locations. Only one discount per service per address. All services will be provided by independently owned and operated franchises or corporate-owned offices of Merry Maids® depending on location. Some restrictions may apply. Offer is void if copied or transferred and where prohibited. Any other use may constitute fraud. Cash value 1/100 of 1 cent. Offer expires 12/31/06. **If you are not completely satisfied, we will happily come back and re-clean whatever is in question at no additional charge. At Merry Maids®, the job is only finished when you are completely satisfied.

Subject to Rules of Use. Not valid with other discount offers, unless specified. Coupon VOID if purchased, sold or bartered for cash.

Valid now thru December 31, 2006

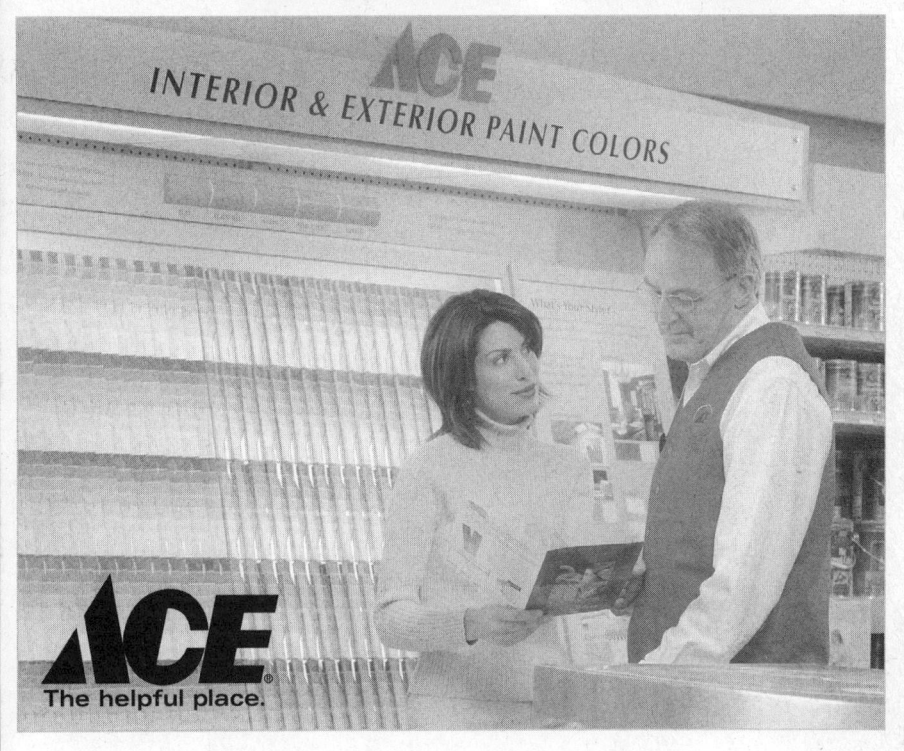

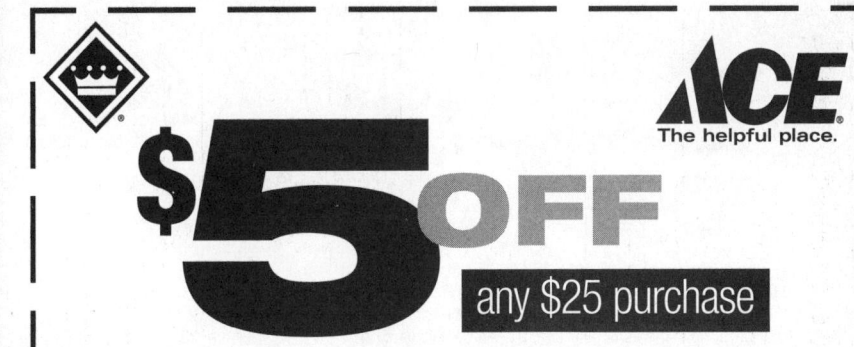

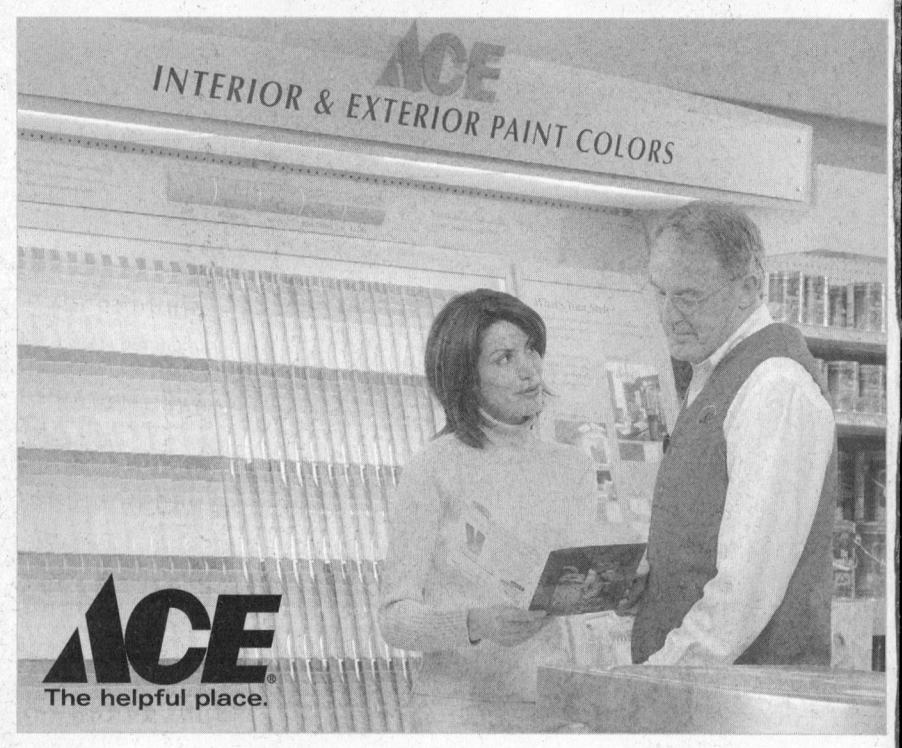

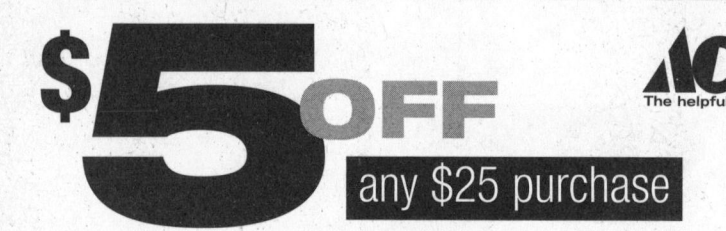

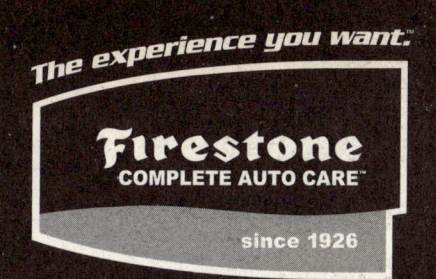

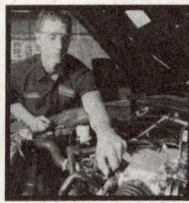

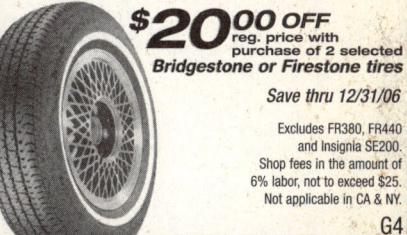

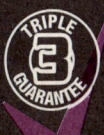

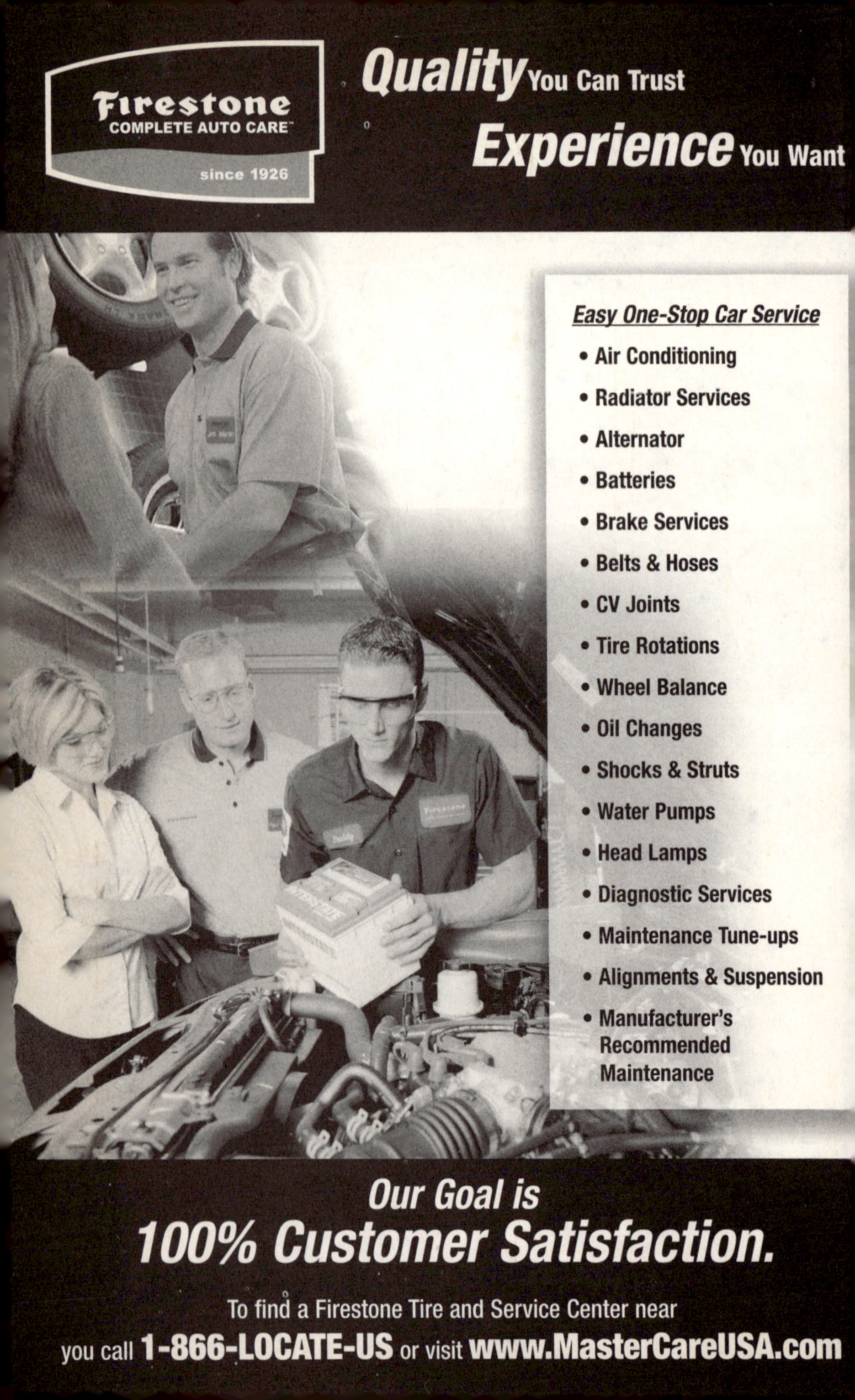
Firestone
COMPLETE AUTO CARE™
since 1926
Quality You Can Trust
Experience You Want
Easy One-Stop Car Service
• Air Conditioning
• Radiator Services
• Alternator
• Batteries
• Brake Services
• Belts & Hoses
• CV Joints
• Tire Rotations
• Wheel Balance
• Oil Changes
• Shocks & Struts
• Water Pumps
• Head Lamps
• Diagnostic Services
• Maintenance Tune-ups
• Alignments & Suspension
• Manufacturer's Recommended Maintenance
Our Goal is
100% Customer Satisfaction.
To find a Firestone Tire and Service Center near
you call 1-866-LOCATE-US or visit www.MasterCareUSA.com

entertainment.
entertainment.com

great place for kids

$10.00 Value

Dick's Sporting Goods

For a store nearest you call 1-866-819-0038

$10.00 OFF a PURCHASE of $50.00 or more.

valid anytime

See reverse for restrictions

EVERY SEASON STARTS AT DICK'S SPORTING GOODS

G5

Valid now thru November 1, 2006

Not valid holidays & subject to Rules of Use. Not valid with other discount offers, unless specified. Coupon VOID if purchased, sold or bartered. Discounts exclude tax, tip and/or alcohol, where applicable.

Bonus Discounts at entertainment.com

entertainment.
entertainment.com

great place for kids

$15.00 Value

Dick's Sporting Goods

For a store nearest you call 1-866-819-0038

$15.00 OFF a PURCHASE of $75.00 or more.

valid anytime

See reverse for restrictions

EVERY SEASON STARTS AT DICK'S SPORTING GOODS

G6

Valid now thru November 1, 2006

Not valid holidays & subject to Rules of Use. Not valid with other discount offers, unless specified. Coupon VOID if purchased, sold or bartered. Discounts exclude tax, tip and/or alcohol, where applicable.

Bonus Discounts at entertainment.com

entertainment.
entertainment.com

great place for kids

$20.00 Value

Dick's Sporting Goods

For a store nearest you call 1-866-819-0038

$20.00 OFF a PURCHASE of $100.00 or more.

valid anytime

See reverse for restrictions

EVERY SEASON STARTS AT DICK'S SPORTING GOODS

G7

Valid now thru November 1, 2006

Not valid holidays & subject to Rules of Use. Not valid with other discount offers, unless specified. Coupon VOID if purchased, sold or bartered. Discounts exclude tax, tip and/or alcohol, where applicable.

Bonus Discounts at entertainment.com

9 11111 11334 6

Limit one coupon per customer. Total amount of coupon must be redeemed at one time. Cannot be combined with any other offers, coupons or Guaranteed In-Stock markdown, or used for layaways, licenses or previously purchased merchandise. Coupon valid on in-store purchases only. Not redeemable for cash, gift cards or store credit. No reproductions or rainchecks accepted. Excludes all Callaway, Odyssey, Titleist, Cobra and select new release TaylorMade products, firearms, electronics, treadmills, championship merchandise, Levi's, Under Armour, Nike Dri-FIT, Therma-FIT, Sphere and Pro Compression, Merrell footwear, Nike Shox, Impax, Air Zoom Generation, Air Zoom Miler, Jordan and LE shoes, Oakley, Maui Jim, Smith, Ray-Ban, Suunto, Arcteryx, The North Face and Columbia merchandise. Upon redemption, scan barcode and take a group discount markdown. Minimum purchase of $50 before sales tax. Valid through 12/31/06.

00504863

®

entertainment.com

00504863

9 11111 11295 0

Limit one coupon per customer. Total amount of coupon must be redeemed at one time. Cannot be combined with any other offers, coupons or Guaranteed In-Stock markdown, or used for layaways, licenses or previously purchased merchandise. Coupon valid on in-store purchases only. Not redeemable for cash, gift cards or store credit. No reproductions or rainchecks accepted. Excludes all Callaway, Odyssey, Titleist, Cobra and select new release TaylorMade products, firearms, electronics, treadmills, championship merchandise, Levi's, Under Armour, Nike Dri-FIT, Therma-FIT, Sphere and Pro Compression, Merrell footwear, Nike Shox, Impax, Air Zoom Generation, Air Zoom Miler, Jordan and LE shoes, Oakley, Maui Jim, Smith, Ray-Ban, Suunto, Arcteryx, The North Face and Columbia merchandise. Upon redemption, scan barcode and take a group discount markdown. Minimum purchase of $75 before sales tax. Valid through 12/31/06.

00576747

®

entertainment.com

00576747

9 11111 11233 2

Limit one coupon per customer. Total amount of coupon must be redeemed at one time. Cannot be combined with any other offers, coupons or Guaranteed In-Stock markdown, or used for layaways, licenses or previously purchased merchandise. Coupon valid on in-store purchases only. Not redeemable for cash, gift cards or store credit. No reproductions or rainchecks accepted. Excludes all Callaway, Odyssey, Titleist, Cobra and select new release TaylorMade products, firearms, electronics, treadmills, championship merchandise, Levi's, Under Armour, Nike Dri-FIT, Therma-FIT, Sphere and Pro Compression, Merrell footwear, Nike Shox, Impax, Air Zoom Generation, Air Zoom Miler, Jordan and LE shoes, Oakley, Maui Jim, Smith, Ray-Ban, Suunto, Arcteryx, The North Face and Columbia merchandise. Upon redemption, scan barcode and take a group discount markdown. Minimum purchase of $100 before sales tax. Valid through 12/31/06.

00576749

®

entertainment.com

00576749

Meadows Farms Nurseries

See reverse side for locations

- Serving you for 44 years
- Farmer says... plant a little happiness
- Free plant delivery - see store for delivery
- Open 8 a.m. Mon. - Sat.

Bonus Discounts at entertainment.com

entertainment. entertainment.com

20% OFF

Meadows Farms

Enjoy 20% off any one plant.

valid now thru Dec. 24th, 2006

Retail sales only; Not valid with any other offer; Not valid on landscape installation

www.meadowsfarms.com

G8

Valid now thru November 1, 2006

Not valid holidays & subject to Rules of Use. Not valid with other discount offers, unless specified. Coupon VOID if purchased, sold or bartered. Discounts exclude tax, tip and/or alcohol, where applicable.

Meadows Farms Nurseries

See reverse side for locations

- Serving you for 44 years
- Farmer says... plant a little happiness
- Free plant delivery - see store for delivery
- Open 8 a.m. Mon. - Sat.

Bonus Discounts at entertainment.com

entertainment. entertainment.com

20% OFF

Meadows Farms

Enjoy 20% off any one plant.

Valid March 1st thru July 31, 2006

Retail sales only; Not valid with any other offer; Not valid on landscape installation

www.meadowsfarms.com

G9

Valid now thru November 1, 2006

Not valid holidays & subject to Rules of Use. Not valid with other discount offers, unless specified. Coupon VOID if purchased, sold or bartered. Discounts exclude tax, tip and/or alcohol, where applicable.

Meadows Farms Nurseries

See reverse side for locations

- Serving you for 44 years
- Farmer says... plant a little happiness
- Free plant delivery - see store for delivery
- Open 8 a.m. Mon. - Sat.

Bonus Discounts at entertainment.com

entertainment. entertainment.com

20% OFF

Meadows Farms

Enjoy 20% off any one plant.

Valid Aug. 1, 2006 thru Dec. 24, 2006

Retail sales only; Not valid with any other offer; Not valid on landscape installation

www.meadowsfarms.com

G10

Valid now thru November 1, 2006

Not valid holidays & subject to Rules of Use. Not valid with other discount offers, unless specified. Coupon VOID if purchased, sold or bartered. Discounts exclude tax, tip and/or alcohol, where applicable.

MARYLAND

Burtonsville
15930 New Columbia Pk.
(301)384-3730

Clarksburg
11406 Hawkes Rd.
(301)353-0098

Frederick
5432 Old National Pike.
(301)473-5411

Leonardtown
49010 Merchants Ln.
(301)475-1500

Mitchellville
18301 Central Ave.
(301)249-2933

Severna
470 Jumpers Hole Rd.
(410)544-0606

Westminster
1731 Littlestown Pk.
(410)857-6160

VIRGINIA

Annandale
4808 Backlick Rd.
(703)941-5656

Chantilly
43054 John Mosby Hwy.
(703)327-3940

Culpeper
16417 Brandy Rd.
(540)825-4888

Falls Church
6561 Arlington Blvd.
(703)538-3100

Fredericksburg
5043 Plank Rd.
(540)784-8171

Herndon
11254 Leesburg Pk.
(703)450-4240

Leesburg
1360 E. Market St.
(703)777-1900

Manassas
8677 Plant Place
(703)361-4769

Stafford
597 Garrisonville Rd.
(540)659-0606

Vienna
10618 Leesburg Pk.
(703)759-3900

Warrenton
5074 Lee Hwy.
(540)341-0020

Winchester
1725 Berryville Pk.
(540)722-4141

Woodbridge
14135 Jefferson Davis Hwy.
(703)494-0444

00596319

entertainment.com

00596319

MARYLAND

Burtonsville
15930 New Columbia Pk.
(301)384-3730

Clarksburg
11406 Hawkes Rd.
(301)353-0098

Frederick
5432 Old National Pike.
(301)473-5411

Leonardtown
49010 Merchants Ln.
(301)475-1500

Mitchellville
18301 Central Ave.
(301)249-2933

Severna
470 Jumpers Hole Rd.
(410)544-0606

Westminster
1731 Littlestown Pk.
(410)857-6160

VIRGINIA

Annandale
4808 Backlick Rd.
(703)941-5656

Chantilly
43054 John Mosby Hwy.
(703)327-3940

Culpeper
16417 Brandy Rd.
(540)825-4888

Falls Church
6561 Arlington Blvd.
(703)538-3100

Fredericksburg
5043 Plank Rd.
(540)784-8171

Herndon
11254 Leesburg Pk.
(703)450-4240

Leesburg
1360 E. Market St.
(703)777-1900

Manassas
8677 Plant Place
(703)361-4769

Stafford
597 Garrisonville Rd.
(540)659-0606

Vienna
10618 Leesburg Pk.
(703)759-3900

Warrenton
5074 Lee Hwy.
(540)341-0020

Winchester
1725 Berryville Pk.
(540)722-4141

Woodbridge
14135 Jefferson Davis Hwy.
(703)494-0444

00597544

entertainment.com

00597544

MARYLAND

Burtonsville
15930 New Columbia Pk.
(301)384-3730

Clarksburg
11406 Hawkes Rd.
(301)353-0098

Frederick
5432 Old National Pike.
(301)473-5411

Leonardtown
49010 Merchants Ln.
(301)475-1500

Mitchellville
18301 Central Ave.
(301)249-2933

Severna
470 Jumpers Hole Rd.
(410)544-0606

Westminster
1731 Littlestown Pk.
(410)857-6160

VIRGINIA

Annandale
4808 Backlick Rd.
(703)941-5656

Chantilly
43054 John Mosby Hwy.
(703)327-3940

Culpeper
16417 Brandy Rd.
(540)825-4888

Falls Church
6561 Arlington Blvd.
(703)538-3100

Fredericksburg
5043 Plank Rd.
(540)784-8171

Herndon
11254 Leesburg Pk.
(703)450-4240

Leesburg
1360 E. Market St.
(703)777-1900

Manassas
8677 Plant Place
(703)361-4769

Stafford
597 Garrisonville Rd.
(540)659-0606

Vienna
10618 Leesburg Pk.
(703)759-3900

Warrenton
5074 Lee Hwy.
(540)341-0020

Winchester
1725 Berryville Pk.
(540)722-4141

Woodbridge
14135 Jefferson Davis Hwy.
(703)494-0444

00597548

entertainment.com

00597548

EB Games

Valid at All Participating Locations

- Awesome savings & the best selection of pre-owned video games & video systems that are 100% guaranteed
- The newest, hottest releases at excellent prices
- Incredible, fast game/CD reconditioning service
- Game rentals at many locations

Bonus Discounts at entertainment.com

entertainment® entertainment.com

great place for kids

$5.00 Value

EB GAMES™

Enjoy $5 off any ONE PREPLAYED VIDEO GAME priced $29.99 or higher.

valid anytime

Not valid on hardware; Cannot be combined with any other offers or discounts

G11

Valid now thru November 1, 2006

Not valid holidays & subject to Rules of Use. Not valid with other discount offers, unless specified. Coupon VOID if purchased, sold or bartered. Discounts exclude tax, tip and/or alcohol, where applicable.

EB Games

Valid at All Participating Locations

- Awesome savings & the best selection of pre-owned video games & video systems that are 100% guaranteed
- The newest, hottest releases at excellent prices
- Incredible, fast game/CD reconditioning service
- Game rentals at many locations

Bonus Discounts at entertainment.com

entertainment® entertainment.com

great place for kids

$5.00 Value

EB GAMES™

Enjoy $5 off any ONE PREPLAYED VIDEO GAME priced $29.99 or higher.

valid anytime

Not valid on hardware; Cannot be combined with any other offers or discounts

G12

Valid now thru November 1, 2006

Not valid holidays & subject to Rules of Use. Not valid with other discount offers, unless specified. Coupon VOID if purchased, sold or bartered. Discounts exclude tax, tip and/or alcohol, where applicable.

EB Games

Valid at All Participating Locations

- Awesome savings & the best selection of pre-owned video games & video systems that are 100% guaranteed
- The newest, hottest releases at excellent prices
- Incredible, fast game/CD reconditioning service
- Game rentals at many locations

Bonus Discounts at entertainment.com

entertainment® entertainment.com

great place for kids

$5.00 Value

EB GAMES™

Enjoy $5 off any ONE PREPLAYED VIDEO GAME priced $29.99 or higher.

valid anytime

Not valid on hardware; Cannot be combined with any other offers or discounts

G13

Valid now thru November 1, 2006

Not valid holidays & subject to Rules of Use. Not valid with other discount offers, unless specified. Coupon VOID if purchased, sold or bartered. Discounts exclude tax, tip and/or alcohol, where applicable.

EBC3008315

Valid at All Participating Locations

00547066

entertainment.com

00547066

EBC3008315

Valid at All Participating Locations

00547066

entertainment.com

00547066

EBC3008315

Valid at All Participating Locations

00547066

entertainment.com

00547066

FYE
Valid at All Participating Locations

Bonus Discounts at entertainment.com

entertainment
entertainment.com

great place for kids

$3.00 Value

$3 off any CD OR DVD regularly priced $12.99 and up.

valid anytime

Limit 1 per transaction; Not to include electronics, game hardware, CD singles, gift cards/coins, sale items or special orders; Attention TWE Associate: Redemption instructions: Press discount key. Enter $3. Scan item. Select TWE coupon and enter promotion code 803800000000

f.y.e.
for your entertainment
music • movies • games • more

G14

Valid now thru November 1, 2006

Not valid holidays & subject to Rules of Use. Not valid with other discount offers, unless specified. Coupon VOID if purchased, sold or bartered. Discounts exclude tax, tip and/or alcohol, where applicable.

FYE
Valid at All Participating Locations

Bonus Discounts at entertainment.com

entertainment
entertainment.com

great place for kids

$3.00 Value

$3 off any CD OR DVD regularly priced $12.99 and up.

valid anytime

Limit 1 per transaction; Not to include electronics, game hardware, CD singles, gift cards/coins, sale items or special orders; Attention TWE Associate: Redemption instructions: Press discount key. Enter $3. Scan item. Select TWE coupon and enter promotion code 803800000000

f.y.e.
for your entertainment
music • movies • games • more

G15

Valid now thru November 1, 2006

Not valid holidays & subject to Rules of Use. Not valid with other discount offers, unless specified. Coupon VOID if purchased, sold or bartered. Discounts exclude tax, tip and/or alcohol, where applicable.

FYE
Valid at All Participating Locations

Bonus Discounts at entertainment.com

entertainment
entertainment.com

great place for kids

$3.00 Value

$3 off any CD OR DVD regularly priced $12.99 and up.

valid anytime

Limit 1 per transaction; Not to include electronics, game hardware, CD singles, gift cards/coins, sale items or special orders; Attention TWE Associate: Redemption instructions: Press discount key. Enter $3. Scan item. Select TWE coupon and enter promotion code 803800000000

f.y.e.
for your entertainment
music • movies • games • more

G16

Valid now thru November 1, 2006

Not valid holidays & subject to Rules of Use. Not valid with other discount offers, unless specified. Coupon VOID if purchased, sold or bartered. Discounts exclude tax, tip and/or alcohol, where applicable.

f.y.e.

for your entertainment

music • movies • games • more

Valid at All Participating Locations

00593867

entertainment.com

00593867

f.y.e.

for your entertainment

music • movies • games • more

Valid at All Participating Locations

00593867

entertainment.com

00593867

f.y.e.

for your entertainment

music • movies • games • more

Valid at All Participating Locations

00593867

entertainment.com

00593867

Sunny's

See reverse side for locations

- Ready for a little adventure?
- Casual and outdoor apparel
- Camping and outdoor equipment
- Footwear
- Official Boy & Girl Scout merchandise
- Workwear
- Military
- For a location nearest you call 1-800-4-SUNNYS

Bonus Discounts at
entertainment.com

entertainment
entertainment.com

great place for kids

Up To $25.00 Value

Enjoy any purchase at 25% off the regular price - maximum discount $25.00.

Excludes boats, kayaks, and official scout merchandise

valid anytime

SUNNY'S SM

www.sunnysonlime.com

G17

Valid now thru November 1, 2006

Not valid holidays & subject to Rules of Use. Not valid with other discount offers, unless specified. Coupon VOID if purchased, sold or bartered. Discounts exclude tax, tip and/or alcohol, where applicable.

Sunny's

See reverse side for locations

- Ready for a little adventure?
- Casual and outdoor apparel
- Camping and outdoor equipment
- Footwear
- Official Boy & Girl Scout merchandise
- Workwear
- Military
- For a location nearest you please call 1-800-4-SUNNYS or visit www.sunnysonline.com

Bonus Discounts at
entertainment.com

entertainment
entertainment.com

great place for kids

Up To $25.00 Value

Enjoy one ITEM at 50% off the regular price - maximum discount $25.00.

Excludes boats, kayaks, and official scout merchandise

valid anytime

SUNNY'S SM

www.sunnysonline.com

G18

Valid now thru November 1, 2006

Not valid holidays & subject to Rules of Use. Not valid with other discount offers, unless specified. Coupon VOID if purchased, sold or bartered. Discounts exclude tax, tip and/or alcohol, where applicable.

Sunny's

See reverse side for locations

- Ready for a little adventure?
- Casual and outdoor apparel
- Camping and outdoor equipment
- Footwear
- Official Boy & Girl Scout merchandise
- Workwear
- Military
- For a location nearest you call 1-800-4-SUNNYS

Bonus Discounts at
entertainment.com

entertainment
entertainment.com

great place for kids

Up To $25.00 Value

Enjoy $25.00 off your choice of any canoe or kayak - maximum discount $25.00.

valid anytime

SUNNY'S SM

www.sunnysonline.com

G19

Valid now thru November 1, 2006

Not valid holidays & subject to Rules of Use. Not valid with other discount offers, unless specified. Coupon VOID if purchased, sold or bartered. Discounts exclude tax, tip and/or alcohol, where applicable.

SUNNY'S℠

DELAWARE
Rehoboth
4575 Hwy 1
(302)644-2123

MARYLAND
Annapolis
3 Old Solomons Island Rd
(410)841-6490

Bel Air
5 Bel Air South Pkwy
(410)515-2044

Dundalk
1549 Merritt Blvd
(410)284-4020

Ellicott City
9291 Baltimore - Nat'l Pike
(410)461-9122

Frederick
1003 W. Patrick St
(301)620-1070

Glen Burnie
7324 Ritchie Hwy
(410)761-3511

Laurel
13718 Baltimore Ave.
(301)604-5771

Parkville
7906 Harford Rd
(410)668-8050

Randallstown
8139 Liberty Rd
(410)922-3622

Timonium
2157 York Rd
(410)561-7885

Towson
7 West Chesapeake Ave
(410)825-8050

Westminster
625 Baltimore Blvd
(410)840-8701

VIRGINIA
Alexandria
370 S.Pickett St
(703)461-0088

Manassas
11650 Sudley Manor Dr
(703)257-7069

00499733

entertainment.com

00499733

SUNNY'S℠

DELAWARE
Rehoboth
4575 Hwy 1
(302)644-2123

MARYLAND
Annapolis
3 Old Solomons Island Rd
(410)841-6490

Bel Air
5 Bel Air South Pkwy
(410)515-2044

Dundalk
1549 Merritt Blvd
(410)284-4020

Ellicott City
9291 Baltimore - Nat'l Pike
(410)461-9122

Frederick
1003 W. Patrick St
(301)620-1070

Glen Burnie
7324 Ritchie Hwy
(410)761-3511

Laurel
13718 Baltimore Ave.
(301)604-5771

Parkville
7906 Harford Rd
(410)668-8050

Randallstown
8139 Liberty Rd
(410)922-3622

Timonium
2157 York Rd
(410)561-7885

Towson
7 West Chesapeake Ave
(410)825-8050

Westminster
625 Baltimore Blvd
(410)840-8701

VIRGINIA
Alexandria
370 S.Pickett St
(703)461-0088

Manassas
11650 Sudley Manor Dr
(703)257-7069

00499809

entertainment.com

00499809

SUNNY'S℠

DELAWARE
Rehoboth
4575 Hwy 1
(302)644-2123

MARYLAND
Annapolis
3 Old Solomons Island Rd
(410)841-6490

Bel Air
5 Bel Air South Pkwy
(410)515-2044

Dundalk
1549 Merritt Blvd
(410)284-4020

Ellicott City
9291 Baltimore - Nat'l Pike
(410)461-9122

Frederick
1003 W. Patrick St
(301)620-1070

Glen Burnie
7324 Ritchie Hwy
(410)761-3511

Laurel
13718 Baltimore Ave.
(301)604-5771

Parkville
7906 Harford Rd
(410)668-8050

Randallstown
8139 Liberty Rd
(410)922-3622

Timonium
2157 York Rd
(410)561-7885

Towson
7 West Chesapeake Ave
(410)825-8050

Westminster
625 Baltimore Blvd
(410)840-8701

VIRGINIA
Alexandria
370 S.Pickett St
(703)461-0088

Manassas
11650 Sudley Manor Dr
(703)257-7069

00499810

entertainment.com

00499810

Cartoon Cuts

See reverse side for locations

- "Hair! We can really cut it"
- Cartoons at every station
- Friendly elephant shampoo
- Quality, fun & value

entertainment.
entertainment.com

25% OFF

Enjoy a CHILD'S HAIRCUT at 25% off the regular price.

Bang trims excluded

valid anytime

Not valid with any other offer

07

CARTOON Cuts
Hair. We can really cut it.™

www.cartooncuts.com

G20

Valid now thru November 1, 2006

Not valid holidays & subject to Rules of Use. Not valid with other discount offers, unless specified. Coupon VOID if purchased, sold or bartered. Discounts exclude tax, tip and/or alcohol, where applicable.

Cartoon Cuts

See reverse side for locations

- "Hair! We can really cut it"
- Paul Mitchell
- Systeme Biolage By Matrix
- Amplify by Matrix
- Cartoon Cuts
- Bed Head

entertainment.
entertainment.com

Up To $5.00 Value

Enjoy a HAIR CARE PRODUCT at 25% off the regular price.

valid anytime

Not valid with any other offer

08

CARTOON Cuts
Hair. We can really cut it.™

www.cartooncuts.com

G21

Valid now thru November 1, 2006

Not valid holidays & subject to Rules of Use. Not valid with other discount offers, unless specified. Coupon VOID if purchased, sold or bartered. Discounts exclude tax, tip and/or alcohol, where applicable.

Cartoon Cuts

See reverse side for locations

- "Hair! We can really cut it"

entertainment.
entertainment.com

25% OFF

Enjoy an ADULT HAIRCUT at 25% off the regular price.

valid anytime

Not valid with any other offer

09

CARTOON Cuts
Hair. We can really cut it.™

www.cartooncuts.com

G22

Valid now thru November 1, 2006

Not valid holidays & subject to Rules of Use. Not valid with other discount offers, unless specified. Coupon VOID if purchased, sold or bartered. Discounts exclude tax, tip and/or alcohol, where applicable.

FLORIDA
Coral Springs
9481 W. Atlantic Blvd.
(Coral Sq. Mall)
(954)341-4221

Hialeah Gardens
9300 NW 77th Ave.
(Hialeah Gardens - inside Wal-Mart)
(305)231-9006

Kendall
8412 Mills Dr.
(Town & Country Ctr.)
(305)270-2325

Miami
8888 136th St. #110
(The Falls)
(305)278-1211

Pembroke Pines
11401 Pines Blvd.
(Pembroke Lakes Mall)
(954)435-7166

Wellington
10300 W. Forest Hill Blvd.
(Mall at Wellington Green)
(561)383-6500

GEORGIA
Kennesaw
400 Ernest Barrett Pkwy.
(Town Ctr. at Cobb)
(770)795-0014

MARYLAND
Baltimore
8200 Perry Hall Blvd.
(White Marsh Mall)
(410)931-1588

Bel Air
696 Baltimore Pike
(Harford Mall)
(410)399-9939

Columbia
10300 Little Pautuxent Pkwy.
(The Mall at Columbia)
(410)740-6665

Gaithersburg
701 Russell Ave.
(Lakeforest Mall)
(301)948-7020

Glen Burnie
7900 Governor Ritchie Hwy.
(Marley Station Shpg. Ctr.)
(410)768-9606

Laurel
327 Montrose Ave.
(Laurel Shpg. Ctr.)
(301)317-4444

Rockville
1619 Rockville Pike
(Congressional Plaza)
(301)816-3098

VIRGINIA
Chesapeake
1401 Greenbrier Pkwy.
(Greenbrier Mall)
(757)420-9576

Dulles
21100 Dulles Town Center
(703)433-1440

Fairfax
Fair Oaks Mall
(703)359-2887

Reston
1472 North Point Village Center
(Kool Klips)
(703)689-2665

Springfield
Springfield Mall
(Kool Klips)
(703)719-9791

Sterling
46262 S. Cranston St.
(Kool Klips - Cascades Marketplace)
(703)444-5855

Virginia Beach
701 Lynnhaven Pkwy.
(Lynnhaven Mall)
(757)631-1100

Woodbridge
14066 Shoppers Best Way
(Smoketown Stations)
(703)670-3400

00201327

entertainment.com

00201327

FLORIDA
Coral Springs
9481 W. Atlantic Blvd.
(Coral Sq. Mall)
(954)341-4221

Hialeah Gardens
9300 NW 77th Ave.
(Hialeah Gardens - inside Wal-Mart)
(305)231-9006

Kendall
8412 Mills Dr.
(Town & Country Ctr.)
(305)270-2325

Miami
8888 136th St. #110
(The Falls)
(305)278-1211

Pembroke Pines
11401 Pines Blvd.
(Pembroke Lakes Mall)
(954)435-7166

Wellington
10300 W. Forest Hill Blvd.
(Mall at Wellington Green)
(561)383-6500

GEORGIA
Kennesaw
400 Ernest Barrett Pkwy.
(Town Ctr. at Cobb)
(770)795-0014

MARYLAND
Baltimore
8200 Perry Hall Blvd.
(White Marsh Mall)
(410)931-1588

Bel Air
696 Baltimore Pike
(Harford Mall)
(410)399-9939

Columbia
10300 Little Pautuxent Pkwy.
(The Mall at Columbia)
(410)740-6665

Gaithersburg
701 Russell Ave.
(Lakeforest Mall)
(301)948-7020

Glen Burnie
7900 Governor Ritchie Hwy.
(Marley Station Shpg. Ctr.)
(410)768-9606

Laurel
327 Montrose Ave.
(Laurel Shpg. Ctr.)
(301)317-4444

Rockville
1619 Rockville Pike
(Congressional Plaza)
(301)816-3098

VIRGINIA
Chesapeake
1401 Greenbrier Pkwy.
(Greenbrier Mall)
(757)420-9576

Dulles
21100 Dulles Town Center
(703)433-1440

Fairfax
Fair Oaks Mall
(703)359-2887

Reston
1472 North Point Village Center
(Kool Klips)
(703)689-2665

Springfield
Springfield Mall
(Kool Klips)
(703)719-9791

Sterling
46262 S. Cranston St.
(Kool Klips - Cascades Marketplace)
(703)444-5855

Virginia Beach
701 Lynnhaven Pkwy.
(Lynnhaven Mall)
(757)631-1100

Woodbridge
14066 Shoppers Best Way
(Smoketown Stations)
(703)670-3400

00201354

entertainment.com

00201354

FLORIDA
Coral Springs
9481 W. Atlantic Blvd.
(Coral Sq. Mall)
(954)341-4221

Hialeah Gardens
9300 NW 77th Ave.
(Hialeah Gardens - inside Wal-Mart)
(305)231-9006

Kendall
8412 Mills Dr.
(Town & Country Ctr.)
(305)270-2325

Miami
8888 136th St. #110
(The Falls)
(305)278-1211

Pembroke Pines
11401 Pines Blvd.
(Pembroke Lakes Mall)
(954)435-7166

Wellington
10300 W. Forest Hill Blvd.
(Mall at Wellington Green)
(561)383-6500

GEORGIA
Kennesaw
400 Ernest Barrett Pkwy.
(Town Ctr. at Cobb)
(770)795-0014

MARYLAND
Baltimore
8200 Perry Hall Blvd.
(White Marsh Mall)
(410)931-1588

Bel Air
696 Baltimore Pike
(Harford Mall)
(410)399-9939

Columbia
10300 Little Pautuxent Pkwy.
(The Mall at Columbia)
(410)740-6665

Gaithersburg
701 Russell Ave.
(Lakeforest Mall)
(301)948-7020

Glen Burnie
7900 Governor Ritchie Hwy.
(Marley Station Shpg. Ctr.)
(410)768-9606

Laurel
327 Montrose Ave.
(Laurel Shpg. Ctr.)
(301)317-4444

Rockville
1619 Rockville Pike
(Congressional Plaza)
(301)816-3098

VIRGINIA
Chesapeake
1401 Greenbrier Pkwy.
(Greenbrier Mall)
(757)420-9576

Dulles
21100 Dulles Town Center
(703)433-1440

Fairfax
Fair Oaks Mall
(703)359-2887

Reston
1472 North Point Village Center
(Kool Klips)
(703)689-2665

Springfield
Springfield Mall
(Kool Klips)
(703)719-9791

Sterling
46262 S. Cranston St.
(Kool Klips - Cascades Marketplace)
(703)444-5855

Virginia Beach
701 Lynnhaven Pkwy.
(Lynnhaven Mall)
(757)631-1100

Woodbridge
14066 Shoppers Best Way
(Smoketown Stations)
(703)670-3400

00201364

entertainment.com

00201364

Meineke Car Care Center

Offer is valid at any participating Meineke Car Care Center location.

Bonus Discounts at entertainment.com

entertainment. entertainment.com

25% OFF

Valid for 25% Off Any Lifetime Muffler.

Offer valid on in-stock parts only when installed at Meineke. Discount applies to regular retail pricing. Not valid in conjunction with any other special offer or warranty work. Coupon must be presented at time of estimate.

meineke® car care center

valid anytime

G23

Valid now thru November 1, 2006

Not valid holidays & subject to Rules of Use. Not valid with other discount offers, unless specified. Coupon VOID if purchased, sold or bartered. Discounts exclude tax, tip and/or alcohol, where applicable.

Meineke Car Care Center

Offer is valid at any participating Meineke Car Care Center location.

Bonus Discounts at entertainment.com

entertainment. entertainment.com

25% OFF

Valid for 25% Off Any Lifetime Brake Pads and Shoes.

Offer valid on in-stock parts only when installed at Meineke. Discount applies to regular retail pricing. Not valid in conjunction with any other special offer or warranty work. Coupon must be presented at time of estimate.

meineke® car care center

valid anytime

G24

Valid now thru November 1, 2006

Not valid holidays & subject to Rules of Use. Not valid with other discount offers, unless specified. Coupon VOID if purchased, sold or bartered. Discounts exclude tax, tip and/or alcohol, where applicable.

Meineke Car Care Center

Offer is valid at any participating Meineke Car Care Center location.

Bonus Discounts at entertainment.com

entertainment. entertainment.com

$5.00 OFF

Valid for $5.00 Off Any Oil Change.

One coupon per vehicle. Discount applies to regular retail pricing. Not valid in conjunction with any other special offer or warranty work. Coupon must be presented at time of estimate.

meineke® car care center

valid anytime

G25

Valid now thru November 1, 2006

Not valid holidays & subject to Rules of Use. Not valid with other discount offers, unless specified. Coupon VOID if purchased, sold or bartered. Discounts exclude tax, tip and/or alcohol, where applicable.

Offer is valid at any participating Meineke Car Care Center location.

00662355

entertainment.com

00662355

Offer is valid at any participating Meineke Car Care Center location.

00662377

entertainment.com

00662377

Offer is valid at any participating Meineke Car Care Center location.

00662386

entertainment.com

00662386

Mr. Wash Car Wash

See reverse side for locations

- Every Mr. Wash Super Wash includes full-service - all soft cloth brushless wash, interior vacuum, windows washed - inside & out, full wipedown
- Undercarriage wash, clearcoat protectant, 3-color clearcoat treatment & wheel cleaner

Bonus Discounts at
entertainment.com

entertainment.
entertainment.com

50% OFF

Enjoy one SUPER WASH at 50% off the regular price.

valid anytime

S-654

MR WASH®
FULL SERVICE
BRUSHLESS
CAR WASH

www.mrwash.com

G26

Valid now thru November 1, 2006

Not valid holidays & subject to Rules of Use. Not valid with other discount offers, unless specified. Coupon VOID if purchased, sold or bartered. Discounts exclude tax, tip and/or alcohol, where applicable.

Mr. Wash Car Wash

See reverse side for locations

- Every Mr. Wash Super Wash includes full-service - all soft cloth brushless wash, interior vacuum, windows washed - inside & out, full wipedown
- Undercarriage wash, clearcoat protectant, 3-color clearcoat treatment & wheel cleaner

Bonus Discounts at
entertainment.com

entertainment.
entertainment.com

50% OFF

Enjoy one SUPER WASH at 50% off the regular price.

valid anytime

S-654

MR WASH®
FULL SERVICE
BRUSHLESS
CAR WASH

www.mrwash.com

G27

Valid now thru November 1, 2006

Not valid holidays & subject to Rules of Use. Not valid with other discount offers, unless specified. Coupon VOID if purchased, sold or bartered. Discounts exclude tax, tip and/or alcohol, where applicable.

Mr. Wash Express

See reverse side for locations

- Outside only includes:
- Brushless car wash
- 3 color clear coat treatment
- 3 coat protection
- Undercarriage wash
- Wheel cleaner

Bonus Discounts at
entertainment.com

entertainment.
entertainment.com

50% OFF

Enjoy one OUTSIDE ULTIMATE CAR WASH at 50% off the regular price.

valid anytime

Code: 755

MR WASH®
EXPRESS

www.mrwash.com

G28

Valid now thru November 1, 2006

Not valid holidays & subject to Rules of Use. Not valid with other discount offers, unless specified. Coupon VOID if purchased, sold or bartered. Discounts exclude tax, tip and/or alcohol, where applicable.

MR WASH®
FULL SERVICE
BRUSHLESS
CAR WASH

1311 13th St. NW
Washington, DC
(202)462-5573

812 Geipe Rd.
Catonsville, MD
(410)744-1090

3407 Mt. Vernon Ave.
Alexandria, VA
(703)683-6930

101 N. Glebe Rd.
Arlington, VA
(703)243-7735

540 Maple Ave. West
Vienna, VA
(703)242-0540

00090972

entertainment.com

00090972

MR WASH®
FULL SERVICE
BRUSHLESS
CAR WASH

1311 13th St. NW
Washington, DC
(202)462-5573

812 Geipe Rd.
Catonsville, MD
(410)744-1090

3407 Mt. Vernon Ave.
Alexandria, VA
(703)683-6930

101 N. Glebe Rd.
Arlington, VA
(703)243-7735

540 Maple Ave. West
Vienna, VA
(703)242-0540

00090972

entertainment.com

00090972

MR WASH®
EXPRESS

3817 Dupont Ave.
(Behind Savannah's Restaurant)
Kensington, MD
(301)933-4858

7996 Georgia Ave.
(1/3 of a block south of E-W hwy)
Silver Spring, MD
(301)495-9335

420 S. Van Dorn St.
(corner of S. Van Dorn & Edsall Rd.)
Alexandria, VA
(703)751-4138

00481176

entertainment.com

00481176

Sport Clips
Valid at All Participating Locations

entertainment. entertainment.com

$3.00 Value

Enjoy $3 off any HAIRCUT.

valid anytime

Valid at all participating Sport Clips locations; Not valid with any other discounts or promotions; One coupon/card per customer per visit; Mens 720; Boys 721

Sport Clips HAIRCUTS

sportclips.com

G29

Valid now thru November 1, 2006

Not valid holidays & subject to Rules of Use. Not valid with other discount offers, unless specified. Coupon VOID if purchased, sold or bartered. Discounts exclude tax, tip and/or alcohol, where applicable.

Bonus Discounts at entertainment.com

Great Clips
See reverse side for locations

- Great haircuts. Every time. Everywhere.
- Haircuts & perms
- Salon quality at a down-to-earth price
- Licensed, professionally trained stylists
- Call 888-78-CLIPS for the location nearest you!

entertainment. entertainment.com

great place for kids

Up To $25.00 Value

Enjoy 20% off any regular priced HAIRCUT OR SERVICE - maximum discount $25.00.

valid anytime

Great Clips for hair.®

Guaranteed Satisfaction. Guaranteed Style.™

www.greatclips.com

G30

Valid now thru November 1, 2006

Not valid holidays & subject to Rules of Use. Not valid with other discount offers, unless specified. Coupon VOID if purchased, sold or bartered. Discounts exclude tax, tip and/or alcohol, where applicable.

Bonus Discounts at entertainment.com

Glamour Shots
Springfield Mall
Springfield, VA
(703)922-3900

entertainment. entertainment.com

great place for kids

Up To $25.00 Value

Enjoy 20% off the regular price of any PURCHASE (sale items excluded) - maximum discount $25.00.

valid anytime

GS Glamour Shots℠

www.glamourshots.com

G31

Valid now thru November 1, 2006

Not valid holidays & subject to Rules of Use. Not valid with other discount offers, unless specified. Coupon VOID if purchased, sold or bartered. Discounts exclude tax, tip and/or alcohol, where applicable.

Bonus Discounts at entertainment.com

Sport Clips® HAIRCUTS

Valid at All Participating Locations

00650283

entertainment.com

00650283

Great Clips for hair.®

Guaranteed Satisfaction.
Guaranteed Style.™

1464A N. Beauregard St.
(The Shops of Mark Center)
Alexandria, VA
(703)931-8070

3544-B S. Jefferson St.
(Crossroads Place)
Bailey's Crossroads, VA
(703)820-5500

8971 Ox Rd.
(Shops at Lorton Valley)
Lorton, VA
(703)495-9995

00665476

entertainment.com

00665476

GS Glamour Shots℠

Springfield Mall
Springfield, VA
(703)922-3900

00651294

entertainment.com

00651294

Great Clips

See reverse side for locations

entertainment. entertainment.com

great place for kids

Up To $25.00 Value

Great Clips for hair.®

Enjoy 20% off any regular priced HAIRCUT OR HAIRCARE PRODUCT PURCHASE - maximum discount $25.00.

Sale items excluded

valid anytime

Not valid with any other discounts or promotions

www.greatclips.com

G32

Valid now thru November 1, 2006

Not valid holidays & subject to Rules of Use. Not valid with other discount offers, unless specified. Coupon VOID if purchased, sold or bartered. Discounts exclude tax, tip and/or alcohol, where applicable.

Bonus Discounts at entertainment.com

Xtra Mart Convenience Stores

Valid at All Participating Xtra Mart Locations

entertainment. entertainment.com

ONE 20 OZ. SPORT TOP WATER

Valid for one FREE 20OZ. SPORT TOP WATER.

valid anytime

Valid at any Xtra Mart Convenience Store

100% NATURAL Xtramart CONVENIENCE STORES SPRING WATER

G33

Valid now thru November 1, 2006

Not valid holidays & subject to Rules of Use. Not valid with other discount offers, unless specified. Coupon VOID if purchased, sold or bartered. Discounts exclude tax, tip and/or alcohol, where applicable.

Bonus Discounts at entertainment.com

Harbor Freight Tools

Valid at All Participating Locations

entertainment. entertainment.com

10% OFF

Enjoy 10% off your entire PURCHASE.

valid anytime

One coupon per customer per visit; Valid at Harbor Freight Tools Retail Stores only

HARBOR FREIGHT TOOLS®

www.harborfreightusa.com

G34

Valid now thru November 1, 2006

Not valid holidays & subject to Rules of Use. Not valid with other discount offers, unless specified. Coupon VOID if purchased, sold or bartered. Discounts exclude tax, tip and/or alcohol, where applicable.

Bonus Discounts at entertainment.com

Great Clips for hair®

1477 Carl D Silver Pkwy.
(in Central Park)
Fredericksburg, VA
(540)785-2522

4228 Plank Rd.
(Ukrop's)
Fredericksburg, VA
(540)785-9300

309 Worth Ave., Ste. 105
(Doc Stone Commons)
Stafford, VA
(540)657-7117

00656673

entertainment.com

00656673

100% NATURAL Xtramart CONVENIENCE STORES SPRING WATER

Valid at All Participating Xtra Mart Locations

00665618

entertainment.com

00665618

HARBOR FREIGHT TOOLS®

Please tell us about yourself to validate coupon

Name: ______________________

Address: ______________________

City: ______________________

State: ____________ ZIP: ____________

Email: ______________________

Copies of this coupon will not be accepted

00659116

entertainment.com

00659116

Pawsenclaws & Co.

See reverse side for locations

- Pawsenclaws & Co. is a fun & interactive specialty store where guests choose an animal to stuff, dress & adopt for themselves or give as a special gift
- Pawsenclaws & Co. parties are great for any occasion
- Birthday parties
- Scout troop parties
- School parties & field trips
- We supply the fun

Bonus Discounts at entertainment.com

entertainment. entertainment.com — great place for kids

Up To $25.00 Value

Enjoy 20% off the regular price of any PURCHASE (sale items excluded) - maximum discount $25.00.

valid anytime

Not valid on birthday parties; One coupon/card per customer per visit

1024

Pawsenclaws & Co.™ CUSTOM BEAR MAKERS

www.pawsenclaws.com

G35

Valid now thru November 1, 2006

Not valid holidays & subject to Rules of Use. Not valid with other discount offers, unless specified. Coupon VOID if purchased, sold or bartered. Discounts exclude tax, tip and/or alcohol, where applicable.

Pawsenclaws & Co.

See reverse side for locations

- Pawsenclaws & Co. is a fun & interactive specialty store where guests choose an animal to stuff, dress & adopt for themselves or give as a special gift
- Pawsenclaws & Co. parties are great for any occasion
- Birthday parties
- Scout troop parties
- School parties & field trips
- We supply the fun

Bonus Discounts at entertainment.com

entertainment. entertainment.com — great place for kids

20% OFF

Enjoy 20% off the regular price of any BIRTHDAY PARTY.

valid anytime

One coupon/card per customer per visit

1026

Pawsenclaws & Co.™ CUSTOM BEAR MAKERS

www.pawsenclaws.com

G36

Valid now thru November 1, 2006

Not valid holidays & subject to Rules of Use. Not valid with other discount offers, unless specified. Coupon VOID if purchased, sold or bartered. Discounts exclude tax, tip and/or alcohol, where applicable.

Music & Arts Center

Valid at All Participating Locations

- Band & orchestra instruments
- Guitars, amps & keyboards
- Sheet music & accessories
- Private music lessons
- Instrument repairs

Bonus Discounts at entertainment.com

entertainment. entertainment.com — great place for kids

$5.00 Value

Enjoy $5.00 off your purchase of $25 or more - maximum discount $5.00.

Valid on sheet music & books

valid anytime

Not valid with any other discounts or promotions

Ent05

Music & Arts Centers

Riccardo's Music Center

Ted Herbert's Music

www.musicarts.com

G37

Valid now thru November 1, 2006

Not valid holidays & subject to Rules of Use. Not valid with other discount offers, unless specified. Coupon VOID if purchased, sold or bartered. Discounts exclude tax, tip and/or alcohol, where applicable.

Pawsenclaws & Co.™
CUSTOM BEAR MAKERS

7000 Arundel Mills Circle
(Arundel Mills Mall)
Hanover, MD
(443)755-8851

310 Daniel Webster Hwy.
(Pheasant Ln. Mall)
Nashua, NH
(603)897-0020

436 Franklin Ave.
Hewlett, NJ
(516)295-7307

1400 Willowbrook Blvd.
(Willowbrook Mall)
Wayne, NJ
(973)237-0090

238 Lehigh Mall
(Lehigh Valley Mall)
Whitehall, PA
(610)264-1900

21100 Dulles Twin Circle
(Dulles Town Centry)
Dulls, VA
(703)430-7900

00593009

entertainment.com

00593009

Pawsenclaws & Co.™
CUSTOM BEAR MAKERS

7000 Arundel Mills Circle
(Arundel Mills Mall)
Hanover, MD
(443)755-8851

310 Daniel Webster Hwy.
(Pheasant Ln. Mall)
Nashua, NH
(603)897-0020

436 Franklin Ave.
Hewlett, NJ
(516)295-7307

1400 Willowbrook Blvd.
(Willowbrook Mall)
Wayne, NJ
(973)237-0090

238 Lehigh Mall
(Lehigh Valley Mall)
Whitehall, PA
(610)264-1900

21100 Dulles Twin Circle
(Dulles Town Centry)
Dulls, VA
(703)430-7900

00593031

entertainment.com

00593031

Music & Arts Centers

Riccardo's Music Center

Ted Herbert's Music

Valid at All Participating Locations

00615890

entertainment.com

00615890

Molly Maid, Inc.

Check your Yellow Pages for the number of your local MOLLY MAID® service, or call toll-free 1-800-MOLLYMAID (1-800-665-5962).

Bonus Discounts at entertainment.com

entertainment® entertainment.com

SAVE $25.00

Save $10 on your first regularly scheduled visit and save $15 on your fourth regularly scheduled visit. www.mollymaid.com.

Identify yourself as an Entertainment® Member when making arrangements for cleaning. This offer is available at participating locations only. New customers only. Not valid with any other discount offer. Check your Yellow Pages for the number of your local MOLLY MAID® service, or call toll free 1-800-MOLLYMAID (1-800-665-5962).

valid anytime

MOLLY MAID®

www.mollymaid.com

G38

Valid now thru November 1, 2006

Not valid holidays & subject to Rules of Use. Not valid with other discount offers, unless specified. Coupon VOID if purchased, sold or bartered. Discounts exclude tax, tip and/or alcohol, where applicable.

Maid Brigade

Call 800-515-MAID (6243) to schedule your initial cleaning service

- Rated #1 in reliability
- Satisfaction guaranteed
- Bonded, insured & documented maids
- Weekly, bi-monthy, or for special occasions
- HEPA vacuums collect 99.7% of allergens
- Cheerful office staff at your service, live 8 a.m. to 5 p.m., Mon. thru Fri.

Bonus Discounts at entertainment.com

entertainment® entertainment.com

Up To $25.00 Value

Enjoy 20% off INITIAL CLEANING SERVICE.

Call 800-515-6243 (maid) to schedule your initial cleaning service

valid anytime

·MAID BRIGADE·®

G39

Valid now thru November 1, 2006

Not valid holidays & subject to Rules of Use. Not valid with other discount offers, unless specified. Coupon VOID if purchased, sold or bartered. Discounts exclude tax, tip and/or alcohol, where applicable.

Closet Factory

3 JP Morgan Ct.
Unit J Waldorf MD
(301)893-1605 OR
(888)256-7587

- If only your life were this organized
- Custom storage solutions for every room in the house
- Professionally trained designers & installers
- Closets, office, garage, entertainment center - any where
- Organizing homes since 1983

Bonus Discounts at entertainment.com

entertainment® entertainment.com

Up To $100.00 Value

Enjoy 20% off the regular price of any PURCHASE (sale items excluded) - maximum discount $100.00.

valid anytime

Not valid with any other discount offer

closetfactory

www.closetfactory.com

G40

Valid now thru November 1, 2006

Not valid holidays & subject to Rules of Use. Not valid with other discount offers, unless specified. Coupon VOID if purchased, sold or bartered. Discounts exclude tax, tip and/or alcohol, where applicable.

MOLLY MAID®

www.mollymaid.com

Check your Yellow Pages for the number of your local MOLLY MAID® service, or call toll-free 1-800-MOLLYMAID (1-800-665-5962).

00441283

entertainment.com

00441283

MAID BRIGADE®

Call 800-515-MAID (6243) to schedule your initial cleaning service

00599296

entertainment.com

00599296

closetfactory

3 JP Morgan Ct. Unit J Waldorf MD (301)893-1605 OR (888)256-7587

00530464

entertainment.com

00530464

Annie Sez

Valid at All Participating Locations

- The latest looks from today's top designers
- New styles every week, amazingly low prices every day
- A vast selection of sportswear, separates, dresses, seasonal outerwear, active wear & lingerie
- Famous name shoes & hand bags & the latest trends in accessories
- A wonderful array of home decor & theme gifts

Bonus Discounts at entertainment.com

entertainment. entertainment.com

Up To $25.00 Value

Enjoy 20% off the regular price of any PURCHASE (sale items excluded) - maximum discount $25.00.

valid anytime

May not be used on previous purchases or on the purchase of gift cards; Must redeem at time of purchase; Offer cannot be combined with Obsession card discount; Limit one per customer; May not be combined with any other coupon discount or special offer; Coupons must be surrendered at the time of purchase

Annie sez

87 G41

Valid now thru November 1, 2006

Not valid holidays & subject to Rules of Use. Not valid with other discount offers, unless specified. Coupon VOID if purchased, sold or bartered. Discounts exclude tax, tip and/or alcohol, where applicable.

Annie Sez

Valid at All Participating Locations

- The latest looks from today's top designers
- New styles every week, amazingly low prices every day
- A vast selection of sportswear, separates, dresses, seasonal outerwear, active wear & lingerie
- Famous name shoes & hand bags & the latest trends in accessories
- A wonderful array of home decor & theme gifts

Bonus Discounts at entertainment.com

entertainment. entertainment.com

Up To $25.00 Value

Enjoy 20% off the regular price of any PURCHASE (sale items excluded) - maximum discount $25.00.

valid anytime

May not be used on previous purchases or on the purchase of gift cards; Must redeem at time of purchase; Offer cannot be combined with Obsession card discount; Limit one per customer; May not be combined with any other coupon discount or special offer; Coupons must be surrendered at the time of purchase

Annie sez

87 G42

Valid now thru November 1, 2006

Not valid holidays & subject to Rules of Use. Not valid with other discount offers, unless specified. Coupon VOID if purchased, sold or bartered. Discounts exclude tax, tip and/or alcohol, where applicable.

Annie Sez

Valid at All Participating Locations

- The latest looks from today's top designers
- New styles every week, amazingly low prices every day
- A vast selection of sportswear, separates, dresses, seasonal outerwear, active wear & lingerie
- Famous name shoes & hand bags & the latest trends in accessories
- A wonderful array of home decor & theme gifts

Bonus Discounts at entertainment.com

entertainment. entertainment.com

Up To $25.00 Value

Enjoy 20% off the regular price of any PURCHASE (sale items excluded) - maximum discount $25.00.

valid anytime

May not be used on previous purchases or on the purchase of gift cards; Must redeem at time of purchase; Offer cannot be combined with Obsession card discount; Limit one per customer; May not be combined with any other coupon discount or special offer; Coupons must be surrendered at the time of purchase

Annie sez

87 G43

Valid now thru November 1, 2006

Not valid holidays & subject to Rules of Use. Not valid with other discount offers, unless specified. Coupon VOID if purchased, sold or bartered. Discounts exclude tax, tip and/or alcohol, where applicable.

Annie sez

Valid at All Participating Locations

00532556

entertainment.com

00532556

Annie sez

Valid at All Participating Locations

00532556

entertainment.com

00532556

Annie sez

Valid at All Participating Locations

00532556

entertainment.com

00532556

entertainment.
entertainment.com

great place for kids

20% OFF

Coconuts

Valid at All Participating Locations

Enjoy 20% off any CD OR DVD regularly priced at $12.99 and up.

valid anytime

Limit 1 per transaction; Not to include electronics, game hardware, CD singles, gift cards/coins, sale items or special orders; Attention TWE Associate: Redemption instructions: Press discount key. Select %. Key in percentage off. Scan item. Select TWE coupon and enter promotion code 803910000000

G44

Valid now thru November 1, 2006

Not valid holidays & subject to Rules of Use. Not valid with other discount offers, unless specified. Coupon VOID if purchased, sold or bartered. Discounts exclude tax, tip and/or alcohol, where applicable.

Bonus Discounts at entertainment.com

entertainment.
entertainment.com

great place for kids

Up To $25.00 Value

Up Against the Wall

See reverse side for locations

Enjoy 20% off the regular price of any PURCHASE (sale items excluded) - maximum discount $25.00.

valid anytime

www.upagainstthewall.com

G45

Valid now thru November 1, 2006

Not valid holidays & subject to Rules of Use. Not valid with other discount offers, unless specified. Coupon VOID if purchased, sold or bartered. Discounts exclude tax, tip and/or alcohol, where applicable.

Bonus Discounts at entertainment.com

entertainment.
entertainment.com

great place for kids

Up To $25.00 Value

Commander Salamander

1420 Wisconsin Ave. NW
Washington, DC
(202)337-2265

Enjoy 20% off the regular price of any PURCHASE (sale items excluded) - maximum discount $25.00.

valid anytime

G46

Valid now thru November 1, 2006

Not valid holidays & subject to Rules of Use. Not valid with other discount offers, unless specified. Coupon VOID if purchased, sold or bartered. Discounts exclude tax, tip and/or alcohol, where applicable.

Bonus Discounts at entertainment.com

Valid at All Participating Locations

00593832

00593832

CALIFORNIA

Concord
130 SunValley Shpg. Ctr.
(SunValley Shpg. Ctr. Bldg. B, Level 1)

Culver City
114 Foxhills Mall
(Foxhills Mall)
(310)397-7901

Hayward
0324 Southland Mall
(Southland Mall)

Lakewood
#48 Lakewood Ctr. Mall
(Lakewood Ctr. Mall)
(562)630-1638

Los Angeles
8500 Beverly Blvd., Ste. 788
(Beverly Ctr. - 7th Floor)
(310)659-1321

Redondo Beach
1815 Hawthorne Blvd. #238
(Gallaria at South Bay)
(310)921-6341

DISTRICT OF COLUMBIA

Washington
2301-M Georgia Ave. NW
(Howard University)
(202)234-4153

3219 M St. NW
(Georgetown - M St.)
(202)337-9316

MARYLAND

Annapolis
146 Annapolis Mall
(Annapolis Mall)
(410)897-0721

Hyattsville
3500 East-West Hwy.
(PG Plaza)
(301)559-6780

Marlow Heights
3743-G Branch Ave.
(Iverson)
(301)899-1294

Waldorf
5000 Rt. 301 S. #201
(St. Charles Town Ctr.)
(301)705-8021

Wheaton
11160 Viers Mill Rd. P103
(Wheaton Plaza)
(301)949-6123

VIRGINIA

Arlington
1100 S. Hayes St.
(The Fashion Ctr. at Pentagon City)
(703)413-4590

Glen Allen
10101 Brook Rd. #308
(Virginia Ctr. Commons)
(804)264-2647

Hampton
1800 W. Mercury Blvd. C-9
(Coliseum Mall)
(757)826-5274

Norfolk
300 Monticello Blvd. #103
(MacArthur Ctr.)
(757)623-4445

880 N. Military Hwy. #1121
(Military Circle)
(757)466-7668

Richmond
7201 Midlothian Tpke. E-14
(Cloverleaf)
(804)745-9710

Springfield
6399 Springfield Mall
(Springfield Mall)
(703)922-8623

Virginia Beach
701 Lynnhaven Pkwy. #1080
(Lynnhaven Mall)
(757)463-6164

Woodbridge
2700 Potomac Mills Circle, Ste. 139
(Wearhouse - Unit 975)

00612184

00612184

1420 Wisconsin Ave. NW
(Georgetown)
Washington, DC
(202)337-2265

00612165

00612165

entertainment.com

entertainment.com

entertainment.com

Masters Tuxedo

See reverse side for locations

- Designer tuxedos
- Huge selection
- 14 area locations
- Prom specials
- Visit our website to see our on-line catalog

Bonus Discounts at
entertainment.com

entertainment.
entertainment.com

Up To $25.00 Value

Enjoy 20% off the regular price of any TUXEDO RENTAL.

valid anytime

MASTERS TUXEDO

www.yourtuxedo.com

G47

Valid now thru November 1, 2006

Not valid holidays & subject to Rules of Use. Not valid with other discount offers, unless specified. Coupon VOID if purchased, sold or bartered. Discounts exclude tax, tip and/or alcohol, where applicable.

S & K Men's Stores - Formalwear

See reverse side for locations

- Offering a wide selection of brand name suits, formalwear, sport coats & casual wear
- From contemporary to classic tuxedo styles
- Over 235 locations in 27 states
- Visit us at www.skmenswear.com
- For the store nearest you, call 1-800-644-SUIT

Bonus Discounts at
entertainment.com

entertainment.
entertainment.com

Up To $20.00 Value

Enjoy $10.00 off any BASE TUXEDO RENTAL OF $69.99 OR HIGHER OR $20.00 off any BASE TUXEDO RENTAL OF $89.99 OR HIGHER.

Additional charges for accessories may apply; $10.00 off use code - C078344; $20.00 off use code - C078351

valid anytime

Not valid with any other discounts or promotions

S&K men's stores Demand value.®

www.skmenswear.com

G48

Valid now thru November 1, 2006

Not valid holidays & subject to Rules of Use. Not valid with other discount offers, unless specified. Coupon VOID if purchased, sold or bartered. Discounts exclude tax, tip and/or alcohol, where applicable.

Chariots For Hire

13164 lazy Glen Lane
Oak Hill, VA
(703)481-0496

- The Premier Limousine service in the area
- For reservations call us at (703)481-0496 or 1(866)4-limoos
- Stretch limos for all occasions
- Safe, reliable service

Bonus Discounts at
entertainment.com

entertainment.
entertainment.com

Up To $25.00 Value

Enjoy 20% off any LIMOUSINE RENTAL - maximum discount $25.00.

valid anytime

On availability basis

Chariots For Hire

www.limoos.com

G49

Valid now thru November 1, 2006

Not valid holidays & subject to Rules of Use. Not valid with other discount offers, unless specified. Coupon VOID if purchased, sold or bartered. Discounts exclude tax, tip and/or alcohol, where applicable.

MASTERS TUXEDO

MARYLAND
Annandale
Annandale Tuxedo & Costumes 7008 Columbia Pike
(703)354-7500
Bowers
15415 Emerald Way #D-03
(301)805-9877
Gaithersburg
16514 S. Westland Drive
(301)258-9305
Sterling
Sterling Tuxedo & Costumes
(Countryside Center)
(703)444-2300
Warrenton
Warrenton Tuxedo & Costume 250 W. Lee Highway
(540)341-2700
Woodbridge
Woodbridge Tuxedo & Costume 2924 Prince William Pky.
(Smoketown Stations)
(703)580-8863
VIRGINIA
7713 Sudley Rd.
Manassas Tuxedo & Costumes
(703)369-7100
Arlington
3836 S. Four Mile Run Dr.
(703)845-0111
Arlington Tuxedos & Costumes 3840 S. Four Mile Run Dr.
(703)820-8880
Fair Oaks
Fair Oaks Mall
(703)385-2241
Falls Church
Falls Church Tuxedo 362 W. Broad St.
(703)534-2331
Forestville
Forestville Tuxedo 6611 Marlboro Pike
(301)568-7661
Kensington
10530 Connecticut Ave.
(301)949-4800
Kingstowne
Kingstowne Tuxedo
(703)313-8866
Silver Spring
Sears White Oak Tuxedos 11255 New Hampshire Ave.
(301)681-1705

00532455

entertainment.com

00532455

S&K men's stores
Demand value.®

645 Prime Outlets Blvd.
(Prime Outlets at Hagerstown)
Hagerstown, MD
(301)714-0991

1281 Carl D. Silver Pwy.
(Central Park)
Fredericksburg, VA
(540)786-0738

241 Fort Evans Rd. NE
Suite 1137
(Leesburg Corner Premium Outlets)
Leesburg, VA
(703)669-1943

1150 Stafford Market Place Suite 107
(Stafford Marketplace)
Stafford, VA
(540)720-3175

2700 Potomac Mills Circle #518
(Potomac Mills)
Woodbridge, VA
(703)494-5641

2700 Potomac Mills Circle Suite 840
(Men's Market)
Woodbridge, VA
(703)491-8011

00635412

entertainment.com

00635412

Chariots For Hire

13164 lazy Glen Lane
Oak Hill, VA
(703)481-0496

00566530

entertainment.com

00566530

Dick's Sporting Goods

For a store nearest you call 1-866-819-0038

entertainment.
entertainment.com

great place for kids

$10.00 Value

EVERY SEASON STARTS AT DICK'S SPORTING GOODS.

$10.00 OFF a PURCHASE of $50.00 or more.

valid anytime

See reverse for restrictions

G5

Valid now thru November 1, 2006

Not valid holidays & subject to Rules of Use. Not valid with other discount offers, unless specified. Coupon VOID if purchased, sold or bartered. Discounts exclude tax, tip and/or alcohol, where applicable.

Dick's Sporting Goods

For a store nearest you call 1-866-819-0038

entertainment.
entertainment.com

great place for kids

$15.00 Value

EVERY SEASON STARTS AT DICK'S SPORTING GOODS.

$15.00 OFF a PURCHASE of $75.00 or more.

valid anytime

See reverse for restrictions

G6

Valid now thru November 1, 2006

Not valid holidays & subject to Rules of Use. Not valid with other discount offers, unless specified. Coupon VOID if purchased, sold or bartered. Discounts exclude tax, tip and/or alcohol, where applicable.

Dick's Sporting Goods

For a store nearest you call 1-866-819-0038

entertainment.
entertainment.com

great place for kids

$20.00 Value

EVERY SEASON STARTS AT DICK'S SPORTING GOODS.

$20.00 OFF a PURCHASE of $100.00 or more.

valid anytime

See reverse for restrictions

G7

Valid now thru November 1, 2006

Not valid holidays & subject to Rules of Use. Not valid with other discount offers, unless specified. Coupon VOID if purchased, sold or bartered. Discounts exclude tax, tip and/or alcohol, where applicable.

9 11111 11334 6

Limit one coupon per customer. Total amount of coupon must be redeemed at one time. Cannot be combined with any other offers, coupons or Guaranteed In-Stock markdown, or used for layaways, licenses or previously purchased merchandise. Coupon valid on in-store purchases only. Not redeemable for cash, gift cards or store credit. No reproductions or rainchecks accepted. Excludes all Callaway, Odyssey, Titleist, Cobra and select new release TaylorMade products, firearms, electronics, treadmills, championship merchandise, Levi's, Under Armour, Nike Dri-FIT, Therma-FIT, Sphere and Pro Compression, Merrell footwear, Nike Shox, Impax, Air Zoom Generation, Air Zoom Miler, Jordan and LE shoes, Oakley, Maui Jim, Smith, Ray-Ban, Suunto, Arcteryx, The North Face and Columbia merchandise. Upon redemption, scan barcode and take a group discount markdown. Minimum purchase of $50 before sales tax. Valid through 12/31/06.

00504863

entertainment.com

00504863

9 11111 11295 0

Limit one coupon per customer. Total amount of coupon must be redeemed at one time. Cannot be combined with any other offers, coupons or Guaranteed In-Stock markdown, or used for layaways, licenses or previously purchased merchandise. Coupon valid on in-store purchases only. Not redeemable for cash, gift cards or store credit. No reproductions or rainchecks accepted. Excludes all Callaway, Odyssey, Titleist, Cobra and select new release TaylorMade products, firearms, electronics, treadmills, championship merchandise, Levi's, Under Armour, Nike Dri-FIT, Therma-FIT, Sphere and Pro Compression, Merrell footwear, Nike Shox, Impax, Air Zoom Generation, Air Zoom Miler, Jordan and LE shoes, Oakley, Maui Jim, Smith, Ray-Ban, Suunto, Arcteryx, The North Face and Columbia merchandise. Upon redemption, scan barcode and take a group discount markdown. Minimum purchase of $75 before sales tax. Valid through 12/31/06.

00576747

entertainment.com

00576747

9 11111 11233 2

Limit one coupon per customer. Total amount of coupon must be redeemed at one time. Cannot be combined with any other offers, coupons or Guaranteed In-Stock markdown, or used for layaways, licenses or previously purchased merchandise. Coupon valid on in-store purchases only. Not redeemable for cash, gift cards or store credit. No reproductions or rainchecks accepted. Excludes all Callaway, Odyssey, Titleist, Cobra and select new release TaylorMade products, firearms, electronics, treadmills, championship merchandise, Levi's, Under Armour, Nike Dri-FIT, Therma-FIT, Sphere and Pro Compression, Merrell footwear, Nike Shox, Impax, Air Zoom Generation, Air Zoom Miler, Jordan and LE shoes, Oakley, Maui Jim, Smith, Ray-Ban, Suunto, Arcteryx, The North Face and Columbia merchandise. Upon redemption, scan barcode and take a group discount markdown. Minimum purchase of $100 before sales tax. Valid through 12/31/06.

00576749

entertainment.com

00576749

Party Land

Valid at All Participating Locations

- One of the largest party supply store chains
- Carrying a full line of party supplies for anniversaries, weddings, bridal & baby showers, sweet sixteens & birthdays
- Largest selection of children's party supplies & accessories

Bonus Discounts at entertainment.com

entertainment.
entertainment.com

$2.00 Value

PARTY LAND

Enjoy $2.00 off a purchase of $10.00 or more.

Balloons & balloon decorations excluded

valid anytime

Limit one offer per person; Please present coupon/card at time of purchase; Cannot be combined with any other offer

www.partyland.com G50

Valid now thru November 1, 2006

Not valid holidays & subject to Rules of Use. Not valid with other discount offers, unless specified. Coupon VOID if purchased, sold or bartered. Discounts exclude tax, tip and/or alcohol, where applicable.

Party Land

Valid at All Participating Locations

- One of the largest party supply store chains
- Carrying a full line of party supplies for anniversaries, weddings, bridal & baby showers, sweet sixteens & birthdays
- Largest selection of children's party supplies & accessories

Bonus Discounts at entertainment.com

entertainment.
entertainment.com

$5.00 Value

PARTY LAND

Enjoy $5.00 off a purchase of $25.00 or more.

Balloons & balloon decorations excluded

valid anytime

Limit one offer per person; Please present coupon/card at time of purchase; Cannot be combined with any other offer

www.partyland.com G51

Valid now thru November 1, 2006

Not valid holidays & subject to Rules of Use. Not valid with other discount offers, unless specified. Coupon VOID if purchased, sold or bartered. Discounts exclude tax, tip and/or alcohol, where applicable.

Party Land

Valid at All Participating Locations

- One of the largest party supply store chains
- Carrying a full line of party supplies for anniversaries, weddings, bridal & baby showers, sweet sixteens & birthdays
- Largest selection of children's party supplies & accessories

Bonus Discounts at entertainment.com

entertainment.
entertainment.com

Up To $10.00 Value

PARTY LAND

Enjoy $10.00 off a purchase of $50.00 or more.

Balloons & balloon decorations excluded

valid anytime

Limit one offer per person; Please present coupon/card at time of purchase; Cannot be combined with any other offer

www.partyland.com G52

Valid now thru November 1, 2006

Not valid holidays & subject to Rules of Use. Not valid with other discount offers, unless specified. Coupon VOID if purchased, sold or bartered. Discounts exclude tax, tip and/or alcohol, where applicable.

PARTY LAND

Valid at All Participating Locations

00083855

entertainment.com

00083855

PARTY LAND

Valid at All Participating Locations

00584699

entertainment.com

00584699

PARTY LAND

Valid at All Participating Locations

00584736

entertainment.com

00584736

The Red Apple

2922 Chain Bridge Rd.
Oakton, VA
(703)281-1701

- Featuring clothing for boys & girls newborn to size 20
- Seasonal items available

Bonus Discounts at
entertainment.com

entertainment
entertainment.com

Up To $25.00 Value

Enjoy 20% off the regular price of any PURCHASE (sale items excluded) - maximum discount $25.00.

valid anytime

Sale items excluded

the red apple
Clothing for Boys and Girls

www.redapple1.com

G53

Valid now thru November 1, 2006

Not valid holidays & subject to Rules of Use. Not valid with other discount offers, unless specified. Coupon VOID if purchased, sold or bartered. Discounts exclude tax, tip and/or alcohol, where applicable.

The Bike Lane

9544 Old Keene Mill Rd.
Burke, VA
(703)440-8701

- Committed to finding the right bike for every adult & child
- Come in & check out all our great bikes & accessories
- Open Mon.-Fri. 10 a.m.-8 p.m., Sat. 10 a.m.-6 p.m. & Sun. 12 noon-5 p.m.
- For more info - check out our web site

Bonus Discounts at
entertainment.com

entertainment
entertainment.com

great place for kids

Up To $25.00 Value

Enjoy 20% off the regular price of any PURCHASE (sale items excluded) - maximum discount $25.00.

valid anytime

Sale items excluded

The Bike Lane
your neighborhood bike shop

www.thebikelane.com

G54

Valid now thru November 1, 2006

Not valid holidays & subject to Rules of Use. Not valid with other discount offers, unless specified. Coupon VOID if purchased, sold or bartered. Discounts exclude tax, tip and/or alcohol, where applicable.

Spokes Etc. Bicycles

See reverse side for locations

- Voted Washingtonian Magazines "Best Bike Shop" in the DC area
- Area's best selection of bikes, parts & accessories
- The friendliest & most knowledgeable sales & service staffs
- Open Mon.-Fri. 11 a.m.-8 p.m., Sat. 10 a.m.-6 p.m. & Sun. Noon-5 p.m.

Bonus Discounts at
entertainment.com

entertainment
entertainment.com

great place for kids

Up To $25.00 Value

Enjoy 20% off the regular price of any PURCHASE (sale items excluded) - maximum discount $25.00.

valid anytime

Spokes Etc. BICYCLES ®
Best Wheels Goin' Around

www.spokesetc.com

G55

Valid now thru November 1, 2006

Not valid holidays & subject to Rules of Use. Not valid with other discount offers, unless specified. Coupon VOID if purchased, sold or bartered. Discounts exclude tax, tip and/or alcohol, where applicable.

the red apple
Clothing for Boys and Girls

2922 Chain Bridge Rd.
(Oakton Shopping Center)
Oakton, VA
(703)281-1701

00574614

entertainment.com

00574614

The Bike Lane
your neighborhood bike shop

9544 Old Keene Mill Rd.
(Burke Town Plaza)
Burke, VA
(703)440-8701

00528061

entertainment.com

00528061

Spokes Etc.
BICYCLES ®
Best Wheels Goin' Around

1506 Belle View Blvd.
Alexandria, VA
(703)765-8005

1545 N. Quaker Lane
Alexandria, VA
(703)820-2200

224 E. Maple Ave.
Vienna, VA
(703)281-2004

00570412

entertainment.com

00570412

Capital Soccer

6230 I Rolling Rd.
Springfield, VA
(703)866-4625

- A premier soccer specialty store
- Featuring all major brands
- Closed Sunday

entertainment. entertainment.com

great place for kids

Up To $25.00 Value

CAPITAL SOCCER

Enjoy 20% off the regular price of any PURCHASE (sale items excluded) - maximum discount $25.00.

valid anytime

sale items excluded

G56

Valid now thru November 1, 2006

Not valid holidays & subject to Rules of Use. Not valid with other discount offers, unless specified. Coupon VOID if purchased, sold or bartered. Discounts exclude tax, tip and/or alcohol, where applicable.

Soccer Plus

6230 I Rolling Rd.
Springfield, VA
(703)866-4625

- Largest selection of soccer shoes in Virginia
- Everything a soccer & field hockey player needs to have fun
- Visit our website for directions, hours of operation & upcoming store promotions & sales

Bonus Discounts at entertainment.com

entertainment. entertainment.com

great place for kids

Up To $25.00 Value

SOCCER PLUS
LARGEST SELECTION OF SOCCER SHOES IN VIRGINIA
FIELD HOCKEY

Enjoy 20% off the regular price of any PURCHASE (sale items excluded) - maximum discount $25.00.

valid anytime

www.soccerplusfieldhockey.com

G57

Valid now thru November 1, 2006

Not valid holidays & subject to Rules of Use. Not valid with other discount offers, unless specified. Coupon VOID if purchased, sold or bartered. Discounts exclude tax, tip and/or alcohol, where applicable.

Play It Again Sports

5750 Union Mill Rd.
Clifton, VA
(703)266-8677

- We buy, sell, trade & consign used & new sports equipment
- Play it smart, Play it Again Sports
- Locally owned & operated

Bonus Discounts at entertainment.com

entertainment. entertainment.com

great place for kids

Up To $25.00 Value

PLAY IT AGAIN SPORTS®

Enjoy 20% off the regular price of any PURCHASE (sale items excluded) - maximum discount $25.00.

valid anytime

www.playitagainsports.com

G58

Valid now thru November 1, 2006

Not valid holidays & subject to Rules of Use. Not valid with other discount offers, unless specified. Coupon VOID if purchased, sold or bartered. Discounts exclude tax, tip and/or alcohol, where applicable.

CAPITAL SOCCER

6230 I Rolling Rd.
(West Springfield Ctr.)
Springfield, VA
(703)866-4625

00579679

entertainment.com

00579679

SOCCER PLUS

LARGEST SELECTION OF SOCCER SHOES IN VIRGINIA FIELD HOCKEY

6230 I Rolling Rd.
Springfield, VA
(703)866-4625

00634740

entertainment.com

00634740

PLAY IT AGAIN SPORTS®

5750 Union Mill Rd.
(The Colonnade at Union Mill)
Clifton, VA
(703)266-8677

00618597

entertainment.com

00618597

The Cellular Phone Store

See reverse side for locations

entertainment.

entertainment.com

Up To $25.00 Value

Enjoy 20% off the regular price of any PURCHASE (sale items excluded) - maximum discount $25.00.

valid anytime

G59

Valid now thru November 1, 2006

Not valid holidays & subject to Rules of Use. Not valid with other discount offers, unless specified. Coupon VOID if purchased, sold or bartered. Discounts exclude tax, tip and/or alcohol, where applicable.

Wireless Jungle

See reverse side for locations

- Cell phones, Pagers & Satellite Systems
- Join the King of the Jungle
- Northern Virginia's largest wireless provider
- Sales, service & repairs available
- When you're hooked up with the jungle...you're covered for life

entertainment.

entertainment.com

Up To $25.00 Value

Enjoy 20% off the regular price of any PURCHASE (sale items excluded) - maximum discount $25.00.

valid anytime

www.wirelessjungleonline.com

G60

Valid now thru November 1, 2006

Not valid holidays & subject to Rules of Use. Not valid with other discount offers, unless specified. Coupon VOID if purchased, sold or bartered. Discounts exclude tax, tip and/or alcohol, where applicable.

Jungle Tan

11199 B Lee Hwy
Fairfax, VA
(703)383-0422

- Come tan in the jungle
- All types of packages available
- Open daily

entertainment.

entertainment.com

Up To $25.00 Value

Enjoy 20% off any Salon or Spa services - maximum discount $25.00.

valid anytime

G61

Valid now thru November 1, 2006

Not valid holidays & subject to Rules of Use. Not valid with other discount offers, unless specified. Coupon VOID if purchased, sold or bartered. Discounts exclude tax, tip and/or alcohol, where applicable.

THE CELLULAR PHONE STORE

247 S. Van Dorn St.
Alexandria, VA
(703)778-1888

5890 Kingstowne Ctr.,
Ste. 120
Alexandria, VA
(703)313-7599

9526 Liberia Ave.
Manassas, VA
(703)777-1212

4483 Cheshire Station
Plaza
Woodbridge, VA
(703)730-5959

Valid at Future
Locations

00607631

entertainment.com

00607631

Wireless Jungle

dish NETWORK

cingular WIRELESS

13848-A Lee Hwy
Centreville, VA
(703)830-1889

11199-B Lee Hwy
Fairfax, VA
(703)383-0023

8128 Sudley Rd
Manassas, VA
(703)335-8797

181 W. Lee Hwy
Warrenton, VA
(540)341-8700

00510112

entertainment.com

00510112

JUNGLE TAN

11199 B Lee Hwy
Fairfax, VA
(703)383-0422

00557712

entertainment.com

00557712

Hollywood Tans

Valid at All Participating Locations

- The Worlds best UV Free 6 second tan

Bonus Discounts at entertainment.com

entertainment.com

Up To $25.00 Value

Enjoy 20% off any Tanning Package - maximum discount $25.00.

valid anytime

HOLLYWOOD TANS
TANNING SALON

www.hollywoodtans.com

G62

Valid now thru November 1, 2006

Not valid holidays & subject to Rules of Use. Not valid with other discount offers, unless specified. Coupon VOID if purchased, sold or bartered. Discounts exclude tax, tip and/or alcohol, where applicable.

Sun Splash Mega Tan

See reverse side for locations

- The Region's Premier Tanning Salons
- The most distinguishing & innovating thing about us is the effectiveness of the many types of tanning systems we feature
- Offering the latest "Mystic-Tan" sunless tanning in a matter of seconds - Centreville & Herndon

Bonus Discounts at entertainment.com

entertainment.com

Up To $25.00 Value

Enjoy 20% off the regular price of any SALON and/or SPA SERVICES - maximum discount $25.00.

valid anytime

Sun Splash Mega Tàn

www.sunsplashmegatan.com

G63

Valid now thru November 1, 2006

Not valid holidays & subject to Rules of Use. Not valid with other discount offers, unless specified. Coupon VOID if purchased, sold or bartered. Discounts exclude tax, tip and/or alcohol, where applicable.

Elany Image Salon & Day Spa

**8091 F & G Alban Rd.
Springfield, VA
(703)440-8073**

- Feel the need to be pampered, rejuvenate your body, revitalize your mind
- On beauty, health & image - we are committed to excellence
- We have hair designs, skin care, massage, body treatment, manicures & pedicures & more
- Call us today

Bonus Discounts at entertainment.com

entertainment.com

Up To $25.00 Value

Enjoy 20% off the regular price of any SALON and/or SPA SERVICES - maximum discount $25.00.

valid anytime

Elany Image
Salon & Day Spa

elanyimage.com

G64

Valid now thru November 1, 2006

Not valid holidays & subject to Rules of Use. Not valid with other discount offers, unless specified. Coupon VOID if purchased, sold or bartered. Discounts exclude tax, tip and/or alcohol, where applicable.

Fashion Time, The Time Store

See reverse side for locations

entertainment® entertainment.com

Up To $100.00 Value

Enjoy 20% off the regular price of any PURCHASE (sale items excluded) - maximum discount $100.00.

valid anytime

FASHION TIME®
The Time Store

G65

Valid now thru November 1, 2006

Not valid holidays & subject to Rules of Use. Not valid with other discount offers, unless specified. Coupon VOID if purchased, sold or bartered. Discounts exclude tax, tip and/or alcohol, where applicable.

Fast-Fix Jewelry & Watch Repairs

Valid at Participating Locations

- The only nationwide chain of stores devoted to while-you-watch jewelry & watch repairs!
- Ring Sizing, mountings, watch repairs, chain repairs & more!

entertainment® entertainment.com

Up To $25.00 Value

Enjoy 20% off the regular price of any SERVICES OR REPAIRS - maximum discount $25.00.

valid anytime

Valid at participating locations; Each Fast-Fix Jewelry & Watch Repairs location is independently owned & operated

FAST-FIX JEWELRY AND WATCH REPAIRS®
www.fastfix.com

G66

Valid now thru November 1, 2006

Not valid holidays & subject to Rules of Use. Not valid with other discount offers, unless specified. Coupon VOID if purchased, sold or bartered. Discounts exclude tax, tip and/or alcohol, where applicable.

All Around Art

See reverse side for locations

entertainment® entertainment.com

Up To $25.00 Value

Enjoy 20% off the regular price of any PURCHASE (sale items excluded) - maximum discount $25.00.

Some original & limited edition pieces may be excluded

valid anytime

Not valid with any other discount offer

ALL AROUND ART

G67

Valid now thru November 1, 2006

Not valid holidays & subject to Rules of Use. Not valid with other discount offers, unless specified. Coupon VOID if purchased, sold or bartered. Discounts exclude tax, tip and/or alcohol, where applicable.

FASHION TIME®

The Time Store

DISTRICT OF COLUMBIA
Washington
Ronald Regan National Airport
(next to United Airlines terminal)
(703)417-0610

MARYLAND
Annapolis
Annopolis Mall
(Food Court entrance, next to American Eagle)
(410)266-5404

Bethesda
Montgomery Mall
(next to Bebe)
(301)767-0026

Columbia
Mall in Columbia
(Hecht's wing, 2nd floor)
(410)715-9150

Gaithersburg
Lakeforest Mall
(301)330-0016

Glen Burnie
Marley Station
(410)766-2644

Hanover
Arundel Mills
(Neighborhood 2)
(410)799-8003

Waldorf
St. Charles Town Ctr.
(next to American Cafe)
(301)705-8161

VIRGINIA
Arlington
Fashion Ctr. at Pentagon City
(next to Kenneth Cole)
(703)415-2266

Charlottesville
Charlottesville Fashion Square
(center of the mall, near Kay Jewelry)
(434)974-5500

Chesapeake
Chesapeake Square
(near Food Court, center of mall)
(757)405-6074

Dulles
Dulles Town Ctr.
(next to Lord & Taylor, 2nd floor)
(571)434-8875

Glen Allen
Virginia Ctr. Commons
(near the Food Court)
(804)261-3894

Harrisonburg
Valley Mall
(center of the mall)
(540)433-2112

Manassas
Manassas Mall
(near Sam Goodies)
(703)369-7446

McLean
Tysons Corner Ctr.
(next to Bloomingdale's, 2nd level)
(703)893-9005

Norfolk
MacArthur Mall
(757)616-0777

Spotsylvania
Spotsylvania Mall
(next to Kay Jewelry)
(540)785-5921

Springfield
Springfield Mall
(entrance #1 next to JC Penney & American Cafe)
(703)922-8859

Winchester
Apple Blossom Mall
(near Gadzooks)
(540)535-9072

Woodbridge
Potomac Mills Mall I
(Neighborhood 8)
(703)491-0709

Potomac Mills Mall II
(Neighborhood 1)
(703)490-1556

Potomac Mills Mall III
(Neighborhood 3)
(703)490-5682

For Location Nearest You, Call 800-285-9571

00617987

entertainment.com

00617987

FAST-FIX
JEWELRY AND WATCH REPAIRS®

Valid at Participating Locations

00656196

entertainment.com

00656196

ALL AROUND ART

3620 King St.
Alexandria, VA
(703)379-9800

454-A S. Pickett St.
Alexandria, VA
(703)370-2170

3102 Columbia Pike.
Arlington, VA
(703)521-2496

5723-B Lee Hwy.
Arlington, VA
(703)237-2170

10623 Braddock Rd.
Fairfax, VA
(703)278-8900

2599-A John Milton Dr.
Herndon, VA
(703)390-9120

00584378

entertainment.com

00584378

T.G.S. Children's Shoes

9564 Old Keene Mill Rd.
Burke, VA
(703)451-3069

- For more than 80 years, Stride Rite has been committed to designing & developing the finest shoes available for growing children
- Stride Rite offers style-smart, trend-savvy products that kids love to wear with features parents want from the brand they trust

Bonus Discounts at entertainment.com

entertainment. entertainment.com

great place for kids

Up To $25.00 Value

T.G.S. Children's Shoes

stride rite® Life's waiting. Let's go.

Enjoy 20% off the regular price of any PURCHASE (sale items excluded) - maximum discount $25.00.

valid anytime

G68

Valid now thru November 1, 2006

Not valid holidays & subject to Rules of Use. Not valid with other discount offers, unless specified. Coupon VOID if purchased, sold or bartered. Discounts exclude tax, tip and/or alcohol, where applicable.

Pro-Tek Our Kids

12164 Darnley Rd.
Lake Ridge, Va
(866)227-6686 Ext. 7274

- Purchase includes a 2 year video & photo registration for your child
- We provide the only missing child prevention program
- An investment in your peace of mind
- Call us today for more details

Bonus Discounts at entertainment.com

entertainment. entertainment.com

great place for kids

Up To $25.00 Value

Enjoy 20% off the regular price of any PURCHASE (sale items excluded) - maximum discount $25.00.

valid anytime

Pro-Tek Our Kids

A *Child Shield, U.S.A.* ™ Registered Agent

G69

Valid now thru November 1, 2006

Not valid holidays & subject to Rules of Use. Not valid with other discount offers, unless specified. Coupon VOID if purchased, sold or bartered. Discounts exclude tax, tip and/or alcohol, where applicable.

Game Crazy

See reverse side for locations

- The ultimate neighborhood gaming store
- World's largest selection of new, used & classic games & consoles
- Play ANY game before you buy
- Get more for your trade - GUARANTEED
- Always 12 FREE rentals at Hollywood Video ($72.00 value) with a new or used console purchase

Bonus Discounts at entertainment.com

entertainment. entertainment.com

Up To $25.00 Value

Enjoy 20% off the regular price of ANY USED GAME purchase - maximum discount $25.00.

valid anytime

game crazy

G70

Valid now thru November 1, 2006

Not valid holidays & subject to Rules of Use. Not valid with other discount offers, unless specified. Coupon VOID if purchased, sold or bartered. Discounts exclude tax, tip and/or alcohol, where applicable.

T.G.S. Children's Shoes

stride rite®

Life's waiting. Let's go.

9564 Old Keene Mill Rd.
Burke, VA
(703)451-3069

00637294

entertainment.com

00637294

Pro-Tek Our Kids

A *Child Shield, U.S.A.* ™ Registered Agent

12164 Darnley Rd. Lake Ridge, Va (866)227-6686 Ext. 7274

00579470

entertainment.com

00579470

game crazy

Valid at All Participating Locations

Log on to www.gamecrazy.com for store locations, tournaments, news, chat and more

Game Crazy is located at select Hollywood Video stores

00400430

entertainment.com

00400430

Discount Driving Clinic

See reverse side for locations

- Classroom or internet courses available
- Fast, fun & easy
- Valid for point count reduction & insurance discount
- Approved by Virginia DMV

Bonus Discounts at entertainment.com

entertainment. entertainment.com

Up To $25.00 Value

Enjoy 20% off the regular price of any PURCHASE (sale items excluded) - maximum discount $25.00.

INTERNET COURSES EXCLUDED

valid anytime

NOT VALID WITH ANY OTHER DISCOUNTS OR PROMOTIONS

Discount Driving Clinic

www.discountdrivingclinic.com

G71

Valid now thru November 1, 2006

Not valid holidays & subject to Rules of Use. Not valid with other discount offers, unless specified. Coupon VOID if purchased, sold or bartered. Discounts exclude tax, tip and/or alcohol, where applicable.

Ukrop's

See reverse side for locations

- Visit us at ukrops.com to find the Ukrop's nearest you & a listing of store features
- Full-service Ukrop's Pharmacy
- First Market Bank
- Photofinishing
- Dry Cleaning
- Full-service Floral Department
- US Mail & UPS services
- Grill & Cafe
- Ukrop's Helpline 1-800-868-2270
- Carryout Catering 1-888-793-3663

Bonus Discounts at entertainment.com

entertainment. entertainment.com

$5.00 Value

Enjoy $5.00 off a PRESCRIPTION TRANSFERRED to UKROP'S PHARMACY.

valid anytime

Not valid on prescriptions transferred from other Ukrop's Pharmacy locations. To redeem, present coupon with your Valued Customer Card. Valid anytime. One coupon per customer per visit. Valid at Ukrop's Pharmacy locations.

PLU #1154

Ukrop's™

www.ukrops.com

G72

Valid now thru November 1, 2006

Not valid holidays & subject to Rules of Use. Not valid with other discount offers, unless specified. Coupon VOID if purchased, sold or bartered. Discounts exclude tax, tip and/or alcohol, where applicable.

Pittsburgh Paints

Valid at All Participating Locations

- We earn our stripes everyday
- Visit www.pittsburghpaints.com for locations near you

Bonus Discounts at entertainment.com

entertainment. entertainment.com

$5.00 Value

Enjoy $5 off any PURCHASE of $25 or more.

valid anytime

Sale items excluded; Offer applies to retail pricing only

PITTSBURGH PAINTS

www.pittsburghpaints.com

G73

Valid now thru November 1, 2006

Not valid holidays & subject to Rules of Use. Not valid with other discount offers, unless specified. Coupon VOID if purchased, sold or bartered. Discounts exclude tax, tip and/or alcohol, where applicable.

Discount Driving Clinic

For Classroom Call (800)252-6551 www.discountdrivingclinic.com

00528985

entertainment.com

00528985

Ukrop's

Ashland
253 N. Washington Hwy.

Colonial Heights
3107-15 Boulevard

Fredericksburg
4250 Plank Rd.

Glen Allen
10150 Brook Rd.

10250 Staples Mill Rd.

9645 W. Broad St.

Mechanicsville
7324 Bell Creek Rd. S.

Midlothian
1220 Sycamore Sq.

13700 Hull Street Rd.

Petersburg
3330 S. Crater Rd.

Richmond
11361 Midlothian Tpke.

2250 John Rolfe Pkwy.

3000 Stony Point Rd.

3460 Pump Rd.

4346 S. Laburnum Ave.

500 N. Harrison St.

5201 Chippenham Crossing Ctr.

5700 Brook Rd.

7045 Forest Hill Ave.

7803 Midlothian Tpke.

9600 Patterson Ave.

Williamsburg
4660 Monticello Ave.

00663639

entertainment.com

00663639

PITTSBURGH PAINTS

Valid at All Participating Locations

00662029

entertainment.com

00662029

Made By You

See reverse side for locations

- Let your creativity soar
- You pick the piece, you design it & we'll glaze & fire it
- No studio fees
- Ceramic, glass, terracotta painting, work shops, parties & special events
- Open daily

Bonus Discounts at entertainment.com

entertainment. entertainment.com

great place for kids

Up To $25.00 Value

MADE BY YOU™

Enjoy 20% off the regular price of any PURCHASE (sale items excluded) - maximum discount $25.00.

valid anytime

Not valid with any other discount offer or gift certificate

G74

Valid now thru November 1, 2006

Not valid holidays & subject to Rules of Use. Not valid with other discount offers, unless specified. Coupon VOID if purchased, sold or bartered. Discounts exclude tax, tip and/or alcohol, where applicable.

Self Storage Plus

See reverse side for locations

- Resident managers
- 24 hour security
- Month to month lease
- Climate controlled storage spaces
- Full line of boxes & packaging supplies
- Open daily

Bonus Discounts at entertainment.com

entertainment. entertainment.com

50% OFF

SELF STORAGE PLUS

Enjoy YOUR FIRST MONTH OF STORAGE at 50% off the regular price.

valid anytime

Subject to availability & May be limited to selected sizes; Subject to customer's execution of standard rental agreement; Requires purchase of 2nd month rental at lease signing; Not valid with any other discounts or promotions

www.selfstorageplus.com

G75

Valid now thru November 1, 2006

Not valid holidays & subject to Rules of Use. Not valid with other discount offers, unless specified. Coupon VOID if purchased, sold or bartered. Discounts exclude tax, tip and/or alcohol, where applicable.

Alexandria Black History Museum

902 Wythe St.
Alexandria, VA
(703)838-4356

- Enriching the lives of Alexandria's residents & visitors
- Housed in the Robert H. Robinson Library
- Open Tues.-Sat. 10 a.m.-4 p.m.; Sun. 1 p.m.-5 p.m.

Bonus Discounts at entertainment.com

entertainment. entertainment.com

Up To $25.00 Value

ALEXANDRIA BLACK HISTORY MUSEUM

Enjoy 20% off the regular price of any PURCHASE (sale items excluded) - maximum discount $25.00.

valid anytime

www.alexblackhistory.org

G76

Valid now thru November 1, 2006

Not valid holidays & subject to Rules of Use. Not valid with other discount offers, unless specified. Coupon VOID if purchased, sold or bartered. Discounts exclude tax, tip and/or alcohol, where applicable.

MADE BY YOU™

3413 Connecticut
Cleveland Park, DC
(202)363-9590

4923 Elm St.
Bethesda, MD
(301)654-3206

209 N. Washington St.
Rockville, MD
(301)610-5496

2319 Wilson Blvd.
Arlington, VA
(703)841-3533

00404607

entertainment.com

00404607

SELF STORAGE PLUS

MARYLAND
Annapolis
2005 Trout Rd.
(410)266-6100

Baltimore
1100 Interstate Ave.
(410)633-7111

3634 Falls Rd.
(410)662-6464

9810 Pulaski Hwy.
(410)686-8494

Bel Air
423A N. Main St.
(410)638-5001

Cockeysville
11150 York Rd.
(410)771-1211

Edgewood
1306 Pulaski Hwy.
(410)676-4474

Elkridge
7025 Kit Kat Rd.
(410)799-5400

Gaithersburg
18830 Woodfield Rd.
(301)963-7500

501 East Diamond Ave.
(240)632-0062

Gambrills
790 Maryland Route 3 South
(410)923-2392

Glen Burnie
7519 Solley Rd.
(410)360-8834

Lanham
10108 Greenbelt Rd.
(301)794-8440

Laurel
9515 Lynn Buff Ct.
(301)470-1430

Rockville
14690 Southlawn Lane
(301)610-0009

851 E. Gude Dr.
(301)762-1956

Silver Spring
11105 New Hampshire Ave.
(301)754-2105

Timonium
16 W. Aylesbury Rd.
(410)561-1049

VIRGINIA
Alexandria
2520 Oakville St.
(703)548-3311

35 S. Dove St.
(703)836-0656

4650 Eisenhower Ave.
(703)751-8100

Arlington
605 South Ball St.
(703)413-4833

Fairfax
3179 Draper Dr.
(703)352-7795

Fredericksburg
21 Commerce Pkwy.
(540)371-3355

Leesburg
847 Trailview Blvd., SE
(703)777-8211

Vienna
300 Mill St., NE
(703)255-0185

00455600

entertainment.com

00455600

ALEXANDRIA BLACK HISTORY MUSEUM

902 Wythe St.
Alexandria, VA
(703)838-4356

00656725

entertainment.com

00656725

entertainment.

Magruder's

Washington's Original Quality Grocer
Serving the Community since 1875

Party Trays & Fruit Baskets for All Occasions

The Freshest Produce at Low-Low Prices
Local Produce available in season

Certified Angus Beef at the Lowest Prices

Visit out Wine & Beer Shoppe at our
Gaithersburg, DC and Virginia Stores

www.magruders.com

See Reverse Side For Locations

Enjoy $5.00 OFF any PURCHASE of $50 or more - maximum discount $5.00.

(One coupon per month for 12 months) (Cigarettes, alcohol & lottery excluded)

Enjoy $5.00 OFF any PURCHASE of $50 or more - maximum discount $5.00. valid May 2006 PLU #985 (see reverse side) Magruder's	Enjoy $5.00 OFF any PURCHASE of $50 or more - maximum discount $5.00. valid Nov. 2005 PLU #985 (see reverse side) Magruder's
Enjoy $5.00 OFF any PURCHASE of $50 or more - maximum discount $5.00. valid June 2006 PLU #985 (see reverse side) Magruder's	Enjoy $5.00 OFF any PURCHASE of $50 or more - maximum discount $5.00. valid Dec. 2005 PLU #985 (see reverse side) Magruder's
Enjoy $5.00 OFF any PURCHASE of $50 or more - maximum discount $5.00. valid July 2006 PLU #985 (see reverse side) Magruder's	Enjoy $5.00 OFF any PURCHASE of $50 or more - maximum discount $5.00. valid Jan. 2006 PLU #985 (see reverse side) Magruder's
Enjoy $5.00 OFF any PURCHASE of $50 or more - maximum discount $5.00. valid Aug. 2006 PLU #985 (see reverse side) Magruder's	Enjoy $5.00 OFF any PURCHASE of $50 or more - maximum discount $5.00. valid Feb. 2006 PLU #985 (see reverse side) Magruder's
Enjoy $5.00 OFF any PURCHASE of $50 or more - maximum discount $5.00. valid Sept. 2006 PLU #985 (see reverse side) Magruder's	Enjoy $5.00 OFF any PURCHASE of $50 or more - maximum discount $5.00. valid March 2006 PLU #985 (see reverse side) Magruder's
Enjoy $5.00 OFF any PURCHASE of $50 or more - maximum discount $5.00. valid Oct. 2006 PLU #985 (see reverse side) Magruder's	Enjoy $5.00 OFF any PURCHASE of $50 or more - maximum discount $5.00. valid April 2006 PLU #985 (see reverse side) Magruder's

entertainment.
One coupon per month for 12 months; Cigarettes, alcohol & lottery excluded; PLU #985

entertainment.
One coupon per month for 12 months; Cigarettes, alcohol & lottery excluded; PLU #985

entertainment.
One coupon per month for 12 months; Cigarettes, alcohol & lottery excluded; PLU #985

entertainment.
One coupon per month for 12 months; Cigarettes, alcohol & lottery excluded; PLU #985

entertainment.
One coupon per month for 12 months; Cigarettes, alcohol & lottery excluded; PLU #985

entertainment.
One coupon per month for 12 months; Cigarettes, alcohol & lottery excluded; PLU #985

entertainment.
One coupon per month for 12 months; Cigarettes, alcohol & lottery excluded; PLU #985

entertainment.
One coupon per month for 12 months; Cigarettes, alcohol & lottery excluded; PLU #985

entertainment.
One coupon per month for 12 months; Cigarettes, alcohol & lottery excluded; PLU #985

entertainment.
One coupon per month for 12 months; Cigarettes, alcohol & lottery excluded; PLU #985

entertainment.
One coupon per month for 12 months; Cigarettes, alcohol & lottery excluded; PLU #985

entertainment.
One coupon per month for 12 months; Cigarettes, alcohol & lottery excluded; PLU #985

DISTRICT OF COLUMBIA
Washington
3527 Connecticut Ave. N.W.
(202)237-2561

5618 Connecticutt Ave. N.W.

5626 Connecticut Ave. N.W.
(202)244-7800

MARYLAND
Bowie
6810 Racetrack Rd.
(301)262-8229

Gaithersburg
602 A Quince Orchard Rd.
(301)948-2165

Rockville
15108 Frederick Rd.
(College Plaza)
(301)315-0703

981 Rollins Ave.
(301)230-3000

VIRGINIA
Alexandria
4604 Kenmore Ave.

Annandale
7010 Columbia Pike
(703)941-8864

Falls Church
2800 Graham Rd.
(703)280-0440

Vienna
180 Maple Ave. W.
(703)938-4700

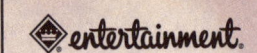

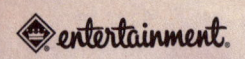

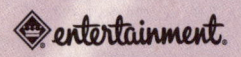

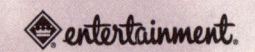

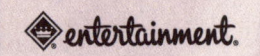

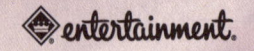

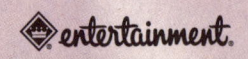

entertainment®

The Well-Oiled Machine®

Jiffy Lube
Signature Service® Oil Change

59 Washington, DC Area Locations
(see reverse side for locations)

Each Jiffy Lube Signature Service® Oil Change includes:

up to 5 quarts of quality motor oil & a new oil filter

Exterior window wash

Interior vacuum

Tire pressure check

Window washer fill up

Check all fluid levels (where applicable)

www.jiffylube.com

The Well-Oiled Machine®

Enjoy $4.00 off any JIFFY LUBE® SIGNATURE SERVICE® OIL CHANGE.

see reverse side
offer expires 11/1/06
Code # E0106

Participating Washington Area Jiffy Lube

The Well-Oiled Machine®

Enjoy $4.00 off any JIFFY LUBE® SIGNATURE SERVICE® OIL CHANGE.

see reverse side
offer expires 11/1/06
Code # E0206

Participating Washington Area Jiffy Lube

The Well-Oiled Machine®

Enjoy $4.00 off any JIFFY LUBE® RADIATOR SERVICE.

see reverse side
offer expires 11/1/06
Code # FR506

Participating Washington Area Jiffy Lube

The Well-Oiled Machine®

Enjoy $5.00 off any JIFFY LUBE® FUEL SERVICE.

see reverse side
offer expires 11/1/06
Code # EF506

Participating Washington Area Jiffy Lube

entertainment.

Valid only at participating stores; Cash value $1/100; Must present coupon at time of service; Not valid with any other offer

entertainment.

Valid only at participating stores; Cash value $1/100; Must present coupon at time of service; Not valid with any other offer

entertainment.

Valid only at participating stores; Cash value $1/100; Must present coupon at time of service; Not valid with any other offer

entertainment.

Valid only at participating stores; Cash value $1/100; Must present coupon at time of service; Not valid with any other offer

MARYLAND

Beltsville
10537 Baltimore Blvd.
(301)595-5823

Bethesda
7103 Democracy Blvd.
(301)469-5154

Bladensburg
4307 Bladensburg Rd.
(301)864-7773

Bowie
2325 N.W.. Crain Hwy.
(301)218-1222

Capitol Heights
31 Hampton Park Blvd.
(301)350-7879

Clinton
6415 Coventry Way
(Rt. 5 & Coventry Way)
(301)856-1432

College Park
8808 Baltimore Blvd.
(301)982-2999

Forestville
5917 Silver Hill Rd.
(301)736-5823

Frederick
1210 W. Patrick St.
(301)663-6666

5500 Buckeystown Pike
(Francis Scott Key Mall)
(301)682-5566

Gaithersburg
116 N. Frederick Ave.
(301)330-4090

8031-H Snouffer School Rd.
(301)990-9600

Germantown
19520 Walter Johnson Dr.
(301)916-9400

Kensington
3825-C DuPont Ave.
(301)942-8600

Lanham
7571 Annapolis Rd.
(301)456-8886

Laurel
13559 Baltimore Ave.
(301)210-5823

301 Second St.
(Rt. 1 & Montgomery St.)
(301)498-5823

Lexington Park
21540 Great Mills Rd.
(301)863-0077

Oxon Hill
5518 St. Barnabas Rd.
(301)630-7308

Rockville
15121 Frederick Rd.
(301)762-8777

5535 Nicholson Ln.
(301)984-8880

806 Rockville Pike
(301)424-9531

Silver Spring
11259 New Hampshire Ave.
(White Oak Shopping Ctr. in Sears)
(301)681-5207

3251 Automobile Blvd.
(301)890-8487

Takoma Park
6510 New Hampshire Ave.
(301)270-4900

Waldorf
3160 Crain Hwy.
(301)843-5823

VIRGINIA

Alexandria
2912 Duke St.
(703)823-5823

2950 Southgate Dr.
(703)768-2023

511 S. Van Dorn St.
(703)370-8987

6001 Duke St.
(703)941-4250

Annandale
4301 Backlick Rd.
(703)941-5365

Arlington
4148-B S. Four Mile Run Dr.

950 N. Jackson St.
(703)522-6768

Ashburn
43910 Farmwell Hunt Plaza
(703)724-3985

Burke
5653 Burke Center Pkwy.
(703)503-5305

Centreville
13821 Lee Hwy.
(703)263-0143

Chantilly
13701 Lee Jackson Hwy.
(703)263-9366

Culpeper
560 James Madison Hwy.
(540)829-9052

Dumfries
17440 Jefferson Davis Hwy.
(703)221-7261

Fairfax
10535 Lee Hwy.
(703)591-5439

12000 Lee Jackson Memorial Hwy.
(Fair Oaks Mall in Sears)
(703)383-1694

Falls Church
1014 W. Broad St.
(703)532-5823

6220 Wilson Blvd.
(703)533-0445

Falmouth
724 Warrenton Rd.
(540)310-4893

Fredericksburg
3300 Plank Rd.
(540)786-4740

5310 Jefferson Davis Hwy.
(540)891-2332

Herndon
604 Elden St.
(703)435-2220

Leesburg
509 E. Market St.
(703)771-2600

Manassas
8786 Centreville Rd.
(703)361-4050

Mt. Vernon
8540 Richmond Hwy.
(703)619-9000

Springfield
6701 Backlick Rd.
(703)569-0990

Stafford
204 Garrisonville Rd.
(540)720-3497

Sterling
46210 Potomac Run Plaza
(703)433-0460

Vienna
210 W. Maple Ave.
(703)242-0691

Warrenton
300 Broadview Ave.
(540)341-8663

Winchester
1517 S. Pleasant Valley Rd.
(540)662-7800

Woodbridge
13300 Minnieville Rd.
(703)492-1189

13319 Occoquan Rd.
(703)491-9098

WEST VIRGINIA

Martinsburg
1109 N. Queen St.
(304)263-5516

entertainment®

Backlick Cleaners
Burke Cleaners
Cardinal Cleaners
Catalano Cleaners
Cleaners America
Connell's Valet
Countryside Cleaners
Elden St. Cleaners
Fair City Cleaners
Jon-Son Cleaners
Merrifalls Cleaners
Noble Signature Cleaning
South Valley Cleaners
Superior Cleaners
Tyson's Station Cleaners
Tyson's Super Cleaners
Village II Cleaners
Yorkshire Cleaners

See Reverse Side For Locations

Enjoy any DRY CLEANING ORDER at 50% off the regular price - maximum discount $5.00.

One coupon per month for 12 months

Maximum discount $5.00

Leather, silk, suede, furs, repairs & box storage excluded

Present coupon with incoming order

Not valid holidays and subject to Rules of Use.

Enjoy any DRY CLEANING ORDER at 50% off the regular price - maximum discount $5.00.

See reverse side
valid May 2006
VA ONLY

Enjoy any DRY CLEANING ORDER at 50% off the regular price - maximum discount $5.00.

See reverse side
valid Nov. 2005
VA ONLY

Enjoy any DRY CLEANING ORDER at 50% off the regular price - maximum discount $5.00.

See reverse side
valid June 2006
VA ONLY

Enjoy any DRY CLEANING ORDER at 50% off the regular price - maximum discount $5.00.

See reverse side
valid Dec. 2005
VA ONLY

Enjoy any DRY CLEANING ORDER at 50% off the regular price - maximum discount $5.00.

See reverse side
valid July 2006
VA ONLY

Enjoy any DRY CLEANING ORDER at 50% off the regular price - maximum discount $5.00.

See reverse side
valid Jan. 2006
VA ONLY

Enjoy any DRY CLEANING ORDER at 50% off the regular price - maximum discount $5.00.

See reverse side
valid Aug. 2006
VA ONLY

Enjoy any DRY CLEANING ORDER at 50% off the regular price - maximum discount $5.00.

See reverse side
valid Feb. 2006
VA ONLY

Enjoy any DRY CLEANING ORDER at 50% off the regular price - maximum discount $5.00.

See reverse side
valid Sept. 2006
VA ONLY

Enjoy any DRY CLEANING ORDER at 50% off the regular price - maximum discount $5.00.

See reverse side
valid March 2006
VA ONLY

Enjoy any DRY CLEANING ORDER at 50% off the regular price - maximum discount $5.00.

See reverse side
valid Oct. 2006
VA ONLY

Enjoy any DRY CLEANING ORDER at 50% off the regular price - maximum discount $5.00.

See reverse side
valid April 2006
VA ONLY

entertainment.

Maximum discount $5.00; Leather, silk, suede, furs, repairs & box storage excluded; Present coupon with incoming order

entertainment.

Maximum discount $5.00; Leather, silk, suede, furs, repairs & box storage excluded; Present coupon with incoming order

entertainment.

Maximum discount $5.00; Leather, silk, suede, furs, repairs & box storage excluded; Present coupon with incoming order

entertainment.

Maximum discount $5.00; Leather, silk, suede, furs, repairs & box storage excluded; Present coupon with incoming order

entertainment.

Maximum discount $5.00; Leather, silk, suede, furs, repairs & box storage excluded; Present coupon with incoming order

entertainment.

Maximum discount $5.00; Leather, silk, suede, furs, repairs & box storage excluded; Present coupon with incoming order

entertainment.

Maximum discount $5.00; Leather, silk, suede, furs, repairs & box storage excluded; Present coupon with incoming order

entertainment.

Maximum discount $5.00; Leather, silk, suede, furs, repairs & box storage excluded; Present coupon with incoming order

entertainment.

Maximum discount $5.00; Leather, silk, suede, furs, repairs & box storage excluded; Present coupon with incoming order

entertainment.

Maximum discount $5.00; Leather, silk, suede, furs, repairs & box storage excluded; Present coupon with incoming order

entertainment.

Maximum discount $5.00; Leather, silk, suede, furs, repairs & box storage excluded; Present coupon with incoming order

entertainment.

Maximum discount $5.00; Leather, silk, suede, furs, repairs & box storage excluded; Present coupon with incoming order

Alexandria
South Valley Cleaners
7732-E Richmond hwy.
(703)780-3130

Burke
Burke Cleaners
9411- B Burke Lake Rd.
(703)978-4400

Village II Cleaners
9570 K Burke Rd.
(703)239-2092

Chantilly
Cleaners America
14240-Q Sullyfield Circle
(703)968-6482

Dale City
Catalano Cleaners
4810 Dale Blvd.
(703)590-4040

Fairfax
Fair City Cleaners
9647 Lee Hwy.
(703)273-5477

Jon-Son Cleaners
8640 Lee Hwy.
(703)204-0606

Falls Church
Merrifalls Cleaners
7810 H Lee Hwy.
(703)698-4417

Tyson's Station Cleaners
7459 Patterson Rd.
(703)734-5768

Fredericksburg
Cardinal Cleaners
503 Jefferson Davis Hwy.
(Fredericksburg Shpg. Ctr.)
(540)899-3800

Herndon
Elden St. Cleaners
767 Elden St.
(703)435-8626

Manassas
Yorkshire Cleaners
7569 Centreville Rd.
(703)361-1770

Montclair
Catalano Cleaners
4388 Kevin Walker Dr.
(703)680-6584

Catalano Cleaners
5167 Waterway Dr.
(703)583-8853

Quantico
Catalano Cleaners
512 Broadway St.
(703)640-6400

Springfield
Backlick Cleaners
6715-I Backlick Rd.
(703)451-9852

Superior Cleaners
8081-F Alban Rd.
(703)440-9277

Stafford
Noble Signature Cleaning
1495 Stafford Market Place #107
(540)658-9996

Sterling
Countryside Cleaners
122 Edds Ln.
(703)444-2000

Vienna
Cleaners America
266 Cedar Lane
(703)205-9800

Connell's Valet
148 Maple Ave. West
(703)255-9481

Tyson's Super Cleaners
8413 Old Courthouse Rd.
(703)893-2277

Woodbridge
Catalano Cleaners
13309 Occoquan Rd.
(703)494-6016

Catalano Cleaners
13841 Foldger Sq.
(703)680-2500

Catalano Cleaners
16677 River Ridge Rd.
(703)221-2200

entertainment®

American Valet
Parkland Cleaners
Parklane Cleaners

See Reverse Side For Locations

Enjoy any DRY CLEANING ORDER at 50% off the regular price - maximum discount $5.00.

One coupon per month for 12 months

Maximum discount $5.00

Leather, silk, suede, furs, repairs & box storage excluded

Present coupon with incoming order

Not valid holidays and subject to Rules of Use.

Enjoy any DRY CLEANING ORDER at 50% off the regular price - maximum discount $5.00.

See reverse side
valid May 2006
DC ONLY

Enjoy any DRY CLEANING ORDER at 50% off the regular price - maximum discount $5.00.

See reverse side
valid June 2006
DC ONLY

Enjoy any DRY CLEANING ORDER at 50% off the regular price - maximum discount $5.00.

See reverse side
valid July 2006
DC ONLY

Enjoy any DRY CLEANING ORDER at 50% off the regular price - maximum discount $5.00.

See reverse side
valid Aug. 2006
DC ONLY

Enjoy any DRY CLEANING ORDER at 50% off the regular price - maximum discount $5.00.

See reverse side
valid Sept. 2006
DC ONLY

Enjoy any DRY CLEANING ORDER at 50% off the regular price - maximum discount $5.00.

See reverse side
valid Oct. 2006
DC ONLY

Enjoy any DRY CLEANING ORDER at 50% off the regular price - maximum discount $5.00.

See reverse side
valid Nov. 2005
DC ONLY

Enjoy any DRY CLEANING ORDER at 50% off the regular price - maximum discount $5.00.

See reverse side
valid Dec. 2005
DC ONLY

Enjoy any DRY CLEANING ORDER at 50% off the regular price - maximum discount $5.00.

See reverse side
valid Jan. 2006
DC ONLY

Enjoy any DRY CLEANING ORDER at 50% off the regular price - maximum discount $5.00.

See reverse side
valid Feb. 2006
DC ONLY

Enjoy any DRY CLEANING ORDER at 50% off the regular price - maximum discount $5.00.

See reverse side
valid March 2006
DC ONLY

Enjoy any DRY CLEANING ORDER at 50% off the regular price - maximum discount $5.00.

See reverse side
valid April 2006
DC ONLY

entertainment.

Maximum discount $5.00; Leather, silk, suede, furs, repairs & box storage excluded; Present coupon with incoming order

entertainment.

Maximum discount $5.00; Leather, silk, suede, furs, repairs & box storage excluded; Present coupon with incoming order

entertainment.

Maximum discount $5.00; Leather, silk, suede, furs, repairs & box storage excluded; Present coupon with incoming order

entertainment.

Maximum discount $5.00; Leather, silk, suede, furs, repairs & box storage excluded; Present coupon with incoming order

entertainment.

Maximum discount $5.00; Leather, silk, suede, furs, repairs & box storage excluded; Present coupon with incoming order

entertainment.

Maximum discount $5.00; Leather, silk, suede, furs, repairs & box storage excluded; Present coupon with incoming order

entertainment.

Maximum discount $5.00; Leather, silk, suede, furs, repairs & box storage excluded; Present coupon with incoming order

entertainment.

Maximum discount $5.00; Leather, silk, suede, furs, repairs & box storage excluded; Present coupon with incoming order

entertainment.

Maximum discount $5.00; Leather, silk, suede, furs, repairs & box storage excluded; Present coupon with incoming order

entertainment.

Maximum discount $5.00; Leather, silk, suede, furs, repairs & box storage excluded; Present coupon with incoming order

entertainment.

Maximum discount $5.00; Leather, silk, suede, furs, repairs & box storage excluded; Present coupon with incoming order

entertainment.

Maximum discount $5.00; Leather, silk, suede, furs, repairs & box storage excluded; Present coupon with incoming order

Washington

American Valet
4519 Wisconsin Ave., N.W.
(202)364-9440

Parkland Cleaners
3811 McKinley, NW
(202)966-2411

Parklane Cleaners
4034 Connecticut Ave., NW
(202)363-5510

entertainment®

VIDEO WAREHOUSE

See Reverse Side For Locations

Enjoy one complimentary MOVIE/ GAME RENTAL when a second MOVIE/GAME RENTAL of equal or greater value is purchased.

(one coupon per month for 12 months)

Not valid holidays and subject to Rules of Use.

Enjoy one complimentary MOVIE/GAME RENTAL when a second MOVIE/GAME RENTAL of equal or greater value is purchased.

valid May 2006
Code # ER1G1

Video Warehouse

Enjoy one complimentary MOVIE/GAME RENTAL when a second MOVIE/GAME RENTAL of equal or greater value is purchased.

valid Nov. 2005
Code # ER1G1

Video Warehouse

Enjoy one complimentary MOVIE/GAME RENTAL when a second MOVIE/GAME RENTAL of equal or greater value is purchased.

valid June 2006
Code # ER1G1

Video Warehouse

Enjoy one complimentary MOVIE/GAME RENTAL when a second MOVIE/GAME RENTAL of equal or greater value is purchased.

valid Dec. 2005
Code # ER1G1

Video Warehouse

Enjoy one complimentary MOVIE/GAME RENTAL when a second MOVIE/GAME RENTAL of equal or greater value is purchased.

valid July 2006
Code # ER1G1

Video Warehouse

Enjoy one complimentary MOVIE/GAME RENTAL when a second MOVIE/GAME RENTAL of equal or greater value is purchased.

valid Jan. 2006
Code # ER1G1

Video Warehouse

Enjoy one complimentary MOVIE/GAME RENTAL when a second MOVIE/GAME RENTAL of equal or greater value is purchased.

valid Aug. 2006
Code # ER1G1

Video Warehouse

Enjoy one complimentary MOVIE/GAME RENTAL when a second MOVIE/GAME RENTAL of equal or greater value is purchased.

valid Feb. 2006
Code # ER1G1

Video Warehouse

Enjoy one complimentary MOVIE/GAME RENTAL when a second MOVIE/GAME RENTAL of equal or greater value is purchased.

valid Sept. 2006
Code # ER1G1

Video Warehouse

Enjoy one complimentary MOVIE/GAME RENTAL when a second MOVIE/GAME RENTAL of equal or greater value is purchased.

valid March 2006
Code # ER1G1

Video Warehouse

Enjoy one complimentary MOVIE/GAME RENTAL when a second MOVIE/GAME RENTAL of equal or greater value is purchased.

valid Oct. 2006
Code # ER1G1

Video Warehouse

Enjoy one complimentary MOVIE/GAME RENTAL when a second MOVIE/GAME RENTAL of equal or greater value is purchased.

valid April 2006
Code # ER1G1

Video Warehouse

entertainment.
Membership rules apply; Free membership; Additional day fees acrue at regular rates

entertainment.
Membership rules apply; Free membership; Additional day fees acrue at regular rates

entertainment.
Membership rules apply; Free membership; Additional day fees acrue at regular rates

entertainment.
Membership rules apply; Free membership; Additional day fees acrue at regular rates

entertainment.
Membership rules apply; Free membership; Additional day fees acrue at regular rates

entertainment.
Membership rules apply; Free membership; Additional day fees acrue at regular rates

entertainment.
Membership rules apply; Free membership; Additional day fees acrue at regular rates

entertainment.
Membership rules apply; Free membership; Additional day fees acrue at regular rates

entertainment.
Membership rules apply; Free membership; Additional day fees acrue at regular rates

entertainment.
Membership rules apply; Free membership; Additional day fees acrue at regular rates

entertainment.
Membership rules apply; Free membership; Additional day fees acrue at regular rates

entertainment.
Membership rules apply; Free membership; Additional day fees acrue at regular rates

DISTRICT OF COLUMBIA

Washington
4300 Connecticut Ave.
(202)237-0700

MARYLAND

Bowie
6950 Laurel Bowie Rd.
(301)805-2266

Clinton
7730 Old Branch Ave.
(301)877-0277

District Heights
6471 Marlboro Pike
(301)735-9878

Frederick
1305 W. 7th St.
(301)620-0500

Gaithersburg
19226 Montgomery Village Ave.
(301)963-6900

Gambrills
2616 A Chapel Lake Dr.
(410)451-9800

Germantown
13408 D5 Kingsview Village Rd.
(301)540-8001

Hagerstown
102 Railway Ln.
(301)733-1700

43 Eastern Blvd.
(301)733-0776

Laurel
361 Montrose Ave.
(240)568-9993

VIRGINIA

Arlington
2301 S. Jefferson Davis Hwy
(703)418-3950

3411 S. 5th St.
(703)521-6512

Ashburn
43330 Junction Plaza #110
(703)729-9292

Bristow
12721 Braemar Village Center.
(703)335-7400

Burke
5747 B. Burke Center Pkwy.
(703)250-2900

Falls Church
7235 Arlington Blvd
(703)560-5367

7810 A Lee Hwy.
(703)207-9738

Harrisonburg
227 Burgess Rd.
(540)432-1771

Herndon
13354 Franklin Farm Rd.
(703)464-7400

Leesburg
13 Catoctin Circle N.E
(703)443-2500

Reston
12050 D. North Shore Dr.
(703)481-9017

Stafford
1495 Stafford Market Place Ste. 101
(000)000-000

Sterling
20789 Great falls Plaza #188
(703)450-1661

Winchester
1851 S. Pleasant Valley Rd.
(540)545-8040

Woodbridge
4300 A. Merchant Plaza
(703)583-0497

entertainment®

great place for kids

Dollar Video
Power Video
Vid-Mark Video
Video Connection
Video Corner
Video King
Video Outlet
Videopix

See Reverse Side For Locations

Enjoy one complimentary VIDEO RENTAL when a second VIDEO RENTAL of equal or greater value is purchased.

One coupon per month for 12 months members & non-members welcome no security deposit required with valid credit card

Not valid holidays and subject to Rules of Use.

G82

Enjoy one complimentary VIDEO RENTAL when a second VIDEO RENTAL of equal or greater value is purchased.

See reverse side
valid May 2006

Enjoy one complimentary VIDEO RENTAL when a second VIDEO RENTAL of equal or greater value is purchased.

See reverse side
valid Nov. 2005

Enjoy one complimentary VIDEO RENTAL when a second VIDEO RENTAL of equal or greater value is purchased.

See reverse side
valid June 2006

Enjoy one complimentary VIDEO RENTAL when a second VIDEO RENTAL of equal or greater value is purchased.

See reverse side
valid Dec. 2005

Enjoy one complimentary VIDEO RENTAL when a second VIDEO RENTAL of equal or greater value is purchased.

See reverse side
valid July 2006

Enjoy one complimentary VIDEO RENTAL when a second VIDEO RENTAL of equal or greater value is purchased.

See reverse side
valid Jan. 2006

Enjoy one complimentary VIDEO RENTAL when a second VIDEO RENTAL of equal or greater value is purchased.

See reverse side
valid Aug. 2006

Enjoy one complimentary VIDEO RENTAL when a second VIDEO RENTAL of equal or greater value is purchased.

See reverse side
valid Feb. 2006

Enjoy one complimentary VIDEO RENTAL when a second VIDEO RENTAL of equal or greater value is purchased.

See reverse side
valid Sept. 2006

Enjoy one complimentary VIDEO RENTAL when a second VIDEO RENTAL of equal or greater value is purchased.

See reverse side
valid March 2006

Enjoy one complimentary VIDEO RENTAL when a second VIDEO RENTAL of equal or greater value is purchased.

See reverse side
valid Oct. 2006

Enjoy one complimentary VIDEO RENTAL when a second VIDEO RENTAL of equal or greater value is purchased.

See reverse side
valid April 2006

entertainment.

Members & non-members welcome; No security deposit required with valid credit card

entertainment.

Members & non-members welcome; No security deposit required with valid credit card

entertainment.

Members & non-members welcome; No security deposit required with valid credit card

entertainment.

Members & non-members welcome; No security deposit required with valid credit card

entertainment.

Members & non-members welcome; No security deposit required with valid credit card

entertainment.

Members & non-members welcome; No security deposit required with valid credit card

entertainment.

Members & non-members welcome; No security deposit required with valid credit card

entertainment.

Members & non-members welcome; No security deposit required with valid credit card

entertainment.

Members & non-members welcome; No security deposit required with valid credit card

entertainment.

Members & non-members welcome; No security deposit required with valid credit card

entertainment.

Members & non-members welcome; No security deposit required with valid credit card

entertainment.

Members & non-members welcome; No security deposit required with valid credit card

DISTRICT OF COLUMBIA

Washington
Video King
1845 Columbia Rd., NW
(202)483-8801

MARYLAND

Capitol Heights
Video Outlet
8801 Hampton Mall Dr.
(301)336-0101

Hyattsville
Video Outlet
5502 Landover Rd.
(301)864-5858

Suitland
Video Outlet
4910 Silver Hill Rd.
(301)735-5895

Upper Marlboro
Vid-Mark Video
7589 South West Crain Hwy.
(301)952-0010

VIRGINIA

Alexandria
Power Video
1628 A Belleview Blvd.
(703)768-2877

Fairfax
Video Corner
10014 Main St.
(703)385-3314

Herndon
Video Connection
372 Elden St.
(703)471-7232

Manassas
Videopix
7688 Streamwalk Lane
(Walmart & Home Depot Shpg. Ctr.)
(703)369-6281

Manassas Park
Video Connection
8466 Centreville Rd.
(703)369-5927

Woodbridge
Dollar Video
14087 Noblewood Plaza
(703)670-0625

Dollar Video
14511 Jefferson Davis Hwy.
(703)497-1256

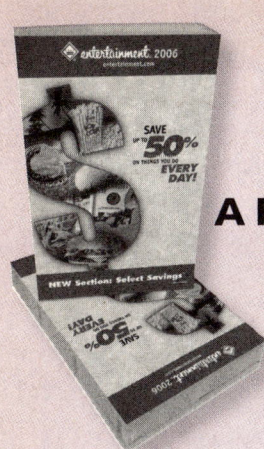

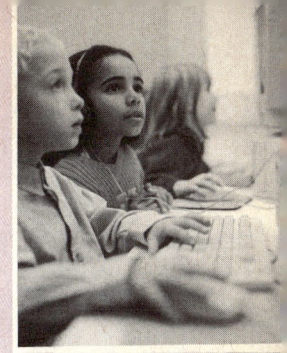

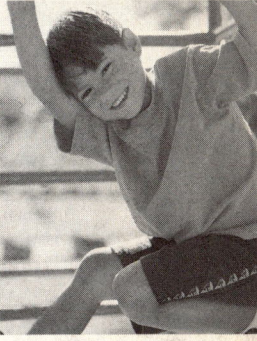

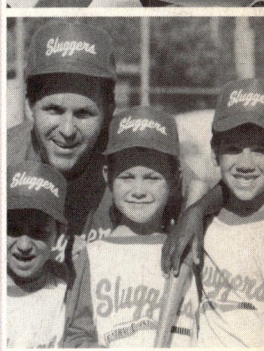

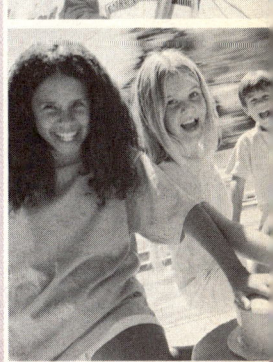

Neighborhood Index

Multiple Locations

kids **Great Place for Kids!** NEW **New Merchants Added This Year**

kids **Great Place for Kids!** NEW **New Merchants Added This Year**

Neighborhood Index

District Of Columbia

Washington

MARYLAND

VIRGINIA

NEIGHBORHOOD INDEX

Neighborhood Index

kids Great Place for Kids!

NEW New Merchants Added This Year

Neighborhood Index

Neighborhood Index

kids **Great Place for Kids!**

NEW **New Merchants Added This Year**

1

A

B

D

E

F

G

H

I

Alphabetical Index

N

O

P

Q

R

S

T

U

V

W

X

Y

Z

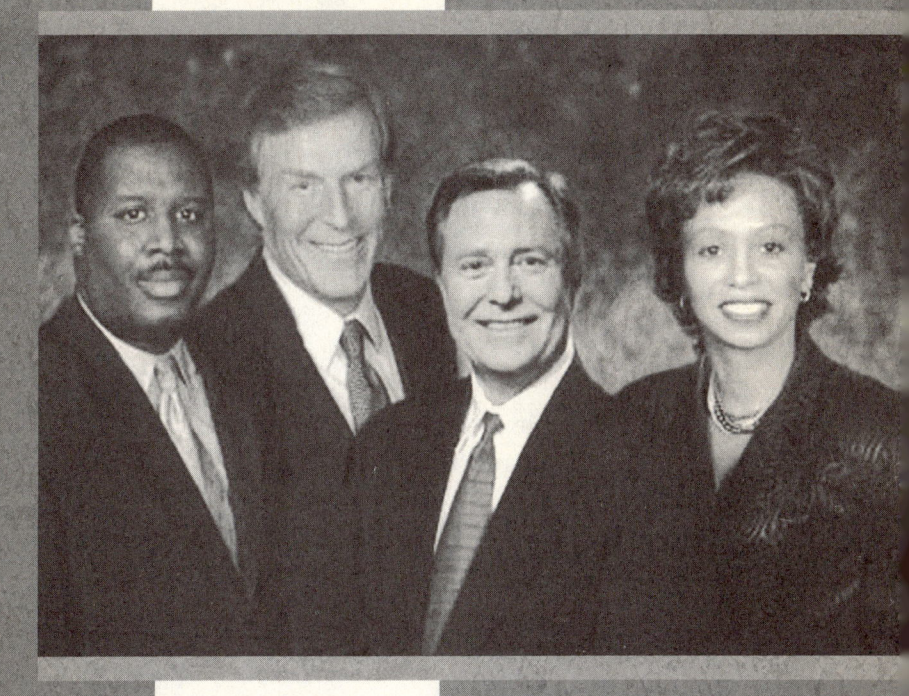

Rules of Use

The membership card and coupons are valid now through November 1, 2006, unless otherwise stated on the discount offer.

1. **Entertainment® Membership Card**...Remove your membership card from the front of this book and register online at **www.entertainment.com/register** to receive full membership benefits and begin using the membership card right away. The membership card is used to obtain the offers found in the Fine & Casual Dining section that have [card icon] in the upper right-hand corner of the offer page and with car rentals, select hotels, and participating Frequent Values® merchants.

2. **Additional Conditions**...Read the offer carefully for stated conditions, restrictions, and exclusions. All offers are valid anytime except on defined holidays or unless the offer states otherwise. Certain offers are restricted to one offer per party, per visit. These additional conditions supersede other Rules of Use.

3. **How To Redeem Discount**...Present your coupon/membership card to a participating merchant at the time you request your bill to receive your discount. The merchant will retain your coupon or remove the card number from the back of your membership card to indicate you have used the discount offer. The least expensive item(s), up to the maximum value stated, will be deducted from your bill, or you will receive a percentage off the designated item(s), up to the maximum value stated, depending on the discount offer. For restaurants offering one complimentary "menu item" when a second is purchased, a "menu item" is a main course or entrée item. You may only use an offer once, and you may not combine the offer with any other discount or awards program/offer.

4. **Valid Dates and Times/Holidays**...Read the offer carefully for valid dates and times. Major holidays, including those below, and regional holidays observed by participating merchants, are excluded, even if the offer states "valid anytime":

New Year's Eve/Day	Valentine's Day	St. Patrick's Day	Easter
Mother's Day	Father's Day	Thanksgiving	Christmas Eve/Day

Please check with the merchant regarding other holidays.

5. **Dining Discount Details**...Only one coupon/membership card may be used for every two people, up to a maximum of three coupons/membership cards per party, and separate checks are not allowed. Some restaurants include a "when dining alone" option in their offers. These offers are valid only when dining alone. Dining offers cannot be applied to children's menu items, discount-priced daily specials, senior citizen rates, Early Bird specials, carryout/takeout (except in the Family Restaurants, Informal Dining & Carryout section), and buffets, unless otherwise noted. Discounts on alcohol are prohibited. The discount will be applied only to the food portion of the bill.

6. **Tipping**...Tipping for satisfactory service should be 15-20% of the total bill **before** the discount amount is subtracted.

7. **Discounts**...Discounts exclude tax, tip and/or alcohol, where applicable.

8. **Hotel Discounts**...Please see the "Hotel Rules of Use" located in the Travel & Hotels section.

9. **Movie Theater Discounts**...Some movie theaters are obligated by studio contracts to exclude discounts on certain movies. ***Please check with the theater for exclusions.***

10. **Free Offers**...In most cases, to qualify for a free offer or complimentary item, you must purchase goods or services from the merchant making the offer. Such offers may not be used in conjunction with any other discount or awards program/offer.

11. **Frequent Values®**...Register at **www.entertainment.com/register** for a list of participating merchants and program details.

12. **Merchant Information**...All merchant information is valid as of May 1, 2005. Go to www.entertainment.com for important updates.

The barter, trade, sale, purchase, or transfer for compensation of this book, in whole or in part or any of its offers, is strictly prohibited, unless expressly authorized by ENTERTAINMENT PUBLICATIONS, INC. This book and its offers are intended for the personal use of the individual purchaser of this book and are not valid with other discount offers or in other cities unless otherwise specified. The use of this book or any of its offers for advertising purposes, in any form or fashion, is strictly prohibited. Any use of an offer in violation of these Rules will render the offer VOID and ENTERTAINMENT PUBLICATIONS, INC. will pursue all legal remedies available to it by the law. Offers may not be reproduced and are void where prohibited, taxed or restricted by law.

ENTERTAINMENT PUBLICATIONS, INC., and or its parent or subsidiaries, will not be responsible if any establishment breaches its contract or refuses to accept the membership card/coupons; however, it will attempt to secure compliance.

ENTERTAINMENT PUBLICATIONS, INC. disclaims all alleged liability for bodily injury or property damage resulting from any accident, event or occurrence on, or resulting from the use of, the premises of the participating businesses. ENTERTAINMENT PUBLICATIONS, INC. disclaims all warranties express, implied or otherwise imposed by law, regarding the condition of those premises or the safety of same. ENTERTAINMENT PUBLICATIONS, INC. disclaims all alleged vicarious liability for bodily injury or property damage resulting from the acts or omissions of the participating businesses.

Membership Information

www.entertainment.com
Your comprehensive source for information about your Entertainment® membership and related products.

MEMBER SERVICES

(You must register your Membership Card and log in to access these services.)

TO REGISTER YOUR BOOK/MEMBERSHIP CARD
Go to www.entertainment.com/register

FOR QUESTIONS REGARDING YOUR ENTERTAINMENT® MEMBERSHIP AND ITS MANY BENEFITS
Go to www.entertainment.com/questions

TO PURCHASE ADDITIONAL ENTERTAINMENT® BOOKS AT MEMBER-ONLY PRICES (FOR GIFTS OR TRAVEL)
Go to www.entertainment.com/books

FOR OUR HOTEL PROGRAMS, GUARANTEED BEST RATE, OR DIRECT TO HOTEL
Go to www.entertainment.com/hotels for Guaranteed Best Rate and www.entertainment.com/directtohotel for Direct to Hotel information

FOR THE LATEST MEMBER UPDATES AND OFFER INFORMATION
Go to www.entertainment.com/hotline

FUNDRAISER/BUSINESS SERVICES

IF YOU ARE INTERESTED IN SELLING OUR PRODUCTS AS A FUNDRAISER
Go to www.fundraising.entertainment.com/2006

IF YOU ARE INTERESTED IN ADVERTISING IN THIS BOOK OR ON OUR WEB SITE
Go to www.entertainment.com/advertise

IF YOU ARE INTERESTED IN CREATING A CUSTOM COUPON BOOK OR ONLINE SAVINGS PROGRAM
Go to www.entertainment.com/pmd

If our web site does not address your question, or if you need to speak to one of our customer care representatives, please call
1-888-231-SAVE (7283)

Published by: Entertainment Publications, Inc. • International Headquarters
1414 E. Maple Road • Troy, MI 48083

Order Extra Editions & Out-of-Town Editions

Prices listed below reflect regular retail price and are shown in U.S. dollars. When completing the **order form** on the reverse side or when calling **1-866-592-5991** toll free to order extra editions, you will receive $5 off the prices listed below. If you choose to order online at **www.entertainment.com**, you will receive $5 off the price listed below plus **FREE SHIPPING** (a $5 value). You must have registered your membership at www.entertainment.com/register and be signed in to take advantage of this free shipping offer. Please refer to the 3-digit code and edition name below when ordering.

Regular Retail Price listed below.

ALABAMA
- 106 Birmingham $25

ARIZONA
- 047 Phoenix $30
- 068 Tucson $40

ARKANSAS
- 082 Little Rock $30

CALIFORNIA
- 104 Bakersfield $30
- 055 East Bay Area $30
- 086 Fresno/Central Valley $35
- 097 Inland Empire/Riverside/ Palm Springs $30
- 110 Lake Tahoe/Reno $30
- 016 Los Angeles West $30
- 102 Modesto/Stockton $35
- 084 Monterey Peninsula $30
- 014 Orange County $40
- 042 Sacramento/Gold Country $45
- 017 San Diego $45
- 012 San Fernando Valley $30
- 073 San Francisco/San Mateo $30
- 096 San Gabriel Valley $30
- 010 San Jose/Santa Clara $30
- 088 Santa Barbara/Ventura $30
- 126 Sonoma/Marin $35

COLORADO
- 141 Colorado Springs $30
- 038 Denver $30

CONNECTICUT
- 080 Fairfield County $30
- 046 Hartford $35
- 144 New Haven $30

DELAWARE
- 157 Delaware $35

FLORIDA
- 137 Brevard County $30
- 035 Ft. Lauderdale/ West Palm Beach $35
- 075 Ft. Myers/Naples $35
- 037 Gainesville $30
- 036 Jacksonville $30
- 154 Miami/Florida Keys $35
- 153 Orlando $30
- 204 Pensacola $30
- 118 Sarasota $35
- 139 St. Petersburg/Clearwater $30
- 045 Tampa $30

GEORGIA
- 028 Atlanta $30
- 201 Augusta $30

HAWAII
- 146 Hawaii $35

IDAHO
- 085 Boise $30

ILLINOIS
- 008 Chicago North/Northwest $30
- 027 Chicago South/Southwest $30
- 015 Chicago West/Central $30

INDIANA
- 078 Ft. Wayne/NE Indiana $35
- 039 Indianapolis/ Central Indiana $30
- 058 Northwest Indiana $30
- 159 South Bend/Michiana $35

IOWA
- 053 Des Moines $30
- 302 Quad Cities $35

KANSAS
- 105 Kansas City $30
- 057 Wichita $30

KENTUCKY
- 122 Lexington $30
- 056 Louisville/Southern IN $25

LOUISIANA
- 202 Baton Rouge $30
- 321 Lafayette $35
- 121 New Orleans $30

MARYLAND
- 024 Baltimore $30
- 022 Washington, D.C./ Maryland $30

MASSACHUSETTS
- 030 Boston $30
- 124 Springfield/Western MA $30
- 108 Worcester County/ Central MA $30

MICHIGAN
- 001 Detroit Area $30
- 150 Grand Rapids $40
- 303 Saginaw $30

MINNESOTA
- 091 Twin Cities Happenings $35
- 123 Twin Ports Happenings $30

MISSISSIPPI
- 304 Jackson $30

MISSOURI
- 105 Kansas City $30
- 134 Springfield/Branson $30
- 013 St. Louis $30

NEBRASKA
- 138 Omaha/Lincoln $30

NEVADA
- 149 Las Vegas $25
- 110 Reno/Lake Tahoe $30

NEW HAMPSHIRE
- 128 Southern New Hampshire $30

NEW JERSEY
- 048 Central/Middlesex $30
- 094 Central/Monmouth $30
- 052 North/Bergen $30
- 026 North/Essex $30
- 093 North/Morris $30
- 076 NJ South $35

NEW MEXICO
- 083 Albuquerque/Santa Fe $40

NEW YORK
- 060 Albany $35
- 109 Binghamton $25
- 011 Buffalo $30
- 111 Cortland/Ithaca $25
- 033 Long Island/Nassau/ Suffolk $30
- 087 Mid-Hudson Valley $35
- 034 New York City $30
- 044 Rochester $30
- 074 Syracuse $30
- 040 Westchester/ Lower-Hudson Valley $35

NORTH CAROLINA
- 043 Charlotte $30
- 222 Fayetteville $30
- 113 Greensboro $30
- 112 Raleigh/Durham $35

OHIO
- 006 Akron $35
- 069 Canton $35
- 002 Cincinnati Area $35
- 004 Cleveland $30
- 003 Columbus/Central OH $35
- 005 Dayton/Springfield $35
- 018 Toledo/NW Ohio/ SE Michigan $35
- 131 Youngstown $30

OKLAHOMA
- 160 Oklahoma City $30
- 151 Tulsa $30

OREGON
- 051 Oregon $35
- 029 Portland/Vancouver $35

PENNSYLVANIA
- 136 Erie $30
- 162 Harrisburg $30
- 072 Lancaster/York $30
- 062 Lehigh Valley $25
- 156 NE Pennsylvania/Poconos $35
- 031 Philadelphia North $30
- 079 Philadelphia West $30
- 007 Pittsburgh $30
- 120 Pittsburgh and East $30
- 081 Reading/Pottsville $30

RHODE ISLAND
- 155 Providence $30

SOUTH CAROLINA
- 261 Charleston $30
- 021 Columbia $30
- 129 Greenville/Spartanburg $30

TENNESSEE
- 116 Memphis $25
- 064 Nashville $25
- 205 Tri-Cities $30

TEXAS
- 142 Austin Passbook $30
- 140 Corpus Christi $30
- 145 Dallas Passbook $30
- 125 El Paso $30
- 147 Ft. Worth Passbook $30
- 019 Houston Area $30
- 152 San Antonio $30

UTAH
- 092 Utah Happenings $35

VERMONT
- 095 Vermont $35

VIRGINIA
- 063 Norfolk/VA Beach $30
- 070 North Virginia/ Washington, D.C. $30
- 158 Richmond $30
- 301 Roanoke $30

WASHINGTON
- 143 N. Puget Sound $35
- 050 S. Puget Sound $35
- 023 Seattle/Eastside $35
- 090 Spokane/N. Idaho $35

WEST VIRGINIA
- 115 Charleston Area $35
- 117 Huntington $30

WISCONSIN
- 077 Appleton/Green Bay $35
- 049 Madison $30
- 032 Milwaukee $40

CANADA
- 065 Calgary $36
- 066 Edmonton $36
- 130 Halifax $28
- 059 Hamilton/Burlington/ Oakville $32
- 089 Montréal et environs $28
- 101 Okanagan Valley $28
- 067 Ottawa/Outaouais $32
- 135 Saskatchewan $28
- 054 Toronto Area $32
- 025 Vancouver $41
- 107 Victoria/ Mid Vancouver Island $28
- 161 Winnipeg $24

PUERTO RICO
- 100 San Juan $45

EUROPE
- 0IG Gothenburg† $45

AUSTRALIA
- 327 Adelaide $45
- 326 Brisbane/Gold Coast $45
- 332 Canberra $45
- 387 Geelong $45
- 324 Melbourne $45
- 330 Newcastle $45
- 388 Parramatta/ Blue Mountains $45
- 336 Perth $45
- 328 Sydney $45

NEW ZEALAND
- 331 Auckland $45
- 400 Christchurch $45
- 338 Wellington $45

Some editions will not be available until 11/1/05. Offer subject to availability. Credit card transactions are processed in U.S. funds and are subject to applicable exchange rates. Offer expires 9/1/06.

†Published in language other than English.